D0355516

A Refugee from His Race

To my beloved husband, Martin,
and to my beloved mentors,
H. Bruce Franklin and Jane Franklin,
inspiring models all of courageous and
principled struggle for a just world

Contents

Figures

Preface

During one of the darkest periods of U.S. history, when white supremacy was entrenching itself throughout the nation, the white writer-jurist-activist Albion W. Tourgée (1838–1905) forged a remarkable alliance with African Americans. Acclaimed by blacks as "one of the best friends of the Afro-American people this country has ever produced" and reviled by white Southerners as a "pestiferous mouther who for years has labored to incite an uprising of the negroes in the South," Tourgée offers an ideal lens through which to examine relations between progressive whites and African Americans.[1] In a career stretching over four decades, he won fame in so many arenas that scholars increasingly rank him as a major actor in U.S. history and culture.

An Ohio carpetbagger, Tourgée figured prominently in North Carolina's Reconstruction from 1865 till 1875. Creating an effective interracial and cross-class coalition that elected a Radical Republican government, he helped write a democratic constitution for the state that still bears his impress. In addition, he distinguished himself as a superior court judge who insisted that "justice should at least be 'color blind,'"[2] ensured that juries included African Americans, and vigorously pursued indictments of the Ku Klux Klan at the risk of his life.

A prolific novelist with a readership of "five to ten millions,"[3] Tourgée influenced the outcome of the 1880 presidential election with two fictionalized accounts of the turbulent era he had lived through. The first, *A Fool's Errand. By One of the Fools* (1879), which exposed the depredations of the Klan as powerfully as Harriet Beecher Stowe had the horrors of slavery, sold almost 150,000 copies within a year and 600,000 in Tourgée's lifetime.[4] The second, *Bricks Without Straw* (1880), sold 50,000 copies within a year and opened new literary horizons by dramatizing Reconstruction from the perspective of the South's recently emancipated slaves.[5]

A byliner for a leading Republican newspaper, the *Chicago Daily Inter Ocean*, which published his weekly column "A Bystander's Notes" (1888–98) on its Saturday editorial page, Tourgée boasted an interracial audience of 200,000 subscribers.[6] The "Bystander" commented on a broad array of political, economic, and cultural topics, foregrounding the race question at a time when politicians were seeking to bury it and most white mainstream newspapers were avoiding it. Not only did Tourgée consistently denounce such racist abuses as disfranchisement, segregation, lynching, and the qua-si-reenslavement of agricultural workers, but he also refuted the claims of white superiority and black inferiority that his contemporaries invoked to justify all these forms of racial oppression. The column elicited hundreds of letters a week from fans and foes—letters that Tourgée regularly quoted and answered in it. Extending its reach even further, two African American newspapers in particular, the *Cleveland Gazette* and the *Detroit Plaindealer*, frequently reprinted the column.

In launching the National Citizens' Rights Association (NCRA) in 1891 as an interracial civil rights organization, Tourgée simultaneously harked back to the abolitionist movement, which disbanded while the country was in the throes of Reconstruction, and anticipated the NAACP, which a coalition of black and white activists founded four years after his death. Through the NCRA, Tourgée sought to abolish what he called "caste," the systematic subjection of people of color to white domination, and thus to complete the work his abolitionist predecessors had left unfinished. Although the organization failed to accomplish its goal, it enrolled some 250,000 members at its peak—a figure that equals the membership of the American Anti-Slavery Society in the 1830s and dwarfs that of the NAACP in the 1910s.[7]

Paradoxically, Tourgée achieved his greatest success in a phase of his career that has been all but forgotten: the campaign against lynching that he initiated in his "Bystander" column as early as 1888 and continued in collaboration with Ida B. Wells and Harry C. Smith, the leaders of the African American antilynching movement. The antilynching law Tourgée framed for Ohio, which Smith shepherded through the state legislature in 1896, served as a model for those in nine other states, as well as for the NAACP.

Climaxing Tourgée's crusade against caste, he encouraged New Orleans people of color to contest segregation in what became the *Plessy v. Ferguson* case, which he argued pro bono. His visionary brief exposing racial distinctions as arbitrary and unscientific constructs did not prevent the Supreme Court of 1896 from endorsing segregation in a seven-to-one ruling but impressed the justices who overturned *Plessy* more than half a century later in *Brown v. Board of Education* (1954).

A Refugee from His Race covers all these facets of Tourgée's career, concentrating on its most exceptional feature: his steadfast alliance with African Americans during a time of extreme racial separatism—a subject no other scholar has investigated in depth. Tourgée's papers contain a treasure trove of letters by African Americans of the 1890s, which, along with editorials in the African American press, provide an intimate view of the cross-racial dialogue and collaboration in which he and they engaged. The African American voices that emerge from the archives tapped in *A Refugee from His Race* bespeak a community in cultural and political ferment—a community harboring a variety of opinions while resisting white supremacy by many different means, among them alliances with white progressives. In sum, delving into Tourgée's career sheds new light on African American history as well as on turn-of-the-century race relations.

The book takes its title from a question raised by the white Southerner Joel Chandler Harris, compiler of the Uncle Remus stories and editor of the *Atlanta Constitution*, in his review of Tourgée's 1890 novel *Pactolus Prime*: "What shall we say of such a writer? Is he a monomaniac, or simply a refugee from his race?" To Harris, as to other white Southern commentators, Tourgée's sympathy for African Americans could only be explained by what they interpreted as his "narrow, burning hatred of his own race."[8]

African Americans, on the other hand, often marveled at how well Tourgée understood and expressed their sentiments. "No suffering black man could speak in more emphatic tones, and cut with a keener lash," editorialized the African American feminist Josephine St. Pierre Ruffin in her newspaper, the *Boston Courant*.[9] Another African American feminist, the scholar Anna Julia Cooper, similarly credited Tourgée with "presenting truth from the colored American's standpoint," speaking "with all the eloquence and passion of the aggrieved party himself," and surpassing "any living writer, white or colored," in the "fervency and frequency" of his protests against his country's racist ideology and practice.[10] "I some times wonder if you was a colord [*sic*] man," confided one of Tourgée's African American "Bystander" fans, struck by Tourgée's ability to write as if he had personally "felt the sting" of racism.[11] Convinced of his unshakable commitment to winning justice for them, African Americans retained their admiration for Tourgée even when he castigated them mercilessly and took stands they judged impolitic.

Readers today may react with skepticism to the notion that any white man could have inspired, let alone deserved, the tributes from African Americans quoted above. Both reflecting and reinforcing the widespread tendency to look askance at whites who espoused the cause of African Americans, most of the scholarship about them has highlighted their paternalism. This focus, growing out of the civil rights and Black Power movements of the 1960s, originated as a necessary corrective to previous historiography, much of which had uncritically glorified white progressives, overlooked the racism many (though not all) of them betrayed, and neglected the crucial role African Americans played in the struggle for justice and equality. While seeking to correct the errors of the past, however, the scholarship of the last few decades has produced an overwhelmingly negative portrayal of white progressives' relations with African Americans. The relentless emphasis on the failure of white progressives to measure up to present-day standards of political correctness has forced a diverse group of people into a single mold, flattened out historical complexities, eliminated nuances and distinctions, and not infrequently ignored the countervailing testimony of the African Americans who worked most closely with the antiracist activists all too many scholars now characterize as, at best, inadvertent racists.

True, in a culture that has made "race" so fundamental to identity, it may be hard for anyone, white or black, to be entirely immune to perceiving people through a racial lens. Yet the term "racist" blurs the distinction between subjective and objective manifestations of racism, between the psychological racism that exists in the mind of an individual or the culture of a society—a type of racism that can also be internalized by its victims—and the systemic racism built into the structure of a society, which maintains the dominance of one group over others through policies designed to distribute economic, political, social, and educational resources unequally. Unlike psychological racism, systemic racism does not inhere in individuals, although individuals may strive to abolish it, as did some white progressives. Conversely, traces of psychological racism may linger in individuals and in the culture even after the establishment of a systemically egalitarian society. By riding roughshod over such distinctions, we empty the term "racist" of specificity and thus deprive ourselves of the tools required to eradicate racism. Worse, we lump together African Americans' allies and their adversaries, defining both sides as equally racist, whether they have consistently repudiated racial discrimination or have consistently practiced or excused it.[12]

The blanket disparagement of white progressives not only homogenizes them and impedes the struggle against racism but substitutes one form of condescension for another. That is, present-day scholars condescend to the past when they judge the activists of earlier generations by present-day standards that do not take into account such factors as the crafting of messages for particular circumstances and audiences or the changing connotations of language over time. They condescend to activists of both races, for they discount the sacrifices each made, devalue their collaboration, and disregard the tributes activists of color have paid to their white partners. Far from enabling later activists to avoid the pitfalls of their predecessors, the negative thrust of current scholarship can actually disempower them. After all, if no white person, no matter how dedicated, can ever succeed in overcoming racism, why should anyone engage in cross-racial collaborations or participate in interracial coalitions? If even individuals who have devoted their lives to combating racism have not escaped its taint, how can we expect to create a society, let alone a world, free of racism?

The Tourgée archive opens an alternative window into cross-racial alliances. Tourgée and his African American correspondents managed to carry on an honest dialogue about race at the height of the white supremacist era and to do so in a manner that allowed sharp disagreements to coexist with mutual respect. They also managed to collaborate fruitfully in fighting against segregation and lynching, despite the obstacles they faced in a climate that deterred interracial socializing. As the archive reveals, moreover, tens of thousands of white activists joined the interracial movement Tourgée sparked, some of whom may well have forged lasting relationships with African Americans—a topic that awaits exploration. It is my hope that by recovering the model Tourgée and his African American allies embodied, this book can empower present and future activists to cultivate the cross-racial alliances vital to transforming our society.

A Refugee from His Race consists of seven chapters, each isolating a single strand of Tourgée's intertwined exertions for racial justice, but all highlighting his dialogue with African Americans. Chapter 1 introduces Tourgée and illuminates his ethos, first, by tracing his career from the Reconstruction era to 1890, when he entered on his most intensive collaboration with African Americans, and, second, by sampling his exchanges with selected African American correspondents, including both those requesting his assistance and those with whom he developed the strongest bonds. Chapter 2 focuses on Tourgée's novel *Pactolus Prime* and the responses it evoked from African Americans, many of whom felt that Tourgée spoke for them when he blasted white racism and hypocrisy through the mouth of his title character, an African American bootblack. Chapter 3 surveys Tourgée's "Bystander" column, showing how it fostered a national dialogue about the race question by incorporating long extracts from the private letters and public statements of African Americans and whites representing an array of political opinions and regional identities. Chapter 4 examines the NCRA, the pioneering interracial civil rights organization Tourgée founded to agitate for equal citizenship and provide an alternative to black separatism—an organization that leading African American editors publicized in their newspapers.

Chapter 5 centers around the least-known aspect of Tourgée's career: his collaboration with Wells and Smith in a three-way campaign against lynching. Chapter 6 reconsiders the best-known, but perhaps most misunderstood, aspect of Tourgée's career: his collaboration with Louis A. Martinet, editor of the *New Orleans Crusader*, in the *Plessy v. Ferguson* case. Chapter 7 reflects on Tourgée's last years as U.S. consul to Bordeaux and assesses his legacy. Finally, a brief afterword suggests the implications of *A Refugee from His Race* for future scholarship on civil rights movements.

Acknowledgments

The dedication to my husband, Martin, and to my mentors, H. Bruce Franklin and Jane Franklin, reflects my deepest and most longstanding debts, both personal and intellectual. Martin has unstintingly supported my work for half a century, reading and rereading drafts, offering helpful suggestions at every step, and even immersing himself in the authors about whom I was writing. Bruce started teaching me how to write and think critically in his 1963 freshman English course at Stanford and has been doing so ever since. His tough-minded comments on the entire manuscript forced me to reformulate key portions. Jane brought her expertise on Cuba to bear on chapter 7 by suggesting both sources to consult and refinements in the text. More fundamentally, Bruce and Jane have shaped my perspective on the world through their activism in the anti–Vietnam War movement and their engaged scholarship, which has provided a model for my own.

Others who helped me improve specific chapters are Sally Greene, whose legal training and familiarity with the *Plessy* case proved indispensable in chapter 6; Dorothy Ross, who read an early version of chapter 4; Carolyn Sorisio, who read early versions of chapters 1 and 4 and skillfully guest-edited my article "Albion W. Tourgée and Louis A. Martinet: The Cross-Racial Friendship behind *Plessy v. Ferguson*" for a special number of the journal *MELUS*; and Mark Elliott, who not only read early versions of chapters 1 and 4 but shared many research leads. Showing a generosity rare in our profession, Mark also invited me to participate in a panel he was chairing at the American Historical Association and procured invitations for me to the Tourgée conferences in Westfield, New York, and Raleigh, North Carolina, at which he delivered keynotes. I am indebted as well to three anonymous readers of the manuscript for valuable suggestions on how to sharpen the argument and above all to associate editor Lucas Church for his meticulous cutting of chapters 1 and 6, which I tried to emulate in other chapters.

Without the assistance of archivists and librarians, I could never have completed the extensive research this book required. I especially thank Christopher Harter of the Amistad Research Center and the late Beth Howse of the Special Collections division of Fisk University's John Hope and Aurelia E. Franklin Library for sending me copies of items relating to the New Orleans

Citizens' Committee, the *Crusader,* and Charles W. Chesnutt's correspondence with Tourgée. At my home institution, the Library of Congress, Sheridan Harvey and Thomas Mann also greatly facilitated my research.

Finally, I thank the Chautauqua County Historical Society for permission to quote from the Albion W. Tourgée Papers, the Amistad Research Center for permission to quote from the Charles Rousseve and Nils R. Douglas Papers, and the journals *Prospects, Comparative American Studies, MELUS: The Journal of the Society for the Study of the Multi-Ethnic Literature of the United States,* and *Elon Law Review* for permission to reprint the portions of the manuscript they previously published as articles.

A Refugee from His Race

CHAPTER ONE

A Straight-Talking Advocate

The true interests of an oppressed people were never yet served by apology, petition or submission. . . . Good-temper is an excellent thing when we speak of the wrongs of *others*. . . . But when one *feels* the iron of oppression and has the cause of a people on his heart, it is the hot fire of resentment flowing through his speech that convinces the world of his sincerity. . . . [W]hen next you have a chance to strike a blow for your people, hit hard and let the world know that the gall of oppression is not changed to honey by the color of the skin.
—Albion W. Tourgée to J. Gray Lucas, 28 February 1891

A week before receiving the above letter, J. Gray Lucas, an African American who had recently been elected to the Arkansas State Legislature, had sent a copy of his speech against the Jim Crow car bill that his colleagues were debating—one of many sprouting up all over the South in the 1890s— to Albion W. Tourgée, then the foremost white champion of African Americans. Lucas probably knew that Tourgée had been encouraging New Orleans people of color to challenge the constitutionality of a similar law Louisiana had passed requiring segregated railway travel, and he sought Tourgée's endorsement of his own efforts. Instead of praising the "pacifica-tory" tone Lucas had struck in his speech, however—a tone adapted to the lethal conditions of white supremacist rule under which African Americans lived in the Deep South—Tourgée had objected that the strategy of trying to "kill a cat" by "overfeed[ing] it with sweetened cream" merely "wasted a deal of good cream." "It is useless to appeal to the conscience of the Southern white man," Tourgée argued. "The only hope lies in continued appeal to the conscience of the North, which though dull and apathetic is still open to appeal." Because white Northerners had succumbed to the myth that "the colored man is content with his debasement," Tourgée emphasized, African Americans must jolt them out of their illusions with militant demands for justice.[1]

Lucas did not reply for almost a year, but his next letter indicates that far from having taken offense at Tourgée's brutally frank criticism, he had greeted it as the gesture of a "friend." Thus, he reciprocated by addressing Tourgée as "Dear Sir and Friend." He confided, "I have many a time and oft thought to write you how heartily I appreciate your endeavors to not only awaken public sympathy and conscience *towards* the oppressed, but also to awaken the intelligence and manhood *of* the oppressed that they might not through the many years of suffering forget to oppose and agitate and 'lose the name of action'" (in the words of Hamlet's famous "To be or not to be" soliloquy [italics mine]).[2] Lucas went on to lead the struggle against the disfranchisement of African Americans in Arkansas, eventually moving to Chicago and achieving a distinguished career as a lawyer, during which he pleaded cases before the U.S. and Illinois Supreme Courts and obtained several landmark decisions.[3]

The exchange between Lucas and Tourgée typifies the extensive correspondence that the man nineteenth-century African Americans widely regarded as their most reliable white ally carried on with the people whose cause he advocated. This correspondence challenges us to rethink our assumptions about relations between white progressives and African Americans. The bulk of it dates from approximately 1889 to 1897, a period marked by extreme racial separatism, as well as by such atrocious repression of African Americans that the historian Rayford W. Logan branded it "the nadir"—worse even than the era of slavery.[4] Yet in defiance of both the racial codes that prohibited socializing across the color line and the white supremacist ideology that came to rule the nation, Tourgée maintained contacts, either by mail or in person, with more than a hundred African Americans from all walks of life: field hands, housewives, students, teachers, college professors, ministers, businessmen, journalists, newspaper editors, writers, artists, lawyers, officials, legislators, activists, race leaders. The majority, like Lucas, trusted him deeply, sought his opinions, valued his outspoken criticism almost as much as they did his passionate defense of their rights, and freely aired their disagreements with him whenever occasion arose. They also recognized that Tourgée had nothing to gain and much to lose by aligning himself with them long after the nation had consigned African Americans to neo-slavery in the South and second-class citizenship in the North—hence, that they could truly consider him a "friend" rather than a patron.

Undertaking a "Fundamental Thorough and Complete Revolution"

The record of dedication to fighting for racial equality that Tourgée had set by the time he wrote to Lucas in February 1891 shows why African Americans believed they could count on him to advocate their rights unstintingly.

Retracing that record from its starting point during the Civil War up to 1890, the year his correspondence with African Americans ballooned, furnishes insight into the interracial dynamics of the letters examined in the second half of the present chapter—letters that articulate the ethos shaping Tourgée's career, introduce some of his main correspondents, and illustrate the relationships he developed with them.

In explaining how he came to embrace the African American cause, Tourgée himself always credited his service in the Union army with transforming his consciousness by exposing him to African Americans as fellow soldiers and self-empowered agents. Although born in 1838 in Ohio's Western Reserve, a region burning with antislavery fervor, Tourgée did not question stereotypes of African Americans as inferior until he rubbed shoulders with the fugitive slaves who flocked to his regiment, the 105th Ohio Volunteer Infantry. The bravery, resourcefulness, and political awareness these men displayed projected an image of black manhood that Tourgée never forgot. His new respect for African Americans turned into identification when capture in an ambush and a four-month ordeal as a Confederate prisoner of war taught him the meaning of "bondage." "It is chagrin, humiliation—insult—fused in fierce flash of misery," he wrote to his wife-to-be, Emma Kilbourne. Tourgée emerged from the war committed to a "fundamental thorough and complete revolution & renovation" of American society—one that would sweep away all vestiges of slavery and its racist underpinnings.[5]

This commitment impelled Tourgée to devote the next fourteen years of his life to the enterprise known as Reconstruction: rebuilding the post–Civil War South on a foundation of freedom and equality rather than on slavery. With Emma and her extended family, he settled in Greensboro, North Carolina, in October 1865. Initially, he intended primarily to offer a model of how free labor and just relations between the races could benefit Southern society. Establishing a nursery business, he hired previously enslaved workers at good wages; helped them to buy land of their own; set up a school for them on his property, at which Emma and her family members taught; occasionally attended black churches; hosted African American guests at his table; and even adopted a formerly enslaved child. As if defying all the racial proscriptions of the white South did not suffice, events soon propelled Tourgée into direct involvement in politics.[6]

All over the South, emboldened by President Andrew Johnson's lenient terms for swift restoration of the pre–Civil War Union, the dispossessed slaveholders sought to nullify emancipation through draconian Black Codes that guaranteed them a captive labor force. In response, the U.S. Congress

FIGURE 1 Photo of Emma Kilbourne Tourgée and Albion W. Tourgée taken in 1865, the year they moved to North Carolina. Courtesy of the Chautauqua County Historical Society, Westfield, N.Y.

mandated that the ex-Confederate states hold conventions to rewrite their constitutions and allow African Americans to elect, and to be elected as, delegates to those conventions. Meanwhile, African Americans were enlisting in organizations called Union Leagues and demanding land, education, political rights, and protection against de facto reenslavement.[7]

Tourgée stepped into the thick of the brewing conflict between the South's awakened black masses and intransigent white ruling class when he joined an interracial chapter of the Union League in 1867. North Carolina African Americans were then registering to vote for the first time. Forging an effective coalition that united African Americans with poor whites, Quakers, and upper-class converts to radical Republicanism, he won election as a delegate to the 1868 constitutional convention. At age twenty-nine, Tourgée distinguished himself as both the youngest and the most influential member of the body, playing such a key role in drafting the new democratized constitution that nearly every article bore his imprint. Tourgée went on to win election as a superior court judge, serving from 1868 until his defeat in 1874 by resurgent white supremacists. Determined to uphold equal rights in the courtroom despite constant vilification by the white supremacist press, he practiced "color blind" justice, included African Americans on juries, fined lawyers for using the epithet "nigger," and set aside guilty verdicts based on flimsy evidence.[8]

Tourgée's judicial term coincided with the tidal wave of Ku Klux Klan terrorism that overwhelmed the South and ultimately destroyed Reconstruction.[9] Besides administering countless beatings, shootings, rapes, and home attacks, in 1870 the Klan savagely murdered two of Tourgée's close associates: Wyatt Outlaw, an African American town commissioner and president of an interracial Union League chapter; and John W. Stephens, a white state senator, magistrate, and trusted ally of the black population. Disregarding plots against his own life, Tourgée doggedly collected evidence against the perpetrators, confronted hostile juries made up of Klan members who refused to indict or convict their coconspirators, lobbied for passage of the federal Ku Klux Klan Act (1871), and fed names of witnesses to subpoena to the congressional committee investigating the Klan.

The nation lacked the stomach, however, to prevent the Klan and its elite white supremacist patrons from derailing Reconstruction. By 1877, Northern public opinion had shifted decisively in favor of letting white Southerners run their internal affairs without federal interference.[10] The shift resulted in a disputed election decided by a backroom deal that awarded the presidency to Republican Rutherford B. Hayes in exchange for his agreement to end Reconstruction.

With white supremacists again in power throughout the South and the Republican Party in flight from all the principles it had proclaimed since embracing emancipation, Tourgée found himself "dead politically,"[11] yet he could not abandon African Americans. His turbulent years in North Carolina had marked him too profoundly. He had observed the ruthlessness of the white Southern ruling class firsthand. He had seen his colleague Wyatt Outlaw's body twisting in the wind a few steps from the courthouse. He had taken testimony from hundreds of Klan victims who described the outrages to which they and their children had been subjected and showed him their lacerated flesh. He had marveled at the rapid progress the newly freed slaves had made in prospering as farmers and artisans, forming self-sufficient communities, erecting their own churches and schoolhouses, and acquiring education. He had worked with black activists in the Union League, participated in Republican meetings at which black orators had spoken, strategized with black community leaders in election campaigns, interacted with black delegates at the 1868 constitutional convention, and shared guard duty with black volunteers massing against anticipated Klan raids. In the process, he had developed enormous admiration for a people he had come to feel "almost like calling . . . [*his*] people."[12] He knew the country owed an immeasurable debt to black soldiers for saving the Union and would benefit greatly from the integration of African Americans as equal citizens.

A Fool's Errand and *Bricks Without Straw*

Blocked from championing African Americans in the political or judicial sphere, Tourgée turned to literature as a medium for mobilizing the public to demand that the nation fulfill its obligation to the emancipated slaves it had left at the mercy of their vengeful former masters. In November 1879, a few months after quitting the South forever, Tourgée published *A Fool's Errand. By One of the Fools*, an anonymous novel based on his experiences as a Radical Republican in Reconstruction-era North Carolina. Its graphic exposé of the Klan terrorism he had witnessed, culminating in thinly fic-tionalized accounts of Outlaw's and Stephens's grisly murders, caused a sensation. Acclaimed as the *Uncle Tom's Cabin* of Reconstruction, *A Fool's Errand* sold almost 150,000 copies within a year, a figure putting it in a league with Stowe's best seller.[13] Moreover, it quickly attracted the attention of Republican Party members disenchanted by the failure of President Hayes's conciliatory policy to stem violence in the South—chief among them pres-idential candidate James A. Garfield, a boyhood friend of Tourgée's. During the run-up to the 1880 election, speakers quoted the novel on the stump, and the Republican Campaign Committee reprinted and circulated "whole sections of the book . . . as campaign documents."[14]

Before hitting the campaign trail himself, Tourgée finished a comple-mentary novel that he had actually begun earlier than *A Fool's Errand* but had laid aside in frustration.[15] *Bricks Without Straw*, published under his own name and identifying him as "Late Judge of the Superior Court of North Carolina" and "Author of 'A Fool's Errand,'" appeared in October 1880 and at first sold even faster than its predecessor, though it peaked at 50,000 copies. By presenting Reconstruction through the eyes of the South's black masses as they struggled to define the meaning of freedom for themselves and to determine their own future, *Bricks Without Straw* broke new historical and literary ground. The historical insights it displayed anticipated those of *Black Reconstruction in America* (1935), the African American scholar W. E. B. Du Bois's monumental revisionist study of a period hitherto inter-preted as a conflict between Northern and Southern whites. The literary achievement of *Bricks Without Straw* lay in centering a novel on realistically portrayed African American characters, conceived not as menials attached to whites but as autonomous agents rooted in a community of their peers. No white writer had yet attempted such a feat, and not until Howard Fast's *Freedom Road* (1944), also about Black Reconstruction, would any match it. Indeed, only a handful of African Americans—William Wells Brown, Frank J. Webb, Martin Delany, and Frances E. W. Harper—had so far published novels similarly focused on the collective liberation struggle of the African American community: *Clotel* (1853), *The Garies and Their Friends* (1857), *Blake; or, The Huts of America* (1859, 1861–62), and *Minnie's Sacrifice* (1869).[16] Small wonder, then, that Tourgée's twin best sellers gained an appreciative African American readership whose ranks encompassed a number of his future correspondents.

On the national level, *A Fool's Errand* and *Bricks Without Straw* reawakened sympathy for the black subalterns whom white Northerners had gone to war to liberate. The two novels also countered the white supremacist propaganda that had discredited Reconstruction as an orgy of misrule by ignorant ex-slaves, greedy "carpetbaggers," and villainous "scalawags." Instead, they unmasked the brutality of the white gentlemen who claimed to be the Negro's "best friends" but resorted to lynching, murder, rape, mutilation, and arson to crush a people's aspirations for freedom and enforce abject submission. At the same time, both novels held out the hope that the nation could still salvage the goals of the Reconstruction program it had bungled so calamitously. A massive federal education project, Tourgée argued, could reconstruct the South by alternative means, eradicating racism along with ignorance, spreading enlightenment along with literacy, and teaching good citizenship to whites and blacks alike.

A Fool's Errand and *Bricks Without Straw* helped decide the hotly contested 1880 election and exerted an impact on Republican policy as well as on public opinion—an accomplishment not even *Uncle Tom's Cabin* could boast. Garfield credited Tourgée's novels with securing his narrow victory, and his inaugural address reprised several of their major themes. The new president hailed the "elevation of the negro race from slavery to the full rights of citizenship" as a major advance and reminded those who "resisted the change" that "under our institutions there was no middle ground for the negro race between slavery and equal citizenship," no place for a "permanent disfranchised peasantry in the United States." Praising the "remarkable progress" the "emancipated race" had already made, he pledged to ensure, within the limits of his authority, that "they shall enjoy the full and equal protection of the Constitution and the laws." Most significantly, Garfield echoed Tourgée's call for a nationally funded public education system to wipe out illiteracy in the South and thus combat "the danger which arises from ignorance in the voter."[17]

Sadly, we will never know to what extent Garfield might have implemented the advice Tourgée continued to proffer in detailed letters and face-to-face meetings over the next few months, because an assassin's bullet felled him in July 1880, barely four months after his inauguration and fifteen years after Lincoln met the same fate.[18] The tragedy ended both Tourgée's fleeting access to political power and the revival of the Republican Party's progressive wing. Garfield's successor, Chester A. Arthur, a member of the party's conservative faction, quickly indicated his intention to lay Southern affairs to rest, as did the Republicans' 1884 presidential candidate, James G. Blaine.

Convinced that neither the party nor the nation could afford to leave the racial conflict in the South unresolved and that education provided the only viable long-term solution, Tourgée expanded the plan he had presented to Garfield into a full-length book, *An Appeal to Caesar* (1884), which the historian George M. Fredrickson has called "the most profound discussion of the American racial situation to appear in the 1880s."[19] In it Tourgée proposed that Congress set up an annual fund to be applied to teachers' salaries and distributed directly to Southern schools; he further proposed tying the amounts disbursed to the number of illiterates and the school's record of good management, as certified by regular inspection, and conditioning grants on the willingness of the state, county, municipality, or private donors to match the federal appropriation. Such a method of financing education in the South, Tourgée contended, would eliminate fraud and waste, circumvent state governments' tendency to steer funds toward white rather than black schools, encourage local initiative, and avoid charges of imposing federal control. As with *A Fool's Errand* and *Bricks Without Straw*, Tourgée timed *An Appeal to Caesar* to sway the American people (the Caesar of the title) as they went to the polls. The book garnered a large crop of reviews and "prompted speeches and debates," according to Tourgée's biographer Otto H. Olsen, but lacking the drama of his novels, its carefully elaborated argument, bolstered with statistics, failed to move an electorate weary of the race problem. For the first time since the Civil War, a Democrat, Grover Cleveland, won the presidency, and the country continued its headlong retreat from the ideals of Reconstruction.[20]

As white voters and politicians lost interest in the plight of the emancipated blacks, readers lost interest in Tourgée's writings. Sales declined markedly for *A Fool's Errand* and all but ceased for *Bricks Without Straw*. The waning of Tourgée's literary popularity occurred at the very moment when he most needed the income from his books. Having invested his entire savings in an overambitious literary magazine, *Our Continent*, which he edited from 1882 to 1884, and having borrowed heavily to keep it afloat, he plunged into bankruptcy when it collapsed. The crash swept away "his fortune, his ambition, his hopes—everything but his wife," recalled Emma ruefully. It also precipitated a mental and physical breakdown from which Tourgée took months to recover and saddled him with debts totaling more than $100,000, which he would struggle for the rest of his life to pay off.[21] Meanwhile, the audiences that had once gobbled up his novels and flocked to his lectures had melted away.

"I have simply outlived my time—the world has forgotten my thought and almost my existence," lamented Tourgée in one of many letters to Emma bemoaning the sparse attendance at his lectures, which often yielded too little to cover his expenses.[22] "I am a man that *was*," he concluded grimly.[23] Newspaper accounts bear out Tourgée's complaints about the poor turn-out at his lectures, though they also note that his "easy, fluent, conversational style," enlivened by humor and drama, held hearers "with a charmed power."[24] Tourgée's publishers likewise confirmed that "his *great* popularity is a thing of the past" and "there is no sale for his books now."[25] The firm that had enjoyed such spectacular profits from *A Fool's Errand* reported "very little demand for '[An Appeal to] Caesar,'" and when Tourgée floated an article on the "Negro Question" to the McClure syndicate in March 1888, the director replied that he would shop it around to periodicals but could not judge whether any market existed for the subject.[26] Nothing could better indicate how inextricably Tourgée's fate was linked with that of African Americans.

Starting a New Dialogue on the Race Problem

Just as Tourgée's reputation and white Northern sympathy for African Americans seemed to reach their lowest ebb, however, the tide turned. Perhaps prompted by the hope that the literary talents Tourgée had put to such good use in the campaign of 1880 could help Republicans recapture the White House in 1888, the *Chicago Daily Inter Ocean*, a liberal Republican newspaper with a circulation of 200,000 subscribers,[27] contracted with him for a weekly column titled "A Bystander's Notes," starting in April. Tourgée had already contributed several well-regarded anonymous and pseudonymous series to the *Inter Ocean*,[28] but his "Bystander" column would far eclipse them. Published over his own name, it would quickly win him a mass readership among African Americans as well as among whites. Many African Americans subscribed to the *Inter Ocean* for the sake of the "Bystander" column alone, and major African American newspapers frequently reprinted it—among them the *Cleveland Gazette*, the *Detroit Plaindealer*, the *New Orleans Crusader*, the *Chicago Conservator*, the *New York Age*, the *Washington Bee*, and the *Indianapolis World*.[29]

Tourgée initially oriented the "Bystander" column toward the needs of the electoral campaign, for example by demonstrating statistically how much the "violence, intimidation, and fraud" used to suppress the black vote in the South diminished Republican totals nationwide.[30] Once Republican Benjamin Harrison had secured the presidency (albeit with so little Southern support that he lost the popular vote), the "Bystander" began agitating for laws to ensure fair elections throughout the country, guarantee "equal and exact justice" for all citizens, and punish mob violence against African Americans.[31] Tourgée now found the Northern white public awakening from its apathy, spurred partly by "an upsurge in lynchings" aimed at terrorizing black Southern voters and agricultural workers and partly by Southern spokesmen's calls for laws instituting segregation and disfranchising African Americans, in effect nullifying the Fourteenth and Fifteenth Amendments.[32] Only a year after McClure had cast doubt on the possibility of marketing an article on the "Negro Question," three important periodicals—the *Forum*, *Frank Leslie's Illustrated Newspaper*, and, most surprising of all, the *New York Tribune*, which had been leading the Republican defection from the cause of racial justice—solicited Tourgée's views on this very topic.[33] He obliged with the articles "Shall White Minorities Rule?" (*Forum*, April 1889), "Our Semi-Citizens" (*Frank Leslie's*, 28 September 1889), and "The American Negro: What Are His Rights and What Must Be Done to Secure Them?" (*Tribune*, 16 February 1890), all of which commanded a wide audience and expressed the ethos African Americans had recognized in Tourgée's novels about Reconstruction. By late 1889 Tourgée could write happily to Emma from the lecture circuit, "Big house last night—the Race Problem—as usual."[34]

The aspect of the race problem on which Tourgée concentrated in these three influential articles, as their titles announce, was African Americans' debasement to the status of "semi-citizens" since the overthrow of Reconstruction—a debasement that their disfranchisement threatened to consummate. Although the demand for disfranchisement had originated in the South, its chief rationale—the allegation that ignorant voters cor-rupted the political system—also appealed to elite Northerners, some of whom favored literacy tests and poll taxes as means of purging the "unfit" from electoral rolls nationwide.[35] Hence, Tourgée devoted special attention to countering the argument that white elites deserved to govern ignorant black masses. To question majority rule was to subvert "the fundamental principle of our government," he pointed out. Moreover, the issue was "not whether the colored man shall be allowed a new privilege, but whether he shall be permitted to exercise a right already guaranteed by law"—the right to vote conferred in the Fifteenth Amendment of 1870. Nor did the pretext of the black voter's ignorance hold water. Despite the handicap of public schools' being open only a hundred days a year, illiteracy among Southern blacks had been "rapidly decreasing" in comparison to illiteracy among the region's poor whites. What most clearly betrayed the hypocrisy of citing ignorance as the ground for disfranchising blacks, Tourgée emphasized, was that white Southerners regarded the "educated negro . . . as far more obnoxious, in a political sense, than the ignorant one," and that "those who object[ed] to the negro as a political factor" likewise objected to "the white man . . . chosen by [black] votes." Tourgée also exorcised the bugbear of "negro domination" that white Southerners perpetually conjured up in their distorted accounts of Reconstruction. "The negro has never asked for domination or control," he insisted, but only for "a voice in the gov-ernment." While discounting the supposed evils of black suffrage, Tourgée warned against the dire consequences of unremitting oppression. African Americans would not submit indefinitely to being "kept in a subordinate position and despoiled of their guaranteed rights . . . through the instru-mentality of the shot-gun, the cow-hide, the falsified return, or perjured election officials," he predicted. The American people could not afford to leave the race problem unresolved, he concluded, because there would never be "any security for our institutions or any guarantee of domestic peace" until the nation adopted the sole reliable remedies: "justice and knowledge."[36]

Tourgée's articles on the race question generated passionate responses pro and con. He himself considered "Shall White Minorities Rule?" a par-ticular "hit," based on the praise he was receiving from readers for the "strik-ing" and "original" perspective it offered. "It is the best presentation of the subject yet made," affirmed a correspondent from Missouri. Tourgée's "hint" that "a box of matches" might suffice to overthrow white supremacy was making the chivalry's "hair rise and [their] flesh creep," gleefully confided a Reconstruction-era ally from North Carolina.[37] An editorial by "an old enemy" in a Wilmington, North Carolina, newspaper accused Tourgée of "hound[ing] the Southern whites," wanting "to turn loose the dogs of war upon them," and inciting blacks to revolt if they were not allowed to "control wherever they [were] numerically in the ascendant." Tourgée's article was "vigorous, even eloquent in a certain way," conceded the Wilmington editor, but it exposed him as a racial renegade who had either blackened himself by association or betrayed his tainted ancestry: "No white man of self-respect and of genuine Aryan stock could have written his malignant and plausible plea for negro supremacy in the South."[38]

African Americans apparently did not begin responding to Tourgée's articles on the race question until late 1889, but when they did, their communications showed that they had been paying them close attention. "I read with much interest your stirring weekly letters in the Inter-Ocean," wrote Charles W. Chesnutt, who had recently made his debut on the literary scene with the story "The Goophered Grapevine" (*Atlantic Monthly,* August 1887).[39] African Americans "over the whole length & breadth" of the nation were "looking to [Tourgée] as their noblest, grandest & most powerful champion," wrote the secretary of the newly formed Wisconsin Civil Rights League.[40] The most dramatic attestation of African Americans' faith in Tourgée came from Robert Pelham Jr., manager of the *Detroit Plaindealer,* which had just reprinted "Our Semi-Citizens."[41] Treating him almost as an honorary member of the race, Pelham invited Tourgée to comment on an exchange of correspondence the paper had published regarding the timeliness of founding an organization for "race unity, protection, and the . . . promotion of all interests pertaining to the dignity and welfare of our people" (the soon-to-be-launched National Afro-American League).[42] Pelham even highlighted Tourgée's reply under the headline "The Time Has Come for the Race to Show Itself Worthy of Liberty."[43]

A quintessential expression of Tourgée's ethos, his letter to the *Plaindealer* exemplifies the tone he habitually struck in his interactions with African Americans during the 1890s—militant yet patronizing (to a twenty-first-century ear), respectful yet hectoring. It also illustrates the stance he adopted as an insider-outsider who could negotiate between the black and white worlds, interpreting each to the other. While recognizing that to counsel African Americans on a matter they were "capable of deciding wisely for themselves" would be "manifestly improper," Tourgée enthusiastically endorsed the proposed organization as "the first step the race has attempted *of its own motion* towards self-assertive freedom—the only freedom that can ever be relied on to give good results." Establishing a foothold in the South would surely breed martyrs, he predicted, but the "colored race" had arrived at a point where it needed a "martyrology . . . of those suffering in the endeavor *to achieve* liberty, to counterbalance the rather over crowded one which testifies to their long-suffering endurance of oppression." (Tourgée seems to have forgotten his colleague Wyatt Outlaw and the countless other African Americans who had died fighting for their rights during Reconstruction—the heroes he had memorialized so powerfully in *A Fool's Errand* and *Bricks Without Straw*. Perhaps he could not bear to realize that the federal government and white Northern public, whose abandonment had made the martyrdom of Reconstruction's many Wyatt Outlaws unavailing, showed fewer signs than ever of suppressing white supremacist violence or of supporting an African American resistance movement in the 1890s.) Tourgée nonetheless discerned an important new development when he posited that the white leadership of the past must now give way to African American leadership: "There is no doubt in my mind that the colored man must take the laboring oar in the movement for his real enfranchisement." Such a movement must contend with enormous obstacles and might well fail to accomplish "tangible good," he acknowledged, "but *any sort* of effort under present conditions is better than *no* effort." As their first priority, Tourgée urged the organization's founders to procure testimony from Southern blacks—without endangering them—about the day-to-day oppression they faced, so as to enlighten "the intelligent thinking people of the North." He ended by underscoring that it was "high time the Negro race in America did something—*as a race*—" to show their white compatriots they were determined to "exercise the privileges granted them" and to "preserve for their children the liberties so many shed their blood to secure."[44]

Tourgée versus African Americans

As Tourgée was cheering African Americans on in their renewed struggle for racial justice, he was working with congressmen and senators to draft a bill providing for federal aid to education in the South and an election law that would protect voters against intimidation. Simultaneously, he was pushing white reformers to engage in a dialogue on the race question that included African Americans as partners rather than objects of white benevolence. In these endeavors he carried on a lively dialogue of his own with African Americans, one that reveals a different manifestation of Tourgée's ethos in his stubborn refusal to heed African Americans who cautioned against his stand.

The opportunity for Tourgée to shape legislation on his two cherished measures arose in September 1889, when he received a fan letter from a newly elected House of Representatives member, Harrison Kelly of Kansas, who applauded his "fearless" advocacy of "equal rights and equal protection to citizens" and offered to help advance these goals.[45] Tourgée immediately suggested introducing "an educational measure on the plan proposed in 'An Appeal to Caesar'" and a law giving the federal government and U.S. courts the power to "take charge of national elections," in accordance with the Fourteenth Amendment. Kelly did so, letting Tourgée frame both bills.[46]

Initially it looked as though Tourgée might succeed in getting his legislation through Congress in the form he favored. House Speaker Thomas B. Reed gave Kelly's bills strong backing, President Benjamin Harrison expressed his support, and Tourgée was invited to testify before congressional committees on education and electoral reform.[47] Nevertheless, both bills fell prey to compromises in the Senate that seriously weakened them.

Senator Henry Blair of New Hampshire had been sponsoring a federal aid to education bill since 1881 that differed from Tourgée's in granting funds to state governments to distribute—a course that would have left them free to route the lion's share toward white schools—whereas Tourgée's plan called for bypassing state governments and allocating federal funds directly to schools on the basis of illiteracy rates, which would have ensured that black and white schools each received amounts proportionate to the number of illiterate pupils enrolled. (Neither Tourgée's nor Blair's bill challenged segregation, but Tourgée's mitigated its effects by dividing resources equitably between the races.) The Blair bill had won passage in the Republican-controlled Senate three times, but Democrats had so far defeated it in the House. Now that Republicans enjoyed a majority in both houses, it stood a good chance of passing. To the dismay of African Americans, however, Tourgée opposed the Blair bill so bitterly that he not only devoted three "Bystander" columns to itemizing its flaws but actually lobbied against it in person. As formulated, the Blair bill reinforced the doctrine of states' rights, risked the "waste" or mismanagement of funds by corrupt state officials, and "would make the colored man of the South wholly dependent for opportunity and hope upon the [region's] usurping 'white-line' Democrats," Tourgée asserted in a "Bystander" article of 23 November 1889. Responding to "scores of inquiries, especially from leading colored men," he reprinted a copy of his own bill in his "Bystander" column of 7 December. Just before the final vote on the bill, Tourgée "enjoin[ed]" readers "to earnestly support the *purpose* and with equal earnestness denounce and abjure the *methods* of the Blair bill," averring that "the Nation should never attempt to do justice" rather than "attempt it in a way certain to result in a fresh and glaring injustice to the colored race."[48]

Unlike Tourgée, however, most African Americans realistically judged half a loaf to be better than none. "We understand the evils pointed out by one of the best friends our race has ever known," editorialized William H. Anderson in the *Detroit Plaindealer*, "yet with all its defects we are for the Blair bill still." He spelled out why: "In many districts the school houses are so badly fitted, the teachers so poorly equipped and the time so short, that no benefit arises from their work. In more than one place all the 'colored schools have been entirely suspended for the want of funds.' ... The Blair bill cannot fail to rectify some of these evils if not all."[49]

Alex G. Davis, head of the Afro-American News Bureau, agreed with Anderson's assessment and could hardly contain his astonishment over Tourgée's opposition to the Blair bill, which almost made him wonder whether "his friendship for the race is growing less."[50] Joseph C. Price, president of the recently formed National Afro-American League, pointed out that African American children would gain from having their school term doubled even if whites controlled and "misappropriated" the federal funds. A still more compelling reason for endorsing the Blair bill, Price underscored, was "the absence of any thing tangible to take its place."[51] This consideration led African American radicals who shared Tourgée's misgivings or objected (as he did not) to sanctioning segregated schools to rally behind the bill in the end.

Tourgée turned a deaf ear to all the reasons African Americans urged for supporting a bill they recognized as seriously flawed. He even impugned their motives.[52] Behind the scenes, Tourgée collared every lawmaker who would listen to push for voting down the bill. Because "schools for the two races are everywhere separate" in the South, he argued, and because whites outnumbered blacks in most states, at best "the *colored* schools of the South would have received one-third and the *white* schools two-thirds of the fund, though the colored schools represent *two-thirds* of the illiteracy." Moreover, the Blair bill gave "the whites of the South control of even that modicum of the national gratuity" allotted to the education of "colored" pupils.[53] Tourgée's lobbying convinced at least five Republican senators to reject the Blair bill, which failed by six votes as he and Emma watched triumphantly from the Senate gallery.[54] But far from paving the way for the alternative measure he preferred, defeat of the Blair bill killed the prospect of federal aid to education for decades to come. Thus, Tourgée ironically helped block the very solution to the race problem that he had been advocating since the Reconstruction era.

In the months that followed, he continued unrepentantly to justify his stand. Addressing an audience of white reformers who had all backed the Blair bill, Tourgée avowed: "*I* do not hesitate, in the name and on behalf of the colored people of the United States, to express here the most profound gratitude that this measure failed to become a law. Why? Because it was the most amazing piece of injustice which ever resulted from unwise methods linked to kindly purposes."[55] Contrary to his brash allegation, however, African Americans universally lamented the Blair bill's rejection as a major setback and tried for years to resuscitate some version of it.[56]

Tourgée would never admit that he had failed African Americans by refusing to accept their leadership on a matter so crucial to them (though the more self-effacing role he later adopted in the campaign against lynching may indicate that he learned better). Nor would he ever admit that he had disastrously miscalculated by contributing to the defeat of the only federal education bill that could have obtained congressional approval in his lifetime. Nonetheless, he did not repeat the error with the election bill. Originally he had recommended separating national and state elections, putting the former under federal control and leaving the states in charge of the latter—a strategy intended to increase Republican representation in Congress by preventing violence and fraud in national elections and at the same time to circumvent Southern resistance by not overtly threatening local white supremacy. Instead, Senate Republicans opted for holding national and state elections simultaneously, as usual, but having federal supervisors oversee elections and count ballots wherever the electorate petitioned Congress for such intervention, an approach that had already been tried unsuccessfully in 1871.[57] A "Supervisor's Law . . . cannot be *enforced at the South*," Tourgée warned its sponsor, Henry Cabot Lodge. "I have never been accused of any lack of courage," he pursued, "but I frankly admit that I *would not*" volunteer to supervise a Southern election "unless I desired to find an honorable end for an ill-spent life."[58] After fruitless efforts to amend the Lodge bill by working privately through his Senate allies, Tourgée went public and used his "Bystander" column to hammer away at the defects of a "Supervisor's Law," first in his own voice and then by quoting the criticisms his African American correspondents had made of it. Black Southerners "*will be expected to furnish the corpses to prove its inefficiency*," one had complained. Any Southern Republican, black or white, who signed a petition for federal oversight, let alone acted as a supervisor, would be branded "an enemy to the South . . . and so treated," Tourgée elaborated. A white man would be subjected "[a]t the very least" to a "social and business boycott" and might find himself "set upon by unknown parties and killed" or beaten to a pulp. To grasp the fate a black man would risk, a reader must "multiply the danger" and the viciousness of the reprisal "by ten."[59]

Yet ultimately, having perhaps realized the futility of uncompromising adherence to principle, Tourgée reluctantly "endorsed the Lodge bill as better than nothing." His capitulation to political pragmatism in this case proved as unavailing as had his quixotic campaign against the Blair bill. Faced with a Democratic filibuster that not only whipped up public hysteria about restoring the alleged "Negro rule" of Reconstruction but also prevented the Senate from considering any other legislation, Republicans finally jettisoned the Lodge bill in January 1891 and devoted themselves to fulfilling their economic agenda. Excoriating the eight Republican senators whose votes sealed the doom of a federal election law, Tourgée editorialized in his "Bystander" column, "In one day these representatives of the Republican party have sold into bondage, oppression, and hopelessness more men and women than *all the slave-catchers and slave-dealers of the earth ever offered for sale in a quarter of a century!*"[60]

Presenting "The Negro's View of the Race Problem"

Amid the sparring over the Lodge bill, Tourgée received an invitation to attend a prestigious conference of white reformers called to discuss the "Negro Question"—an invitation that gave him an opportunity to display his ethos at its best. Hosted by the Quaker Albert K. Smiley in June 1890 on the shores of Lake Mohonk in upstate New York, where he had long held annual colloquies on the Indian Question, and chaired by former U.S. president Rutherford B. Hayes, the assembly gathered together the luminaries of the Social Gospel movement, the North's leading "editors, educators, and pastors," and a few liberal Southerners but deliberately excluded African Americans themselves. The Mohonk Conference on the Negro Question, like the abortive education and election bills, revealed at once the white Northern public's revived desire to tackle the race problem and the stark limitations of that desire. The anomaly of seeking to address the "Negro Question" without consulting those who lived it did not escape all of the invitees. Tourgée and three other radicals—George Washington Cable of New Orleans, whose articles in defense of African American rights had alienated his fellow white Southerners and forced him into exile; William

Hayes Ward, editor of the abolitionist-founded Congregationalist weekly, the *Independent*; and Joseph Cook, editor of the influential reform journal *Our Day* and a popular Social Gospel minister—vainly urged the conference organizers to include at least some prominent African American participants. The rationale that the Reverend Lyman Abbott, one of the main organizers, gave for refusing typified the condescension with which most white reformers of the time regarded African Americans: "A patient is not invited to the consultation of the doctors on his case."[61] The disease that racked American society with recurrent eruptions of violence, these reformers believed, emanated from the black body, not the white mind, and only white experts knew how to cure it.

African American editors, who were following the controversy through the white press, exposed the fallaciousness of their would-be benefactors' analogy, as well as the hypocrisy and arrogance of their stance. "While the doctors do not call the patient to the consultation he is always questioned concerning his complaint bearing on the symptoms, and his answers control the diagnosis," noted Anderson of the *Detroit Plaindealer*.[62] T. Thomas Fortune of the *New York Age* went further. "The assumption that the entire Afro-American race is a patient, whose desperate case must be diagnosed behind closed doors, so to speak, is refuted" by thousands of black doctors more competent than their white colleagues to wield a "scalpel" on the "anatomy" of the race problem, he retorted. The real reason behind the exclusion of African Americans from the Mohonk Conference, he emphasized, was "fear of offending the white participants from the South."[63]

Aware that Cable and Cook planned to boycott the "Negro" conference (a word he put into quotation marks both to highlight its inapplicability to an all-white event and to indicate his preference for the term Afro-American), Anderson asked whether Tourgée meant to attend it.[64] Yes, Tourgée answered, "not with any expectation of doing any good or getting any, but simply for the fun" of seeing emergent New South spokesmen and "know-all-about young Northern pacificators . . . beslaver each other with mutual admiration." As for him, he would "say nothing: do nothing except absorb whatever absurdity there may be in the air."[65] Anderson made clear, however, that he wanted Tourgée to defend African Americans' interests at what he sarcastically called "Podunk." "*Don't be silent* at Podunk if views contrary to justice are likely to prevail," he exhorted Tourgée.[66]

As Anderson hoped, Tourgée did in fact "disrupt the complacent consensus" of the Mohonk gathering. First, he intervened in a session on "industrial education" to criticize the participants for focusing on Southern blacks' "deficiencies" and overlooking their "achievements." Having employed "hundreds" of previously enslaved blacks as both "agricultural and mechanical laborer[s]" during his years in North Carolina and having closely followed their subsequent progress, Tourgée asserted, "I do not hesitate to say that *the colored people of the South have accomplished more in twenty-five years, from an industrial point of view, than any people on the face of the earth ever before achieved under anything like such unfavorable conditions.*" For example, Tourgée specified, "five times" as many blacks as "'poor whites'" had become self-employed homeowners.[67] Next, he joined another radical participant in condemning the pervasive racial discrimination that barred African Americans from all but the most menial jobs throughout the North. "We do not give the colored man a white man's chance industrially and commercially," and "when he goes into a respectable white church," he is relegated to corners "as far out of sight and hearing as he can be stowed," charged Tourgée. Even the editorial practices of Northern journals reinforced prejudice, he commented in another session. Transmitting a grievance frequently articulated in the black press, he complained that only one "high-grade" white publication—a Catholic literary magazine—deigned to spell "'Negro' . . . with a capital 'N.'" Finally, on the last morning, Tourgée delivered a rousing thirteen-page address foregrounding the missing element of the conference: "The Negro's View of the Race Problem." Appropriately, a terrific storm burst overhead as he spoke, and flashes of lightning and peals of thunder "dramatically punctuated" his remarks.[68]

"The testimony of the Negro in regard to his past and present conditions and aspirations for the future is worth more than that of all the white observers that can be packed upon the planet," Tourgée insisted. "The man who wears the shoe knows better than anybody else just where it pinches." Tourgée clarified that he did not presume to speak for African Americans, nor did he claim always to understand them. "I am not certain that anyone can who has not suffered with [them]," he acknowledged. Because he recognized the difficulty of bridging the experiential gap between the privileged white philanthropist and the victim of slavery and racism, Tourgée continued, "I have never been so sure as many of our friends what was the very best thing *to be done for* the colored man; but I have never doubted that the most exact justice and the fullest recognition of his equality of right must be the prime elements of any successful policy which has for its purpose the elevation of the race and the development of his individual manhood. Wrong is never cured by fresh injustice, and manhood is never ennobled by being compelled to wear the brand of inferiority." Tourgée then shifted the onus from African Americans, whose defects had preoccupied conference participants for the past three days, to whites. "So far as the peaceful and Christian solution of the race problem is concerned, indeed," he proclaimed, "I am inclined to think that the only education required is that of the *white* race. The hate, the oppression, the injustice, are all on our side." He ended with a series of "resolutions" he thought the conference should endorse instead of those officially adopted. The one that best encapsulated the thrust of his address affirmed that the nation owed its wealth, prosperity, and industrial might to African Americans' 250 years of uncompensated labor—a debt it could discharge only by enabling them to exercise their rights and to enjoy equal opportunities.[69]

Tourgée's speech, Emma recorded in her diary, "was the sensation of the Conference. He covered himself with honor." Corroborating her judgment, former president Hayes praised the address in his own private journal as "pungent, dramatic, original, and daring." Yet so little did it influence the reformers convened at Mohonk that they persisted in excluding African Americans from their second and last "Conference on the Negro Question," which Tourgée boycotted. African Americans applauded Tourgée's performance at Mohonk. The *Plaindealer* published a conference précis in which both his speech and his comments at other sessions received detailed coverage. It also reprinted his "Bystander" column on the conference, as did the *Cleveland Gazette*. Overlapping with his speech, Tourgée's retrospective in the "Bystander" broadcast his critique of white reformers' paternalism and his call for racial justice to a much larger audience.[70]

Thus, by mid-1890 Tourgée was enjoying constant visibility in the black press. With black newspapers disseminating his "Bystander" column and articles on the race question to their subscribers, publicizing his positions on federal aid to education and protection of voters, and celebrating his eloquent championship of African Americans on such occasions as the Mohonk Conference, Tourgée's African American correspondents multiplied exponentially. They began writing to him at that juncture not only because he had emerged as the race's most ardent defender against the white supremacist juggernaut, having proved his dedication over a career that stretched back a quarter of a century, but because they sensed in his writings the ethos of a man they could approach on familiar terms.

Tourgée's Responses to Typical African American Correspondents

Who were Tourgée's African American correspondents, what did they want from him, and how did he relate to them? Many were obscure individuals seeking advice, financial or career assistance, or protection for their communities. Despite a dauntingly busy schedule interrupted by frequent bouts of illness, Tourgée generally replied, typically drafting letters by hand and relying on Emma to type final copies. Thanks to her meticulous filing, a remarkable number of his drafts survive, providing a fascinating window on his interactions with African Americans. Tourgée treated his black correspondents with the same brutal frankness he displayed when addressing his white audience at Mohonk. The letter to J. Gray Lucas with which I opened this chapter is only one of countless examples. A sampling of others will serve to convey the combination of uncompromising honesty and personal generosity that led so many African Americans to consider him their friend as well as their advocate, even when he wounded their feelings.

The first of these sample letters answers a nameless woman who had solicited Tourgée's "candid opinion" of her manuscript, apparently a novel about slavery. Knowing how much his reply would disappoint his correspondent, he revealed that he had "examined many hundred manuscripts at the request of inexperienced writers"—hence, she was not alone in receiving an unfavorable verdict from him. "It is sometimes hard to realize the fact but the real friend of a writer is not the one who praises but the one who warns," Tourgée stressed. He proceeded to caution her that publishers would not find the manuscript acceptable "in any form." In his sole reference to her African American identity, Tourgée expressed surprise that so soon after the demise of slavery, "a descendant of the race" should find it "so difficult to portray" the relations between master and slave realistically, especially from the slave's point of view. "Your ideas do not lack smartness," Tourgée consoled the writer, but "your characters are not like any men and women I have ever known." He advised her to burn her manuscript, "practice portraying known characters and every day conversations with the least possible explanation and description," and "let such brief sketches, after some years, grow into larger work by almost imperceptible degrees." Despite having taken the trouble to read and critique a novel he clearly found wooden, as well as to offer four pages of constructive suggestions on how the writer might perfect her craft, Tourgée exhibited a disconcerting lack of empathy for a novice's fragile ego. No aspiring novelist could have helped being devastated by such a harsh judgment of her work.[71]

Like this frustrated novelist, a young man from Indianapolis who requested a loan to pay for his last year of college must have hoped for a more encouraging response. Though Tourgée's "very straightened [*sic*] circumstances" forced him to refuse the loan, he gave the young man the benefit of his own experience. "I know the task [of financing one's education] is not an easy one for I worked my own way through college mainly with my hands," Tourgée confided. Still, he counseled the young man to "earn . . . rather than borrow" the sum required, in order to "start on life free of debt." Avoiding debt was all the more important, Tourgée went on, because the student could not expect immediate employment at a black college after graduation: "You will find the competition much sharper than you seem to think." Again holding himself up as an example, Tourgée related, "In earning money for my college course, I did whatever came to hand,—worked on a farm, in a shop, did little jobs and big ones; worked with my hands whenever they could earn more than my brain and with brain when the odds were in its favor." The student would be a "better and stronger man" if he completed his education at age twenty-five instead of age twenty-one and gave his "body a chance to do its share as well as [his] brain," Tourgée opined. Finally, he reminded the young man that college was only a "means," not an "end" in itself. "Stand on your own feet whenever you can; keep your back stiff," he urged.[72] While reverberating with echoes of Emerson and Thoreau, Tourgée's advice was striking for its lack of race consciousness. He referred to his correspondent's race only in implying that qualified black graduates had become so numerous as to create fierce competition for jobs at black schools and colleges. In addition, he put himself on the same level as a needy black college student. Tourgée knew, of course, what an obstacle prejudice and discrimination posed for African Americans—indeed, the very fact that African American teachers could not hope for employment except at black colleges spoke volumes—but he chose to empower this student by showing how he himself had overcome the obstacle of poverty they both shared rather than belabor the limited opportunities available to African Americans, whatever their educational attainments.

Tourgée's African American correspondents included not only humble supplicants for personal assistance but also prominent intellectuals. Often avid readers of his novels and "Bystander" column, intellectuals respected Tourgée as a fount of knowledge about every aspect of the race question from slavery times to the present. Accordingly, they turned to him for guidance on their research projects. For example, the "outstanding and accomplished" Chicago lawyer Hale Giddings Parker, a former school principal, asked Tourgée for a bibliography on political conditions and public education in the South during Reconstruction. Tourgée obliged with an eight-page survey of primary sources to consult at area libraries, prefaced by a list of generally overlooked facts. Wishing Parker success, he admonished him, "The work you have undertaken is a great one. Well done, it will be valuable: half done it will be worth nothing."[73] Implicitly, Tourgée was holding Parker to the standards he himself had set in such works as *An Appeal to Caesar*. He was additionally putting his wealth of accumulated knowledge at the disposal of African American researchers and enabling them to carry on the scholarly investigations needed to win equality.

Tourgée's legal and political expertise likewise prompted African American officeholders to seek his aid in framing and securing passage of civil rights legislation. Tourgée's correspondence with one such officeholder, Charles W. Anderson, head clerk of the treasurer's office in Albany, furnishes insight into how African American perceptions of their needs differed from Tourgée's and how the parties handled such divergences. Anderson wanted to present a civil rights amendment to New York's state constitution at the forthcoming 1894 convention and requested Tourgée to draft it for him. Fearing that Tourgée might consider it an "imposition" to be asked to spend more of his "time and treasure" on an endeavor African Americans ought to accomplish on their own, Anderson assured him, "However imperfectly repaid your efforts in behalf of the Negro have been, they are highly appreciated, and affectionately remembered. In my melancholy moments, I sometimes am inclined to the belief that my chief and only pride in belonging to the race, is that we can claim such loyal friends as yourself."[74] No apology was necessary, Tourgée answered: "My services are always freely rendered to the extent of my ability for anything that promises a fuller liberty." Nevertheless, he confessed he did not see anything to be gained by inserting a civil rights amendment into the state constitution, because New York's courts had been "pretty strait-backed on this subject." If Anderson still wished to propose one, Tourgée recommended the following: "There shall be no distinction of right or privilege in this state based on race or color." Such an innocuously worded clause "might slip through without much opposition" from those who would vote against the threat of school integration, Tourgée thought. In any case, he regarded "specific provisions in a constitution [as] dangerous."[75] Anderson disagreed. The real danger, he argued, lay in leaving civil rights so ill defined as to "confer upon judges a legislative, as well as a judicial function." He cited a recent case that had generated much publicity in the black press: T. Thomas Fortune's suit against a restaurant owner who had refused to serve him a glass of beer and had him "beaten and ejected from the premises" for standing his ground. As Anderson reminded Tourgée, the judge had validated the owner's right to refuse service and use force to eject an undesired customer and had instructed the jury to decide only whether or not "excessive force" had been used. Nothing but a clause in the constitution that "cannot, and will not, be disregarded" could prevent such judicial lawmaking, Anderson insisted.[76] Tourgée apparently remained unconvinced, but he hailed Anderson's spirit. "I am very glad . . . to see that the young colored men are taking up the work of asserting and defending the rights of their race," he wrote.[77]

The fullest picture of Tourgée's relations with African Americans emerges from his exchanges with long-term correspondents. All of these correspondents will reappear in subsequent chapters, where we will find them collaborating with Tourgée in such endeavors as building a biracial civil rights movement, campaigning against lynching, and challenging Jim Crow laws. Here I would like to explore the personal side of their interactions with Tourgée as a means of laying the groundwork for better evaluating the achievements and limitations of the cross-racial alliances through which he and they sought to transform their society.

Tourgée and Chesnutt

The first of these long-term correspondents was Charles W. Chesnutt, whose praise of Tourgée's "stirring" articles on the race question I quoted earlier. As Chesnutt's journal indicates, during the period when he was contemplating a literary vocation, Tourgée had loomed large in his consciousness. A long entry of 16 March 1880 suggests that he viewed the older man as simultaneously a model and a rival. Noting with envy that Tourgée had reportedly sold *A Fool's Errand* for $20,000, Chesnutt commented:

> Judge Tourgee is a Northern man, who has lived at the South since the war, until recently. He knows a great deal about the politics, history, and laws of the South. . . . Nearly all his stories are more or less about colored people, and this very feature is one source of their popularity. . . . And if Judge Tourgee, with his necessarily limited intercourse with colored people, and with his limited stay in the South, can write such interesting descriptions, such vivid pictures of Southern life and character as to make himself rich and famous, why could not a colored man, who has lived among colored people all his life; who is familiar with their habits, their ruling passions, their prejudices; their whole moral and social condition; their public and private ambitions; their religious tendencies and habits;—why could not a colored man who knew all this, and who, besides, had possessed such opportunities

FIGURE 2 Photo of Charles W. Chesnutt at age forty, taken in 1898, a year after his correspondence with Tourgée ended. Courtesy of the Cleveland Public Library Digital Gallery.

for observation and conversation with the better class of white men in the south as to understand their modes of thinking; who was familiar with the political history of the country, and especially with all the phases of the slavery question;—why could not such a man, if he possessed the same ability, write a far better book about the South than Judge Tourgee or Mrs. Stowe has written?[78]

As we can see from this journal entry, Chesnutt already had a remarkable awareness of his literary gifts for a young man of twenty-two, along with a sound assessment of the many qualifications that could enable him to portray African American life and race relations in the South more authentically than Tourgée had. In linking Tourgée with Harriet Beecher Stowe, Chesnutt was perhaps referring not only to the phenomenal success *A Fool's Errand* and *Uncle Tom's Cabin* had enjoyed but also to the subordinate roles black characters play in these two novels and to the racial stereotyping that mars them. The sole other Tourgée novel he could have read by March 1880 would have been the pseudonymous *Toinette* (1874), whose light-skinned heroine would not have appealed to the future creator of Mandy Oxendine and Rena Walden. We do not know whether Chesnutt would have judged *Bricks Without Straw* more favorably, since he never mentions it either elsewhere in his journal or in his correspondence, but it seems to have influenced his own masterpiece, *The Marrow of Tradition* (1901), which anatomizes the 1898 coup d'état and massacre in Wilmington, North Carolina, much as *Bricks Without Straw* does the overthrow of Black Reconstruction in the same state.

A similar mixture of admiration and rivalry, as well as a degree of racial tension, is discernible in Chesnutt's and Tourgée's letters to each other.[79] Chesnutt initiated their correspondence when he thanked Tourgée for the "compliment paid" in his widely noticed December 1888 *Forum* article, "The South as a Field for Fiction." Besides hinting that Chesnutt came closer to depicting Southern life accurately than did Joel Chandler Harris, the popular white Southern compiler of the Uncle Remus stories, Tourgée had prophesied that "the children ... of slaves" would soon "advance American literature to the very front rank" by exploiting "the richest mine of romantic material that has opened to the English-speaking novelist" since Sir Walter Scott: "the life of the Negro as a slave, freedman, and racial outcast." In the process, they would create "an altogether new character in fiction"—the free African American as a "man with hopes and aspirations, . . . hot passion, fervid imagination," and ambition to be "equal to the best." Elaborating on the new elements the descendants of slaves would bring to American literature, Tourgée had again compared Chesnutt with Harris, though without mentioning either by name: "The traditions of the freedman's fireside are richer and far more tragic than the folklore which genius has recently put into his quaint vernacular." He could only have meant that stories such as Chesnutt's "The Goophered Grapevine" and "Po' Sandy," recently published in the *Atlantic Monthly*, better conveyed the harsh reality of slavery and its aftermath, as well as the complex culture that had helped slaves to survive, than did the Brer Rabbit tales Harris had collected and put into the mouth of the faithful slave Uncle Remus.[80]

Chesnutt must have been gratified by this flattering acknowledgment of his talent from a writer he had long esteemed, but we have to deduce the contents of his letter, which is no longer extant, from Tourgée's reply of 8 December 1888.[81] Tourgée's opening sentence—"Few things have given me greater pleasure than your letter"—indicates that Chesnutt had thanked him warmly. Chesnutt may also have inquired whether he correctly understood the indirect allusions to his fiction, for Tourgée confirmed, "Of course, it was to you that I referred." He had couched his remarks cryptically, Tourgée explained, because "I did not dare make the reference more explicit lest it should do you an injury. The fact of color is yet a curse the intensity of which few realize." The editors of the *Atlantic* had not revealed Chesnutt's racial identity to the public, and Tourgée may have assumed that he wanted to keep it secret to further his literary career. He himself had guessed, however, that only an African American could have rendered the "traditions of the freedman's fireside" so knowledgeably and insightfully. "I have kept track of your work and have noted the growth," he told Chesnutt. "Its realism is unique and true—true to nature and not to the fettering ideas of the narrow rules which makes our so-called realism the falsest and sorriest of fiction."[82]

The "so-called realism" Tourgée dismissed so contemptuously was the form prescribed by the school's leading American theorist, William Dean Howells, with whom Tourgée had been carrying on a running quarrel. Unlike Howells, who had set up a "false standard of the truth" by alleging that "only the average, every-day, common-place happenings . . . are true" or "'real'" (as Tourgée objected in his March 1889 *North American Review* article, "The Claims of 'Realism'"), Chesnutt drew on the slaves' belief in conjuring—the very opposite of the commonplace—to reveal truths invisible to superficial white observers. And unlike Howells, who banished "hope, aspiration, and triumph" from realist fiction and stigmatized literature "with a purpose" as inartistic,[83] Chesnutt devoted his art to celebrating an oppressed people's struggle to maintain hope, fulfill the aspirations slavery denied them, and triumph as best they could over their masters' dehumanization of them. Apparently divining the "high, holy purpose" Chesnutt had confided to his journal—to contribute to the "moral progress of the American people" by liberating them from racial prejudice[84]—Tourgée encouraged him to hew to his course: "You may do much—I trust you will do much—to solve the great question of the hour—the greatest question of the world's history—the future of the Negro race in America. It involves American liberty—American civilization, and Protestant Christianity. All of these are failures unless . . . the white American, Christian freeman is true enough and brave enough and strong enough to be just to the colored man on American soil." Having endorsed the political aims encoded in Chesnutt's stories, Tourgée reiterated and amplified the prophecy he had made in "The South as a Field for Fiction": "I incline to think that the climacteric of American literature will be negroloid in character,—I do not mean in form—the dialect is a mere fleeting incident, but in style of thought, intensity of color, fervency of passion and grandeur of aspiration. Literature rather than politics, science or government, is the arena in which the American negro—not the African for there is really but little of the African left—will win his earliest perhaps his brightest laurels."[85] In predicting that African Americans would carry their country's literature to its apogee by stamping it with their own character, Tourgée was paying a double tribute, for he ranked his chosen field of literature higher than politics, science, or government—professions he had acerbically critiqued.

Tourgée had more than one reason for taking special pleasure in Chesnutt's letter: Chesnutt had thanked him not only for boosting his career but for defending the rights of African Americans. Touched by this "recognition of [his] labors," Tourgée responded volubly: "I do not know what made me take up so firmly the cause of the colored man—*as a man*. I am not a philanthropist nor a professional reformer. I do not like weakness nor whining; but I do love *justice* and am anxious above all things for my country's glory—that her fame may be spotless." He then complained about how little gratitude African Americans had shown toward their rare white allies: "I think very few colored men at all realize what I have done. The race is yet too near to slavery to understand its collective obligations. Even John Brown yet lacks a monument." He would repeat such complaints often in years to come. However misplaced his sense of grievance may have been, it was true that in December 1888 Tourgée had not yet acquired the vast following among African Americans he would gain by 1890. Hence, Chesnutt's familiarity with the range of writings and activities through which Tourgée had been championing African Americans since Reconstruction marked him as unusually politicized.

It took Chesnutt almost a year to acknowledge "receipt of [Tourgée's] kindly letter," which he did on 26 September 1889, indirectly apologizing for his remissness by saying he did not know whether he had yet performed that courtesy. Both the long delay and the tone his answer occasionally struck give the impression that some of Tourgée's comments may have irritated him. Chesnutt devoted only one sentence to expressing the "great pleasure" and "much encouragement" he had derived from Tourgée's praise. Immediately afterward, he reacted defensively to the intimation that African Americans had not properly repaid their debt to John Brown. Although he conceded they had not so far "attained, as a class, that pitch of enlightenment, that degree of confidence in themselves" needed to organize the financing of a monument to Brown, Chesnutt noted drily that "the example set by their white fellow-citizens in the matter of the Washington and Grant monuments is not exactly an inspiring one."[86] (Commissioned in 1848, the Washington Monument had not been completed until 1885; the Grant Memorial would not be completed until 1924.)

Tourgée's assertion that color was a "curse" also seems to have rankled Chesnutt. As if to show how much he had achieved despite the "curse," he enclosed a copy of the October 1889 *Atlantic*, containing his story "Dave's Neckliss," and listed his other recent successes: an article and a forthcoming story in the *Independent* ("What Is a White Man?" [30 May 1889] and "The Sheriff's Children" [7 November 1889]) and another story in the *Overland Monthly* ("The Conjurer's Revenge" [June 1889]). Chesnutt also took issue explicitly with Tourgée in a postscript. "You said to me that you thought the fact of color would hurt me in literature—the knowledge of the fact rather" (correcting Tourgée's phrasing): "Perhaps it might with the public. It has not with the *Independent*—on the contrary I think it has helped me with that journal. I do not think it has hurt me with the *Atlantic*. The editors of both journals are aware of my connection with the colored race. The road to success in literature is not, I imagine, an easy one, and perhaps, if I have the patience and the industry to pursue it, the fact of color may in the course of time prove to be a distinction instead of a disadvantage."

The note of annoyance detectable in these two passages disappeared in the rest of the letter, where Chesnutt identified himself as an enthusiastic "Bystander" reader, particularized the intentions governing his craft, echoed the aesthetic tenets Tourgée had articulated both in "The South as a Field for Fiction" and in his letter of 8 December 1888, and asked advice on whether it would pay to publish a collection of his stories. He was sending "Dave's Neckliss," he specified, because he hoped Tourgée would consider it "the best of the series" featuring Uncle Julius McAdoo, Chesnutt's answer to Harris's Uncle Remus. One of Chesnutt's bitterest and most powerful stories, "Dave's Neckliss" projects a view paralleling Tourgée's of the lasting damage slavery inflicted on the Southern psyche, both black and white; thus, Chesnutt's expectation that Tourgée would like it attests to his sense of their political affinity. "Dave's Neckliss" differed from the other Uncle Julius stories, Chesnutt indicated, in that he had "tried . . . to get out of the realm of superstition into the region of feeling and passion—with what degree of success the story itself can testify." He also disclosed that he had "about used up the old Negro who serves as mouthpiece" and would "drop him in future stories, as well as much of the dialect." In announcing his desire to move away from dialect and superstition and to accentuate "feeling and passion," Chesnutt was "self-consciously describing himself as an African-American artist in the terms employed by Tourgée in his 8 December letter," as Joseph R. McElrath Jr. and Robert Leitz III have pointed out.[87] Yet in the next breath, he declared his allegiance to an aesthetic principle that differentiated his fiction from Tourgée's: "I tried to write as an artist and not as a preacher."

If Chesnutt hoped for a detailed response to his story, Tourgée's perfunctory statement that he had been "much interested" in it must have disappointed him. Instead of saying anything further about "Dave's Neckliss," Tourgée veered off into a tirade against a story that had just appeared in *Century Magazine*, "Ben and Judas" by the Georgian local colorist Maurice Thompson, about a master and slave who grew up inseparable and spent their lives in loving companionship. Tourgée did congratulate Chesnutt on his "success," however, which he found "positive and encouraging" enough to convince him that the current trend would indeed make Chesnutt's "racial affinity an advantage rather than a hindrance." He also offered to write a preface to Chesnutt's proposed collection of stories, wryly opining that his imprimatur "would do the volume no harm." (By the time Chesnutt's *The Conjure Woman* finally appeared ten years later without the promised preface, Tourgée's imprimatur would have done no good, for he had fallen into literary obscurity and was serving as U.S. consul to Bordeaux.) Was there a hint of rivalry in the account that followed of Tourgée's own publications—two consecutive serials in a religious weekly, the *Chicago Advance* (the novels later titled *Pactolus Prime* [1890] and *Murvale Eastman, Christian Socialist* [1890])?[88] Tourgée could hardly have avoided noticing that the contrast between the prestigious *Atlantic* and the parochial *Advance* marked Chesnutt's star as ascendant and his own as declining. Might this contrast, rather than his busy schedule, help explain why he said so little about Chesnutt's story? We can only speculate about the reasons for Tourgée's reticence, but we do know that Chesnutt chose George Washington Cable and not Tourgée as his literary mentor and that, unlike Tourgée, Cable provided him with in-depth critiques of his manuscripts and enjoyed connections with top-ranking publishers from which Chesnutt hoped (vainly, as it turned out) to benefit.[89]

Still, Chesnutt felt sufficiently drawn to Tourgée to visit him twice while vacationing on Lake Chautauqua. "He is a very interesting fellow, and improves on acquaintance," Chesnutt reported to his wife, implying that he found Tourgée more congenial in person than in his letters.[90] The two must have shared their literary projects, for Tourgée lent Chesnutt a manuscript. They continued to correspond until 1897. Chesnutt continued as well to value Tourgée's committed championship of African American rights. "You will never get an adequate reward in this world for your efforts in behalf of the oppressed and the humble," he said in one of his last letters to Tourgée.[91] Not only did Chesnutt write Tourgée an effective recommendation for a consular position and deliver a moving eulogy at the memorial service Emma held for her husband in November 1905, but as McElrath and Leitz and Sally Ann Ferguson have noted, he rendered homage to Tourgée in his novel *The Colonel's Dream* (1905), dedicated to "those who are seeking . . . to bring the forces of enlightenment to bear upon the vexed problems which harass the South."[92] Its hero, Colonel French, a progressive Southern version of Tourgée's Northern autobiographical persona Colonel Servosse in *A Fool's Errand*, fails as tragically to transform the North Carolina of the 1890s as Servosse and Tourgée had the North Carolina of the Reconstruction era. Indeed, Chesnutt's final comment on Colonel French's decision to leave his native South forever applies equally well to Tourgée, who chose to die in Bordeaux rather than return to his native land after losing the fight against segregation in the *Plessy v. Ferguson* case: "And so the colonel faltered, and, having put his hand to the plow, turned back. But was not his, after all, the only way? For no more now than when the Man of Sorrows looked out over the Mount of Olives, can men gather grapes of thorns or figs of thistles. The seed which the colonel sowed seemed to fall by the wayside, it is true; but other eyes have seen with the same light, and . . . other hands have taken up the fight which the colonel dropped."[93]

Tourgée and William H. Anderson

Tourgée's long-term African American correspondents included one other literary man: William H. Anderson, who besides editing the *Detroit Plaindealer* also coauthored the antilynching novel *Appointed* (1894) with Walter H. Stowers. Anderson typified the contradictions of what Kevin Gaines has dubbed "racial uplift ideology," the political philosophy through which "black ministers, intellectuals, journalists, and reformers sought to refute the view that African Americans were biologically inferior and unassimilable" by citing "class distinctions, indeed, the very existence of a 'better class' of blacks, as evidence of what they called race progress." As Gaines details, the "black elites" who shaped racial uplift ideology held that "the improvement of African Americans' material and moral condition through self-help would diminish white racism" and, consequently, that black leaders must strive "to rehabilitate the race's image by embodying respectability, enacted through an ethos of service to the masses."[94] Anderson gave classic expression to these tenets: "My theory is that while each Afro-American should do what he can to uplift his fellows, the whites likewise need educating on certain lines, and . . . this work . . . should fall on those best fitted by circumstances to do it." What fitted Anderson especially well for the mission he described was his membership in a wealthy Episcopal parish, which allowed him to make his way unobtrusively among whites of "the better classes" and thus to change "public opinion concerning the Afro-American."[95]

FIGURE 3 Photo of the "Plaindealer Boys." *Standing, left to right:* Robert A. Pelham Jr. (manager), Walter A. Stowers (coauthor of *Appointed*), William H. Anderson (editor of the *Plaindealer* and coauthor of *Appointed*). *Sitting, left to right:* Benjamin B. Pelham, Byron G. Redmond. The *Detroit Plaindealer* reprinted many of Tourgée's "Bystander" columns, and Tourgée corresponded extensively with Anderson and briefly with Pelham. From the *Michigan Manual of Freedmen's Progress,* 1915. Courtesy of Matthew Siegfried.

Anderson conducted a spirited dialogue with Tourgée on elitist versus egalitarian models of "race progress." It was Tourgée who initiated the correspondence, not to hail Anderson's literary talent, as with Chesnutt, but rather to excoriate him for an April 1890 article recommending as part of a general "solution of the race problem" that Congress impose an "educational qualification upon the right of suffrage"—a perfect example of racial uplift ideology's elitist strategy.[96] "It is with the greatest grief that I see a colored man advocating an educational qualification for voters," Tourgée fired back. "Have not your race learned that the great peril to free government is not to be looked for from ignorance but from educated injustice? . . . An educational qualification is just as unjust [as] and even more cowardly, than a property qualification." Both forms of discrimination, Tourgée argued, made a mockery of the liberty for which John Brown, Lincoln, and a "host of martyrs died." In the name of that liberty, Tourgée firmly rejected the concept of "race progress" to which Anderson and his fellow proponents of racial uplift ideology subscribed. "My dear Sir," he expostulated, "will your people *never* see that the measure of progress with your race is not the apt iteration of the fallacies by which they have been so long oppressed"—the fallacies of "privilege and superiority" invoked to justify the rule of the "rich and wise" over the "poor and ignorant," and of the "white man" over the "black man"? Tourgée went on to warn that by placating rather than fiercely resisting their oppressors, African Americans merely courted reenslavement in all but name. It was to save African Americans from such a fate that he had devoted so "many volumes" to pleading their cause to the detriment of his career, Tourgée explained, but he was now wondering whether he had wasted his efforts: "Somehow, as time goes on, I am almost sorry I have fought so hard and hoped so much for the Negro. A good deal that I have seen and heard of him of late—and I do my studying at first hand—inclines me to fear that he would rather be flattered by being called a 'good nigger' than respected as a free man."[97]

Despite his adherence to racial uplift ideology, Anderson did not deserve to be accused of truckling to whites, for he militantly demanded racial justice, not only in his editorials for the *Plaindealer* but in his role as vice president of the Afro-American League's Michigan chapter. Nevertheless, rather than retort angrily to Tourgée's diatribe, he patiently clarified his position. He did not favor an educational qualification for African Americans alone or under prevailing conditions, he stipulated—only under a "complete system of education, in every state *accessible to all*." Given "equal conditions and equal opportunities," he was sure the Afro-American would be "willing to submit to the *same tests* that are applied to the rest of the people in the Republic." This position was neither "'cowardly'" nor contrary to Brown's and Lincoln's ideals, Anderson insisted. He believed an educational qualification would put a "premium upon suffrage," "act as a spur upon the colored people," and "draw the lines as they should be, between the worthy and the unworthy." In the process, Anderson tellingly claimed, it would disfranchise many more ignorant whites than blacks, among them the thousands of immigrants who landed on American shores every week. "From their ranks" came the preachers of "communism and anarchy," the "cohorts" of the Democratic Party, and the bitterest enemies of the "Afro-American as a laborer," he reminded Tourgée.[98]

While parrying Tourgée's charges and declaring his own independence, Anderson gave African Americans' renowned "champion" his due. Yet he also chided Tourgée for being "a man of strong opinions, perhaps impatient with those whose views you may understand to deviate from the strict lines of your own, but who like yourself are fighting for the same purpose." With unerring insight, Anderson identified the character trait that gave Tourgée both his tenacity in the face of opposition and his intransigence in situations requiring tact and compromise (as when he torpedoed the Blair bill). Still, unlike Chesnutt, Anderson did not bristle at Tourgée's criticism of African Americans. Instead, he admitted to feeling a similar disappointment in the results of his sacrifices for the race. "My own experience with the mass has not been encouraging," he confided to Tourgée, "and many a time have I been tempted to give it up and pursue my own way quietly." Although he had "sometimes thought too much is expected from a class of the people emerging so recently" from slavery, he had simultaneously resented all African Americans' being "heaped unjustly together, not because of race for they have in them the blood of most of the European and African races (no two families possessing the same mixture) but because they have suffered from like causes." Nothing could better encapsulate the contradictions in racial uplift ideology between embracing and disdaining the black folk, between espousing an ethos of service and indulging an impulse toward stratification—or as Gaines phrases it, between "a pejorative notion of race and an affirming concept of cultural distinctiveness."[99]

Tourgée's reply barely acknowledged Anderson's reproof and once again proclaimed his own thoroughgoing egalitarianism. "Perhaps I am impatient," he conceded grudgingly, but "right is right and wrong is wrong." Only compulsory education for all could spur literacy. As for the immigrant vote, Anderson was confusing "suffrage and citizenship": "No immigrant should be allowed to become a *citizen* until he can read and write and understands something of our laws and government. . . . We are not responsible for *his* ignorance and should not be endangered by it." But this reasoning did not apply to African Americans, because they were already citizens, who had been deliberately forbidden education under the slave system and were still not getting their fair share.[100]

Tourgée may not have succeeded in changing Anderson's mind on the merits of requiring an educational qualification, but the two men remained on excellent terms and kept in touch until Tourgée's departure for Bordeaux in 1897. Indeed, Anderson could take partial credit for Tourgée's appointment to the Bordeaux consulship, having contributed one of several hundred letters of recommendation sent by African American and white admirers.[101] Illustrating the tenor of their relationship, Anderson wrote in 1892, "The good you are doing for the cause of freedom and our pleasant personal correspondence makes it appear as we were personal friends." When Tourgée fell seriously ill in 1895, Anderson "wish[ed he] was near at hand so that [he] could help" with the editorial work that was burdening the invalid. He also recommended books on self-cure. "You are too valuable a man to spend so much time on a bed of suffering," he admonished Tourgée.[102]

Meanwhile, Anderson regularly published or reprinted Tourgée's articles, until the *Plaindealer* succumbed to the Panic of 1893. He and Tourgée additionally reviewed each other's novels, *Pactolus Prime* and *Appointed*. As was his wont, privately Tourgée gave the neophyte author an honest assessment of his work's literary execution. "I am sorry you did not let me have it in the proof-sheets. I think a free use of my pencil would have improved it," he told Anderson, adding apologetically, if patronizingly, "You must not blame me for writing so freely. I have almost the same interest in the literary work of a colored man as I would in that of a son and perhaps, manifest it somewhat too freely." Tourgée praised the novel's "general plan" of portraying an interracial friendship between two young men, and he recognized that Anderson had potential worth cultivating, but he urged him to study the art of rendering "dialogue" with "variety" and "naturalness." Should Anderson "attempt another novel," offered Tourgée, "I would be glad to have you consult me about the plot before beginning and let me see the ms before it is printed." In his review of *Appointed* for the *Inter Ocean*, Tourgée avoided commenting on its literary quality but emphasized its value as a window into the mind of the educated African American: "To those who wish to know the other side of that separatism which underlies the 'Jim Crow' car, a 'Jim Crow' government, and a 'Jim Crow' church, the Bystander most earnestly commends the perusal of this work."[103]

Anderson responded gratefully to both the review and the private criticism. The review was already helping to sell the book, he rejoiced. As for the criticism, "I was conscious of all the defects that you speak of when [the novel] was first written and I didn't know how to correct them." Consequently, he had kept the manuscript in his desk drawer for three and a half years, and only his coauthor's persuasion had induced him to seek out a publisher. He had actually considered asking Tourgée to vet the manuscript of *Appointed* before publication but had decided against doing so out of fear that it would "look too much like imposition." Next time he would be "pleased to have the free use of [Tourgée's] blue pencil."[104] There would not be a next time, however, because Anderson seems never to have fulfilled his intention of writing another antilynching novel.

Tourgée and T. Thomas Fortune

Tourgée's relationship with Anderson's fellow editor T. Thomas Fortune of the *New York Age* got off to a much rockier start. A lifelong Republican, albeit one increasingly marginalized by his racial egalitarianism, Tourgée

could not forgive Fortune for switching his political allegiance as a protest against the party's abandonment of African Americans. He might have
tolerated Fortune's defection to the Prohibitionists in 1884, an election in
which he himself had not campaigned for presidential candidate James
G. Blaine because party leaders had banned any mention of racial issues,
but when Fortune threw his support to the Democrats in 1888, despite the
Republican platform upholding a "free and honest popular ballot and the
just and equal representation of all the people,"[105] Tourgée's disgust knew
no bounds. Convinced that only "a restless self-seeking, ambitious, dema-
gogue" could have urged his people to vote for a party long identified with
white supremacy, Tourgée went so far as to warn the newly elected president
of the National Afro-American League, Joseph C. Price, against allowing
Fortune to influence the organization he had played a key role in founding.
"He approves and favors nothing except what he conceives to reflect himself," Tourgée alleged, "and, consequently, is not a man who for any great
length of time can command confidence."[106] The charge was grossly unfair,
as any reader of Fortune's thoughtful book *Black and White: Land, Labor,
and Politics in the South* (1884) can judge.

This said, by 1893 Tourgée had completely changed his mind. As he confessed in a postscript he deleted from a letter to Fortune, the principled,
consistently radical course Fortune had been following in the intervening
years had not only dissipated Tourgée's former "distrust" but given him the
"firmest confidence in [Fortune's] high purpose and sincere conviction."[107]
He particularly complimented Fortune on a scathing editorial of February
1893 occasioned by the recent deaths of Blaine and ex-president Rutherford
B. Hayes, both of whom had cruelly betrayed African Americans. "I do not
quite agree with you as to Hayes," Tourgée quibbled. "He was simply of the
neuter gender which begets good motives that hatch out evil consequences."
(To another African American editor, probably Anderson of the *Plaindealer*,
Tourgée more frankly characterized Fortune's "denunciation of Hayes" as
"too virulent.") Still, he underscored, what mattered most was that "the
colored people have grown big enough and strong enough and brave enough
to condemn openly, boldly and emphatically those who betray the liberties
of their people."[108]

Having noted how closely Fortune's political positions and militant
rhetoric resembled his own, Tourgée now ventured to ask an extraordinary
favor: Could Fortune palm off as one of his *New York Age* editorials an article Tourgée could not afford to publish in the *Inter Ocean* as a "Bystander"
column? The article in question execrated lame-duck president Benjamin

FIGURE 4 Engraved portrait of T. Thomas Fortune, editor of the *New York Age*, dating from the period of his correspondence with Tourgée. Courtesy of the State Archives of Florida, Florida Memory.

Harrison for appointing a white supremacist, states' rights Democrat, Howell Jackson of Tennessee, to the Supreme Court. Tourgée explained, "I am not afraid to speak my views, as you know, but my position as counsel in the Jim Crow Car cases now pending in the Supreme Court, puts upon me a check I ought not to disregard. Such language traced to me might prejudice the cause I represent, which is far more important than any expression of my views upon the subject could be." Harrison nonetheless deserved to be raked over the coals, and if a prominent African American editor voiced the rebuke, "it would do good. It is time it was fully understood that the colored race will judge public men by their attitude to its liberties and will appeal to the world through their press." Harrison would "squirm to his last day over such a farewell from the party he thought he owned," Tourgée crowed. To maximize the article's distribution, Fortune should send proof sheets to "the leading papers." Many would surely reprint the editorial, and Tourgée planned to "*quote* it in the Bystander as an indication of race-sentiment."[109] In short, he was asking Fortune to help him pass as a black man by serving as his mouthpiece.

Fortune happily obliged. He, too, recognized the affinity between his journalistic style and Tourgée's. He was pleased to "*father*" Tourgée's article because he had intended to editorialize in the same "temper" on the

Supreme Court appointment, and he offered to continue their collaboration. The piece was already in press when Tourgée suddenly panicked and asked, too late, to withdraw it, but Fortune consoled him: "Your original view is the entirely correct one."[110]

Published in the *Age* under the provocative title "Ben Harrison a Traitor, Too!" and retitled "Negroes Condemn Harrison" by the *Troy Press*, a mainstream Democratic organ, the jointly "fathered" and widely circulated article indeed passed as a black man's. Tourgée so thoroughly melded his voice with Fortune's that he even adopted the term "Afro-American," though he himself preferred the term "colored American." During Harrison's administration, Tourgée-as-Fortune pointed out, more than a dozen Afro-American citizens had been "openly burned alive," beginning "the day after his inauguration" and culminating in the latest "demoniac" incident, for which "excursion trains were run to bring professing Christian thousands to view the revolting spectacle," just as the president was about to elevate to the Supreme Court a "virulent supporter of the very theory by which such infamies are excused and protected." The last of a long "line of Judases" who had "sold American liberty, in order to continue the oppression and debasement of Afro-Americans," "Harrison, the Little," as Tourgée-Fortune derisively dubbed him, had "won the distinction of having sold the freedom he professed to prize for the least price and the meanest motive"—"spite." As incendiary as these charges may sound to modern ears accustomed to a press that treats presidents with greater deference, Tourgée had made similar accusations before. The one he had never publicly broadcast, however, was that Harrison had refused a minor judgeship to an African American applicant on the ground that "I would not like to practice before a Negro judge and do not think I ought to require others to do what I would not like to do myself." Tourgée alone had heard Harrison say this in a private conversation no one else could have known about, and he must have feared the anecdote would immediately give him away, though there is no evidence that it did.[111]

Shortly afterward, Fortune solicited Tourgée's opinion on whether or not he should try to reach "friendly whites" of the "better class" by "launching a high class monthly," because he had given up hope of inducing them to read a "race newspaper."[112] Tourgée nixed the idea. Very few whites would subscribe to a magazine "run by a colored man" with primarily African American contributors, Tourgée pointed out, and very few African Americans could afford to subscribe to a "'first-class Monthly.'" Exclusionary sentiment among whites had worsened to such a degree and become so "insanely bitter," he added, that only "a crystallized colored sentiment and constant aggression" could "make any impression" on the white public: "The class or race which has the power to kill and shows a disposition to use it is the only one civilization respects." Under current conditions, Tourgée asserted, Fortune could achieve more by militant appeals to African Americans through the *Age* than through any other instrumentality. "Make your fight on the color line just as bitter as you can," he advised. "Attack the trucklers of your own race. . . . Lash your people unmercifully for the 'cake-walk' spirit in everything. *This* will attract the attention of the whites" and win the *Age* "ten times" the audience of a "colored paper . . . that tries to conciliate by pleasant and respectful language."[113]

While discouraging Fortune from starting a magazine that could "serve as a sort of interpreter between the races," Tourgée hinted that he himself was contemplating an enterprise of this nature. (He would unveil these plans to Fortune nine months later and ask him to help obtain African American financial backing for such a magazine.) "Though I blush to write it," Tourgée avowed, "if it is to reach the white people to any great extent, it will have to be a *white* publication, for a time at least."[114]

Fortune thanked Tourgée for a letter from which he had derived "unusual pleasure and profit" but professed to discern "a liberal undercurrent" in white racial attitudes that reinforced his optimism about his prospects of obtaining white subscribers if he founded a "high class monthly." As for the line Tourgée recommended that he take in the *Age*, the combative editor admitted having learned that it was "tough for the business end of the machine, since our people run away from strong radicalism as madly as white men denounce it."[115] In fact, unbeknown to Tourgée, Fortune was having trouble keeping the *Age* afloat. Thus, after he failed to interest Tourgée in a joint editorship of the racial crossover magazine both dreamed of, the two men's correspondence ceased in late 1893, and Fortune sought the assistance of his friend Booker T. Washington, who would subsidize the *Age* from 1895 on.

Tourgée and Ida B. Wells

Unlike Fortune, who hired her to write for the *Age* in June 1892—and unlike Anderson and Chesnutt—Ida B. Wells never expressed any ideological disagreement with Tourgée. Equally uncompromising in their radicalism, the fiery antilynching crusader and the militant advocate of racial equality repeatedly endorsed each other's stances and admired each other unreservedly.[116] Yet their surviving correspondence with each other, largely mediated through Emma, reveals the constraints that the racial separatism of the era imposed on social relations.

Wells first encountered Tourgée through his novel *Bricks Without Straw*, which she spent "all day" reading on 1 March 1886, six years before their correspondence began. As she noted in her diary, "The writer is actuated by a noble purpose and tells some startling truths."[117] Then teaching school and experimenting with journalism, the twenty-four-year-old Wells was already preoccupied with the issues that would engage her as an activist: "lynching and other atrocities, the segregation of public facilities, unjust laws and unfair sentences."[118] She was also seeking models for the craft best suited to her as a newspaperwoman. She would soon find one in Tourgée's "Bystander" column, which she probably started reading by late 1889, when African American newspapers started reprinting it. Not Wells but Tourgée would initiate their correspondence—and their alliance against lynching— when he wrote to compliment her on her first major exposé of this national crime, published in the *New York Age* in June 1892.

Wells and Tourgée had been collaborating for less than a year in the campaign against lynching when she turned to him for legal advice on her defamation by Southern editors. Not content with having "exiled" her and her coeditor from Memphis and destroyed their press in retaliation against her outspoken editorials, Memphis elites sought to prevent Wells from gaining a hearing from white Northerners. To discredit her testimony against lynching, the *Memphis Commercial* assassinated Wells's moral character and impugned her professional standing. Dismissing "this Wells wench" as nothing but a "black harlot" angling for a white husband, the *Commercial* did not even deign to acknowledge her as a journalist but denigrated her as "the mistress of the scoundrel" who had authored the editorials it found so offensive.[119] Incensed, Wells decided to sue the *Commercial* for libel and asked Tourgée to serve as her lawyer. "I wanted the opinion of one who was not a member of the race," she specified in a letter of 22 February 1893, because black lawyers were "too partisan to give cool unbiased counsel" when the race's honor was at stake: "I had confidence some how in your professions, more than any of your race."[120]

To Wells's disappointment, Tourgée refused. He was no longer practicing law, he explained, except in special public interest cases like the pending suit against the "Jim Crow Car," which he was handling "wholly gratuitously." He elaborated, "I could not afford to do more gratuitous work, being as you may know not only poor but very deeply in debt; and you could not afford to pay me enough to make good the time and expense it would require to engage" in a drawn-out suit. What dismayed Wells more than Tourgée's unwilling-ness to take on her case was the prudential tone of his reply to her question regarding her chances of winning a "vindication of [her] character." To com-bat aspersions on her virtue in a court of law, he warned in a heavily revised draft letter, Wells would have to do more than refute the charge of being her coeditor's mistress; she would have to "sustain a denial of impropriety *with any man.*" She would also need to arm her lawyer with more facts than she had so far supplied, including information about the African American witnesses who had agreed to testify against her (some of whom held per-sonal grudges against her).[121] Stung, Wells answered, "I know not whether to impute your conservative replies to native caution on the subject, or the intimation that there are those of my own race who are ready to perjure themselves in an effort to gratify their spirit of revenge." If a third possibility occurred to her—that Tourgée might suspect some indiscretion lay behind her enemies' slander—Wells did not say so. Instead, she furnished Tourgée with the information he requested, so that he could better advise her on how to proceed.[122]

Tourgée passed the case on to Ferdinand L. Barnett, an African American lawyer and newspaper editor in Chicago, with whom he had been in contact since September 1891—an introduction that fortuitously led to the couple's marriage. He also shared his misgivings with Barnett, who agreed that "it would be a serious mistake to begin the case and then lose it." After meet-ing Wells and interviewing the witnesses she named, Barnett (who seems already to have been falling in love with her) elatedly reported to Tourgée that he was convinced the *Commercial*'s "libelous article was wholly with-out foundation." Yet he and Wells eventually reached the same conclusion Tourgée had—that it would be safer to drop the case, given the presumption of guilt an African American woman would inevitably confront in a white male court, especially when she had violated strictures against feminine decorum by publicly addressing the tabooed issues of lynching and volun-tary sexual relations between white women and black men.[123]

Wells's consultation with Tourgée about a matter so sensitive for a nine-teenth-century woman tested their relationship to the limit. Tourgée's judiciously worded draft, with its many crossed-out sentences, shows that he not only respected Wells's sensibilities but also dared to give her tough advice rather than treat her with condescension. (As he put it in one of those crossed-out sentences, "I would be a very bad friend should I do as you wish.") Wells's letters of 10 and 22 February 1893 show that she trusted

Tourgée enough not to take offense at his seeming reservations and that she felt able to "expose the weaknesses of [her] race" to him, knowing that he would not exploit them. Their political partnership weathered this challenge, which increased their confidence in each other.[124]

They confronted another challenge two years later, when Wells decided to take advantage of a March 1895 lecture engagement in Rochester to visit Tourgée at his home in Mayville, New York, on the same train line from Chicago. She had not made the decision casually, for frigid opposition to "social equality" between the races barred African American guests from white homes, except on rare occasions.[125] Yet Wells had met Tourgée during one of his lecture engagements in Chicago, at which time he had given her "such a cordial invitation to visit him" on her next trip East that she had "treasured it to be acted upon." She got cold feet as soon as she received Emma's (no longer extant) reply to her letter announcing her travel plans. The "formal tone" of what appears to have been a hasty note granting "permission to stop and consult the Judge on matters touching race welfare" and providing "instructions touching the trains to take" made Wells fear Emma did not feel the same comfort level with African Americans that her husband did and would not welcome her presence.[126] Consequently, she changed her itinerary without telling the Tourgées, to their chagrin.

Wells could not have known that the Tourgées had been hosting African Americans at their home since their days in Greensboro and that they had in fact legally adopted an African American adolescent and brought her up as a daughter.[127] Nor could she have realized how overburdened Emma was with her responsibilities for handling Tourgée's correspondence, typing up his articles, arranging his lecture tours, and nursing him and other family members through incessant illnesses—burdens that easily account for her businesslike note. In any event, Emma's reproachful letter charging her with a "breach of etiquette" and expressing "disappointment" at her "failure to come" convinced Wells she had been mistaken. "I can see clearly . . . that you did not think . . . I was trying to force myself socially upon you," she wrote Emma penitently. Knowing that the Tourgées "would rather have the truth than an evasion," Wells tried to convey how painful it was for African Americans to contend with white racism at every turn and how difficult it was for them as a result to interpret white behavior in any other light. "It may be wrong to seem so sensitive," she granted, "but I seriously doubt if others whose skins are not colored would not feel as keenly the air of social condescension which the Negro generally meets even from his friends among the white people. On the other hand we meet it so constantly that we are liable to imagine it where it is not meant."[128]

While the misunderstanding reveals what monumental barriers stood in the way of natural, egalitarian social interactions between the races during the nadir, Wells's strategies for surmounting those barriers reveal how much she valued both Tourgée's advocacy for African Americans and her relationship with him. She could "sympathise greatly" with the Tourgées' hurt feelings, she responded, because she too had "so often been made to feel that [she had] become . . . '[An] Enemy of the People'" (the title of an 1882 play by Henrik Ibsen) through her very efforts to "help them." She added, "I am inspired to keep up the fight for principle's sake by such examples as your noble husband's and your own. I know that you do not labor for the applause of the multitude any more than did our Savior who was denied, betrayed and forsaken by his own whom he had taught and loved, and crucified by those He came to save; and hence none of these things move you from championing the cause of right."[129] By likening the Tourgées' and her own experiences of being ill-requited by the people whose rights they were defending, Wells was putting herself on an equal footing with them and bridging the social chasm between white and black activists. She was also acknowledging the tie that bound her to the Tourgées—all three had gone against "the multitude" to "fight for principle's sake," at the price of being pilloried as "An Enemy of the People." At the same time, by hailing the Tourgées as inspiring models and true disciples of "our Savior," Wells was gracefully expressing the appreciation that they and other white allies frequently complained of not receiving from African Americans. The comparison Wells drew between the Tourgées' self-sacrificing work for humanity and that of Jesus not only sanctified them but summoned them to persist as Jesus had, even if it meant being "crucified by those" they would "save." Portraying herself, the Tourgées, and "our Savior" alike as seeking to help "the People," uphold "principle," champion "the cause of right," and teach and love suffering humanity, Wells further contributed to eliminating barriers and distinctions between whites and blacks by studiously avoiding racialized language. This extraordinary letter illustrates the depth of Wells's commitment to forging an honest relationship with the white ally she admired more than any other.

Anxious to make up for the misunderstanding—and perhaps to test her white friends' professions—Wells called at Tourgée's office in Buffalo when her business again took her to western New York the following August. "I was very much disappointed" to find him absent, she wrote Emma, "for in a dim way I hoped to get to see you and learn if you still thought hardly of me for a seeming lack of appreciation of your kindness." Instead of the second chance she craved, she once more found herself obliged to apologize for a breach of etiquette. Upon the announcement of Wells's marriage to Barnett, Emma had sent her a "handsome present"—"a set of George Eliot's works & Judge Tourgee's novels" that Wells had always coveted and proudly showed off to her friends. Two months had gone by without the customary thank-you note, however, and Emma was now inquiring whether the books had arrived. Mortified, Wells explained that four days after the wedding, she had taken charge of her husband's newspaper, the *Chicago Conservator*, and that the demands of acting as "business manager, editor etc all rolled into one" had prevented her from fulfilling the "pleasant duty" of thanking people for their gifts. She had listed the gifts in the *Conservator* while waiting for an opportunity to acknowledge them "more properly," but had somehow neglected to send the Tourgées a copy of the marked issue.[130]

Because the segregated society of the 1890s did not allow for day-to-day collegial contact between the races, without which normal human relations cannot flourish, every such personal contretemps mushroomed into a racial incident. Yet despite the awkward miscues that dogged Wells's intercourse with the Tourgées, she persisted in her attempts to surmount the racial barriers impeding their friendship. As we shall see, she loyally supported the interracial civil rights organization Tourgée founded, helped publicize and circulate its organ, the *Basis*, and in turn drew on his support for her crusade against lynching. She joined fifty other African Americans in attending Tourgée's obsequies and delivered an eloquent eulogy that she later had printed as a pamphlet.[131] Emma felt enough of a bond with Wells to send her a clipping that both women agreed was the "best estimate" of Tourgée's work. Wells also shared Emma's commitment to preserving Tourgée's legacy, for she promised that if Emma succeeded in reprinting *A Fool's Errand*, "our people . . . stand ready to help" with the funding and distribution.[132] The project of reviving *A Fool's Errand* eluded the two women, sadly, thwarted by the white supremacist consensus that consigned Tourgée to oblivion, and their correspondence ended with this letter. Nevertheless, more than two decades later Wells memorialized Tourgée in the autobiography she wrote to preserve her own legacy.

Tourgée and Louis M. Martinet

Of all Tourgée's long-term correspondents, none formed a closer bond with him than Louis A. Martinet, the Creole-of-color[133] editor of the *New Orleans Crusader* and a key member of the Citizens' Committee that challenged segregation in what became the *Plessy v. Ferguson* case. Indeed, Tourgée and Martinet recognized each other as kindred spirits. Their letters to each other convey better than any others in the Tourgée archive the flavor of a cross-racial friendship during the nadir. Interweaving personal details into discussions of legal and political strategy, these letters also furnish insight into how two men divided by race, but united by similar personalities and values, interacted and worked together in pursuit of common goals. Martinet's letters additionally afford an intimate glimpse into the experience of living under Jim Crow and reveal a rare inclination to share the pain of that experience with a white ally. Unfortunately, because Martinet's papers, unlike Tourgée's, were never collected, most of Tourgée's letters to Martinet have disappeared.[134] Despite the resulting imbalance in the surviving correspondence, Martinet's twenty-one letters to Tourgée and the four letters to Martinet of which Tourgée kept drafts illuminate a friendship based on trust, mutual respect, reciprocity, and honesty, as well as on fundamental affinities.

The two men's correspondence began in October 1891, as Martinet and his associates were launching their legal battle with Tourgée's encouragement and Tourgée was toying with the idea of founding a national civil rights organization modeled partly on one Martinet had helped establish. By then, Martinet, like Tourgée, had already spent decades fighting for racial justice, having entered politics during the Reconstruction era. White supremacist violence raged even more fiercely in Louisiana than in North Carolina, and as a man of color, the son of an emancipated slave and a Belgian carpenter, Martinet ran greater risks than Tourgée in agitating for racial equality.[135] Yet he, too, had stood up against gangs of armed thugs. "I was often threatened, & several times saw guns levelled at me, but I never flinched and always maintained my ground & used to carry openly an arsenal about me," he related proudly, adding, "It was then that I learned that there was a good deal of cowardice & braggadocio in the Southern character."[136] Elected a state representative from St. Martin Parish at age twenty-three, Martinet served three years, refusing to yield to the terrorism that impelled most of his Republican colleagues to flee.[137]

Martinet also told Tourgée about a phase of his past that he looked back on with less pride: his brief stint as a Democrat. He had switched his allegiance to the Democrats at a time when "Republican leaders thought a division of the Negro vote [between the two parties] would secure the Negro a measure of protection & bring about a corresponding division of the white vote which in time would make the South habitable." But he had soon learned his mistake. Though the "more liberal" Democrats who then dominated the party in Louisiana had started out by being "fair and just to colored men" and denouncing racist "outrages," they had quickly caved in to white supremacist rabble-rousers. "The disappointment was bitter, but I am glad the experiment was made," concluded Martinet. It had shown him the worst side of white Southerners—"their inborn & ingrained hypocrisy & treachery"—and thus convinced him once and for all that cooperation with them could not secure "harmony & friendly relations between the two races."[138]

Amid his Reconstruction-era politicking, Martinet attended Straight University Law School and was admitted to the bar in 1875.[139] According to Tourgée, however, he "became dissatisfied at the lack of opportunity the profession offered for assisting the colored people" and therefore "set about studying medicine." Meanwhile, he supported his family as a notary public and later supplemented his income by giving anatomy lecture-demonstrations at his alma mater, Flint Medical College. Martinet started the *Crusader* in 1889, partnering with what Tourgée described as a "little company of colored men desiring to promote self-respect and manly independence among their colored fellow citizens." "I have been familiar with the enterprise, in a sense, ever since its initiation," wrote Tourgée to William E. Chandler, the Republican senator from New Hampshire, to whom he was secretly appealing on Martinet's behalf for financial assistance to the *Crusader*, "and I must say I have never seen such dogged resolution and such cheerful self-sacrifice displayed by any body of men as a mere matter of principle, and for the benefit of others." He added, "They have kept the paper afloat by simply giving part of their life every day to its support." Characterizing Martinet as "the glowing heart of the whole enterprise," Tourgée spelled out what his self-sacrifice had entailed. Martinet had received an undreamed-of offer from ex-president Rutherford B. Hayes, on Tourgée's recommendation—a chance to study in Paris for three years with expenses paid—but he had replied that "his duty to his people" and to his colleagues at the *Crusader* "required him to forego [*sic*]" this "tempting" opportunity "with many thanks and regrets."[140]

No one knew better than Tourgée how dearly the sacrifice cost his friend, for Martinet poured out his heart to him in letters that occasionally reached more than twenty pages in length. "You wrote sometime ago that I was despondent," Martinet recalled in one of those marathon letters, dated 4 July 1892. Wondering how Tourgée had guessed his feeling, Martinet surmised that his white friend was wrestling with doubts and fears much like his own as he resisted the juggernaut of segregation and the neo-slavery it portended, knowing that he and his comrades on the Citizens' Committee might lose their appeal to the Supreme Court. "I notice you are as low-spirited as I am sometimes. Your last letter to me showed a depth of discouragement that was painful," observed Martinet sympathetically. "'What have I to gain in fighting this battle?'" he quoted Tourgée as asking, perhaps in this no-longer-extant letter. "Like you, I have asked myself this question a thousand times. Certainly I gain nothing, but spend time, labor & money in it. There is no doubt that if I turn my attention to, or put my energies in professional or some private pursuits, I would get along much better in this world." Why, then, did he keep fighting?, Martinet asked again. "Like you, I believe I do it because I am built that way," he answered.[141]

True, Martinet, unlike Tourgée, was defending the rights of his own people, not of another oppressed group, yet being light-skinned enough to pass, and having been "brought up under some more favored circumstances than the general mass of the colored people," he had "always enjoyed a degree of consideration" that set him apart from his fellows.[142] Thus, he could have chosen a less arduous path and reaped the (limited) rewards African Americans could expect when they accommodated themselves to the South's racial code.

Both men realized that they risked undermining their marriages by sacrificing financial security on the altar of their ideals—another shared concern that drew them together. Hinting at his wife Leonora's dissatisfaction with his course, Martinet described his single-minded dedication to the struggle for civil rights as "too great a sacrifice, not to me, but to my wife & child." Tourgée likewise reproached himself for the privations that his idealistic undertakings and consequent inadequacies as a wage earner inflicted on Emma and their daughter, Aimée. We do not know whether he confessed such worries to Martinet, but the strains on his marriage surface clearly in his letters to Emma and in her diary. Both wives ultimately rebelled, Emma by withdrawing her support for Tourgée's activism and insisting that he seek remunerative employment, Leonora by divorcing Martinet around 1900.[143]

Further commonalities that cemented the bond between Martinet and Tourgée included their fiery rhetorical styles, uncompromising adherence to principle, contempt for trucklers, and fearless disregard of threats against their very lives. "Intransigent in his ideas, invincible in his perseverance, precise and varied in his style, he reflected in the columns of his newspaper the aspirations of the people in all their force and in all their purity," and "he made himself respected for his courage and his fidelity to republican principles," wrote Martinet's Creole-of-color associate on the *Crusader*, Rodolphe Desdunes, paying tribute to his editorship in words that could apply with little modification to Tourgée.[144]

Encapsulating the quintessence of a friendship that defied all the racial codes of the nadir, frank exchanges of opinion punctuate the two men's letters to each other. Martinet obviously regarded Tourgée as a political soul mate to whom he could safely express views that might offend other white men. For example, after the Republican convention of 1892 nominated Harrison for a second term as president, Martinet noted with satisfaction that Tourgée's "Bystander" column "did not enthuse much" over either the party's chosen candidate or its platform. He knew, of course, that like himself, Tourgée would have preferred Thomas Reed of Maine, a strong defender of African American rights, but Harrison was an incumbent president about whom most white Republicans might have expected an African American to speak with deference, especially in an election year. Still, Martinet did not mince words, branding Harrison "narrow-minded, selfish & unscrupulous in his own interest" and deriding his "reputed personal honesty" as mere "Presbyterian cant." Martinet felt no need to muffle his criticism of his fellow African Americans either, treating Tourgée more like an insider than like an outsider from whom family squabbles must be hidden. The "Negro delegates" at the convention held the balance of power between the Harrison and Reed factions, charged Martinet, but instead of shedding "lustre . . . on their people," they "obeyed the master's whip or were bought with gold or bribed with office or the promise of office. The scoundrels!" All too many African Americans who attained positions of power betrayed their people, making the battle for equal rights harder than ever, he complained. "If the Negro politicians North are in 'for revenue only,'" as Tourgée alleged, "those in the South," Martinet informed Tourgée, "are positively corrupt & devoid of manhood & dignity, with but *few* [double-underlined] exceptions. And then again one is surrounded by so much petty jealousy & envy that it's quite disgusting."[145]

Like Tourgée, Martinet looked down on career politicians, whether black or white, and preened himself on not "belong[ing] to that class of cattle." If he wished, he pointed out, he could easily become a "'big man'" by allying himself with "some of the unscrupulous white men to whom the Republican Administration entrusts the government service & its political interests" (a reminder that white politicians were as self-seeking as black ones). "But . . . I do not train with the 'gang'; . . . and therefore the 'leaders' and the 'bosses' have no use & no love for me."[146] As Martinet was well aware, Tourgée had often voiced analogous sentiments, notably through his favorite personas, the "Fool" of his famous novel and the "Bystander" of his newspaper column.

On only one issue did the two men disagree. Tourgée, a devout Methodist, had urged African Americans to hold a national day of prayer and fasting for justice, but Martinet, a Catholic imbued with Gallic anticlericalism, balked: "I am not a hypocrite. I did not like then, & I don't now, feel like praying for the injustices & outrages heaped upon us in this country. No just God should permit such abominations."[147] So fiercely did Martinet object to religious hypocrisy that, as he announced in a *Crusader* editorial Tourgée may have read, he had "long ago ceased going to church owing to the prejudice shown in the churches" and had determined "if he cannot go to Heaven by the same gate as others, he will go to sheol."[148]

Tourgée and Martinet set their friendship on an equal footing not only by allowing each other the freedom to disagree but by engaging in gestures of reciprocity. Shortly after Tourgée volunteered to donate his services to the Citizens' Committee, he asked Martinet to back his candidacy for a position on the Interstate Commerce Commission, an appointment for which President Benjamin Harrison was considering him. Martinet promptly did so through articles in the *Crusader*, which he sent to the president on the committee's behalf. "I am glad you were pleased with my mention of your name," he wrote to Tourgée. He went on to apprise Tourgée of the racial politics behind the scene: "In fact I thought of mentioning you for the Court of Appeals bench, but then the colored journals were asking the appointment of a colored man, & I thought the one might antagonize the other." Martinet had recommended the African American lawyer Augustus Straker for the appeals court and was now coordinating a campaign for Tourgée's nomination to the Interstate Commerce Commission. "I hope that the colored papers will take it up & press it," he added, drawing Tourgée's attention to a "nice little article in your favor" that the editor of the *New Era* had published at Martinet's suggestion and enclosing a copy of one he himself had just placed in the "*Standard-Pelican*, which the editor made his 'leader.'"[149] Ultimately, Tourgée did not receive the nomination, but what matters is that he valued the public support of the African American community enough to request Martinet to orchestrate it, reversing the roles of benefactor and debtor. He apparently sought to reinforce Martinet's sense of the reciprocity governing their relationship by keeping his own appeals for Martinet to Hayes and Chandler confidential.

The same reciprocity is discernible in the two men's promotion of each other through their respective newspapers. As we shall see, Tourgée frequently showcased Martinet and the *Crusader* in his "Bystander" column. Martinet similarly showcased Tourgée in the *Crusader*, though the disappearance of this influential journal's files, along with the rest of Martinet's papers, forces us to rely for evidence on the few remnants that have survived.[150] One of these remnants, containing a brief editorial by Martinet and a fragmentary article by Tourgée, illustrates with particular clarity the way in which the two journalists collaborated through the press. Martinet's editorial of 19 May 1894 welcomed with "exceeding pleasure" the contribution by "our great friend, Judge Tourgee," to which it directed "special attention." In parallel fashion, Tourgée's article hailed the newly launched *Daily Crusader* (upgraded from a weekly). Pointing out that "self-government, as a political principle based on equal right and privilege, is to-day on trial in the United States as it never was before," Tourgée described the *Daily Crusader* as key to bringing that trial to a successful outcome. "It will be an interpreter to the white people of all classes, of the best hope and aspiration of the colored race,—an exponent of the best there is in the colored American," Tourgée predicted. But he went on to warn that the paper would not "prosper" unless the "colored people of Louisiana" gave it "a good patronage" and that if they let the *Daily Crusader* die for want of their support, "the friends of liberty throughout the North [would] lose much hope and the enemies of equal rights, security and justice for all, throughout the country, [would] rejoice."[151] Martinet could hardly have wished for a stronger endorsement.

Tourgée and Martinet maintained a long-distance friendship by mail for a year and a half before they finally met in May 1893. Their paths converged in Chicago, where Martinet spent several weeks taking a special course for physicians and Tourgée went for a lecturing engagement. Like Wells, Martinet found Tourgée as warm and genuine in person as on the page. The meeting meant so much to him that he prolonged his stay on learning that Tourgée might return to Chicago for an antitrust convention. "Not that I have any business," Martinet confessed, ". . . but only for the pleasure of seeing you once more & shaking your hand. I feel that you are our *one* friend in this land of oppression." Whether inspired by Tourgée's sympathy or by the liberating atmosphere of the North, Martinet unburdened himself more frankly now than ever before. For the first time, he invited Tourgée to peer beneath the veil of the militant persona he cultivated—a veil that concealed the terrible toll the struggle against white supremacy exacted: the vulnerability, the fear, the suffocation, the sense of imprisonment. "Dear Judge, I return South with a heavy heart," he confided:

> I have lived here a new man—a free man. Of course, I am a free man in
> the South, and, knowing it, to a great extent, I act as a free man—that

is, I ride in any car, or go in any public place I want, &c. But I know too how often I carry my life in my hands in doing so, for I will not be ejected without physical resistance. You don't know what that feeling is, Judge. You may imagine it, but you have never experienced it—knowing that you are a free man & yet not allowed to enjoy a freeman's liberty, rights & privileges unless you stake your life every time you try it. To live always under this feeling of restraint is worse than living behind prison bars. My heart is constricted at the very thought of returning to these scenes.[152]

While acknowledging the gulf that separated him from his sympathetic white friend, Martinet offered Tourgée a bridge across it.

Intensifying his anguish at the prospect of going back to Louisiana, Martinet admitted, was his fear that he and his allies were "fighting a hopeless battle—a battle made doubly hopeless by the tyranny & cruelty of the Southern white & the Negro's lack of appreciation, his want of energy & his submissiveness." He could not help wondering, he added, "are the Negroes progressing, or are they not retrograding under the yoke of the Southern barbarians, and are not our efforts for their betterment put forth in a method & manner calculated to do little good, or perhaps harm?" While he worried on the one hand that the message of resistance the *Crusader* was preaching risked endangering rather than firing up the South's black masses, he objected on the other hand that the message of accommodation Booker T. Washington and his ilk were preaching did not seem to be equipping the graduates of such institutions as Tuskegee for anything but "menial employment." Yet Martinet conceded that if teachers at black industrial colleges "sought to instil [sic] in the youthful minds committed to their training the spirit of true manhood, of manly courage & resistance to oppression, they would not be tolerated in the communities where they are." Though unable to see any way out of the impasse, Martinet hailed Tourgée's tireless advocacy: "You [are] doing an immense good to the blacks of the South by enlightening the country on their pitiable & oppressed & well-nigh hopeless condition, and perhaps to many of them directly by instilling in them a spirit of resistance to oppression & wrongs inflicted on them & truer manhood which may some day explode to awaken this sinful Nation to its duty."[153] Martinet could have addressed these comforting words as much to himself as to Tourgée.

We cannot know from the surviving archival evidence whether or how Tourgée answered this gut-wrenching letter. In lieu of a private reply, history has preserved only a "Bystander" column of 12 August 1893, in which Tourgée anonymously reproduced a different passage from Martinet's letter, excoriating the nation's galling racial arrogance.[154] Before its publication, Tourgée did in fact return to Chicago, where he and Martinet again spoke in person, as a later letter of Martinet's makes clear.[155] Though no record remains of their conversation, we can perhaps glean a hint of what Tourgée may have said, either in person or in a missing letter, from his response to another outburst by Martinet. "Hardly anything has gone to my heart like your despairing cry, 'Let us get out of this hell of the United States!'" Tourgée replied on this subsequent occasion. "I do not blame you. I know I should feel so in your place—or rather much more desperate. I could not be so temperate and patient as many of you who I know realize the truth are."[156] We may cringe at the presumptuousness of a white man's claiming that he would feel "much more desperate" than African Americans themselves were he in their place. Still, it was Tourgée's ability to "imagine" what he had "never experienced," to put himself in the shoes of his African American friends, to listen when they bared their wounded psyches to him, to transmit their messages to a deaf white world, that won him the love and trust of Martinet and of all the other men and women who regarded him as a beacon lighting the darkest decade of U.S. race relations.

WHAT INSIGHTS CAN we cull from eavesdropping on the private exchanges between Tourgée and his chief African American correspondents and from peeping into the personal aspects of his relationship with each? How might these insights help us evaluate his collaboration with African Americans in efforts to reverse the white supremacist trends of the 1890s by fighting for equality and justice? First, we might note the diversity of viewpoints expressed by Chesnutt, Anderson, Fortune, Wells, and Martinet, notwithstanding the commitment they all shared to ending racial oppression. Second, we might observe the wide variations in the tone and tenor of Tourgée's letters to each, showing that he perceived them as individuals, not as racial stereotypes, and treated them accordingly. Third, we might take stock of the enormous difficulties that men and women of different races had to overcome in forging friendships across the color line during the nadir—and of the remarkable persistence they demonstrated by refusing to let social constraints discourage them. Fourth, we must surely be struck by the honesty both Tourgée and his African American correspondents displayed in their communications with each other—honesty about their disagreements, their feelings, and the racial barriers that divided them. Might we not then apply these insights to elaborating new paradigms of cross-racial collaborations as we examine Tourgée's interactions with Chesnutt, Anderson, Fortune, Wells, Martinet, and other African Americans in his main endeavors of the 1890s: promoting a national debate on the race question through his novel *Pactolus Prime* and his newspaper column "A Bystander's Notes"; founding an interracial civil rights organization, the National Citizens' Rights Association; campaigning against lynching; and challenging segregation in the *Plessy v. Ferguson* case?

CHAPTER TWO

Passing for Black in *Pactolus Prime*

I know of nothing that could give me greater pleasure than the "*disgust*" you say your readers are expressing in regard to Pactolus Prime. . . .

Please tell your readers for me, with all kindness and sincerity, that if they will get upon their knees and study their own hearts as Christians and American citizens, . . . they will do more than any human genius can toward determining what the sequel of the lives of . . . millions . . . shall be.

—Albion W. Tourgée to H. S. Harrison, editor,
  Chicago Advance, 26 March 1889

Tourgée's novella *Pactolus Prime; or, The White Christ* had been running since 13 December 1888 as an extended "Christmas Story" in the *Chicago Advance*, a Congregationalist weekly, when it ended abruptly on 14 March, leaving its African American title character dead and the fates of the two other African American protagonists unresolved. Besieged by angry subscribers who felt "imposed upon" by a truncated plot, the *Advance*'s editor warned Tourgée that unless he agreed to furnish a "sequel" tying up loose ends, the journal would have to break its contract with him for another serial. Tourgée's truculent reply spelled out his aesthetic philosophy with crystalline precision. He did not intend "merely to please—and certainly not to instruct" readers, he underscored, for to do so would be to treat them as passive consumers of literature. Nor did he intend to fulfill readers' desire for a story to "end as they had mapped out that it should," for they derived their expectations from the very status quo he sought to change. Thus, he had purposely provoked their "disgust" as a means of spurring them to imagine—and create—new possibilities for "tomorrow." In short, Tourgée conceived of literature as a vehicle for promoting social transformation, and he defined the relationship between author and reader as a dynamic partnership in that endeavor.[1]

Responding to a request for clarifications of the plot from a critic assigned to review the serialized novella for a literary society, Tourgée elaborated still more explicitly on the aesthetic philosophy guiding his formal choices. He had indeed meant that "much should be read between the lines" and even "*outside* the lines," he confirmed. Instead of "coddling" readers, he sought to awaken in them "an unsatisfied questioning impulse." He had deliberately left his novella "*not incomplete* but suggesting" questions that readers would feel "irresistibly compelled to answer." As for the "sequel" everyone was badgering Tourgée to write, only God could write it, using "the American people as tools."[2]

Notwithstanding his commitment to making readers write their own endings in accordance with their views as to whether, and how, prevailing racial mores might evolve, Tourgée ultimately compromised with current literary convention when he published *Pactolus Prime* as a book in March 1890. The serialized version had forced readers to infer—or guess—the details of Pactolus's past from his conversations with others, but in the book version, much to the satisfaction of the *Advance*'s reviewer, Tourgée tacked on "A True Record," an autobiographical narrative allowing Pactolus to "impart the secret of [his] life" to his survivors.[3] Similarly, the serial had prompted readers to envision futures for its two phenotypically white protagonists— Pactolus's publicly unacknowledged daughter, Eva, and his assistant, Benny, the son of Pactolus's estranged wife by their former master—that would burst the limits both literature and society placed on African Americans, but the book confined Eva squarely within those limits, reserving its original open ending only for Benny. In lieu of the serial's ragged-edged plot, the book's striking cover—"half black and half white, like the people whose condition it portrays," as reviewers noticed—took over the function of jarring readers' aesthetic tastes.[4]

Pactolus Prime's Critique of White Christianity

Regardless of the formal differences between them, the two versions of *Pactolus Prime* pose the same key questions: Can the U.S. race problem be solved, and if so, how? Speaking primarily through Pactolus, but also through Eva and Benny, Tourgée identifies white racism as the root of the problem, charging that it permeates all aspects of U.S. society and especially contaminates the Christianity preached and practiced by white Americans—hence the subtitle, "The White Christ." The "worship of the White Christ," a Christ reinterpreted as "the white man's Saviour," is the state religion, asserts Pactolus (13, 67). It has perverted "the Christ who came to bless and cure" the entire human race, the Christ "to whom all men are alike," into "the defender of caste" (296, 297). Descanting on the distortions of white Christianity, Pactolus fulminates, "This religion excuses the white man's license and suppresses the colored man's complaint. For every wrong done the colored man, it finds some palliation; for the evil he suffers, it urges only patient endurance and offers no hope of remedy this side the grave. It is a religion of injustice and inequality. . . . It administers soporifics rather than purgatives, to the troubled conscience" (296–97). Pactolus does not limit this critique to the white Christianity of the United States but applies it to all countries colonized by white people. Throughout the world, the "religion of the white Christ" has been "the accompaniment of bondage, or the precursor of destruction" to colored races, he observes, citing the examples of the Sandwich Islanders, the natives of Africa, and American Indians (298). Nevertheless, Pactolus pointedly distinguishes the cult of the "white Christ" from the message of universal love proclaimed by the historical Jesus. Precisely because he "revere[s]" the "teachings" of Jesus as articulating "God's ideal" of how human beings should relate to each other, "both individually and collectively," he "would rather suffer eternal torture than accept a God who would measure one man's right by the yard and another's by the barleycorn, or accord to one license to do evil because he is white, and impose on another intolerable wrong because he is black," Pactolus emphasizes (297).

Oriented toward white readers, Pactolus's critique of white Christianity does not pertain to black Christianity. We know from Tourgée's other writings, however, that he celebrated black Christianity insofar as it intertwined "political thought" with "religious conviction" in the pursuit of freedom and that he excoriated it insofar as it advised worshipers to "praise God and make money" rather than demand justice.[5]

By setting *Pactolus Prime* on Christmas Day in the nation's capital at a hotel symbolically named the "Best House," Tourgée depicts the problem of white racism as simultaneously religious and political. Located within sight of both the Capitol and the church of St. Aloysius, the Best House evokes at once the houses of government and of worship. It evokes as well Americans' "complacent" certainty that they have achieved the best political system the world has ever seen, "founded in justice," "embosomed in righteousness," and rewarded for its virtue by an "overflowing treasury" (2–3). Yet ironically, this "crowded inn" recalls "the one at Bethlehem, some nineteen centuries ago," that had "no place for the mother of our Lord" (5). It thus provides the perfect setting for determining whether the "Christian people" registered at the Best House apply the teachings of Jesus or the religion of the "white Christ" to the challenge of solving America's race problem (2, 13).

Tourgée stages the preponderance of the novel's action around Pactolus's bootblack stand in the hotel basement, where a series of customers representing a spectrum of white opinion come to get their shoes shined and, while waiting, debate the race question with Pactolus and his assistant,

Benny, who also debate it between themselves. Through these dialogues, which continue in other venues as the characters go about their business, Tourgée explores a range of possible remedies for the inequities, prejudices, and bitterness that two and a half centuries of black slavery have legated to the nation. He also tests practitioners of various occupations for their willingness and ability to repudiate white racism: a doctor, a lawyer, a minister, a traveling salesman, a judge, a former soldier, a plantation owner, a senator, and a journalist. At the same time, he probes the discourses of religion, law, science, and journalism.

Pactolus as Tourgée's Persona

For most of the novel, Pactolus serves as Tourgée's chief mouthpiece. The "colored bootblack" is "none other than the powerful, impassioned, convinced and convincing lecturer, Judge Tourgee himself, done over in ebony," notes the African American scholar-educator-activist Anna Julia Cooper, the most insightful of the book's contemporary reviewers: "His caustic wit, his sledge hammer logic, his incisive criticism, his righteous indignation, all reflect the irresistible arguments of the great pleader for the Negro; and all the incidents are arranged to enable this bootblack to impress on senators and judges, lawyers, and divines, his plea for justice to the Negro."[6] Commenting from a late twentieth-century perspective on the "doubleness" of this literary strategy, Brook Thomas points out, "Tourgée, a white lawyer, speaks out on race by adopting the voice of a black man, who in the novel needs a white lawyer to act as his agent."[7]

Tourgée's identification with his black hero goes far beyond borrowing his voice. He gives Pactolus his own Civil War experiences, his own combat wounds, his own ordeal as a target of white supremacist rage during Reconstruction, and his own status as a surrogate politician with an independent mind, who impresses "statesmen" as a "close observer, and not seldom . . . a sound adviser" (25). Tourgée even fulfills his own thwarted aspirations through Pactolus.

When we first meet Pactolus on his way to his bootblack stand, we find him walking with a "heavy cane" and a "curious shuffling gait" that results from his right leg's being "turned outward below the knee," so that it "drag[s] after the other" (8, 28). A doctor who examines him later, after he is "knocked down by a horse" (233) while heading toward his daughter Eva's house, discovers that though Pactolus's "injury is nervous rather than physical," the "concussion" has exacerbated what appears to be a "previous injury of the spine" (230–31). Examination of the "patient's hip and right leg" also reveals "gun-shot wounds—from the rear" (233). Because the accident comes on top of "former injuries," the doctor predicts that "paraplegia may supervene—partial paralysis" (231, 233). These details closely parallel accounts of Tourgée's medical condition. Hit in the back by a gun carriage during the Union army's frenzied rout from the battlefield of Bull Run, Tourgée had undergone almost a year of partial paralysis. On regaining some mobility, he could at first move his legs only by "swinging [his] body" and "dragging with staff and crutch." When he at last succeeded in walking without crutches, "'a little drag' in the movement of his right leg" remained. Tourgée attributed his cure to a "prescription . . . that contained 'strychnine in large quantities.'"[8] He would subject Pactolus to an equally drastic course of treatment: "nitrate of silver in such stiff, old-fashioned doses as to produce . . . silver-poisoning" (251). Like Pactolus, Tourgée reinjured his spine. Pactolus's gunshot wound in the hip further echoes the shrapnel wound in the hip that Tourgée received at the battle of Perryville.

Many details of Pactolus's military career also invite comparison with Tourgée's. Passing for white under the name P. P. Smith, Pactolus had "enlisted as a private in the —th Indiana Volunteer Infantry, near Shell Mound, Tenn., on the 17th day of June, a.d. 1862, and was discharged 'for promotion,' on the 6th day of December, a.d. 1863, at Chattanooga," when he was elevated to a "Lieutenancy in a colored regiment" (254, 310). Tourgée, who had served as a private in the Twenty-Seventh New York Infantry at Bull Run, reenlisted as a lieutenant on 20 August 1862 in the 105th Ohio Volunteer Infantry, which fought in the vicinity of Shell Mound and Chattanooga; he was discharged on the same day as his hero: 6 December 1863. Unlike his hero, on the other hand, Tourgée not only failed to obtain either the promotion or the transfer to a black regiment for which he had applied but, worse still, endured the humiliation of being forced to resign because his superiors judged him physically unfit for active duty. Tourgée's reinjured spine prevented him from participating in his regiment's most celebrated battle, the storming of Missionary Ridge east of Chattanooga, which he had to observe from below.[9] In contrast, under the appropriate guise of the white "color-bearer" P. P. Smith—a guise that conceals his identity as the sole colored soldier in an all-white engagement—Pactolus charges up Missionary Ridge, saves his commanding officer from bleeding to death after losing an arm, and wins recognition as a "gallant fellow" (96). Although Tourgée did not share the military glory he bestowed on his hero, he did share Pactolus's fate as a Confederate prisoner of war. Captured in January 1863, Tourgée spent four months in Richmond's Libby prison, among others—an experience he looked back on as formative. Pactolus, too, would count it a "real privilege, strange as that may seem," to have been incarcerated in a wartime "prison-pen" where soldiers were "kept on half-rations for months." For him, the significance of his stint as a POW lay in the bonds it forged among soldiers who had sacrificed their liberty, their health, and frequently their lives to liberate others from bondage—a significance Tourgée likewise saw in his Civil War service. "It is the grandest thing I ever knew," reminisces Pactolus, "—those men who did not know who might see the morning, singing in quivering tones as the sun went down: 'As He died to make men holy, let us die to make men free!'" (124).[10]

The parallels between Tourgée's career and his hero's extend beyond the war into the Reconstruction era, during which Tourgée leased an orchard in North Carolina and Pactolus / P. P. Smith buys a plantation in South Carolina. Pactolus's daughter, Eva, remembers that "he employed a number of laborers and worked with them," as did Tourgée, and that she "used to ride behind him on horseback," as did Tourgée's daughter, Aimée (195). Like Tourgée, Pactolus / P. P. Smith becomes "active in politics" and makes himself "'obnoxious,' as the saying is in that section, to the 'respectable people' of the region by the free expression of his opinions" (278). Yet once again, Tourgée embellished the record he projected onto his hero. He himself had forestalled several plots against his life and escaped physically, if not psychologically, unscathed, but Pactolus is actually "shot and left for dead upon the highway" (312). Moreover, Pactolus attributes the enmity of his neighbors to jealousy of his "prosperity" as well as resentment of his "politics" (312), whereas Tourgée's business enterprises in North Carolina had failed.

The detail that most suggestively links Tourgée with Pactolus—the poison used to restore both to a semblance of health after the crippling injuries they suffer during the war and its violent aftermath—indicates that Tourgée identifies with his hero above all as a racial outcast. Light enough to pass for white as a soldier, plantation owner, and advocate of radical Reconstruction, Pactolus darkens so much as a result of the nitrate of silver his physician has prescribed to lower the fever caused by his wounds that his complexion turns a "peculiar leaden-gray" (28). Even his lips and the whites of his eyes have acquired this unnatural tint. In addition to the congenital skin color that marked him as "white," Pactolus has lost all the hair on his body, including his eyelashes, hair being another feature commonly used to ascertain a person's "race." The transformation in racial appearance that Pactolus has undergone is directly traceable to his having defied "respectable" public opinion, which has consigned him to being "left for dead" (312) as a white man, and allowed him to survive only at the price of what the white world considers social death: being branded as "black."[11]

In discussing Pactolus's case, the doctor, who recognizes him as the "white" victim of silver poisoning described in a pathbreaking medical article, wonders "why a white man should wish to be thought a Negro"—a fate he regards as so dreadful that he himself "would rather not be, than be black" (255). Pactolus's lawyer supplies an answer: "Don't you see, Doctor, the man's whole life has been a struggle against the curse of color? . . . — the curse which makes the Negro a hopeless inferior and invokes the law of God—the religion of Jesus of Nazareth—to keep him so!" (261). As this dialogue reveals, Tourgée displayed remarkable self-awareness about the nature of his identification with his "black" hero. His life, too, had been a "struggle against the curse of color," and he, too, had metaphorically turned black in the process. "One who takes the part of an oppressed and despised people, especially if they be of another race, must, in a sense, lose caste with his own," he would observe several years later in a "Bystander" column.[12] He would express the insight even more plainly when publishers and editors turned their backs on him and started rejecting his manuscripts after his defeat in the 1896 *Plessy v. Ferguson* case sealed the doom of his lifelong campaign for racial equality: "I am in effect a Negro so far as literary opportunity is concerned."[13] In sum, Tourgée knew exactly what he was doing in *Pactolus Prime* by posing as a man who could no longer pass for white.

Of course, these autobiographical resonances do not exhaust the novel's meaning or explain its literary strategies. For example, by making Pactolus his white master's half brother and rival for the love of the equally light-skinned slave Mazy, the mother of Eva and Benny, Tourgée creates a family romance plot to symbolize the psychosexual perversions of slavery. Pactolus's shifts in racial identity also serve the larger purpose of calling racial categories into question. As the doctor argues, a "drop" of "colored blood"—"even a suspicion of a drop"—may be enough "for the world, society," and perhaps the church, to classify someone as a "Negro," but this social fiction cannot hold up "medically" or "scientifically" (262). The novel demonstrates the illusoriness of "race" both through characters who are light enough to pass— Pactolus, Eva, and Benny—and, more subversively, through the medical treatment that blackens Pactolus. If skin color, facial features, and hair type do not provide foolproof means of determining racial identity—if a person can flip from "black" to "white" and back again depending on social circumstances and the effects of chemicals on the body—then "race" is not a stable fact of nature, and the rigid distinctions society maintains between the dominant race and its Other(s) threaten to collapse at any moment, Tourgée shows (anticipating the argument he would develop in the *Plessy* case).[14]

Pactolus's Dialogue with Benny about Passing

While dismissing "race" as a construct that has no scientific basis, Tourgée recognizes white racism as an intractable political problem derived from the legacy of slavery. He sets readers the task of solving that problem by inviting them to participate in the dialogues his characters conduct about it.

Pactolus's dialogues with Benny, through which Tourgée seems to be addressing and responding to African Americans, pronounce the prospects of reforming white racial attitudes to be so remote that passing for white—an option only a few can exercise—offers the sole escape from a life of humiliation. Having "tried once, to help in the lifting up of a race and securing its rights," confides Tourgée through his fictional mouthpiece, and having been defeated by violence, he has become "content to help individuals" (141). Pactolus's recipe for helping individuals is enabling those who can to pass, yet he fails to persuade either Benny or Eva to choose this path. Clearly, Tourgée realizes that most African Americans find the idea of passing repugnant.

The arguments Pactolus urges in favor of passing are that the peer pressures preventing whites from recognizing African Americans as equals "are not likely to change in a good many years—perhaps not in a good many centuries, and [Benny] cannot afford to wait" (136); that anyone "known to have a drop of Negro blood in his veins" will always be a "nigger" in white eyes, no matter what his (or her) talents or attainments, and consequently that none of the avenues of upward mobility available to whites are of any use for raising the status of blacks (43); and that by passing, Benny can give his "children the advantage of being regarded as superior beings to whom all opportunities are open," whereas by identifying himself as black, he will be entailing on them a "degrading curse" (45, 135). In addition to arguments, Pactolus presents Benny with a plan: he will take the young man into partnership in the shoeshine business through which he has accumulated a small fortune; once Benny has made enough money, he should relocate, "take a new name . . . and keep right on makin' money, never lettin' on that you're not as white as anybody" (40).

Benny indignantly rejects what he views as an attack on his race pride. "I'm a Negro, sir, . . . and I do not care who knows it: I've no wish to be anything else," he tells Pactolus "proudly, raising his head" (39). Embracing his identity, he equates blackness with manhood and whiteness with dehumanizing greed: "I'd rather be a man and black, than a mere money-bags and white" (43). Although Benny has experienced discrimination, having lost his previous job as a cashier when his employer learned of his race (134), he "hate[s] the very thought" of becoming a "white man," as Pactolus advises, not only because "he hate[s] the very thought" of his white father (using the identical phrase) but because passing "seems like deserting my race" (136, 138).[15] The desire to "do something for the race" (140)—a desire Benny believes "we ought all to think of now, before anything else" (133)—has impelled him to study law with the white lawyer Mr. Phelps, who has been handling Pactolus's legal affairs. Pactolus insists, however, that Benny should aim to be a "*white* lawyer," because he can do more for his race "as a white man . . . than a thousand colored men" could (140, 143). Pactolus cannot specify, however, what Benny can contribute as a white man to transforming "*white* sentiment, white civilization, white Christianity" (140). If he means that Benny will be able to speak to whites with more authority as one of them, Tourgée's notable lack of success in inducing the majority of his fellow whites to overcome their racism would seem to contradict him. Like Tourgée, Pactolus can only predict that "the essential equality in right, power, privilege and opportunity of the Negro in America is sure to be established" eventually, but he cannot foresee "when or how," whether "within a generation" or in "centuries," whether "by reason" or "by force," whether "by a change of Christian ideals" or "by a message from heaven written in blood," such as the Civil War (142).

We never find out how Benny chooses to "work out his own destiny" (358). Tourgée leaves the dialogue between the idealistic young spokesman for race pride and the jaundiced old proponent of passing—who may or may not voice the sentiments of the white author—unresolved.

Eva's Rejection of Passing

Tourgée conveys African Americans' distaste for passing as a solution to the race problem not only through Benny's passionate outbursts against it but also through Eva's rejection of the course Pactolus has plotted for her by bringing her up in ignorance of her parentage, placing her in a Montreal convent and a New England college for education as a white lady, and bequeathing her the fortune he has amassed with hard work, thrift, and astute investments in real estate under his white alias, P. P. Smith. Unlike

Benny, Eva objects to the plan not out of race pride—since she has grown up cut off from African Americans, though dimly suspecting that she is "somehow connected with that unfortunate people" (150)—but out of loyalty to the man she considers "more than a father to her," whom she has known as "Uncle Pac," allegedly the faithful servant of her deceased father (148). Thus, when Pactolus sends his lawyer, Mr. Phelps, to tell Eva of the bequest by "P. P. Smith," she refuses it, unless she can share her new wealth and her home with her "Uncle Pac." As Phelps reports to Pactolus, "She feels certain that you have supported, cared for and educated her, and she is determined that where you are, she will go. In the words of Ruth, she is ready to say, 'Your people shall be my people and your God my God'" (150).

Because Pactolus has delegated Phelps as his agent to avoid identifying himself as Eva's father, which would "ruin" her chances of being classed as white (151), Eva engages Phelps, rather than Pactolus, in a dialogue on the choice she faces: passing for white at the cost of denying the man she loves as a father, or casting her lot with African Americans at the cost of sacrificing all the pleasures she has hitherto enjoyed in life. In this dialogue, aimed at white readers, Eva echoes Pactolus's "diatribes" against white racism and the "white Christ," and Phelps illustrates the limitations of late nineteenth-century white liberals. Phelps himself notices that Eva must have "listened to more than one of [Pactolus's] diatribes on the status of the colored race" before she could have learned to reproduce them so exactly (150), and Pactolus confirms that he influenced her racial views: "While I wished her to be white, I could not bear that she should be taught to despise the race with which she is even remotely allied" (322). Accordingly, as Eva anticipates white society's ostracism of her, should she reveal her ancestry, she reproaches Phelps in accents similar to Pactolus's: "You yourself, would not dare treat me as an equal. You would not think of introducing me to your daughter, of asking me to your table. Perhaps you would not even care to be seen ringing the bell at my door! Oh, I understand what it is to be considered a colored person, more especially a colored woman! I know that no merit, no ability, no refinement, no accomplishment, can put me on a level with even the lowest born and most vulgar white woman of the land" (202). Being "considered . . . a colored woman," Eva implies, means being perceived by whites as tainted by a heritage of rape and concubinage that defines her as immoral, regardless of how chaste her life may be. Hence, "no white woman can call such an one her friend; no white man offer her love that is not an insult!" (202). That is why Phelps would not wish to introduce her to his daughter or be caught ringing her doorbell. For the same reason, if his son ever became "insane enough" to marry Eva, Phelps would order the "door shut in his face and pass him by unrecognized on the streets!" (203).

Like Pactolus, Eva extends her arraignment of white society's racism to its practice of Christianity: "You are a good Christian, but if Christ were black you would not dare ask Him to your table!" No longer distinguishing, as Pactolus does, between the "ideal" articulated in the teachings of the historical Jesus and the white man's "distortion of that ideal" (297), Eva charges, "The Christ may be the Saviour of both races; but He will never make the white man willing to do justice to the Negro. He may perhaps change the colored man's skin—even if he has to blanch it with shame—but he will never change the white man's heart" (209–10).

Reluctantly, Phelps admits that Eva is right. "Society is stronger than any man, and society is—white!" he acknowledges (203). Indeed, he has demonstrated his unwillingness to challenge society in an earlier scene, in which he has invited Pactolus to share a meal with him while they are conferring in his office, but has "securely locked" the door to avoid the "odium" he would "incur" if he were seen eating with a "black pariah" (165). Like most white liberals of his day, including those Tourgée would berate at the Mohonk Conference a few months after the publication of *Pactolus Prime*, Phelps shifts the burden of changing these conditions onto African Americans, without promising that whites will ever lift their social proscriptions.

Tellingly, he does not finish the sentence he begins: "When the colored race shall have acquired wealth, intelligence and power—." In reply to Eva's question—"Will it make them white?"—Phelps prophesies not that African Americans will win acceptance in white society as equals but that "the colored race will form a society of its own, and know how to recognize each other's merits" (204).

Tourgée surely knew that African Americans did in fact already form a society of their own, nowhere more conspicuously than in Washington. In his judgment, this did not absolve whites of their duty to repudiate racism and cease discriminating against their African American brothers and sisters. Speaking through Eva, Tourgée sarcastically denounces the segregation Phelps seems to endorse and denies that separate can ever mean equal: "Then you think society will assume a dual form; there is to be a white aristocracy and a black aristocracy, a white people and a black people, a white church and a black church! . . . Will you go farther and have a Black Christ as well as a White Christ? I suppose they will maintain 'fraternal relations,' while strictly avoiding all approach to equality. Shall we have a dual millennium, too? And a separate heaven for each?" (204–5).

As bitterly as Eva condemns white racism and segregation, the white world is the only one she has ever known. Unlike Benny, she can imagine no dignified or fulfilling life outside it. Hence, she contemplates the social landscape through white eyes, discerning nothing but privation and stigma beyond the precincts of white privilege: "*My* world—the world of ambition, art, literature, society, the world that contains all that one loves to enjoy— the world which it is life to be a part of, and worse than death to be shut out from—this is white—all white—pure white! All else is foul, inferior— tolerated only!" (205–6).

Ultimately, Tourgée cannot provide a satisfactory solution to Eva's dilemma. Literary realism, Tourgée's chosen mode (despite his rejection of its leading proponent's tenets), by definition operates within the bounds of the possible.[16] Within those bounds, the racist society of nineteenth-century America allowed no means for a young woman in Eva's circumstances to live with her visibly black father on an equal footing—let alone to fulfill her pledge "Your people shall be my people and your God my God"—except by forfeiting the privileges of whiteness. Thus, Tourgée kills Pactolus off and immures Eva in a convent, where she honors her father's memory not by assimilating into white society as he wished but by taking the name Sister Pactola and devoting her fortune and her life to working for the uplift of her father's people without openly identifying herself as one of them. As Phelps explains, "She sees no other way to avoid either [the] deception" of passing for white "or the confession of inferiority" that assuming an African American identity would entail (358).

The denouement of Eva's story is the least successful aspect of *Pactolus Prime*. Contrived and defeatist, it shows that Tourgée was right to prefer letting his readers decide for themselves how to remove the racial barriers preventing African Americans from participating in the world of culture and politics on equal terms with their white fellow citizens. The novel accomplishes this purpose far more successfully through Pactolus's dialogues with his white shoeshine customers. By relying so heavily on polemical dialogues, rather than on a romantic plot, Tourgée once again flouts the literary conventions of his time in order to plumb the depths of racism. He substitutes a portrait of American society constructed around a series of deft character sketches and exchanges in which the principals reveal their personalities, ethical values, and racial attitudes as they interact with Pactolus—a literary achievement in its own right.[17]

Pactolus's Dialogue with Lawyer Phelps

Pactolus's first customer, his lawyer, Mr. Phelps, preaches the "Gospel of Wealth" as a solution to the race problem. "You know my feeling in regard to your race," Phelps tells Pactolus: "Money is the secret of success, and the power to make money the test of merit. The ladder on which your race must rise has golden rounds. When they become the owners of railroads they will be able to travel first-class anywhere. As soon as they own the majority of acres in any State, they will control its legislation. Power is regulated by the dollar-mark; so are privilege and esteem" (154). Writing at the height of the Gilded Age and its robber barons, Tourgée no doubt recognized the threat to American democracy embedded in the assertion that those who own the most property control the government and frame its legislation (a threat more dire than ever in the wake of the 2009 and 2014 Supreme Court decisions legalizing unlimited corporate and personal contributions to elections). Pactolus, however, exposes Phelps's advice as impious and hypocritical. Its implication, he points out, is that "niggers ought to worship Mammon" (60)—a clear violation of Jesus's precept, "Ye cannot serve God and mammon" (Matt. 6:24). He also hints that under their pretense of worshiping God, white Americans worship Mammon. Moreover, notes Pactolus, without "knowledge," African Americans cannot acquire property, yet whites refuse to pledge either to educate African Americans or to change their discriminatory practices once the race has obtained "learning" and wealth. He has heard the president himself (the newly elected Republican Benjamin Harrison) respond to requests for help by exhorting African Americans simply to "wait and work until we got as much money as white folks," promising "nothing" when they had done so (60–61). As a result, Pactolus has concluded, "Money makes a white man, that's true: but even money can't help a 'nigger': he's nothing but a 'nigger,' no matter how rich. The only thing for him to do is to get to be white or pretend to be white" (155).

Pactolus's Dialogue with a Minister

While Phelps represents the secular liberals who preach the "Gospel of Wealth," Pactolus's second customer, a minister in the adjacent seat of his bootblack stand, represents white Christianity. Throughout their discussion, the minister displays more concern with defending the reputation of the church than with assuaging the oppression of African Americans, which he accuses them of exaggerating. "Your people" are "too impatient," he admonishes Pactolus; "you want everything at once" (70). He believes Pactolus's identity as a "colored man" biases him to "fancy" that his "race has suffered" grave "wrongs," but the minister cannot see how his own identity as a white man might bias him to discount those wrongs (72). He remains unable to put himself in the place of African Americans, even with the help of the analogy Pactolus draws by asking the minister how he feels when someone owes him money but does not repay it, despite numerous requests. Translating the analogy back into the language he favors, Pactolus proclaims, "I feel as if Christianity—the followers of the white Christ—had robbed my people of two hundred and fifty years of bodily toil and rightful opportunity, taking the proceeds to add to their own wealth, their own luxury, the education of their children, the building of churches and colleges.... Not a dollar nor a cent came back to us in any form. We gave and you took.... No shuffling or evasion can avoid the responsibility" (72–73). Under the weight of Pactolus's arguments, the minister at length breaks down and admits African Americans "cannot be blamed for feeling that they have been bitterly wronged" (an admission that still falls short of recognizing that they *have* in fact been "bitterly wronged"), but he insists Christianity should not be held responsible for the misdeeds of its "votaries" (77, 78). "Why not?" retorts Pactolus: "You hold Mahometanism responsible for all the ills of Turkish life and government, and credit heathenism with the woes that befall the people who practice idolatry. In like manner, Christianity is responsible for every evil it permits to exist among a Christian people—or that results from a Christian government" (78). Pactolus finally manages to shake the minister's complacent faith. The man of God walks to church asking himself, "Can it be that the followers of the Christ have made Him seem to be only the friend and Saviour of the white man? Is Prime right in calling Him the 'White' Christ?" (79). Terrified at the thought, the minister wonders "what would have been his own religious status had the *Man* Jesus Christ been black, and the circumstances of his life and that of Pactolus Prime been reversed" (80). Notwithstanding his newfound empathy, the minister proves impotent to suggest any remedy for racial injustice. "What can we do?" he muses. "God help us—*it is a terrible problem!*" (80).

Pactolus's Dialogues with White Racists about Reparations

Ironically, a customer who makes no pretensions to either Christianity or sympathy for African Americans sparks consideration of a remedy still

being passionately debated today: reparations.[18] Voicing majority sentiment in the North, this customer, a traveling salesman, rages, "I wish you
niggers would find out just how much the country owes you, or how much
you would be satisfied with, and let us pay you off and quit fussing about it!
I don't seem to have heard of much else in my day except, the wrongs of the
nigger, and I'm tired—sick of the whole matter! I'd like to have the account
settled and be done with it!" (73). He brushes off Pactolus's warning that the
country's debt to African Americans can never be adequately estimated, still
less repaid. "Oh, we wouldn't be particular about the amount," declares the
salesman, ". . . if we could only stop the race's whining. . . . I'd like to see the
account squared and start fresh, with the understanding that each race was
to keep up its own end hereafter and ask no favors" (73–74).

In what may well be the earliest attempt to set a monetary figure on the
reparations owed African Americans for their two and a half centuries of
unremunerated labor (unless we include the legendary "40 acres and a mule"
that the newly freed slaves believed the government had promised them),
Pactolus and Benny proceed to calculate the "whole value of the Negro's
work in the United States as a slave" (74). Though they fix the ridiculously
inadequate price of ten cents on a day's work and "three-fifths of each life
as work-time"—a rate even the salesman pronounces "too low"—the total
comes to *"more than ten billions of dollars!"* (75, 76). Benny specifies that he
has arrived at that sum by multiplying "two hundred and forty-seven years of
bondage" by "twenty-six slaves at first and five millions at the last" and "counting only three hundred days to the year" (76). Incredulous, the salesman finds
when he recalculates the amount that Benny has understated it by "fully a
half billion" (76). "Blamed if I ever snarl at a nigger for grumbling, again,"
he exclaims (77). But the salesman's behavior demonstrates the unlikelihood
that the mass of white Americans will agree to discharge their debt to African
Americans. He makes a quick exit, saying, "Don't want to hear any more; I've
had enough" (77), as Pactolus tries to explain why $10 billion amounts to
"only a tithe of what Christianity" and a "Christian government" owe his people: "Who shall estimate the damages for lost opportunity, to say nothing of
violated right? Who shall state the money value of two centuries of enforced
ignorance and depravity? What sum could compensate a people for the stain
of universal illegitimacy, the denial of fatherhood, the violation of maternal
right, the debasement of female virtue, the utter effacement of all family ties
and family relations, the refusal of even a family name?" (78). To answer these
questions, white Americans would need to examine their country's history
honestly, but none of Pactolus's interlocutors indicates any desire to do so.

The customer who takes the salesman's place, one of several Southerners and Southern sympathizers to harangue Pactolus in the course of the day, reflects the entrenchment and pervasiveness of the racism that prevents any solution to African Americans' predicament. The heavy pro-Southern presence around Pactolus's bootblack stand also reflects the South's diffusion of its white supremacist ideology throughout the nation. Claiming to "know something about the facts of history, and something about niggers too," the new customer rejects the notion of a white debt to African Americans as "nonsense" and the calculations of Pactolus and Benny as "humbug" (81). Pactolus easily disposes of his adversary's efforts to portray slavery as a benevolent institution under which slaves received more than their "work was worth" in food, clothing, housing, medical care, and education (81), but the apologist now accuses him of "harping on" a "dead" issue (85). In answer to Pactolus's charge that white Americans are "flaunting the fruits" of the slaves' stolen labor, he shouts, "Who's got the money the nigger earned? . . . Can anybody trace it? Does anybody know how much it is? Where is it deposited? In what is it invested? . . . If a man can prove his property, he has a right to take it, not otherwise. That is the law!" (86).

At this juncture Benny intervenes to clarify the legal basis for demanding reparations. "That is the law; but it is not equity, and our case is in equity," he argues: "Our demand is for an equivalent, or a partial equivalent, for what has been wrongfully taken from us and converted to the use of the taker" (86). He proceeds to parry the objections raised by a "kindly" judge in the audience who acts as a stand-in for Tourgée. Because "the slave's labor has gone into the national wealth," Benny reasons, "that immense aggregate . . . is, in equity, charged with whatever sums may be necessary to recompense our people, so far as may be, for the wrong done them in the past" (87–88). Granted that many Americans "remonstrated against the injustice of slavery" (88), as the judge notes, all Americans nevertheless share the political and moral responsibility for allegiance to a Constitution that protected slavery against any legal interference (89). Benny ends by citing a precedent for taxing the nation to compensate African Americans for the damages they sustained from slavery: "If property is destroyed in a riot, the municipality which did not afford sufficient protection is responsible for the damages" (90). Benny's performance as a lawyer in training wins him the highest commendation a judge can bestow: "I hope to see you at the bar very soon, sir, and do not doubt you will have occasion to express your views upon these matters more effectually when I am dead and gone" (91).

Thus, readers may well conclude that Benny does not need to pass for white the better to serve his people, contrary to Pactolus's insistence.

Though Benny has won the debate over reparations, Pactolus objects that no such remedy for racial injustice has any chance of being implemented by white Americans. "What white people would think it worth their while to pay any claim the Negro might have against them?" he asks. "The Christian idea of justice never gets across the color line. . . . Right is always white in Christian law" (93–94). Consequently, Pactolus believes African Americans have properly contented themselves with appealing for justice and not demanding reparations. "Justice to-day pays all the debts of yesterday, and nothing else will," he contends (94). As we shall see, however, he later advocates an alternative form of reparations: federal aid to education.

Pactolus's Dialogue with a Civil War Union Veteran

Meanwhile, before Pactolus broaches this subject with a customer who has the power to legislate on it, another stand-in for Tourgée appears on the scene: a maimed Civil War veteran. Pactolus immediately recognizes him as the major whose life he saved, in his guise as the color-bearer P. P. Smith, when the officer lost his arm during the battle of Missionary Ridge. The major, on the other hand, does not recognize his "white" color-bearer in the dark-skinned bootblack. Tourgée eschews the dramatic possibilities of letting Pactolus reveal his identity to the major—a choice that keeps the scene focused not on the two men's personal relationship but on the broader political issues their dialogue raises. Having eavesdropped on the debate over reparations, the veteran complains that "you colored folks . . . don't state the case fairly when you charge up all your wrongs against us and omit to give credit for what you have received from us," namely, freedom and citizenship rights (94). He expresses the sentiments of many white Northerners who had fought against slavery both as abolitionists and as Union soldiers and wanted "credit" for their contributions. Pactolus readily acknowledges that men like the veteran deserve "double credit" for their sacrifices (94), but he questions whether African Americans have received the value of the blood they themselves shed for the nation as soldiers. After depriving African Americans of the freedom with which "God and nature" originally endowed them, whites have no right to claim credit for giving it back, points out Pactolus (97). As for citizenship, "you gave us a *legal* right . . . and then permitted its exercise to be made a matter of mortal peril to the colored man who seeks to benefit himself or his people, thereby" (98). The veteran not only concedes the justice of Pactolus's criticisms but promises to continue their conversation when he has "more time." Exemplifying the best hope of solving the nation's race problem, he shows "how community of peril,—the comradeship of battle,—fuses lives together so closely as to burn away even the barriers between black and white manhood" (99). Tourgée had learned precisely this lesson from his own experience as a Union soldier, which had inspired him to devote his life to championing African Americans.

Pactolus's Dialogue with Proponents of Black Expatriation

Just as the nation's sympathy for African Americans in the wake of the Civil War had quickly given way to promoting reconciliation with former Confederates, the veteran has hardly left Pactolus's shoeshine stand before two spokesmen for white supremacy come to the fore. The first, an "elegantly dressed young man" sporting a cigar, who turns out to be the brother of Pactolus's former master, though he does not recognize the bootblack, wishes "every 'nigger' could be sent back to Africa where they belong" (100). The second, "a sallow, narrow-faced man with a long beard who sat scowling behind a paper he had pretended to be reading in another chair," wishes "as Henry Clay did, that 'the foot of the Negro had never rested on American soil'" (100, 101). Clay, a Whig senator from Kentucky, had been a leading antebellum proponent of "Colonization," or deportation to Africa, as an ostensible means of ending slavery—a scheme that had been denounced as racist and fraudulent by black and white abolitionists.

Defunct since the Civil War, the idea of ridding the nation of its race problem by ridding it of African Americans had been regaining traction among white supremacists in the 1880s. During the very months when Tourgée was expanding *Pactolus Prime* into a full-length novel, a book by the Charleston newspaper editor and Confederate veteran Carlyle McKinley titled *An Appeal to Pharaoh* resurrected the idea of inducing African Americans to emigrate "voluntarily" by promising them free transportation to Africa and implicitly threatening them with intensified oppression if they refused. Modeled on Tourgée's *An Appeal to Caesar* with a view to countering it, this travesty of his plea for justice to African Americans quoted him only to turn his warning against disregarding the "laws of God" on its head. As if to add insult to injury, *An Appeal to Pharaoh* bore the imprint of the firm that had published *An Appeal to Caesar*, as well as *A Fool's Errand* and *Bricks Without Straw*. Tourgée replied to it in his article "Shall We Re-Barbarize the Negro?" (1889). Although he shared McKinley's mistaken assumption that native Africans were barbarians who needed to be civilized (as the term "re-barbarize" indicates), Tourgée rejected McKinley's claim that promoting emigration to Africa offered a solution to the U.S. race problem. "The obligation arising from centuries of enslavement cannot be discharged by returning [the Negro] naked to the wilds of Africa," retorted Tourgée:

> For every dollar of unrequited toil that went into our wondrous aggregate of wealth, he has a right to claim a just and fair equivalent in intelligence and opportunity. When by his labor he made it possible for schools and colleges to be built, where the sons of the masters might enjoy the blessings of knowledge; when his labor helped pay for churches and court-houses, and all those monuments of progress of which our nation boasts— . . . he established an indefeasible equity, for himself and his descendants, in their enjoyment.[19]

We will of course recognize these arguments as identical to the ones Benny and Pactolus urge in favor of African Americans' entitlement to reparations.

Yet instead of reiterating them, Pactolus acknowledges that "it was a great advantage to the colored race to be brought to this country" because it raised them above the level of "the Negroes on the Congo coast" and introduced them to "Christianity and civilization" (102–3).[20] Tourgée's faith in a beneficent Providence, his confidence in the Christian religion's superiority to all others, and his belief in European "civilization" as the acme of human development left him in a weak position to refute the notion that slavery had in some degree benefited African Americans. Few African Americans conceded as much, but one who did was Booker T. Washington, with whom Tourgée disagreed on most other matters. Despite the institution's "cruelty and moral wrong," Washington would write in *Up from Slavery* (1901), "the ten million Negroes inhabiting this country, who themselves or whose ancestors went through the school of American slavery, are in a stronger and more hopeful condition, materially, intellectually, morally, and religiously, than is true of an equal number of black people in any other portion of the globe."[21]

Pactolus's Dialogue with a Senator about Federal Aid to Education

This said, it was not the Booker T. Washingtons that Tourgée sought to represent in *Pactolus Prime*. Through Pactolus and Benny, he sought rather to voice the militant demands for equal rights that were issuing from the

National Afro-American League and from black newspapers like the *Detroit Plaindealer* and the *Cleveland Gazette*. The novel succeeds best at speaking for African American militants in the dialogues it stages about reparations, which climax with Pactolus's efforts to convince a U.S. senator that federal aid to education, allotting African Americans the largest share, would constitute the most effective form of reparations.

The unnamed senator, obviously Henry Blair of New Hampshire, against whose education bill Tourgée had been campaigning while writing and revising *Pactolus Prime*, arrives as the brother of Pactolus's former master storms away from the bootblack's taunting. Once again reflecting the influence white Southerners were exerting over Northern opinion, the senator immediately shows where his sympathies lie in any racial dispute. The "Southern people" should not be blamed for atrocities that only "a small portion" of them commit or condone, he rebukes Pactolus, while flourishing his credentials as a spokesman "very far from being an apologist for the wrongs that have been done your race" (110). Pactolus rejoins that a "'nigger,' who studies Southern life every day he lives, at first hand and short range, is apt to know more about it than a Northern man who never gets nigh enough to it to *feel* it" (111). He proceeds to explain how ignorance of the South flaws the National Aid to Education bill that the senator touts as a "measure designed" to "compensate your people for enforced ignorance" (111). Though blacks "would have no voice in the control or application" of the federal education funds allocated to the states for distribution, underscores Pactolus, they would be held responsible for failing to progress in inferior schools (113).

Defending his bill against Pactolus's criticism, the senator protests, "The fact that a man is black does not prove that he knows what is best for the colored race" (116). Pactolus argues to the contrary that no one can know "what is best for the colored race" without walking in the shoes a colored person wears in a racist society and feeling where they pinch. Of course, Pactolus does not literally speak for African Americans but for a white author who is passing as black through a fictional persona. In fact, Tourgée's stubborn opposition to the Blair bill, notwithstanding the African American community's decision to support it, ironically aligned him more with the senator's contention that black people do not necessarily know what is best for them than with Pactolus's retort, "I know what it is *to be a 'nigger,'* . . . and *you don't*" (116).

Still, Pactolus's dialogue with the senator accurately captures the positions that Blair, Tourgée, and some African American spokesmen took in debates over the education bill. The parallels are especially striking in the passages Tourgée inserted into the book version of *Pactolus Prime*. Just as the fictional senator tells Pactolus, "But your people, hundreds and thousands of them, have asked for this very measure which you denounce" (124), Blair "claimed that every black newspaper in the country had endorsed his bill" and cited statements of support he had received from black church congregations and teachers.[22] Pactolus replies to these claims much as Tourgée did in private conversations with Blair and his Republican supporters: "The colored people . . . have been starved so long and are so eager for knowledge that they are willing and glad to get even the scraps they hope they may receive by this measure. Besides, a good many of them have despaired of anything like justice. . . . They think they cannot get anything better, and so say: 'Even half a loaf is better than no bread'" (125–26). As Tourgée's mouthpiece, Pactolus is directly quoting National Afro-American League president Joseph C. Price, who recognized the defects of the Blair bill but urged his organization to unite behind it with the plea, "Our people are hungering and thirsting for education. If we can't get the whole loaf don't, in heaven's name, withhold the half loaf that is offered us." Like Tourgée, Pactolus is disregarding the conclusion a majority of Afro-American League members drew when they voted to heed Price's plea: "A hungry man knows what he wants better than a man with a full stomach can tell him."[23]

In addition to the debates over the Blair bill, Tourgée inserted into the expanded novel the alternative he had suggested in the education bill he himself had written: disbursing federal funds directly to the "schools of each township," so that "wherever separate schools for the two races are maintained, every dollar granted on account of white illiteracy should be applied in aid of white schools, and every one granted on account of colored illiteracy should be applied to the maintenance of colored schools" (123, 126). As Pactolus spells out, this plan would ensure equitable distribution of federal funds without "compel[ling] the Southern states to admit colored children to their white schools," which he agrees the U.S. government should not try to do. "Prejudice, whether right or wrong, can rarely be legislated out of existence," he reasons, "and the schools of the South would be valueless to the colored people if they were opened by compulsion to them" (118). In another irony, Pactolus here echoes Chief Justice Lemuel Shaw of the Massachusetts Supreme Court, whose famous verdict in the 1849 case of *Roberts v. City of Boston*—a case in which an African American plaintiff unsuccessfully challenged school segregation—laid the basis for the "separate but equal" principle that Tourgée would soon challenge in *Plessy v. Ferguson*.[24]

Pactolus once again speaks for Tourgée, not for African Americans, when he accepts separate schools. Those African Americans who had opposed the Blair bill had objected particularly to its endorsement of separate schools. As T. Thomas Fortune put it, "If national funds are to be used for educational purposes, let it not be for separate schools, but" for schools "thrown open" to all alike.[25] In contrast, Tourgée contended, "Separate schools are not a positive *wrong*: they are only bad policy—double expense. A colored man is not *wronged* or hurt if on one corner is a white school and on the other a colored one. The wrong is when there is *none*."[26] Convinced that Southern states would shut down public schools rather than be forced to integrate them, Tourgée preferred to devise a method of funding education that would equalize black and white schools. Like Blair, the fictional senator rejects this method as politically unworkable (129). And like Tourgée, Pactolus blames the North more than he does the South for the nation's failure to pass an effective education bill: "I can understand the motive of a Southern white man in opposing National Aid to education. . . . He wants to keep [the Negro] a menial. He is profitable in that position, and the degree of profit depends on his helplessness. . . . But I can see no reason why the North should be unwilling to do plain and simple justice to the Negro except the mere fact of his color" (129). Ultimately, concludes Tourgée, racism rather than economics lies at the root of the nation's paralysis. He thus leaves readers facing a tautology as well as an impasse: only by eradicating racism can the nation solve its race problem, yet racism is the very obstacle it must surmount to achieve this goal.

Tourgée's Indictment of the White Press

Of the various representatives of U.S. society whom Tourgée exposes as impediments to solving the race problem, none comes off looking worse than a journalist on the staff of the *Index*, a newspaper whose title suggests that it serves as the index of white public opinion. The journalist, Mr. Stearns, is the only person in the crowd gathered around Pactolus's shoeshine stand who never enters into dialogue with the bootblack. Instead, after overhearing snatches of Pactolus's conversation with his lawyer, Mr. Phelps, about the intended bequest to Eva, Stearns asks Phelps to supply the details of what appears to be a juicy story for the *Index*. When Phelps refuses to violate his client's confidentiality, the reporter rushes off to ferret out the details for himself. Nothing could better indicate the role the white press played in closing its columns to the African American voice and feeding the white public stories about African Americans obtained from white sources—a practice that obviously reinforced white prejudices and stereotypes. As a columnist for the *Chicago Daily Inter Ocean*, Tourgée was taking a great risk in shedding such a harsh light on the profession that supported him financially.

By tracking Stearns to Eva's house, to which he gains admittance on false pretenses in pursuit of his story, Tourgée develops his indictment of reporters as unprincipled scoundrels who cater to their readers' worst instincts and of the newspaper press as a purveyor of sensationalism rather than fact. Speaking through Eva, Tourgée differentiates the "printing-press"—an invention with "wonderful power for good or evil"—from "that other thing that calls itself 'the press,' the great scandal-monger with its army of thieves and spies—which feeds on filth and misfortune" (185–86). Eva accuses Stearns of not scrupling to "blast [her] good name . . . to give the readers of the *Index* a sensation" and of systematically looking for "something mean— something sinister—something unworthy" in the noblest actions (186).

The story Stearns publishes in the *Index* distorts the truth in a worse manner than Eva anticipates, however. Instead of sensationalizing and derogating Pactolus's motives, it sentimentalizes them. Turning the trenchant critic of the "white Christ" into a sycophant, it reaffirms the very ideology of slavery and white supremacy against which Pactolus had railed so bitterly:

> The *Index* had told with flaming headlines, and that skill which so readily weaves fact with fancy, the story of the bootblack of the Best House, who had given a lifetime of labor and self-sacrifice to restore his old master's daughter to ease and luxury. It was a beautiful story, and the lame, dark-visaged Thoth made a peculiarly attractive hero. . . .
>
> He had done . . . just what a Negro ought to do,—been patient, humble, respectful, and never sought to thrust himself forward or claimed to be the equal of white folks, though he had been so much more successful than many of them. . . . If there were only more like him among the "niggers," it would not be so hard for white people to get along with them! (347–48)

In short, Tourgée shows that the *Index* publishes fiction in the guise of fact. Though a newspaper, it paints a picture of slavery indistinguishable from the one produced by the nostalgic plantation romances that were flooding the market of the 1880s. Not only does the press glorify the oppressive institution that had cost the country hundreds of thousands of lives to abolish, but in the process it fosters public contempt for the black soldiers who fought for the Union. Thus, Tourgée charges, those who sing the praises of the fictional hero memorialized by the *Index* would "mock and spurn the dead, if the true record of his heroism were told!" The white public considers it "a grand thing for a slave to be true to a master" but a disgrace for a black man to have "fought for Liberty and Union" and saved his country's flag from "dishonor" (351, 352). Moreover, if the *Index*'s readers knew that Pactolus had sacrificed himself not to "restore his old master's daughter to ease and luxury" but to enable his own daughter to pass for white, they would explode with "wrath" (347, 352).

Tourgée completes his exposé of the journalist by revealing how he both benefits from and participates in fortifying white supremacy. His ability to fulfill the press's function of promulgating the dominant ideology earns the reporter promotion to "city editor" and marks him as a future "luminary in his profession" (356). Meanwhile, after laying "siege" to Eva's heart and "demand[ing] a surrender" (353), as he puts it in the language of conquest masquerading as love, Stearns quickly drops his proposal of marriage when she makes him read her father's narrative before giving him her answer, but he continues to pursue her as sexual prey. His lust reveals her to have been all too prescient in predicting the impact that being identified as a "colored woman" would have on her moral standing in white eyes: "no white man [can] offer her love that is not an insult" (202). She doubtless views the convent as a refuge from the dishonorable intentions of white men like the *Index*'s star reporter, as well as from the burdens of passing or discrimination.

The bleakest of Tourgée's novels, *Pactolus Prime* seems to arrive at a dead end in its search for solutions to the race problem. The most promising remedies it explores—reparations and equitably distributed federal aid to education—cannot be implemented because white Americans lack the political will or the financial generosity to do so, as the fictional senator and the majority of Pactolus's customers demonstrate. Pactolus's life drives home the message that acquiring wealth cannot buy African Americans political or social equality, nor can it protect them against white violence, nor can it free them from dependence on whites as long as whites rule U.S. society. Passing, which Benny, like most African Americans, views as desertion of his race, may help a few individuals to escape discrimination, at the cost of abandoning darker family members, denying their own cultural heritage, and sometimes even joining the ranks of white racists in order to protect themselves against discovery, as African American classics of the genre have brilliantly shown.[27] Yet passing essentially preserves the hierarchy of white over black, even while subverting the racial distinctions that uphold it.

Intermarriage is taboo, as the reporter's withdrawal of his proposal to Eva confirms. Transformation of white racial attitudes appears virtually hopeless with two exceptions: the judge who applauds Benny's legal acuity and the Union veteran who has transcended the barriers between blacks and whites in the "comradeship of battle" (99). Otherwise, even the characters most sympathetic to African Americans—notably Phelps and the doctor who treats Pactolus after he is knocked down by a horse—prove unwilling or unable to challenge their society's racist proscriptions.

The White Reception of *Pactolus Prime*

The novel's reception helps explain why Tourgée found the conundrum of racism impossible to resolve, at least within the constraints of literary realism. Yet the sheer number, diversity, and tenor of reviews the novel prompted suggest that it contributed to intensifying and conceivably advancing the national debate on the race question—a debate Tourgée fostered most successfully in his "Bystander" column, as we shall see. Southern newspapers predictably blasted *Pactolus Prime*. "In its pages the sores of slavery are re-opened, the Negro and the white man are contrasted to the disadvantage of the latter, Christ is blasphemed as merely a white Christ, and fanciful calculations are made the basis for a claim by the descendants of the slaves," fumed the *Memphis Commercial*, unconsciously echoing Pactolus's most hostile customers. "The effect of this upon the Negroes, for whom the book is evidently written, will be to deepen their dissatisfaction with themselves and their hate of the race which stands in the way of what they are thus taught is their full development," added this reviewer.[28] Both the *Memphis Commercial* and Joel Chandler Harris of the *Atlanta Constitution* accused Tourgée of being motivated solely by "personal hate for the people of the South, among whom he failed to make his home." Complained Harris: "Each gloomy page makes it appear that in this fair land of the south the ruling race is cold-blooded and cruel, while the blacks are patient martyrs, barred out from their rightful place in society." He judged the thesis he attributed to the novel so self-evidently absurd that he could only ask, "What shall we say of such a writer? Is he a monomaniac, or simply a refugee from his race?"[29]

Contrary to Southern reviewers' allegations, however, Tourgée aimed his sharpest barbs at Northern rather than Southern racial attitudes. The reactions of Northern reviewers confirmed his diagnosis of racism as a national rather than a Southern disease, so deep-seated and widespread as almost to defy cure. "The . . . prejudice . . . denounced by Judge Tourgee in the person of Pactolus Prime is one of those realities which cannot be overcome by legislation, or by persuasion, or by logic, or by rhetoric, or by reproaches, or by sarcasm. If it can be overcome at all, or by any means, the slow incidence of time, but not necessarily the influence of education, may effect the change," pontificated the *New York Daily Tribune*, which had long since renounced the abolitionist sympathies it had displayed during the Civil War era.[30] "That evil was done to the colored race no one will deny, but that the nation should be held responsible for it forever is open to doubt," whined the *San Francisco Chronicle*.[31] The *New York Commercial Advertiser* accurately summarized the sentiments *Pactolus Prime* ascribed to African Americans but confessed itself unmoved by them: "He [the Negro] wishes for the time when black and white shall be members of the same social circle, meet in the same drawing-room, dine at the same table; but the highest hope offered to him is of a time when the social position of the white race and of the black race shall be indisputably equal, while their social circles are at the same time kept indisputably distinct."[32] Like Phelps in the novel, the *Commercial Advertiser* did not regard segregation as humiliating or social integration as desirable. "It is naturally hard to rouse men's indignation" against the maintenance of barriers between the races as long as they are "indisputably equal," admitted this reviewer, apparently oblivious to the contradiction between exclusiveness and equality. If the *Commercial Advertiser* spoke for Northern liberals, the *Chicago Times* spoke for the hard-core Northern racists who typically belonged to the Democratic Party. Like those of Pactolus's customers who favored repatriation to Africa, the *Chicago Times*' reviewer faulted Tourgée for not realizing that the "original wrong" of "bringing the negro here at all" could "not be atoned for fully until he is put back where he came from and aided there to become self-sustaining." Whether or not the black race flourished after being replanted in its native soil, concluded the *Times*, at least "the white race would be freed from an endless cause of discord."[33]

Several Northern reviewers commented on the "apparent hopelessness of the condition of the negro."[34] "Although the story is powerful in places, and quite clever at times, our impression upon closing the volume is . . . that Judge Tourgée seems in these pages to feel that he is powerless to definitely prescribe any remedy for the racial evil," complained the *Christian Union*.[35] Tellingly, the *Catholic World* came closer to understanding Tourgée's intentions than did any Protestant or secular journal. While noting with gratification that "Judge Tourgée explicitly exempts Catholics from his sweeping censure" of white Christianity, this Catholic organ sermonized,

"It behooves all of us . . . to consider how we may mend our ways, and by act and prayer and penance help to expiate and repair a national crime whose consequences were too far reaching to be obliterated by a civil war and an emancipation proclamation. Christianity, in a word, needs to permeate our minds, to mould our convictions, to get hold of our prejudices, if it is to be a working force in our civilization." Yet even the *Catholic World* inadvertently reinforced the prevailing pessimism when its reviewer acknowledged that Tourgée was "ploughing a desperately stubborn soil."[36]

Most reviews credited Tourgée with having at least shaken readers out of their complacency—precisely the aim he had avowed to the editor of the *Advance*—and many praised *Pactolus Prime* as one of his best performances. The *Inter Ocean* pronounced it "a most remarkable book, destined to provoke controversy, to make people uncomfortable, and to stir the hearts of many as they have been stirred by few of the arguments on the race question."[37] The *Harrisburg Telegraph* lauded *Pactolus Prime* even more fulsomely: "The book is a master piece, eloquent, analytical, full of keenest reasoning and with a pathetic story that excites the warmest sympathies and disturbs the complacent legislative moralist with the pointed and as yet unanswered question of what shall be done for the negro?" "*Pactolus Prime* . . . strikes us as perhaps the most able of all [Tourgée's] writings thus far . . . and its moral lesson ought to be heeded," affirmed the *Congregationalist*. "Judge Tourgée has written no story founded on 'the negro problem' so forcible as 'Pactolus Prime.' Indeed, none so impressive has appeared since 'Uncle Tom's Cabin,'" averred the *Philadelphia Bulletin*.[38] The *Springfield Republican* ranked it as "by far the best work [Tourgée] has done since 'A Fool's Errand'" and predicted it would achieve a "large sale."[39] Even reviewers who repudiated the novel's premises often commended its style as "nervous, energetic," and "powerful."[40] Assessments of the characters and plot varied, however. The *Inter Ocean* hailed Pactolus as a character "new in fiction," the story as "fresh," and "the method" as virtually "unique"—judgments reiterated by the *Harrisburg Telegraph*, the *Rochester Herald*, the *Omaha Bee*, the *Boston Traveller*, the *Jamestown (N.Y.) Journal*, and the *San Francisco Daily Evening Bulletin*.[41] On the other hand, the *New York Daily Tribune*, the *New York Commercial Advertiser*, and the *Baltimore Sun* found there to be "a great deal too much argumentation for a novel," branded Pactolus an unconvincing and "impossible hero," and decried the plot as "improbable" and "sensational."[42]

Perhaps the most nuanced evaluation came from the *Independent*, a journal sympathetic to both Tourgée's aesthetic preferences and his indictment of racism. "The difference between romance proper and that lifeless parody of life known as analytical realism, was never more clearly shown" than in *Pactolus Prime*, asserted this reviewer, who identified it as "a romance of one phase of American life set forth with boldness, breadth and vigor." Yet he lamented that Tourgée "shortens and weakens his strokes at race prejudice" by putting them in the mouth of a near-white hero: "This gives his opponents full room to say that it was the white blood, not the black, that spoke through Pactolus Prime. . . . The romance would have been of firmer texture and of finer fiber if Prime had been a pure-blooded Negro, the hero of his race and representative of one side of the race-question."[43]

The African American Reception of *Pactolus Prime*

We may well wonder to what extent African Americans shared this opinion, but few reviews from the black press survive. Tourgée's scrapbook of clippings contains only two from African American newspapers, since the wire service he used culled reviews almost entirely from white ones.[44] "Have you seen nothing of Pactolus in the *Afro American* papers? I am anxious to know what they will say," Emma wrote to her husband a few weeks after the novel's publication.[45] She made strenuous efforts to have review copies of *Pactolus Prime* sent to them. In one case she assured Tourgée's publisher that she had not confused the *Detroit Plaindealer* with the *Cleveland Plain Dealer*. In another case, she contacted the *New York Age*, which had recently commented on William Dean Howells's novel about passing, *An Imperative Duty* (1891), to suggest that the paper review *Pactolus Prime*.[46] It promised to do so, but unfortunately the relevant issues of the *Age* are missing from its files.

The main surviving African American reviews, William H. Anderson's in the *Detroit Plaindealer* and Anna Julia Cooper's in the journal the *Southland* and her book *A Voice from the South* (1892), did not dwell on the novel's passing plot. Anderson simply noted that Pactolus's life, "common to men of his race, . . . explains [his] cynicism," his "bitterness" against white Christianity, and his desire to "keep the identity of his daughter a secret in order that she might escape the proscription placed upon all in whose veins courses one drop of African blood."[47] Cooper criticized the "mixture of silent deception and inward self-sacrifice" for which Eva opts as untrue to her "spirit" and out of keeping with either of the choices that a "heroic few" or "the average colored woman of her complexion would almost invariably" have elected.[48] Both Anderson and Cooper highlighted the book's argument rather than its plot. Characterizing Pactolus as an "intelligent Afro-American" who cogently articulates the "claims that the Afro-American has upon the Republic," Anderson summarized his ripostes to his white customers. Cooper awarded the novel the highest accolade it received:

> In Pactolus Prime Mr. Tourgee has succeeded incomparably, we think, in photographing and vocalizing the feelings of the colored American in regard to the Christian profession and the pagan practice of the dominant forces in the American government. And as an impassioned denunciation of the heartless and godless spirit of caste founded on color, as a scathing rebuke to weak-eyed Christians who cannot read the golden rule across the color line, as an unanswerable arraignment of unparalleled ingratitude and limping justice in the policy of this country towards the weaker of its two children, that served it so long and so faithfully, the book is destined to live and to furnish an invaluable contribution to this already plethoric department of American literature.[49]

Cooper also conveyed her enthusiasm for the novel in a letter to Tourgée of 5 June 1891. She and her friends had read it aloud to each other "at one sitting barely stopping for lunch," and she had dashed off her review the "same night, while the inspiration was fresh," she confided.[50]

If Cooper had expected a gratified response when she sent Tourgée a copy of the fledgling literary journal the *Southland* in which her review first appeared, she must have been sorely disappointed.[51] Far from expressing appreciation for what he called her "pleasant words," Tourgée reproached her for the "eleven months" that had intervened before a "magazine claiming to represent the best thought of the colored people in the United States, first [found] opportunity to notice a book" by an author who had devoted six novels and years of weekly columns to advocating justice for African Americans when everyone else was advocating "charity and dole." Clearly the paucity of African American reviews since the novel's publication had wounded Tourgée's ego and exacerbated his nagging fear of having lost caste to no avail. "It is useless for a white man to attempt to fight your peoples [*sic*] battles for them. He simply awakens the contempt of his own race and the suspicion of yours," he groused, sounding an all too frequent refrain in his correspondence.[52]

Because the *Southland*'s founding editor was none other than Joseph C. Price, president of the National Afro-American League, Tourgée had been especially galled that the magazine "commended the resolutions of the Mohonk Conference of 1890—a conference of white men held to concoct advice for colored men . . . based upon the assumption of inferiority, pauperism and immorality upon one side and superiority, wisdom and purity on the other." He himself had been "stirred . . . to such indignation" by his fellow delegates' condescension that he was "forced to protest," Tourgée reminded Cooper, and his friend the Reverend Jeremiah Rankin, the white president of Howard University, "so felt the insult of the race's exclusion [from the Mohonk Conference] that he would not attend," yet here was a prominent African American organ "quietly ignor[ing]" white reformers' racism and "beg[ging]" an "invitation . . . for two or three colored men to enter the charmed circle!" When he saw African Americans exhibit this kind of ser- vility, it made him "lose confidence in the manhood of the race," Tourgée scolded. Yet he hastened to clarify that his censure applied to a few male leaders, not to the race as a whole: "I am so firm a believer in the Negro's capacity and see so clearly his magnificent opportunity that I cannot but be angry when I see their leading men striving for the reputation of being 'good niggers'" or pleading for crumbs from white tables. He ended by declaring that African American women rather than men represented the best hope for the race's advancement: "In courage, in aspiration, in virtue and in that determination to do for their race which is the hope of the future, they have far excelled their brothers and it is my conviction that it is to the colored women of the country more than to any other influence that the race must look for whatever betterment tomorrow may bring."

Regardless of how she felt about having her eulogistic review met by such a tirade, Cooper replied graciously, thanking Tourgée for his "sugges- tive words (the bitter no less than the sweet)" and "still more . . . for the inspiration [his] whole life & personality ha[d] been to [her]." She could understand the "dissatisfaction" with which he measured the "results" of having championed African Americans "so heroically and unflinch- ingly, so devotedly and untiringly," Cooper assured Tourgée, because the "prophet is seldom a satisfied man." While massaging his ego, she tactfully directed him away from objectionable racial generalizations by noting that "human nature—as well as Negro nature—is an unsatisfying com- modity to manipulate." She then explained that although her review had been scheduled to appear in the August 1890 number of the *Southland*, a "shortage of funds" had reduced the magazine from a monthly to a quarterly and delayed its publication. Perhaps to make amends for his curmudgeonly letter, Tourgée warmly reviewed Cooper's *A Voice from the South* in his "Bystander" column of 8 April 1893, describing it as "a culti- vated woman's view of the gulf" between white and black Christians and praising its polished literary style, "deft but stinging satire, and keen but not ill-tempered wit."[53]

Besides Cooper and Anderson, the Reverend J. C. Embry, editor of the African Methodist Episcopal Church organ the *Christian Recorder*, hailed *Pactolus Prime* as "one of the best books ever written on the race subject in this country."[54] Another African American writer who apparently gave *Pactolus Prime* a glowing review was the journalist John Edward Bruce, better known by his pen name Bruce Grit. In a letter of 27 July 1891, he told Tourgée he had read the novel "eagerly" and considered it to be "in your happiest vein." "It will make the people of your race, think on the great wrongs they have done to my race in all the years we have labored and suffered in our weakness and ignorance," he predicted, no doubt with Pactolus's and Benny's demands for reparations in mind. Bruce volunteered to review *Pactolus Prime* for his "syndicate letter" (as yet unlocated) and to do everything he could to "increase its sale."[55]

Among Tourgée's rapidly growing number of African American correspondents, the Louisiana minister Alexander S. Jackson and the Chicago businessman Mack W. Caldwell likewise greeted *Pactolus Prime* as a novel that spoke for them. "I have read and reread [it] with peculiar interest," wrote Jackson, perhaps hinting that he identified with Pactolus's experiences as well as with his sentiments. Caldwell, too, enjoyed the novel so much that he "inten[ded] to read it through again."[56]

Two dissenting voices stood out from the African American chorus of praise, however. "The only real criticism I have ever made of the writings of that grand advocate of the rights of the Negro, Judge Tourgee," wrote Ohio state senator John P. Green, is that *Pactolus Prime* accords too salient a role to those misguided "colored brethren" who perpetually grieve about not being white and who "go through the world as if their relation to the Negro race were a great misfortune—an insuperable barrier to all progress." Quoting Pactolus's repeated advice to Benny—"Be as much of a man as you can, but be a white man; don't transmit the degrading curse to your children"—Green avowed, "I am sure that the foregoing do not represent the sentiments of any considerable portion of the right-minded colored people in the United States."[57]

In a similar vein, the near-white Charles Chesnutt, who took pride in his African American identity and who had been wrestling with a novel of his own about a heroine light enough to pass, strongly objected to Tourgée's portrayal of Eva and resolution of her fate. "Judge Tourgée's cultivated white Negroes are always bewailing their fate and cursing the drop of black blood which 'taints'—I hate the word, it implies corruption—their otherwise pure race," complained Chesnutt to his literary mentor George Washington

Cable, referring not only to Eva but to the heroine of Tourgée's earlier novel *Hot Plowshares* (1883). In a sentence he deleted from the final draft of his letter, Chesnutt additionally faulted Tourgée for feeling "obliged to kill off his [African American] characters," as he did Pactolus, "or immerse them in convents, as [he] does his latest heroine, to save them from a fate worse than death, i.e., the confession of inferiority by reason of color."[58]

Yet Chesnutt's reproof acquires a poignant irony in the light of his private journal and his novel of passing, *The House behind the Cedars* (1900). As a young man in Fayetteville, North Carolina, Chesnutt had faced the very barriers Tourgée evoked in Eva's agonized cry: "*My* world—the world of ambition, art, literature, society, the world that contains all that one loves to enjoy—the world which it is life to be a part of, and worse than death to be shut out from—this is white—all white—pure white!" (205–6). Chesnutt had indeed known the social death of being "shut out from" the world of culture. As he had recorded in his journal, "I love music. I live in a town where there is *some* musical culture. I have studied and practiced till I can understand and appreciate good music, but I never hear what little there is to be heard. I have studied German and have no one to converse with but a few Jewish merchants who can talk nothing but business. As to procuring instruction in Latin, French, German, or Music, that is entirely out of the question. First class teachers would not teach a 'nigger' and I would have no other sort."[59]

Chesnutt had found greater freedom in the North, but even there he had chafed against racial barriers. By 1897 he would confide to Tourgée that he hoped to move to France because he "look[ed] forward with horror" to having his daughters live "under the conditions that await them in the United States."[60] As an aspiring novelist, Chesnutt confronted racial barriers of a different sort. "The kind of stuff I could write, if I were not all the time oppressed by the fear that this line or this sentiment would offend some-body's prejudices, jar on somebody's American-trained sense of propriety, would, I believe, find a ready sale in England," he told Cable. Not until 1900, after countless revisions to accommodate the tastes of the white men who ruled the American literary establishment, did he find a publisher for *The House behind the Cedars*. One of the accommodations he felt "obliged" to make was "to kill off" his phenotypically white heroine after her unsuccessful attempt to pass.[61]

Chesnutt was not the only person to rebel against the idea that taking refuge in a convent was the sole option for a young woman of African American ancestry who wanted neither to pass for white nor to submit to discrimination. Tourgée's friend the Reverend Rankin likewise hinted at his discomfort with this outcome when he suggested an alternative: "I rather wish you would take a heroine, with some shadow of colored blood, & make her devote herself to the elevation of the race." Recognizing that Tourgée had intended *Pactolus Prime* "to quicken the conscience of the Anglo Saxon," he asked, "Can you not write a book, which shall give courage & inspiration to some struggling colored man or woman, who would rise above the situation, & be ready to help others?" Perhaps sensitized by his immersion in the black world of Howard University, Rankin understood that African Americans needed to build their own institutions as well as to fight for inclusion in all of U.S. society's benefits. "It seems to me, that we want to cultivate in colored people a sense of *independence* of the white race: not antagonism but of independence," he argued. "This sense only will make that individual development into teachers, writers, preachers possible."[62]

Tourgée replied that he had written *Pactolus Prime* "not for the sake of the colored man, but to save . . . civilization, Christianity, and our country" from the race war he feared would erupt if white Americans did not repent. Nor did he consider it necessary to "cultivate . . . independence" in African Americans because the "*self-dependence* of the colored race in the United States excels that of any people of which we have any knowledge." In Tourgée's view, self-dependence did not suffice without "equality of right, privilege and opportunity"—in short, justice—and the only way African Americans could "obtain justice" was "by the display of power and purpose to resent injustice."[63]

Novelistic Dialogues with *Pactolus Prime*

Within two years, two other novelists would respond in different ways to the challenge of imagining alternative solutions to America's race problem. The first response came from William Dean Howells, whose concept of literary realism Tourgée had repeatedly castigated for painting life as "essentially mean and petty," "aspiration . . . [as] ridiculous, and self-sacrifice an attribute to be ashamed of."[64] True to that concept, Howells's *An Imperative Duty* (1891), which may actually have been written with *Pactolus Prime* in mind,[65] makes light of the dilemma its phenotypically white heroine faces on learning of her African American ancestry. At the same time, by depicting African Americans through her eyes, the novel reinforces white readers' racist stereotypes. Unlike Eva, Howells's Rhoda Aldgate recoils with disgust from her newfound blood brothers and "grovel[s] in self-loathing and despair" at the revelation of her kinship to them: "She never knew before how hideous they were, with their flat wide-nostriled noses, their out-rolled thick lips, their mobile, bulging eyes set near together, their retreating chins and foreheads, and their smooth shining skin." Howells satirizes the sense of "duty" that drives Rhoda to feel she ought to repress her disgust and "try to educate them, and elevate them; give [her] life to them," as Eva does. He also intimates that the high-minded white Dr. Olney who stifles his "race instinct" of "repulsion" and marries Rhoda—in contrast to the unprincipled journalist who turns his back on Eva—acts out of a similarly misguided sense of duty masquerading as love. Though the two settle in Italy and conceal the secret of Rhoda's ancestry, the marriage proves unhappy, leaving the impression that the race problem can neither be transcended by idealism nor escaped by going abroad.[66]

Commenting on *An Imperative Duty* in the same essay, "One Phase of American Literature," that contains her assessment of *Pactolus Prime* and of Tourgée's oeuvre generally, Anna Julia Cooper objected that Howells "had no business to attempt a subject of which he knew so little." Howells was basing his impressions of African Americans on those he had encountered as "menials" in hotels or observed in the streets, Cooper pointed out:

> He has not seen, and therefore cannot be convinced that there exists a quiet, self-respecting, dignified class of easy life and manners (save only where it crosses the roughness of their white fellow countrymen's barbarity) of cultivated tastes and habits, and with no more in common with the class of his acquaintance than the accident of complexion,— beyond a sympathy with their wrongs, or a resentment at being socially and morally classified with them, according as the principle of altruism or self love is dominant in the individual.

Among this class, noted Cooper, Howells's heroine could have met "young women of aspiration and intellectual activity with whom she could affiliate without nausea and from whom she could learn a good many lessons." Cooper added tartly that had Howells's heroine "followed her first gushing impulse to go South and 'elevate' the race with whom she had discovered her relationship," she may not have "found even them so ready to receive her condescending patronage."[67]

Despite her contrasting appraisals of *An Imperative Duty* and *Pactolus Prime*, Cooper could hardly have helped noticing that an African American community of "cultivated tastes and habits" is equally absent from both. Whether because Tourgée did not yet have sufficient contact with this class of African Americans, whose churches would frequently host him as a lecturer after he founded the National Citizens' Rights Association in October 1891, or simply because he had framed *Pactolus Prime* to probe racism through a representative cross-section of white characters, he portrayed his three African American protagonists in isolation from their peers.

It would be an African American novelist who would supply what the Reverend Rankin called for: a novel aiming to "give courage & inspiration" to a "struggling" people by featuring a "heroine, with some shadow of colored blood," who "devote[s] herself to the elevation of the race."[68] Frances Ellen Watkins Harper's *Iola Leroy; or, Shadows Uplifted* (1892), published the same year as Cooper's *A Voice from the South* and sometimes reviewed together with it, positions itself explicitly as an African American view of the race problem, offering its own people role models to emulate and providing both races with correctives to white misconceptions.[69] "Out of the race must come its own thinkers and writers," emphasizes one of these role models, the phenotypically white Dr. Latimer, who has refused an opportunity to pass: "Authors belonging to the white race have written good racial books, for which I am deeply grateful, but it seems to be almost impossible for a white man to put himself completely in our place." Accordingly, he urges Iola to "write a good, strong book" that would be "of lasting service for the race"—a book like *Iola Leroy* itself. Such a book's hero and heroine, agree Dr. Latimer and Iola, must act as examples to those "trying to slip out from the race and pass into the white basis" and must inspire readers to want to "cling" more closely to their race precisely because it is weak—just as both of them have done. Having earned his medical degree from the University of P—thanks to the sacrifices of his mother, a freedwoman, Dr. Latimer has turned down his white grandmother's proposal to "adopt him as her heir, if he would ignore his identity with the colored race." Out of the same loyalty to her mother and her mother's people, Iola turns down the marriage proposal of the white Dr. Gresham who loves her. Though Dr. Gresham insists he sees no use in her claiming she is "colored when [her] eyes are as blue and complexion as white" as his, Iola rejects passing as abhorrent: "I am not willing to live under a shadow of concealment which I thoroughly hate as if the blood in my veins were an undetected crime of my soul." And when Dr. Gresham tells Iola (as Howells's Dr. Olney tells Rhoda) that her "education has unfitted [her] for social life among" former slaves, she replies with an argument similar to the one Pactolus makes in favor of reparations: "It was . . . through their unrequited toil that I was educated, while they were compelled to live in ignorance. I am indebted to them for the power I have to serve them."[70]

Yet unlike Tourgée—and unlike Howells, whose *An Imperative Duty* she seems to be directly countering, as numerous critics have pointed out[71]—Harper roots her phenotypically white characters in an African American community that she portrays as richly diverse, ranging from illiterate but wise and resourceful folk to highly qualified intellectuals. She shows them embracing their African American heritage out of love for their families and identification with a shared experience of enslavement and discrimination, rather than hiding in a convent or fleeing to Europe. She also shows them choosing to serve their people not out of a self-sacrificing impulse—whether sincere, as in Eva's case, or supercilious and melodramatic, as in Rhoda's—but out of a genuine desire for self-fulfillment. While revealing the benefits African Americans derive from the "self-dependence" Tourgée praised in them, Harper simultaneously presents a less pessimistic picture of white Americans' capacity for change. Dr. Gresham, in particular, evolves from trying to "banish [Iola] from his mind" after he learns of her racial background, to deciding to "win her for his bride" but "hide from his aristocratic relations all knowledge of her mournful past" as a slave, to proffering her the possibility of combining marriage with working for her race.[72] True, Iola opts for marrying Dr. Latimer instead. Nevertheless, by suggesting that whites *can* overcome their prejudices, Harper empowers readers to keep striving for a society free of racism.

More than any other novel of the era, *Iola Leroy* meets the challenge Tourgée threw out to the readers of his original Christmas story in the *Advance*, when he urged them to "get upon their knees and study their own hearts as Christians and American citizens" in order to write a proper "sequel" to his characters' lives.[73] Harper not only imagines a meaningful future for the class Benny and Eva represent but additionally prompts both black and white readers to envision a "brighter coming day" for the nation as a whole.[74] It is thus a sad irony that Tourgée, who followed African American life and letters so closely, apparently remained unaware of *Iola Leroy*, despite its having received favorable reviews in two white journals sympathetic to African Americans, the *Independent* and the *Nation*.[75] It is likewise curious that Harper, who had extensive contacts with white reformers, does not appear among Tourgée's African American correspondents. Still, even though the two authors' paths seem never to have crossed, their novels speak to each other and illuminate the complementary perspectives that a white and an African American progressive brought to the race question in one of the darkest decades of U.S. history.

While the conversation between Tourgée's and Harper's novels remains metaphorical, Tourgée was simultaneously engaging in his "Bystander" column in a literal and very public dialogue on the race question with African Americans and whites of diverse persuasions. The next chapter focuses on the interracial dialogue Tourgée sought to promote through this innovative newspaper column.

CHAPTER THREE

The "Bystander"

"Oftimes a bystander seeth better than one having part in the fray." . . .
The law . . . counts the evidence of the onlooker better than that of the actor.

So opened the article of 21 April 1888 that inaugurated "A Bystander's Notes,"
the weekly column Tourgée published in the Saturday edition of the *Chicago
Daily Inter Ocean* until October 1898. Introducing the persona Tourgée
sported for the rest of his career as a journalist, during which he would consistently refer to himself in the third person as "the Bystander," the quotation
from an "ancient chronicler" that prefaced this article articulated the rationale validating the heterodox political commentary he would offer in the
column.[1] As a bystander detached from the "fray," Tourgée argued, he saw
more clearly than the leaders and party bosses who shaped national policy.
He also furnished testimony a court of law would rank superior in accuracy
to theirs as "actor[s]." Hence, he implied, politicians involved in the "fray"
should heed his advice instead of dismissing it as utopian. In short, from its
inception "A Bystander's Notes" claimed authority precisely from the position on the sidelines to which practical politicians had relegated Tourgée.

Over its ten-year life span, punctuated by several interruptions, "A
Bystander's Notes" would cover an array of topics amounting to an archive
of nineteenth-century American culture. This archive would include disqui-
sitions on literary realism and historical fiction; reviews of novels, political
biographies, religious works, and pseudoscientific treatises on race; historical retrospectives analyzing the legacies of the slave system, the abolitionist movement, the Civil War, and Reconstruction; interventions in current
electoral politics; and discussions of such economic issues as free trade versus protectionism, the gold standard versus bimetallism, and the respective
merits of monopoly capitalism, unions, and strikes.

No subject would receive more extensive—or more passionate—
coverage in "A Bystander's Notes" than the race question. Tourgée delved
into every aspect of the unresolved controversy over African Americans'
rightful place in the United States that was still roiling the nation more
than twenty years after the Thirteenth Amendment had abolished slavery.
He reprobated the tactics being used to disfranchise African Americans in
the South, from voter intimidation and fraud to poll taxes, biased literacy

FIGURE 5   Photo of the Bystander in his study at his home in Mayville, New York, ca. 1890. Courtesy of the Huntington Library, San Marino, Calif.

tests, and grandfather clauses. He denounced the separate car laws that were imposing segregated railway travel in one Southern state after another. He highlighted the informal modes of segregation and discrimination that prevailed throughout the North and urged both whites and African Americans to challenge them. He unsparingly documented the horrific incidents of lynching and massacre that most white newspapers ignored or explained away. And he refuted the claims of white superiority and black inferiority that his contemporaries invoked to justify all these forms of racial oppression.

The most remarkable feature of "A Bystander's Notes" consisted in the platform it provided readers for airing their views and engaging in dialogue with Tourgée. Tourgée frequently summarized and quoted letters his correspondents sent him, which numbered in the hundreds, if not, as he asserted, in the thousands. He also incorporated extracts from rival newspapers, be they Northern or Southern, Republican or Democratic, secular or religious, white- or black-edited. In the process, he set readers in dialogue with each other, allowed those who contested white supremacist ideology to rebut those who upheld it, and broadcast the voices of African Americans to a white public that lacked exposure to the thriving black press and rarely, if ever, interacted with blacks, except as menials. The multivocal dialogue Tourgée encouraged in "A Bystander's Notes," along with the range of stylistic devices he cultivated, made it the most innovative and literarily distinguished journalistic column of its time. As a forum for national debate on the race question at a key historical moment, moreover, "A Bystander's Notes" stood unrivaled. On both literary and historical grounds, the column repays close attention, as I hope to demonstrate in this chapter.

Tourgée, Nixon, and the *Inter Ocean*

How did a column as radical as "A Bystander's Notes" find a home in the *Chicago Daily Inter Ocean*, which the leading historian of American journalism, Frank Luther Mott, describes as "a newspaper for the solid, respectable classes, and . . . an uncompromising party organ" whose "motto was 'Republican in everything, independent in nothing'"?[2] Part of the answer, of course, lies in Tourgée's long-standing association with the Republican Party, climaxed by the role *A Fool's Errand, Bricks Without Straw, The Invisible Empire* (1880), and *Figs and Thistles* (1879) had played as campaign literature contributing to James A. Garfield's victory in the election of 1880.[3] Though excluded by conservative party bosses from the electoral campaign of 1884, Tourgée published four series of anonymous or pseudonymous articles in the *Inter Ocean* during the mid-1880s, all of which won accolades from the Republican faithful.[4]

No wonder, then, that the *Inter Ocean*'s managing editor and part owner, William Penn Nixon, recognized Tourgée as an eloquent spokesman for the Republican Party's founding ideals, harking back to its antislavery origins and its record of promoting racial justice during Reconstruction.[5] Nixon, indeed, shared some of those ideals. Descended from antislavery Quakers on his father's side and from an interracial union on his mother's, who traced her ancestry to a Cherokee forebear, Nixon prided himself on having been "born an abolitionist" with "little or none of the prejudices against color which most people converted to abolitionism have." He accordingly developed the *Inter Ocean* into a newspaper reputed for "extreme friendliness toward the colored race."[6] Thus, far from discerning any incompatibility

between Tourgée's stand on racial matters and the *Inter Ocean*'s, Nixon probably hoped that a new column by the Republicans' best-known political
writer would build the paper's subscription list, enhance its prestige among
the former abolitionists and Union veterans who made up the party's rank
and file, and help ensure a Republican victory in 1888. In addition, as Mark
Elliott has suggested, Nixon may well have expected Tourgée to attract to
the *Inter Ocean* the degree of "attention that Henry Demarest Lloyd had
brought to its Democratic rival, the *Chicago Tribune*."[7]

Despite the seeming fit in their profiles, Tourgée's relationship with
Nixon and the *Inter Ocean* would prove stormy. Again and again, Tourgée's
deviations from Republican orthodoxy and his stinging criticisms of the
party for betraying African Americans would provoke Nixon's ire. Not only
did Nixon fruitlessly implore Tourgée to confine himself to attacking the
Democrats, but he occasionally censored utterances to which he objected,
refused to print at least one "Bystander" article he considered incendiary,
and twice suspended the column for long periods (1893–94, 1895–96),
finally dropping it altogether.[8] Until October 1898, however, the wide popularity of the "Bystander," combined with Tourgée's pertinaciousness, kept
the *Inter Ocean* from permanently terminating the column.

Much of the credit for preserving good relations with Nixon and the *Inter
Ocean*'s other principal editor, William H. Busbey, belongs to Emma, who
conducted the bulk of her husband's correspondence with them and served
as his representative. Emma deserves credit as well for helping to produce
the "Bystander" column. As her diary entries frequently mention, she vet-
ted, typed up, and mailed every installment, even those Tourgée wrote
when traveling the lecture circuit.[9] She also furnished vital research assistance. "Copy and send to me out of the scrap-book the extract from Grady's
Texas speech about the South remaining solid against the negro," Tourgée
instructed Emma while on tour. In the same scrapbook, he told her, she
would find an "extract from the report of a Committee of Colored Ministers
in Charleston, S.C.," in which they said that the master could never understand the slave. "I want that, too," he specified.[10] As we can see, Tourgée knew
Emma was thoroughly familiar with the scrapbooks of clippings on which
he relied for his articles. We can thus deduce that she helped compile them.

Emma's diary, Tourgée's letters to her, and the couple's detailed correspondence with Nixon and Busbey form part of the exceptionally rich
collection of material that facilitates the close study "A Bystander's Notes"
merits. A virtually unbroken file of the "Bystander" column, both in microfilm and online, constitutes the core of the collection. Scores of letters from

readers praising or damning Tourgée for particular articles round out the cache. Among the most valuable are a few surviving manuscript versions of the countless letters Tourgée incorporated into his "Bystander" articles—manuscripts that invite comparison with the published texts.

Drawing on these resources, the present chapter explores Tourgée's sustained dialogue with the *Inter Ocean*'s readers about the race question, as he conducted it from April 1888 through January 1895, when he transferred the "Bystander" column to his short-lived magazine the *Basis*. While analyzing selected "Bystander" articles in the context of Tourgée's correspondence, this chapter tells the story of how Tourgée enlisted white Northern Republicans, the *Inter Ocean*'s main constituency, in the dialogue on the race question that earned the "Bystander" column its distinction; how he brought African Americans and white supremacists into the dialogue and orchestrated their clashing voices; how he wrestled with the *Inter Ocean*'s editors and patrons as he defied the edicts of the party bosses seeking to bury the race question; and how he at last went down to defeat.

Phase One of the "Bystander": Electoral Politics

Perusing the "Bystander" column chronologically, we can discern six phases in its dialogue with readers. The first, dating from 21 April 1888, addressed white Northern Republicans, seeking to convince them that their party could not afford to ignore the disfranchisement of the South's African American voters. The second, dating from 15 December 1888, appealed to the same audience, now with the aim of arousing sympathy for the racial oppression endured by African Americans in the South. The third, dating from 4 May 1889, actively involved African Americans in the dialogue about race, which it extended to white supremacists as well. The fourth, dating from 31 October 1891, privileged the members of Tourgée's newly founded National Citizens' Rights Association; the fifth, spanning from 10 December 1892 to 12 August 1893, gave African American voices their greatest prominence; and the sixth, spanning from 5 May 1894 to 5 January 1895, attempted to placate the *Inter Ocean*'s editors and Republican Party bosses by foregrounding economic issues, at the same time that it precariously maintained the dialogue about race.

Constrained by the needs of a major Republican organ during an election year, Tourgée at first presented racial justice as a matter of party self-interest. For example, his column of 28 April contended that only by embracing rather than burying the legacy of equal citizenship rights inscribed in the

Fourteenth and Fifteenth Amendments could the party win the election of 1888. Republicans owed their victory in 1880 to their forthright defense of federal aid to education and of every citizen's right to vote without being subjected to intimidation or fraud, Tourgée insisted. Conversely, he alleged, they owed their defeat in 1884 to having "relegated all ... questions of principle to the background, and mounted the hobby-horse of economics."[11]

Over the months leading up to the November election, Tourgée repeatedly tried to show that African Americans constituted a strength, not a liability, of both the party and the nation, and that by neglecting to protect blacks in the South from violence at the polls, Republicans were depriving themselves of votes that could make the difference between carrying or forfeiting the election. Unlike white Southerners and the Northern urban rabble who frequented "grog-shops, dives," and socialist or anarchist meetings, Tourgée pointed out in his column of 5 May, catering to the Inter Ocean's "solid, respectable" readers, African Americans had caused "no turmoil, no violence, no bloodshed, no peril," but had been "peaceful, industrious, sober." They had supported not only themselves but their oppressors, created much of the nation's wealth with their labor, and contributed "225,000 able and efficient soldiers" to the Union army, "of whom the proportion killed and wounded in action" far exceeded the average for whites.[12] Moreover, in the twenty-three years since their emancipation, black Southerners had accumulated property worth tens of millions of dollars, achieved a literacy rate of more than 20 percent, and built impressive church membership rolls. In view of such facts, asked Tourgée, "is it not about time that the Republican party ceased to blush for their colored allies?"[13]

A few weeks later, Tourgée spelled out the exact price Republicans would pay for letting Southern states suppress the black vote: "SIXTY per cent of the voters of South Carolina, FIFTY-EIGHT per cent of the voters of Mississippi, and FIFTY-TWO per cent of the citizens of Louisiana will be silent on the 5th of next November." The franchise that Southern blacks would "not be permitted to exercise," he elaborated, would strengthen the power of their white oppressors and thereby falsify electoral returns throughout the country.[14] The "unfairness to the Northern voter" was "even greater" than in slavery times, explained Tourgée in another column, because now Southern states could count their entire black population in determining their representation in Congress, whereas previously the Constitution had allowed them only to count three-fifths of their slaves.[15]

Exasperated by party leaders' failure to heed his admonitions, Tourgée intensified his rhetoric. The Republican Party had "the power to set the seal of condemnation on violence, intimidation, and fraud," yet it had "done nothing" he complained.[16] Instead of writing off the South, the party ought to "wage an aggressive campaign" there "by sending Northern speakers of eminence and ability to discuss the issues of the pending conflict—organize the vote and prepare to contest at the ballot-box the solidity of the South." Such a strategy, Tourgée argued, would serve the double purpose of injecting "Northern ideas and Northern intelligence" into the hermetically sealed South and giving Northern Republican politicians "actual personal knowledge of the condition of affairs in those States"—knowledge that might convince them to act.[17]

Ultimately, Benjamin Harrison won the election despite losing both the "solid South" and the national popular vote—and despite ignoring Tourgée's exhortations. Undeterred by an outcome that seemingly gave the lie to his warnings, Tourgée predicted that the "question of one free vote for every free man, a fair count," and an end to the "bulldoz[ing]" of black and white Republican voters would remain "the most important question of American politics" until it was "settled."[18]

Phase Two of the "Bystander": Publicizing "Lawless Violence"

Harrison's narrow victory nevertheless freed Tourgée to cease subordinating his passion for justice and equality to pragmatic issues of electoral politics. His column of 15 December 1888 marked the shift to the second phase of "A Bystander's Notes." In it Tourgée focused on publicizing and condemning the many forms of "lawless violence" directed against African Americans. He initiated his treatment of the subject not with finger-pointing at the South but with an injunction to white Northerners to confront and root out their own propensity toward "lawless violence."

The most recent manifestation of this propensity had occurred in the midwestern states of Illinois, Indiana, and Ohio, where, according to Elliott, "a shadowy group of vigilantes calling themselves the White Caps had lynched and threatened dozens of blacks in a rash of incidents . . . designed to drive off black residents."[19] The *Cleveland Gazette*, one of the many African American newspapers Tourgée regularly read, had been covering the White Caps since July, when it observed that these roving mobs were "causing the white people" of the region "about as much trouble as the 'Ku-Klux' did our people in some parts of the South." By December, the White Caps were targeting African Americans rather than whites and were centering their depredations in Tourgée's native Ohio, as two *Gazette* articles of 8 December 1888

titled "Ohio's Ku Klux—the White Caps" and "Fighting for Rights in Felicity [Ohio]" reported. Tourgée's column of 15 December apparently took its
cue partly from the preceding week's *Gazette.*[20]

While similarly noting continuities between the White Caps and the
Klan, however, Tourgée interpreted the outbreak of mob violence in the
North as a case of chickens coming home to roost. In his view, Northerners had smugly dismissed the Klan as a Southern phenomenon that did not
require national soul-searching or federal intervention. "'Why do you permit such things to take place?'" they had lectured Southerners. "Now let
[Northerners] answer the question themselves," Tourgée shot back. By cor-
rupting "public sentiment," the nation's "tolerance" of the Klan's "outrages"
during Reconstruction had fueled the spread of lynch law throughout the
land, he charged. Northern states had seen an "amazing increase" in lynchings since 1880, yet Northern papers remained "almost universally silent"
about these atrocities in their home territory. "Before the disease assumes
further proportions," urged Tourgée, Northern states should pass laws to
snuff out vigilante violence.[21]

When Tourgée first named lynching a national crime in his column of
15 December on the White Caps, he eschewed identifying the victims as
primarily black, but he changed tactics within a week. His column of 22
December 1888 and its sequel of 5 January 1889—stellar examples of the stylistic devices Tourgée used to educate his readers—graphically described
a racial confrontation in Kemper County, Mississippi, that culminated in a
massacre of black farmers. The white Southern press had misrepresented
the episode as a "bloody" attack on "white men by an infuriated negro mob"
seeking to unleash a "nigger insurrection." Through parody, sarcasm, comic
exaggeration, and role reversal, Tourgée invited readers to dissect the contradictions in Southern newspaper accounts that endlessly repeated formu-
las serving to "prevent a true version of the facts from reaching the Northern
press":

> We have again the old, old story of the eager mustering of armed men
> from half a State to put down the revolt of a dozen negroes at some
> country cross-roads! The same sickening tale of murder of those who
> dared resist unlawful violence; the same hunting of the refugees in the
> swamps and hills as if they were wild beasts; . . . the same impudent
> avowal of the necessity of protecting innocent and saintly whites against
> the barbarous brutality of black demons who are threatening to destroy
> all that is lovely and of good report in the civilization of the South!

Tourgée's language emphasized the disproportion between the alleged provocation—"the revolt of a dozen negroes" in an obscure rural locality— and the retaliation: a "mustering of armed men from half a State" ("brought by special trains from all directions," he went on to specify). He also created sympathy for the black victims by redefining their action not as a "revolt" but as a courageous attempt to "resist *un*lawful violence" (italics mine) and by portraying them as "refugees" from a ferocious white mob that was "hunting" fellow human beings "as if they were wild beasts." Having primed readers to question the stereotype of beleaguered whites forced to defend their "civilization" against the "barbarous brutality of black demons," Tourgée slid into parody that exposed the absurdity of Southern propaganda. If white supremacists considered blacks to be "demons" and brutes, as they so frequently avowed, then they must consider themselves "innocent and saintly," Tourgée implied. If the defense of white Southern "civilization" against the threat of black barbarism necessitated lynch mobs, as their apologists claimed, then lynch mobs must be one of the "lovely" features of this civilization.[22]

After presenting the Kemper County incident as one more version of an "old, old story," Tourgée proceeded to reconstruct the "facts" leading up to the "man-hunt." Once again, he poked holes in the Southern press dispatch he summarized. The racial confrontation had begun when the cart of a "negro 'desperado'" had collided with that of a "white boy (age not given)" and his father, causing the two vehicles' wheels to "become interlocked." The black man had used "'insolent language'" to the boy, the father had objected, and the black man had knocked down the father "with a pistol" instead of shooting him and had immediately taken to his heels—behavior that hardly suggested a "desperado." Tourgée commented:

> Any one who is at all familiar with southern life can easily imagine the character of the brawl. The negro, of course is a "desperado"—nearly all negroes are desperadoes. Those who own carts, and mules, and houses, and plantations are almost sure to be desperadoes! The Southern white man is invariably very tender and considerate of the rights and feelings of the negro! . . . The Southern negro always takes the middle of the road, and with brutal violence and raging threats compel[s] the meek and long-suffering white man to drive into the ditch!

Tourgée signaled his use of parody with the proliferation of exclamation points, the quotation marks around "desperado," the phrase "of course," and the sweeping generalization "nearly all negroes are desperadoes." The common definition of "desperado" as an outlaw or bandit did not apply in the South, he indicated. There, what almost infallibly branded a black man as a desperado was ownership of "carts, and mules, and houses, and plantations"—the qualifications that established a white man as an economically stable, successful member of society. A black man who acquired such status symbols threatened the South's social order as much as an outlaw did other regions'.

By appealing to those "familiar with southern life" to reimagine the scene, Tourgée drew attention to the distortions in the press account. Southern protocol dictated that blacks give way to whites on the road and entitled whites to drive blacks "into the ditch" both literally and figuratively, as Tourgée no doubt expected readers to know. Thus, in reversing the roles of black and white, he underscored the improbability that a black man would force a white man off the road and into a ditch "with brutal violence and raging threats," as the press account intimated, or that a white man would meekly accept such treatment. At the same time, Tourgée's parody of Southern protocol highlighted the ugliness of a social system that permitted one race to humiliate and degrade another with complete impunity, regardless of which race dominated.

As he reconstructed the subsequent stages of the "lurid drama," Tourgée continued to expose the contradictions in white Southern propaganda through parody and sarcasm. First, a "score or so of indignant white men" armed with guns rather than with a "warrant" entered the premises of the "'nigger desperado'" to "remonstrate with him upon his conduct" in a "peaceful and friendly" manner. They found the "'desperado'" barricaded in his cotton shed with a group of equally "fiendish" friends who met the "charitable errand of the aggrieved whites" by firing at them, killing "two or three," and wounding "several," forcing them to retreat. Next, when the "devoted white remonstrants" returned the following morning, "the 'desperado,' his family and everything movable about the premises had disappeared"—a provocation that compelled the "tender-hearted white Christians of Kemper County" to burn the "house, kitchen, smoke-house, barn and cotton-sheds" of the "'desperado'" and to kill "all his stock," as he "deserve[d]." (That a man who "did not even own himself" twenty-three years earlier had managed to accumulate so much property, remarked Tourgée, showed him to be an "industrious 'nigger,' despite his desperate character.")

The Kemper County episode ended with the killing of an indeterminate number of black men, many of them uninvolved in the original confrontation. In his follow-up column of 5 January 1889, framed as a reply to a Southern newspaper that had accused him of overlooking the region's progress, Tourgée sarcastically commended the county for having "put itself in the very van of 'Southern progress'" by managing the affair with "such prudence and sagacity" that the official record of it no longer referred to "killings" but to "'disappearances'"—a term the perpetrators literalized by disposing of the bodies with no trace. He then accentuated the most telling aspect of the episode: "ALL THE NEGROES KILLED OWNED LITTLE FARMS." One of the murdered men had fought under Grant at Vicksburg, he noted for the benefit of the Union veterans among his readers. The state document justifying the "'disappearances,'" added Tourgée, reported "with brutal frankness" that "all the dead men's farms" had been reallocated to "*white men!*" These facts, Tourgée instructed readers, revealed the true explanation for the perennial racial violence that white Southern newspapers blamed on "negro 'desperadoes'": only by preventing blacks from prospering as independent farmers could white supremacists guarantee the cheap, abject labor force essential to maintaining their hegemony.[23]

In a column of 2 March 1889, Tourgée adduced further evidence both of how Southern whites conspired to keep blacks in slavelike conditions and of how blacks resisted. In North Carolina and Mississippi, he informed readers, black agricultural workers were quitting in droves, instigated by employment agents who promised them "better wages, surer pay, and more liberal treatment elsewhere." In response, North Carolina planters were flooding the state legislature with petitions for a law criminalizing the promotion of emigration—petitions that had in turn prompted African Americans to hold a "mass-meeting . . . openly, defiantly and insolently declar[ing] their right to go whithersoever they chose." Unlike their North Carolina peers, Mississippi whites did not bother with legislative niceties but simply lynched the "offensive emigration agent," an African American minister. Parodying the rationale Southern apologists offered for such actions, Tourgée editorialized, "The proceedings were a little irregular, but . . . if the negro is allowed to go where he pleases and demand what wages he sees fit[,] it would mean starvation and bankruptcy to the greater part of the South."[24]

Phase Three of the "Bystander": Initiating a Multivocal Dialogue on Race

Before long, Tourgée's sympathetic accounts of mob attacks on Southern blacks and his incisive refutations of white Southern propaganda started garnering him appreciative letters from African American readers. He began quoting extracts from their letters in his column of 4 May 1889, which inaugurated the interracial third phase of the "Bystander" column's dialogue on the race question by showcasing two of his African American correspondents. The first, a New York Union veteran who had "learned to write with the left hand, having lost the right as a boy of 16 or 17" during his army service, contended that commemorations of the war ought to give "special recognition" to African Americans because they had "'furnished *more than one-ninth of the enlisted men*'" in Union ranks. The second, a Southerner who asked for anonymity, shared details of a local meeting at which fifty "prominent colored men" had unanimously decided to observe the centennial of the U.S. Constitution not with "thanksgiving" but with prayers for release from the "injustice and oppression" their country meted out to them. Russia's freed serfs fared better than their African American counterparts, commented this correspondent.[25] Thereafter, such extracts became a regular and defining feature of "A Bystander's Notes."

By 29 June 1889, Tourgée was receiving such a volume of correspondence from "Bystander" readers of both races, North and South, that he introduced his column of that date by listing the categories the letters fell into: "words of commendation" and gratitude; "stories of wrong"; expressions of hope and fear for the future; "request[s] for information"; "virulent invective"; and calls for the "Bystander" to discuss particular subjects. His correspondents, Tourgée confided, were shaping his "Bystander" column by impelling him to address their concerns, either directly or surreptitiously. When possible, he specified, he answered their letters in print, but a "considerable proportion" of his correspondents asked him *not* to refer to their communications in a manner that might cast "suspicion" on them. "Freedom of thought or freedom of action in political matters" was not "permitted to any man, white or black," in the South, he explained.[26]

Defending the "Bystander" against Nixon

As the race question came to dominate Tourgée's "Bystander" column to the exclusion of the economic issues Republican leaders considered central to their redefinition of the party's agenda, the *Inter Ocean*'s managing editor, William Penn Nixon, apparently grew nervous. In a letter of 14 June 1889, he proposed dropping the "Bystander" column in July to "reduce expenses." "I do not like to lose you as a contributor," he wrote mollifyingly, "and hope to be able to take you on in some other way after I have got the ship trimmed and lightened."[27] His desire to exploit Tourgée's literary talents "in some other way" gives the impression that much as he valued the luster the author of *A Fool's Errand* shed on the *Inter Ocean*, Nixon worried that the "Bystander" column was costing the paper more in party sponsorship than it was earning in subscriptions. In reply, Tourgée emphasized the publicity the "Bystander" was generating for the *Inter Ocean*. "You may wonder that I keep banging at that Negro matter," he wrote Nixon. "If you have noticed how the Bystander has been quoted of late you will not wonder. Of course that means the *Inter-Ocean* [(double-underlined) has been quoted,] only you get the credit and I take the '*cussing!*'"[28]

After several more exchanges of letters with the tenacious Tourgée, on 23 August Nixon suggested the compromise of transforming rather than eliminating "A Bystander's Notes."[29] Tourgée met it with the same argument as he had Nixon's earlier proposal but elaborated that the "system of correspondence" he had devised with "Bystander" readers supplied him with press clippings and "information from every part of the country," enabling the *Inter Ocean* to offer better coverage of race issues than any other newspaper.[30] There could be no mistaking his purpose in opening his column of 31 August 1889 with an allusion to the "big box of letters which greeted the Bystander's return from his vacation"; nor could there be any doubt about why he singled out as the one he most "highly prized" the message from an illiterate "colored Mississippian" who had asked his daughter to write "that he subscribed for THE INTER OCEAN in order that his children might read to him what the Bystander has to say in vindication of [his] race's rights and encouragement of its hopes."[31]

For the time being, Tourgée succeeded in allaying Nixon's qualms. Accordingly, his "Bystander" column continued to foreground the race question, publicize incidents of white supremacist violence and black resistance, agitate for justice and equality, and broadcast the voices of African Americans. On 21 September, Tourgée credited a correspondent "who dare not let his name be known" with providing an inside view of a massacre in Leflore County, Mississippi, that the white supremacist press was misrepresenting as an insurrection. This correspondent set the number of black victims at "*more than 100*" and revealed that their crime had consisted in organizing "'labor alliances'" and demanding "'payment of the wages agreed upon by strikes during the cotton-picking season.'"[32]

Five months later, in a column of 22 February 1890, Tourgée took up another aspect of white supremacy: the Southern prison system. He had seen its horrors close up, both as a prisoner of war in 1863 and as a judge in Reconstruction-era North Carolina, though he seemingly did not realize that the Northern prison system exhibited many of the same horrors.

The "barbarity" of the South's "prison methods" and, indeed, of its "whole penal system," argued Tourgée, arose from "generations of the hardening, embruiting [*sic*] influences of slavery." He asked, "Can not one see in such a condition of legalized and unrestricted control of bodies and souls the seeds of that new barbarity which shows itself in the 'convict camps' and prisons of the Southern States to-day?" During his judgeship, Tourgée recalled, he had found North Carolina whites so inured to the sufferings of prisoners that many had opposed his order to heat prison cells in winter, ridiculing it as "Yankee sentimentalism." He also attributed the gaping disparities between the sentences imposed on blacks and whites for the same crimes to the legacy of slavery, which had necessitated the total subordination of blacks to whites. As an instance, he cited a "five-years' sentence imposed on a young colored man for a very doubtfully proved theft of a cheap pair of gloves" from a store counter, while an older white man proved guilty "beyond question" of having "broken into a dwelling-house . . . and stolen about all the clothing he could carry away" received a suspended sentence. The South's penal system and "prison terror" rivaled those of Siberia in harshness, Tourgée declared, referring to a recent series of articles on Siberian conditions by the journalist George Kennan. Tourgée went so far as to intimate that because racial bias so thoroughly permeated the South's judicial practice, its black victims could be likened to Siberian political prisoners. He exhorted "national associations of colored men" to gather data on Southern prisons that "would shock all the world's heart" as deeply as Kennan's Siberian revelations had.[33]

The "Bystander" and the Black Press

Well before this "Bystander" article appeared, influential African American newspapers had started reprinting Tourgée's column on their front pages, in the process simultaneously familiarizing their subscribers with his ideas, attracting new subscribers to the *Inter Ocean*, and creating a black forum for the interracial dialogue Tourgée had sparked. The *Cleveland Gazette*, which had been quoting and alluding to Tourgée's writings since 1884, even advertising subscription packages that included some of his books, reprinted its first "Bystander" column on 3 August 1889, one in which Tourgée disputed common white misconceptions about the nature, causes, and solution of the "Negro Problem."[34] Both the *Gazette* and the *Detroit Plaindealer* reprinted Tourgée's "Bystander" of 2 November 1889 hailing the project of founding a "National league of colored men . . . to promote the interests of the colored race in the United States" (the organization that became the

National Afro-American League).[35] Subsequently, the *Gazette* featured Tourgée's *Inter Ocean* articles at intervals, the *Plaindealer* on almost a weekly basis, especially from August 1891 on. Given the close relationship Tourgée developed with Louis A. Martinet, editor of the *New Orleans Crusader*—and given the extraordinary number of letters Tourgée received from black Southerners—the *Crusader*, too, must have reprinted the "Bystander" with some frequency, though the extreme paucity of the paper's surviving remnants makes such a conjecture impossible to document.

However much they admired Tourgée and appreciated his impassioned advocacy of racial equality and justice, African American editors did not always agree with his views. As we have seen, they engaged him in dialogue on such matters as whether or not to support the seriously flawed bills for federal aid to education and supervision of elections that Senators Henry Blair and Henry Cabot Lodge were shepherding through Congress. Thus, they, too, helped shape Tourgée's "Bystander" column by pushing him to articulate more clearly why he opposed those bills and what alternatives he advocated.[36]

The "Bystander" and White Racist Ideologues

From the antipodal end of the spectrum, racist ideologues, by inciting him to refute their theories, likewise shaped the interracial dialogue Tourgée's "Bystander" column fostered. Notwithstanding Nixon's desire to rein in his troublesome contributor, he heartily approved of Tourgée's attacks on these ideologues. "I do not think such people can be hit too hard," he opined, congratulating Tourgée on a "timely" article of 13 July 1889 that dressed down a "Scientific Negrophobist" from Massachusetts who advocated disfranchisement as a prelude to the mass deportation of African Americans and who justified both to prevent the evils of "amalgamation." "In all the world's history there is not a more relentless and intolerant bigot than the scientific theorist," editorialized Tourgée.[37]

Few scientific theorists of race exerted greater influence in the late nineteenth century than Nathaniel Southgate Shaler, professor of paleontology and geology at Harvard. In antebellum days an avowed proslavery apologist and promulgator of polygenesis (the human races' separate origins), he nonetheless enjoyed a reputation for scholarly objectivity, as attested by the publication of his article "Science and the African Problem" in the *Atlantic Monthly* of July 1890. Reviewing this article in a "Bystander" column of 19 July, Tourgée reminded readers that "the most willing servants of the injustice of slavery were the guild of American scientists" who "buttressed" the

institution in a manner "singularly at variance with" the discipline's "present claims" to unbiased investigation. Shaler proposed to solve the "African
problem in the United States" by forming "a great anthropological society . . .
to study the American negro" for the sake of determining "what he is fit for
and what can be made of him." Yet just as proslavery apologists had done,
noted Tourgée, "Professor Shaler discredits himself and his proposed remedy in advance by prejudging the whole question, deciding that the negro is
a racial inferior and that the white race is authorised to dominate and control him." Tourgée dismissed Shaler's "so-called 'scientific' deductions" as
"simple 'rot'" unsupported by any evidence. "Science can never determine"
African Americans' rightful status in the United States, he underscored,
because "in the first place the *facts* can never be established" independently
of social constraints, and in the second place, "the American negro will neither admit himself a racial inferior of the white man, nor recognize the right
of the white scientist to sit in judgment on that question."[38]

Intriguingly, however, Tourgée found confirmation in Shaler's article of
an idea that had long been germinating in his mind. A society should indeed
be formed to study the race question, he ventured, but it should be an "equal
rights association, having for its object the collection and dissemination of
information in regard to the present conditions of the colored people, and
how they may be improved." It should rely not on "scientific dogma, but [on]
simple justice and Christian teaching as a sure and safe solution of the 'African
Problem.'" Tourgée envisaged this equal rights association as collaborating
with the National Afro-American League but encompassing "every one who
recognizes the gravity of the problem and is willing to aid in its solution"—a
description that suggests an interracial coalition. It "should be organized
throughout the country without delay," he urged twice in his review of Shaler's article.[39] Yet Tourgée would delay for another fifteen months before
founding the nationwide organization he called for. Meanwhile, he laid the
intellectual groundwork for it by setting his white and African American
readers in dialogue with each other through his "Bystander" column, both to
promote greater understanding across racial barriers and to demonstrate that
African Americans themselves offered the best refutation of racist ideology.

*Transmitting an African American's Message
to "Bystander" Readers*

Tourgée first adopted the strategy of letting African Americans answer
white racists in a column of 17 January 1891 denouncing the eight Republican senators whose sellout in the face of a Democratic filibuster had just

doomed the federal election law. To illustrate "how these things appear to the colored man, who is the victim of this great transaction in human rights," Tourgée quoted copious extracts from the letter of an African American correspondent he characterized as having "made himself eminent for scholarly attainment." He prefaced the extracts by contrasting his correspondent with the politicians who glibly consigned African Americans to civic impotence: "Intellectually, very few Senators are his superior. Not one in that body has shown the manhood he has displayed— . . . has achieved so much in the face of obstacles—has shown such dogged resolution—has practiced such rigid economy—is indebted in so slight a degree to the State, to public sentiment and to general environment, for the fact that he is what he is." Such a man deserved to be honored by his country, but conditions in the South instead necessitated protecting his anonymity—a bitter commentary on the failure of American democracy, implied Tourgée. He then vivified for his readers the threat of white supremacist violence that shadowed every African American in the South, no matter how distinguished: "The Bystander would no more dare to reveal his correspondent's name or in any way designate his identity than point out a victim to a murderer. If it were known that he had written such a letter, he would be an exile within a fortnight even if permitted to escape alive." After this preface, Tourgée let his correspondent speak for himself through sentences drawn from his letter.[40]

Because the original letter survives in Tourgée's papers—unlike most of the ones he quotes in his "Bystander" column—it presents a rare opportunity to examine his approach toward transmitting the voices of African Americans to a predominantly white audience. Writing on his institution's departmental stationery, headed "A. O. Coffin, Ph.d., Natural Science," its author, Alfred Oscar Coffin, was a professor at Wiley University in Marshall, Texas. BlackPast.org identifies him as the first African American to earn a Ph.D. in biological sciences (at Illinois Wesleyan) and the author of a book on the origins of the mound builders. Coffin was responding not to the Senate vote on the election bill, which had not yet occurred, but to Tourgée's "Bystander" column of 30 December 1890 in the *Weekly Inter Ocean* (27 December in the *Daily*), which had made him "feel like shaking hands with" a man who showed "stamina enough to speak the truth though the heavens fall." He wrote:

> Legislation, Colormania, Corporations and the Devil are all in league against us, and if my race had half the daring of the Indian, something would happen but as it is they meekly submit to what your house-dog

would resent, and trustingly look forward to the millennial day when the their [sic] Messiah: the Republican Government will come to finish his work of emancipation begun in 1863.

The brutal, yea, ultra-brutal atrocities of this Sunny South-land will never be published, for they would read so like a romance no one so far away as you are, would give them credence.

There is a cloud that hangs like a pall over every possible avenue that opens to us any possible competence than menial labor, and an armed foe that stands ready at a moment's notice to emphasize every clause of the unwritten Ku Klux Code.

To assert our rights as freemen means a telegram to every militia organization in the south to kill all Negroes at sight and the White Caps bringing up a prompt second.

Of course our *Glorious Government* will see to those small matters when the matters of importance are off the calendar but it interferes a little with our family relations to have several thousand of our best men murdered every year while waiting for our guardian to assume responsibilities. It is true that only two of my family have been killed, but think of the poor unfortunates that left no one to tell the tale!

We do indeed have a great country: there is none other like unto it.[41]

In the "Bystander" Tourgée omitted Coffin's initial words of gratitude and made some significant editorial changes in the passages he reproduced, rearranging the order of sentences, inserting phrases, and intensifying the sarcasm of the original. For example, he transformed the second and third clauses into full sentences and began his extracts with them—a revision that had the effect of goading African Americans to fight for their own rights; he also spelled out the prophecy of an imminent revolutionary upheaval (a frequent theme in his writings) that Coffin had barely hinted at: "If my race had the desperation of the Indian something would *soon happen which would make the world's heart stand still with horror*" (italics mine). Moving the third clause further down the series of paragraphs, after the sentences about the "brutal atrocities" practiced in the South, Tourgée dropped the word "Messiah" and inserted a taunt directed at Republicans: "Our people still hope that a millennial day will come when a Republican government will complete the emancipation begun in 1863, *and of which they have boasted ever since*" (italics mine). The taunt acquired a sharper edge from the new context, which highlighted white supremacists' methods of keeping blacks in subjection despite their legal emancipation. Tourgée further injected a sexual element unarticulated in the original: "To assert one's rights as a free-man, *or to protect the honor of a colored woman*" (italics mine). An attentive reader will notice many other editorial changes in the "Bystander" version.

These alterations of a letter from an African American correspondent Tourgée purported to be quoting raise the question, To what extent did he genuinely give voice to the people whose cause he championed? I would argue that Tourgée's revisions neither muffled Coffin's voice nor modified his sentiments. Rather, they remained faithful overall to Coffin's language and style while successfully adapting his message to a broader audience that lacked the inside knowledge and political perspective Coffin could take for granted in Tourgée—an audience Coffin could never otherwise have reached. In that sense, Tourgée indeed offered African Americans a channel through which to speak to the white public.

Letting African Americans Talk Back

African American correspondents eagerly seized the opportunity to talk back to racist whites via Tourgée's "Bystander" column. When a white Southern Republican chided Tourgée for "wasting [his] sympathy upon a people who have neither gratitude nor capacity" for advancement, as his "Bystander" of 11 April 1891 reported, the insult generated a flood of "indignant" retorts, notwithstanding Tourgée's reply to the slur. "The Bystander is not aware that he ever asked or expected 'gratitude' from any one on account of his advocacy of measures which he believes to be for the common good of all—black and white alike," Tourgée had rejoined. He gained enough satisfaction, he added, from letters like the following: "Ten of us who work on three adjoining plantations put in a dime apiece to get THE WEEKLY INTER OCEAN, in order that we may have the reading of your 'Notes.' We get together every Saturday night and read them to a big house full." Still, Tourgée acknowledged that he had "not unfrequently" heard former abolitionists complain of feeling forgotten by the people "for whom they had toiled and suffered."[42]

Rankled by the charge of ingratitude, Tourgée's African American correspondents besieged him with letters "so numerous" and incisive that Tourgée decided to let them "speak for themselves." In his column of 25 April he quoted extracts from nine letters that countered the charge of ingratitude with such arguments as these:

Is it the negro or the white man who is ungrateful? We did the work of the South for generations. We built the churches, the colleges, made the farms valuable and enabled the white people of the South to live in ease and luxury and the North to grow rich by manufacturing the products of our toil. When [the war] was over they turned us out without farms, homes, money, education—with nothing but our lives and our hands.

. . . .

I believe we have been *too grateful*. I was born a slave and do not know as much about history as those who have had a better chance to learn; but I have never heard of any people who amounted to much who sat down and counted over their blessings, and give [*sic*] thanks for the scraps when they ought to have had the whole loaf.[43]

Tourgée carefully refrained from identifying those who risked reprisal, but he did provide useful biographical information about others. For example, he prefaced an especially bitter reply to the accusation of ingratitude by noting that the writer "was driven out of the home he had purchased with the pittance he had saved as a soldier" and that he had since "acquired [a] competence by honest industry in another land." This correspondent fulminated: "The American flag represents to me injustice. Whenever I see it I curse it. I am sorry I gave my blood to support it. I do not think the American people have any sense of justice toward the colored man." In a second case, Tourgée quoted a "young man in college" as saying, "It is harder for a colored man to rise than for a white man. Everything is against him." The student's complaint pertained to segregation and discrimination in the North, which threatened an African American who wanted to participate in a patriotic ceremony with "loss of his own self-respect."[44] In a third case, Tourgée quoted a teacher who insisted that African Americans *were* grateful to abolitionists, Union soldiers, and "those who have advocated for us equal and exact justice and equal opportunity."[45] By allowing his African American correspondents to articulate their own grievances through his "Bystander" column, Tourgée sought to breach the color line that kept whites ignorant of black sentiments.

Promoting Dialogue across the Color Line

Tourgée clearly sympathized with the views of the African American correspondents whose denials of ingratitude he quoted, but he remained convinced that white abolitionists deserved more recognition than they had received from the black community. Both in his "Bystander" column and in private letters, he sought to enlist African American opinion-makers in a campaign to educate the black masses about the sacrifices their white benefactors had made for them—a campaign Tourgée considered vital to rebuilding a cross-racial alliance strong enough to complete the work of the abolitionist movement by winning equal rights for all U.S. citizens, not simply on paper but in practice. Toward this end he revisited the subject of black ingratitude in a "Bystander" column of 12 September 1891 that engaged African American editors in a dialogue while setting white and black readers in dialogue with each other. It opened by addressing white Southern newspaper editors and closed by addressing their African American counterparts.

A white Southern newspaper, Tourgée reported, had dismissed his accounts of recent atrocities as "'campaign lies' from Northern newspapers." To the contrary, Tourgée riposted, he had drawn all these accounts directly from "Southern Democratic papers," which portrayed the black "agricultural laborers" in their states as "the most contented and prosperous . . . in the world," even as they matter-of-factly recorded the "lynchings and unrebuked public killings" of any who dared to resist oppression. Tourgée urged readers who truly wished to gain a "keener realization of the anomalous condition in which one-eighth of our population find themselves placed" to subscribe to one or more of the "newspapers published and edited by colored men." He listed five political weeklies and one religious journal: three already familiar to us—the *Detroit Plaindealer*, the *Cleveland Gazette*, and the *New Orleans Crusader*—along with the *Richmond Planet*, the *Indianapolis World*, and the *Southwestern Christian Advocate*, a periodical with a special claim on Methodists as the "official organ" of their church in the New Orleans region.

Tourgée singled out the *Crusader* for praise as "the most earnest and active" of African American newspapers "in promoting organized legal resistance" to Jim Crow transportation laws. In the next breath, however, he took its unnamed editor (Louis A. Martinet) to task for not doing enough. A month earlier, in his "Bystander" column of 15 August, Tourgée had charged that although African Americans were "justly proud" of "more than a hundred newspapers owned and edited by colored men," these newspapers were not performing their duty to the race. "Not one of them publishes a blacklist which tells the terrible tale of Christian savagery each year. Not one of them has ever had the courage and the enterprise to learn and publish the names" of massacre victims and other "martyrs to unholy persecution," Tourgée had alleged.[46] He now criticized Martinet for responding, "If the Bystander realized the difficulties and dangers attending such a course he would perhaps have more charity for their apathy." No, answered Tourgée: "It is precisely because he *does* know the difficulty attending such a course that the Bystander blames [black editors] for not adopting it. What is the use of watchmen if they do not sound an alarm? And how shall a race reach a higher level of manhood if its leaders are silent when their rights are trampled upon?" Tourgée hastened to add that he "meant no reproach to any one—certainly not to one who has shown the courage of the editor of the *Crusader.*" Yet he expressed the belief that African Americans were "advertising very urgently for heroes—men who think more of their race than of themselves"—and that their editorial spokesmen should "unflinchingly" lead the van.[47] This public dialogue marked the beginning of his relationship with Martinet, which would soon flower into their collaboration in the *Plessy v. Ferguson* case.

A Public-Private Dialogue with Ferdinand L. Barnett of the Chicago Conservator

Having berated African editors for failing to risk their lives to liberate their people, Tourgée appealed to them to memorialize the heroism of the white men and women who had "faced obloquy and danger" in fighting against slavery and teaching the newly emancipated blacks. He cited the poignant example of Calvin Fairbank, who had "liberated *forty-seven*" slaves and paid for his philanthropy with "*seventeen years* imprisonment" and "more than *thirty thousand stripes*" in the Kentucky penitentiary but who now languished "broken, worn and scarred, . . . in loneliness and want, forgotten by the race in whose behalf he suffered" and scorned by his fellow whites. Faring little better in public memory, the thousands of Northern teachers who had braved the violence of the Reconstruction-era South to equip "an outcast and despised people" with "knowledge and power" also awaited due acknowledgment, Tourgée asserted. "As yet not a single one of the newspapers edited by colored men has taken any pains to inform its readers" of the role these teachers had played in the race's history, he claimed. African Americans could better find allies among Northern whites if they showed appreciation for their white allies of the past, he implied. He predicted, nevertheless, that in the future, a different dynamic would govern such cross-racial alliances. The "colored man" must fight his own battles, "make his own appeals," and "compel attention to his just demands," "not as a pauper begging for aid, but *as a man demanding his rights.*" The question of equal civil and political rights for all citizens throughout the country, "*not only awarded in the statute but enforced and protected by the courts,*" must override any other issues for African Americans, concluded Tourgée.[48]

This "Bystander" column stung at least one African American editor, Ferdinand L. Barnett of the *Chicago Conservator*, into writing to Tourgée the very same day, initiating what became a decade of correspondence between them that later included Barnett's future wife, Ida B. Wells, and Emma Tourgée. Barnett identified himself at the outset as a regular reader of Tourgée's "inspiring utterances." He and his people always weighed them carefully, he assured Tourgée. Barnett's reason for writing, he explained, was to ask Tourgée to correct the statement that "not a single one of the newspapers edited by colored men" had paid homage to Calvin Fairbank, because the *Conservator* had in fact publicized Fairbank's story and raised a fund for him more than a year ago. Barnett's sensitivity to his people's reputation as a "race of ingrates," however, apparently led him to misread the statement he quoted.[49] As Tourgée quickly pointed out, in context it referred not to Fairbank but to the teachers of the freedmen's schools.

Tourgée's letter did little to assuage an African American's hurt pride at being held responsible for his people's shortcomings. As if freed from the constraints of writing for public consumption, Tourgée abandoned any effort at tact and belabored the charge of ingratitude in a nakedly personal manner. "You know as well as I that the colored people have lost friend [*sic*]—true friends, I mean—very rapidly during a few years past," he hectored Barnett. "The *people* of the North do not regard them as kindly as they did." Although historians have ascribed this shift of public sentiment to the postwar longing for reconciliation between Northern and Southern whites, which necessitated sacrificing African Americans,[50] Tourgée ascribed it to disappointment with African Americans' "lack of appreciation"—a disappointment he admitted to sharing. Hardly any African Americans attended his lectures on the race problem, Tourgée complained: "Now, when a man is fighting the battles of a people, he has a right to expect at least a manifestation of their approval while engaged in it. You no doubt wonder why I keep on. Candidly, so do I."[51] (It evidently did not occur to Tourgée that many African Americans may not have been able to afford the price of admission to his lectures and that some may have feared being made to feel unwelcome in predominantly white venues.) African Americans' seeming apathy not only disheartened their friends but also armed their enemies, Tourgée contended, instancing the deduction a hostile newspaper had drawn from the paucity of black faces in his audience: "The Judge might as well give it up. The Negro is—a 'nigger,' and always will be." Nothing could better counteract such views or accomplish more to "tie your people to the true-hearted ones of the North," Tourgée suggested, than an African American tribute to "Our Race's Benefactors." Why not publish such a tribute, first as a series of syndicated newspaper articles, afterwards as a book? Begin with "the

Abolition movement and its leaders," he instructed Barnett. "Leave out their quarrels; extol their merits." Then tell the stories of the teachers who had been devoting themselves to the race's uplift since emancipation. "Do it neatly: don't slobber nor inflate." Naming Charles Chesnutt as an ideal candidate for writing or editing the volume, which required a "skilled pen," Tourgée held up the prospect that the venture might even "be profitable if well done." Only after riding roughshod over the sensibilities Barnett's letter had revealed did Tourgée apologize—halfheartedly at that—for "lecturing—or seeming to do so." He did not apologize for intimating that African American writers needed to be warned not to "slobber nor inflate." If Barnett took offense at Tourgée's officious condescension, he left no trace of it. The two men's correspondence remained cordial, and Barnett continued to regard Tourgée as "one of our best friends." Yet neither he nor any other African American editor took up the idea of publishing a tribute to "Our Race's Benefactors."[52]

A Public-Private Dialogue with Journalist John Edward Bruce

Tourgée displayed similar crotchetiness toward another African American correspondent with whom he conducted a public-cum-private dialogue, the journalist John Edward Bruce, better known by his pen name, Bruce Grit. In his "Bystander" column of 15 August 1891 (the one to which Martinet had responded by pleading for greater awareness of the dangers that muzzled African American spokesmen in the South), Tourgée used a much-disguised version of a letter from Bruce as a pretext for goading race leaders to preach militant resistance rather than patient submission. "A colored man whose record of persistent effort in securing an education and whose worthy use of the same are a credit to his people," editorialized Tourgée, had maintained "with a spirit of pardonable exultation, that the hope of the negro in the future lies chiefly in the patience and good temper of the race—the fact that they 'write the memory of favors in marble and the memory of wrongs in water.'" Tourgée categorically rejected this notion. "Submission to oppression stimulates the desire to oppress. Only those people who stubbornly and persistently assert their rights, ever rest secure in their possession," he retorted: "The man who forgives the fellow who has him down and is gouging him is not only a fool but a coward, and the people who hope for prosperity by kissing the rod of injustice will be sorely disappointed. The hope of the oppressor lies in the submissiveness of the oppressed." What incited him to argue so vehemently against his correspondent's valuation of patience and forgiveness, Tourgée noted, was that it had arrived during a week marked by four lynchings and a massacre.[53]

In exploiting Bruce's letter as an opportunity to rebuke religious leaders who advised African Americans to "'praise God and make money'" while awaiting divine rescue from their plight, Tourgée disregarded Bruce's actual reason for writing: to congratulate him on the publication of *Pactolus Prime*, to offer to review and promote the novel, and to thank him for his tireless advocacy. Tourgée had directly influenced his own career, Bruce recalled. As a youth newly freed from slavery, he had heard Tourgée's name "in the mouth of every Negro who could read." Taking advantage of a chance encounter, Bruce had introduced himself and asked for Tourgée's autograph, and above his signature Tourgée had inscribed the motto from *A Fool's Errand* that had launched his campaign for federal aid to education: "Make the spelling book the sceptre of national power." "I have that sentiment and autograph pasted on the first page of my scrap book and prize it more than you can ever know," Bruce wrote, adding that it had inspired his continuing struggle to "make a place for myself in the domain of intellect" and to devote his life to advancing "the interests of my race." Bruce's touching expression of gratitude did not earn him a gesture in kind from a man who had confessed to a craving for gratitude. Instead, Tourgée focused his "Bystander" article almost solely on the statement to which he objected: "I have an abiding faith in the promises of our dear Lord and in the future of my race. '*The meek shall inherit the earth.*' We have the patience and the courage to wait for the coming of the morning—to bide our time to suffer contumely and we are magnanimous enough to write our 'benefits in marble and our injuries in dust.'"[54]

Tourgée pursued his dialogue with Bruce in a letter marked "Personal." Confirming that he remembered meeting Bruce, Tourgée praised his articles in the *Cleveland Gazette* but quickly shifted to criticism. The "greatest danger" menacing African Americans, he opined, was that the "spirit of assertion and resistance [would] die out" among them and that they would "become the Jews of the new world—submissive inferiors whom it [would] be a pleasure and an almost irresistible temptation to oppress." Rather than "dwelling gleefully upon [their] prospects and achievements," Tourgée scolded, African Americans should "make 'the hollow vault of hell resound' with denunciation of [their] wrongs, past and present." They should also "patronize each other . . . in business" and be "just as clannish as the German[s]" in order to present a "coherent force" against racism. He used "plain words," Tourgée specified, because he believed he could best serve the people and the causes he defended by telling the "truth, even when it was not wholly pleasant to those who heard."[55]

Bruce replied to Tourgée's private and public communications in two separate letters dated 1 September 1891. The first, a six-page typed letter, is remarkable for its honesty, acuity, and historical consciousness. "Some of your *bricks* have spikes in them and they hurt," he admitted (playing on the title of Tourgée's famous novel), "but I am not going to complain because I sometimes indulge in that pastime myself." While conceding that Tourgée's cross-cultural examples sufficed "to convince any Negro that manhood pays," Bruce pointed out the unique obstacles his people faced in a white supremacist nation:

> The Englishman who is outraged in this country has a strong and powerful government behind him to demand reparation for injuries sustained. . . . To whom, can the Negro look for protection when his home is invaded, his life threatened, his liberty abridged and his rights as a citizen denied? Certainly not to the Federal Government or to Congress, or to the Supreme Court, for each and all these branches of Government have tacitly refused to admit that Negroes have any rights which white men are bound to respect. . . . Tell me if you will or can, how 8[,]000,000 Negroes may obtain justice and fair treatment from the 54,000,000 white people in this country who own the railroads, steamship, telegraph lines, manufacture and own all the firearms and ammunition, in fact own everything worth having in this country? The press with some notable exceptions is prejudiced against us and the white American church piously loves God and hates "niggers."[56]

Apparently referring to Tourgée's claim (in an earlier article) that the race needed martyrs willing to fight to the death for freedom,[57] Bruce went on to remind Tourgée that African Americans had already contributed their share of martyrs, whose fate indicated that "they do not seem to thrive in this climate." He cited the case of the 1831 Nat Turner insurrection in Virginia, the largest in U.S. history, which not only had been brutally put down in reprisals victimizing hundreds of innocent blacks but also had fed persistent stereotypes of black savagery. "A similar uprising among the Negroes would produce upon the public mind in our day" the same deleterious effect, argued Bruce: "The Negro hating press and the Negro hating orators in and out of Congress would deal with us" as they had with Turner, "and every man of us would be characterized as a murderous black brute—fiends incarnate, Devils from Hell." These propagandists would "so intensify the feelings against us as a race for daring to strike for our liberties that I fear we would soon be exterminated or our ranks so decimated that we wouldn't hanker after another such opportunity for a century at least." Though he could not agree that "your race would change its methods of dealing with my race, if my race would show some sign to indicate that it will retaliate when imposed upon," Bruce did agree with Tourgée's criticisms of black religious and political leaders. Evincing no need to close ranks with his racial confreres against a white ally's censure, Bruce pronounced the black clergy an "incubus of ignorance[,] superstition, immorality and rascality" that had proved a "positive hindrance" to his people's intellectual development. He judged "our so-called leaders in politics, with here and there an honorable exception," equally harshly, branding them as "a set of unscrupulous merce-naries ... who have sold us out to the highest bidder." He also acknowledged Tourgée's "kindly spirit" and "sincere ... friendship for my race," which no doubt convinced Bruce he could unburden himself without inhibitions.[58]

Even when he ruefully recognized his own words used against him in Tourgée's "Bystander" column of 15 August 1891, Bruce did not doubt the genuineness of Tourgée's commitment to African American liberation. "I notice in the Detroit Plaindealer [which had reprinted the column], that you have jumped on a colored man who wrote you a letter some time since and have preached him a most interesting sermon," Bruce commented in his second letter of 1 September, this one dashed off by hand:

> The aforesaid Colored man feels hurt, his bones are sore his feelings don't feel right. Yet despite his dilapidated condition he read after you with his accustomed admiration and pleasure and voted you are the "*Grandest* white man in this glorious land of '*Coon hunters*'" and mid-night marauders. You certainly pumped the sentimentalities out of that colored man.
>
> I have a faint suspicion that the quotation you have discussed with so much vigor, emphasis, and elaborateness, was contained in my reply to your first letter to me. You emasculated the original quote with so much skill and deftness that the remains almost defy identification. I fellicitate [*sic*] myself however upon having given you something to talk about though I regret that you wiped the sidewalk up with me.

As if to confirm that he bore Tourgée no ill will, Bruce signed this letter "Faithfully your friend."[59]

With its frank avowal of hurt feelings, its self-deprecating humor, and its perceptive description of the literary techniques Tourgée used to incorporate his correspondents' messages into his "Bystander" column, Bruce's letter stands out among the hundreds of responses Tourgée received from African American readers. It offers particularly valuable insight into the reasons African Americans continued to trust and admire a man who harangued them mercilessly and sometimes gave them advice they could not accept. They knew Tourgée had risked his own life to uphold equal citizenship rights in the teeth of Klan violence. They knew he was paying a heavy price for championing their cause amid a national backlash against egalitarian ideals. They knew they could count on him. And they knew he respected them.

Bruce's career provides a fascinating footnote to his correspondence with Tourgée. True to his pen name, Bruce indeed demonstrated "grit" in his writings and speeches, which sounded much more like Tourgée than like the "colored man" chastised in his "Bystander" column. African Americans threatened with racist violence, Bruce urged in an 1889 speech, should "meet force with force," defend their homes and families to their last breath, and retaliate in kind for murder, arson, and property damage. Like Tourgée, Bruce argued that "wherever and whenever the Negro shows himself to be a man he can always command the respect even of a cutthroat." And like Tourgée, he advocated "organized resistance" as the "best remedy" for white supremacist terrorism.[60]

Transmitting African American Criticisms of the Republican Party

The public dialogue Tourgée conducted with African Americans through his "Bystander" column did not always cast him as preceptor and them as tutees. A "Bystander" article of 9 May 1891 instead reveals how Tourgée's African American correspondents educated him. Citing a resolution passed by the convention of Republican clubs that had recently taken place in Cincinnati, they had expressed fears that party bosses were preparing to mute or "ignore . . . altogether" the issue of citizens' rights in the 1892 electoral campaign. Tourgée quickly realized his African American informants were right and apologized "with some confusion" for his oversight. The Cincinnati Republicans' decision to assign "almost the last place" in their platform to a statement about national citizenship rights vindicated African Americans' concerns, admitted Tourgée.[61]

One of the correspondents who alerted Tourgée to the deficiencies of the Cincinnati platform was A. M. Middlebrooks, a deputy revenue collector in Pine Bluff, Arkansas, who had begun writing to him in January 1891. "Say Judge!! *Now listen and think* [double-underlined]," he exhorted Tourgée in a letter of 29 April. To counter the ominous trends they had observed in Cincinnati, Middlebrooks confided, African Americans planned to hold a "Convention of Constitutional Liberty" in Indianapolis, the home of presidential incumbent Benjamin Harrison: "We want the old school of White Republicans . . . to meet with us as delegates and we want you as the leader to . . . make a Speech *remedial* of the wrongs perpetrated upon the Negroes in the South and also to have Mr. George W Cable to do likewise," specified Middlebrooks, asking Tourgée to reply through his "Bystander" column.[62] We do not know whether Tourgée spoke at the proposed convention, which was held on 30 June in Cincinnati rather than in Indianapolis, but his "Bystander" column of 11 July reprinted its chief resolutions. These resolutions castigated the Republicans for their "studied and prearranged silence . . . on the infamous frauds and brutal outrages" against African Americans in the South and for their failure to pass the federal elections bill despite their majority in the Senate; accused President Benjamin Harrison of conniving to found a Lily White Southern branch of the Republican Party; charged him with ingratitude to the "colored voters of Ohio, whose ballots gave [him] twenty-three electoral votes"; and pledged that African Americans would keep agitating for "political justice and equality, unconditioned and unqualified," until they won it. "The negro begins to see that he has his own way to make in securing his rights as a citizen," Tourgée editorialized in support of the insurgent African American Republicans whose rage at the party he conveyed to his white readers.[63]

Reprinting the New Orleans Citizens' Committee's Challenge to Jim Crow

While fostering interracial dialogue among the readers of his "Bystander" column and engaging in his own public and private dialogue with African American opinion-makers, Tourgée eagerly watched for signs of increasing black militancy. The latest such sign—the spirited stand black Republicans took at their Cincinnati convention on 30 June—followed on the heels of two others Tourgée had cited in earlier "Bystander" articles. On 7 February 1891, he had hailed the formation by "colored voters" of the American Citizens' Equal Rights Association (ACERA). So far the only organizations devoted to securing to all U.S. citizens "the peaceful enjoyment of their civil and political rights" owed their creation to "the earnest and manly efforts of colored men," Tourgée editorialized on 2 May, referring to the National Afro-American League as well as to the ACERA.[64] With each new manifestation of African Americans' readiness for a major new initiative, Tourgée inched closer to launching the interracial equal rights association for which he had called the previous January.

The final impetus came from Creoles of color in New Orleans, led by Martinet. Meeting in the offices of Martinet's *Crusader* on 1 September 1891, eighteen members of the Creole-of-color and African American elite founded the "Citizens' Committee for the Annulment of Act No. 111 Commonly Known as the Separate Car Law." They promptly issued "An Appeal" in which they announced their intention of challenging the "obnoxious" law's constitutionality and asked for contributions to the fund they were setting up for that purpose.

Greeting the enterprise with jubilation, Tourgée reprinted the entirety of the committee's "Appeal" in his "Bystander" column of 3 October. "It would be hard to find in all the literature of resistance to oppression a more calm, dispassionate, and sensible appeal to the best interests of the citizen," he commented. The "'Jim Crow' car law" was self-evidently "unconstitutional and in conflict with the fundamental principles of free government," averred Tourgée, predicting that the campaign against it would pay dividends beyond its immediate goal: "The habit of concerted appeal to the law for the protection and enforcement of legal rights is the most important lesson of self-government." Tourgée especially commended African American newspapers for "urging upon their people unity of action" in carrying the case to fruition. Still, he emphasized, the movement for citizens' rights should not be "exclusively confined" to African Americans, because "citizenship and its rights are a common heritage." Addressing himself to readers of both races, he besought African Americans to invite the aid of trustworthy white allies and whites to "unite with the colored men of the South" in demanding their lawful rights.[65] Yet Tourgée stopped short of establishing the interracial organization he deemed so desirable.

He took that decisive step two weeks later in his "Bystander" column of 17 October. He had "endeavored in every possible way to avoid" the "burden" of leading such an interracial organization, Tourgée confessed, but a "singular fatality" had "strangely and unaccountably thrust" the role "upon him." Three factors had combined to force his hand. "First, a flood of letters from all over the country ha[d] come pouring in," endorsing his statement of support for the Citizens' Committee. Second, the treasurer of that committee had just written to inform him that its fund now totaled $1,412.70—a remarkable sum for a people in precarious circumstances to have donated. Third, a white supremacist newspaper, the *Times* of Shreveport, Louisiana, had warned African Americans that no matter what the federal courts ruled, the "white people of the South" would never accept "social equality" but would inflict disastrous punishment on those seeking it. Tourgée did not mention a fourth consideration: that he had already volunteered to serve pro bono as legal counsel to the Citizens' Committee in its court challenge. Confronting readers with the opposing messages of African Americans and white supremacists, he asked them to determine "whether the law of the land or the appeal to assassination shall control public conduct"—whether readers would "stand by the colored citizen in his appeal to law or the red-handed bulldozer in his defiance." He also asked them to furnish "positive evidence" of their willingness to join a citizens' rights movement by signing and mailing in the statement he appended to his "Bystander" article, together with a two-cent stamp to cover the cost of return postage for a circular about the organization and a numbered membership certificate:

> I hereby approve the object of forming a "Citizens' Equal Rights Association" for the purpose of securing and disseminating information and encouraging and assisting in the legal assertion of the rights of National citizenship, and agree to co-operate with the same when organized.
>
> Postoffice . . . .
>
> County . . . .
>
> State . . . .

If enough readers answered his appeal, Tourgée promised, he would set up the organization. Tourgée received his reply within three days: "nearly a hundred letters" encouraging him to go ahead with the project.[66]

Phase Four of the "Bystander": Guiding the National Citizens' Rights Association

The founding of the National Citizens' Rights Association or NCRA (as it came to be called) initiated the fourth phase of the "Bystander" column. No longer did Tourgée target the broad audience of *Inter Ocean* subscribers, encompassing mainstream Republicans as well as former abolitionists and Civil War veterans. Rather, he oriented his articles primarily toward the members of his organization. His column of 31 October, for example, answered a variety of questions new recruits had raised: Could women join the NCRA? (Yes, because they, too, were citizens, responded Tourgée, although agitating for women's suffrage was beyond the scope of the organization.) Did the organization need funds? (So far not yet, but eventually it would need to defray the costs of "printing, stationery, and, perhaps, by and by, a secretary.") What would its "ultimate work" consist in? (For the present, recruitment should be its prime task, since "showing the oppressed the number of their friends, and the oppressors the number who disapprove" could accomplish more than any other method of protesting against injurious measures and "harmful prejudices.") Who exactly had joined so far? ("Nearly half" were "old soldiers," but members came from "every rank of life; from shop and home and farm," with "editors of country papers strongly represented, and college students unexpectedly numerous.")[67]

In the weeks that followed, Tourgée quoted extracts from members' letters, so that they could "speak directly to each other."[68] Specifically, he devoted his columns of 7, 14, and 21 November to letters from former abolitionists, Civil War veterans, and African Americans in turn.[69] By giving voice to each of these marginalized groups, Tourgée forged them into a united movement. Yet he also used their letters to correct misconceptions the general public held about the legacy of the struggle against slavery, and thus to attract converts from the *Inter Ocean's* mainstream Republican constituency. Accordingly, quotations from elderly abolitionists who wished to "enlist again under the banner of liberty in the Citizen's Rights Association" served to dispel the fashionable view that the slave's "champions" had "outlived whatever influence they ever possessed."[70] In the same vein, the words of Civil War veterans who had sacrificed limbs, eyes, and health to free the nation from slavery summoned the "people of the North" to act lest "the better part of what we fought for . . . be lost."[71] Most obviously, of course, samples from "the hundreds of letters received from colored men and women all over the country" drove home the message that a "people who are wronged feel it as no one else can" and showcased African Americans as the NCRA's earliest and most enthusiastic recruits. "I am now 36 years old and I enlist for the balance of my life of usefulness with whatever brain, money, and physical ability I possess," Tourgée quoted a "distinguished graduate of a leading university" as vowing.[72] He also noted that a "colored man" had contributed the "first dollar" to the NCRA and that another "colored man who ha[d] shed his blood for the Nation's safety" had pledged "a dollar a month" as long as his donations could be kept secret.[73] Tourgée gave special prominence to his African American women correspondents, the most eloquent of whom wrote, "If you can in this work find any use for a woman who brings youth, strength, an absorbing desire to live for some high purpose and a determination to do whatever of good comes to her hand—pray command me." Nearly all the African Americans Tourgée quoted expressed their "deepest gratitude" to him, allowing him tacitly to lay to rest, once again, the hackneyed charge of ingratitude that bedeviled the race.[74]

With few exceptions, Tourgée's columns continued for months to focus on the NCRA. Some did so in a parochial manner, as when Tourgée described the NCRA's Administrative Council, answered questions about the organization's aims and strategies, directed members to form local citizens' unions and to hold weekly meetings at each other's homes, or announced plans to publish an NCRA newsletter to be titled the *National Citizen*.[75] In other cases, Tourgée adapted long-standing features of his column, such as incorporating the voices of hostile white Southerners and angry African Americans, to the new end of commenting on the NCRA.

"You are the very worst enemy the negro ever had," he quoted a white Southern correspondent as fulminating. "What you are doing will merely encourage the negro to equalize himself with the whites. As soon as he does that he will have to be put down." In reply, Tourgée acknowledged the likelihood that an "epidemic of murder" might sweep the South before African Americans succeeded in obtaining their rights. The death toll might well reach the horrific figure of 100,000 brandished by this Southern ideologue. With his trademark reckless bravado, Tourgée opined that it would be preferable for "even 100,000 [to] be killed" than for "7,000,000 [to] be crowded back into serfdom and helplessness for an indefinite period." Nevertheless, he immediately qualified this statement by arguing that if both the Northern public and Southern blacks proved themselves "in earnest" about "demanding and achieving" equal citizenship, "it would be granted, not willingly, of course, not instantly, but ultimately and fully."[76]

To show how much "in earnest" black Southerners actually were, Tourgée dedicated his column of 12 December 1891 to extracts from their letters. One hailed the NCRA as "the first glimmer of hope" for the "educated negro," whose "life in the South" was otherwise "hardly worth living." Another declared that when "our rights as free men" were at stake, "we should contest every inch of ground." Tourgée did not limit himself to unambiguous expressions of support but also included a long extract from a black Southerner who challenged the Bystander's oft-reiterated faith in education, questioned the efficacy of the NCRA, and ruffled white Americans' patriotic sentiments. "They are always saying, 'When you niggers get education things will be different,'" wrote this correspondent:

The statement is literally true—how true no Northern man can conceive. I achieved an education [the writer won distinguished honor

at a Northern university, interjected Tourgée] and came back home
ten times more distinguished a mark for race prejudice and hate than
before. * * * [Tourgée's ellipses] It is the educated negro who is the
especial eye-sore of the race-hating Bourbon, whose argument for
"inferiority" is a blow or a bullet. . . . [America] is not the "land of the
brave and free," but of the coward and the oppressor and is ruled by the
braggart and the assasin [sic]. * * * It is possible that the Citizens' Rights
Association may do some good; but I have not much confidence. I do
not think there are many Northern people who care what becomes of a
few million negroes. I will do what I can for it, however, and trust that
your hope may not be in vain.[77]

By transmitting this black Southerner's bitter message, Tourgée implicitly
appealed to his white Northern readers to prove that they did care about the
fate of their African American compatriots. If even a man who had suffered
so much from his country's broken promises could commit himself to working with the NCRA, albeit with "not much confidence," surely the comfort-
able subscribers of the *Inter Ocean* could do so, Tourgée intimated. Unless
white Americans made a serious effort to transform their society, he warned
through the mouth of his black spokesman, they would reap the hatred of
eight million fellow citizens who had every reason to consider their native
country the land of the "coward and the oppressor."[78]

Competing Definitions of the "Negro Problem"

Despite having narrowed the purview of the "Bystander" column and
reduced its target audience to NCRA members, Tourgée still included occasional articles on other subjects. Just as he had exposed the speciousness
of Harvard professor Nathaniel Southgate Shaler's "Science and the African
Problem" when it appeared in the *Atlantic Monthly* of July 1890, he scath-
ingly attacked the British historian James Bryce's "Thoughts on the Negro
Problem" as soon as he saw it in the *North American Review* of December
1891. Bryce's views carried weight with the U.S. public because his 1888
book, *The American Commonwealth*, offered a friendly perspective on the
nation's institutions that updated Alexis de Tocqueville's *Democracy in
America* (1835). Yet as Tourgée pointed out in a double "Bystander" column
of 19 and 26 December, Bryce did not deserve his reputation as an objective "foreign observer," because he had taken his information only from the
"Southern gentlemen who . . . loaned him their eyes and furnished him with
ears." As a result, Bryce defined the "'Negro Problem' . . . with the negro's

rights and interests left out." The sole question he examined was "whether the negro can be held in subjection and made profitable to the white man, as a laborer." Tourgée ended by stressing that the heartless economic premises on which Bryce based his analysis of the "Negro Problem" ultimately threatened workers of all races: "Professor Bryce represents, in its highest perfection, the English economic idea of civilization—of a harsh immutable destiny whose ideal of justice is that of the hog-pen—a right to get and hold without regard to other lives or other fates. It is well for the [white] American worker . . . to keep in mind the fact, that the very same philosophy, which justifies injustice and degradation to the colored man to-day, will parcel out the same to his [the white American worker's] children to-morrow."[79]

Tourgée returned again to his pre-NCRA framing of the "Bystander" column in an article of 16 April 1892 critiquing the exclusion of African Americans from the planning of the upcoming Chicago World's Fair. Timed to celebrate the fourth centenary since Columbus had landed in the Western Hemisphere, the fair was also intended to advertise the United States' progress to the world. Yet despite the key role African Americans had played in the nation's economic development, despite the degree to which their progress as a race since emancipation illustrated that of the nation, and despite African Americans' own vociferous demands, the managers of the World's Fair refused to accord them any representation in the exhibits, the administrative committees, or even the construction crews.

Tourgée raised the issue by staging a dialogue between two of his white correspondents. The first, "a thoughtful lady to whom the problem of Southern conditions seem[ed] well nigh insoluble," asked why he kept insisting that African Americans' economic advancement in the South depended on their exercise of "political rights." Tourgée's position, she noted, deviated from the consensus that the "best thing" for the Negro "would be entire exclusion from the field of politics until he has become thoroughly fitted to discharge its duties by the acquisition of wealth and education." In contrast, the second correspondent expressed astonishment that the World's Fair provided no evidence of either "the progress made by the colored man" or "the capacity of republican institutions to solve" the problem of racial and social inequality—an omission that foreign visitors would surely notice. How did Tourgée explain such neglect by a Republican-led government?, inquired this correspondent. The two questions answered each other, replied Tourgée, by proving that "whenever the political rights of any class of citizens of a republic are taken from them their civic and individual rights are sure to follow." If black voters had not been disfranchised in the Southern states, and hence eliminated as claimants in the impending 1892 campaign, no Republican president could have "forgotten" to appoint at least one African American commissioner to the fair's board, Tourgée emphasized. He went on to challenge the economic ideology that influenced Harrison (as well as other Republican Party leaders). Though the president sought to "promote the business interests of the exposition" by putting wealthy white financiers in charge of it, asserted Tourgée, he did not seem to realize that capital was "merely the gilded roof of National prosperity," while labor constituted its foundation. Tourgée concluded by reminding both the president and *Inter Ocean* readers at large that of all laborers, none had contributed more to American prosperity than African Americans: "In short, they are the only class of American citizens who paid a century in advance for the right and privilege of an honorable place in the world's great congress of labor to be held in the world's most wonderful city next year."[80]

The "Bystander," the NCRA, and the 1892 Election

Still, the NCRA remained Tourgée's chief preoccupation during the fourth phase of "A Bystander's Notes." In a poignant column of 14 May 1892, he acknowledged secret doubts about whether the NCRA would succeed in its mission. "Like many people, the Bystander has his periods of depression," he confided. While wrestling with this demon, he could not help quailing before the "magnitude of the work which had almost unwittingly devolved upon him," suspecting that the methods he envisaged might prove inadequate, and fearing that a bloody revolution might afford "the only road to liberty and justice." It did not help, he added, "to be told a hundred or more times a week that the course one has adopted is hopeless; that neither churches, nor parties, nor people desire that justice should be done." Under the circumstances, he had felt relieved "to cut loose from" the responsibility of running the NCRA when he set out on a six-week lecture tour from which he had just returned. "It was almost like waking in a new world, therefore," to find thousands of letters from NCRA members waiting for him, with the news that the organization had spread into "nearly fifty new counties," all with their own "advisory committees equipped for work."[81]

As the Republican convention drew nearer, Tourgée more and more frequently addressed questions from his correspondents about what they should do if the party turned its back on the NCRA and shrugged off the issue of citizens' rights during the 1892 electoral campaign.[82] Although he at first counseled a wait-and-see attitude and cited reasons for optimism, he could no longer dodge the quandary after the platform approved at the convention took the most anemic stand possible on the protection of black Southerners. NCRA members must decide for themselves how and whether to vote, Tourgée advised, but they should weigh the probable consequences of a "general refusal to vote at all."[83]

In subsequent weeks, Tourgée published letters from NCRA members relaying their decisions. "A lawyer of eminence in a Western State" whom Tourgée identified as a "life-long Republican" proclaimed that he had "no confidence in the honesty of the intentions of those who apparently control the Republican party"; as a result, he had "withdrawn from it and . . . cast in [his] lot" with the Populists. "A Wisconsin divine, whose voice has always been for liberty and justice alike to all," found the Republicans no better than the Democrats; he, too, now planned to vote for the Populists. Another disillusioned Republican who contemplated bailing out had ceased to believe his party would ever "pass a National election law or do anything to secure the rights of the citizen at the South." Clearly, Tourgée hoped their voices would serve as a wake-up call to the party bosses who were trying to win the election by burying the unsolved problem of racial justice.[84]

As usual, he published a Southern opponent's threat alongside the protests of NCRA members. This Southern spokesman complained that blacks in Florida, hitherto "quiet and orderly," were "getting to be rather too 'mouthy'" since "emissaries of Judge Albion W. Tourgée" had begun "organizing societies among them." The Southerner boasted, "One of the agitators was recently notified to leave and never be seen here again. He has gone." Tourgée drew the obvious inference: that "the rights of free speech, public assemblage, and personal liberty are scarcely more secure in the South than in Russia." The mission of the NCRA consisted precisely in exposing the true nature and purpose of the "barbarism springing out of slavery," editorialized Tourgée: "Profit on the negro's labor is the real motive for his subjection and intimidation to-day. As long as he can be prevented from learning, asserting, and maintaining his rights he is a cheap and 'manageable' laborer, and a saving of $1 a month on his wages adds $25,000,000 a year to the net profits of his white employers." Whatever the result of the election, Tourgée implied, the NCRA must redouble its efforts to abolish this latter-day slavery.

By September, Tourgée realized that the prospects of a Republican victory were dimming. Two constituencies would determine the party's fate: African Americans and NCRA members in what we would now call swing states, all located in the North and Midwest. "The mere refusal of the colored citizen to vote at all makes it *absolutely certain that the Republican*

party can not win in, at least six . . . probably in eight" of these states, prophesied Tourgée. Only if Republican candidates committed themselves to
fighting for the protection of citizens' rights could they motivate their key
constituents to go to the polls, he stressed, urging NCRA members to seek
such pledges from their congressional representatives.[85]

The Republicans' massive electoral defeat in the House and Senate, as
well as in the presidential contest, bore out Tourgée's dark prophecies. In
a postmortem calling the realignment the "most important political event"
since the election of 1860 that brought Lincoln to power and ushered in the
Civil War, Tourgée warned that the next four years would see the proliferation of legal measures aimed at depriving African Americans of their constitutional rights, the entrenchment of the "solid South," and the indefinite
postponement of "a peaceful and just solution" to the race problem.[86]

As comments on the election poured in from his correspondents,
Tourgée incorporated their voices into his postmortems. "I cannot see any
light before us," he quoted a black Southerner as writing in a letter typical
of the "heartrending" messages "piled high upon the Bystander's desk": "So
far as our rights as men and women are concerned, we are no better off than
in the old slave times. So far as security of life is concerned, we are even
worse off than then. No man is punished for killing any of us. . . . Now that
all fear of the National Government ever doing anything to secure our rights
is gone, we shall be without any hope. . . . I wish 10,000 Northern white
men could have black skins and be put in our places for a while." Tourgée
juxtaposed this grim assessment with a question from a white Northern
minister: "Is there not some way in which the Christian spirit of the South
may be aroused to remedy these evils?" Replied Tourgée, "Unfortunately,
'the Christian spirit of the South' approves of the subjection of the colored
citizen to the absolute control and dominion of the white race." Another
white correspondent wondered why "the Bystander [was] able to predict
with such certainty that the Republican party could not win" on an economic platform that promised to protect U.S. industries but not the rights
of U.S. citizens. Tourgée answered at length, highlighting the principle that
the "appeal to mere material self-interest *alone* tends to weaken the sense of
moral obligation and patriotic duty." As if to reinforce the point, he quoted
a defeated Republican candidate from Indiana who conceded, "You were
right . . . and I was wrong. I think your course as the head of the National
Citizens' Rights Association has been very wise, judicious and commenda-
ble. I see no hope for the future but in the adoption of the course you have
suggested in that organization. Please enroll my name, and tell me what I

can do to promote its purpose." Tourgée let members already active in the NCRA respond: "Now, is the time to go to work as the anti-slavery people did," when they circulated petitions and distributed abolitionist tracts. Emulating these tactics, Tourgée's followers requested more NCRA membership forms and copies of his pamphlet *Is Liberty Worth Preserving?* (1892) to use in their recruitment efforts. Tourgée summed up his column by articulating his method of setting his readers in dialogue with each other: "Thus one correspondent answers another. If only each could read the other's words!"[87]

Phase Five of the "Bystander": Letting African Americans Educate the White Public

Once the dust of the election settled, Tourgée again expanded the conversation among "Bystander" readers beyond NCRA ranks, and the column entered a fifth phase. As if to follow up his black Southern correspondent's wish that Northern white men could be "put in our places for a while," Tourgée accorded more space than ever to African American spokesmen equipped to educate the white public about life under Jim Crow. The "colored man . . . is the best and practically the only authority" on his wrongs, "since he suffers them in his own person" as "part and parcel of his daily experience," Tourgée pointed out in a column of 10 December 1892. Besides quoting extracts from correspondents whose testimony revealed "how widespread" was the "terrorism" blacks endured in the South, Tourgée partially reprinted an article from the *Detroit Plaindealer* by an African American who had "traveled all through the South, carefully studying conditions." Its author, Mack W. Caldwell, a native of Chicago, had undertaken this dangerous mission at Tourgée's suggestion, shortly after contacting him in January 1890 to ask "what he could do for the benefit of his race." Caldwell's investigation had proved "instrumental in uncovering some of the most atrocious features" of recent lynchings, massacres, and other Southern "barbarisms," noted Tourgée, opining that through such fact-finding, he was "doing more for his race and the cause of liberty and justice than any, or perhaps all, who assume to be 'leaders' and pose as 'representatives' of the colored people." Although Caldwell had courageously signed his article in the *Plaindealer*, originally titled "The Order System. How the Southerner Manages to Keep the Afro-American Poor," Tourgée protected him against possible reprisals by suppressing his name and editing out details that might reveal his identity to white Southern readers of the *Inter Ocean*.[88]

"It is impossible for any person in the North to understand the actual relations existing between the white and colored people in the rural districts of the South," affirmed Caldwell. Journalists sent by Northern newspapers "invariably" ensconced themselves in white Southern circles and transmitted their hosts' views, he charged: "They never go among the colored people, never hear their side of the case, never see how they live, and never consult them about their wrongs" (nor could they have, even if so inclined, without exciting suspicion and imperiling the lives of any African American interlocutors willing to talk to them). Caldwell had accomplished exactly this feat. Citing interviews with black sharecroppers, he showed how systematically they were "robbed by white employers and merchants" and why they could not defend themselves. "One man and his wife had raised ten bales of good cotton," weighing a total of five thousand pounds, Caldwell reported. They had been promised seven cents per pound, which should have amounted to $350, but the merchant claimed their cotton was worth only $310 and then deducted $295 for supplies. Another sharecropper had been billed $315 for supplies, without being told how much he was going to be paid for the fourteen bales of cotton he had raised. Caldwell had asked his informants whether they could request itemized bills for all their purchases, or better still, whether they could have a literate African American keep a record of their purchases, to prevent their being cheated. *"'If we did that,' they both said, 'we could not live here . . . We would all be killed. . . because a white man don't allow a colored person to dispute his word.'"* Tourgée editorialized:

> It ought not to take any man of average common sense very long to understand from such plain pictures of every-day life as these why it is that the colored man is so utterly helpless in those States. . . . What is needed for the cure of colored serfdom at the South is the very thing that had to precede the abolition of slavery—the common, honest, law-abiding, justice-loving Northern man must have a chance to look into the caldron of oppression, barbarism and greed at the South with the cover off.

In short, Tourgée wanted his "Bystander" column and the testimony of his African American correspondents to mobilize white Northern readers by opening their eyes and arousing their consciences—the function abolitionist newspapers, tracts, and slave narratives had fulfilled a generation earlier.

Through his extracts from Caldwell's article, Tourgée sought both to celebrate the unsung heroes who were risking their lives for their people's liberation and to herald the African American press as a crucial mouthpiece of black opinion. Nowhere did he more prominently carry out these aims than by featuring Louis A. Martinet at the head of his 7 January 1893 "Bystander" installment, which doubled as a New Year's column. This journalistic genre typically passed judgment on the year that had just closed. Tourgée ceded that privilege to Martinet, whose New Year's column in the *Crusader* he quoted. Marked by a record number of lynchings, the Republican Party's shameless betrayal of African Americans, and its electoral trouncing by the Democrats, whose ascendancy promised to complete the triumph of white supremacy, 1892 stood out for infamy, observed Martinet:

> It has been a year of disappointment, strife, and blood. In spite of victories won by means fair and just, we find the heart of the enemy as hardened as ever and still busy plotting new schemes to fill the chalice of injustice and rivet the chains of oppression, on the limbs of the weak and unprotected. With another year like 1892, with victories barren of permanent results and no advance in the cause of right and humanity, we shall begin to despair of ever achieving our rights as citizens of the great Republic, except by a resort to more drastic measures for the amelioration of our conditions.

As editor of the *Crusader*, Tourgée underscored, Martinet had "stood nobly and squarely by the rights of his people under conditions which few men would have the courage to confront." He had not only turned down an offer of "seductive personal advantage" in order to "fight the battle of the weak for the sake of the weak"—a battle that involved enormous danger—but he had forged Louisiana African Americans into "the most intelligent, the most persistent, the most manly, and the most hopeful" champions of their people's cause. Because he was uniquely "qualified to speak ... [for] the better element of the colored race," his veiled threat of a "lesson written in blood" if the nation stuck to its injustice deserved "serious consideration," stressed Tourgée.[89]

Continuing the public dialogue with Martinet that he had begun in his "Bystander" column of 12 September 1891, Tourgée nevertheless acknowledged that he himself was "not inclined to so gloomy a foreboding as that of the editor of the *Crusader*." The divergence arose from their different geographical vantage points, he surmised. Martinet witnessed at close range the hardening of white attitudes and the vertiginous deterioration of blacks' status in the South, while Tourgée discerned "healthful tendenc[ies]" among both African Americans and Northern whites. "The year 1892 has seen more growth in manhood upon the part of the colored citizenship of the United States than any other since the very first marvelous years after his emancipation," claimed Tourgée. He found "an amaz[ing] . . . change of spirit" exhibited both in the black press and in such militant gestures as the refusal of a "colored congregation in Chicago . . . to sing 'America.'" Northern whites, in turn, had responded to African Americans' new assertiveness "with that regard which well-tempered self-respect always secures." For example, "when a colored woman wrote a substitute" for "America," a white "Episcopal bishop of rare literary attainment pronounced" her "burning words" "'worthy of Whittier.'" NCRA enrollments offered the best proof that African Americans' display of backbone was inspiring a solidarity movement among white Northerners. Hence, Tourgée concluded, "when the colored people of the United States shall urgently, unitedly, wisely and persistently make manifest their desire for, and determination to, achieve equal rights and to be satisfied with nothing less, they will find that the sentiment which animated the white people of the North to abolish slavery is still alive, and ready at like sacrifice to establish liberty and secure justice to all."

The Last "Bystander" Column of Phase Five

Tourgée quoted Martinet even more extensively, though this time anonymously, in what would prove to be his last "Bystander" column for nine months. Dated 12 August 1893, it reflected national developments that had considerably dampened the optimism expressed in his New Year's column. The Panic of 1893, the worst economic depression the country had yet seen, erupted that spring. A spiral of railroad and other corporate bankruptcies, bank failures, massive layoffs, and collapsing farm prices caused widespread hardship. As had occurred in earlier depressions, the economy's free fall not only diverted attention from the issue of racial justice but unleashed a surge of racism. It also strengthened the hand of those Republican leaders who had long advocated purging the party of its abolitionist heritage, the better to implement their plutocratic agenda. Tourgée contested both the economic and racial components of that agenda.

The plutocrats' economic ideology led them to condemn "paternalism in government," which their twenty-first century heirs refer to as "big government." In particular, they objected to regulations that interfered with the right of "every man . . . to do what he chooses with his own [property] whatever may be the effect upon the means of livelihood, comfort, or even the lives of others," as Tourgée put it. They further objected to taxes that "confiscate one man's possession for the benefit of another." Tourgée noted drily that the "loudest outcry against 'paternalism' is heard" from "the very men in whose behalf" the power of government "has been most freely exercised" through the creation of banks, "mortgages, stocks, [and] bonds," the granting of "charters, shares, [and] corporate privileges," and the subsidization of railroad building. Accusing the plutocrats of favoring *"the promotion of special advantage for restricted classes,"* which he dubbed *"false 'paternalism,'"* Tourgée instead advocated *"true 'paternalism,'"* which he defined as the use of government to enhance the general welfare, equalize opportunity, and prevent the abuse of power and wealth.[90]

The form of paternalism that some Republican Party leaders most wanted to eliminate was the body of law designed during the Reconstruction era to help African Americans overcome the legacy of slavery. These leaders did not wait long to make their move. As early as mid-June, anti-black Republicans joined forces with Democrats in a bipartisan campaign to repeal the Fourteenth and Fifteenth Amendments, which conferred U.S. citizenship on African Americans, prohibited states from denying them equal protection of the law, and granted voting rights to African American men. In a pair of "Bystander" articles dated 10 and 17 June, Tourgée condemned the attempt to repudiate the Republican Party's main legislative achievements. "To thrust seven millions of free citizens back into disfranchisement, serfdom, dependency, and despair" would be a "crime against God and man infinitely more atrocious and terrible even than American slavery," he protested. The real shortcoming of Reconstruction lay not in enfranchising ignorant ex-slaves, argued Tourgée, but in failing to provide them with land, education, and direct access to federal courts. He attributed this failure to Republicans' "overwhelming cowardly fear" of being labeled a "'nigger party,'" their anxiety to avoid piling more expenditure onto the war debt, and their naive belief that the ballot would enable African Americans to obtain education and secure economic independence.[91] When an Iowa Republican who favored repeal asked whether black suffrage had yielded "any great benefits," Tourgée reminded him that without the "vote of the negro citizen there would be no adequate public school system in any State of the South to-day."[92]

Despite Tourgée's efforts to stem it, the racist tide rose apace. As one white correspondent bluntly caviled, "The American people have tired of color politics, and race legislation." The conflict with the Southern states over "negro rights" had "come near breaking the back of the Republican party, and ha[d] done the negro no good," he opined, and the country ought now to turn its attention to "graver and more important" issues.[93] By 12 August, Tourgée had received so many letters from white correspondents mouthing racist clichés that he felt compelled to devote his valedictory "Bystander" column to refuting them. He subtitled it "'Don't You Know—?'" because they all posed such questions as "Don't you know . . . that the whites are a superior race and that it is the law of nature and of God that the strong and wise shall rule and the weak shall serve or disappear?" or "Don't you know that the colored man is not fit to vote and that his enfranchisement was a great mistake?" After answering ten such belligerent inquiries in turn, Tourgée countered with questions of his own. Were not "the very evils we now suffer . . . the fruit and consequence of our failure to do justice[?] . . . If there had been a free ballot and a fair count at the South would the laborers of the North be facing a period of idleness, want, and suffering to-day?" "Can a Nation hope to be prosperous when one eighth of her population" is thoroughly disaffected? He let two of his most eloquent African American correspondents, whose identities he cloaked, articulate the rage and hatred that white racism incited in them and thus turn the tables on those who branded them as inferior. In the process, Tourgée merged his voice with theirs, much as he had in his novel *Pactolus Prime*.[94]

Tourgée drew the first extract from an eight-page letter Martinet had written to him in May.[95] Describing his visit to the Chicago World's Fair, Martinet had confided that "its very grandeur" had "filled [him] with bitterness." "If there be a just God, how can he permit such an iniquitous people to prosper?" he demanded, adding, "I felt that if the whole thing should sink in Lake Michigan and disappear I would rejoice." Martinet knew he did not have to tell Tourgée why the fair had aroused such "resentment" in him. For the benefit of *Inter Ocean* readers, however, Tourgée inserted two sentences, purporting to be Martinet's, that charged the fair with making room for "all other peoples" but reserving "no place for the American negro, his history, his sufferings, his wrongs, or his achievements!" Tourgée went on to quote Martinet's retrospective account of how his feelings toward whites had evolved since his younger days:

When a boy, a youth[,] I hated almost every white man I met. I wished, longed, for a chance to fight, to kill—but I have never had occasion to kill in self-defense and would not murder. . . . I no longer hate the individual, but the whole people, the Nation [here Tourgée inserted "—the white race which claims a monopoly of God's favor and would compel me to defer until after death the claim of equal right and freedom."] I sometimes feel as if I could tear the flag—the Stars and Stripes—into shreds.

Hatred of white people, the U.S. flag, and the entire nation, not to speak of the urge to kill white men, were sentiments almost any white reader would have found shocking, indeed downright frightening—sentiments that few, if any, African Americans had ever trusted a white person enough to avow. Martinet had certainly not intended to share them with anyone except Tourgée. Yet he did not object to the use Tourgée made of his letter, nor did he cease to write as frankly in subsequent communications. He seems to have agreed with Tourgée that white people needed to be faced with the consequences of their racial arrogance.

Tourgée ended his long extract from Martinet's letter with a passage that addressed whites' phobia of "social equality"—the mingling of the races in private as well as public spaces that conjured up the bugbear of intermarriage. "I do not hanker for companionship or social relation with those who do not want to associate with me," Martinet specified; "nor do I desire unduly the personal advantages that accrue from unreserved association with one's fellow beings." Far from betraying any consciousness of inferiority, Martinet characterized whites simply as "fellow beings" and asserted his superiority to those who allowed racism to cloud their judgment: "I am foolish enough to think that I am above those who view a man's worth through the glasses of color prejudice." Rather than social equality, he clarified, he wanted civil equality, not merely for himself but for everyone: "All I want is my simple rights as a man and lawful privileges as a citizen. And with this I want simple justice for all to whom it has been denied. I want to *enjoy rights* and do not *want to be tolerated merely*."[96] For good measure, Tourgée amplified the unpatriotic tone that permeated the quotation by inserting another sentence of his own in Martinet's voice: "And I cannot be proud of or rejoice in a country which refuses me my rights and bids me cringe and fawn for the barest privileges of life, simply because my cheek is a shade or half a shade darker than another's!" In his own voice, Tourgée then turned back to the racist correspondents whose white supremacist contentions he had rejected at the outset: "Is it any wonder to you, white citizen of the United States, that this man who is inferior in intellect, in culture, in all that makes a man estimable, to no one whose eye will rest upon these lines, is it strange to you that he feels as he does, or can you expect a nation to prosper whose injustice stirs even to hate the blood of such a son?"

Next, Tourgée quoted a letter from an African American "college graduate, a man of intellect and power, whose life had been recently put in extreme peril at the hands of a Southern mob." This man had initially sought Tourgée's "aid in getting a foothold in a Northern city" but had since changed his mind: "I ought to [leave] now, if I considered only myself and my children's interest," he explained. "But to leave my people here in the house of bondage looks like cowardice and desertion. I will stay and if they perish I will die with them. . . . I mean now to stand steadfastly for the right and for them to whom right is denied and then—*to keep on standing!*" Again collaring his white racist correspondents, Tourgée asked, "How many such men will it take to relieve the colored race of the imputation of 'inferiority'?"

Through his quotations from the letters of two African Americans whose intellectual and moral superiority demonstrated the falsity of claims that the "law of nature and of God" destined the black race for servitude and the white for dominance, Tourgée discredited the white supremacist ideology that the Panic of 1893 had revived. Through his final example, Tourgée exposed the secret terror the ideology masked—the terror that whites might not be superior to blacks after all. The treatment of the African American elite flatly contradicted the oft-reiterated notion that whites disliked associating with ignorant, uncouth ex-slaves. As Tourgée pointed out, "the nearer a colored man approaches to what is most commended in a white man the more odious he becomes" to white supremacists. The case of Martinet's wealthy, cultured friend Paul Bonseigneur proved this point. Bonseigneur had bought and remodeled a house in a resort where he had been renting a cottage for several years, but when the renovations were finished, the white residents of the community, who felt outclassed by him as a property owner, blocked him from moving into it, demanded that he sell it at a loss, and drove him and his invalid wife out of town. Because Bonseigneur was the treasurer and financial angel of the New Orleans Citizens' Committee, his colleagues had decided to publish a pamphlet denouncing the outrage as "an attack on each and all of us." Martinet requested Tourgée to help increase the pamphlet's circulation by contributing one of the articles. Tourgée not only obliged but publicized the Bonseigneur incident in his "Bystander" column and urged readers to order the pamphlet.

Tourgée's account of Bonseigneur's persecution drove home the mendaciousness of white supremacist ideology. Had Bonseigneur conformed to the stereotype of the black man, he would not have run afoul of his white neighbors, emphasized Tourgée:

> If he were poor and mean and "humble," taking off his hat with a grin
> as soon as the majesty of a white "superior" rose upon his vision, and
> receiving a kick or a "tip" with equal complacency, he would be indorsed
> as a "good nigger" and highly approved by the "best citizens."

But Mr. Bonseigneur is rich, respectable and better able to bestow favors than many of his neighbors who have only the "inherent superiority" of the white race of which to boast. This is disgusting! Shall such a man be allowed to parade his devotion to his wife, his fine horses, his wealth and his courtly manners in the presence of white men to whom they are a reproach?

Not while violence is able to subvert the law![97]

To maintain their sense of superiority, white supremacists needed the stereotypical "good nigger," hinted Tourgée. They boasted of their race's "inherent superiority," he suggested, because they lacked the forms of superiority achieved by one's own efforts: wealth and stylish accoutrements, yes, but more important, respectability, generosity, "courtly manners," and the "devotion" of a model husband—in short, good character. A man of Bonseigneur's attainments made poor whites feel inadequate and rich whites feel less superior. The sole recourse against such a living testimony to the lies on which their society was built was violence. Yet nothing better revealed the hollowness of whites' pretensions to superior culture than their habit of resorting to "violence . . . to subvert the law."

Tourgée ended his column by once more turning his guns against Northern racists of the ilk whose "Don't-you-know"'s he had begun by disputing: "Will not some servile Northern apologist explain why it is that a rich and cultivated colored man is so much worse than an ignorant and dependent one?" This fusillade served as his leave-taking from the *Inter Ocean*, which had just "unceremoniously dropped" "A Bystander's Notes" from its editorial page.[98]

The Quarrel with Nixon

It is easy to understand why Nixon decided to suspend Tourgée's weekly column. One wonders, in fact, why he waited so long to take this step. Tourgée's use of the *Inter Ocean* to promote the NCRA, turning "A Bystander's Notes" into little more than an NCRA newsletter for much of 1892, as we have seen, had increasingly strained his relations with Nixon. The two had engaged in a spat in March of that year over a misunderstanding as to whether the *Inter Ocean* had agreed to foot the entire bill for printing 25,000 copies of the NCRA manifesto *Is Liberty Worth Preserving?*, as Tourgée contended, or to split the expenses with him, as Nixon insisted. Nixon finally agreed not to press Tourgée to pay his share, but he bristled: "Just what this Society is doing for The Inter Ocean I really cannot say. The most that I hear in regard to it is that it is attracting very considerable attention to your articles, and probably has added some subscribers to our list."[99]

Nixon's displeasure had intensified as Tourgée stepped up his criticism of the party during the 1892 nominating convention and as he continued during the electoral campaign to agitate the racial justice issues Republican leaders had chosen to mute. In July, Nixon refused to print a "Bystander" column he judged incendiary, because it predicted that "unless the attitude of the South towards the colored race changes, we shall have within the next ten years a massacre which has not been parelled [*sic*] since the French Revolution." Such an outbreak was as "inevitable" as the "explosion" of a "powder magazine" when ignited by a spark, Tourgée claimed, though no one could anticipate what event would trigger it. Nixon objected that he could "see no possible good," but "considerable harm . . . to the colored people themselves," in "prophesying or talking about a bloody insurrection in the South." Indeed, by indulging in reckless predictions of this sort, the press could inadvertently foment an insurrection "in which thousands and thousands of blacks would be slaughtered, and those that survived have their condition ten times worse." Nixon then spelled out the limits Tourgée must not transgress: "I would be very sorry to have The Inter Ocean considered the organ and promoter of anything bordering a bloody revolution in the South." He also made clear that he could not allow Tourgée to impugn the moral character of those who did not share the views of NCRA members but who were "perhaps just as good and just as patriotic." Most ominously, Nixon hinted that the *Inter Ocean* might have to dispense with Tourgée if he persisted in "injuring the past work of the 'Bystander' by giving expression to radical and mere prophetic ideas."[100]

Tourgée's truculent reply could hardly have mended matters. He was trying to avert, not precipitate, the cataclysm he feared, he explained, and to induce the Republican Party to help prevent it. "However, what may clearly be for the interest of humanity or the country may not be for the interest of a newspaper. Its prosperity depends on its telling people what they *want* to hear rather than what they *ought* to hear." Although Nixon accused him of using the NCRA against the party, Tourgée went on, he had actually done everything possible to head off a third party movement by NCRA members, only to have the convention confirm their worst suspicions. The "policy" Republican leaders had adopted was "practically kicking 200,000 active, earnest, men who would have worked night and day for [its] success" in the coming election, Tourgée fumed: "It is the supremest folly I have ever known." He climaxed this outburst with a blast of withering sarcasm: "Of course, I will not write what you do not want and will never mention 'the press' or the N.C.R.A. again and will make no further reference to the rights of the citizen or the denial of justice. They are lewd words. I sincerely regret that I was ever inclined to use them. I realize the difficulty of your position in trying to make people understand why it is necessary to protect a man's hat and shoes and leave the citizen who wears them unprotected."[101]

Tourgée did not abide by his sneering promise to cease crusading for citizens' rights, but he did stop conducting NCRA business in his column, as noted earlier. Still, he ignored other warning signals that ought to have prompted him to exhibit greater tact toward Nixon. When the *Inter Ocean* reacted to the economic crisis by cutting his pay for the "Bystander" column from seventy-five dollars to fifty dollars a week, first temporarily, then permanently, Tourgée rebelled. Judging from the complimentary letters he received, his column was not "decreasing in attractiveness," claimed Tourgée. Unless he was rewarded commensurately, with an "increase of the price of the Bystander, and a permanent arrangement" for all his contributions to the *Inter Ocean*, he would take his work elsewhere. Nixon did not sufficiently appreciate all the "advantages" the paper derived from the "Bystander" column, Tourgée complained. Thanks to the views published over his name, the *Inter Ocean* stood "entirely alone . . . in American journalism" for advocating "full and impartial" justice on the "race question."[102]

As might be expected, Tourgée's "tone" incensed Nixon. What especially infuriated him was the charge that he had undervalued his petted columnist. "We have made as much as we could of you as a member of The Inter Ocean family," he retorted.

> You have been allowed the broadest kind of latitude, in fact, have had the least possible restraint. A few times I thought that you over-stepped the bounds, but generally our relations have been cordial because I have always fully sympathized with your objects, though I sometimes did not with your methods. During all these years I have continued you as a contributor, much of the time contrary to the wishes of some of those interested with me, not because they did not like your articles, but because the price we paid you was many times greater than that which we paid anybody else.

He had now reached the limits of his tolerance, Nixon implied, and if Tourgée wanted to sell his work where he could obtain a higher price for it, he was free to "part company with The Inter Ocean."[103]

Over the next few weeks, Tourgée tried in vain to conciliate Nixon. Emma even wrote secretly to him, apologizing abjectly for "annoying" him and disclosing the financial straits that had led her husband to protest the cut in remuneration. She depended on the seventy-five-dollar check from the *Inter Ocean* to pay the mortgage, she confided, and as a result of the diminished amount, she had missed a payment. Far from yielding to her plea, Nixon announced on 8 August that because the dire economic emergency required "reducing expenses and discharging employes [sic]," he had been directed to notify Tourgée that the *Inter Ocean* was suspending the "Bystander" column for at least sixty days, and possibly forever.[104]

An Outcry from "Bystander" Fans and a Reversal by Nixon

However pompous, Tourgée's boast that the *Inter Ocean* owed its "distinction" to his "Bystander" column did not wait long for verification. The editorial page immediately sank into dullness. "Bystander" fans soon began expressing their disappointment both to Tourgée and to the *Inter Ocean*. "I valued ["A Bystander's Notes"] more than all the rest of the paper," wrote Joseph Cook, editor of *Our Day*, a Social Gospel periodical based in Boston.[105] "The principal interest in your paper, for me, and I believe for hundreds if not thousands of your readers, centres in Judge Tourgee's powerful articles, in fact, it was on account of them that I first subscribed for the paper," wrote a white Northern teacher who had devoted her life to educating Southern blacks.[106] "These articles voiced the sentiment of a *very large* Northern constituency," echoed a doctor, asking, "Has the Inter Ocean abandoned the cause of justice?"[107] "Where now will I find your sentiments on 'The Race Problem' . . . since The Inter Ocean no more contains them?" inquired an NCRA member from Bath, Indiana.[108] "Can it be that you have deserted us when we need you most? I pray not," wrote an African American school principal from Fayetteville, Arkansas, who had "always looked . . . for advice" to Tourgée's column. He would subscribe for whatever journal Tourgée published in, he ventured.[109]

Understandably, the flood of letters Nixon received from aggrieved "Bystander" fans did not mollify him. Quite the contrary, the "insinuation" some voiced that "the paper had . . . abandoned its stalwart republicanism, wounded and offended" him, as his colleague William H. Busbey, the *Inter Ocean*'s other principal editor, told Emma. Given his "reputation for extreme friendliness toward the colored race," Nixon found it "impertinent and gratituously [sic] offensive for anyone to intimate" that the *Inter Ocean* had retreated from its "advanced position simply because" it had dropped one of its contributors. Both Nixon and Busbey suspected, not without reason, that an organized "campaign" had fueled the letters, to which the two editors had sent angry replies. If so, Busbey stressed, it had backfired and "provoked a resentment that is not easy to quiet."[110]

Whether "Bystander" fans' importunities delayed or hastened Nixon's about-face, he finally reinstated the column on 5 May 1894, almost nine months after its suspension. He imposed two conditions: Tourgée must cease all mention of the NCRA (a restriction he had been observing well before his banishment) and stop criticizing the Republican Party.[111]

Phase Six of the "Bystander": Foregrounding Economic Issues

The pair of articles that inaugurated the "Bystander" column's sixth phase seemingly indicated Tourgée's willingness to turn over a new leaf by shifting his focus from the race question to the economy. The first, subtitled "The Approaching Economic Crisis—Protection to the Citizen" (5 May 1894), commented sympathetically on Coxey's Army, a workers' march on Washington protesting unemployment and appealing to the government to create public works jobs. The second, subtitled "The Theory of Malthus and Its Bearing on the Question of Wages" (12 May 1894), attacked free trade, a Democratic Party panacea, and upheld "protection," the Republican policy of protecting U.S. industry with tariffs on imports. As in his earliest "Bystander" articles of 1888, however, Tourgée in fact sought to integrate his commitment to racial (and social) justice into current Republican doctrine, this time by arguing that "liberty and justice and prosperity are an inseparable trinity" and that "the rights of the colored citizenship of the South are inseparably linked with the prosperity of the white citizenship of the North."[112] He also sought to redefine protection as "the duty of every government to protect the opportunity of the weak from the invasion and repression of the strong."[113] Conditions in the United States, where poverty existed despite an abundance of agricultural products, proved Thomas Malthus wrong, asserted Tourgée. They showed that "poverty, instead of being mainly the fault of the weak [whom Malthus blamed for overpopulation and scarcity], has in all ages been chiefly the consequence of the unrestricted exercise of power by the strong." Thus, Tourgée contended, the "protection" of U.S. industry must be "linked with strenuous restriction of the power of combined capital," including "trusts, syndicates, and the consolidation of corporations." Tourgée's sympathy with the poor and weak embraced white Northern workers along with their Southern black counterparts but did not extend to foreign immigrants—a blind spot he shared with most of his white abolitionist predecessors. Accordingly, he favored equally "strenuous restriction" of immigration to protect the wages of native-born American workers against competition from "ignorant and debased" foreigners.

After this pair of articles Tourgée alternated between discussions of the race question and the economy. His two most notable articles on economic issues concerned the Pullman strike, which dominated the *Inter Ocean*'s headlines for much of July 1894. In both, Tourgée departed significantly from the pro-business stand of the *Inter Ocean*, whose editors applauded Democratic president Grover Cleveland's use of U.S. troops to suppress the strike and excoriated Illinois governor John Altgeld, a progressive Democrat who had opposed this move, for his "sympathy with anarchy." In "Wage Tyrants and Profit Tyrants" (14 July 1894), a title equating labor unions with corporations as oppressors blind to the public interest, Tourgée maintained that "it is cheaper, wiser, and better every way to avoid [strikes and other "civil convulsions"] than to put them down." He proposed a "labor code" designed with "careful regard for the rights" of employers and workers alike and including provisions for "compulsory arbitration"—a proposal that prompted many correspondents to ask him to formulate such a code. In "To Prevent Strikes by Removing the Inducement to Strike" (21 July 1894), Tourgée advocated adjusting "the relative shares of labor and capital in the profits of business . . . to give labor an assured part of the profits and not require it to bear an undue proportion of the losses."[114] Never enacted, the legislation he recommended would still be radical today.

Thus, while ostensibly conforming to his agreement with Nixon for the reinstatement of his "Bystander" column, Tourgée was often subtly and not so subtly violating it. This subversiveness even marked his article "Colored Men and the Democratic Party" (4 August 1894), which answered an African American call for throwing the race's support to the Democrats. The call's author had misquoted Tourgée as claiming that "the Democratic party of the South is just as friendly to the negro's interest as the Republican party of the North." Tourgée replied categorically: "Not only did the Bystander never utter the words attributed to him but *he never could have uttered them*," because they "give the lie to every word and act of his life." After noting that every law in favor of African Americans owed its passage to Republicans in the teeth of fierce Democratic resistance, Tourgée nevertheless conceded that "only . . . a minority of the party" remained committed to protecting the "life and rights of the colored citizen." He went so far as to say that if ever this minority entirely lost its ability to shape Republican policy, the party would be "no more worthy of support by the lovers of liberty than if it explicitly indorsed the theory and practice" of its Democratic rival—a statement that must have made Nixon cringe.[115]

Tussling with the Inter Ocean's *Editors*

No wonder, then, that Busbey finally laid down the law. Doubtless in the hope that Emma would make her husband listen to reason, Busbey wrote first to her on 13 August. He reminded her that before approving resumption of the "Bystander" column, he had "emphasize[d] the point that the notes should be in accord with the Republican policy of THE INTER OCEAN." He added, "If I remember rightly, I did make this point strong. Mr. Nixon said at the time that he would not publish any articles that were apparently written to find some fault with Republican leaders or with the Republican party as it now stands. The plain truth is that the party, as now organized, has no sympathy with 'kickers' or 'grumblers.'" The *Inter Ocean's* stockholders had "always objected" to paying Tourgée "a higher rate per column than is received by any other political writer in the country," elaborated Busbey. Joining them now, "the very best sentiment in the Republican party" had voiced an "emphatic protest" against heading into an election "with the most radical newspaper of the party publishing every week inuendos [*sic*] and criticisms of the party management. These people say they will not stand it and instead of making friends for THE INTER OCEAN the Judge is making enemies." Apparently believing that nothing else would ensure Tourgée's compliance with the editors' wishes, Busbey announced the paper would "not pay for articles from the Judge, which coming as contributions from any one else, it would not publish for any amount of money." He enclosed proofs of a section Nixon had cut from Tourgée's column of 11 August, subtitled "The Evolution of Parties." The offending passage had avowed that corruption, once confined to the Democrats, had become common among Republicans, too (if anything an understatement, given the scandals that had rocked the party since Ulysses S. Grant's presidency), and had cited the selling of votes in party caucuses. In truth, Busbey and Nixon could have chosen similar passages in almost any "Bystander" column. Busbey ended,

> I hope you can find a way to make it clear to the Judge that the tone of
> the "Bystander's Notes" must be strongly and earnestly republican. . . .
> There was never a better opportunity for criticism of the Democratic
> party than just now and any one wielding such a pen as the Judge has a
> fine opportunity for analytical, satirical and critical work. It seems to me

that if he "turns his guns" on the right party, he can do us a great deal of good, but he must remember that the success of THE INTER OCEAN depends on its fight FOR the Republican party and its fight AGAINST the Democratic party.[116]

Busbey's letter to Tourgée the following week reinforced this plea by explaining that Nixon was surrounded by enemies ready to pounce on any sign that his allegiance to the "protection wing of the party" could be construed as "luke warm."[117]

Nixon himself revealed further details in a "Strictly Confidential" letter of 5 October, which he wrote by hand to keep it from the eyes of his colleagues, including Busbey. The *Inter Ocean* was teetering on the edge of bankruptcy, he disclosed, not only because the "Cleveland hard times" had "made July & August the worst two months for business" that Chicago newspapers had yet experienced but also because he had been forced to incur large debts the previous spring, when he had bought out the *Inter Ocean*'s co-owner, Herbert H. Kohlsaat. Nixon had already laid off scores of staff members, but a major stockholder was pressing him to "cut down the pay roll and all expenses" even more drastically. Hence, he was asking Tourgée to accept a 50 percent pay cut. By writing "fully and confidentially," Nixon hoped to obviate the kind of "misunderstanding" that had arisen between them in August 1893, when Tourgée's refusal to accept a pay cut had necessitated eliminating the "Bystander" column altogether.[118]

Tourgée "cheerfully" acquiesced—at least until the *Inter Ocean* terminated the column on the expiration of his contract just after New Year's.[119] Then, instead of sparing Nixon another "misunderstanding," he caused one. In a private letter to a "Bystander" fan who indiscreetly published it, Tourgée speculated that the *Inter Ocean* may have discontinued the column because its managers objected to his "views" regarding "labor, capital, and the regulation of their relations by law." Contrasting his position with the *Inter Ocean*'s, he commented that the paper upheld the "ultra let alone side," according to which "a man's power to restrict, control and make a profit from the labor of his fellows, shall never be impaired or regulated"; he, on the other hand, found this principle "just as repulsive as it would be to repeal law against murder and assaults and leave every man to beat his fellow into acquiescence as he chose."[120]

The *Cleveland Gazette* offered another explanation for the *Inter Ocean*'s discontinuance of "A Bystander's Notes." "The proprietors of that paper have tired of the judge's pleading our cause in its columns," charged the

Gazette's editor, Harry C. Smith. In retaliation, he urged "our people all over the country" to "make it a point to drop the Inter Ocean." Yet almost in the same breath, he implicitly vindicated Nixon's claim to having earned African Americans' loyalty: "We do not know a single daily paper in the country brave and manly enough to publish Judge Tourgee's contributions as the Inter Ocean has been doing."[121]

Notwithstanding these perceptions of the gulf between the paper and its star contributor, in the months before the *Inter Ocean* terminated the "Bystander" column for the second time Tourgée apparently made strenuous efforts to comply with Busbey's request that he hew to the organ's political line. He published a striking number of articles on the economy, all of which criticized free trade and promoted the tariff in orthodox Republican fashion.[122] Although he interspersed these eminently forgettable articles with powerful denunciations of lynching, he studiously refrained from attacking the Republican Party for its failure to do anything to stop this national crime. He also refrained from arguing, as he had in every prior electoral cycle, that the party was signing its own death warrant in the Solid South by allowing the disfranchisement of the region's African American voters.

Breaking New Ground on the Race Question

Despite the muzzling he endured in the waning days of the "Bystander" column, Tourgée broke new ground on the race question in two articles. The first, subtitled "Colored People and Christianity" (27 October 1894), juxtaposed comments on a recent speech by Booker T. Washington with an account of the valiant struggle for justice that "colored Republicans of Louisiana" were waging.[123] Washington and Louisiana's "colored Republicans" offered opposing strategies for African American advancement in the South, implied Tourgée; he left no doubt about which strategy he considered most promising. Washington had asserted that "the only way for the colored people to 'have the most of Jesus is to have a good bank account.'" Tourgée pronounced Washington right in concluding that Christianity had "substituted pity for justice and exalted economic theory above the golden rule" but "wrong in thinking that" African Americans could improve their situation merely by acquiring wealth. As proof, Tourgée cited the case of a "wealthy and refined colored man, the head of a respectable and cultivated family," who had "recently bought a house upon a fashionable street" in Brooklyn, renowned as the "City of Churches." The news that a "colored family who were not menials" was moving into the neighborhood touched off an "uproar," Tourgée reported. The white residents "roundly denounced" the new homeowner for refusing $12,000 to "surrender his purchase." Whether or not the man stood his ground to the last, remarked Tourgée drily, "he certainly discovered a new way in which 'Christianity and a bank account' may be made to operate for 'a brother in black.'" Rather than rely on a bank account to procure justice, Tourgée advised, African American Christians should integrate white churches and thus remind them that "God made 'of one blood all the nations of the earth,' and that Christ died to make earth tolerable for us as well as to make heaven accessible for all."

Unlike Washington, Tourgée indicated, Louisiana's "colored Republicans" were defending political principles with "self-respectful firmness." A group of five hundred white Louisiana sugar planters had agreed to join the Republican Party and support the tariff in exchange for a subsidy of their crop, but only on condition that the party endorse their inalterable opposition to "equal power for black and white citizens, especially in State affairs." The party was accordingly asking "colored Republicans"—hitherto its most "devoted" adherents—to "sacrifice" themselves by voting for representatives who planned to exclude them. Tourgée quoted their response, probably published in the *Crusader*: "If this is not a Republican fight—if it does not mean the success of Republican government and Republican principles— justice to all and equality before the law, equal privilege and equal opportunity for all—it means to us *absolutely nothing.*" Commending the "colored Republicans" for simultaneously holding "equal right . . . too sacred . . . to be bartered for gold" and agreeing "to yield non-essentials for the public good," Tourgée credited them with "making history" not only for their race but for the "whole country." History would in fact elevate Washington over the "colored Republicans," at least in the short run. But by giving voice to both in his column, Tourgée was once again, and for the last time, fostering dialogue among his readers, within and across racial lines.

In his farewell column for the *Inter Ocean*, "White-Line Republicans in the Southern States" (5 January 1895), Tourgée returned to the issue that was confronting the Republican Party as it sought to gain a foothold in the South at the price of disfranchising its African American members.[124] Even if the Republicans succeeded in winning a few Southern states through such tactics, Tourgée opined—a possibility he found dubious—their victory would only amount to a "'choice between stinking fish,'" that is, between two different methods of "depriving the colored citizen of his rights." He then replied to a white Republican from Texas who accused him of perceiving the South of the 1890s through the lens of the 1870s. On the contrary,

Tourgée retorted, ever since leaving the South, he had continued to study the race question there and elsewhere "in every manner he could devise": "Scarcely a column has been printed touching the relation of black and white in the whole country in a dozen years that has not passed under [the Bystander's] eye. The letters he has received on this subject during the last year alone number at least a thousand. The white and colored Republicans of the South have poured into his ears their 'tale of woe' without restraint; while the white Democracy of the South have offered him no end of good advice." Even without the knowledge gained from these diverse sources, Tourgée emphasized, anyone who could "add, subtract, and multiply" could see that the white-line Republican plan "smells insufferably of the foul taint of slavery, injustice, and inequality of right."

Tourgée nonetheless recognized that under existing conditions, "separate caucuses" for black and white party members might help restore black voters' "confidence in the Republican party" and reduce racial conflict. He thus suggested letting white and black delegates vote separately but requiring a "majority of each . . . to bind the convention." As he pointed out, it was a compromise akin to the plan he had presented for funding schools in the South—a plan that allowed segregation but ensured equal funding. He asked both white and black Southern Republicans to "consider" his suggestion.

No transition led into the concluding sentence that abruptly announced, "With this the Bystander bids adieu both to the subject and his readers in THE INTER OCEAN." True, Tourgée's adieu would prove less final than the word implies. Two and a half months later, he would inaugurate a new series of "A Bystander's Notes" in the *Basis*, the periodical he founded as an organ for the NCRA. It would run until the demise of the *Basis* in April 1896. Following the 1896 election, the column would resume in the *Inter Ocean*, continuing after Tourgée's departure for Bordeaux in July 1897, only to be terminated once and for all in October 1898. The reincarnations of "A Bystander's Notes" would all lack the features it exhibited in its heyday, however: the in-depth coverage it provided of the race question, exploring aspects of it seldom or never seen in the mainstream press; the platform it accorded to African Americans from all regions and walks of life; the broad range of voices it incorporated, representing an extraordinary diversity of political viewpoints; and the lively dialogue it fostered between Tourgée and his readers, between whites and blacks, between progressives and reactionaries, between racists and egalitarians. Along with Tourgée's passion, eloquence, insight, and scathing irony, these features made "A Bystander's

Notes" one of the most innovative columns that American journalism ever produced.

RECEIVING FREQUENT MENTION in Tourgée's "Bystander" articles for more than half of the period covered here, and dominating the column for well over a year, the NCRA has threaded its way through this chapter. It nevertheless requires a chapter of its own to do it full justice—the undertaking to which we next turn.

CHAPTER FOUR

The National Citizens' Rights Association

There must be a *revolution* in the Republican party which shall bring to the
front again the idea of personal liberty and the equal rights of the citizen.
—Albion W. Tourgée to Marriott Brosius, 24 January 1891

In January 1891, nine months before founding the National Citizens' Rights
Association, Tourgée took into his confidence a Republican congressman
from Pennsylvania and fellow Civil War veteran named Marriott Brosius, with
whom he shared the plans he was revolving to "inaugurate" a mass movement.
By then, he admitted to Brosius, he could no longer avoid recognizing that
"lust of gain" had destroyed the Republican Party's commitment to racial
justice and sapped it of vitality. "The vigor, persistence, determination of the
Senate seem to be almost entirely on the other side," that is, on the side of
white supremacist Democrats, observed Tourgée. "*They* mean business, and
will do or sacrifice anything to carry their point." In contrast, dissension, apathy, and timidity were eating away at the Republicans, whose leaders merely
wanted "*power*" for the sake of controlling the government. "There must be
a *revolution*" in Republican ranks, Tourgée concluded, to "bring to the front
again the idea of personal liberty and the equal right of the citizen." He considered himself ideally suited to inaugurating such a "revolution," precisely
because he was a political outsider with "no future to be harmed and no past
to be mended—nothing to fear and nothing to hope for."[1]

Tourgée launched the NCRA in his "Bystander" column of 17 October
1891, where he challenged readers to match the "civic instinct" displayed by
African Americans of New Orleans. Though "oppressed and impoverished"
and "asserted to be incapable of self-government or co-operation," Tourgée
pointed out, these African Americans had managed to collect over $1,400
"by dimes and half-dimes" to "test the constitutionality of the infamous 'Jim
Crow car' law." The outcome of their test case would show "whether justice is still color-blind or National citizenship worth a rag for the defense of
right or not." Would the "people of the North" demonstrate their solidarity
with their "colored" fellow citizens of the South by joining a "Citizens' Equal
Rights Association"?[2] Responses poured in by the thousands, and within less
than a year the renamed National Citizens' Rights Association claimed over
100,000 members, ultimately peaking at 250,000.[3] Its ranks encompassed

Civil War Union veterans, scions of abolitionist families, African American intellectuals and activists, and barely literate plantation hands.

No one expressed greater astonishment than Tourgée at the myriads who answered his call for an interracial solidarity movement. "I expected a few score of responses," he confessed, but "300 or 400 applications" a day, along with "100 to 200 letters," had inundated him. "At first I signed the certificates and numbered them. Then Mrs. T. helped me; then one of her sisters and her mother; then we had to hire a clerk. Now the whole household work at it, servants and all when they have any spare time. We procured a numbering machine. It only ran up to 100,000. . . . We have had to start a new series more than once." The miraculous resurgence among both whites and blacks of a determination to fight side by side for equal rights—a shared militancy not seen since the abolitionist crusade had culminated in the emancipation and enfranchisement of the slaves—convinced Tourgée that God must be behind the phenomenon. "If the Lord must impose such work on one why did he not find a man not racked with pain or tired of vain attempts to accomplish good—," he grumped.[4]

Tourgée communicated with NCRA members not only through the public forum of his "Bystander" column but also through private letters that span the three to four years of the organization's operative existence. Filling up a vast file that occupies three reels of microfilm, these letters detail the methods by which members enlisted new recruits, offer opinions on how to achieve the NCRA's aims, comment on political developments, express candid views on race, apprise Tourgée of local atrocities unreported in the national press, and convey frustration with his refusal to move beyond recruitment to a concrete plan of action. In turn, Tourgée's responses provide insight into the obstacles that prevented the NCRA from fulfilling its ambitious goals: his deficiencies as an organizer, his lack of access to the capital needed to mount lawsuits against white supremacist practices, the ferocious repression that confined the NCRA's African American members in the South to underground activities, the inadequate enrollment of African Americans from Northern states, the growing trend toward black separatism, and the discomfort many whites felt at the prospect of publicly socializing with African Americans on an equal footing.[5]

African American Newspaper Editors' Role in Publicizing the NCRA

African American newspaper editors played the most visible role in publicizing the organization and shepherding their readers into it. Chief among them, of course, stood Louis A. Martinet, whose organ, the *New Orleans Crusader*, was spearheading the battle against Jim Crow transportation that had prompted Tourgée to start the NCRA. Tourgée had consulted with Martinet before proposing the idea of a "national organization, without the color or race line, to speak for the oppressed & defend their rights," and Martinet had "heartily approve[d]" it. "When organized on the lines you indicate & for the purpose you name—which embrace those I had in mind—it will be a success, I firmly believe; *it will have influence, dignity & effectiveness,*" Martinet predicted. He proceeded to sketch out the complementary roles that he saw his associates in New Orleans and the NCRA as playing: "While we need resist the encroachment on our rights in the South, the North needs to be educated as to conditions in the South & its disloyalty & rebellious tendencies. And we need do the work soon."[6]

A second early champion, Ida B. Wells, endorsed the NCRA in the *Memphis Free Speech* around November 1891, six months before she rose to national prominence through her campaign against lynching. Wells also continued to promote the organization among the network of contacts she cultivated as she began lecturing on lynching.[7] Other African American editors whose newspapers advertised the NCRA included Harry C. Smith of the *Cleveland Gazette*, who as a state legislator later solicited Tourgée's help in passing Ohio's antilynching law, the first in the nation; Josephine St. Pierre Ruffin of the *Boston Courant*, who would go on to found and preside over the Woman's Era Club, closely allied with Wells's antilynching campaign; Ferdinand L. Barnett of the *Chicago Conservator*, a well-respected attorney who would marry Wells in 1895; and William H. Anderson of the *Detroit Plaindealer*.

Only the *Plaindealer* and the *Gazette* survive, but they amply convey the enthusiasm with which these African American editors supported Tourgée and the NCRA. Both reprinted more than a year's worth of Tourgée's "Bystander" column, frequently on the front page. Both conspicuously featured and warmly seconded "A Personal Letter to Afro-Americans, from Judge Tourgee," in which he defined the goals and methods of the NCRA and urged blacks to unite behind it. Both devoted many editorials to praising "the most popular white man in the country to-day with Afro-Americans ... that staunch *friend* of the race, Judge Albion W. Tourgée," and to commending the NCRA as the organization best able to "arouse and obtain the sympathy of the whites." The *Plaindealer*, in particular, portrayed Tourgée as completing the work of William Lloyd Garrison, Wendell Phillips, and John Brown by transmitting the sentiments of the "intelligent self-respecting

Afro-American . . . to the world" through a civil rights organization that embraced "all classes of citizens . . . irrespective of race."[8] In addition, all of these newspapers printed copies of the same application for NCRA membership Tourgée appended to his weekly "Bystander" column in the *Inter Ocean*, which they prefaced by notices exhorting "every colored person man and woman" to join.[9] Attesting to the influence African American editors wielded, many of Tourgée's correspondents specified from which newspapers they had clipped the membership applications they enclosed, among which the *Crusader*, the *Conservator*, and the *Plaindealer* received most frequent mention.

The NCRA's Southern Black Membership

Of the NCRA's African American members, Southerners made up the largest contingent. Some identified themselves as longtime readers of Tourgée's novels and "Bystander" articles. "Your last book 'Pactolus Prime,' I have read and reread with peculiar interest," wrote Alexander S. Jackson, a minister in New Orleans. He added, "Your proposition to organize a National Citizens' Equal Rights League brought joy and strength to my heart . . . looking as it does to unifying all classes—true white men and true colored men," rather than perpetuating racial separatism.[10] Likewise based in New Orleans, the Illinois-born Baptist missionary S. T. Clanton echoed, "Your . . . 'Bricks without Straw,' [']Fool's Errand,' Pactolus Prime, etc., I have read with delightful profit."[11] Charles W. Cansler of Knoxville, Tennessee, recalled, "I read your great book, 'A Fool's Errand' when quite small and no other book save the Bible has impressed me as it did."[12] The Land and Loan Company president Jno. M. Nimocks from Meridian, Mississippi; the "colored farmer" and schoolteacher Jno. G. Monroe from Percy, Mississippi; and the deputy revenue collector A. M. Middlebrooks from Pine Bluff, Arkansas, all described themselves as "constant reader[s]" of Tourgée's "Bystander" column. "With what ability and sagacity you are battling for the rights of a race whose oppressions have increased despite the fact that we have reached a higher round in both the numerical and intellectual ladder," marveled Monroe.[13]

The ranks of the NCRA's educated black Southern members also included the Creole-of-color journalist Rodolphe L. Desdunes, a close associate of Martinet's on the *Crusader* staff and the Citizens' Committee that was filing the test case against Jim Crow transportation; the minister Thomas R. Griffin and his brother Charles, who had recently moved back to their native New Orleans from Chicago; and the schoolteachers F. B. Hood and his brother A. P. Hood, friends of Martinet's, both in Bolivar County, Mississippi. "I believe that in the course of a few years, you shall have changed the current of ideas in the Negro race," prophesied Desdunes as he rejoiced over the influence the "Bystander" and the *Crusader* exerted over delegates attending a recent state Republican convention, where "questions of right, of justice, of citizenship" gained a hearing for the first time.[14] Initiating his correspondence with Tourgée in 1890, Thomas Griffin noted that African Americans suffered from contemptuous treatment in the North as well as in the South and that the Republican Party unfailingly relegated the "sacred question of *Human rights*" for citizens of color "to the rear of our platform" during election campaigns. "But I hasten to beg your pardon," he interjected. "A grateful people remembers that the eloquent pen of Heaven's inspired servant, Albion W. Tourgee has already drawn attention to this fact."[15] Eager "to help along in the stupendous, yet noble work in which you and other humanitarians are engaged, in behalf of *Liberty*," F. B. Hood introduced himself with a character sketch: "While I have a considerable sprinkling of the Anglo-Saxon's much vaunted blue-blood, the major part of my make-up is of African lineage. That *brand* [double-underlined] on my forehead, like Cain's, forms an almost impassible barrier to the pursuit of happiness along the highway of liberty. I have always been an ardent and uncompromising lover of justice (of the *heaven-like* [double-underlined] order) to all men— regardless of hue or conditions." Articulate, highly qualified, yet barred from professional advancement and subjected to unremitting humiliation, this class of black Southern NCRA members used their letters to Tourgée as outlets for their frustration and as opportunities to reach sympathetic whites.[16]

Most of the NCRA's black Southern members came from less literate sectors of society, however. They often clustered in nodes, as if around a central recruiting point, suggesting that word of mouth may have supplemented local African American newspapers like the *Crusader* or the *Free Speech* in spreading accounts of the NCRA. New Orleans and its environs, where the Creole-of-color elite predominated, doubtless boasted the largest black Southern NCRA enrollment, though no numbers are available. Pine Bluff, Arkansas, harbored 250 members, probably recruited by A. M. Middlebrooks, one of Tourgée's most frequent correspondents since January 1891.[17] Bolivar County, Mississippi, held another 200 NCRA members, perhaps thanks to the Hood brothers' efforts.[18] Adjoining Bolivar to the north, Coahoma, Mississippi, also showed a significant NCRA presence. Beyond these nodes, scattered correspondents mailed in applications from Georgia, Alabama, Tennessee, and Kentucky.

The threat of deadly white supremacist reprisals imposed severe constraints on the activities of black Southern NCRA members and forced them to operate in secrecy, whether canvassing, reporting incidents of violence against their fellows, or simply sending letters to Tourgée. Again and again, they reminded Tourgée of the need for the utmost discretion to protect them from martyrdom at the hands of lynch mobs, even as they risked their lives to supply him with material he could use to enlighten white Northerners about the plight of African Americans in the South.

Passing on information about a schoolteacher in Bolivar County who had received an anonymous warning to leave town or "be swung to a limb" for having published an article in an out-of-state newspaper exposing the "deplorable" oppression endured by Mississippi blacks, A. P. Hood underscored that if Tourgée referred to the case in the "Bystander," he should mention no names, lest it "endanger either one of us." He also acknowledged that he had canceled an engagement to speak about the NCRA to a "crowd of Negroes" for fear of sharing this teacher's fate. "My God! how long will the Negroe's education be only a source of torture to him?" he exclaimed.[19] His brother F. B. Hood matter-of-factly remarked that he had "met with several reverses" for having agitated against the "'Jim Crow' car" and proceeded to explain what had caused so much unrest among Southern blacks: "Wages are at starvation points, and increasing cruelties more atrocious." As evidence, he enclosed an article from a white Southern newspaper that justified the shooting in cold blood of a black man who had been caught "cursing" a white man's children.[20] Two years later, F. B. Hood would meet his own death at the hands of a mob "variously estimated at from 150 to 300 men, if men they can be called," reported his brother. "The 'crime' for which his life was forfeited consisted in" writing two letters to the county superintendent of education that were "construed . . . as insulting or, at least impudent." Gunned down in his schoolhouse at noon, Hood fought back "as long as he could 'use his right hand'" and killed one of his assailants with his revolver. Although his brother took satisfaction in believing that F. B. Hood's valiant self-defense "had the effect of breaking up white-capism" in the county, he curtailed his own canvassing to avoid a similar doom.[21]

Another correspondent from Bolivar County, S. R. Kendrick, spelled out in equally graphic terms the price of defying white supremacy in the South: "The man or woman who attempts to Strike a Blow here for Freedom must be killed outright or he must be Exiled from all he possesses at once as Miss Ida B. Wells of the Memphis Free Speech have been." Throughout the South, he specified, "Standing armies" of "Negro haters" drove home the message that blacks "*must* obey the white man." Kendrick stressed that defeating the Confederates had required four years of war, hundreds of thousands of troops, "modern artilry," and a vast treasury. Thus, it was "simply absurd" to think African Americans without arms, troops, or money could overthrow "these same men," now back in power. Nevertheless, Kendrick told Tourgée, Bolivar County NCRA members had decided, in accordance with instructions in a recent "Bystander" column, to form "Local unions," "even if we are exterminated." Requesting fifty leaflets to distribute, and asking whether women could join the NCRA, he attached a page of signatures by ten men pledging to participate in a local union.[22]

H. W. Winans of Lake Village, Arkansas, expressed the same resolve, despite having already been driven from his home in Gloster, Mississippi, because his leadership prevented whites from exerting their accustomed control over the black population. "I have not been silent!" he assured Tourgée. "Many a day have I walked streets expecting every moment to be shot down for the defense of my people's rights. . . . A free country is it! if so, God forbid that I shall ever live to see a slave country." Few black NCRA members wanted to court death, however, and even the bold Kendrick objected acerbically, "We are a little tired of having to show our corpse to prove to the world that the Laws of this Country is not sufficient to protect the Black man as well as the white."[23]

Elsewhere in the South, NCRA members admitted to finding the perils of canvassing more daunting than they could manage. "We Collored people in this part of North Georgia have to be very carefull about who we speak to about the association," because local whites were "dead down on" it, cautioned Henry A. Fowler from Raccoon Mills.[24] A. N. Jackson, a Methodist pastor in La Fayette, Alabama, concurred, regretting that he and his peers could not "be of *very* much help" notwithstanding their "full sympathy" with the NCRA's aims. African Americans in Alabama and indeed in "every other Southern state," he elaborated, were "knocked and cuffed and kicked around" like slaves, "and if they resent this treatment the mob steps in and its the end of that person."[25] The draconian surveillance and ever-present danger of lynching hobbled NCRA recruitment, attested Jam[es?] Mosly of Spring Ridge, Louisiana: "Our people is very slow in giving there names on account of being intered ferred [interfered] with [by] the white people. Some of our letters has been open and our [enrollment] lists taken out before it left the office. . . . & when we write to you we are questioned by the whites verry much."[26] Seeking to circumvent such obstacles, Jane and Minnie Evans of Waynesboro, Mississippi, announced that they were shielding their menfolk by testifying in their place, "as the men was afraid . . . to let it be known . . . the white people of this county are taking the colored men and beating them and putting them in Jail."[27] Other correspondents signed their communications only with their membership certificate numbers.[28]

At least one, "John Branch" of Shreveport, Louisiana, assumed a pseudonym. To highlight the continuities with slavery times, he enclosed a poster paralleling the fugitive slave advertisements of the pre–Civil War era: "$500 Reward! Will be paid for the capture and delivery of the negro, Henry Patterson." Patterson, an "industrious" tenant farmer who "attended to his own business," had had the "manhood" to "talk back" to a white man and to defend himself against a "crowd of six toughs" who had broken into his house at midnight, recounted "Branch": "The negro leveled his double barrelled shot gun, killed one, and shot and [sic] arm off another. He made the battle so warm that the rest retreated. After trying to dislodge the negro for some time, in vain, they withdrew for reinforcement. When they returned the negro was gone. *He still goes—*." While celebrating this act of heroic resistance and successful escape, "Branch" tallied its cost: Patterson had had to leave behind his wife and possessions, including a "fine span of mules." The rest of the letter described how a "howling mob of '*white-supremacist*'" attacked the "leading colored men of this city" for promoting the Republican ticket—the same tactics used to deter African Americans from voting in 1874 and 1876, the years of the Reconstruction era's worst massacres. "Will the southern white man ever be emancipated from the spell of prejudice which has so 'abnormalized' his nature? What say you By-Stander?" "Branch" challenged Tourgée.[29]

Although most black Southern members appear to have joined the NCRA because they hoped it could spark a national campaign to end the white supremacist reign of terror under which they were living, some wanted the organization to provide military, financial, or legal assistance. Walter H. Griffin, who belonged to a club in Panther Burn, Mississippi, that alternately called itself the "sons of liberty" and the "Friends of protection," appealed to Tourgée to send arms: "Don't certify what is in the Box Just say hard ware," he directed.[30] Pliny J. Weels and A. A. Tompkins in Coahoma County requested confirmation of rumors that Tourgée was going to "furnish gun & Ammunition" for those who signed up for the NCRA "at reduce rates," that Republican president Benjamin Harrison was going to intervene, and that "this country will soon belong to the North." Weels's NCRA chapter had been paying the fare "from one club to another" of an organizer who had been spreading these rumors. "If he is humbug let us hear," he wrote (he received an immediate answer, according to a notation at the top of the letter).[31] Willis Reese, representing a desperate group planning a mass exodus from Grand Lake, Arkansas, implored the NCRA to "healp us out of the State."[32] F. Bass, W. C. Freeman, and J. H. Johnson of Alligator Lake, Mississippi, asked whether "the constitution of the U.S. is at our Back" with "its written guarantee to protect us" if they were assailed by their enemies. "We are half Living and do not want to Live Worst," they explained: "We are in favor of Liberty, and will make abreak [?] every time for Liberty But do not want to make abreak [?] in vain. . . . We do not want to engage in athing that will cause a number of our people to get kill up as we feel that there are enough of [us] being kill all ready. . . . Therefore we want to hear from you . . . If you mean Business." They added that two of their comrades had already been "attacted by some of the leading white and for biden ever be caught on certain plantation any more Just for advocating the cause of association."[33] NCRA members in other Mississippi towns reported being shot at, having their homes broken into at night, and being jailed or set at hard labor on the state farm for their outreach activities.

Tourgée publicized some of these cases in a "Bystander" article of 15 October 1892, aimed at countering white press accounts claiming that the victims were "'conspiring to kill the whites.'" He knew such charges to be false, Tourgée retorted, because the accused belonged to the NCRA, whose sole purposes were to help members "'seek by lawful and peaceful means' redress of grievances" and "consider how they might lawfully improve their condition and learn the duties of citizens." As proof, Tourgée quoted one of the many letters he had received from NCRA members who had been threatened with death when caught meeting together: "What they are afraid of is that we will talk about wages and the constitution that takes away our votes." Tourgée commented, "This correspondent, knowing the fate before them, bravely declares that even if the worst comes, it will be better for his people than to submit silently to be deprived of every right."[34] Through such articles, Tourgée sought to build support for the NCRA and its black Southern members.

Their own letters naturally articulated a broader range of tones, attitudes, and motives than any of Tourgée's "Bystander" columns captured. "Is there any thing that is in your power that you can do, for we poor helpless people as a protection," pleaded one. "I Want you to get me out of this fix," raged another from his prison cell, demanding that Tourgée send him a lawyer and warning that all the people working for the NCRA were "Waiting to see What you Will Do for me in this trubel." (By appealing to wealthy NCRA members, Tourgée succeeded in hiring a lawyer who procured the prisoner's release, as detailed in a "Bystander" article of 1 October 1892.)[35] Several correspondents from Mississippi also inquired whether their NCRA membership certificates would enable them to vote, notwithstanding the 1890 state law that disfranchised African Americans.[36]

Few of Tourgée's replies to such letters survive, but one addressing the question about voting sums up both his aspirations for the NCRA and his view of how black Mississippians should conduct themselves while awaiting their delivery from oppression. NCRA membership certificates did "not confer any right to vote at state elections," Tourgée clarified, but the organization did plan to challenge the constitutionality of the Mississippi election law in court, once it raised sufficient funds. Meanwhile, NCRA members could "serve the cause of liberty not less by submitting to law . . . than by doing all in [their] power to have it tested and overthrown by lawful means." Tourgée's emphasis on "lawful means" implies that he discountenanced resorting to arms, contrary to the hopes of his correspondents in Panther Burn and Coahoma County. Indeed, he specifically asserted, "The colored citizens of Mississippi can now do little more than pray and wait for redemption from the bondage that has overwhelmed them until the conscience and patriotism of the Nation shall bring them relief. They should stand together; let their wrongs be known; raise what funds they can to carry the questions involved to the Supreme Court of the United States, and especially do nothing to destroy the confidence of the people of the North in their worthiness to enjoy the equal citizenship of which they have been deprived." As slaves, black Mississippians had shown by "faith and self-restraint" that they deserved freedom, Tourgée continued. "The same qualities are now certain to win justice and equal right." Tourgée did recognize the right to use violence in self-defense, however. "Defend your lives if attacked; your homes if invaded," he advised. "Resist the mob—the lyncher and the ravisher and the Kuklux, though you lose your lives—but bow always to the forms of law though it take away your dearest right. This is the duty of the citizen: the part of the patriot."[37]

Tourgée's advice to black Mississippians conveyed mixed messages. Were they entitled by the constitution to equal citizenship, or must they prove themselves worthy of it? Would resisting oppression prove them worthy only if it cost them their lives? Did they depend as much on white Northerners for rescue as they had under slavery, and did white Northerners want them to do nothing but "pray and wait for redemption"? Or did these capricious rescuers require such proofs of "worthiness" as the ability to raise funds and publicize "their wrongs" and the willingness to die standing up to the "mob"? Perhaps Tourgée was expressing buried conflicts of his own about black rebellion and the capacity of the South's black masses to exercise their citizenship rights effectively.

The NCRA and Black Northerners

Unlike African Americans in the South, those in the North could recruit openly for the NCRA without fear of retaliation. Yet to Tourgée's chagrin, black Northerners, especially on the Eastern Seaboard, lagged far behind their Southern counterparts on the NCRA's membership rolls, despite his allies' efforts to herald the organization in their newspapers. "The colored people of the South send me their piteous tear-stained appeals for aid. The colored people of the North remain indifferent, unresponsive,—doing nothing. . . . What does it mean?" Tourgée harangued the African American former abolitionist Charlotte Forten Grimké, whose church in Washington, D.C., had hosted him as a lecturer in May 1892. "Do not the colored people [of the North] care for liberty and justice? Do they expect to wait like gaping young robins and have justice, equal right and equal opportunity dropped into their mouths? Or are they willing to sit still until bound hand and foot, as in Mississippi?" Worse yet, were they willing to lend credence to the racist theories of Kentucky-born Harvard professor Nathaniel Southgate Shaler, who claimed that the Negro lacked "the capacity, the confidence and the devotion to a high purpose, necessary . . . to co-operate with others even for his own prime advantage"? While rejecting Shaler's theories, which he had dismissed as "rot" in his "Bystander" column of 19 July 1890, Tourgée confessed that "the apathy, the indifference, the distrust, the selfish quer- ulousness manifested by the most intelligent, the assumed 'leaders' [of the race], discourage[d] and depresse[d] [him] very greatly," giving him the impression that Northern African Americans felt "very little the wrongs of the colored people of the South." If so, Tourgée underscored, they needed to realize they themselves held the key to ending racial oppression in the United States:

> The colored people of the South *will never receive justice* nor enjoy equal
> rights before the law and equal opportunity in the industrial world, until
> the colored men and women of the North come to feel these wrongs
> so keenly that they think of them, pray for them, speak of them and
> labor for them, more earnestly, more continuously and more zealously

than for anything else. It must become the *one* thought of the colored race before it will *become the purpose of God or the effectual desire of the American people.*[38]

Grimké might have been expected to take offense at Tourgée's tirade, especially since it came in response to her thanks for his "noble and powerful address" to her church, which had "stirred our souls to their depths, and made us feel, more strongly than ever before, that we, the colored people, *must* bestir ourselves, instantly and insistently, in this matter." Yet instead of retorting angrily, she arranged to have Tourgée's letter read aloud at a mass prayer meeting. Furthermore, she and her husband, the Reverend Francis Grimké, immediately set about circulating application forms. The reason so few black Washingtonians had joined the NCRA, she discovered, was that they had either not heard of the organization or had supposed it was intended only for whites. Once they understood that Tourgée was seeking to create an interracial movement for equal citizenship, they "entered heartily" into the endeavor, she affirmed.[39]

Another correspondent to whom Tourgée grumbled about the slow pace of Northern black recruitment, Florence A. Lewis of Philadelphia, herself the first "colored woman" to join the NCRA in November 1891, agreed that if African Americans of the "Eastern and Middle States" were not flocking to the association, it was mainly because "*They have not heard of the movement.*" The *Chicago Inter Ocean* did not circulate in Philadelphia, she pointed out, offering to write an account of the NCRA for the *A.M.E. Church Review*, a periodical "seen by colored people in all sections of the United States." Although prevented by the flu from fulfilling her intention before the next issue went to press, she did publicize the NCRA among her contacts in Washington and Boston, as well as in Philadelphia, and sent Tourgée a list of twenty-three Washingtonian recruits, including such prominent figures as John R. Lynch, former congressman from Mississippi, now an auditor of the U.S. Treasury; Lewis H. Douglass, son of Frederick Douglass; and Robert H. Terrell, a Harvard- and Howard-trained lawyer heading the Navy Pay Division. More would join the organization, Lewis ventured, once Tourgée unveiled a "definite plan of work" for members. "*What* is to be done? *How?* These two queries meet me at every turn," she nudged. (Indeed, many of Tourgée's correspondents, white as well as black, raised the same questions, as we shall see.)[40] At Lewis's behest, the prominent doctor Nathan F. Mossell started a Philadelphia chapter of the NCRA, which he characterized as a reincarnation of the "old abolition movement" and "the most important [organization] that has been inaugurated since the war for the benefit of the colored people."[41] Perhaps because Mossell cautiously sought to keep "the political side of our fight . . . in the back ground," however (contrary to Tourgée's advice), the Philadelphia chapter did not take off until October 1893, when the painter Henry O. Tanner, son of AME bishop Benjamin Tucker Tanner, returned from art studies in Paris and energized his denomination's preachers.[42]

Like Florence Lewis and Charlotte Forten Grimké, Josephine St. Pierre Ruffin threw her support behind the NCRA almost at its inception, only to have Tourgée complain that she and other Northern African Americans were not doing enough. While expressing "pleasure" at seeing "several notices in the 'Courant' of the National Citizens' Rights Association," along with complimentary references to himself, Tourgée stressed that enrollments mattered more than favorable publicity. "Do you realize that it is *your* cause much more than mine that I am fighting for? If so why dont you *do* something," he hectored Ruffin in a "personal" letter to the editor, whom he assumed to be a man. "What we want is men—men with souls—men who will stand up and be counted." If the NCRA could display a membership list of "a million white names and a million black ones—especially *men*," it could institute racial equality "without firing a gun." How many members could Ruffin furnish from Boston?, Tourgée demanded, promising to send twenty lists for her to fill with signatures. "Dont wait to be carried over the hard places in the road. The manhood of your race never was on trial as it is now. Let us hear from it," he urged.[43]

Less deferential than Lewis and Grimké, Ruffin replied tartly that though she and her staff were not men but "only overworked, anxious, women," they had the "requisite souls" to "help all we can in this discouraging effort to make white men feel and act that 'a man's a man for a that and a that,'" in the words of the Scottish poet Robert Burns. The chief obstacle lay in white men's racism rather than in black men's lack of manhood, she intimated. Nevertheless, she committed herself to recruiting for the NCRA.[44]

Ruffin would remain a staunch ally of Tourgée's, yet one wonders how she reacted to his long letter in answer to hers, in which he not only reiterated his aspersions on the "Northern colored man" but also assigned women a subordinate role in the NCRA. Ruffin should take it as a "great compliment" that he "mistook [her] sex," Tourgée told her, "since I knew you only by your work and when a woman's work is mistaken for a man's, it is a sure testimony that it is not inferior to a man's." Although both men and women were welcome to join the NCRA, he specified, "it is most desirable at this time not to have too great a proportion of women on our lists" because they could not vote in U.S. elections and thus critics might say "women do not count." African American women could best serve the cause by "acting as solicitors" for the NCRA, in which capacity they could "be the most efficient agents for promoting its spread among their people." Ignoring Ruffin's pointed censure of white racism, Tourgée redirected responsibility for fighting racism back toward African Americans: "Of course, a race that will not work for its own rights and liberties does not deserve to have them and will not long retain them. The colored people of the South know this and they are alert to take advantage of anything that promises relief. The same is true of the masses of them in most of the cities of the [Mid]West. At the East they are yet apathetic." As he speculated about the reasons for this seeming apathy, Tourgée considered two possible explanations. Was the educated "colored man of the North . . . ashamed of his poor relations"? Or had the reigning scientific racism convinced him that "he is an ethnic inferior and will remain so until he is so bleached as to be undistinguishable from the Caucasian"? He was advancing these speculations privately, Tourgée emphasized in a lengthy postscript, because he felt he could "say . . . confidentially" to an African American supporter "what it might be inexpedient to publish." Besides, the *Courant* would more successfully mobilize readers in a campaign that required "earnest and universal co-operation" if it relied not on his words but on those of "its own best author" to win converts. "I am . . . willing to trust the advocacy of the N.C.R.A. to your woman's instinct and good sense," Tourgée assured Ruffin.[45]

Whether through the *Courant* or through other channels, the NCRA did gain adherents in the Boston area. For example, the Cambridge Afro-American League, numbering fifty or sixty members, decided to form itself into an NCRA chapter and change its name accordingly. As the league's secretary informed Tourgée, Northern African Americans were not indifferent to the plight of their Southern brothers and sisters—they simply did not know about either the extent of white supremacist repression beneath the Mason-Dixon line or the "good work" the NCRA was accomplishing in New Orleans, because local newspapers were not adequately covering these topics.[46]

Of course, no reader of Tourgée's "Bystander" column could plead similar ignorance. Thus, Chicago, home of both the *Inter Ocean* and the *Conservator*, held the largest and most enthusiastic cohort of African American NCRA members in the North. Mack W. Caldwell, who had been corresponding with Tourgée since 1890, typified their spirit. Eager to share "equally" in sustaining the organization, he proclaimed, "Whenever money is needed count me, whenever a burden is to be borne count me, and whenever any fighting is to be done to vindicate the rights of the members of the association or those it aims to protect count me in as an able-bodied soldier ready and willing at all times to fall over and die in the interest of the *Right*." He pledged to send "at least five names each week to add" to the NCRA's membership list, to sell fifty copies of Tourgée's pamphlet on citizenship, *Is Liberty Worth Preserving?*, and to "leave nothing undone . . . to advance the interest of the organization."[47]

Another black Chicagoan, William Lewis Martin, who identified himself as an Oberlin student slated to graduate with the class of 1892, greeted the NCRA as the "consummation of [his] fondest hopes and earnest prayers." He volunteered to target ministers and teachers, through whom he hoped to recruit five hundred members within two months. Tourgée should try to enlist the influential bishops of the AME church, suggested Martin. Although they "dislike to 'mix politics and religion,'" they could be "aroused" because of their concern for the "wellfare of the race," especially if Tourgée solicited them personally. Promising to devote all his spare time to building the organization, Martin wrote, "I want to see you get a million voters or members enlisted and shall do my part to swell the number."[48]

No less enterprising, Chicago collector of customs Robert McCoomer sent Tourgée a circular showing that he had called a mass meeting of African Americans in his congressional district, under the auspices of the Banneker League, of which he was the president. It exhorted those who "value the future welfare of our race" not only to come themselves but to "induce [their] friends to come." "The colored people of this district will do all they can for the citizens rights Association having profound Confidence in all of your works Consequently where you Lead we will follow," McCoomer vowed to Tourgée.[49]

Even the most energetic of the NCRA's promoters never managed to generate notable grassroots participation in it among their fellow African Americans of the North, however. In a desperate bid to increase Northern black NCRA enrollment, Tourgée finally addressed "A Personal Letter to Afro-Americans," which the *Plaindealer*, the *Gazette*, and probably other "race journals" published in early June 1892. Perhaps acting on his allies' promptings, Tourgée stressed the organization's interracial character and elaborated on its methods: "It advocates prayers, petitions, argument, law, remonstrance, and if need be when all other means shall fail, resistance to oppression." He then warned that if educated black Northerners refused to join the NCRA, not only would they discourage the "hundreds of thousands of white men who have rallied as if by magic" to the cause of equal rights, but they would fuel their enemies' claims that African Americans were "not fit for self-government." He climaxed his appeal by replying for the first time to critics of "Tourgeeism"—African Americans preaching accommodation to the racist status quo, a faction that would soon flock to the banner of Booker T. Washington: "The man who counsels voluntary submission to wrong rather than protest, remonstrances and peaceful united effort for its overthrow, is simply deficient in that manhood on which alone equal citizenship can be securely based."[50]

Two editorials in the *Plaindealer* seconded Tourgée's appeal. The first urged readers to "see that every Afro-American is enrolled in this Grand Army of liberty," so as to prove the charge of "apathy" unwarranted. "Judge Tourgee is so intense in his advocacy of freedom, that any thing less than a degree of intensity that approaches his own appears to him as apathy," wrote editor William H. Anderson diplomatically. The second editorial emphasized the need for supplementing racial self-help with black-white collaboration. "It is time we must do for ourselves, but we must do it in connection with and when necessary under the leadership of just such able and true white friends as now proffer us aid," argued Anderson, underscoring that "Judge Tourgee has done more for the cause of liberty than any Afro-American living outside of [Frederick] Douglass."[51] Nonetheless, neither Tourgée's "Personal Letter to Afro-Americans" nor Anderson's endorsement gained the NCRA the desired mass following.

Possible Reasons for Lower Northern Black Enrollments in the NCRA

What accounts for the failure of black Northerners to embrace the NCRA with the excitement their Southern counterparts displayed? Did they feel less driven to clutch desperately at almost any solution to their predicament, because white supremacy in the North took less virulent forms? Did they wish to know more about how and by whom the NCRA was going to be run and what plan of action it would propose before they committed themselves to working for it? Did their agenda differ from Tourgée's? Or as Tourgée suspected, did black Northerners, and especially their religious and political leaders, not "desire the co-operation of white people to secure" their rights?[52]

NCRA archives furnish evidence partially supporting all these explanations, but no decisive answers. Arthur B. Lee, a black Civil War veteran from Wisconsin, for example, echoed Florence Lewis: "I am met with the question on all sides, . . . but what are you going to *do*."[53] Samuel G. Hicks of Clay City, Illinois, voiced dissatisfaction with signing up recruits merely to demonstrate the existence of broad public sentiment in favor of guarantee-ing all Americans equal citizenship. He had enrolled in the NCRA because he had expected it to do "real work," he complained.[54] Tourgée replied that the NCRA was designed not to indulge in "buncombe" but to obtain leg-islation protecting "free speech, equal rights, and a free ballot" throughout the United States; only a "great national party" could sponsor such leg-islation and then only if the public demanded it vociferously enough, he argued—hence, NCRA members must concentrate for the time being on redoubling recruitment.[55] Apparently unconvinced, Hicks did not pursue the correspondence.

Many Northern African Americans—like those in the South who besieged Tourgée with requests for arms, protection, emigration assistance, and access to voting—seem to have shared Hicks's desire for concrete action against the white racist practices that victimized them. Topping the list of evils they wanted the NCRA to tackle was lynching. Calls for exer-tions against this national crime grew to a crescendo after Wells launched her international antilynching campaign with a lecture tour of the British Isles in the spring of 1893. That July, when C. J. Miller of Springfield, Illinois, was lynched in Bardwell, Kentucky, for a crime he did not commit, the *New Orleans Crusader* erroneously announced that the NCRA was collecting contributions to help Miller's widow sue for damages. Picked up by the *Philadelphia Evening Herald*, the announcement triggered a spurt of new NCRA enrollments. Among them, D. D. Weaver of Philadelphia eloquently articulated his reasons for waiting until this moment to send in the appli-cation for NCRA membership that he had left blank on his desk for many months. He had involved himself in so many "schemes . . . inaugurated to protect and defend" his race, only to see them "defeated," that he had "almost lost courage" and decided to leave the "wrongs done [his] people for time to rectify," he confided, but the (inaccurate) news that the NCRA was raising funds to take a lynching case to court had encouraged him to join the organ-ization and begin recruiting for it.[56]

Tourgée had in fact been speaking out forcefully against lynching in his "Bystander" column since December 1888, when he had first advocated the passage of antilynching legislation, and he had been collaborating with Wells for over a year by the time the Miller lynching occurred.[57] Still, he resisted taking up the Miller case because he saw it as a distraction from the NCRA's mission, which he defined as "manufacturing right sentiment until it ripens into just deeds." Thus, he initially answered Weaver by saying that the NCRA had "no funds to carry on" a lawsuit for a lynching victim. No doubt because he had been "so widely importuned to take action," Tourgée reversed himself in the postscript and agreed to "act as trustee" for the Miller fund. As he had anticipated, however, the amount of money collected proved entirely inadequate, and he returned it to the donors.[58]

Perhaps the chief factor impeding the large-scale recruitment of black Northerners lay in the deep chasm that had opened up between the races since the demise of the abolitionist movement after the collapse of Reconstruction. Before the war, the struggle against slavery had brought whites and African Americans together for the first time, and participants like the young Charlotte Forten had succeeded in bridging the black and white worlds and cultivating cross-racial friendships. Yet even at the height of the abolitionist movement, only a handful of whites had shown themselves immune to the racist tendencies of their culture. Black abolitionists had frequently charged their white collaborators with arrogance and condescension and complained of being excluded from leadership roles. In response, white abolitionists had charged blacks with disloyalty or ingratitude. Differing priorities had also provoked racial tensions.[59]

Mutual distrust had greatly increased by the 1890s, when few survived who had experienced the freedom of socializing across the color line and working in integrated activist groups to eradicate racism. The tide of reaction that had swept the country in the wake of Reconstruction had all but erased the abolitionist movement from general public memory, repudiated its ideals of racial equality and impartial justice, and substituted white supremacy in their place.[60] Disillusioned by the impotence of their staunchest white allies to stem this tide—and by the defection of all too many who succumbed to white Southern propaganda and concluded that legislation could not raise the status of a race branded by nature as inferior—African Americans devoted themselves to building their own institutions. Black churches, newspapers, religious periodicals, and self-help organizations flourished as never before. A vastly expanded black middle class supported these institutions, its intelligentsia emerging from the colleges and universities established for African Americans during and after Reconstruction, as well as from the rare white schools to admit African Americans, such as abolitionist-founded Oberlin.[61] Two developments exemplify the trend among African Americans toward separatism as a strategy for countering white supremacy: first, the formation in 1890 of the all-black National

Afro-American League to fight against disfranchisement, lynching, virtual reenslavement under the Southern penitentiary system, discriminatory education, and segregation—an initiative led by the militant journalist T. Thomas Fortune, editor of the *New York Age*;[62] and second, the creation in 1893 of the International Migration Society to promote the return of blacks to Africa, sponsored by AME bishop Henry McNeal Turner, who had begun his career as a Radical Republican but had abandoned hope that African Americans would ever achieve justice in the United States.

Tourgée had warmly supported the founding of the National Afro-American League. In addition, he devoted his "Bystander" column of 2 November 1889 to celebrating the announcement of the national league's forthcoming inaugural convention, to be held in Chicago on 18 January 1890. "It is high time the colored man took up the cudgels for the assertion of his rights himself. There will never be any more Garrisons or Phillipses to fight his battles for him," he editorialized. Two requisites for the success of this enterprise, Tourgée contended, were "martyrs . . . brave enough to die . . . in every county of the South to secure their liberty"; and a leader with the "nerve and power and self-forgetfulness . . . to ruthlessly put down the horde of self-seekers who always spring to the front in such a movement" and at the same time with "tact enough to make them all work toward one end." Tourgée had also sent a letter to be read at the convention, listing the objectives toward which he believed the association should strive: to organize African Americans into a united pressure group; to collect information on the disabilities and abuses they endured throughout the United States; and to agitate for just laws and fair administration of those laws—objectives remarkably similar to those he would soon lay out for the NCRA, but tamer than those Fortune had announced for the league.[63] To Tourgée's outrage, some members of the league, *not* including Fortune, had wanted to return the letter unopened, but the newly elected president of the group, Joseph C. Price, president of Livingston College in North Carolina, had prevailed on his colleagues to acknowledge it politely. "I would thank you, . . . were it not a matter of far more importance to the race than to me," Tourgée told Price. The race could not "afford to allow its representative men to offer the almost unprecedented insult of returning the letter of a man who has published half a dozen volumes in advocacy of their rights, which have been read by ten millions of American citizens." African Americans depended on winning the support of the white majority "because majorities rule," Tourgée pointed out. "So it will not pay to kick a faithful champion because he is white."[64] Initially Tourgée rejoiced that Price had been chosen to head the league, rather than Fortune, whom he then distrusted as a "self-seeker." Congratulating Price on his accession, Tourgée wrote, "Only once in an age is such a chance to flex the world's thought and destiny made possible to *any individual*. It is not your race alone but the world's civilization, political systems and the quality of Christian thought that is liable to be affected by the operations of the League, if skilfully and wisely directed." He went on to warn Price against letting Fortune sow dissension in the league and derail the fledgling organization through "indiscretion."[65] Tourgée quickly soured on Price, however, whom he accused of scattering his energies by starting a literary magazine instead of educating the white Northern public about the brute force that kept African Americans in neo-slavery. "It will hurt his work in the League. The man at its head should know no other interest— worship no other God but liberty until his race is free," Tourgée opined to the *Plaindealer's* Anderson, vice president of the league's Michigan chapter.[66] The disappointment he met in his efforts to form a broad alliance with the Afro-American League and later with Bishop Turner would seem to justify Tourgée's suspicion that black Northerners, or at least some of their leaders, did not "desire the co-operation of white people to secure" their rights.[67]

Although the trend toward black separatism may have played a role in hampering the NCRA's growth, the separatist Afro-American League did not succeed any better than the NCRA in inspiring a grassroots movement among black Northerners and may actually have fallen short of the NCRA's recruitment of black Southerners. Indeed, the league's racial exclusivity alienated the Creoles of color who so enthusiastically promoted the NCRA. Refusing to affiliate with an organization whose very title drew the "color line" they were seeking to eliminate through their defiance of the Jim Crow car, Creoles of color had patronized an alternative organization in July 1890 called the American Citizens' Equal Rights Association, but it had turned into nothing more than a "political resolution machine," according to Martinet, and had lasted only a year.[68] As for the league, already "languishing" by the time Tourgée founded the NCRA, it dissolved in August 1893, and Fortune blamed its dissolution on the same problems Tourgée lamented: "fail[ure] to win a following among the Negro masses" and "lack of support from race leaders."[69]

Whatever the reason for which "race leaders" kept aloof from the Afro-American League, Tourgée attributed their coolness toward the NCRA to political ambition, petty jealousy, and resentment at a white man's having presumed to launch a civil rights organization without seeking their endorsement. "A lot of the so-called 'leaders' are going to make a kick because they are not consulted," he confided to Martinet, who shared his disdain for them. "They are so intoxicated with the idea of being 'leaders' that I fear they are willing to sell their brethren into Egypt for the tinsel of a cheap notoriety."[70]

The "so-called 'leaders'" Tourgée perhaps had in mind may have been such politicians as John M. Langston, Blanche K. Bruce, and P. B. S. Pinchback—men dependent for their positions on Republican Party bosses and thus reluctant to associate themselves with a radical movement steered by a political gadfly. Like Martinet, he may even have numbered Frederick Douglass among those who *"have grown rich in fighting the race's battles"* but who "never make the slightest sacrifice, or do anything to help unless it benefits them."[71] Tourgée may also have been targeting editors of the more conservative race papers. As reported in the *Plaindealer*, the *Gazette*, and the *Conservator*, for example, Edwin H. Hackley, editor of the *Denver Statesman*, "spen[t] much of his spare time in writing harsh criticisms of Judge Tourgee, the best friend to-day that the colored man has in this country."[72] Hackley insisted that "'no white man' could 'lead or direct' the colored population and specifically repudiat[ed] agitation, political action, and remedial legislation" because he believed such methods only worsened "race hatred."[73] The editor of the *Indianapolis Freeman*, Edward E. Cooper, attacked "Tourgeeism" even more vituperatively, calling Tourgée a "blatherskite," deriding his "ill-seasoned vaporings," and rejecting his "inflamable . . . advice to the colored people."[74] Tourgée would continue to carp about "ill-natured, little flings" from "colored editors" as late as 1895.[75] He could conceivably have avoided antagonizing these leaders by inviting them to join the NCRA's Administrative Council, but he opted instead "to disarm them by appointing colored men and women who are representatives but *not* 'leaders,'" among them Charles W. Chesnutt, Rodolphe Desdunes, Ida B. Wells, and Florence Lewis. As he explained to Martinet, if African American leaders were "thrust forward, the white people [would] draw out," and the NCRA would lose its character as an interracial organization modeled on the abolitionist movement: "White men will not join a colored League, to any extent that is. Yet it is white votes and sentiment we must rely on at the North."[76]

The NCRA's White Membership

When Tourgée sent out his call in the *Inter Ocean* for a "Citizens' Equal Rights Association," he had expected to have far more trouble attracting whites than African Americans to such an organization. After all, the white

Northern public had acquiesced with dismayingly little protest in President Hayes's dismantling of Reconstruction and the subsequent rollback by Congress and the Supreme Court of equal rights legislation that represented the fruits of a forty-year antislavery struggle and a murderous Civil War. To Tourgée's astonishment, however, white Northerners initially outnumbered African Americans ten to one on the NCRA's enrollment lists and eventually constituted 200,000 of the association's 250,000 members.[77] It was this gaping disparity that spurred him to badger his Northern black supporters to increase the rate of recruitment in their communities. As he admitted to Charlotte Forten Grimké, he worried that if the "hundreds of thousands of white voters who [had] pledged themselves to demand justice and equality for the colored man" realized African Americans were not doing their share of the NCRA's work, they would soon cease their own efforts, finding it useless to "force liberty and equality upon a people who are indifferent" to their rights.[78] The conundrum Tourgée thought he faced was that whites would neither join a black-led or black-dominated civil rights organization nor make sacrifices blacks themselves seemed unwilling to make in the battle against racial oppression.

Yet white Northerners responded in such overwhelming numbers to Tourgée's appeal that we may well wonder whether he underestimated the legacy the abolitionist movement had left.[79] Hundreds identified themselves as children of abolitionists or Civil War Union veterans who, like Tourgée himself, had fought in abolitionist regiments dedicated to freeing African Americans from bondage and who had remained faithful to their ideals despite the nation's betrayal of them. H. Farmer of Jefferson County, Illinois, a former captain in the Wisconsin infantry, offers a typical example. His abolitionist father, he proudly recalled, had sent him to war when General John C. Frémont issued the first emancipation proclamation of 30 August 1861 (countermanded by Lincoln to the disgust of abolitionists): "He Said to me now is the time to go & I went." Disabled in combat and living on a "pittance," Farmer nevertheless asked for NCRA circulars and a copy of *Is Liberty Worth Preserving?* to distribute. He ended his letter, "May the Spirit of John Brown help you."[80]

Another representative Civil War veteran, A. Ryall from South Haven, Michigan, wrote that along with a "Million Comrades," he had braved "rebel bullets" to free the slaves, only to see slavery persist in other guises. He had been eagerly "watching the progress" of the NCRA because it promised to right wrongs that "Cry aloud for redress." If these wrongs were not "speedily redressed," he feared, they would "bring to our ears a cry for vengeance the mere imaginary contemplation of which makes one shudder."[81]

J. H. Wimpey from Splitlog, Missouri, described his enlistment in the NCRA as an extension of his Union army service and a fulfillment of its mission. He wanted to pass his NCRA membership certificate down to his grandchildren along with his military discharge, he asserted, "to show them that, in the conflict for Nationality and freedom, I stood on the right side, and to show them that my gratitude or manhood was not so shriveled up . . . as to oppose extending equal rights and protection to my colored comrades in arms that stood beside me when rebel cannon was hurling missiles of death into our ranks." In Wimpey's opinion, doing justice to his "colored comrades" deserved even higher priority than obtaining pensions for old and disabled Civil War veterans—a cause Tourgée had been agitating in his "Bystander" column to great applause among former soldiers.[82]

The ranks of Northern white NCRA members also included women of abolitionist background like Jannice Page of Blue Springs, Nebraska, who had long ago subscribed to Tourgée's defunct literary magazine, *Our Continent* (1882–84), and now cherished his "Bystander" column. "My blood boils with indignation and my nerves quiver in sympathy when I read of the indignities, cruelties, and sufferings to which this slave born people are subjected," she wrote. Although uncertain about whether the NCRA accepted women, she sent in her application less than a week after Tourgée launched his challenge to "Bystander" readers. Women in "isolated farm houses and quiet homes" appreciated the "valiant strokes of [Tourgée's] pen" as much as men did, Page assured him, aware that "each encouraging voice" would fortify his "sword, which it almost seems is the only defence the black man has in this unequal battle."[83]

The NCRA appears to have aroused particular enthusiasm on college campuses, then as now hotbeds of progressive activism. In his lecture tours Tourgée regularly included college towns, where he "always manage[d] to spend an hour . . . with the students."[84] The personal interest he took in them won him both their adulation and their support for the NCRA. Announcing that he was "thoroughly in sympathy with the cause for which you are doing such heroic and effective work," Fred Meyers, a student at the University of Iowa, asked Tourgée for a letter he could read at an organizing meeting he planned to hold with the aim of starting a campus NCRA chapter. "Hundreds of young men here . . . would be willing to join the Citizens Rights Assoc. if the matter was properly presented to them," he declared. Tourgée obliged with a powerful statement characterizing the NCRA as "a new Army of Liberty" whose "purpose [was] to substitute public opinion for armed strife; prevention for cure; the ballot for the bullet." By contributing two cents each to cover the cost of mailing a certificate of membership, Tourgée told Iowa students, they could show whether they "care[d] as much as two-cents for the maintenance of liberty and justice and the equal rights of American Citizens."[85]

Students at Grinnell College, also in Iowa, were already deeply engaged in advocating equal rights for African Americans when Tourgée started the NCRA. The leaders of Grinnell's debating team, Charles L. Fitch and Charles D. Seaton, had asked Tourgée to send them material they could use to defend the propriety of "Federal Interference in the Negro Problem," and he had treated them "magnificently." After two and a half months of study, during which they had "prepared digests of arguments" from Tourgée's *Bricks Without Straw*, *A Fool's Errand*, and *An Appeal to Caesar*, they had won their debate handily. They now proposed to canvass for the NCRA, requesting fifty membership forms and paying for them with the same number of two-cent stamps. Many students at Grinnell "would be anxious to join," they predicted.[86]

NCRA Members' Frustrations

However much white Northern NCRA members may have outnumbered their African American counterparts, they shared the same belief that they could recruit more sympathizers if Tourgée could formulate the organization's agenda, plan of action, and structure with greater clarity. As A. Ryall, the war veteran from Michigan, put it, "Thus far I am unable to gain from the 'Bystanders Notes' . . . the precise line of action in view in order to make the 'Association' effect the desired purpose." He was writing on behalf of the *"few pronounced friends"* of the NCRA in his community, who had deputed him to ask whether the organization was supposed to "take the form of a party—with a platform of principles—" or whether it aimed to collect and present the signatures of all "lover[s] of Justice & freedom . . . in one monster petition and remonstrance to Congress or the Executive—*with an ultimatum*—." His comrades also wanted to know whether Tourgée favored having members publicize the NCRA and advertise its meetings in the local press. They all agreed that *"very many"* adherents would be "ready to declare themselves should any feasable" modus operandi be enunciated.[87]

White NCRA members like Ryall probably found Tourgée's vague answers to their inquiries as frustrating as did black NCRA members like Samuel Hicks. So far the organization had only two purposes, he replied: "(1) To get as many names of the liberty-lovers of the land on its rolls as can be found by its active and earnest members. (2) To be ready to do whatever may require to be done to promote the desires of its members and secure equal rights for all citizens." Neither he nor his Administrative Council wanted to "prescribe any specific method" or course for local communities to adopt, Tourgée indicated. Instead, leaving each free to act as it deemed best would encourage participation by those who quailed at being stigmatized as a beleaguered minority of "pioneers." It would additionally avoid the "bickerings, jealousy, distrust and excess of machinery" to which Tourgée attributed the failure of analogous enterprises attempted by African Americans (an oblique reference to the Afro-American League and the ACERA). On the one hand, the system of enrollment lists and circulars allowed "every one an opportunity to work according to his own inclination and capability and in his own way." On the other hand, the requirement that "the names of all members secured be sent to headquarters for registration" made "every member directly accessible for consultation on information of any sort" and thus facilitated "unity and harmony of action." Tourgée did not say so, but the combination of decentralized local action and centralized control at "headquarters" prevented divisiveness by blocking direct communication between the various NCRA chapters and channeling it through him. He may not have been able to admit to himself that he was acting like a possessive father unwilling to let his child grow up and that the NCRA could never flourish as a grassroots organization if he treated it as his personal preserve. He simply convinced himself that he alone could keep the NCRA unified. As far as publicity and public meetings were concerned, Tourgée warned that "a good cause is sometimes 'talked to death' before it is fairly on its feet."[88]

Tourgée more explicitly spelled out his reasons for shrinking from publicity to Nathan Mossell. Previous organizations, he claimed, had generated "wind enough to make a cyclone and eloquence enough to move a gate post" through their "meetings and speeches" yet had not produced "tangible" results. Moreover, "hunting game with a bass-drum" tended to scare off "shy" quarry. Rather than chase away indecisive recruits through vain boasts, he urged, "let us land our catch and 'holler' afterwards."[89]

Even when NCRA members agreed that quiet personal solicitation proved more effective than press coverage and mass meetings in building the organization, they often seem to have felt a need for more structure than Tourgée favored. They may not have known that the Administrative Council whose authority Tourgée frequently invoked consisted only of hand-picked appointees with no responsibilities, but they persistently requested copies of the NCRA's nonexistent constitution, "rules and regulations," bylaws, and minutes. Perhaps harking back to such precedents as the abolitionist societies of the antebellum era or the Afro-American League and the ACERA of the recent past, some also advocated collecting dues, holding monthly meetings, and planning a national convention.[90]

Tourgée, on the contrary, viewed the NCRA's lack of structure as one of its chief strengths. Both his observation of the Afro-American League's internal conflicts and his cognizance of the political schisms and power struggles that had bedeviled the abolitionist movement convinced him that introducing such "machinery" as formal codes, procedures, elected officers, regular meetings, and annual conventions would open the door to factional disputes. Because the NCRA had no "'leaders'" but only "members and a servant" (himself), it could neither be torn apart by rivalry nor manipulated by outsiders seeking to create "disaffection," he argued, "for there is nothing to act on." A convention, by contrast, would "yield 200 speeches and twenty factions."[91]

Tourgée especially feared racial strife, which would doom joint efforts to end systemic discrimination—an enterprise "no one should ask or expect" African Americans to carry out successfully on their own. "Meetings, speeches talk and clamor" would inevitably breed "dissension between black and white," and "all jarring on the question of color ... *must be avoided* until the sentiment of duty and the policy of justice become sufficiently well established to override the sin and crime of prejudice and caste," he emphasized to the successive heads of the Philadelphia NCRA chapter, Nathan Mossell and Henry O. Tanner.[92] He unburdened himself most frankly on this issue to the white Quaker Phillip C. Garrett: "Very many [white] people who believe in justice are very shy of practicing it and thousands who say they are willing the colored citizen should have equal rights, would abandon all idea of it, if they had to attend a public meeting and accord it to him" by sitting and dining side by side, giving African American speakers the same prominence as their white counterparts, or electing African American officers. "This is foolish and wrong *but true*," Tourgée underscored, reminding Garrett of how the philanthropists who had organized the 1890 and 1891 Mohonk Conferences on the Negro Question had excluded African Americans but invited white Southerners. African Americans, for their part, were "very jealous" of their independence and sensitive to anything that smacked of white domineering. Rather than confront the problem of race relations head-on and "endanger good results by trying to compel compliance with my notions," Tourgée confided to Garrett, he was seeking to "walk around it." That was why he was responding to the widespread demand for more structure by recommending the establishment of "local 'Unions'" or "Liberty Leagues" of about thirty members who should meet weekly at each other's homes and why he was leaving these small groups free to decide for themselves whether their membership should be integrated or segregated. After working separately toward the same goal for several years, African Americans and whites would develop a "common interest" and be ready to "act with each other without friction," Tourgée believed. Indeed, some groups had already formed local advisory committees consisting of "white and black, male and female" members who seemed to "work heartily together." Once interracial cooperation became more general, the chances of organizing successfully on a national scale would be greater, if such an endeavor proved necessary. Meanwhile, however, local unions should concentrate on arousing "the public conscience in that part of our country where men are free and votes are counted."[93]

Two models apparently suggested the idea of local unions or Liberty Leagues to Tourgée: the Union Leagues of the Reconstruction era, like the interracial one he had joined in Greensboro, North Carolina, in 1867, and the Chautauqua Circles of the 1880s and 1890s, originating in the Lake Chautauqua region of upstate New York, where he had lived for the past decade. Both empowered the masses to educate themselves, whether politically, as had the Union Leagues, or culturally and spiritually, as did the Chautauqua Circles. Thus, Tourgée conceived of his local unions or Liberty Leagues as enabling participants to learn citizenship through study and practice. Just as members of Union Leagues had done so by conning the U.S. Constitution and Declaration of Independence, reading Republican newspapers together, and debating how to stand up to exploitative employers and defend themselves against Klan attacks, members of NCRA local unions would read and discuss Tourgée's "Bystander" articles and his pamphlet *Is Liberty Worth Preserving?*, delve into the history of slavery, and try to determine "*how* justice may be done and equal right and adequate security be peacefully obtained for all." In the process, they would turn the NCRA into a "great popular School of Liberty," a gigantic Chautauqua for training citizens in self-government.[94] Many such groups, often calling themselves Tourgée Clubs, were already functioning in Louisiana and other Southern states, and two existed in Chicago, Tourgée informed an unidentified African American correspondent.[95]

Unlike their prototypes of the Reconstruction era, however, Tourgée's local unions, at least as he described them, seemed oriented more toward the study than the practice of citizenship. Granted, in the South such actions as striking for higher wages or collectively defying white mobs had become even more dangerous than during Reconstruction, when African Americans could hope for at least some federal protection. Yet in the North local unions could have targeted such prevalent instances of discrimination and segregation as the refusal of restaurants and hotels to serve African Americans. If they did so, they left no record of it. When NCRA members sued discriminatory establishments, as did Tourgée's ardent champion Mack Caldwell, they acted as individuals, not as representatives of either the national association or its chapters.[96] Tourgée himself never provided guidelines on how to apply the lessons on citizenship his followers might glean from his writings.

Even the manifesto that presents the fullest statement of the NCRA's principles, *Is Liberty Worth Preserving?*, devotes twenty-five out of twenty-nine pages to detailing the formidable threats to liberty the nation faced—Southern states' "wholesale nullification" of African Americans' constitutional rights, the consequent subjection of black laborers to "starvation wages" and of all blacks to murder or lynching if they dared to resist, the disproportionate representation Southern whites acquired in Congress by disfranchising African Americans while counting them in their total population base—and only four pages to sketching the NCRA's proposed methods of tackling these threats. Indeed, Tourgée admitted that the NCRA had "no specific remedy for the evils it desire[d] to ameliorate." It sought simply to maximize its membership, and thus its leverage on public opinion; to procure and publish "reliable information" on "political and economic conditions at the South," as "regarded from the standpoint of those who suffer injustice"; to challenge discriminatory state laws in federal court, especially Louisiana's Separate Car Act and Mississippi's constitution disfranchising African Americans; and to "urge by every means in its power, the enactment . . . of National legislation" enforcing equal citizenship rights throughout the country.[97]

Tourgée's Vision of the NCRA

Though unwilling to outline a concrete plan of action, a constitution, or a structure for the organization, Tourgée did articulate a remarkably modern twofold vision of the NCRA that we can recognize as anticipating both the civil rights movement of the 1960s and the twenty-first century's e-mail lists. At times, he characterized the NCRA as a mass mobilization "applying the moral force" of "millions" of committed participants to individuals, parties, elected officials, society at large, and "the world." "Put 2.000.000.

Northern freemen in front of Southern prejudice demanding justice and a million colored men *who know they have friends* behind it, and the South will listen to reason very quickly," he told Mossell. Of course, Tourgée was wildly optimistic in claiming that the "Negro Problem [could] be settled" almost overnight by an army of peaceful citizens numbering "as many as it required soldiers to put down the [Confederate] rebellion." Still, he dimly foresaw the collapse of Southern segregation, albeit seven decades later, under the onslaught of black and white protesters relying on marches, sit-ins, boycotts, and civil disobedience in lieu of weapons.[98]

Tourgée's own métier lay not in the tactics of mass mobilization but rather in writing and political lobbying. Hence, he more often envisaged the NCRA as a precursor of today's social media pressure groups. The mere existence of a roster of people committed to equal citizenship rights for all, he asserted, would serve as a "potent force" for shaping national policy through the Republican Party. If Republican leaders and "weak-kneed members of Congress" knew that he could "reach by mail tomorrow and every day 100.000 or 200.000 or more voters all of whom [were] more or less in accord with the sentiments [he] advocate[d]," they would realize that they could not afford to alienate such a sizable block of adherents.[99] This was the vision Tourgée held out to the countless NCRA members who pressed him to supply them with clearer goals and strategies.

This was also the vision that prompted him to attend the June 1892 Republican national nominating convention, with the aim of brandishing the NCRA membership list to show that the association held "the balance of power in seven northern states."[100] Such a demonstration of electoral strength, he hoped, would earn the NCRA a role in selecting the party's presidential candidate and framing its platform. NCRA members supported House Speaker Thomas B. Reed of Maine, a consistent defender of African American rights, but the convention renominated President Benjamin Harrison, who had not only angered African Americans by declaring himself helpless to act against lynching but was secretly conspiring with other Republican power brokers to redefine theirs as a "White Man's Party," according to rumors Tourgée had heard.[101] To the dismay of African American NCRA members, one of whom had written to the convention's black delegates exhorting them to convey "the feeling of our people" that they would bolt the party if it continued to flout their concerns, even some of these delegates had voted for Harrison.[102] Adding insult to injury, the convention approved a platform that unmistakably announced the party's fealty to big business and its indifference to racial justice. Nine planks upheld the main

Republican priorities: protecting manufactures through tariffs, expanding trade and commerce, and maintaining the value of "standard money." In contrast, only two affirmed the principle of a "free and unrestricted ballot in all public elections" and denounced the "inhuman outrages perpetrated upon American citizens for political reasons in certain Southern States of the Union"—statements carefully formulated to dodge the divisive "race question" and avoid mention of legal remedies. Moreover, all but two white Republican newspapers refused to print the NCRA's "respectful protest to the convention"—a snub the *Inter Ocean's* publisher compounded by accusing Tourgée of having "become soured at everybody except the members" of the NCRA.[103]

The negligible outcome of Tourgée's lobbying at the 1892 convention bitterly disappointed his followers. Replying to one complainant, he insisted that had he not pushed so hard, "no allusion to a free ballot or outrages on citizenship would have been found in the platform at all,"[104] but he knew very well how little such a plea would satisfy NCRA members. Even Martinet had concluded, "The Republican party will continue to act its cowardly part as long as the people of the North are not aroused to the emergencies of the situation," which he argued "ought to be the chief work of the association for the present."[105] Many other NCRA members had tried to persuade Tourgée to emulate the abolitionists who had founded the Liberty Party in 1840, which by 1854 had evolved from a fringe group into the Republican Party.[106] At least one, the Chicago lawyer George R. Gaines, had floated the idea of encouraging his fellow African Americans to form a party of their own, so that Republicans could no longer take the black vote for granted. A white correspondent had also suggested exploring the merits of teaming up with the Farmers' Alliance, or Populist Party, which was gathering strength in the South and West. Tourgée balked at all these proposals. Aware that the Liberty Party and its Free Soil successor had siphoned off antislavery voters, thereby helping to elect rabidly proslavery Democrats several times before the Republicans' first victory in 1860, Tourgée did not relish the prospect of repeating the cycle. Nor did he think the country could afford to wait so long to do justice to African Americans, for he feared a massive uprising. He never dreamed that almost three quarters of a century would elapse before the U.S. Congress passed a voting rights act like the one for which he had been agitating.

Tourgée reacted even less sympathetically to the alternatives of black political separatism or partnership with the Populists. "Any distinctively *colored* political movement will alienate every white friend of equal rights and protected citizenship in the country" and will "generally be regarded as a blackmailing, selling out movement," he warned Gaines, reminding him that "it is to the conscience, the humanity and the patriotism of the *Northern white voter alone,* that the colored citizen can look for justice." Instead of inciting the Republican Party to guarantee the exercise of equal rights, a mass defection by African Americans might have the "contrary effect" of strengthening the faction calling for "the repeal of the 14th and 15th Amendments" and "the disfranchisement of the colored man" throughout the nation. "You must remember that the power to defeat a party does not imply the power to control its subsequent action," Tourgée added. He did, however, endorse another tactic Gaines was considering—interrogating candidates and voting only for those who pledged "in writing to support the proper legislation" (a classic abolitionist tactic)—as long as it was carried out by "*citizens without regard to color*" and was done "without clamor" to avoid backfiring against progressive candidates. If Gaines went ahead with the African American mass meeting he had called, Tourgée advised, the most expedient course would be for the participants to ask the NCRA to "hold a council" for the purpose of ascertaining members' "general sentiments" on how best to achieve the association's goals under current conditions.[107]

As for the Populists, Tourgée gave them short shrift. Though he "quite agree[d]" with several items on their platform, he had "no hope of any good" from their party, because he had seen its Southern members in action during his long sojourn in North Carolina and knew them to be "the worst enemies labor ever had," especially black labor. At best, the Populists could "encourage free speech and independence of thought among the Southern whites" and perhaps "lessen Southern intolerance." Competition from the Populists might also "spur the Republican party up to its duty"; nonetheless, progressive Republicans could better accomplish this by working within the party than by deserting it.[108]

Tourgée gave cogent reasons for opposing the various third party initiatives his followers were calling for, but in truth, his loyalty to the Republican Party did not allow him to contemplate breaking with it. He had joined it to campaign for John C. Frémont in 1856, he had fought for it during Reconstruction, and to him, it would always be the party that had abolished slavery and amended the Constitution to mandate equal citizenship rights. Furthermore, he depended on the party for his livelihood. As a columnist for the solidly Republican *Inter Ocean,* he could chastise the party (within limits) for policies he deemed self-defeating, but he could not abandon it for a rival without forfeiting any possibility of ever again writing for a Republican publication. Over the years, Tourgée had also applied for a number of patronage positions—so far unsuccessfully—and he did not want to close the door to such an opportunity to escape from his increasingly precarious financial circumstances. Thus, he remained within the fold and counseled NCRA members to vote for Harrison as the lesser of the two evils.

The NCRA's Accomplishments

Though the NCRA proved ineffectual as a vehicle for influencing electoral politics, Tourgée did not limit it to this purpose. As president of the association and spokesman of its 250,000 members, he addressed letters to key opinion makers and religious bodies, in which he refuted racist ideology and demanded justice for African Americans. For example, when press dispatches summarized a lecture by Cornell University professor of political economy Jeremiah W. Jenks, alleging that "history and science" revealed the Negro to be "of an inferior race and incapable of advanced civilization," Tourgée fired off an immediate response on NCRA stationery. "I know of no scientific formula by which superiority and inferiority may be determined," he asserted, pointing out that science had previously justified slavery and was now justifying white supremacy. Tourgée vigorously contested the Southern-derived myths about black misrule during Reconstruction that Jenks cited as his main proof of the race's inferiority. "Does financial mismanagement of public affairs imply racial inferiority?" asked Tourgée. "If so what shall be said of the people of New York who during those very years lost more by Tweed and Tammany than any Southern State by 'Negro' government." He flatly denied that the so-called Negro governments, in most of which African Americans were in the minority, ever "passed 'shameful and oppressive laws against the whites'"—unless Jenks, like Southern whites, considered "the grant of equal privileges to colored citizens to be 'shameful' and the taxation 'oppressive.'" Unlike the white governments both before and after Reconstruction, Tourgée emphasized, African Americans had never passed a "scrap of legislation" discriminating against another racial group, nor had they "deprived" anyone of "life, liberty or property through oppressive laws or oppressive conduct of public officials." He went on to list examples of "beneficent legislation" by Reconstruction governments: the "establishment of free public schools," hitherto unknown in the South; "the abolition of whipping, branding, clipping, maiming and other barbarous forms of punishment"; "the reduction of the number of capital crimes from *SEVENTEEN* to two or three"; and "the abolition of property-qualifications" for voters, officeholders, and jurors. Jenks had damaged the "repute of a great university" by teaching bad history and bad science, Tourgée charged. He ended with the hope that those who formed the minds of students might learn to recognize "justice, equal right and equal opportunity for all the children of our common Father" as higher truths than "the survival of the fittest."[109]

Tourgée also replied in the name of the NCRA to the manager of the *Atlanta Times*, who based his allegations of African American inferiority on the race's current condition and who lamented that Southern states could do nothing to change it. "The colored man has little responsibility for his present condition," countered Tourgée, reminding the Georgia newspaperman that the master class, the church, and the nation had all failed to educate and equip the slaves for citizenship and that "the colored man is not equal before the law with the white man of Georgia, because the law is not enforced to secure his rights or redress his wrongs." Despite these disadvantages, he noted, African Americans had progressed more since the Civil War than had poor whites in "intelligence, enterprise and accumulation" of property. They were now "awakening to a sense of [their] wrongs," which would make them "desperate" if not redressed. "The only remedy for injustice is *justice*," stressed Tourgée, "and the people who will not grant it must suffer for their own neglect."[110]

The most fruitful of the letters Tourgée wrote as NCRA president was the one he addressed to the Methodist Episcopal General Conference meeting in Omaha in May 1892, to which he gave special prominence by publishing it in his "Bystander" column. It opened by alerting the church to the upcoming day of "fasting and prayer" African Americans had set aside (at Tourgée's suggestion) "for the deliverance of their race from the oppression and injustice which they experience at the hands of the white Christians of the great Republic." Would the bishops of the church take time out from their proceedings to join with African Americans in this fast and prayer?, Tourgée asked. Were the "white Christians of America willing to indorse the petitions of our colored fellow Christians for justice"—not for mercy? Shifting from "they" to "we" and speaking as a long-standing member of the Methodist Episcopal Church, Tourgée underscored, "There is no middle ground. We must either join in the prayer for justice or pray for the continuance of injustice. To be silent is to ask God to perpetuate wrong and prosper oppression."[111] In what many contemporaries hailed as a triumph for both Tourgée and the NCRA, the Methodist Episcopal General Conference unanimously "approved a strong resolution denouncing prejudice and segregation and calling for remedial action by churches, the press, and all levels of government."[112] At the request of Charlotte Forten Grimké, Tourgée addressed a similar letter to the Presbyterian General Assembly, her own denomination, which approved a weaker resolution.[113]

Tourgée's Vision of an NCRA Organ

These achievements notwithstanding, Tourgée faced an impasse at the end of the NCRA's first year. Not only did the organization fail to stem the Republican Party's rightward march, but the election of November 1892 resulted in a Democratic victory. Meanwhile, Tourgée had been coming under increasing pressure from the *Inter Ocean*'s editors and stockholders to cease promoting the NCRA in "A Bystander's Notes" and to bring the column in line with the party's dominant ideology. As a result, he began to pursue an alternative avenue for advancing the organization's aims: founding a journal that would serve as the NCRA's organ, just as the *National Anti-Slavery Standard* had served as the organ of the American Anti-Slavery Society. Martinet had in fact advocated such a publication in his earliest extant letter to Tourgée. A newspaper whose "own trusty correspondents" provided firsthand reports "gathered all over the South" would furnish a "powerful lever in educating the North" about the oppressiveness of Jim Crow and thereby inspire "remedial national legislation," argued Martinet. To maximize its impact, he recommended, such a newspaper should be "under the auspices of men of national reputation" and should observe "no color line" but include "colored men as editors."[114] Tourgée had "carefully considered," but not acted on, Martinet's suggestion at the time, because he wanted to wait until the need for an NCRA organ became "undeniable and the way open for carrying it into effect."[115] That moment arrived in August 1893, when the *Inter Ocean* suspended his "Bystander" column on the plea of financial exigency. In what proved to be his next-to-last column for nine months, Tourgée quoted a correspondent he described as voicing a widespread sentiment: "The war for justice is on and it can no more be shirked than could the war for liberty. We need . . . an official organ that shall express our views and put the cause of the rights of the citizen clearly before the people of the country."[116] Martinet immediately reminded Tourgée that he had "often" reiterated the urgency of issuing an NCRA organ.[117] Indeed, in a letter written in July 1892, he had spelled out what ought to be its mission— not merely "giving lessons in the duties of the citizen" but "expos[ing] continually to the people of the North the hideous sores of the South & the ever-recurring outrages to which we are subjected."[118]

Impelled by the loss of the imperfect vehicle the *Inter Ocean* had furnished and excited by prospects that enough NCRA members would subscribe to a periodical of their own to make it self-supporting, Tourgée threw himself into the project with enthusiasm. He had already settled on a title for the journal—the *National Citizen*—when Martinet first broached the subject. Now he embraced a movement organ as the best solution to the problem with which he had wrestled when he had decided against holding a convention, lest the NCRA fall prey to racial strife. Elaborating on the vision his friend had originally held out to him, he wrote Martinet, "We must have a *great journal* which shall voice the needs of your people, the duty of mine and the obligations and interests of both with authority. It must be great enough to be heard by all the world and strong enough to defy clamor and party. Such a journal should be in the control of both white and colored men, in order that it may speak with confidence to and for both races and illustrate the truths it advocates." The journal he proposed to create, Tourgée specified, would fill a niche that neither the mainstream media nor the black press had so far managed to fill—the former because white-run newspapers and wire services either ignored atrocities against African Americans or covered them in biased and stereotyped ways, the latter because black newspapers rarely if ever entered white homes. Due to this lacuna, the Northern white public "had to take the testimony of [crossed out: your] the oppressors in relation to the oppressed." Mindful of Martinet's able editorship of the *Crusader*, Tourgée tactfully explained why no black newspaper could accomplish the purpose he thought the *National Citizen* could: "The mere race-journal, however well-conducted, desirable and brave it may be, is *necessarily restricted* in its influence and circulation by the fact that it is a race-journal." Yet rather than compete with or eliminate the need for race journals, Tourgée hastened to add, an "organ of human rights" under biracial editorship would "greatly enlarge the circulation and enhance the influence of the colored press" by attracting readers who would not normally subscribe to a race journal and by reprinting articles from black newspapers and thus "sending [their] utterances into white homes they [could] never reach otherwise."[119]

Tourgée wanted the *National Citizen* to model the ideal of racial integration at every level—its joint white-black editorship, its juxtaposition of black- and white-authored articles, and its financial ownership—so that it would serve as "a practical exponent" of the views the NCRA promulgated. By "accustoming the people to the idea of white and colored working together on the most advanced plane of human action," Tourgée believed, a high-quality integrated journal would counteract racial prejudice and promote racial equality far more efficaciously than any open attempt to challenge deeply rooted habits of white entitlement and black resentment that led both peoples toward separatism.[120]

For associate editor, Tourgée wooed Charles Chesnutt, whom he had hailed in a "Bystander" column of 8 April 1893 as the most distinguished African American writer to appear on the literary scene. Chesnutt had as yet published only a half dozen stories in the *Atlantic Monthly* and other periodicals—"The Goophered Grapevine," "Po' Sandy" (1888), "The Sheriff's Children," "The Conjurer's Revenge," "Dave's Neckliss," and "A Deep Sleeper" (1893)—and he was then concentrating on his legal stenography business in the hope of accumulating enough money to support a full-time literary career. Chesnutt responded with cautious interest. "I am free to say that I should like" the position of associate editor, he wrote. "I have always looked forward to the literary life, although not specially in the direction of journalism." He set several conditions for accepting the offer, however. First, he wanted Tourgée's assurances that the two would share responsibilities on an equal footing. "I certainly would not care to be a mere figurehead in such an enterprise, even for the honor of having my name coupled with such a distinguished one as your own," he stipulated. Second, he would not be ready to undertake the job for the next eight months, being in the midst of his busiest season. Third, he could invest at most $500 in the journal, payable in several installments—far short of the $2,500 Tourgée was seeking from a partner who could contribute part of the capital needed to start the journal. Chesnutt also expressed reservations about whether the *National Citizen* could succeed. While he "recognize[d] the need of such a journal," in common with "colored people who think at all," he "would doubt the existence" of sufficient demand among white readers to sustain it, "were it not for the large roll of the Citizens' Rights Association." If Tourgée thought it useful, Chesnutt volunteered, they could discuss the matter in person at Tourgée's home in Mayville, New York, an easy train ride from Chesnutt's home in Cleveland.[121]

"I should be glad to have you come down [Saturday, as Chesnutt proposed] and stay over Sunday with me," Tourgée replied. They could "talk business" on Saturday evening, because Tourgée never did so on the Sabbath, "no matter how pressing" the imperative, and Chesnutt could read through "some thousands of letters" from NCRA members that might resolve his doubts about whether the *National Citizen* would find a large enough white audience. Meanwhile, Tourgée addressed Chesnutt's concerns at length.

He gave a number of reasons for his confidence that the venture *could* succeed: his "own power to command and hold the attention of the public"; the new African American consensus that the only hope of abolishing racial oppression lay in educating and mobilizing sympathetic whites; and "the wide spread alarm" that "the best classes of white people" were already feeling about the South's addiction to disfranchisement, lynching, and mob violence. Tourgée then unveiled his plans for financing the journal. He hoped to form a joint stock company in which African Americans would take half the promoter's stock, "1,000 shares of $5. each for $25,000," and he wanted to be able to announce, both to the upcoming "colored convention" in Cincinnati and to white NCRA members, that African Americans "were the first" to provide capital toward launching the *National Citizen*. Whether the number of African American stockholders amounted to "one or two, or ten or twenty or a hundred," was immaterial, as long as the investment was "made reasonably secure." The directorate of the company would reflect African Americans' approximate share of the investment, with three out of seven directorships going to them. Tourgée was asking Chesnutt to help round up African American investors, with the option of becoming associate editor once he accomplished this task. For the first year, he need only "write something every now and then to let the readers get acquainted with him." After that the job would "require his whole time."[122]

Chesnutt apparently never made the trip to Mayville. He remained skeptical that the *National Citizen* would find as large a white audience as Tourgée believed. "While you have infinitely better opportunities for feeling the public pulse than I have," Chesnutt countered, his own daily business contacts with "the best white people of one of the most advanced communities" in the North left him much less optimistic. Whenever he brought up the "wrongs of the Negro," Chesnutt noted, his white acquaintances "dismissed" the subject "as quickly as politeness [would] permit. They admit that the present situation is all wrong, but they do not regard it as their personal concern, and do not see how they can remedy it." Chesnutt worried, moreover, that a journal "devoted entirely to a discussion of one topic, so to speak, even so important a one as citizenship, would have a tendency to repel the average white man rather than attract him." Chesnutt conceded that Tourgée "could make such a venture successful, if any one could," but he clearly did not think anyone could—and the future would prove him right. Aside from the racial politics involved, Chesnutt deemed a "newspaper venture, even under the most favorable auspices," to be "always a speculation." Though "willing to risk something" in a worthy cause, he "would regard it as a risk and would prefer to confine [his] investment to what [he] could afford to lose." He was currently too busy to commit himself to raising $2,500, "especially in view of the present 'hard times,'" but he promised to write to two wealthy friends who were "constant reader[s] and admirer[s]" of Tourgée's articles and could probably be "induced to subscribe for stock" if Tourgée contacted them. Chesnutt ended by expressing his regret that he could not "immediately and fully accept" Tourgée's "very flattering offer . . . for I consider it a great honor to be asked to co-operate with you so closely" and by pledging to do everything he could to help Tourgée "without assuming any burdensome responsibility."[123]

Chesnutt's reference to "hard times" points to a major obstacle Tourgée faced as he tried to line up investors in the *National Citizen*. The Panic of 1893, which had begun in May, was in full swing at the very time he decided to go ahead with plans for founding the journal. In fact, it had played a role in the *Inter Ocean*'s suspension of Tourgée's "Bystander" column in August. The economic crisis almost guaranteed that Tourgée would not be able to secure sufficient capital to build the *National Citizen* on a firm foundation. The case of F. J. Loudin, one of the two men Chesnutt had recommended that Tourgée contact, vividly illustrates the impact of the panic. As manager of the Fisk Jubilee Singers and proprietor of a shoe manufactory, Loudin had amassed a small fortune, but he lost $50,000 in bank failures and tens of thousands more through the bankruptcies of his customers and of other firms in which he owned stock. Now he could barely keep his head above water. Thus, though he "ardently desire[d]" to invest $500 to $1,000 in the *National Citizen*, which met with his "hearty approval" and was just the sort of endeavor he had "longed to see," he could no longer afford to. At best, he could subscribe to the journal himself and distribute circulars advertising it at Fisk Jubilee Singers' concerts outside of the South.[124]

Two weeks before Tourgée heard from Loudin and in the midst of his fruitless courtship of Chesnutt, he received an astounding proposal from T. Thomas Fortune that might have solved the problem of financing the *National Citizen*, had he been willing to consider it. By now, Tourgée had completely reversed his previous low opinion of Fortune. Accordingly, he had apprised Fortune of his plans for the *National Citizen* and appealed to him, too, for help in mobilizing enough African American investors to make the journal truly a joint racial enterprise. "I am anxious to unite the forces of liberty—*not have them dissipated*," Tourgée explained in his long letter to Fortune. Only a journal "recognized as an authoritative exponent and advocate" of both races, he insisted, could convince the nation that unless its black citizens' rights were guaranteed, neither its democracy nor its Christian civilization would survive.[125]

Fortune responded the same day. Unlike Chesnutt, he thought the *National Citizen* "ought to succeed," as long as the "literary and business management" were "in the control of not more than three persons, every one of whom" was "thoroughly experienced in newspaper management." To help the journal get off the ground, Fortune suggested, "it would be good business policy to absorb an established newspaper." He offered Tourgée the *New York Age*. Its advantages included location in New York, "the publication field of the newspaper"; "a plant capable of sending out an eight page paper," the size Tourgée contemplated for the *National Citizen*; "a standing of thirteen years' continuous publication," during which it had won "the confidence of the colored people and the respect of the leading editors of the country"; a subscription list of 5,000, which the "addition of [Tourgée's] prestige and influence would undoubtedly double . . . within a reasonable time"; "a fair advertising constituency"; and Fortune's own expertise as editor of the nation's top-ranking African American newspaper, which made him an ideal candidate for associate editor of the *National Citizen* (though he modestly refrained from spelling this out). If Tourgée agreed, Fortune would "devote [his] best efforts to placing the $5,000 of stock . . . apportioned as the share of Afro-Americans."[126]

Tourgée turned Fortune down the same day he wrote to Chesnutt asking for an "immediate" reply to the tender of the associate editorship, which Chesnutt had so far been sitting on. Why Tourgée preferred an emerging fiction writer to a seasoned newspaper editor at first seems mysterious, but his answer to Fortune sheds some light on his reasons. The *National Citizen* would "not be a *news*paper in any sense except with regard to events bearing on" equal rights and racial justice, Tourgée indicated. Instead, he seems to have conceived of it as a cross between a literary magazine and a vehicle of political advocacy. The model he had in mind, he intimated, was Gamaliel Bailey's *National Era*, the antislavery weekly that had serialized Harriet Beecher Stowe's *Uncle Tom's Cabin* and was widely praised as the most literarily distinguished abolitionist organ, thanks to its associate editor, the poet John Greenleaf Whittier. Tourgée's ambition was to make the *National Citizen* be to the present struggle "what the old '*National Era*' was to the conflict for liberty—a journal so strongly edited as to command not only the respect but the attention both of those opposed and those indifferent."[127] "It must be of the highest literary tone and quality," he specified. "It must be wise as well as firm in its treatment of [racial] prejudice which however deplorable is still a fact and like all prejudice must be overcome by patience and example quite as much as by argument."[128]

In view of this description, Tourgée's choice of Chesnutt makes perfect sense. Chesnutt's stories appealed to a broad spectrum of white readers, as their publication in such journals as the *Atlantic Monthly* and the praise they received from such bellwethers of the literary establishment as William Dean Howells attested. Their light touch and deft use of humor and pathos undermined readers' prejudices rather than openly attacked them. Indeed, Chesnutt had deliberately adopted this strategy, as he had confided to his journal long before publishing his first story:

> The object of my writings would be not so much the elevation of the colored people as the elevation of the whites,—for I consider the unjust spirit of caste which is so insidious as to pervade a whole nation, and so powerful as to subject a whole race and all connected with it to scorn and social ostracism—I consider this a barrier to the moral progress of the American people. . . . But the subtle almost indefinable feeling of repulsion toward the negro, which is common to most Americans—and easily enough accounted for—, cannot be stormed and taken by assault; the garrison will not capitulate: so their position must be mined, and we will find ourselves in their midst before they think it.[129]

Tourgée, of course, did not have access to the ruminations in Chesnutt's journal that tallied so closely with his own designs for the *National Citizen*, but as a fellow fiction writer motivated by very similar aims, he surely recognized the thrust of the stories in which Chesnutt "mined" the "garrison" of white prejudice.

In contrast to Chesnutt, Fortune practiced a militant, hard-hitting style of journalism much like that of Tourgée's "Bystander" column. The two would have reinforced, not complemented, each other, and Tourgée may have feared that Fortune's strident tone would alienate the white readers who needed to be won over. The reason he gave Fortune for refusing a merger with the *Age*, however, was that he did not want the *National Citizen* to be perceived as a "race journal" because that would "defeat its . . . purpose" and end up "spoiling both" papers. "*THE AGE* has its own field," Tourgée elaborated. As a race journal, it performed the vital function of defending African Americans against the relentless defamation of a hostile white society by fostering collective resistance and affirming pride in their cultural identity. He saw the mission of the African American press as different from the one he envisaged for the *National Citizen*. The race journal must promote race unity and plead for African Americans "as a distinct class." The *National Citizen*, on the other hand, "must be a journal of equal citizenship without regard to color."[130]

Both Tourgée and Fortune felt it would be worthwhile to continue their discussion in person. Fortune, who had "become dissatisfied with race journalism" precisely because it could not reach a white audience, hoped to convince Tourgée that a merger with the *Age* would benefit the *National Citizen*. "We so fully agree upon so many points," he urged, that "a good talk over the matter" would bring them to an understanding. Tourgée hoped to retain Fortune's support for his project and thought that if Fortune could come to Mayville, each would quickly "get a just comprehension of the other's notions."[131] But Fortune could not make time for the visit before Tourgée left for a lecture tour of the Midwest, and they went their separate ways.

Turning down Fortune's offer proved to be a colossal mistake. It cost Tourgée the only chance he ever received to enter into partnership with an African American as coeditor and investor, and ultimately it doomed the enterprise of endowing the NCRA with a genuinely biracial organ through which to make the case for equal citizenship to the American people. As Tourgée's first major biographer, Otto H. Olsen, concludes, "By his decision Tourgée surrendered a substantial basis for operation and a rare opportunity to secure support in the vital Northeast, where his influence was weak."[132] Tourgée's most recent biographer, Mark Elliott, concurs: "It might have been wiser to exchange his vague hope of capturing the moderate white audience for uniting Northern black leadership behind the NCRA."[133]

Why did Tourgée throw away the extraordinary opportunity Fortune held out to him? As persuasive as his explanations for doing so may sound, unconscious motives may also have impelled him. Did his commitment to forging an abolitionist-style interracial movement (by definition white-dominated) prevent him from realizing that he faced a trade-off between courting moderate whites and gaining a solid base in the Northern black community? Did he fear that he would lose caste and forfeit his influence over whites if he aligned himself with a controversial black editor? Did he simply feel less confident of being able to work harmoniously with the truculent Fortune than he would have with the younger Chesnutt, whom he may have perceived as more amenable to guidance? We can only speculate about the causes of Tourgée's wrongheaded decision, but we know that it speeded the demise of the NCRA. That said, even at its height, the NCRA had failed to halt the Republican Party's drift away from its Reconstruction-era ideals. Given this stubborn fact, it is hard to believe that any journal, no matter how

well edited, well financed, widely read, or broadly based in a biracial constituency, could have influenced the Supreme Court. Nor is it at all clear that
absorbing the *New York Age* into the *National Citizen* with Fortune as associate editor would either have put the journal on a secure financial footing
or brought an influx of black Northerners into the NCRA; after all, Fortune
was already struggling to keep the *Age* afloat, and neither the Afro-American
League nor its successor, the Afro-American Council, ever attracted a mass
following among black Northerners.[134]

Confronting Opposing Forces in the Black Community

Had Tourgée chosen the path that a partnership with Fortune would have
opened up, he would necessarily have oriented the *National Citizen* as much
toward fortifying African Americans' commitment to fighting for justice and
equality in their homeland as toward overcoming white prejudice, for by
1893 that commitment was starting to waver. As the racial climate worsened,
not only were the voices preaching accommodation growing louder, but
interest in emigration was surging.[135] With lynchings skyrocketing in number and ferocity, legalized disfranchisement spreading from one Southern
state to another, the Republican Party determined to jettison African
Americans, the Democrats back in power, the Supreme Court edging ever
closer to endorsing white supremacy, and Northern voters indifferent, even
Martinet was beginning to view emigration more favorably. When Martinet
defended it in the *Crusader* as a viable option, Tourgée argued passionately
against the illusion that emigration could release African Americans from
their desperate plight in the United States. "The American Negro will have
to make his contest for equality of right and opportunity with the Negro-
hating white man of the United States *wherever* he may be upon the planet,"
Tourgée rejoined in a letter published in the *Crusader*. Whether African
Americans took refuge in Mexico, as Martinet apparently envisaged, or in
Africa, as AME bishop Henry McNeal Turner advocated, whites would
follow them and enlist the "power and flag of the Republic [in] protecting
and supporting the white man's wrong-doing." Only by winning equality
at home could African Americans go abroad secure in the expectation that
their country's power would guard their rights, not "deliver [them] up to the
white man's rapacity." "There is no other way, my friend," Tourgée admonished Martinet: "The colored man *must work* out his deliverance here in the
United States. . . . The battle of liberty justice and equal opportunity must
be fought out *here*. The colored man and those white men who believe in

liberty and justice—who do not think Christ's teachings a sham—must join hands and hearts and win with brain and patience and wisdom and courage."[136] It was in the same letter that Tourgée held out the *National Citizen* as the means of unifying African Americans and progressive whites in a victorious battle for freedom and equality in the United States—the alternative to emigration.

If Tourgée aspired to persuade African Americans to join forces with him rather than prepare for emigration, no one would be more important to win over than Bishop Turner. Accordingly, Tourgée had written Turner on 30 October to propose that they collaborate with each other. "Heartily" commending Turner's outraged denunciation of *The Barbarous Decision of the Supreme Court Declaring the Civil Rights Act Unconstitutional* (1893), Tourgée emphasized that he and Turner agreed on many more points than they disagreed on. They parted company mainly on "means" rather than on ends: "You do not think it possible that the government and people of the United States can ever be brought to deal justly with the colored increment of our population, while I believe that they can." Hence, "you believe that the colored people of the United States ought to be" seeking a refuge from the "injustice and oppression to which they are subjected here," while "I contend that no effort . . . at all commensurate with the magnitude and importance of the task . . . has yet been made" to "wipe out the indifference and apathy of the white people of the North" by educating them *"week by week"* until they induce the nation to guarantee African Americans their constitutional rights. Tourgée then shared with Turner the same vision of the *National Citizen* articulated in his letters to Martinet, Fortune, Chesnutt, and Loudin. What support for this project could he expect from African Americans?, Tourgée queried. "I do not ask them to accept my 'leadership,' for I want none," he clarified; "but they can either double the value of my work by joining in it or take away half by witholding their confidence and support." The future of African Americans in the United States depended on whether the "forces of liberty" could act effectively together to transform white attitudes, Tourgée argued: "In that way only can the wrongs of exile, expatriation, extinction or practical re-subjection be avoided." He added, "If I believed it hopeless I would join hands with you and say 'Go, in God's name!' But I cannot think that God will permit the American people to stain the future with such shame and crime."[137]

Turner replied graciously, expressing his "exalted esteem" for Tourgée's "friendship to my race and . . . fidelity to justice" but regretting that Tourgée stood almost alone in championing African Americans. Despite his conviction that there was "no future in this country for the Negro," he pledged to "support [Tourgée] to the fullest extent." He made good his pledge by sending a list of potential subscribers to the *National Citizen*; forwarding Tourgée's letter to the AME organ the *Christian Recorder*, which had been publishing a series of articles weighing the pros and cons of emigration; and inviting Tourgée to attend and address the convention he had called in Cincinnati to debate how African Americans should meet the racial crisis that confronted them.[138] Tourgée demurred, because he considered it inappropriate for him to speak at a "colored" convention, let alone publicly "oppose the purpose for which it is called," yet he ended up exerting quite an influence on the delegates.[139] His letter to Turner appeared in both the *Christian Recorder* and the *New York Age*, generating much favorable comment. The AME ministers who managed the *Recorder* gave it their "unanimous" endorsement and promised to "do all in [their] power to sustain" the *National Citizen*, and Fortune greeted the letter as an "inspiring bugle note."[140] The letter was also read aloud to the convention on the second day and was "received with great enthusiasm," reported one delegate, who judged it "the best paper" he had ever heard and praised it for "pricking . . . the African Colonization bubble." He confided as well that Bishop Turner "felt the force of [Tourgée's] anti-emigration arguments" so strongly that he requested the delegates not to "discuss the paper," although he "spoke in the highest terms" of Tourgée's "indefatigable efforts in behalf of the race." This delegate, who edited a Methodist journal with a circulation of 20,000, titled the *Christian Educator*, enrolled in the NCRA and volunteered to "help in arousing public sentiment."[141]

All in all, Tourgée had so far found gratifying support among African Americans for his enterprise, but when he returned from his lecture tour, he had not yet lined up either substantial investors or an associate editor. Without African American business partners, he could not fulfill his vision of the *National Citizen*.

A Compromise with Emma

At home Tourgée confronted an equally serious threat to his project. Emma, who had been handling his vast NCRA correspondence since 1891, as well as his communications with editors, publishers, and lecture bureaus, and who had been managing the couple's finances to boot, no longer approved of his work. Tourgée should be concentrating on earning enough money to keep his family solvent, she felt, not "wasting" so much of his time on activities that brought in no revenue. For months, she had been recording in her diary her mental "distress" at the diminution in Tourgée's royalties, his dispute with William Penn Nixon, the suspension of the "Bystander" column that provided his only reliable income, and her unavailing endeavors to bring her husband around to her point of view. Emma adamantly opposed Tourgée's starting the *National Citizen*, "seeing nothing but disaster in the scheme if he attempts it alone." She had good grounds for her premonitions, having lived through the debacle of his previous effort to run a magazine without adequate financial backing—the ill-fated *Our Continent*—whose bankruptcy had burdened him with more than $100,000 of debt that he was still straining to pay off. As she lamented in her diary, however, Tourgée would "listen to no reason or persuasion on [her] part," leaving her with little choice but to copy and send out circulars advertising the *National Citizen*.[142] She could hardly have been reassured by Chesnutt's warning that "a newspaper venture, even under the most favorable auspices, is always a speculation." The opinion of the *Inter Ocean*'s managing editor, William H. Busbey, must have strengthened her doubts. "It is a bad time to start any new venture in journalism," he wrote, and he would counsel Tourgée against doing so unless guaranteed "the necessary capital" and a "good salary" as editor.[143]

In April 1894 Emma at last got her way, "much to [her] gratification." After suffering a serious illness, Tourgée agreed to return all the subscriptions to *National Citizen* stock that he had received to date and to defer publishing the journal—a deferral he extended indefinitely several months later.[144] The resumption of the "Bystander" column in May helped soften the blow but did not resolve the need Tourgée saw for an NCRA organ.

Unwilling to renounce his dream completely, Tourgée eventually settled on a "compromise" with Emma by founding a journal that operated on a shoestring budget and thus avoided driving him further into debt.[145] Sad to say, *The Basis: A Journal of Citizenship*, which debuted on 20 March 1895 and lasted until April 1896, proved no substitute for the *National Citizen* and achieved almost none of the aims Tourgée had described so eloquently to his African American correspondents. The small group of investors who laid out the $4,000 needed to start the journal included no African Americans, nor did the editorial staff. Tourgée wrote most of each thirty-two-page number himself. Supplementing his editorial matter and pseudonymous fiction, his daughter, Aimée, furnished a column titled "In a Lighter Vein"; the popular white writer Ada C. Sweet, an associate of Jane Addams's in Chicago, took charge of the "Our Women Citizens" column; and the white minister Thomas Slicer, one of the investors, contributed a weekly lesson on citizenship. Issued from Buffalo by an obscure publisher, McGerald & Son, the *Basis* could never have reached a national audience; in fact, although such loyal African American supporters as Martinet, the brothers Thomas and Charles Griffin, William H. Anderson, Ida B. Wells, Harry C. Smith, and Charles W. Chesnutt went out of their way to promote the journal, its subscription list barely reached 1,200, below the level of most antebellum abolitionist organs and of many current African American newspapers. As a result, the *Basis* could not have significantly increased the white public's exposure to race journalism. Even more disappointingly, little or nothing came of the prizes the *Basis* offered for "sketches and stories by colored writers" illustrating the "common life of the colored people," perhaps because eligibility to compete depended on procuring "five yearly subscribers to THE BASIS."[146]

Despite these shortcomings, the *Basis* offered much of value. Its prime attraction, of course, was Tourgée's "Bystander" column, which remained as incisive as ever. In addition, it featured a monthly "Mob Record," tabulating by race and sex the people hanged, shot to death, burned, beaten, raped, or threatened by mobs and listing their names and the locales when available. It also printed extracts from African American newspapers and communications from African American correspondents—among them one who suggested that "while you are giving the depressing facts concerning lynching and wrongs, past and present endured, give us also some facts concerning the progress of the colored race so as to give them a new inspiration to work for a better tomorrow."[147] Finally, the *Basis* not only provided extensive coverage of race matters but also highlighted aspects of them rarely treated with sensitivity in the white press, such as the struggle over the "color question" in the women's club movement; the demeaning use of the term "negresses" to "sneer at" the "conference of colored women's clubs" that represented a milestone for the race; the racial segregation practiced by white churches, which Tourgée advised African Americans to combat by periodically attending them; and the refusal of hotels in Boston and Connecticut to lodge visiting African American dignitaries—hotels that deserved to be "blacklisted in every religious paper in the United States," Tourgée proclaimed.[148]

Tourgée had founded the NCRA and its organ the *Basis* with one overriding goal: to arouse public sentiment against Jim Crow while the Supreme Court was considering the *Plessy v. Ferguson* case. During the five years since he had called on "Bystander" readers to show their solidarity with the New Orleans citizens who were challenging the Jim Crow car, racial attitudes had hardened rather than softened, however. Meanwhile, far from building into a countermovement powerful enough to sway both "the people" and their judicial arbiters, the NCRA had petered out as an activist organization, and the intended trumpet blast of the *National Citizen* had devolved into the impotent squeak of the *Basis*.

Clearly, Tourgée lacked two of the main requisites for realizing the potential of the NCRA: organizing skills and access to capital. He was a visionary, not a grassroots mobilizer or fund-raiser, and conditions may not yet have been ripe for the broad interracial alliance he envisioned.[149] Only in 1909—eighteen years after the founding of the NCRA, thirteen years after the *Plessy* verdict, and four years after Tourgée's death—would African American and white reformers jointly establish an effective, well-funded, and lasting association dedicated to achieving racial justice and equality: the NAACP. Its organ, the *Crisis*, would boast an African American as chief, not associate, editor: W. E. B. Du Bois. Nevertheless, its inaugural convention would not escape the racial conflicts Tourgée had tried to duck by not letting the NCRA hold a convention.[150] Like the NCRA, moreover, the NAACP would fail ever to win passage of a national antilynching law. And another forty-five years would elapse before it at last achieved the objective that eluded Tourgée and the NCRA—a Supreme Court verdict declaring segregation unconstitutional.

HAUNTING THE HISTORIES of both the NCRA and the "Bystander," the specter of lynching loomed too large for inclusion in either. Yet during the very years when Tourgée was frustrating many of the NCRA's African American members by refusing to devote the organization to fighting against lynching, he was trenchantly condemning this national crime in his "Bystander" column, even as he was contending with threats of censorship or dismissal if he defied the dictates of the *Inter Ocean*'s editors. Like the "Bystander" and the NCRA, Tourgée's campaign against lynching demanded a chapter in its own right. To that chapter we now turn.

CHAPTER FIVE

Campaigning against Lynching with Ida B. Wells and Harry C. Smith

Upon the limb of a low-branching oak not more than forty steps from the Temple of Justice, hung the lifeless body of old Jerry. The wind turned it slowly to and fro. The snowy hair and beard contrasted strangely with the dusky pallor of the peaceful face, which seemed even in death to proffer a benison to the people of God who passed to and fro from the house of prayer.

The most notorious scene in Tourgée's 1879 bestseller *A Fool's Errand*, this description of a dead body gyrating in the wind, as it dangled from a tree limb in front of the courthouse, introduced into American literature a subject no white novelist, and only one African American novelist, William Wells Brown, had dramatized before: lynching.[1] Brown's *Clotel; or, The President's Daughter: A Narrative of Slave Life in the United States* (1853) depicted the burning at stake of a fugitive from slavery who had resisted recapture by committing the "unpardonable offence" of "rais[ing] his hand against a white man." His grisly punishment served as a warning to his fellows, "nearly 4,000" of whom "were collected from the plantations in the neighbourhood to witness" it.[2] The lynching of enslaved blacks remained comparatively rare, however, given their monetary value as property.[3] Not until the Reconstruction era did mob murders of African Americans grow rampant, as white supremacists targeted black leaders who defended their people's rights or whose economic success threatened the goal of reenslaving the black masses in all but name.

Tourgée had fought in vain as a superior court judge in North Carolina to stamp out such vigilante violence and to bring the perpetrators to justice. He had actually seen the shocking sight he fictionalized in *A Fool's Errand*—the corpse of his Radical Republican colleague Wyatt Outlaw suspended from a tree a few feet from the entrance of the very courthouse in which Tourgée conducted trials in Alamance County. "Forever seared upon his memory," as he would recall in a "Bystander" column written twenty-two years after Outlaw's summary execution and thirteen years after the publication of *A Fool's Errand*, his firsthand view of a lynching victim he had personally known and admired guaranteed that Tourgée would speak out passionately against this national crime when it assumed epidemic proportions in the

1890s.[4] His familiarity with the circumstances of lynchings like Outlaw's also ensured that Tourgée would present an analysis of the phenomenon entirely at odds with the popular press's.

Although he sentimentalized Outlaw as the saintly preacher Uncle Jerry in *A Fool's Errand* (doubtless with a nod to Harriet Beecher Stowe's Uncle Tom), Tourgée by no means diminished the real-life original's political militancy. As he emphasized in the pages leading up to the lynching, "Uncle Jerry had been noted for his openly-expressed defiance of the Ku-Klux, his boldness in denouncing them, and the persistency with which he urged the colored men of his vicinity to organize, and resist the aggressions of that body. In this he had been partially successful. A considerable number of the inhabitants of the colored suburb had armed themselves, had appointed a leader and lieutenants, and agreed upon signals, on hearing which all were to rally for defense at certain designated points."[5] Tourgée explained Jerry's lynching much as he had Outlaw's, attributing it not only to his having aroused the Klan's antagonism by mobilizing the black community for resistance but also to his having identified the perpetrators of a previous Klan murder.[6] *A Fool's Errand* thus anticipated Tourgée's "Bystander" articles of the 1890s in portraying a lynching victim as a hero rather than a criminal. It also anticipated those articles in highlighting the travesty of justice and the mockery of Christianity that lynching represented. Indeed, in a "Bystander" column of 12 March 1892, Tourgée drew an explicit parallel between the fictional scene he had been "severely criticized" for "painting" in *A Fool's Errand* and a recent newspaper account of an incident that eerily reenacted it: "Two men were taken from jail at Pine Bluff, Ark., charged with murder, but stoutly denying it, and on the Sabbath day swung up in the public street, their bodies riddled with bullets, and left hanging in the soft, spring sunshine, while we are told in the press reports, 'thousands of good citizens wended their way past them to and from the regular church services!'"[7]

Notwithstanding the similarities linking the two scenes, lynching had undergone a striking metamorphosis since the turbulent era *A Fool's Errand* memorialized. During Reconstruction, lynch mobs had wreaked their violence at night, masking their faces and wrapping themselves in long robes to disguise their identities. By the 1880s, they operated openly in broad daylight, and by the 1890s, they staged their performances as increasingly sadistic mass spectacles, advertised in advance in newspapers and attended by thousands of men, women, and children, often transported by special trains. Earlier, white supremacist ideologues defended mob murders like that of

Outlaw as necessary to prevent insurrections and "Negro domination." Once the restoration of iron-fisted white supremacist rule demolished the plausibility of arguing that black rebellion constituted a serious threat, apologists invented the far more insidious claim that lynching served to protect the purity of white womanhood by punishing black rapists. Widely accepted by the white Northern press, this myth fanned the deadly flames of mob violence against African Americans, spreading the wildfires from the South to the North. Such were the challenges Tourgée confronted when he began editorializing against lynching in his "Bystander" column.

Paradoxically, his campaign against a national crime so recalcitrant that it defied all attempts to pass federal antilynching legislation won Tourgée the signal achievement of his otherwise frustrating career as a proponent of racial justice in an age of triumphant white supremacy: the adoption in 1896 by his native state, Ohio, of an antilynching law he drafted, which became a model for those in nine other states, as well as for the NAACP.[8] Tourgée waged his campaign in close collaboration with Ida B. Wells and Harry C. Smith, who led the vanguard of the African American antilynching movement, Wells through her newspaper articles, pamphlets, and speaking tours, Smith through his editorship of the *Cleveland Gazette* and his politicking in the Ohio state legislature, where he steered Tourgée's bill to passage. In partnering with Wells and Smith, Tourgée developed a new style of collaboration with African Americans. Rather than seek to impose his approach on them, as he had in his ill-fated opposition to the Blair bill, Tourgée supported their endeavors, both publicly in his "Bystander" column and in his testimony to the Ohio state legislature and privately by suggesting strategies, furnishing documentary evidence, and contributing two anonymous chapters to Wells's edited pamphlet *The Reason Why the Colored American Is Not in the World's Columbian Exposition* (1893).

Despite the prominent place that antilynching advocacy occupied in Tourgée's career, and despite the recognition his African American contemporaries accorded him for it, historians of lynching have completely overlooked his voluminous contributions to the nineteenth-century debates about mob violence, its causes, and its remedies. None of the standard histories of lynching so much as mentions Tourgée, and only one article (published in an Ohio journal) discusses his role in formulating Ohio's antilynching law.[9] Until recently, no scholar has examined either his alliance with Wells or the influence the two exerted on each other's critiques of lynching.[10] By illuminating the least-known aspect of Tourgée's life work, the present chapter fills a gaping hole in the scholarship on lynching.

FIGURE 6 Ida B. Wells in 1893–94, at the height of her campaign against lynching and her collaboration with Tourgée. Courtesy of the University of Chicago Library Special Collections Research Center.

The "Bystander" and African American Antilynching Rhetoric

Tourgée first warned against the mushrooming of "lawless violence" in a "Bystander" column of 15 December 1888, prompted by the depredations of White Caps in Ohio and Indiana. Until 1880, he noted in that column, "lynchings had been very rare in the States of the North," but since then, "at least one, and usually . . . several" of these "crimes" had occurred in almost every state "west of New York." Only the immediate enactment of "efficient legislation" could stop the spread of lynching, Tourgée asserted. He recommended three types of laws. "The first . . . should carefully define and prescribe extreme penalties" both for "riotous assemblage" aimed at "interfering with the course of public justice" and for "incitement by speech or writing to such assemblage." The second "should make the going about in disguise in the night-time . . . in companies sufficient to produce apprehension or terror on the part of the citizen, a felony." The third should "make every member

FIGURE 7 Harry C. Smith, editor of the *Cleveland Gazette* and member of the Ohio state legislature, where he secured passage of Tourgée's antilynching law in April 1896. Courtesy of the Ohio History Connection.

of such an unlawful organization individually responsible for its deeds, both civilly and criminally."[11] Ultimately, Tourgée would realize that the laws he proposed with the White Caps and their Ku Klux Klan prototypes in mind would not work to prevent lynching, and he would formulate a law for Ohio based on alternative principles.

Meanwhile, Tourgée continued "sounding notes of alarm" about the dangers of tolerating mob violence. In a "Bystander" column of 23 March 1889, he announced that if people threatened by White Caps could not rely on "strict enforcement of the law" to protect them, they should arm themselves and "fill [their] assailants so full of buckshot" that the aggressors would never make another raid. Defending oneself and one's home against "unlawful invasion" was not only a "legal right" but a "public duty," proclaimed Tourgée. He even contended that a few funerals of White Caps touted as "respectable" citizens might "offer the cheapest and most effective remedy for this curious epidemic" of vigilantism.[12] Nor did Tourgée confine such statements to hypothetical cases. On learning of a black army veteran who had refused to "surrender" when a lynch mob broke into his house at three in the morning but had instead shot and killed the mob leader, Tourgée editorialized in a "Bystander" column of 1 December 1894, "Every colored man who kills a lyncher ought to have his name inscribed very high up among the race's heroes and benefactors. Such a man does more to secure the rights of his people than a whole generation of 'eloquent leaders.'"[13]

Tourgée's call for armed self-defense against mob violence struck a sympathetic chord among many African Americans. Wells had barely started her apprenticeship as a journalist when in September 1886 she reacted to the lynching of an African American woman in Jackson, Tennessee, by firing off to a Kansas City newspaper a "'dynamitic article . . . almost advising murder!'"[14] She never backed down from her youthful embrace of "dynamitic" resistance to lynching. The only African Americans to escape lynching when assaulted by mobs, she pointed out six years later in *Southern Horrors. Lynch Law in All Its Phases* (1892), had been those who "had a gun and used it in self-defense." Wells drew the obvious "lesson," which she exhorted "every Afro American [to] ponder well": "that a Winchester rifle should have a place of honor in every black home, and it should be used for that protection which the law refuses to give."[15]

Smith preached an identical message in the *Cleveland Gazette*. Reproducing (and forwarding to the governor) the threatening notices that White Caps in Felicity, Ohio, had sent to African Americans attempting to integrate public schools there, he urged, "Let our people in Felicity provide themselves with weapons for defense, and in cases of emergency, *use them*."[16] Tourgée surely saw this editorial of 12 January 1889, having been following Smith's reporting on the White Caps prior to publishing his own denunciations of them.

Another of Tourgée's correspondents, the journalist John Edgar Bruce, or "Bruce Grit," thundered in an October 1889 speech, "[L]et the Negro require at the hands of every white murderer in the South or elsewhere a life for a life. If they burn your houses, burn theirs. If they kill your wives and children, kill theirs."[17] Using language almost indistinguishable from Bruce's, T. Thomas Fortune likewise endorsed the "right to retaliate" in an editorial in the *New York Freeman*, pointedly issued on 4 July 1885: "The white man who stabs or lynches a colored man should be stabbed and lynched in return." Even a relatively conservative African American editor, Edward E. Cooper of the *Indianapolis Freeman*, who would later repudiate Tourgée's "inflamable . . . advice to the colored people," celebrated the "manly courage and pluck" of a mob victim named Nelson Jones, who "used his Winchester as long as he could raise it to his shoulders" and thereby saved his family and survived with "29 bullet holes . . . in his body." "If we had more men of the

Nelson Jones stamp, we would be far better off," moralized the author of this article, apparently speaking for Cooper.[18]

In short, by counseling those attacked by mobs to shoot back and "kill the aggressors," Tourgée aligned himself firmly with African Americans. He also presented analyses of lynching that paralleled—and anticipated— many of the insights Wells would soon articulate. Because Tourgée never isolated lynching from other forms of anti-black violence but typically devoted a single "Bystander" article to commenting on a range of incidents, he applied variations of the same explanation to all: on the one hand, vicious persecution of African Americans reflected white racists' inability to recognize blacks as fellow citizens, "entitled of right to equal privilege and equal protection under the law"; on the other hand, anti-black violence served to guarantee a "cheap and 'manageable' labor" force, as much under the employer's heel as slaves had been.[19]

For example, in a "Bystander" column of 7 September 1889, Tourgée discussed "an account of the burning at the stake of a colored man by a mob in Kentucky, on the charge of rape," alongside news stories about black North Carolinians seeking to escape exploitative labor conditions by moving to other states; "colored excursionists" subjected to a hail of bullets by police acting on rumors of "race conflict"; and Mississippi plantation workers massacred for "organizing alliances" to demand better pay. The occurrence of so many incidents in the span of three days showed how anti-black violence had skyrocketed, observed Tourgée. He drove home the significance of the statistics with a telling comparison: more African Americans had been "killed by white mobs during the first eight months of the centennial year" 1889 than "during ten years of the Irish troubles." Only after sketching the big picture into which each of these incidents fit did Tourgée interpret his data: "The manufacture of sentiment against the negro is an habitual function of the Southern press and politicians, because it offers a sure and safe road to popularity. Animosity toward the negro has become an inherited attribute of by far the larger part of the white people of the South." It was in this context that he set the lynching case mentioned in the second paragraph of his article.

To address the rape charge that had allegedly motivated the lynching, Tourgée shifted from economic reasoning toward an exploration of the double standard governing the sexual transgressions of black and white men. "In the twenty-four years since it became unlawful for a white man to compel a colored woman to his will, has a single white man been executed for ravishment of a colored woman?" he asked. As in so many of his "Bystander" columns, Tourgée engaged readers in a dialogue to lead them to a new way of thinking. Thus, he brought onstage an imaginary interlocutor to raise questions and objections he expected from readers: "But the burning at the stake—that certainly was justifiable? The crime charged was a most atrocious one. . . . A colored boy 'nearly grown' is said to have overcome two white girls about his own age and ravished one of them." Tourgée replied in his own voice: "If the charge was true Kentucky law punishes the crime with death." He added sarcastically: "If such barbarity is necessary, why not put burning at the stake among the statutory punishments of the commonwealth?" Readers would instinctively recoil at the idea, he knew, and their revulsion might impel them to realize that nothing could ever justify lynching. His next question—"Was it a horror of the crime or a wild rage for barbaric brutality to the negro that inspired those who conducted this nineteenth century burning?"—brought readers back to the premise he had stated at the outset: that inherited hatred lay at the root of all forms of anti-black violence. Through such Socratic techniques, Tourgée induced readers to consider how their attitudes toward lynching might change "if the girl's face had been black and the 'nearly grown' boy's white"—that is, to acknowledge the sexual-racial double standard.[20]

Early Analyses of Lynching by Tourgée, Smith, and Wells

These early "Bystander" articles already formulated a critique of lynching that countered the myths Southern ideologues peddled to justify the ritualistic torture of African Americans. Until 1891, however, Tourgée referred to lynching only sporadically in his "Bystander" column. (He himself would date late 1890 as the beginning of his "systematic crusade against this new form of barbarism.")[21] Accordingly, he failed even to take note of a much-publicized case in Barnwell, South Carolina—the lynching of eight innocent men in December 1889, which elicited a letter to the *New York Tribune* and a fund-raising appeal for the victims' families by New Hampshire senator William E. Chandler.

In contrast, from April 1889 on, the pages of Smith's *Cleveland Gazette* bristled with editorials and articles about lynching.[22] Unlike Tourgée, Smith generally limited himself to recording rather than analyzing accounts of lynchings, which he often reprinted from other newspapers—a common practice for small, underfunded weeklies. He did, nevertheless, editorialize on an Alabama case in which a white "society leader and wife of a prominent citizen, gave birth to a mulatto child," whose father, "an uncouth farm hand," was being hunted by a lynch mob. "As every intelligent colored man South knows," wrote Smith, "seven out of every ten cases of lynching for alleged [rape] crimes or attempts, are the outcome" of consensual relationships initiated by white women: "The woman of her own free will leads on the man and, if detected, escapes from her predicament at the expense of *his* life by crying rape." Both Tourgée and Wells would later repeat this charge, as would other African American editors.[23] In a second instance, Smith echoed Tourgée's assertion that the hitherto unprecedented "frequency" of lynching in the North "proves that the disease is catching" and "must be stopped" before reaching epidemic levels.[24]

During the months when Smith was tracking lynching, Wells was gaining enough visibility in the black press for him to profile her in the *Gazette* as "one of the brightest geniuses of the rising generation of women" and a "forcible writer" who "is well known among race journalists as 'Iola.'"[25] Yet very little of Wells's apprentice journalism survives, and except for her lost "dynamitic article," none of it pertains to lynching.[26] Tourgée remained unaware of her until she sent him her National Citizens' Rights Association membership application in late 1891. By that time, she was coediting a black Baptist-affiliated weekly, the *Memphis Free Speech*, which she had developed into an extensively circulated and influential organ.

Although the three journalists did not join forces against lynching until 1892, both Smith and Wells were undoubtedly reading Tourgée's "Bystander" column well before then, and Smith was regularly reprinting it. They could hardly have overlooked his widely noticed articles of 15 August and 5 September 1891, which signaled a new urgency in his denunciation of lynching.

Tourgée's article of 15 August cataloged the horrors of a single week: four lynchings involving a total of seven victims; "nine colored hands on a plantation" butchered, allegedly for having tried to rape a white woman, but actually for having demanded the wages due them; and "a white woman and a colored man" whipped "to the verge of death . . . for the crime of having married each other." Once again, Tourgée drew attention to the sexual-racial double standard: "No white man was ever hanged for ravishing a colored woman, though . . . colored men are killed without trial upon the mere imputation of such an outrage upon a white woman." This time he also exposed the rape charge as a convenient pretext for punishing insubordination, deterring labor agitation, and getting rid of witnesses who knew too much about "the accuser's frailty." In addition, Tourgée underscored the glaring disproportion that lynching statistics revealed between white and black deaths: "While it is quite true that white men are sometimes lynched at the South, there are at least ten colored men to one w[h]ite man lynched every year, though the colored people, taking all the Southern States together, are *less than one-third* of the entire population."[27]

Tourgée's article of 5 September opened by alluding to the "blackguard threatenings" he had received from white Southerners in response to his suggestion that the carnage he had tallied in the previous article "amount[ed] to a continuous race war." He had learned to shrug off such epistles after accumulating so many "bushels" of them in his lifetime, remarked Tourgée, but some of the latest crop stood out for "their grotesqueness or extravagance." The one he chose to describe belonged to a newly emergent genre—the lynching postcard—produced to commemorate the lynchers' exploit, and usually shared with like-minded folk, as one would share snapshots of a family picnic. It featured "a photograph of a colored man hanged to a tree with a group of white men and boys standing about evidently proud to constitute the background of an atrocious crime," as Tourgée put it. He commented, "It is a sad spectacle, that of a group of young lads in training to become the hell-hounds of an insensate persecution, but the saddest thing about it, is the unconsciousness of the parties sending this grotesque souvenir, of the truth of their own words," scrawled on the back of the postcard. Tourgée did not transcribe those words verbatim, probably because he regarded their "obscenity" as unfit to print, but perhaps also because they taunted him with his impotence either to help the race he championed or to promote his Christian values: "This S-O-B was hung at Clanton Ala Friday Aug 21st/91 for murdering a little boy in cold blood for 35 ¢ in cash. He is a good specimen of your 'Black Christian hung by White Heathens.' With compliments of, The Committee." The "truth" to which Tourgée was referring, of course, was that the lynchers had proved themselves "heathens." Both the photo and the message have come down to us because Tourgée allowed Wells to reproduce them in her pamphlets *The Reason Why* and *A Red Record: Tabulated Statistics and Alleged Causes of Lynchings in the United States, 1892–1893–1894* (1895).[28]

Tourgée went on to refute the notion that lynchings of this type occurred because "citizens of a Southern town" were aroused to a pitch of "hot indignation" by an appalling crime. "The crime had practically nothing to do with the matter, except to afford a flimsy excuse" for a white mob's "desire *to kill a nigger*," he insisted. The victim "was just as truly a martyr as if he had committed no crime, for if he had not belonged to the colored race he would not have been slain." To support this bold assertion, Tourgée resorted to his favorite techniques of arguing from historical analogy and reversing the roles of black and white. He selected an example familiar to every American Protestant. "Very many" of the Protestants burned at the stake in sixteenth-century England by the Catholic queen "Bloody Mary" Tudor, claimed Tourgée, "were accused of other crimes, some of them even more atrocious than the one alleged against the colored boy" by his lynchers. Whatever the offenses with which they were charged, Queen Mary's victims "were none the less esteemed as martyrs" and listed by the Protestant historian John Foxe in his iconic *Book of Martyrs* (1563), since "the world knew that they suffered *not* because of these offenses, but because of their faith. So this man was lynched not because of his crime, but because of his color." Had the murderer been white and the murdered boy black, the former "would have been in no more danger of lynching than if guarded by an army" and would have stood fewer chances than "one in a hundred thousand" of being legally sentenced to the gallows. Conversely, Tourgée pointed out, no black man tried by a Southern court could escape conviction or punishment: "The odds are all against him even if innocent. He is poor and black. The judges are all white; the jurors mostly if not entirely white; the prosecuting officers are all white; the chief executives of the States are all white." He concluded: "To lynch a colored man under such circumstances is an infinitely more cowardly and infamous crime than any with which he can be charged."

Tourgée devoted the last section of the column to quoting and answering a correspondent who defended lynching as a sacred duty to Southern women. "No Southern woman ever willingly submits to a negro's embraces," pontificated this correspondent, and "immutable" laws prohibited interracial marriage. Dismissing these "vaporings," Tourgée reminded readers that his years of practicing law in the South had taught him how little the "honor" of either poor white or enslaved women was respected by slaveholders and overseers habituated to indulging their "unbridled lusts" at will. He ended by stripping white Southern sexual-racial ideology of its mystifying veil and baring its naked hypocrisy: "No sensible man will believe anything in that pretended horror of miscegenation, which refuses to punish *illegitimate promiscuity* while shrinking in frantic horror at the thought of the *legitimatized* relation. And no one will put any confidence in chivalric boasts of devotion to womanly purity when colored womanhood is left without protection either from the law or public sentiment."[29]

In the weeks and months that followed, Tourgée editorialized regularly on lynching in his "Bystander" column. On 26 September he highlighted a case showing that a black man's "marital dishonor" counted as little in the eyes of white Southerners as a black woman's honor. The black man in question "caught his white employer *flagrante delicto*" bedding his wife and killed him. Had the "wronged husband" been white, noted Tourgée, a court would have ruled this a justifiable homicide; instead, he was seized from jail and "hanged by a mob."[30] On 5 December, Tourgée responded sarcastically to news that the sufferings of Siberian prisoners had prompted half a million Americans in the Philadelphia area to petition the czar on their behalf. "Would these same people as willingly petition" their own government on behalf of their black fellow citizens who fall victim to lynch mobs?, he demanded. "Is it as barbarous a thing to burn an American citizen alive—remember that seven have been burned at the stake within twelve months—to skin him alive, or mutilate, disjoint, and disembowel him for the amusement of a crowd as to allow a Russian's toes to be frost-bitten in a cell in Siberia?"[31]

Tourgée's rhetoric intensified as lynchings multiplied in number and mounted in ferocity. They reached a peak of at least 241 in 1892, while the country was celebrating the quadricentennial of Columbus's landing in the New World.[32] That year also saw the first lynchings conducted as mass spectacles, beginning with that of Edward Coy, in Texarkana, Arkansas, well publicized in the mainstream press. Tourgée's "Bystander" column of 12 March 1892 compared these spectacles to the auto-da-fé rituals of the Spanish Inquisition. "Men are burned at the stake in our free country," just as the Jews were "in Spain 400 years ago," Tourgée editorialized. The American "Christian savages" of 1892 were behaving exactly like their Spanish predecessors of 1492, who had "flocked" to autos-da-fé, "mocked and jeered" as the victims "protested their innocence," and "hooted and laughed, as they writhed in agony amid the flames." Only modern technology distinguished the Texarkana lynching from its fifteenth-century antecedent, with the telegraph and the railroad replacing more primitive means of spreading news and transporting spectators. As in his description of the assembled viewers pictured in the lynching postcard that the Clanton "Committee" had sent him, Tourgée emphasized the sadistic voyeurism that drew multitudes to the spectacle and the blunted moral awareness that blinded the onlookers to their own dehumanization: "Word was sent to the neighboring towns of the entertainment in store for Christian sightseers. The trains were crowded; the enthusiasm was intense. The reports tell us that 'there were many ladies' in the waiting throng."[33] Taking his cue from press accounts, Tourgée conjured up the tableau in graphic detail:

> The protesting prisoner is bound with iron chains to a tree and faggots are heaped about him.... Six thousand of the best people we are told

crowd the streets and struggle for each coign of vantage. . . . They are not cruel, only earnest, brave, chivalric Christian men and tender, refined Christian women, who are anxious to do what God and civilization require them to do. And now they drench the poor wretch's clothing and the wood that is heaped about him with kerosene. A woman steps forward and applies the match! The flames leap upward! The poor wretch writhes and shrieks! The blue flames roar! The flesh crackles and splutters! The crisped clothes fall off and leave the naked body shining in the glare of combustion!

To the last moment he protests his innocence in vain shouts. The crowd makes witty comments! Curses abound! It is infamous the way the poor devil denies his guilt! The smell of burning flesh fills the air! God! what century is this? The fifteenth? No, the nineteenth . . . !

Tourgée took great risks in limning the spectacle so vividly. Historians have characterized lynching as "folk pornography,"[34] and Tourgée indeed accentuated the pornographic elements: the victim's "naked body"; his "shrieks" and writhing; his crackling, spluttering flesh. Tourgée did not allow white readers to indulge their sadism, however. He forced them to confront the protestations of innocence through which the victim exercised his agency in the only way he could. Tourgée also forced readers to turn their attention toward their surrogates: the white "sight-seers" who competed for the best spots from which to gaze at a man they had denuded of his humanity and who reacted with "witty" jests to the unspeakable agony of a fellow human being. These men and women portrayed themselves as "chivalric," "refined," and "Christian" while justifying lynchings in the name of protecting their "civilization." Tourgée asked readers to question these claims and to consider how far nineteenth-century American Protestants had progressed beyond fifteenth-century Spanish Catholics.

Tourgée then shifted his lens to the press, churches, and political parties he accused of authorizing the national crime of lynching through their silence. He indicted each in turn. The "press, pulpits," and intelligentsia of the South kept silent because they did not "esteem the colored man entitled to the same rights, privileges, and immunities as the white man." Northern churches kept silent because "white Christian communities" at home, rather than "brown-skinned heathen ones across the sea," were committing the atrocities. The Democratic Party kept silent because it was by terrorizing blacks that it won elections in the South. Even the Republican Party kept silent; despite "seventeen years of constant promise[s]," it had "enacted not one shred or scrap or syllable of law" serving "to secure justice and assure liberty." Citing the galloping pace at which "these barbarities" had been proliferating, Tourgée predicted that "excursion trains" would soon be "running for such entertainments"—a prediction that would be fulfilled in less than a year. He ended by addressing the question "How can these evils be corrected?" He answered that the newly founded NCRA offered the best vehicle for a political solution and urged readers to increase its membership rolls.

The NCRA proved impotent to stop lynching, however, mainly because it lacked the funds necessary for a major political or legal campaign—a difficulty that also hampered successive African American organizations.[35] In his very next "Bystander" article of 19 March, Tourgée proposed a version of the remedy he would eventually pursue: a law empowering lynching victims or their representatives to sue for damages. "Put the responsibility for due administration of the law upon the *pockets* of the people," he argued, "and you enlist on the side of law and order at once the three great motives which control all public conduct, conscience, patriotism, and greed."[36] At this stage, Tourgée sought a federal law passed by the U.S. Congress. Before long, he would realize that he could more easily win passage of a state law, and he would begin collaborating with Smith to achieve that goal in Ohio.

"Those Memphis Murders"

Fixated on the spectacle of men burned alive, Tourgée apparently overlooked a lynching that substantiated the economic explanation he had originally given for acts of terror as means of trapping African Americans in abject dependency and thereby securing a "cheap and 'manageable' labor" force.[37] Unlike Tourgée, Smith and Wells immediately recognized the significance of what Smith titled "Those Memphis Murders." The *Cleveland Gazette* of 19 March denounced them as the "most shocking and blood-curdling" assassinations that had "ever yet blackened the fair name of a great city or disgraced the southern white people." Their purpose, Smith charged, was to "break up" a prosperous "colored firm," the People's Grocery Company, that had succeeded in gaining the "trade of all the colored people in the surrounding country"—trade formerly monopolized by a white competitor. Accordingly, the "mobocrats" had provoked a riot, "effected the arrest of the managers and some twenty-seven of the customers," and "spent the following Sabbath in pillaging the goods, amounting to some $1,800, and in carousing and hunting down defenseless men of the race." As Smith took pains to establish, the grocery's proprietors, Thomas Moss, Calvin McDowell, and Will Stewart, figured among the "most cultured and well-behaved colored people in the city." They had "committed no crime" but had merely "defend[ed] themselves and their store from the assaults of a villainous mob."[38] Yet they and not their assailants had been jailed. After being denied food, bail, or visits with their families, they had been dragged from their cells in the middle of the night and "inhumanly murdered" with the collusion of "almost every leading white citizen," as Smith revealed in a follow-up editorial of 26 March. Testifying to that collusion, a "patrol wagon" stood ready to carry the men to a railroad yard "just outside of the city," where "steam engines len[t] their whistling noise to hush the report of the murderer's guns." Tipped off ahead of time, journalists waited at the site to capture "the dreadful execution" in "profuse" detail. Their news stories dwelled with relish on how the victims' bodies were shot so full of bullets that they almost defied recognition, though Smith chose not to incorporate such gory particulars into his own account, perhaps out of respect for the victims' manhood. Instead, he emphasized that one of the victims, Thomas Moss, "wore the government uniform, a proud insignia of the nation's pledge," and he demanded that the government fulfill that pledge by "protecting a citizen in her immediate service."[39]

A resident of Memphis who personally knew the proprietors of the People's Grocery and counted Thomas Moss and his wife among her dearest friends, Wells felt the impact of the three men's lynching firsthand. Indeed, it changed the course of her life and converted her into a full-time agitator against this national crime. Her friends' murder, she would recall in her posthumous autobiography, *Crusade for Justice* (1970), "opened [her] eyes to what lynching really was"—not a defense of white womanhood against bestial black rapists but an "excuse to get rid of Negroes who were acquiring wealth and property and thus keep the race terrorized and 'keep the nigger down.'"[40] After all, no one in Memphis had bothered to accuse Moss, McDowell, and Stewart of rape, nor had the leaders of the mob attack on the People's Grocery attempted to disguise their economic motive.

To test her theory, Wells began investigating the circumstances behind every lynching she heard about. She hinted at her findings in a *Free Speech* editorial of 21 May 1892, later reprinted in *Southern Horrors*. "Nobody in this section of the country believes the old thread bare lie that Negro men rape white women," she averred, adding that if "Southern white men" continued to cry rape in the teeth of evidence to the contrary, they would soon "over-reach themselves" and prompt conclusions "very damaging to the moral reputation of their women."[41] Wells's aspersions on the veracity of

Southern white men and the sexual purity of "their women" triggered an explosion among Memphis whites, as she reported in *Southern Horrors*. The city's leading organs, the *Memphis Daily Commercial* and *Evening Scimitar*, declared war on the "black scoundrel" who published "such loathsome and repulsive calumnies." Assuming the "wretch" to be Wells's male coeditor, they threatened to tie "him" to a stake at a major intersection, "brand him in the forehead with a hot iron and perform upon him a surgical operation with a pair of tailor's shears." A lynch mob made up of "leading citizens" responded immediately to this call, but not finding the *Free Speech*'s offending editors, they contented themselves with demolishing the press and enjoining its owners never to try reissuing the paper on pain of death.

Wells had fortuitously left for a vacation in New York before her provocative editorial appeared. There she inaugurated her career as an antilynching agitator with an article on the Memphis incident that filled up the entire front page of T. Thomas Fortune's *New York Age* on 25 June. Having hired her as a columnist, Fortune printed and disseminated ten thousand copies of the piece, which Wells expanded a few months later into *Southern Horrors* (October 1892), her first full-scale pamphlet and the sole remnant of the original text.

Wells's *New York Age* article elicited an immediate tribute from Tourgée: a no-longer-extant letter applauding her for her trenchant journalism. We can conjecture its contents from her reply of 2 July, which thanked him for his "congratulations" and gratefully acknowledged "the approbation of one who has done so much for the race; one to whom, more than all others is the credit due for awaking the sluggish consciences of the great M[ethodist] E[piscopal] Church and the party of great moral ideas." Wells was alluding to Tourgée's role in prompting the Methodist Episcopal General Conference to approve a strong resolution against racial discrimination and in lobbying Republican leaders to defend the citizenship rights of Southern blacks, about which she had been reading in his "Bystander" column. Wells specified that she hoped to reach a nationwide audience so as to vindicate "the Negro race . . . of the foul charge" of rape leveled against black men. Could she count on the *Inter Ocean* to "enlighten the [white] public?," she asked in a postscript.[42] Tourgée would ensure that she could.

Coincidentally, the very day Wells's article came off the press, Tourgée's "Bystander" column of 25 June referred obliquely to the events she had just chronicled: "The editors of a paper which resented the wholesale implication of licentiousness on the part of their race, by intimating that not all the charges against them were true, were driven out of a Southern city, and their paper, a really valuable one to their race, suspended on account of it." True, none but a reader cognizant of Wells's editorial, the *Free Speech*'s destruction, and its owner's threatened castration would recognize the facts masked by Tourgée's elaborate circumlocutions, so different from his graphic description of Edward Coy's lynching. Still, despite their uncharacteristic reticence, his comments show that he was closely following the circumstances that necessitated Wells's exile from Memphis. Tourgée mentioned the incident among several other examples (all summed up in the same circuitous language) of the South's "insane policy" of "promoting obedience to law by destroying all hopes of justice" and of keeping "restiveness under oppression . . . in check" by resorting to "brutality" and "barbarism." "Of course, the ultimate purpose is to so terrify the colored man that he will not dare resist any sort of aggression," he editorialized. "The animating purpose is to drive him out of business, compel him to accept such wages as the 'superior race' may choose to give, and cease to assert in any way his own manhood." Yet Tourgée warned that no amount of repression could succeed in stamping out African Americans' resistance forever. "If the course of the government and people of the United States toward its colored citizens is not speedily modified," he predicted, as he had many times before, "the result is sure to be an epoch of bloodshed rivaling in horror the most sanguinary phase of the French Revolution."[43]

A Three-Way Collaboration

Tourgée's collaboration with Wells in a joint campaign against lynching thus began with an exchange of letters and a convergence of public voices in their respective newspapers. For the next few years, the two militant journalists quoted each other's writings, borrowed each other's arguments, cooperated in compiling and broadcasting information about lynching to an international audience, supported each other's political agendas, paid homage to each other in the face of vilification, and boosted each other's careers. From his editorial tribune at the *Cleveland Gazette*, Smith publicized both Tourgée's and Wells's contributions, provided a forum for the growing antilynching movement, and opened new paths for it while pursuing his own dogged coverage of terrorist strikes against African Americans. After Wells's campaign climaxed with the publication of her comprehensive survey, *A Red Record*, and Tourgée's collapsed with the loss of his "Bystander" column, Smith carried the struggle to eradicate lynching into the legislative arena with Tourgée's help.

Evidence of this three-way collaboration surfaced shortly in *Southern Horrors*, where Wells echoed both Smith and Tourgée in her opening chapter, "The Offense," and cited the *Cleveland Gazette* and "the Bystander in the Chicago Inter-Ocean" as sources in chapter 2, "The Black and White of It." Like Smith, Wells asserted that "Afro-American men do not always rape (?) white women without their consent."[44] Invoking the biblical story of the Hebrew champion Samson, blinded after being seduced by the Philistine courtesan Delilah, she called the men unjustly charged with rape in such cases "Afro-Americans Sampsons [sic] who suffer themselves to be betrayed by white Delilahs." Like Tourgée, Wells went on to expose the hypocrisy of the white South's laws prohibiting interracial marriage. Just as Tourgée had contended that they served only to "encourage illegitimacy" and prevent *"legitimatized"* relationships, Wells argued, "The miscegenation laws of the South only operate against the legitimate union of the races: they leave the white man free to seduce all the colored girls he can, but it is death to the colored man who ... succumbs to the smiles of white women." At the same time that she reiterated points Tourgée and Smith had already made, Wells nonetheless differed from both men in granting white women more agency and defending their right to desire marriage with black men. "There are many white women in the South who would marry colored men," she boldly affirmed, "if such an act would not place them at once beyond the pale of society and within the clutches of the law."[45]

Wells's second chapter documented her claim with many news accounts. Two in particular sympathetically cited instances of white women who had opted for social ostracism rather than betray their black lovers: Sarah Clark of Memphis, who "swore in court that she was *not* a white woman," so that she could live openly with the black man she loved, and Lillie Bailey, a seventeen-year-old girl thrown out of a home for unwed mothers after she gave birth to a black baby and "withh[e]ld its father's name ... [to] prevent the killing of another Negro 'rapist.'" Through such examples, Wells made clear that she condoned voluntary relationships between white women and black men and believed they should be socially and legally sanctioned.

Even as she defined a position on these relationships more liberal than either Smith's or Tourgée's, Wells mined the two men's newspaper columns for ammunition. Her second chapter began with a long summary of a front-page story in the *Cleveland Gazette* of 16 January 1892, about an Ohio minister's wife who had indulged in an affair with an African American, accused him of rape to save her reputation, and finally confessed to her perjury after he had languished in prison for four years. The chapter also featured a two-paragraph extract from Tourgée's "Bystander" column of 24 September 1892, in which he published the results of an investigation his informants had conducted into the facts behind Edward Coy's lynching. That investigation, Tourgée announced, revealed that the white woman "paraded as a victim of violence" had been "criminally intimate with Coy for more than a year previous" and had been "compelled by threats, if not by violence," to charge her black paramour with rape. "When she came to apply the match" to set her hapless lover's body on fire, Tourgée further detailed, "Coy asked her if she would burn him after they had 'been sweethearting' so long!" Once again highlighting the hypocritical double standard that white Southerners applied to interracial sex, Tourgée noted that a "large majority of the 'superior' white men prominent" in Coy's lynching were "the reputed fathers of mulatto children" and that as a member of the "'superior' race," the white woman who had acted as Coy's "willing partner in . . . guilt . . . must naturally have been more . . . guilty" than he. The facts his informants had uncovered, Tourgée commented, indicated that "the so-called 'race question'" actually boiled down to the use of "religion, science, law and political power . . . to excuse injustice, barbarity and crime done to a people because of race and color." Fusing her voice with Tourgée's in this extensive quotation enabled Wells to speak with the authority he possessed as a famous white male writer and former judge.[46]

Tourgée and Mrs. H. Davis versus President Benjamin Harrison

While lending his voice to the antilynching campaign led by Wells and Smith, Tourgée continued to transmit the voices of other African Americans to the white public. His most poignant intervention occurred when a Mrs. H. Davis from Omaha mailed him a draft of a letter she asked him to correct and send on to President Benjamin Harrison for her. "I am a woman, with out sufficient education to carry my aim out" of appealing to the president to use his executive power to stop lynching, she explained to Tourgée, "and from the reading of your writing in print, I trust you are a friend to my people."[47] Tourgée obliged by forwarding Mrs. Davis's letter, typed up by Emma, to Harrison. In a cover note, he assured Harrison that the typescript was "word for word" the same as the handwritten version, "with one exception," where Mrs. Davis had "used 'confessing' evidently meaning 'professing.'"[48]

Notwithstanding the educational deficiencies for which she apologized, Mrs. Davis eloquently described the ordeals African Americans were enduring: "They are shot down as criminals of the lowest grade; they [white Southerners] burned some alive professing ignorance in the burning flames; others are dragged from their homes and hung, and some are beat and stoned to death." She then reminded Harrison of the debt Republicans owed to African Americans: "Where is the party that we gave our life-blood to help gain their victory, when the rebels rebelled against them? Where are they, I say, Mr. President?" She ended with the plea, "And now I call on you, Mr. President, in God's name to help us. It lays in the hands of this Government to protect all citizens of the United States."[49]

To Tourgée's disgust, Harrison replied that the limited powers assigned him by the "Constitution and the laws" did "not extend" to "such cases as those to which [Mrs. Davis] refer[red]," but that he had never "failed . . . to lift [his] protest" against the "outrages" of which she "very justly complain[ed]."[50] Tourgée shot back an indignant handwritten response, sent from Coronado Beach, California, where his lecture circuit had taken him. "During your administration 14 colored citizens of the United States have been burned at the stake: more than 300 have been publicly lynched and more than 1000, murdered by white men at the South," he underscored. "I have not heard any protest which you have made in regard to these things." Disputing Harrison's interpretation of the Constitution and insisting that law and precedent gave the federal government more power than Harrison recognized, Tourgée concluded that if only Harrison *had* "'protested' officially," he could have paved the way toward ending lynching before "many thousand innocent victims" perished.[51]

Mrs. Davis, meanwhile, expressed her own opinion of Harrison's reply: "Now if the head of this goverment can not Control the law then we have no laws so we have got to protect our own selves." Tenaciously, she implored Tourgée to help her make "one more plea" to the president.[52] Instead, he published her letter to Harrison in his "Bystander" column of 23 April 1892, thus giving her a national audience. He prefaced it by editorializing, "Those who are fond of asserting that the common people, especially if they are colored, have neither the ability nor the inclination to think correctly on such subjects, should read it and say whether a more succinct or logical statement of the matter was ever made." And he appended to it another address to "Bystander" readers: "Remember that this letter voices the sentiment of seven millions of citizens of the United States and then say what ought to be the response of the Nation's chief executive, to such a plaint which every one knows to be as true as if written in characters of blood upon the sky."[53]

Tourgée did not let the debate with Harrison over the president's power to act against lynching cease here. In his "Bystander" column of the following week, he criticized what he called the doctrine of "Federal 'futilism,'" which maintained that the federal government could not infringe on the sovereignty of the states. Harrison had just reiterated this doctrine in a speech to a committee of African American spokesmen who, like Mrs. Davis, had demanded that the government protect the rights of all citizens. Tourgée pointed out the similarity between Harrison's views and those of such antebellum proslavery statesmen as Supreme Court chief justice Roger Taney, author of the infamous *Dred Scott* ruling that African Americans could never become U.S. citizens and had "no rights which the white man was bound to respect." "Federal 'futilism' always has been and always will be the chief ally of that 'nullification' of National authority on which slavery rested," Tourgée stressed.[54] He returned to the issue of federal versus state power in a "Bystander" article of 17 September analyzing Harrison's acceptance speech upon his nomination for a second term. "It is admitted by every publicist, every statesman, every lawyer—indeed by every sane man of reasonable intelligence throughout the world—," he declared, "that the only purpose for which any government exists . . . is that it protects or professes to protect the lives, liberties, and legal privileges of its citizens and punishes those who infringe their rights." The U.S. government alone refused to fulfill its responsibility to its citizens. "Is this because of lack of power?" Tourgée asked rhetorically. "Not at all," he answered; "the Constitution grants the power even to redundancy in at least three express and different forms." The obstacle, Tourgée charged, lay not in the Constitution but in a lack of political will: "The Congress of the United States do not exercise the power vested in them. Why not? *Because the people whose servants they are do not demand it of them.*" Their inaction made white Americans and their elected representatives complicit in the "unheeded slaughter" of their black fellow citizens, Tourgée implied. He reinforced the message by listing ten recent victims of a single week's "cowardly" mob murders. Nine out of the ten targeted men had "protested against," resisted, or "advised resistance to the whipping and beating of colored men and women by bands of 'Regulators' who represented white American civilization." The one exception was accused of "having 'attempted' rape," an allegation Tourgée undermined by putting "attempted" in quotation marks.[55]

Starting a Transnational Campaign against Lynching

Marking a new phase in the campaign against lynching that Tourgée waged in collaboration with Wells and Smith—a phase in which they sought allies beyond U.S. borders—this "Bystander" article appeared not only in the

Chicago Daily Inter Ocean and the *Cleveland Gazette* but also in a slim British monthly titled *Anti-Caste*, edited by the Quaker Catherine Impey, a former abolitionist.[56] (The word "caste" referred to color prejudice wherever "our white race habitually ostracises those who are even partially descended from darker races," explained Impey in her journal's March 1888 inaugural issue.) In antebellum days British and American abolitionists had worked closely together, crisscrossing the Atlantic to bear witness against slavery in lecture tours that mobilized the moral authority of a transnational movement.[57] Impey embodied a link to this history and offered Tourgée, Wells, and Smith the opportunity to revive it by carrying the campaign against lynching to Great Britain. Since her first trip to the United States in 1878, when she had stayed for several weeks with the African American novelist William Wells Brown, whom she may have met during his sojourn in England, Impey had been cultivating an "intimate acquaintance with leading coloured Americans." Her "large circle of acquaintances *& friends* [double-underlined]" included the veteran abolitionists Frederick Douglass, Henry Highland Garnet, Robert Purvis, Lewis Hayden, and William Still, coordinator of the Underground Railroad; the poet and novelist Frances Ellen Watkins Harper; the editors T. Thomas Fortune, Benjamin T. Tanner of the *A.M.E. Church Review*, and B. F. Lee of the *Christian Recorder*; the AME bishops Daniel A. Payne and Henry McNeal Turner; and the educator Fanny Jackson Coppin, president of the Institute of Colored Youth, all of whom Impey listed in her inaugural issue. As she confided to Tourgée, Impey considered it "most important to form real friendships if possible to us amongst those whose cause we are defending," because only through such bonds could white allies understand what racism "meant to those who are its *victims*," and only that firsthand understanding could equip them to speak about the race question with the "power" and "confidence" of an advocate who "*knows* whereof" he or she speaks. Impey had been corresponding with Tourgée since 1890, when he had sent her a copy of *Pactolus Prime*. In her letter of thanks, she informed him that she had "read [his] 'Fools Errand' when it first came out with *great* satisfaction—& still more so [his] 'Bricks without Straw.'"[58] She also had at least some familiarity with Tourgée's "Bystander" column, to which she would soon begin subscribing through the *Weekly Inter Ocean*. Hence, she naturally sought him out for a "face to face" meeting at his home on traveling to the United States in the summer of 1892.[59]

Impey's visit with the Tourgées lasted for about a week and apparently took place shortly before he mentioned it in his "Bystander" column of

24 September, which introduced her as the "brave Englishwoman who . . . publishes the pungent little journal . . . *Anti-Caste*" and summarized their conversation. Among the "phases of the race question" that Impey and Tourgée discussed were the recent death of the abolitionist poet John Greenleaf Whittier; the "Christ idea" of freedom and justice that inspired Whittier and his fellow abolitionists; the way in which "science and the church were both enlisted to prove that the Christ philosophy did not apply" to white treatment of other peoples; the double standard that governed sexual relations between the races; the number of "colored men . . . lynched for the crime of having white mistresses"; the "case exactly in point" of Edward Coy's lynching; another massacre in Arkansas of agricultural workers who had gone on strike in cotton-picking season; and the combination of disfranchisement, vagrancy and contract laws, and terrorist attacks that left Southern blacks worse off in many respects than they had been under slavery.[60]

From Impey's account in the October 1892 issue of *Anti-Caste* that featured Tourgée's "Bystander" article of 17 September, we know the two also discussed the NCRA, which Impey hailed as "the new Anti-Slavery Society." Indeed, she avowed, the "crowning" purpose of her trip had been to "meet with some of the leaders of this *new* movement . . . in the cause of liberty."[61] We know as well that Tourgée loaned Impey the lynching photo he had described in his "Bystander" article of 5 September 1891, for she wrote apologizing for having "kept it . . . so long" while having a print made of it.[62] As Tourgée and Impey talked about the NCRA, the "horrors of Negro life in the South," and their many African American contacts, did Tourgée bring up Wells, whose antilynching journalism he had so recently praised?

Alternatively, did Impey hear of Wells from any of the African American hosts with whom she stayed after leaving Mayville, when she spent "several days or a week each" at the homes of Frederick Douglass near Washington and Bishop Tanner and Fanny Jackson Coppin in Philadelphia? Silent about Wells, her editorial "America Re-visited" foregrounded the NCRA instead. "Nearly *everywhere* we went, and with almost *everyone we met*," reported Impey, "the talk worked round to the Caste question OR the Citizens' Rights Association!" So eager were her hosts to hear more about the NCRA from someone who had just "come from its head-quarters" that Coppin invited "about 50 of her coloured friends and acquaintances—clergymen and ministers of several denominations—teachers and students from the schools and colleges—professional and business men and women" to a gathering at which Impey could share her impressions of this "*Civil* Anti-Caste Association."[63] (Ironically, during the very same period, Tourgée was complaining bitterly about the apathy Northern African Americans were allegedly displaying toward the NCRA.) Impey's investigation of the "Caste question" as viewed by African Americans took her to a variety of institutions: "colored churches"; Coppin's "'Institute for Colored Youth,' with its over-flowing classes for children and older students, its trade-school for men and women, and its training classes for teachers"; and the "Coloured Press Convention." It may have been at the press convention that Impey heard Wells lecture. Moved by the power of Wells's presentation, she called on her at the home of their mutual friend William Still, where Wells was staying. The encounter resulted a few months later in Impey's inviting Wells to embark on a lecture tour of Britain that would launch "a worldwide campaign against lynching," as Wells recalled in her posthumous autobiography.[64]

Before Wells left for England in April 1893, Tourgée lent her, too, the lynching photo Impey had returned to him in the meantime. Writing to Emma to thank her for sending it, Wells said she had "used it with good effect" in a lecture to the Moral Education Association of Boston and was making a copy to take with her to England.[65] Prior to Wells's arrival, Impey prepared readers of *Anti-Caste* for her lectures by publishing extracts from Tourgée's latest "Bystander" articles pertaining to lynching. For example, under the titles "That Terrible Lynching Case Investigated" and "Outbreak of Race Persecution in the United States," the November double number of *Anti-Caste* reprinted sections from Tourgée's articles of 24 September and 8 October 1892. The first (partially quoted by Wells in *Southern Horrors*, as we have seen) laid out the facts behind Coy's lynching. The second delved into a massacre billed by the white press as a "TERRIBLE RACE WAR." Typifying Tourgée's practice of giving African American writers a platform in the white press and exposing white readers to the black press, he drew on a report by NCRA member Mack Caldwell that had appeared in the *New York Age* of 1 October. He prefaced it by characterizing Caldwell as one of the NCRA's earliest members and commending him for having "more than once . . . taken his life into his hands and gone into the South to investigate" the facts behind "some peculiarly infamous barbarity." Tourgée quoted at length from Caldwell's reconstitution of the so-called race war, which had started with an altercation between a white and a black farmer over a horse and had snowballed as the white farmer murdered the black, attempted to lynch a black woman who had witnessed the murder—and with whom he had been "living on intimate terms"—and led an "epidemic of whipping, beating, and the usual barbarism" against all the black men who had accompanied the woman to lodge a complaint and vainly request protection from the sheriff and county attorney.[66]

Caldwell interviewed two of the survivors, one of whom showed him his bullet wound in the abdomen, the other the stripes on his back that had "laid open the flesh to the bone," and both of whom had been forced to leave behind their unharvested crops, their homes, and their farm animals in order to save their lives. Tourgée relayed Caldwell's proposal that a fund be raised to relieve the victims' sufferings and agreed to forward all contributions to local parties who could put them "into deserving hands." He also commented that if the perpetrators had been Turks or Arabs and the victims "a half dozen Christian believers" in a Muslim country, "every man and woman on the [U.S.] continent who has a reputation for sanctity or philanthropy to keep up would be making flaming speeches," "every pulpit in the land" would be invoking God's wrath against the persecutors, and a warship might even be dispatched to the region. Abridging Tourgée's diatribe, Impey quoted him as suggesting, "bitterly, that these people should be left to perish [rather] than that our Southern brethren be given any ground of offense by such interference with their management of the negro—whom they 'know all about' and of whom we 'know nothing.'" She ended with his assertion that as president of the NCRA, he had received "more than 5,000 letters from coloured citizens" asking whether the "government of the United States or the people of the North" would "ever do anything to secure us protection in the free exercise of our rights as men and citizens?"[67] In the *Inter Ocean*, of course, Tourgée was confronting white readers and Republican Party leaders with the question his African American correspondents were asking. Transferred to the pages of *Anti-Caste*, however, Tourgée was shaming his country in an international forum and baring to the world the hypocrisy of his compatriots' Christian pretensions.

Tourgée flouted patriotic codes even more boldly by encouraging Impey to publish the lynching photo he had loaned her. It dominated the front page of the January 1893 *Anti-Caste*, captioned "*A LYNCHING SCENE IN ALABAMA. Southern Planters teaching their children how to treat offending (defenceless) negroes. . . .* HOW LONG WILL THE CALLOUS NATION LOOK ON?" Impey informed British readers that "many hundreds of similar lawless scenes" occurred every year and that "NO ONE IS PUNISHED." Her editorial "Our Picture" further informed them that the lynchers had sent the photo to Tourgée with an "insulting message" and that she had "been permitted to reproduce [it] in the hope that it may convey to our readers something of the true state of affairs in the South, in a way that perhaps only a photograph can do."[68] Clearly, Tourgée hoped the photo would shock British viewers, incite an outcry against American barbarism, and thus finally overcome the indifference of the U.S. public. He did not need to spell out these aims. Communicating with the British public from across the Atlantic through Impey, he could let her tell the subscribers of *Anti-Caste* why lynching should matter to them and what they could do to help end it.

Wells's 1893 British Lecture Tour

Like Tourgée, Wells had concluded that only the pressure of world opinion could force her compatriots to act against the national crime of lynching. Until Impey invited her to England, Wells had lectured mainly to African American audiences, except for two engagements in Boston. Neither her lectures nor her articles in the *New York Age* nor her powerful pamphlet *Southern Horrors* had penetrated the sanctum of the white press, "the medium through which [she] hoped to reach the white people of the country, who alone could mold public sentiment." No wonder, then, that she greeted Impey's invitation as "an open door in a stone wall."[69]

In England, Wells nonetheless faced challenges different from any Tourgée encountered. Addressing British audiences in person, she had to answer the question they immediately raised: "why she should have come four thousand miles" to complain to the people of England of grievances that could only be redressed by the "local authorities in America." As a Birmingham city councillor objected, "any interference . . . by English people" in the internal affairs of the United States, not to mention the "local police arrangements" of American towns, "would be an impertinence."[70] Wells responded by capitalizing on what Paul Gilroy has called the "insider-outsider duality" she shared with other African American travelers abroad.[71] Typically, she presented herself to the British as an outsider forced into exile by her native land, which could not accept African Americans as equal citizens, entitled to the same rights and protections as white Americans. She was laying her case before the British people because her white compatriots had refused to hear it, Wells told her audiences. For ten years, she pointed out, the Southern states had been waging a relentless "war against Negro progress." They had "entirely nullified" the black vote by terrorizing all who sought to cast a ballot. They had passed laws criminalizing interracial marriage. White supremacists had imposed a regime of racial segregation that closed the "doors of churches, hotels, concert halls and reading rooms" to African Americans except as menials and obliged them to ride in separate railway carriages. Now, in the "latest culmination" of their "war against Negro progress," they had substituted "mob rule for courts of justice throughout the

South." Over the past decade, Wells underscored, more than "a thousand black men and women and children" had been brutally murdered by white mobs, and within the first few months of 1893 alone, three men had actually been "burned alive." Having provided her British audiences with the facts, Wells explained why she was appealing to them and how she believed they could advance her cause: "The pulpit and press of our own country remains silent on these continued outrages and the voice of my race thus tortured and outraged is stifled or ignored wherever it is lifted in America in a demand for justice." For these reasons she was turning "to the religious and moral sentiment of Great Britain" to "arouse the public sentiment of America," admittedly the sole agency that could secure the "necessary ... enforcement of law." Wells crowned her reply to objections against foreign meddling in domestic concerns by flattering British national pride: "America cannot and will not ignore the voice of a nation that is her superior in civilization, which makes this demand in the name of justice and humanity."[72]

Next, Wells offered proof that British moral leverage had worked in the past. Citing the precedent of the transatlantic abolitionist movement, Wells spoke no longer as an outsider but as an insider who had inherited its mantle. "The moral agencies at work in Great Britain did much for the final overthrow of chattel slavery," she argued. "They can in like manner pray, write, preach, talk and act against civil and industrial slavery; against the hanging, shooting and burning alive of a powerless race."[73]

These arguments, presented in a style British observers described as "quiet" but "educated and forceful," moved audiences to pass "the strongest resolutions of condemnation and protest" and instigated the "leading newspapers of the United Kingdom" to issue "ringing and outspoken editorials" against lynching.[74] "Miss Wells has made an impression on the minds of thousands (perhaps ten thousand *direct*—besides those who read the press accounts)," exulted Impey in a letter to the Tourgées: "We were every where well received—In some places the meetings were packed—*crowded* [double-underlined] & overflow meetings held. . . . She spoke with a cultivated manner—with great simplicity & directness & with a burning intensity of feeling *well controlled*—it was the most *convincing kind* of speaking—it sounded so intensely genuine & real—There was no attempt at oratory—no straining after effects—a persecuted suffering woman come to lay her case before an impartial jury—."[75] By the end of her 1893 British tour, Wells had succeeded in kindling a grassroots movement that pledged to work toward "securing to every member of the human family freedom, equal opportunity, and brotherly consideration," as well as to agitate against all forms of racial oppression, starting with lynching. The movement called itself the "Society for the Recognition of the Brotherhood of Man," and Wells mid-wifed chapters in every city she visited, enrolling hundreds of members after each lecture.[76]

Despite these achievements, Wells's main goal eluded her. The white Northern U.S. press paid no attention to British newspaper accounts of her lectures. Even Tourgée's "Bystander" column never mentioned them. And even African American newspapers gave Wells's 1893 British tour almost no coverage. The only exception, fittingly, was the *Cleveland Gazette*, which had been conducting its own campaign against lynching since 1888, showcasing Wells and Tourgée since 1889, and supporting their antilynching endeavors since 1892. Harry C. Smith's editorial conveyed the energy and persuasiveness of Wells's rhetoric. It also added his voice to hers in a sharp critique of their home country for failing to protect its black citizens, counterbalanced by a warm tribute to their English ally:

> By papers kindly mailed us from England we see that Miss Ida B. Wells . . . is showing our English friends and the humane people of that country what sort of a country this is, particularly the southern portion of it, and also how weak our government is when it comes to protecting its citizens at home, almost under the dome of the nation's capital. The result will be for good, notwithstanding the abuse being heaped upon her and our people by southern papers and some of the chivalry (?) of that section. More power to Miss Wells and that splendid English lady—Miss Catherine Impey, editor of "Anti-Caste," who sent for her.[77]

Smith's crediting of "papers kindly mailed us from England" for information about Wells's tour helps explain why he was the only editor to comment on it. Apparently British news reports of such local events as lectures by obscure visiting foreigners did not get transmitted across the Atlantic except by personal intervention. His reference to Southern newspapers' vilification of Wells suggests that they, at least, took notice of her lectures, but if so, their mudslinging apparently did not reach the white Northern press, as it would when Wells undertook a second lecture tour of England in 1894.[78]

Carrying the Campaign against Lynching to the World's Fair

Before Wells's return from her first tour, Smith started collaborating more actively with her and Tourgée, as well as with several other like-minded radicals, in an ambitious plan to carry their antilynching campaign to an international audience at the Chicago World's Fair. Two impulses motivated the plan: resentment against the U.S. government for excluding African Americans from the fair's exhibits and administrative councils and awareness that the nation's own bid for international attention invited a counterbid. Smith appears to have been the first to think of exploiting the fair as an opportunity to shame the nation. In an editorial of 2 April 1892 titled "Our Civilization's Shame," he noted the glaring contradiction between the highflown rhetoric of the quadricentennial and the sordid facts it ignored: "The four-hundredth year soon to be commemorated for the discovery of the American continent by Christopher Columbus is attended with a greater number of outrages and crimes than were ever known in the annals of the republic." Referring to the fair's purpose of blazoning America's glory to the world, Smith asked sarcastically, "Do the American people propose to celebrate at Chicago the bloody crimes . . . of the southern white people?" He went on to float an idea that would ultimately bear fruit in *The Reason Why the Colored American Is Not in the World's Columbian Exposition*, a collectively authored pamphlet edited by Wells: "Will the historian of to-day, some Albion Tourgee, compile these blackening records of the fourth century of our period and file them as the real exponent of the governing sentiment of the American mind?"[79]

Smith's call went unanswered for months. Then, suddenly, in February 1893, a similar idea occurred simultaneously to Tourgée himself and to F. J. Loudin, the world-renowned leader of the Fisk Jubilee Singers. In his "Bystander" column of 11 February, Tourgée proposed that African Americans "put into the hands of every visitor to the exhibition, printed in all the leading languages of the world," a "solemn protest" against the "inhumanity" and "injustice" that made a mockery of the nation's egalitarian creed, its professed Christian ideals, and its claims to "civilization." For good measure, he also proposed that African Americans petition the fair administrators to allow them "to erect upon the grounds of the exposition a realistic representation of the torture and burning of an unconvicted American citizen by a Southern mob, on fire with the flames of hate."[80]

Given Tourgée's penchant for blistering sarcasm, it is difficult to determine how seriously he meant these suggestions. The second one, in particular, sounds almost like a version of Jonathan Swift's "Modest Proposal," which recommended solving the problem of overpopulation and starvation in Ireland by cooking and eating Irish children. Indeed, Tourgée's main target in his "Bystander" article of 11 February was not the World's Fair but President Benjamin Harrison, as Smith recognized when he reprinted it in the *Gazette* under the headline "Whew!!! Judge Tourgee All but Skins President Harrison Alive for Appointing a Southern Democrat Associate Justice of the United States Supreme Court Almost at the Very Time Southern 'Chivalry' Was Torturing to Death a Texas Afro-American."[81] The article began by connecting the largest spectacle lynching that had yet occurred—the burning at stake of Henry Smith in Paris, Texas, by ten to twenty thousand "white American Christians"—with Harrison's nomination the following day of a judge whose states' rights philosophy predisposed him against federal interference when "one class of citizens" chose to "beat, whip, mutilate, defraud, oppress, hang, shoot, or burn another class of . . . citizens." That the president went through with the nomination after such a shocking exhibition of savagery showed "how lightly" he took the problem of lynching and how little he valued the "lives and liberties" of African Americans, editorialized Tourgée. Thirteen black citizens had been burned alive during Harrison's four years in office, Tourgée emphasized, and these "inhuman displays" had now grown so brazen that they were "duly advertised in advance" and "excursion trains [were] run to accommodate the eager crowds" (just as he had predicted less than a year before).[82] Yet all this while, "the President ha[d] found time for five lines of protest, but not one word of recommendation for restriction or amendment." Tourgée cited several reasons for Harrison's remissness: his concurrence with the states' rights views of his judicial nominee, his desire to "eliminate the 'negro question' from politics," his embrace of the Republican Party's metamorphosis into a "'Millionaires' Club,'" and above all his inability to put himself in the place of African Americans. It was while elucidating this last point that Tourgée introduced his proposals. Harrison "in a black skin," asserted Tourgée, "would be the first" to join in holding his country up to international scorn at the World's Fair, and perhaps even "among the first" to call for exhibiting a "realistic" model of a lynching on the fair ground. If Tourgée expected African Americans to act on his hints, he was proffering them in a curiously roundabout way. Yet act they did.

In prefacing his reprint of this "Bystander" column by "our staunch friend" Judge Tourgée, Smith exhorted "*every* Afro-American . . . to read it *carefully.*" He reiterated the exhortation in an editorial note, pronouncing the article "an exceptionally able one . . . [that] cannot be given too much attention and thought."[83] Smith seems to have been asking his readers to devote as much "attention and thought" to Tourgée's proposals as to his merciless analysis of Harrison's mindset.

Like Smith, F. J. Loudin took Tourgée's proposals seriously. Loudin's letter indicates first and foremost that he regarded Tourgée as both a kindred spirit and a mouthpiece for his own sentiments. Greeting Tourgée as "Dear Friend," he confided that he had "just read your 'Bystanders Notes' in the Inter Ocean of the 11th inst. with keener interest if possible than usual, for I wanted to see in what way you would attempt to express what I *knew* you felt over the . . . Texas horror." The words "what I *knew* you felt" convey an extraordinary sense of intimacy, giving the impression that Loudin related to Tourgée as a personal friend of long standing, and not merely as someone he knew through his writings. Loudin went on to apprise Tourgée of an open letter he had just sent to three African American newspapers—the *New York Age*, the *Detroit Plaindealer*, and the *Cleveland Gazette*—advocating that "steps be taken to lay this whole hell-like business bare before the visitors to the Columbian Exposition."[84]

In this document, addressed to "the Hon. Frederick Douglass and the Oppressed Negro in America," Loudin picked up on a report he had heard that at a lecture by Wells in Washington, Douglass had publicly suggested the same idea he, Loudin, had privately contemplated: "laying before the world at the Columbian exposition in pictures and print the outrages to which we are subjected in this 'land of the free' (?)." He urged, "Let us then compile the accounts of the lynchings, the shootings, the flogging alive, the burnings at the stake, and all the kindred barbarous acts and print them in book or pamphlet form for *free* distribution at the world's fair." He pledged to contribute fifty dollars to the undertaking and recommended forming a committee with Wells on it to oversee the project. Smith enthusiastically seconded Loudin's suggestion, both in his headline to the open letter—"Indorses a Good Idea. Now Let There Be Action and Less Talk—Mr. Loudin Sounds the Key-Note"—and in his editorial on the same page, in which he took credit for having made an analogous suggestion even earlier.[85]

Writing to Tourgée before his open letter appeared in print, Loudin told him, "I see by your notes of the 11th inst. that you have the same thing in mind but on a more extensive scale than I had contemplated." He asked Tourgée to designate "the most practical" means of implementation and to participate in a committee to set the plan in motion.[86] Tourgée apparently replied, volunteering to draft a petition along the lines he had proposed in his "Bystander" article—an idea "approve[d] heartily" by both Wells and Douglass, according to Loudin.[87] Meanwhile, Wells and Douglass had also composed an "address to the people," intended for distribution through the African American press. Loudin enclosed a copy for Tourgée's perusal, along with a letter by Douglass. Tourgée pronounced the address "admirable, short[,] concise, pointed and with no spread-eagle in it." He added,

"I hate feathers in a serious dish." He agreed with Loudin, however, in dis-countenancing Douglass's scheme of holding a month-long "Congress," at which African American spokesmen could air their views on the fair. Instead, Tourgée advised, "Let the colored people put out a strong, brief, compact yet comprehensive pamphlet in two or three languages, circulate it freely at the Fair and then let the matter alone." He also offered to "write the pamphlet if desired."[88]

Ultimately, Wells and Douglass opted for a solution more in keeping with the goal of illustrating African Americans' contributions to the nation's advancement: a pamphlet with chapters by representative race men and women. Work on the project stalled while Wells was lecturing in England, but Smith kept promoting "The Pamphlet Idea" in the *Gazette*. Noting that Loudin and Douglass had each pledged $50 and Wells $10 toward the $5,000 needed to defray the costs of publication, Smith editorialized, "Let *every* Afro-American able to do so . . . forward to Mr. Douglass as large an amount as they possibly can. . . . It is every individual Afro-American's *duty* to aid in this undertaking." He sought as well to pressure Douglass into mak-ing a fund-raising tour of "cities where our people are numerous and fairly prosperous."[89]

Neither Douglass nor Loudin could spare time for fund-raising, or even for compiling the pamphlet, however, and the task fell to Wells on her return from England, at first with meager results. On 1 July she wrote Tourgée that "the outlook for the pamphlet seemed so discouraging," she "hadn't [had] the heart" to contact him earlier, as she had intended. On the one hand, some of the authors she had lined up had "disappointed" her, either by send-ing their chapters late or by "not preparing the work at all"—a delinquency that had prevented her from fulfilling her intention to send the manuscript to Tourgée for editing. On the other hand, the funds collected to date had fallen far short of the necessary amount. Now, however, she saw "the way clear, by personal appeal to raise $500 of the money," which would "nearly" suffice to "publish the pamphlet in the English edition of 20[,]000 copies and electrotype the plates." She was writing to ask Tourgée to fill a gap in the compilation by supplying "a chapter on reconstruction as it affected the Negro." Such a chapter, she specified, should cover "the laws passed by southern states against intermarriage, separate car laws, [and] the opera-tions of the Ku-Klux Klans, White Liners etc to nullify the Negro's vote." She had become acutely aware while in England, Wells explained, that foreign-ers simply could not "understand how state governments can thus nullify the National constitution regarding the right to vote." It was essential that the pamphlet clarify this arcane aspect of the U.S. political system. "You are more likely than any one I know to have the statistics . . . the data and the ability and the zeal for the pamphlet, all rolled in one," Wells told Tourgée. Hence, she "earnestly request[ed]" him to send her "a chapter of not over 15 pages of printed matter on the subject," if possible "by July 15."[90]

Despite the less than two-week turnaround time, Tourgée complied by furnishing two chapters totaling thirteen printed pages titled "Class Legislation" and "The Convict Lease System." He adopted an African American voice speaking as "we" in them, and Wells published them anonymously because she "understood that [he] did not wish to appear" in connection with what was supposed to be the race's endeavor.[91] Wells herself wrote the preface and the chapter "Lynch Law," featuring the photo Tourgée had lent her; Douglass an introduction on the legacy of "prejudice, hate, and contempt" left by slavery; the journalist I. Garland Penn the chapter "The Progress of the Afro-American Since Emancipation"; and Ferdinand L. Barnett one titled "The Reason Why," exploding the white political establishment's rationale for barring African Americans from representation in the World's Fair exhibits. As late as 22 July, Wells still lacked the minimum sum required to print the pamphlet, and she and Smith were still soliciting funds through the *Gazette*.[92] One cause of the financial dearth must have been the Panic of 1893, which had been raging since spring, wreaking such havoc that even Loudin had not yet been able to make good on his fifty-dollar pledge. Another cause can be discerned from Smith's complaints about the "petty opposition of the Indianapolis Freeman" and the waffling of the *New York Age*'s "Editor Fortune."[93] In short, African American opinion leaders did not unanimously support the project. Notwithstanding all the obstacles, *The Reason Why the Colored American Is Not in the World's Columbian Exposition* finally came off the press in September. Smith hailed it in the *Gazette* as a credit to Wells's hard work, "excellent judgment and splendid ability." "More power to her," he cheered.[94] In the end only the preface was translated into French and German, not the entire pamphlet as Tourgée had originally envisaged, but the compilation achieved its purpose of disgracing the nation in the eyes of foreign visitors to the fair and providing them with an alternative perspective on African Americans.

Tourgée's personal copy bears the inscription "To Judge A. W. Tourgee, Whose suggestion it was that originated the preparation of this volume, 20,000 of which were distributed at the World's Fair. Ida B. Wells." Behind Wells's homage to the role Tourgée played in inspiring *The Reason Why* nonetheless lurks a more complicated story. Perennially overburdened, she had delegated the task of mailing the "first bound copy" of the volume to Tourgée, but no one had done so. Wells wondered why Tourgée never expressed his opinion of the pamphlet, even when they met in Chicago. "I hoped he would say how he regarded it, and then thought he ignored it because it was so far from what it should have been," Wells wrote two years later to Emma.[95] The Tourgées, for their part, assumed that Wells had neglected to acknowledge his assistance on *The Reason Why* by sending him a complimentary copy of it—an oversight they chalked up to the "ingratitude" of which white allies so frequently accused African Americans. Testifying to the constraints that bedeviled race relations in an era of such rigid social segregation, neither Wells nor Tourgée had felt free to ask each other the questions that could have cleared up their misunderstanding. Yet hurt feelings did not stop them from collaborating in the campaign against lynching.

Tourgée and Wells on the C. J. Miller Lynching

Besides working together to produce *The Reason Why*, Tourgée and Wells both commented on the lynching of C. J. Miller, which took place on 7 July 1893, just as Wells was finalizing the pamphlet. The particular horror of this case lay not only in the complete absence of any evidence linking the victim to the murder with which he was charged but also in the easy availability of proof that he was more than 150 miles from the scene of the crime. Both Tourgée in his "Bystander" column of 22 July and Wells in *The Reason Why* highlighted Miller's human dignity by quoting in full the speech to the "mob of blood-thirsty murderers" in which he asserted his innocence and described the itinerary he had followed from his home in Springfield, Illinois, to the town of Bismarck, Missouri, where he was on the day he was "'supposed to have committed the offense.'" Both likewise remarked on the "coolness and nerve" Miller had displayed as he "looked into the eyes of those who had already condemned him to death" (in Tourgée's words).[96] Yet the two couched their accounts of the incident in very different styles. Except in one instance where she used italics to convey her outrage at the ostensible self-restraint that led the mob to "give him the benefit of the doubt and *hang instead of burn him*," Wells dispassionately presented the facts: "After a photograph of him was taken as he hung, his fingers and toes cut off, and his body otherwise horribly mutilated, it was burned to ashes. . . . Since his death, his assertions regarding his movements have been proven true."[97] In contrast, Tourgée descanted sarcastically on the "compromise" the mob made by honoring the caveat of the murdered girls' father that *"we are not sure he is the guilty party!"* "The mob of 'superior' white Christians were actually hungry for the spectacle of a colored man writhing and shrieking in the flames," alleged Tourgée. Like the World's Fair, after all, it was a spectacle they might "not have a chance to see again," and one that was "strictly an 'American institution.'" But they had consented to forgo this thrill and to settle for the lesser delight of mutilating a corpse for "a ghastly memento with which to avouch their participation in the horrible debauch of passion and hate!" Opining that Miller and his widow ought to have been properly "grateful" for the concession, Tourgée philosophized, "The compromise was a typical one in which the colored man gained nothing of right or justice and the white man surrendered nothing of power." Reverting to another comparison with the fair, he pointed out that while the "pulpit and the religious press" remained silent about lynching, they had been "stirred to almost universal condemnation" by the policy of keeping the exhibits open on Sunday (condemnation in which Tourgée had joined). As a result, the United States enjoyed the "proud distinction" of being known to foreigners as "the land of Christian murderers." Tourgée devoted the rest of this long "Bystander" article to refuting the "pretense that the colored man is inherently inclined to murder and assault with a lubricious motive because of his African derivation" and to demanding specific measures to end lynching: universal public condemnation of the practice, punishment of lynchers, and a law obliging a locality in which mob violence occurred to pay damages, as he had previously recommended.[98]

The Campaign for an Ohio Antilynching Law

Ten months would go by before Tourgée and Wells would again join their voices against lynching. The *Inter Ocean's* suspension of the "Bystander" column in mid-August 1893—mourned by Smith in the same number of the *Gazette* that celebrated the publication of *The Reason Why*—interrupted Tourgée's collaboration with Wells through the press.[99] During the interval, however, Smith launched the initiative that would climax his collaboration with Tourgée: the campaign for an Ohio antilynching law of the type Tourgée had outlined.

The impetus arose from three converging factors. First, Smith had won election to the Ohio state legislature in November 1893, which empowered him to do more than editorialize in favor of his principles. He wasted no time before attending to his highest priority: an amendment that put teeth into Ohio's civil rights law by fining perpetrators of racial discrimination. No sooner had Smith won this victory than the second factor intervened: a "disgraceful lynching" erupted in West Union, Ohio, a border town "peopled by Kentuckians and West Virginians," and the grand jury refused to indict any of the participants. Smith met three times with Governor William McKinley to no avail but concluded that without an antilynching law, McKinley could do little except denounce the crime and exhort the county officials to perform the duties they balked at—gestures he had already made.[100] The final impetus came from Tourgée, who had no doubt been following developments through the *Gazette*.

Immediately upon learning of the grand jury's defiance, Tourgée had written to McKinley on 22 January 1894 suggesting as a fellow "son of Ohio" that his native state should "take the lead in prescribing an effective remedy for this American epidemic." The decade of 1882–92 had seen more than a 100 percent increase in "fatal lynchings"—a rate that would be much higher if nonfatal mob assaults were included, Tourgée reminded McKinley. Though "alarming" in themselves, lynchings were "only symptoms of a much greater and more dread disease, to-wit, a general contempt for law and disregard for the personal rights of the citizen" that was "national" in scope, Tourgée argued. He noted that according to existing law, "a community [was] liable for the destruction of property by a mob." Should not the same principle be extended to the "destruction of life by a mob?" Tourgée went on to propose that a penalty of $10,000 be imposed on any county in which a fatal lynching occurred, to be paid for by a "tax levy" and awarded to the "legal representative" of the dead victim. Lesser damages could be awarded to mob victims suffering nonfatal injuries that incapacitated them for labor. Were such a law adopted, Tourgée predicted, there would "probably not be more than one or two lynchings in Ohio in the next fifty years—perhaps not one." He closed with a flattering appeal to the pride of a governor who, he knew, harbored presidential ambitions: "Nothing, in my judgment, would add so much to the glory of the great commonwealth whose chief magistrate you are, as to take the lead in this most noble necessary and inevitable crusade against anarchy. I believe every northern state would follow such a lead, and this form of barbarism would be practically eliminated from them in a brief time."[101]

When more than three weeks elapsed with no sign from McKinley, Tourgée concluded that the governor did not "realize how important" the issue was and needed to be goaded into action. On 17 February Tourgée wrote to Smith, enclosing a copy of his letter to McKinley and giving him permission to use it "in any way that seems fit." Smith took the hint and reprinted both letters under the headline "That Lynching. Judge Tourgee Writes Gov. McKinley and the Editor of 'The Gazette,' and Suggests That Ohio Take the Lead in a Crusade against Such Crime. The Judge's Suggestions Relative to a Law to Stop Lynching, Etc.—The Letter of Prime Interest to All Afro-Americans." "It is a fact, generally known that no one person living has worked harder or more incessantly against the lynch disease than has Judge Tourgée," Smith editorialized—a powerful tribute, indeed, considering his own long record of antilynching agitation, not to mention Wells's.[102]

Over the next months, Smith kept *Gazette* readers informed of his bumpy progress toward submitting to the Ohio legislature a bill along the lines of the one Tourgée had proposed to McKinley. Trouble arose at the outset when the other African American representative of Cuyahoga County, William Clifford, not to be outdone by Smith, presented a rival antilynching bill, which sought to define the crime of lynching and provide for the indictment and conviction of the perpetrators. Fulminating against his colleague's violation of "'legislative' courtesy," Smith accused him of having relied on the help of a white person unfriendly "to our race." He asked Tourgée to evaluate Clifford's bill and published his reply in an article of 5 May. Though hardly an unbiased judge of a rival bill, Tourgée raised several perspicacious objections to it. "If you cannot convict a mob of murder," he pointed out, referring to the West Union case, "you could not convict them of lynching." Moreover, "*it is absolutely impossible to indict and convict a mob of two or three hundred or as many thousand people,*" as Clifford's bill required, because such a procedure would define all potential witnesses as defendants. Perhaps the most serious drawback Tourgée saw in Clifford's bill was that it would have "no deterrent effect upon the real source of the evil—those who do not do the acts, but permit or encourage others to do them"—an insight he owed to firsthand observation of how Southern newspapers and community leaders instigated Ku Klux Klan atrocities during Reconstruction. In contrast, asserted Tourgée, holding a county "liable for a penalty," as his own bill did, would "make every citizen a peace-officer to prevent a crime—and prevention is always better than cure." Meanwhile, having read "several hundred press comments" on his letter to McKinley, Tourgée had decided it would be preferable to reduce the penalty from $10,000 to $5,000—the amount railroads generally paid for "fatal negligence"—rather than risk the bill's defeat. He advised Smith to amend the bill accordingly. Tourgée ended with two more pieces of advice: First, "Do not allow any reference to color in the bill. Make it a general law." And second, "Forget yourselves—do not try to make capital—but for God's sake let justice and humanity make you wise and brave enough to push the matter through."[103] From May till December, Smith reprinted Tourgée's letter again and again as he attacked Clifford for not following Tourgée's advice to "*forget yourselves.*" In the same breath, he claimed somewhat contradictorily that he would have supported Clifford's bill if he had been convinced that it was superior to his own.[104]

The resumption of Tourgée's "Bystander" column on 5 May 1894 restored the national platform from which he could best join Smith in advocating for effective antilynching legislation. In an article of 19 May subtitled "The Law and the Mob," Tourgée informed *Inter Ocean* readers that "Hon. H. C. Smith, a colored member of the Ohio Legislature, has recently introduced a bill to impose a statutory penalty upon the county in which a lynching occurs." Without mentioning his own involvement in drafting it, Tourgée described the bill as "carefully drawn," summarized its provisions, and prophesied that it would soon serve as a model for other states. He also showcased African Americans as key players in Ohio politics who would most likely succeed in their endeavor because the Republican Party could not "afford to estrange the colored vote." By building a "movement for the legal restraint of mob violence," African Americans all over the country were "proving [their] capacity for citizenship," Tourgée affirmed. He concluded with a paean to the antilynching movement itself as the work of Providence, which had "mysteriously linked in interest the prosperous white man of the North with the poor and dependent colored citizen of the South."[105] By the time this "Bystander" article appeared, however, it had become clear that Smith's antilynching bill stood no chance in the Ohio legislature, in large part because African American disunity prevented the necessary lobbying of white lawmakers and editors.

Wells's Second British Lecture Tour and the U.S. Press

While awaiting the opportunity to resubmit his bill to the legislature, Smith shifted his energy toward publicizing Wells's second lecture tour of the British Isles in the spring of 1894. Tourgée similarly refocused on forwarding Wells's antilynching campaign through his "Bystander" column. From June through December—during a period when he was under strict instructions from the *Inter Ocean*'s editors to toe the line by emphasizing economic issues and burying the race question, as Republican Party bosses had decreed— he devoted seven "Bystander" articles to inveighing against the Northern press and pulpit for their cowardly silence on lynching. Four of these articles praised Wells and credited her with inducing a change in public sentiment.

Tourgée began backing Wells in the *Inter Ocean* even before she left for England. To ensure that her second British lecture series, unlike her first, would garner attention in the U.S. press, he apparently helped arrange for her to obtain a contract from the paper for a regular column titled "Ida B. Wells Abroad," in which she could report on British reception of her transnational antilynching drive and thus maximize its impact on U.S. public opinion. Despite his strained relationship with William Penn Nixon, the *Inter Ocean*'s editor-in-chief, Tourgée's recommendation still counted heavily, though Wells's future husband, Ferdinand L. Barnett, whose editorship of the *Chicago Conservator* had won Nixon's respect, may also have intervened for her.[106]

A milestone in journalism history, Wells's *Inter Ocean* column made her the first African American hired as a "regular paid correspondent of a daily paper in the United States."[107] It enabled her to cover her own campaign trail as she lectured against lynching throughout England and Scotland; hence, it proved decisive in gaining her cause the national prominence she had vainly sought before winning a hearing across the Atlantic that reverberated all the way home.

From 2 April to 7 July 1894, Wells's dispatches in the *Inter Ocean* broadcast British commentary on her lectures to the American public. Her column's running headlines capture Wells's strategy of highlighting British condemnation of American barbarism to shame her country into eradicating its national crime: "The Nemesis of Southern Lynchers Again in England," "England Sympathizes with the African Race," "Audiences Are Shocked," "Cordial Receptions from Churches of All Denominations— Horrified at Cruelties Perpetrated."[108] The dispatches repeatedly advertised the dozens of antilynching lectures Wells delivered in each city, the venues ranging from churches and public halls to the drawing rooms of "prominent and influential" citizens, the crowds numbering in the thousands flocking to hear her, and the notables presiding over the gatherings or gracing Wells with their presence. Implicitly rebuking the white American press for having hitherto ignored her, Wells underscored that all major British newspapers "contained full accounts" of her lectures, often accompanied by "strong editorials" against lynching, which she reprinted for American readers.[109]

In the same vein, Wells contrasted the Jim Crow treatment she endured in her home country with the equality she tasted in England—a theme on which virtually all African American travelers to Europe expatiated: "Here a 'colored' person can ride in any sort of conveyance in any part of the country without being insulted; stop in any hotel or be accommodated at any restaurant one wishes without being refused with contempt; wander into any picture gallery, lecture room, concert hall, theater or church and receive only the most courteous treatment from officials and fellow-sightseers."[110] Through the litany of privileges she enjoyed in England, Wells educated her British audiences about what it meant to live under a Jim Crow system that permeated every corner of life in the United States, inflicting daily indignities on African Americans, no matter how refined they might be, and barring them from every doorway to intellectual cultivation. Simultaneously, she conjured up for the *Inter Ocean*'s American readers the picture of a world without Jim Crow, presenting it as the fruit of a higher civilization toward which they would do well to aspire.

Like Tourgée, Wells aimed her sharpest barbs at American churches and religious leaders, whom she accused of remaining "silent with a silence which means encouragement" of racial oppression, or worse still, lending "the weight of their influence to the southern white man's prejudices." They were "too busy saving the souls of white Christians from burning in hell-fire to save the lives of black ones from present burning in fires kindled by white Christians," she sarcastically opined. Wells singled out the venerated temperance crusader Frances E. Willard for special opprobrium, quoting her as having all but sanctioned lynching through her endorsement of the myth that bestial, whiskey-sodden black men were menacing the "safety of women, of childhood, of the home."[111] To sting her white American readers into practicing the Christianity they professed, she held up British churches as models for them to emulate. All major denominations, she emphasized, had passed "earnest resolutions . . . in a spirit of Christian love, calling upon the people of the United States to remove the blot upon their good name and put a stop to 'our national crime.'"[112]

Wells pointedly exempted Tourgée from the censure she directed at the chief molders of U.S. public opinion. In two separate lectures, she hailed him as the sole American journalist to pay "systematic attention" to the scourge of lynching "from the standpoint of equal and exact justice" to every U.S. citizen. Only the "voice of the Bystander," which had resounded "so long through the columns of the *Inter-Ocean*," had broken the deafening silence of U.S. moral and political spokespersons on the evil, she contended.[113]

Through her *Inter Ocean* dispatches, Wells finally succeeded in disrupting the complacency of the white U.S. press by confronting her compatriots with the horror and disgust the British public expressed at her revelations about lynching. The *Independent*, a Congregationalist weekly with a heritage of abolitionist advocacy, cheered. "Foreign criticism will affect us here in America when, perhaps, home criticism will not," it admitted.[114] More typically, mainstream newspapers responded with howls of rage at her perfidy in tarnishing her country's image abroad. The *Congregationalist*, a conservative religious weekly, deplored the "exaggerations of Miss Ida Wells, who is stirring up the English Christians."[115] The *New York Sun*, a Democratic Party organ, reiterated the rape myth and redirected censure from white to black morals: "The moment the colored criminal of the South gives up his favorite crime, that moment ninety-nine per cent of the Southern lynchings will cease. Instead of defaming the white women of the South, Miss Ida B. Wells might better try to tame the brutal and bestial natures of too many men of her own color in the South."[116] The Republican *New York Times*, bristling with patriotic indignation, castigated Wells for "shrewdly" arousing the "inherent meddlesomeness . . . in the English nature" through "salacious" and "lurid" allegations that "skillfully mixed" truth with falsehood.[117] Memphis newspapers, of course, reacted the most viciously. The *Memphis Daily Commercial* called Wells a "Notorious Courtesan," a "strumpet," a "malicious wanton," and a "saddle-colored Sapphira"; claimed that "rumors had been rife about her unchastity" throughout her career; and misrepresented her as the "paramour" of her coeditor. Seemingly unaware of exemplifying the sin it denounced, it charged her with "foul and slanderous tirades." Like the *Sun*, the *Commercial* attributed lynching to "a perfect epidemic of outrages perpetrated by negro men upon white women."[118]

In her farewell *Inter Ocean* dispatch, Wells turned these attacks back on her detractors by asserting that the "vulgarity and vileness" of her enemies' smears had "shocked the English people far more than my own recital could do." As proof, she quoted the editorial by Sir Edward Russell in the *Liverpool Daily Post*: "The language is such as could not possibly be reproduced in an English journal." Wells concluded, "If the same zeal to excuse and conceal the facts were exercised to put a stop to these lynchings, there would be no need for me to relate nor for the English press to give ear to these tales of barbarity."[119] Yet it was precisely by going to England to relate tales of American barbarity, and by enlisting the support of the British press, that Wells finally obtained nationwide visibility at home for her crusade against lynching.

Defending Wells against Her Detractors

Besides winning her the notice of the white U.S. press, Wells's *Inter Ocean* dispatches enabled African American newspapers to track her mobilization of British public opinion against lynching as a means of overcoming white American indifference. The *Cleveland Gazette* reprinted several of her columns and pronounced her lecture tour a major coup. "Plucky little Ida B. Wells's success in England, arousing people, press and pulpit of that country . . . to a true realization" of African Americans' plight, had achieved impressive results, exulted Smith. It had incited "the Memphis Commercial and other vile sheets of the south, to not only scream, 'It 'taint so, sah,' but to do their dirtiest to injure her character and standing with the English. . . . They can't do it, however, because her cause is a just one and because she is the right one to plead it." After letting Wells speak for herself in the last paragraphs of her *Inter Ocean* dispatch, Smith marveled, "Her progress abroad has been simply wonderful, and the little woman grows intellectually and in oratorical power with every succeeding week."[120] He continued to quote and celebrate her for weeks. African Americans should give her a "monster ovation and a good fat purse" on her return, so that she could pursue her antilynching advocacy, Smith urged. "She is certainly agitating this country on the lynch question as it has never before been stirred on this subject."[121] Smith also defended Wells against animadversions by both white and black journalists. When a "correspondent in a recent issue of the New York Sun" belligerently asked Wells if she was implying that "southern women are liars," Smith retorted in her place, "Well, considering the fact that many innocent Afro-Americans' lives have been forfeited to mobs as a result of their unlawful relations with willing southern women of weak and loose morals, we are constrained to answer . . . that *some* southern women are all-fired liars of the most dangerous kind. Many a lynched or rather murdered Afro-American has not only been made a 'scapegoat of white men's crime' in the south, but has also been made the foolish victim of white women's lust and passion."[122] Smith responded even more sharply to an African American correspondent in the Beaufort, South Carolina, *New South*, who disparaged Wells for her flight from Memphis. Unlike Wells, sneered this correspondent, "we are compelled to remain in Memphis: indeed we have never fled." "*Indeed!*" huffed Smith. "'*We*' might have added that '*we*' have not done for any of the race's causes what Miss Wells has, either." Smith wound up, "The agitation against lynching, which Miss Wells has given so very much impetus to, goes bravely on, notwithstanding such unkind and miserable little vaporings as the New South's '*we*' indulges in."[123]

Tourgée championed Wells as vigorously as Smith did. He lambasted her white journalistic critics in a scathing "Bystander" article of 16 June 1894, subtitled "In the Glass of English Opinion." Religious organs and the Republican press bore primary responsibility for the "apathy of the Northern mind upon this gravest crime and greatest peril of a Christian government," he stressed, yet "with a few praiseworthy exceptions," they sought merely to undo the damage Wells had inflicted on their country's image. Religious organs, scoffed Tourgée, attempted to palliate the guilt of Southern Christians by "labor[ing] to show that the evil is not so bad as it is represented." Republican newspapers' complaints about Wells's breaches of political etiquette were just as lame: "[They] bewail with almost tearful earnestness the indiscretions of Miss Wells and others, in making such an 'appeal to English prejudice,' especially at this time, 'when the Republican party, which is the true friend of the negro, is about to win a decided victory.'" Rejecting as "ludicrous" the claim that "'the effect of British interference with American affairs will be to deprive the colored man of the sympathy of the Republican party,'" Tourgée exploded, "'Republican sympathy,' indeed!" The Republican platform disclosed no "evidence of 'sympathy' with the wrongs of the colored citizen," he countered, and Republican newspapers had been paying "more attention" to the "colored citizen's rights . . . since the English people and press began to consider them than they had before." He summed up his defense of Wells with a trenchant indictment of white American hypocrisy that upheld every article of the case she had laid before the bar of British opinion:

> The simple truth is that Miss Wells can tell the truth in England and not only live but be listened to by people who believe that it is a shame and disgrace to American Christianity and the American people to permit such oppression of American citizens to continue, simply because they are colored.
>
> If she should make such statements . . . anywhere at the South, she would be mobbed and the colored people who dared go and listen to her would be killed. If she would tell these truths to the white people of the North, the few who would listen at all, would say: "Oh, dear! It is too bad—too bad! But what can we do? The Southern people surely must have some provocation. I know some Southerners myself, and they are most charming people. There must be some mistake!"[124]

In aligning himself with Wells against his racial peers and corroborating her impeachment of their country, Tourgée unmistakably proclaimed himself a rebel against white America, if not "a refugee from his race," as Joel Chandler Harris would have it.[125]

Tourgée followed up his testimony in Wells's favor with several "Bystander" articles in which he symbolically merged his voice with hers as he combined their complementary arguments against lynching. Like her lectures and *Inter Ocean* dispatches, his article of 28 July, subtitled "Christian Thought and the Inherent Rights of Colored Citizens," addressed a dual British and American audience. The proliferation of lynchings and mob attacks forced church members in both countries to face a painful question, argued Tourgée in language that echoed Wells's: "whether any Christian may remain silent in regard to such glaring injustice done by one Christian people against another Christian people and still be blameless." That question now assumed vital importance because "at least four ministers of Christ at the South" had recently "stood forth as public champions or excusants of lynching." All four had either "openly asserted" or "clearly implied, that colored men are only lynched for the ravishment of white women." Branding that allegation a "falsehood," Tourgée cited a statistic he probably drew from Wells's pamphlet *The Reason Why*, since he had never used it before: "In hardly one-third of the cases of lynching of colored men at the South is any such charge made against the victim." He went on to quote a "reverend editor" whose "excuse" for lynch law—that the inferiority of "African citizens" necessitated it—had "inexpressibly shocked the moral sense of his English co-religionists." He ended by asking English Christians, as Wells had, not to "sit still" while their fellow Christians across the Atlantic "demand[ed] that the golden rule be flexed to suit their distorted views."[126]

Tourgée again merged his voice with Wells's in a "Bystander" article of 8 September mocking the "absurd . . . belief that seems to spring eternal in the Northern breast that the South is on the ragged edge of reforming and rebuking the evils that have so long characterized her civilization." On this occasion Tourgée was referring to the hosannas with which the Northern press had greeted the decision of Shelby County, Tennessee, to which Memphis belonged, to convene a grand jury for the purpose of indicting those responsible for lynching six African Americans charged with arson. "Even spasmodic virtue is to be commended and grand juries of that sort are altogether too rare in any State to be allowed to go without praise," conceded Tourgée. Yet he undercut his concession by recalling the lynching that had driven Wells into exile from Memphis: "Has it ever occurred to this body of virtuous citizens to investigate the killing of three good citizens, taken from its jail by a mob and murdered because they dared defend themselves?" His next question uncannily anticipated Wells's most ambitious work, *A Red Record*: "Has it ever occurred to them to make a list of colored men killed by white men who have never been prosecuted?" "Such a list," added Tourgée, "would be more appalling than any study of crime which has been presented to the world in many a day."[127]

As it turned out, the Shelby County grand jury unexpectedly indicted the lynching perpetrators, one of whom proved to be the son of the sheriff and all of whom were jailed while awaiting their trial. Even more surprisingly, local whites "pass[ed] round the hat for the benefit of the families of the murdered men." So reported a "self-complacent citizen of Memphis" who told Tourgée it was "surely time . . . to give us credit for good intentions." Replying to this correspondent in a "Bystander" column of 15 September subtitled "Lynching and Mob Law in the South and North," Tourgée acknowledged that Shelby County's performance surpassed those of Illinois, Ohio, New York, Indiana, Michigan, Wisconsin, Minnesota, and Kansas, "in each one of which lynchings have openly taken place within the past year, and in which grand juries have refused, in violation of their oaths, to permit the law to take its course." Nevertheless, he pointed out, based on his experience in North Carolina, "it is a long road from an indictment to a conviction and a still longer road to punishment." (He proved right: the lynchers were never convicted.) Tourgée noted as well that "Southern subscriptions for the families of colored men slain by mobs" tended to be stingy. Taking advantage of the opportunity to plug his model antilynching law, he insisted that instead of ad hoc local charity, the "people of every county should be taxed for the benefit of the family of every man killed by a mob." Though he granted that Shelby County's actions did indicate portents of change in the South, Tourgée gave all the credit to Wells: "Miss Ida B. Wells had stirred up the brain and conscience of English Christendom upon the murder of American citizens," shaming the people of Memphis into dissociating themselves from lynching.[128]

In a section accidentally omitted from his "Bystander" column of 15 September and attached to that of the following week, Tourgée further expanded on Wells's achievement. The "revulsion of sentiment" toward lynching in the South—exemplified by the *Memphis Appeal*'s corroboration of the "very gist" of Wells's "charges"—had occurred because "English Christian and philanthropic bodies" had at last "stimulated" the Northern public to condemn the "barbarism of mob rule," argued Tourgée. Attributing this result "wholly . . . to the unpretentious courage and tact of Miss Ida B. Wells," he elaborated: "No colored woman, and few women of any sort, have exercised so wide and so beneficent an influence on the civilization of any people." Yet he appended a caveat: "How permanent or effective it may be none can foresee."[129]

Championing Wells against Willard

Tourgée made his ultimate gesture of solidarity with Wells when he sided with her against Frances Willard in a dispute that began during Wells's second British lecture tour. As the founder and president of the Women's Christian Temperance Union (WCTU), an organization that numbered well over 100,000 members in the United States; as the chief proponent of a cause embraced by evangelical and mainline Christians on both sides of the Atlantic; and as the living embodiment of the marriage between moral reform and woman suffrage, Willard was worshiped in the United States and Britain alike.[130] In fact, she counted among her admirers thousands of African Americans, who belonged to separate WCTU chapters in the South but attended national meetings, at which they maneuvered for equal treatment.[131] In drawing African Americans and former white abolitionists into her orbit, Willard capitalized on her own abolitionist heritage. Simultaneously, however, she catered to white Southerners by playing on stereotypes of black drunkenness as a threat to the safety of white women. Willard's near-endorsement of the black rapist myth infuriated Wells, who accused her of "wholesale slander against the colored race and condonation of Southern white people's outrages against us." In turn, Wells provoked a storm of abuse by besmirching an icon of feminine piety and purity. The redoubtable Willard, who happened to be touring England at the same time as Wells, mobilized her British devotees and the entire WCTU for a counterattack. They circulated a statement defending Willard and vouching for her antiracist credentials. Its signatories included such white abolitionist stalwarts as William Lloyd Garrison Jr., Francis Jackson Garrison, Thomas Wentworth Higginson, Julia Ward Howe, and Ednah D. Cheney. Two of the African American community's most respected leaders, Frederick Douglass, whom Wells idolized, and Bishop Henry McNeal Turner, another valued antilynching ally, headed and rounded off the list. Their attestations in Willard's favor reflected the degree to which Wells's declaration of war on the sainted leader of a popular movement divided African American ranks, particularly among WCTU members. Conservative members remained loyal to Willard, while radicals championed Wells.[132]

The two women's hostilities reached a crescendo during the November 1894 annual convention of the WCTU, which met in Cleveland. In her speech at the convention, Willard alleged not only that Wells had "misrepresented" her and the WCTU but that "zeal for her race" had "clouded [Wells's] perception as to who were her friends and well-wishers." She demanded that Wells retract her aspersions on white women's sexual purity as "wholly without foundation."[133] Meanwhile, in deference to white Southern members of the WCTU, Willard prevented the organization from issuing the undiluted resolution against lynching that Wells sought.

Willard considered Tourgée a "good friend," as she boasted in an article written for the temperance newspaper the *Union Signal,* in which she reported on a speech he gave at a WCTU meeting.[134] Tourgée's acquaintance with Wells, on the other hand, was based solely on their common struggle for a just society and kept up almost entirely by correspondence. Nevertheless, he did not hesitate to back Wells rather than Willard, even though Willard pleaded in a personal letter for his seal of approval.[135] In a "Bystander" article of 24 November subtitled "Lynching as a Fad," Tourgée dismissed Willard's allegations that Wells had unfairly maligned her and the WCTU. Wells's assertion was "literally true," Tourgée retorted—the WCTU had indeed been "absolutely silent" about this "monstrous barbarism": "Not until lashed by [Wells's] words and the condemnation of English critics did that organization venture" even a mild censure; "it has not yet uttered any vigorous protest." In his next paragraph, Tourgée also replied to an "Eastern journal" that claimed Wells conveyed a "wholly false impression" when she charged U.S. Christians with encouraging lynching through their silence. "Neither the Christianity, the pulpit, nor the press of the country . . . took any special notice of . . . lynching, until they were driven to it by months and years of earnest and impassioned protest"—his own, the *Inter Ocean*'s, and Wells's—Tourgée rejoined. Given the refusal to date of even a single Northern state to pass an antilynching law, "it is not to be wondered at that a poor colored girl, whose heart is wrung by the unspeakable woes of her race," should judge white American Christians guilty of silence, contended Tourgée. "It is because she speaks the truth that American Christianity withers under her gentle rebuke," he chided. "It does no good to scold or blame her. She is black, but the only way to refute her is" to take meaningful action against lynching.[136] We might assume that the militant Wells cringed at being characterized as a "poor colored girl." The words "gentle rebuke" hardly capture the sting of her tirades against her compatriots—as, indeed, Tourgée recognized when he described her as having "lashed" the WCTU with her tongue. Yet no sign of ambivalence surfaced in the letter Wells immediately wrote to thank Tourgée for his "strong words in defence of [her] and the cause." On the contrary, she assured him, "As always, I feel grateful to you for the only unequivocal expressions in behalf of justice which you alone seemed moved to make."[137]

In the same "Bystander" article that defended Wells against Willard, Tourgée also commented on yet another attempted lynching in Ohio— hence the subtitle "Lynching as a Fad," signifying, as Tourgée explained in the text, that "lynching, wherever it occurs, is a fashionable crime" because "it offers an opportunity to commit murder without fear of blame or punishment." This time, by sending troops of the Ohio National Guard to protect the prisoner, who had pleaded guilty to rape and received a twenty-year sentence, Governor McKinley succeeded in preventing the mob from breaking into the courthouse to seize its intended victim—but at a high cost. When the mob tried to storm the courthouse and refused to disperse, the troops' commander ordered them to shoot through the doors, killing five of the assailants. Indicted for manslaughter, he was ultimately acquitted, although public sympathy lay with the mob. The case illustrated what was "always true of a lynching," editorialized Tourgée, "to wit, it proceeded from, was approved and instigated by, 'the best people' of the town and county." If the Ohio legislature had passed Smith's bill imposing a tax on the county for the "luxury" of indulging in a lynching, Tourgée insisted, the "best people" would never have countenanced the mob attack on the courthouse and the ensuing tragedy "would have been avoided." He inculpated the people of Ohio, black as well as white, in the bill's defeat. The apathy of whites and the failure of blacks to "unite and send in petitions for its passage" had led legislators to conclude that public sentiment favored "mob rule and lynch law, especially when the victims were colored men," opined Tourgée.[138]

For his part, while lamenting the loss of a "golden opportunity" to pass his bill and expressing fear that the backlash against the troops' use of lethal force would block any future antilynching measure, Smith took credit for McKinley's strong stand. His own "persistency" in repeatedly meeting with McKinley to demand action against lynching had prompted the governor to dispatch the National Guard, he claimed.[139] Smith was to show the same persistency by taking his antilynching bill back to the Ohio legislature when it next met in 1896.[140]

During the interim he, like Tourgée, championed Wells against Willard. "Imagine Miss Ida B. Wells telling Miss Francis [*sic*] E. Willard 'to her teeth' . . . in a perfectly lady-like, yet firm and dignified manner, that she had wronged her and our cause in her annual address" at the WCTU conference, Smith crowed.[141] Branding Willard "a temporizer," he accused her of "straddling the lynch question" in a vain effort to "please the anti-lynch people and not displease the south." If Willard hoped to maintain her credibility with African Americans and their allies, she would have to change both her "tune" and her "views," Smith warned.[142] Notwithstanding his bravado, Smith could not help perceiving the ominous fault lines in the African American community that the Wells-Willard confrontation revealed. As he noted both in a headline and in the text of another article in the same number of the *Gazette*, "a few misguided Afro-Americans . . . were foolish enough to want to present Miss Willard a bouquet in the name of the Afro-American ladies of Cleveland, that, too, in the face of her adverse comment upon Miss Wells and the race's cause."[143]

The Backlash from Conservative African Americans

The WCTU hardly constituted the sole forum in which Wells encountered African American opposition to her militancy. Less than two weeks after her triumphal homecoming, she recalled in her posthumous autobiography, "a delegation of the men of my own race . . . asked me to put the soft pedal on charges against white women and their relations with black men"—a request she "indignantly refused." Worse still, leading ministers of the African Methodist Episcopal Church in Philadelphia balked at passing a resolution against lynching that endorsed Wells's work—an "insult" she contrasted with the enthusiastic reception the British had given her. She was destined to endure many more such insults, she wrote bitterly in retrospect.[144]

The winds of conservatism were blowing through the African American community. Even before Booker T. Washington delivered his famous address of 18 September 1895 at the Atlanta Exposition, where he called for "cultivating friendly relations with the Southern white man," some African Americans, battered by decades of white supremacist onslaught, were leaning toward accommodation to the status quo as a safer strategy than agitation for equal rights. Like Wells, Tourgée increasingly found himself muscled aside in the recoil from radicalism, beginning as early as 1892. Not only did such conservative African American editors as Edwin H. Hackley of the *Denver Statesman* and Edward E. Cooper of the *Indianapolis Freeman* denounce "Tourgeeism" that year, but two purported spokesmen of Philadelphia's black community—Robert Purvis, formerly a radical Garrisonian abolitionist, and Isaiah C. Wear, a wealthy, self-made businessman—even deprecated his crusade against lynching. "Won't Indorse Tourgee—Leading Colored Men Regard Him as an Alarmist" gloated the headlines in the 18 June 1892 *Philadelphia Times*, which identified Purvis and Wear as "The Two Most Prominent Representatives of Their Race" in the city and credited them with "national reputations" among "whites and blacks alike." When Tourgée prophesied that if lynching did not cease, a black uprising would necessarily erupt, "rivaling in horror the most sanguinary phase of the French Revolution," Wear sneered that if Tourgée's long "residence in the South" had not given him better insight, "his case [was] hopeless." More egregiously, the *Times* quoted

Purvis as asserting that Tourgée did not "voice the sense of the thinking colored people of the South." "Decent" African Americans could not "afford to make a race war upon the whites in the defense of criminals," Purvis told the *Times'* reporter. He went so far as to reiterate the myth that "lynchings . . . have been almost without exception visited upon colored men who have outraged white women"—a myth Wells, Smith, and Tourgée had all persuasively refuted.[145]

For the time being, however, such conservative cavilers represented a distinct minority of African Americans. Indeed, a week after the *Philadelphia Times* article appeared, "A Negro" from Ravenna, Ohio, probably F. J. Loudin, who owned a shoe factory there, forcefully replied to it. Purvis was ignorantly echoing white apologists' justifications of lynching, Loudin pointed out, but contrary to these justifications, "the facts prove[d] that not more than one-third of the black men who have been burned alive, hanged, shot or disjointed were even accused of assaulting white women." Loudin cited supporting examples drawn from both Wells's and Tourgée's journalism and concluded by saying that much as he "dislike[d]" the prospects of race war, his "observation" led him to agree "with our friend and benefactor, Judge Tourgee, rather than" with Purvis, who had done valuable work for the race in the past but had "lost his bearings now."[146]

The conservative rumblings audible in the attacks on Tourgée, the rallying around Willard, and the nervous attempts to muzzle Wells were drowned out by hosannas in August 1894. Marking the peak of the impact Wells exerted on U.S. public opinion after her second British tour, that month saw the founding of the Massachusetts Anti-Lynching League, the first such organization in the United States, and the introduction by New Hampshire Republican Henry Blair of the first antilynching bill submitted to Congress. Tourgée surely referred to these achievements, as much as to developments in the South, when he judged Wells's influence almost unprecedented for a woman. He nevertheless proved prescient in worrying that it might not last.[147] The Massachusetts Anti-Lynching League left no significant imprint, and the Blair bill went down to defeat, as would every subsequent federal antilynching bill ever proposed.[148] Although Wells's crusade climaxed in 1895 with what we now recognize as her magnum opus, *A Red Record*, she was forced to publish and distribute the book herself. As a result, it reached such a small audience that neither Smith nor Tourgée received review copies, apparently—the only convincing explanation for the two men's failure to mention a book both would otherwise have applauded.[149]

Tourgée's journalistic campaign against lynching suffered a fate similar to Wells's, as the *Inter Ocean* once again terminated his "Bystander" column in January 1895. True, he continued to publicize lynchings in his organ *The Basis: A Journal of Citizenship*, to which he transferred the "Bystander." The "Mob Record" column he introduced into the *Basis* resembled the "Lynch Law Statistics" chapter of Wells's *A Red Record*. It listed all instances of persons hanged, shot, burned, assaulted, wounded, and raped; tallied them; and furnished the names of the victims where available. Like *A Red Record*, however, the *Basis* numbered very few readers. Despite copious advertising in the *Cleveland Gazette* and enthusiastic promotion by Tourgée's African American fans, it attracted only about 1,200 subscribers, compared to the *Inter Ocean's* 200,000.[150]

Passing the Ohio Antilynching Law

With Wells and Tourgée marginalized, it fell to Smith to carry their collective antilynching campaign to fruition. He did so both through the *Cleveland Gazette* and through the Ohio legislature. In the *Gazette* Smith kept up a steady drumbeat of articles tracking lynchings, praising Wells's and Tourgée's contributions, and mobilizing support for his antilynching law. "According to the New Orleans Crusader—an excellent authority on such matters—180 Afro-Americans were lynched in 1894. . . . Many were innocent and defenseless victims of bloodthirsty mobs," Smith reported on 19 January 1895.[151] On 2 February he instructed *Gazette* readers to "drop the Inter Ocean" because it had "dropped" Tourgée's "Bystander" column.[152] On 2 March he heralded the forthcoming inauguration of the *Basis*, "edited by the race's most aggressive friend," and hence deserving "a wide circulation among our people."[153] On 20 July, shortly after Wells's marriage to Ferdinand L. Barnett, Smith announced that she had taken over her husband's newspaper, the *Chicago Conservator*. "We welcome her to the editorial field of journalism," he cheered (forgetting that she had entered that field years ago in Memphis).[154] On 17 August he defended Wells against an "exceedingly narrow-minded" African American editor who had maligned her as "'a notoriety seeker.'" In another editorial of the same date, he endorsed the Woman's Era Club's resolutions in favor of Catherine Impey, Tourgée, and "Mrs. Ida Wells Barnett, as a fearless and unflinching advocate of the humane and just treatment of the Afro-American."[155] He found it deplorable, Smith remarked in an earlier editorial, that any "members of our own race" could disparage Wells's "herculanean efforts" or "question the wisdom of [her] continued

agitation of this 'lynching' matter!"[156] On 19 October Smith again advertised the *Basis* and reprinted from it Tourgée's nuanced analysis of Booker
T. Washington's Atlanta address. (Unlike most interpreters, Tourgée read it
as "a distinct departure" from Washington's usual accommodationist mode
because its "concluding portion . . . demand[ed] for his people security and
justice.")[157] As 1895 ended and 1896 dawned, Smith and Louis A. Martinet
traded editorial tributes to Tourgée. Commenting on the "unique position"
Tourgée occupied as "the most active and constant white friend the race
has," Smith asked, "Have you noticed that there is no great competition for
the position?" Quoting this comment in the *Crusader*, Martinet answered
sarcastically, "Yes, and have you noticed also the gratitude of the race for his
unflagging friendship and devotion to their interests? . . . He is a true friend,
indeed, he who remains faithful when indifference and ingratitude are the
reward of disinterested service and self-sacrifice."[158]

Meanwhile, Smith alerted his constituency to his own campaign for reelection to the state legislature, as a prelude to resubmitting his antilynching
bill. "At the Front. Where His Own Efforts Have Placed Hon. H. C. Smith.
An Orator and Writer. He Has Been Very Successful along Both Lines. . . .
Two Years in the General Assembly and on the Road to Two More"—so
proclaimed the headlines of a biographical sketch of Smith reprinted on 5
October 1895 from the *Cleveland Leader*, which pronounced his chances of
reelection "splendid."[159] A spate of articles followed about states that were
considering antilynching bills modeled on the one Tourgée had drafted for
Ohio, of which he and Smith had sent copies far and wide. South Carolina,
Texas, and Alabama were all debating such bills, Smith noted.[160] In other
editorials Smith hailed McKinley as "the Man of the Hour," celebrated
"throughout the country" for standing up to a lynch mob; described a mass
meeting held at Faneuil Hall by three thousand Bostonians to denounce
lynching; lamented a lynching that had arisen from a mere "accident" and
had victimized the "wrong man"; detailed the latest conflicts between supporters of Willard and of Wells in the British WCTU; and reviewed the
year's record of lynchings, which he characterized as "more cruel, brutal and
horrible" than ever, though slightly fewer than in 1894.[161]

Finally, on 25 January 1896 Smith exultantly informed readers that he
had reintroduced his antilynching bill in the Ohio legislature, where it
had received two public readings before being sent to the judiciary committee. From all indications, he predicted, the bill would be "promptly
passed." Outgoing governor McKinley had strongly recommended an
antilynching law in his last message to the legislature, which Smith claimed

had motivated him to return to the charge. An "overwhelmingly Republican" majority now dominated the legislature. The obstructionist William Clifford had met defeat. Two new African American colleagues in the House of Representatives, William Stewart of Youngstown and William Parham of Cincinnati, whom Smith ranked as "gentlemen of superior ability," could be expected to provide "valuable assistance." And Smith had procured the blessing of the state's two "most prestigious newspapers," the *Ohio State Journal* of Columbus and the *Cleveland Plain Dealer* of his home city. But this time Smith was leaving no stone unturned. "Judge Tourgee, who drew the bill, has promised to appear before the [judiciary] committee in conjunction with Representative Smith," he reported. Moreover, Tourgée had strengthened the bill with an amendment Smith had suggested, "providing against a shifting of the financial responsibility" for lynchings from one county to another.[162] The following week Tourgée advised two further amendments to clarify the "definition of what constitutes a mob" and to allow "persons killed in the defense of prisoners . . . to collect damages from the county." "I can not find words to properly express my appreciation of . . . his well-known and never-tiring interest in the race," Smith enthused. He reciprocated by enjoining *Gazette* subscribers to "read [Tourgée's] splendid books 'A Fool's Errand,' 'Bricks Without Straw,' 'An Appeal to Caesar,' 'Pactolus Prime,' and others . . . of especial interest to our people."[163]

Tourgée duly arrived in Columbus, where he stayed at the "famous Neil [H]ouse" hotel as Smith's guest, and the two dined together in an exhibition of cross-racial solidarity uncommon during the nadir. "What a tour [*sic*] of strength to the race Judge Tourgée is!" exclaimed Smith, buoyed by listening to so "many pertinent statements relative to our people." The next day, 5 February, in a session covered by the *Cleveland Plain Dealer* and *Daily Leader*, whose accounts Smith quoted, Tourgée addressed the judiciary committee before a packed audience that included hundreds of ordinary citizens and "ladies," as well as legislators. They "listened . . . with marked interest" as he "painted the terrors of mob violence in striking colors," decried "with subtle sarcasm the ease with which 'real good people' become exasperated at evil" (a standard rationale for lynching), praised Governor McKinley, and "declared that if the bill was passed there would never be another lynching in Ohio."[164] Calling Tourgée's speech "a treat," Smith pressed Ohio African Americans to do their part: "Go and see your state senator and representative and urge them to support the bill."[165] He kept haranguing them in subsequent weeks. "It does look as if our people throughout Ohio are not much interested in the passage of the anti-lynching bill now pending in the house of representatives," he complained on 22 February, charging that a "large number" of representatives had "not even been approached on the subject by a single one of their constituents" and that not one petition in favor of the bill had yet "been received." Did African American churches "desire mob violence and lynching to continue?" he scolded.[166] "Where are the many so-called race organizations and what are they doing" to lobby for the bill?, Smith demanded again a week later.[167]

The bill had in fact come up for a vote on 26 February, when Smith had made an "able argument" for its passage, according to press accounts he reprinted from the *Columbus Dispatch* and *Cleveland Plain Dealer*. Despite a margin of sixteen votes—fifty for compared to thirty-four against—it fell six votes short of the "necessary constitutional majority." The main opposition, according to historian David A. Gerber, came from legislators of both parties representing the "southern and central counties, where almost all of the recent manifestations of lynch law had occurred."[168] Yet Smith faulted African American apathy as well, and several of his fellow African American editors agreed. "The same old indifference to vital interest seems still to be a characteristic of our people," lamented the *Standard* of Lexington, Kentucky. "Mr. Smith is making strenuous efforts to have a more favorable consideration of the bill. He should have the united support of Negroes at least," editorialized the *Indianapolis Freeman*. As might be expected, Wells spoke out the most vociferously. "If it is true that the indifference of our people to the measure has helped defeat it," she wrote in the *Chicago Conservator*, "it is a shame and disgrace to the race in Ohio." Avowing that the "active opposition or indifference of her own people" to her antilynching campaign had caused "her greatest discouragements," she called on Ohio African Americans to "rally to the support of the anti-lynching bill as one man." Individuals, churches, and associations "should send letters and resolutions to, or call in person upon, their representatives who voted adversely to the bill and urge their support," she specified. "The fate of the race is at stake, and the opportunity may not be theirs again soon."[169]

The tenacious Smith secured a reconsideration of the bill, set for 24 March, and mobilized all the resources at his command—the white press, the black press, churches, race organizations, and community spokespersons—on his second attempt. "Pass the Bill. That Is What Leading Ohio Daily Newspapers Say. . . . They Maintain That Ohio Cannot Afford a Failure to Pass the Bill" and "It Ought To Pass," screamed the *Gazette*'s headlines over articles reprinted from the *Cleveland Leader*, the *Cleveland Daily World*, and the *Ohio State Journal*. At last on the afternoon of the twenty-fourth, Smith's newsletter to the *Gazette* triumphantly announced, "Ohio's anti-lynching bill was passed in the house to-day about 4 p.m., the vote being 61 yeas and 22 nays," four more than the required "constitutional majority."[170] Gerber attributes the gain to "intensive campaigning among house Republicans" but observes that "a relatively large number of southern Ohio Republicans still" withheld their support.[171] Not inclined either to look on the dark side or to rest on his laurels, Smith reminded readers that before becoming law, the bill needed to pass the state senate. "Will our people in Ohio please see their state senators AT ONCE. . . . Don't delay a day," he exhorted them.[172] The bill sailed through the senate on 8 April, with "22 yeas and only 2 nays." Its passage put Ohio in the vanguard of "anti-lynching and anti-mob violence legislation," boasted Smith. No other state legislature had yet approved such a law, nor did bills pending elsewhere "even . . . approach" Ohio's in sophistication. Rejoicing that his "nearly two years labor" had "at last been crowned with success," Smith once again importuned readers to "show some practical appreciation" of the bill's author, Tourgée, "that sterling and constantly aggressive friend of the race," by subscribing to his "splendid magazine THE BASIS."[173] Tourgée returned the compliment in what would prove to be the last number of the *Basis*. To "Mr. H. C. Smith, a colored member of the Ohio legislature," and to "his colored associates, Mr. Stewart and Mr. Parham, the credit for the enactment of this law is chiefly due," he affirmed. "They are entitled to the highest praise, and have nobly attested the wisdom of their party in giving representation in the legislature to the colored people of the state."[174]

The Afterlife of the Ohio Antilynching Law

Contrary to the hopes Smith and Tourgée had invested in it, the Ohio antilynching law was destined for a checkered afterlife. Little more than a year after the bill cleared the state senate, a mob in Urbana, Ohio, gave the lie to Tourgée's confident prediction that "if the bill was passed there would never be another lynching in Ohio."[175] Once again, a young black man already sentenced by the court to the maximum prison term for rape was seized from jail and hanged, this time because a governor and mayor less resolute than McKinley failed to provide adequate troops to keep the assailants at bay. And once again Wells, Tourgée, and Smith joined their voices in condemnation—Wells and Tourgée almost literally, in articles the *Inter Ocean* published the same day.

Responding to another Chicago newspaper, the *Chronicle*, which had touted this "praiseworthy lynching" as an antidote to a crime mainly committed by "human creatures of the African race," Wells retorted, "Lynching is peculiarly an American institution, being unknown in Europe, Asia or Africa. It is 'praiseworthy' nowhere in the civilized world except under the protecting influences of the 'Stars and Stripes.'" She went on to cite two recent trials in Chicago involving white men who had raped juveniles. Would the *Chronicle* advise lynching these men?, she asked.[176]

Tourgée uncannily replicated Wells's critique. "The renaissance of mob-murder, which has come to color all our life . . . is distinctly an American institution," he agreed. Diagnosing it as a "manifestation of hate of the negro, which has festered in our life a foul and perilous residuum of slavery and a slave civilization," he noted that "race antipathy" had by now "come to possess the best as well as the worst elements of our white population." Like Wells, Tourgée ranked his native land at the bottom of a world scale. The "shame of mob murder . . . puts us morally on a level with the Turk in barbarism and below the level of any other people known to history in hypocrisy and false pretense," he contended. Unlike Wells, however, Tourgée vindicated the character of African Americans not by portraying whites as guilty of worse crimes but by highlighting "the proudest achievement of the colored race in America, thus far in its history": the purchase by the French government for the Luxembourg gallery of a painting, *The Raising of Lazarus*, that the Philadelphia African American artist Henry O. Tanner had exhibited in the 1897 "salon," France's prestigious annual art show. "While white Americans are exploiting their savage instincts in such brutal exhibitions as the murder of a condemned prisoner," editorialized Tourgée, "the colored American bearing the burden of disparagement and discrimination which meets him at every turn at home is winning honors for the American name abroad." Such recognition by the nation acknowledged as the art capital of the Western world, Tourgée underscored, was "the highest honor—indeed, one of the very few honors of a tangible sort—which has ever been conferred on an American artist abroad."[177]

Of the three journalists, Smith formulated the most damning indictment by publishing evidence that pointed to the Urbana lynching victim's entire innocence of the crime for which he had been so hastily convicted. His accuser, noted Smith's informant, had changed her story repeatedly and "was never touched," her description of the alleged rapist did not correspond at all to his appearance, and the accused man "never confessed, neither was any crime satisfactorily proven against him."[178]

If the Urbana case seemingly called into question the effectiveness of the Ohio law as a deterrent to lynching, it nonetheless afforded an opportunity for a court test, when the victim's family sued the county for maximum damages. At the trial the leading opponent ridiculed the law as another "fool's errand," and the judge ruled it unconstitutional, but both the county circuit court in 1898 and the Ohio State Supreme Court in 1900 sustained the law's constitutionality.[179] "Ohio's . . . anti-lynch-murder law . . . has been . . . *a grand* [double-underlined] success, thanks to *Judge A. W. Tourgee*, our *grand friend* [quadruple-underlined] for so very many years," Smith exulted in a letter to Emma after her husband's death.[180]

How, ultimately, can we measure the law's success? By one criterion, it fell short of its aims: it did not end lynchings in Ohio, though it did apparently reduce their frequency, from five in the 1890s to two in the decade after 1900. By another criterion—the influence it exerted—the Ohio law deserves to be regarded as Tourgée's greatest triumph. As Gerber documents, South Carolina, Kentucky, Illinois, Minnesota, Nebraska, New Jersey, Pennsylvania, West Virginia, and Wisconsin all passed antilynching laws modeled directly on Ohio's. The legal approach Tourgée had fashioned even served as an inspiration for the campaign against lynching waged by the NAACP.[181] Taking up the banner Tourgée, Wells, and Smith had so long carried, the NAACP would spend decades lobbying for a federal antilynching law but would meet defeat again and again in Southern-led filibusters without ever winning passage. Still, generations of antilynching agitators could take credit when the U.S. Senate at last apologized for this national crime in 2005.

Sadly, Tourgée never had the chance to savor his victory in Ohio, let alone the posthumous vindication of the U.S. Senate's apology. Less than a week after his antilynching bill cleared the Ohio Senate on 8 April, he confronted the hostile U.S. Supreme Court that would destroy his life's work.

CHAPTER SIX

Representing People of Color and Challenging Jim Crow in the *Plessy* Case

The revival of interest in the Jim Crow car matter is owing to you more than
to any one else. . . . We are not, however, without having some obstacles to
surmount among those who should help, as you will see by *the Crusader*, but
we are going ahead.
—Louis A. Martinet to Albion W. Tourgée, 5 October 1891

Why did Louis A. Martinet say in his first extant letter to Tourgée, dated
5 October 1891, "the revival of interest in the Jim Crow car matter is owing
to you more than to any one else"?[1] Answering that question necessitates
delving into the back story of the *Plessy v. Ferguson* case. Martinet used the
word "revival" because the "Jim Crow car matter" had actually begun a year
and a half earlier, in the summer of 1890, when white supremacists and people of color in Louisiana had faced off in a struggle over segregated train
travel. Outraged by the "separate car bill" pending in the state legislature,
which required "all railway companies . . . to provide equal but separate
accommodations for the white and colored races," Martinet had mobilized
opposition to it through the *Crusader*. He had also coauthored an official
protest against such "caste" or "class legislation," addressed to the legislature
and signed by seventeen members of the American Citizens' Equal Rights
Association, an organization he had helped found. Employing language and
arguments Tourgée would later echo in his brief to the U.S. Supreme Court,
the ACERA protest branded the measure "unconstitutional, un-American,
unjust, dangerous and against sound public policy"; invoked the Golden
Rule; pleaded against "unreasonable prejudice"; criticized as "problemati-
cal" theories about the "ethnical origin of color"; and emphasized (based
on the Fourteenth Amendment) that "citizenship is national and has no
color."[2] Besides acting as the opposition's chief spokesman, Martinet had
strategized with the eighteen African American legislators, lobbied their
white colleagues, and appealed to the governor to veto the bill. He remained
undaunted by defeat. Proposing two new means of continuing the battle
against Jim Crow, Martinet urged African Americans to boycott the railways
(as his associate Rodolphe L. Desdunes suggested) and to start contributing

funds toward a legal challenge. "We'll make a case, a test case, and bring it before the Federal Courts on the ground of the invasion of the right [of] a person to travel through the States unmolested," Martinet vowed in a *Crusader* editorial of 19 July 1890.[3]

Early Support from Tourgée

Inspired by this editorial, a young African American member of the ACERA named Eli C. Freeman took it upon himself to seek Tourgée's advice on whether or not to proceed with a test of the new law's constitutionality. He found Tourgée's reply "so encouraging" that he "could not refrain from" publishing it in the *Crusader* without first asking permission, for which he apologized.[4]

Nothing further came of the intended legal challenge for more than a year, however, whether because the ACERA collapsed in the interim or because Louisiana's citizens of color had responded with "apathy" to the *Crusader's* boycott and "test case" campaigns, as a "pessimistic" correspondent of the paper alleged.[5] Martinet and Desdunes kept up the fight in the *Crusader*, but the quest for justice was looking more and more hopeless to many of their readers. Answering such doubts in an article titled "Forlorn Hope and Noble Despair," Desdunes explained why he and Martinet considered it vital to wage a "*guerre à mort*," or war to the death, against the "separate car statute." Both recognized that a formidable list of judicial precedents stood against them yet maintained, in words Desdunes paraphrased from Martinet, that "the *decisions of Courts were the opinions of men*" and as such might be reversed. Both felt certain that history would ultimately vindicate them because their "cause [was] grounded in law, reason, and humanity." Above all, both held that "defeat is more honorable than flight or surrender," as Desdunes put it, and that "'liberty is won by continued resistance to tyranny'"—words he quoted from a lost editorial by Martinet. Desdunes ended, "If the separate car suit is a forlorn hope, we trust to see the people show a noble despair, and be prepared to face any disappointment that might await them at the tray of American justice."[6]

As they contended with defeatists in their ranks, Martinet and Desdunes must have found welcome ammunition in a "Bystander" article by Tourgée that appeared the same day as the *Crusader's* "Forlorn Hope and Noble Despair." Martinet reacted to it by initiating a public dialogue with Tourgée about the need for African American newspaper editors to stand up boldly for their people's rights and fearlessly denounce the crimes committed against them.[7] In another portion of this "Bystander" column of 15 August 1891, Tourgée commented on a "ludicrous" effect of separate car laws: complaints in Texas and Louisiana newspapers about "the inconveniences which the *white people* are compelled to suffer" as a result of the Jim Crow legislation they had demanded and won. Recalling how these two states had "celebrated the victory gained in favor of separate cars for each race" in a Supreme Court verdict on a Mississippi case that he predicted would "one day rank with . . . the Dred Scott" decision, Tourgée chortled, "One or two colored people often have half or the whole of a good car to themselves while every seat is doubly laden and men are even standing in the aisles of the white compartments, cussing the niggers for having the best end of legislation especially intended to degrade and oppress them." (Whites would quickly solve this problem by using the "colored" car as a smoker, in defiance of the rule that each race must ride only in its assigned space.) In the very next section of the same "Bystander" article, Tourgée castigated African Americans who counseled submission rather than resistance to oppression. "Submission to oppression stimulates the desire to oppress," he warned. "Only those people who stubbornly and persistently assert their rights, ever rest secure in their possession."[8] Martinet may well have understood Tourgée to be calling specifically for resistance to Jim Crow laws, in line with the *Crusader*'s position. If so, that may be one reason why he credited Tourgée with doing more than "any one else" to revive the flagging commitment to testing the constitutionality of the Separate Car Law in federal court.[9]

Another reason, no doubt, is that in response to a nationwide appeal by the ACERA immediately after the law's passage, Tourgée had already "offered [his] services and made suggestions" on conducting a constitutional challenge, as Desdunes revealed in "To Be or Not to Be," a letter to the *Crusader* of 4 July 1891. Despite this offer, "indecision," insufficient funds, and lack of "proper . . . direction" were still stymieing proponents of a test case. Desdunes summoned them to act, exhorting his comrades not to give up until they had "exhaust[ed] every legal remedy" against discrimination. If the established political leaders of Louisiana's Creole-of-color and African American communities refused to assume responsibility, hinted Desdunes, he and his fellow militants would "devise their own ways and means."[10] They did so less than two months later on 1 September, when eighteen men, prompted by a Creole-of-color veteran of radical Reconstruction, Aristide Mary, met in the office of the *Crusader* to form the Citizens' Committee for the Annulment of Act No. 111 Commonly Known as the Separate Car Law.

Within four days, the committee issued an "appeal to the citizens of New Orleans, of Louisiana and of the whole Union, . . . without regard to age, color or condition," to help finance a court challenge of this "oppressive law" through a "popular subscription" fund. Listed in the *Crusader* under the heading "Mr. Desdunes's stocking," donations indeed ranged from fifty cents to over a hundred dollars. Most came not from individuals but from groups, many with French titles, including women's and children's organizations, unions, lodges, and churches, the preponderance from Louisiana but a sprinkling from as far away as Washington, D.C., Kansas, and San Francisco. The amount collected would eventually total almost $3,000, and the final report of the Citizens' Committee would include the names of 150 contributors.[11] No wonder, then, that Tourgée hailed the enterprise for laying to rest the libel on people of African descent as "incapable of . . . co-operation . . . and voluntary self-sacrifice for the common good."[12]

The Archival Record of the Tourgée-Martinet Collaboration

Through the *Crusader,* Tourgée closely followed the committee's course. His "Bystander" columns of 12 September and 3 October praised the *Crusader* for its "earnest and active" mobilization of "legal resistance to the 'Jim Crow' car infamy" and reprinted the committee's "Appeal." Some time during these weeks, Tourgée also wrote to Martinet, calling him a "hero" and offering to serve pro bono as counsel to the Citizens' Committee. Martinet's reply on 5 October to this no-longer-extant letter inaugurated the two men's lengthy correspondence, as well as their collaboration in what became the *Plessy v. Ferguson* case. "Do not call me a hero," Martinet admonished Tourgée. "I am a plain, ordinary man. I prefer that. That way I'll not disappoint you." He went on to accept Tourgée's offer in the committee's name, adding that every member to whom he had shown Tourgée's letter had "spontaneously, warmly & gratefully" joined in thanking him "from the deepest of our hearts for all you have done & for the generous tender of your services in the case." Perhaps referring to terms Tourgée had set, Martinet assured him, "You will be the leading counsel & select your own associate. We know we have a friend in you & we know your ability is beyond question. We know you will give more time & attention to the preparation of the case than any other & you shall have control from beginning to end."[13]

Over the next five years, Tourgée and Martinet consulted with each other on every aspect of the case, from devising legal strategy to arousing public support for a court challenge. The twenty-five surviving letters

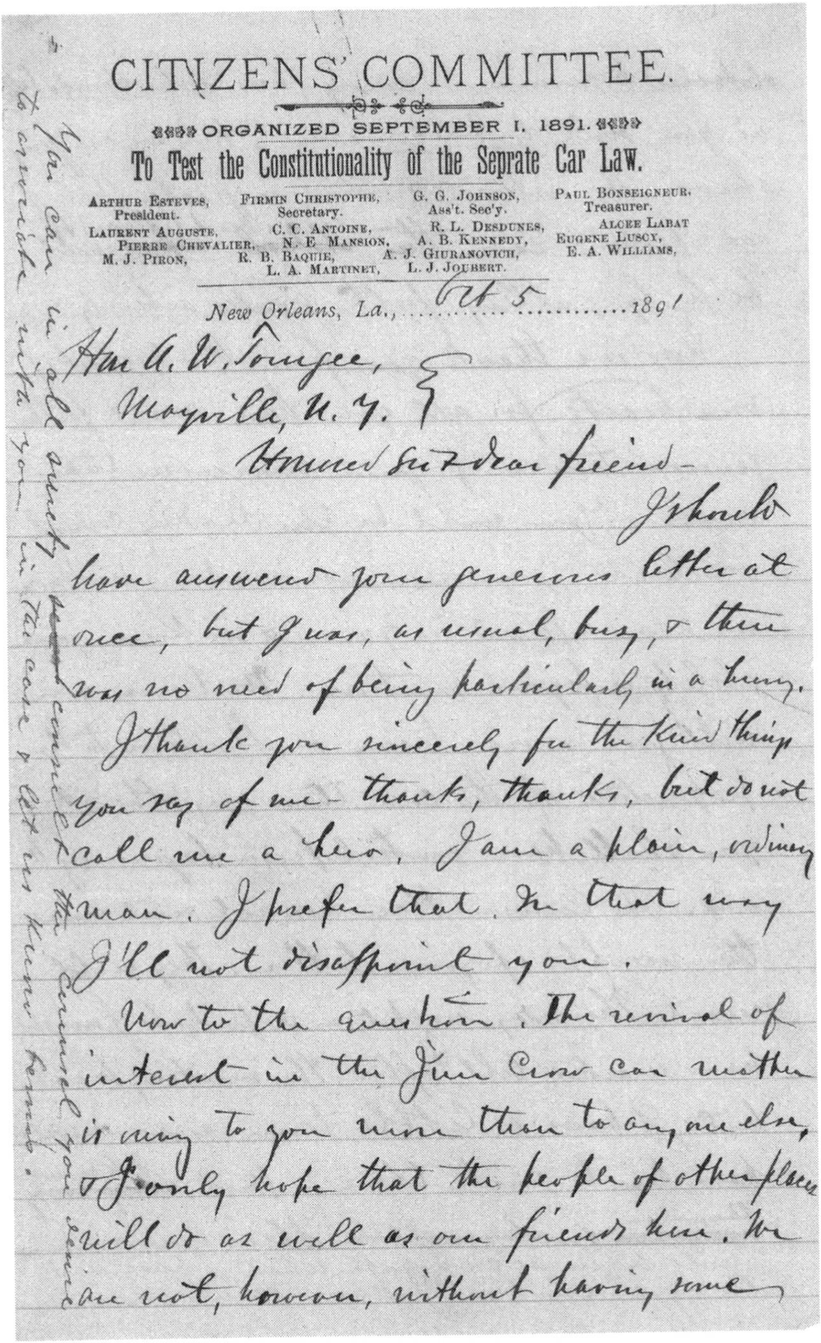

FIGURE 8 The opening page of Louis A. Martinet's first extant letter to Tourgée, dated 5 October 1891. Courtesy of the Chautauqua County Historical Society, Westfield, N.Y. No proven photograph of Martinet exists.

between them provide a rich record of their collegial cooperation and show how it ripened into the most intimate cross-racial friendship either man would ever experience.[14] While affording a unique, behind-the-scenes perspective on the *Plessy* litigation, the Tourgée-Martinet correspondence nonetheless confronts scholars with frustrating asymmetries and gaps. Because Martinet's papers, unlike Tourgée's, have vanished without a trace—reflecting the differential access to repositories that whites and people of color have commanded—most of Tourgée's letters to Martinet have been lost, except for the four of which he kept drafts. In contrast, the Tourgée archive, which encompasses more than 11,000 items, has preserved Martinet's twenty-one letters to him. Often Tourgée's voice reaches us through what appear to be quotations in Martinet's replies. It is in Martinet's letters that we must seek Tourgée.

Interpreting a Key Piece of Evidence

Illustrating how carefully we must scrutinize the abundant, yet partial, sources documenting the two men's collaboration in mounting the case against segregation, Martinet's letter of 5 October obliges us to deduce the legal strategies Tourgée outlined from the questions Martinet raised about their feasibility. After conveying the committee's gratitude and dispensing with other preliminaries, Martinet turned to Tourgée's "suggestions." He numbered the paragraphs he commented on, probably in conformity with Tourgée's own numbering. Apparently, Tourgée had suggested three possible methods of staging a defiance of the Separate Car Law that could lead to an arrest, conviction, and eventual appeal to the U.S. Supreme Court. The first involved arranging to have a "lady ... nearly white refused admission to a 'white' car." Tourgée no doubt specified a "lady" because he presumed a genteel woman would garner more sympathy from the court than a gentleman of similar refinement and standing, and perhaps because he knew from the example of Wells's 1884 lawsuit against the Chesapeake, Ohio, and Southwestern Railroad for ejecting her from the ladies' car that African American women had played a leading role in contesting segregation on trains and streetcars. As Blair L. M. Kelley underscores, "When African American women were ... physically dragged out of their seats in ladies' rail cars," their treatment made a mockery out of the rationale for segregation as a means of protecting "genteel white women" against the "sexual threat" of black male passengers.[15] Tourgée stipulated someone light enough to pass for white because such a choice would most effectively demonstrate the absurdity of segregating passengers by color and the arbitrariness of racial classifications (a long-standing theme in his writings, which his novel *Pactolus Prime* had dramatized the previous year). The second method Tourgée recommended consisted in having "a colored person coming from another State" be compelled by the conductor to move into the Jim Crow car on crossing the Louisiana state line—a situation that would test the applicability of state separate car laws to interstate travel. His third entailed having "a colored person attempt to buy a sleeper ticket & be refused after a white person has secured one"—a tactic that would show how racial discrimination violated the equal citizenship rights guaranteed by the Fourteenth Amendment.

Although he promised to "try & do the best we can" to implement Tourgée's suggestions, Martinet warned that local practices would complicate the effort. "It would be quite difficult to have a lady *too* nearly white refused admission to a 'white' car," Martinet pointed out, because color lines in New Orleans were so fluid that outsiders often could not distinguish between "white" and "colored," and, consequently, people of "tolerably fair complexion, even if unmistakably colored, enjoy here a large degree of immunity from the accursed prejudice." An interstate challenge would pose a different obstacle: "All the surrounding States have the Jim Crow car law." Yet Martinet thought that once in Louisiana, a passenger could sneak "unobserved by the conductor . . . into the 'white' coach, & allow himself to be ejected." He added that he had already "written to a friend in Mississippi," likely F. B. Hood, who would be the right candidate for the experiment. As for Tourgée's third suggestion, Martinet judged it "hardly practical" because railway clerks generally sold first-class tickets and sleeper berths to "all well-dressed persons." Still, Martinet reiterated, "we can try it."

Notwithstanding his repeated assertions of willingness to "try" Tourgée's three proposed methods of staging the case, many scholars have interpreted Martinet's caveats as indicating that he objected to the strategy of using a light-skinned plaintiff to embody the wrongfulness of segregation. Some have even alleged that Tourgée proceeded with this strategy despite "vigorous opposition from organized Black leadership"—an allegation Tourgée's biographer Mark Elliott has pronounced "utterly without foundation."[16] Not only was Martinet far too independent-minded to acquiesce in a strategy he opposed—especially given the high stakes of testing the constitutionality of segregation—but he and his fellow Creoles of color frequently argued, as did Tourgée, that the prevalence of race-mixing and the resulting variety of complexions undermined the racial categories on which segregation depended. One contributor to the *Crusader*, for example, predicted that "the attempt to force class legislation in a free Republic" would fail, "especially in Louisiana, with its cosmopolitan population, and where it is so difficult, sometimes, to tell who is who or which is which."[17] Moreover, far from relying on such arguments to claim privileges for themselves at the expense of darker members of their community (contrary to what some scholars have charged), Creole-of-color radicals denounced the Separate Car Law, in Desdunes's words, as "a slap in the face of every member of the black race, whether he has the full measure or only one-eighth of that blood."[18] Thus, Tourgée could hardly have formulated a strategy more in keeping with his clients' worldview and values.

The very letter we have been examining conclusively dispels the myth that the "colored" leaders who spearheaded the court case against railway segregation fiercely resisted the strategy their dictatorial white lawyer imposed on them. After all, if Martinet and the fellow members of the Citizens' Committee with whom he shared Tourgée's communication objected so strongly to Tourgée's preference for a light-skinned plaintiff, why would they have "spontaneously, warmly & gratefully" accepted his offer to serve as their counsel, much less granted him complete "control" of the litigation and insisted that all other lawyers associated with the case "conform to [his] views"—decisions the full committee formally ratified a few days later? Instead, we can best interpret Martinet's caveats in the light of his follow-up letter of 11 October, in which he wrote, "When we hear from you on . . . what you think of the difficulties I suggested might be in the way to act strictly in accordance with your suggestions, we will go about making the case or cases."[19] That is, Martinet was not rejecting any of Tourgée's legal strategies on principle but simply advising him that they might need to be modified to fit local circumstances.

On one point Tourgée raised in the lost letter that Martinet answered on 5 October, the two men fully agreed. Both believed that the battle against segregation needed to be fought in the court of public opinion as well as in courts of law—a belief grounded in their dual professions as lawyers-turned-journalists. Hence, Martinet eagerly embraced Tourgée's proposal to found a national organization open to both whites and people of color, through which to build broad support for condemning Jim Crow laws as unconstitutional. He particularly approved of the racially integrated membership that would model the ideal of equal citizenship. Martinet and his fellow Creoles of color had wanted "nothing to do with" the Afro-American League because it based membership on race, he confided to Tourgée. Creoles of color differed from Americanized blacks in opposing "segregation of every sort," notes Kelley, "even the establishment of all-black colleges and churches." She clarifies, "Although they wanted to avoid being stigmatized by blackness," they "did not want to become white." Rather, they aspired to preserve their "unique legacy" as Creoles—a legacy that included roots in Francophone culture and the egalitarian ideology of the French Revolution, as well as mixed bloodlines.[20] Martinet recognized in Tourgée a white man whose commitment to the ideal of a racially integrated America matched his own. Having endorsed the concept of Tourgée's projected national organization, he went a step further. To maximize its outreach, Martinet emphasized, the organization would require its own newspaper. He would prod his friend to establish such a paper, support Tourgée's plans for the *National Citizen*, and help distribute the *Basis*, besides participating from the outset in shaping and promoting the National Citizens' Rights Association.

Staging the Case and Choosing a Legal Team

Although Martinet played only an auxiliary role in the NCRA, the two men equitably divided the labor of preparing for the court challenge. Tourgée concentrated on researching and writing the legal briefs, while Martinet assumed responsibility for making the arrangements to set the case in motion: investigating precedents and impediments, negotiating with railway companies to procure their cooperation, selecting a resident lawyer to handle local formalities, hiring private detectives to identify the "colored" passenger in the "white" coach and ensure his or her safety during the arrest, and finding volunteers to disobey the law.[21] In his letter of 5 October, for example, Martinet described two cases into which he was inquiring that might supply precedents for a means of challenging the Separate Car Law: one in which "two colored ladies" had been "forced out . . . of the 'white' coach into the 'colored' while the train was going at the usual rate of speed," and another in which a Pullman conductor had been arrested for "allowing colored persons in the sleeper." He also explained why staging "a *habeas corpus* case . . . would require some tact" in order to avoid "personal danger": the passenger would have to be "refused admission into the 'white' car" and get arrested for entering it before the train's departure, "for if the car starts first, they will simply beat & throw him out, & there will be no arrest"; in addition, it would be crucial to ensure that the person be charged for violating the "separate car law, & not for breach of the peace."

As he went about meeting with railway officials, Martinet reported to Tourgée, he learned that "the roads are not in favor of the separate car law, . . . owing to the expense entailed" of supplying an additional coach for African American passengers. Nevertheless, they hesitated "to array themselves against it" openly because they "dread[ed] public opinion." One official called the law "bad" and "mean" and said the railroads "would like to get rid of it." Another admitted to Martinet that "their road did not enforce the law." They merely observed it formally, by furnishing "a coach for colored persons," posting "the sign required by law," and instructing their conductors to direct "colored" passengers to the coach but not to molest them "if they refused to go into it." Such noncompliance with the law amounted to "a victory already, as you can see," Martinet told Tourgée.[22] Finally, on 28 December Martinet informed Tourgée that the Louisville & Nashville Railroad had agreed to help test the Separate Car Law, on condition that a white passenger on the train (secretly in league with the committee), rather than a representative of the railroad, "object to the presence" of the colored intruder in the "white" coach. "The conductor will be instructed not to use force . . . & *our* white passenger will swear out the affidavit. This will give us our *habeas corpus* case, I hope," Martinet announced.[23]

The process of lining up a resident lawyer took almost as long as reaching an accord with a railway company. After considering two unaffordable candidates, Martinet selected James A. Walker, whom he characterized as "a friend & a conscientious & painstaking lawyer" who would give his clients "solid work." The committee had looked askance at Walker because his expertise lay in criminal law, not in constitutional issues, but Martinet had "faith in his integrity," having worked with him on several cases and known him to have "suffered" for his political convictions as an "active Republican." Moreover, Walker was charging only an economical $1,000 for his services, plus travel expenses to Washington.[24]

Apparently in response to a question by Tourgée, Martinet ruled out including a "colored lawyer" on the New Orleans team. The local ones he knew were of "limited attainments" and "practice[d] almost exclusively in the police" courts. "They would rather obstruct" than assist in the case, he opined. At the outset, as Martinet revealed in a previous letter, he and his associates had thought of hiring a well-known African American attorney named August Straker, even though Martinet had only a "moderate opinion of his attainments," but Straker's reply to a feeler requesting "his endorsement & moral support at least" had indicated that "his heart" was not "much in the cause." Hence, the committee had decided not to have any "colored" lawyer, "unless it be myself." The committee had in fact "unanimously voted" to draft Martinet on the legal team, he confided, but he had refused, unless it proved "necessary to keep some undesirable party out of it." In the first place, he had "no time to attend to" the legal appeal, being already overburdened with his "notarial business," his editorship of the *Crusader*, and his lectures on anatomy at the medical school, not to mention with the mechanics of arranging the habeas corpus case on which the court challenge of the Separate Car Law depended. In the second place, he was afraid "evil-disposed people" might accuse him of "ulterior" motives if he served the committee as a lawyer after playing an "instrumental" role in raising its legal fund.[25]

Ultimately, Tourgée would prevail upon Martinet to change his mind. As a *"regular* member" of both the Louisiana state bar and the federal circuit bar, Martinet had impressive credentials, and Tourgée wanted to bolster the case against segregation by confronting the Supreme Court justices with an able and eloquent African American lawyer. The committee unanimously endorsed Tourgée's recommendation. "They decided that I had no voice in the matter," protested Martinet. Besides, he could not help finding Tourgée's "friendship for & confidence in me, as well as the Committee's, . . .very gratifying," despite his "dread [of] the responsibility" and extra work.[26] Neither Martinet nor the committee relished the alternative Tourgée seems to have suggested without much enthusiasm: to engage John Mercer Langston or another nationally prominent attorney of the race. "Langston is said to be well versed in the law, but he is too vain to add much dignity to the bench," Martinet had told Tourgée in an earlier letter. Langston also figured among the "so-called 'leaders,'" for whom Tourgée and Martinet shared contempt.[27]

In the same letter apprising Tourgée of the reasons for selecting Walker and excluding the possibility of a local "colored lawyer," Martinet complained that an African American clergyman named Alexander S. Jackson was undermining the Citizens' Committee. Jackson had started a rival publication, "the *Legal Defense* (defunct already) ostensibly to wage war on the Jim Crow car, but really to obstruct the Committee." He had also spread "absurd and malicious" rumors that its leaders were "nearly white or wanted to pass for white" and that some had even sought to conceal their racial identity by donating anonymously to the group's legal fund. Martinet indignantly denied these accusations (which the presence on the committee of at least one dark-skinned person, C. C. Antoine, its vice president, likewise refutes, as Elliott has noted). Not being "politicians or preachers" (like the Reverend Jackson), his colleagues were "not seeking notoriety" or indulging in "bluster & buncombe," Martinet retorted. The largest donor, Paul Bonseigneur, had contributed anonymously out of modesty but was listed on the committee's stationery as treasurer. Bitterly, Martinet concluded that "next to the politicians, the preachers . . . are the greatest incumbrance the race has to contend with in its own ranks."[28]

Tourgée must have greeted the news of this feud with dismay because the Reverend Jackson had actually written to him only a few weeks before, not to malign the Citizens' Committee but to express support for the proposed NCRA as an organization "unifying all classes—true white men and true colored men"—precisely the position Martinet took.[29] Tourgée hastened to make peace between the two men, and Martinet accepted the view that Jackson had "been misrepresented."[30] No further signs of the imbroglio surfaced. "Perhaps Jackson's desire to establish a local NCRA chapter with himself at the head fueled" his denigration of the Citizens' Committee, speculates Elliott.[31]

Having chosen a resident attorney, put him in contact with Tourgée, and obtained the cooperation of a railway company, Martinet sought a volunteer for the arrest. "I would try it myself," he avowed, "but I am one of those whom a fair complexion favors. I go everywhere, in all public places, though well-known all over the city, & never is anything said to me."[32] His very ability to pass so easily might appear to identify Martinet as a perfect candidate for challenging the Separate Car Law, but he may not have wished to sacrifice the mobility he enjoyed. His reason for settling on a man rather than a woman, as Tourgée had originally suggested and as Martinet was still contemplating when he wrote on 7 December, is equally open to conjecture.[33] There may not have been any obvious female candidate for the action. Or the committee may have feared exposing a woman to possible violence, of the kind undergone by the "two colored ladies" Martinet had mentioned in his letter of 5 October. Or as Elliott surmises, the committee may have wanted "to project an image of 'manly resistance'" rather than of a damsel "in distress."[34] Whatever the reason, the committee designated Rodolphe Desdunes's nineteen-year-old son, Daniel, a professor of music, who fit the criterion of being light enough to pass for white and who carried out his mission on 24 February 1892.

Because Tourgée and the committee considered it advisable to begin by ascertaining whether the Separate Car Law violated the Constitution's interstate commerce clause, Daniel Desdunes purchased a first-class ticket to Mobile, Alabama. As planned, he seated himself in the "white" coach and "politely refused to comply" when a railway employee alerted to his racial identity ordered him to move to the "coach reserved for colored people." Also as planned, the conductor "stopped the train at the corner of Elysian

Fields and Claiborne streets," where a city Secret Service agent and two detectives hired by the committee arrested Desdunes and took him to the Second Recorder's Court to swear out an affidavit charging him with transgressing the Separate Car Law. The committee's treasurer, Paul Bonseigneur, then paid Desdunes's $500 bond.[35]

Before the Desdunes case came up for trial, however, the Louisiana Supreme Court ruled in a similar case that the Separate Car Law did not apply to interstate travel, which the U.S. Congress alone had the right to regulate. "The Jim Crow car is ditched and will remain in the ditch. Reactionist[s] may foam at the mouth and Bourbon organs may squirm, but Jim Crow is dead as a door nail," exulted the *Crusader* in an article reprinted in the *Cleveland Gazette* under the headline "Justice Wins."[36] The rejoicing proved premature, though, for the intrastate challenge would come to a far bleaker closure.

The committee did not wait for the dismissal of charges against Desdunes before enlisting Homer Adolphe Plessy—a shoemaker by trade, likewise with no discernible trace of African ancestry—in the next battle. (Once again, Rodolphe Desdunes seems to have had a hand in his selection, because Plessy was a friend of his.)[37] Writing a marathon letter to Tourgée that stretched out from 4 July to 29 August 1892, Martinet confessed, "Of course I do not entertain the same favorable result as hopefully as in the Desdunes [case]. But perhaps it is best that the battle be fought. I rely, however, more on the fact that the Negro's right to travel interstate being recognized, & if maintained by him, it will throw the 'Jim Crow' car into disuse, as you say." ("While Martinet's *Crusader* articles invariably predicted victory, his letter to Tourgee sounded a darker and more somber tone," observes Keith Weldon Medley.)[38] Apparently Tourgée shared Martinet's doubts regarding the U.S. Supreme Court's willingness to strike down separate car laws that operated within states. If so, that would explain why both men decided to begin with an interstate challenge that some historians have criticized as a costly detour. Further assessing the ruling that led to the dismissal of the Desdunes case, Martinet elaborated, "The right to travel *through* the State (Louisiana) is thus part of our jurisprudence. The railroads here in most, if not in all, cases so far as we have learned acquiesce in the decision. . . . We have now to fight the Plessy case for our right to travel *in* the State."[39] Clearly, he and Tourgée were counting on the interstate ruling—and the inconsistencies arising from it as railway officials and African American passengers pushed against the boundaries between federal and state policies—to reinforce their argument against the constitutionality of local as well as national Jim Crow laws.

Plessy's ritual protest and arrest on 7 June 1892 proceeded much the way Desdunes's had, except that he purchased a first-class ticket for Covington, Louisiana, on the East Louisiana Railroad, an intrastate line. As the *Crusader* reported, when asked by the conductor "if he was a white man, Plessy, who is as white as the average white Southerner, replied that he was a colored man." Ordered to move to "the coach reserved for colored people," Plessy "determinedly" refused, saying that he "was an American citizen and proposed to enjoy his rights as such and to ride for the value of his money." He added that "he would go to jail first before relinquishing his right as a citizen."[40] In accordance with the Citizens' Committee's arrangements, the conductor then stopped the train and turned Plessy over to a waiting detective who booked him at the police station, where his comrades procured his release on bail.

The Tourgée-Walker Correspondence

Plessy's Louisiana trial would not take place until October 1892, a year after Martinet accepted Tourgée's offer to serve gratis as lead counsel of the Citizens' Committee. In the meantime, Tourgée and resident attorney James C. Walker had been writing back and forth since January, developing the legal strategy and arguments they would use, first in the Desdunes case, then in Plessy's Louisiana trial, and ultimately at the Supreme Court. Tourgée soon found out how well justified Martinet's confidence in Walker had been. "More than impressed with" the generosity and commitment Tourgée had displayed toward his clients, as well as with their "high consideration and esteem" for Tourgée, Walker made clear from the start that he would defer to him in every respect.[41] "Only one motive actuates me," he assured Tourgée, "and that is to conduct our case skilfully [*sic*] towards successful termination. To this end I am schooled to *accept every suggestion, modify every plan*, and sacrifice every conviction. Before I undertake to enter any plea whatever, be assured, you will already have been fully consulted."[42] If one detects a note of defensiveness in the words "sacrifice every conviction," it reflects the two lawyers' initial disagreement over how best to move the case toward the U.S. Supreme Court—whether via the state supreme court, as Walker suggested in order to "exhaust our remedy in the State Courts" before advancing to the federal level, or directly via the federal circuit court for habeas corpus, as Tourgée envisaged to accelerate the process.[43] Sensing Walker's pique, Tourgée disclaimed any "distrust or inclination to override" his new colleague's "judgment on any point." To the contrary, he ventured, "I think we shall enjoy our association and come out of it better friends."[44]

Early in their correspondence, Walker and Tourgée agreed to conduct the case as quietly as possible. Aware that the white supremacist press was already stoking local opinion in favor of ever more stringent segregation laws, the two attorneys thought they stood a better chance of receiving a fair hearing in court if their challenge of the Separate Car Statute did not get leaked to the public through "sensational" articles in the *Crusader*.[45] "Our efforts [should] be looked upon as in no wise political," cautioned Walker.[46] Tourgée promptly concurred: "Our clients should make no clamor at all about the case. . . . Especially let there be no public comment on the proceedings at any stage." Walker should "read this to Mr. Desdunes and ask him to inform Mr. Martinet that this is my wish and judgment," Tourgée instructed.[47] Tourgée's warnings against "clamor" may seem to contradict his rationale for establishing the NCRA as a vehicle for mobilizing public opinion to support a test of the Separate Car Law's constitutionality. The apparent contradiction dissolves, however, when we distinguish, as he surely did, between conditions in New Orleans and in the nation at large. In New Orleans, "clamor" about a case aimed at outlawing segregation could only further inflame the white Southern public and prejudice the court; nationally, on the other hand, generating a massive citizens' movement and press campaign offered the sole prospect of inducing the Supreme Court to rule the Separate Car Law unconstitutional. Hence, Tourgée could simultaneously advocate both raising a national "clamor" through the NCRA and conforming to local sensibilities, as Walker urged, by appearing "in no wise political."

As soon as Walker informed him of Daniel Desdunes's arrest, Tourgée listed the main arguments he wanted made against the indictment and wrote, "I leave the form and character of the plea entirely to your better judgment." Within a week, Walker sent Tourgée a draft of his plea. Tourgée responded immediately, "I like it." He recommended only that Walker delete a reference to passengers "of both white and colored races" because it unnecessarily raised the question of race. Passengers are "simply beings of the human race—who pay fare," Tourgée explained.[48] Already, the two lawyers had learned to work smoothly together. By the time Plessy replaced Desdunes as the committee's plaintiff for testing the Separate Car Law, Tourgée was willing to "approve anything [Walker] may advise," as he wired Martinet.[49] In the end, Walker adopted the strategy he preferred: appealing to the state supreme court, rather than to the federal circuit court, and using a writ of error to "invoke the jurisdiction of the United States Supreme Court."[50]

As the *Plessy* case headed into its final phase, Tourgée beefed up his legal team. Besides Walker and Martinet, whom he had persuaded to join him for oral arguments, Tourgée chose a co-counsel based in Washington, Samuel F. Phillips. The Citizens' Committee unanimously endorsed the choice and sent a check for Phillips's retainer fee of $250. An old friend from Reconstruction days in North Carolina, when he had "bec[o]me radical-ized" while "practicing law in Tourgée's courtroom," Phillips had gone on to a brilliant career as solicitor general under four successive Republican administrations. His long experience of pleading before the Supreme Court had climaxed with the *Civil Rights Cases* of 1883, for which his brief in favor of the plaintiffs had served to underpin Justice John Marshall Harlan's powerful dissent. Tourgée surely hoped Phillips would help influence the verdict, or at the very least "advise [him] on procedure and keep him posted on the case's status before the Court."[51] He was destined to disappointment on both counts.

An About-Face on Strategy

Having completed the filing of the case by late February 1893, Tourgée at first sought to expedite the hearing. He still held to that goal in May, when he and Martinet met in Chicago. As late as August, Martinet and Walker seemed to be expecting to be called to Washington before the end of the year. Walker, reported Martinet, was "anxious" for Tourgée to let him know soon "what part you wish him to take in the Plessy case" because "he wants to have plenty of time to prepare himself." Martinet reminded Tourgée that he had made "the same request for myself before I left Chicago." He added, "Now you have got me into it [the oral argument] & you must help me."[52]

Yet at the very moment when Walker was trying to obtain the Louisiana authorities' cooperation in advancing the case on the Supreme Court's docket, Tourgée was moving in the opposite direction.[53] "I have been having some very serious thoughts in regard to Plessy's Case of late, as my prepa-ration for the hearing has extended," he wrote Martinet on 31 October. He was now wondering whether they should cease to "press for an early hear-ing" and instead "leave it to come up in its turn or even encourage delay?" Knowing that Martinet would be "surprised" by this about-face, Tourgée explained what had impelled it. "When we started the fight there was a fair show of favor with the Justices of the Supreme Court," he asserted. "One, at least, had come to regret" having voted with the majority in ruling the 1875 Civil Rights Act unconstitutional—a change of heart that might have portended a broader shift as justices "not fully committed by participation in" the *Civil Rights Cases* altered the balance of the Court. Over the past two years, however, amid the reactionary tide sweeping the nation—manifested in the spread of lynching and black disfranchisement, the attenuation of the Republican Party's commitment to racial justice, and the triumph of big business—new appointments by both Republican and Democratic presidents had modified the Court's composition for the worse. Currently, "of the whole number of Justices there is but one who is known to favor the view we must stand upon." That one, of course, was Harlan, the sole dissenter in the *Civil Rights Cases.* "There are five who are against us," Tourgée continued. "Of these one may be reached, I think, if he 'hears from the country' soon enough. The others will probably stay where they are until Gabriel blows his horn." Two of the three remaining justices "may be brought over by the argument." The third "is inclined to be with us legally but his political bias is strong the other way." No matter how Tourgée reckoned, he could count only one sure vote and three or four very doubtful ones. History alone gave him reason for hope, as he recalled that "the court has always been the foe of liberty until forced to move on by public opinion." The hope thus lay in arousing public opinion to such a pitch that it would force the Court to yield to the national will. If that endeavor failed, the results would be disastrous, Tourgée warned.[54]

To avert the catastrophe of an adverse decision, Tourgée advised two measures: first, "to leave the case to come up when it will and not attempt to advance it," and second, "to bend every possible energy to secure the discussion of the principle in such a way as to reach and awaken public sentiment." Tourgée conceded that he saw no chance of friendlier judicial appointments in the near future; rather, delaying the case would allow time to educate and mobilize the public. "If we can get the ear of the Country, and argue the matter fully *before the people first,* we may incline the wavering [justices] to fall on our side when the matter comes up," he reasoned. The vehicle through which Tourgée planned to "array the sentiment of the Country against Caste and against the Supreme Court as the ally of Slavery, Secession and Caste" was the *National Citizen,* the journal he was then preparing to launch as an organ of the NCRA. By attacking the Court—an institution the "newspaper press worship[ed]" and "the people" viewed more critically—Tourgée anticipated provoking enough controversy to ensure a national debate on the constitutionality of the Separate Car Law that might influence the verdict. He asked Martinet to call a meeting of the Citizens' Committee, "lay this letter before them," and request them to decide whether or not to accept his advice.[55]

Naturally, the committee accepted it. Indeed, when the *Plessy* case finally reached the Court's docket and appeared to be scheduled for the spring 1896 term, two and half years later, Martinet vainly pushed for a further delay in the hope that the November election might create a more propitious climate for a favorable decision.[56] By then, in any case, no amount of delay would have strengthened Tourgée's hand vis-à-vis the Supreme Court. In the first place, the ally both Tourgée and Martinet dreamed of gaining in the White House—Thomas B. Reed of Maine, a consistent advocate of African American rights—did not stand the slightest chance of winning the Republican presidential nomination, which would go to William McKinley. In the second place, McKinley, despite the strong stand against lynching that won him the loyalty of Harry C. Smith and most other Northern African Americans, gave no sign of foregrounding the issue of racial justice in his electoral campaign, nor would he have won the nomination had he done so. Most crucial, Tourgée had failed to obtain funding for the *National Citizen,* and as a result, the public opinion blitz he had planned as a means of swaying the Court against "caste" legislation had never materialized. Instead of Tourgée, the spokesman who captured public opinion was Booker T. Washington. "In all things that are purely social we can be as separate as the fingers, yet one as the hand in all things essential to mutual progress," Washington announced in his famous "Atlanta Compromise" speech of September 1895, which, as Elliott puts it, "handed the court just the reverse of what Tourgée had envisioned: evidence of public acceptance, even from black leadership, of separate-but-equal segregation."[57] Thus, on the eve of oral arguments, Tourgée occupied an even weaker position than he had feared in October 1893, now with only one reliable vote on the Court.

An Ill-Omened Mix-Up

Tourgée, Martinet, and Walker were still maneuvering to delay the case when Phillips dropped a bombshell on them. "I . . . hoped to see you at the argument which I supposed might be *today* or tomorrow," he wrote on 1 April 1896. "Then I could *hear* you talk about [the case]!" He would "represent the matter orally" in Tourgée's absence, Phillips volunteered, and the Court would accept written briefs from the other attorneys. Thinking that he had missed oral arguments by the time he heard from Phillips, "Tourgée wrote a furious letter to the Supreme Court Clerk." He had been "waiting every day" for "three months" to receive his notification to appear, he raged. Moreover, because the case "*involv[ed] the personal right of half the population of a state*—three other counsel" planned to "take part in the argument and only waited to hear from [him]" before departing for Washington. "I represent an association of about 10,000 colored men of Louisiana who raised the money to prosecute," Tourgée stormed on, "and now by some inscrutable mishap they are deprived of the service they had secured, and I am put in the attitude of neglecting a case over which I have exerted the most scrupulous care and to which I have given years of labor and study."[58] How, he demanded, could the clerk have scheduled the hearing without informing him?

In his reply, the clerk faulted Phillips, who should have known that the Court normally notified only "local counsel" and expected them to pass on the word to their out-of-town associates.[59] Confirming the clerk's imputation, Phillips's correspondence with Tourgée conveys the distinct impression that he was too busy with other concerns to devote sufficient attention to the case. Referring to a package of material Tourgée had sent him two weeks earlier, for example, he promised to read it "attentively" and apologized for not having answered a previous communication: *"mea culpa, &c &c."* He also lulled himself and Tourgée into thinking that the case might not come up until the fall session. Most tellingly, he expressed awareness that the *"screed"* he had prepared for the Court might strike Tourgée as below his usual standard. "I have given more labor to this brief than its contents will suggest to you," Phillips alleged defensively. "I have written a great deal about the topic: written & torn, written and burned!" Phillips's difficulties with the brief do not seem to derive from disagreement with the goal of fighting segregation, for he affirmed "the belief that we are clearly right" and that "general *peace* as well as *right*" would ensue from a decision upholding Plessy's challenge.[60] Perhaps he simply viewed defeat as a foregone conclusion.

Fortunately, it turned out that the case had merely been "called on the Court's docket"; the hearing would not take place until 13 April. The reprieve barely allowed time for Tourgée to travel to Washington from his home in upstate New York. Neither Martinet nor Walker could make the much longer trip from New Orleans on such short notice, however. Walker, in fact, had announced in a letter Tourgée did not receive until his return from Washington that his health would not permit him to undertake the journey (the respiratory illness from which he was suffering would claim his life two years later). "I hope your success will be commensurate with the energy, skill and earnestness which has marked everything you have said and done in the case," he wrote.[61] We can only imagine Martinet's chagrin, for—with the exception of a telegram congratulating Tourgée on his appointment as U.S. consul to Bordeaux in May 1897—he apparently did not continue their correspondence after learning from Emma of the hearing date. Martinet's last extant full-length letter of 4 March—a cry from the depths of his heart—exuded battle weariness: "Must get out of this work, else it will kill me." He hesitated before implicating his Citizens' Committee colleagues in his complaints about the African American community at large, but the need to vent overcame his discretion: "I have so much that I [illegible] want to write to you & yet I hardly know whether I should. What disappointments! How unworthy these people! Is it worth while to fight for them? What corruption! venality! How the best even disappoint you!"[62] Still, having sacrificed so much for the cause, Martinet must have looked forward to testifying in person against segregation alongside Tourgée and thus embodying racial equality and mutually respectful collaboration as the alternative to white supremacy. To be deprived of the opportunity by sheer human error must have been a crushing blow. The outcome of the *Plessy* case would be even more crushing.

A Prophetic Legal Strategy

Boarding the train for Washington on 10 April 1896 after this ill-omened mix-up, Tourgée knew the odds were heavily stacked against him. He faced a Court that included four Democrats: Chief Justice Melville Weston Fuller, who had "denounced the Emancipation Proclamation" and opposed black suffrage; Edward Douglass White, an ex-Confederate and reputed former Klan member from Louisiana, home of the very Separate Car Law the Court would be considering; Stephen Johnson Field, who had voted to strike down the Civil Rights Act, "dissented in two cases that upheld [African Americans'] rights to serve on juries," and equated corporations with "persons" entitled to protection under the Fourteenth Amendment; and Rufus Wheeler Peckham, a corporate lawyer who shared Field's interpretation of the Fourteenth Amendment. Of the Court's five Republicans, none except Harlan (a former Kentucky slaveholder radicalized by Reconstruction) furnished a counterweight. Horace Gray had voted with the majority in the *Civil Rights Cases*, despite his antislavery past. David Josiah Brewer "advocated keeping states free from federal interference"—a position that would have predisposed him to uphold the Separate Car Law, notwithstanding his family's "antislavery roots." (In the end Brewer "did not participate in the *Plessy* decision" because he had missed the oral arguments.) Henry Billings Brown "usually supported a state's right to assert its police powers," the principle at issue in the Separate Car Law. And George Shiras Jr. tended to "side with the majority."[63]

Confronting a Court so "overwhelmingly hostile to his cause," Tourgée formulated a legal strategy that invites two complementary explications. The first is Elliott's: "As a lawyer trying to win a case, he used every favorable argument at his disposal and adopted [a] multifaceted legal strategy on the theory that, as Tourgée put it to his co-counsel Walker, 'it is better to have too many points . . . than not enough.'"[64] The second is one Tourgée himself hints at when he asserts, referring to the Fourteenth Amendment, "The people of the United States were not building for today and its prejudices alone, but for justice, liberty and a nationality secure for all time."[65] Like the architects of the Fourteenth Amendment, I suggest, Tourgée framed his brief and oral arguments not for his time "and its prejudices alone" but for future generations, whom he summoned to rediscover the true meaning of the country's founding ideals and of the Reconstruction amendments that consummated them. He realized, of course, that more than two decades of nefarious Supreme Court decisions since the passage of those amendments had perverted them beyond recognition, rendering them almost useless for protecting victims of discrimination while transforming them into effective tools for maintaining white supremacy, states' rights, and economic privilege. That was precisely why he sought to reclaim for future generations the original intent of constitutional enactments he saw as representing the pinnacle of the American democratic heritage. In short, Tourgée perfectly illustrates Michael Kent Curtis's thesis that antislavery "Republican legal thought" was not "primarily directed at convincing courts" but "served . . . [the] prophetic function . . . of recalling Americans to their commitment to liberty."[66]

The printed brief Tourgée submitted to the Court opened with a page and a half of "Questions Arising" from the facts of the *Plessy* case.[67] In keeping with the rhetorical technique he had so often deployed in his "Bystander" articles, Tourgée resorted to questions as a means of engaging his opponents in dialogue over the fundamental principles at stake. He began with the most fundamental: "Has the State the power under the provisions of the Constitution of the United States, to make a distinction based on color in the enjoyment of chartered privileges within the state" (296)? Assuming that his interlocutor would answer "Yes," Tourgée raised a series of follow-up questions that highlighted the illusoriness of "distinction[s] based on color," undermined color as a reliable indicator of "race," and challenged the very concept of race as unscientific, thus untenable for legal purposes. The most far-reaching of the questions were these:

> Is not the question of race, scientifically considered, very often impossible of determination?
>
> Is not the question of race, legally considered, one impossible to be determined, in the absence of statutory definition? (297)

In the rest of his brief, which he divided into twenty-three numbered "Points of Plaintiff's Contention," Tourgée adopted the more traditional format of quoting the Thirteenth and Fourteenth Amendments and listing the ways in which the Separate Car Law violated their provisions, although he continued to use questions at strategic intervals. The most famous portion of the brief occurs under point 2. To demonstrate that the obnoxious law violated the Fourteenth Amendment's second clause—"No State shall . . . deprive any citizen of life, liberty or property, without due process of law"—Tourgée contended, "In any mixed community, the reputation of belonging to the dominant race, in this instance the white race, is *property*" (299). Accordingly, a passenger forced by a railway conductor to "ride in a 'Jim Crow' car" was deprived without due process "of the reputation of being a white man," and ipso facto of "'property' if such reputation *is* 'property'" (300). As various scholars have pointed out, Tourgée emphasized the threat that the Separate Car Law posed to property rights because "he doubtless hoped thereby to appeal to the preferential treatment the Supreme Court notoriously gave to property rights."[68] More consequentially, as J. Allen Douglas has shown, "by linking Plessy's phenotypically white appearance to reputation and defining reputation for whiteness as a form of property, Tourgée disclosed the racial and cultural dimensions of the connection between property and personality at the law"—a maneuver that laid bare the "plasticity of identity."[69]

To help the Court decide whether or not the reputation of being white was property, Tourgée again resorted to questions. This time he engaged the justices on a personal level by choosing as his example the profession they all practiced: law. "How much would it be *worth* to a young man entering upon the practice of law, to be regarded as a *white* man rather than a colored one?" he asked. He answered with statistics that defined white supremacy in economic terms: "Six-sevenths of the population are white. Nineteen-twentieths of the property of the country is owned by white people. Ninety-nine hundredths of the business opportunities are in the control of white people" (300). He then showed how economic monopoly translated into social exclusiveness and racial prejudice, as evidenced by "the intensity of feeling which excludes the colored man from the friendship and companionship of the white man" (300). Whatever rationalizations they might use to justify their privileges and deny the oppressiveness of white supremacy, avowed Tourgée, "probably most white persons if given a choice, would prefer death to life in the United States *as colored persons*" (300). The words "in the United States" implied that other countries did not condemn "colored persons" to a life worse than death. Tourgée climaxed this section of his brief by asking, "[Is not] the *reputation of being white* the most valuable sort of property, being the master-key that unlocks the golden door of opportunity?" (300). While ostensibly serving to clinch his property argument, the statistics and psychosocial data Tourgée marshaled actually served to indict white supremacy. By inference, Tourgée charged, the "master-key" of white identity "unlock[ed] the golden door of opportunity" only for the master race but kept it firmly locked for subordinate races— an inequity that falsified and sabotaged America's democratic promise. It is because they have missed this radical message that some scholars have misinterpreted Tourgée as articulating "not a defense of the colored man against discrimination by whites, but a defense of the 'nearly' white man against the penalties of color."[70]

Under point 4 of his brief, Tourgée appropriated one of the chief rationales for segregation—that it protected the sanctity of the white family by preventing interracial marriage—but adapted it to the opposite purpose of protecting the sanctity of interracial families. "A man may be white and his wife colored; a wife may be white and her children colored," he hypothesized (301). In such cases the Separate Car Law divided families by compelling the "colored" and "white" spouses and children to ride in different railway carriages.[71]

Tourgée went further under point 5, where he argued that it was both "impossible" and illogical to classify U.S. citizens by race. It was impossible because "in all parts of the country, race-intermixture has proceeded to such an extent" that large numbers of citizens could not be reliably categorized by blood quantum—certainly not "by the casual scrutiny of a busy conductor" (301).[72] The project of classifying citizens by race was also riddled with illogical assumptions. How should one classify people in whom "the race admixture is equal," asked Tourgée. "Are they white or colored?" (301). Merely to pose the question called attention to the arbitrariness of American racial classifications. Tourgée knew, of course, that most white Americans would answer, "All those should be classed as colored in whom appears a visible admixture of colored blood" (302). By turning this rule on its head, however, Tourgée exposed it as based not on science but on white supremacist ideology: "Why not count every one as white in whom is visible any trace of white blood? There is but one reason to wit, the domination of the white race" (302).

Under points 6 through 7, making up the heart of his brief, Tourgée spelled out his interpretation of the Fourteenth Amendment's Section 1: "All persons born or naturalized in the United States, and subject to the jurisdiction thereof, are citizens of the United States and of the State wherein they reside. No State shall make or enforce any law which shall abridge the privileges or immunities of citizens of the United States; nor shall any State deprive any person of life, liberty, or property, without due process of law; nor deny to any person within its jurisdiction the equal protection of the laws."[73] Summing up his understanding of the "plain and universal meaning of the terms employed," Tourgée maintained,

> This provision . . . *creates a new* citizenship of the United States embracing new rights, privileges and immunities, derivable in a *new* manner, controlled by a *new* authority, having a *new* scope and extent, dependent on national authority for its existence and looking to national power for its preservation.
>
> . . . If this provision means anything, it means that the government of the United States will not permit any legislation by the State which invades the *rights* of such citizens. (303)[74]

So revolutionary did Tourgée consider Section 1 that he called it "the *magna charta* of the American citizen's rights" (304).

Having laid out his own interpretation of the Fourteenth Amendment, Tourgée took on the Supreme Court decisions of the past two decades that had erected precedents contradicting him. The first was the *Slaughter-House Cases* of 1873, in which white butchers of New Orleans had invoked the Thirteenth and Fourteenth Amendments to sue the city for passing a public health ordinance safeguarding the water supply from slaughterhouse pollution, at the cost, they alleged, of threatening their livelihood. The Court ruled that the two amendments had been framed specifically to abolish slavery, grant citizenship to African Americans, and protect rights "guaranteed by the federal government"; therefore, they did not apply to the butchers. At the same time, however, the Court denied that the Fourteenth Amendment transferred the protection of citizens' rights "from the States to the Federal government." By validating the power of states to pass "police regulations" for the promotion of public health and morals, even if such regulations potentially "abridge[d] the privileges or immunities of citizens of the United States," the ruling opened the door to state laws abridging the civil rights of African Americans.[75]

Under points 10 through 13, Tourgée boldly disputed not only the legitimacy of justifying the Separate Car Law as a "police regulation" but also the Court's verdict and reasoning in the *Slaughter-House Cases*. A genuine police regulation must promote the "general health or public morals of a whole community, not merely . . . minister to the wishes of one class or another," affirmed Tourgée (309). Did it endanger "public health" or "contaminate public morals," he asked, for a "colored man or woman" to sit in a railway car "in which white men or women [were] sitting," or vice versa (309)? If so, why did such proximity "contaminate any more" in a railway car "than in the house or on the street" (309)? Again highlighting the illogicality of white supremacist ideology by turning it on its head, he feigned ignorance as to whether the authors of the Separate Car Law thought it was "the white who spreads the contagion or the black" (309). He crowned this section of his argument by pinpointing the provision that most nakedly bared the law's true purpose: the exception allowing white children's colored nurses to travel with their charges and employers in the coaches reserved for whites. Contrary to its pretensions, the Separate Car Law was unmistakably "intended to 'keep the negro in his place,'" Tourgée insisted: "The exemption of nurses shows that the real evil lies not in the color of the skin but in the relation the colored person sustains to the white. If he is a dependent it may be endured; if he is not, his presence is insufferable." By sanctioning racial hierarchy, the Separate Car Law violated a cardinal principle, concluded Tourgée: "Justice is pictured blind and her daughter, the Law, ought at least to be color-blind" (310). This famous dictum would find its way into Justice Harlan's even more famous dissent.

Not content with having demolished the Separate Car Law's claim to being a "police regulation," Tourgée mounted a full-scale attack on the Court itself, which he accused of having imposed on Section 1 of the Fourteenth Amendment "a construction absolutely at variance with the plain and unquestioned purport of its words." He elaborated: "No man can deny that the language employed [in the amendment] is of the broadest and most universal character. 'Every person,' 'no State,' 'any law,' 'any person' are the terms employed. The language has no more comprehensive or unmistakable words. Yet in the face of these, the Court arrives at the conclusion that this section was intended *only to protect the rights of the colored citizen from infringement by State enactment!*" (310).

It might seem puzzling that Tourgée should dispute the Fourteenth Amendment's intent as a measure "to protect the rights of the colored citizen," but he specified that such an interpretation was "only half-true" (310): "If [the amendment] protects the colored citizen from discriminating legislation, it protects also, in an equal degree, the rights of the white citizen" (311). The language of the amendment incontrovertibly established its intent to protect the rights of all citizens, Tourgée maintained: "'All' can never be made to mean 'some,' nor 'every person' be properly construed to be only one class or race until the laws of English speech are overthrown" (311).

Tourgée considered it vital to uphold the "universal character" of the Fourteenth Amendment because he believed that law could command the allegiance of all citizens only when it guaranteed them all equal rights and "equal protection." He went so far as to argue, in an original twist, that had the Fourteenth Amendment aimed *"exclusively"* to protect the rights of African Americans, it would have constituted *"class legislation of the rankest sort"* (311), by implication putting it on a par with the Separate Car Law. Far from succumbing to the temptation to substitute one form of "class legisla-tion" for another, however, the framers of the Fourteenth Amendment had deliberately chosen broad, universal language, because they were "not build-ing for today and its prejudices alone, but for justice, liberty and a nationality secure for all time" (312). And so, intimated Tourgée, was he. That was why he launched an even more sweeping attack on the Supreme Court's decision in the *Cruikshank* case of 1876 than he had on its *Slaughter-House* verdict.

"While *Slaughter-House* restricted the scope of the Fourteenth Amendment, the *Cruikshank* decision all but nullified its application to most cases involv-ing the violation of civil rights," explains Elliott.[76] William J. Cruikshank and his terrorist organization, the White League, had perpetrated one of the Reconstruction era's most notorious episodes of white supremacist vio-lence, Louisiana's Colfax massacre of 1873, during which they had butchered somewhere from sixty-nine to over a hundred African Americans who were defending the courthouse against a looming coup d'état by Democrats.[77] Convicted under the 1870 Enforcement Act, which not only prohibited intimidation of voters and conspiracies to deprive citizens of their consti-tutional rights but also gave federal courts the power to enforce the pro-hibition, Cruikshank appealed his conviction. His lawyer, David Dudley Field, the brother of Supreme Court justice Stephen Field, argued that the Fourteenth Amendment clause "No State shall make or enforce any law which shall abridge the privileges or immunities of citizens of the United States" provided federal protection against state action, but not against inju-ries committed by individuals on one another. The Court agreed.[78]

Tourgée had strong personal reasons for objecting to the *Cruikshank* deci-sion on at least two counts. In the first place, he himself had witnessed many comparable incidents of white supremacist violence in North Carolina and taken testimony from both victims and perpetrators; consequently, he felt a visceral investment in having the Colfax massacre's ringleaders brought to jus-tice. In the second place, he had been instrumental in securing passage of the

1871 Ku Klux Klan Act, a sequel of the 1870 Enforcement Act. Hence, we can imagine his outrage when the Court eviscerated the 1870 Enforcement Act because its provisions "overstepped the scope of federal power" and when it ruled that "the protection of all the 'privileges and immunities' of state citizens from infringement by other citizens 'rests alone with the State.'"[79]

Under points 13 to 15 of his brief, Tourgée tore the *Cruikshank* decision to shreds. If the Court's interpretation was correct, the Fourteenth Amendment was "the absurdest piece of legislation ever written in a statute book," he proclaimed (313). Almost sputtering with fury, he reminded the justices that the doctrine of state sovereignty had caused a "war of words" lasting a "quarter-century" and culminating in secession and "years of bloody strife" (313). "Does any one believe" the authors of the Fourteenth Amendment "meant to restore *that very sovereignty* which . . . the bloody tide of war had only just overthrown?" he demanded (313). Yet no matter how much ridicule Tourgée poured over the *Cruikshank* decision, he realized, as he "freely admitted," that it was "squarely against" his client's cause (317). Thus, he took refuge in the plea that it ultimately could not stand because it was based on a "false hypothesis" (317).

As a lawyer and former judge, Tourgée must have known that by covering the *Cruikshank* and *Slaughter-house* verdicts with scorn, he could hardly have persuaded the Supreme Court justices to reconsider them. Why, then, did he flail out so recklessly against the arbiters he was ostensibly seeking to win over? Why did he assail them with the sarcasm he deployed in his "Bystander" column and novels rather than adopt a subtle legalistic approach? He could not have yielded to a sudden burst of pent-up frustration, for he had been writing and revising his brief for months. One can only surmise that by the time Tourgée submitted the document in the fall of 1895, he had lost hope of changing the current justices' minds and that he was speaking not to them but to a future court capable of overturning the *Slaughter-house* and *Cruikshank* decisions and restoring the Fourteenth Amendment's true meaning.

After confronting the Supreme Court verdicts that contradicted his views, Tourgée turned under points 17 through 20 of his brief to the issue of whether a state had the right to force passengers to accept separate accommodations, as long as they were equal in comfort. "The gist of our case is the unconstitutionality of the assortment; *not* the question of equal accommodation," he clarified (319), replying in advance to historians who have faulted him for not trying to show that the accommodations allotted African Americans were not equal.[80]

Next, under point 21, Tourgée cited a rare precedent in his favor, the 1880 Supreme Court case of *Strauder v. West Virginia*, which had invalidated a state law excluding African Americans from juries on the ground that it was a "step toward reducing them to the condition of a subject race." He proceeded to argue that the Separate Car Act, too, violated the Thirteenth Amendment prohibiting slavery. "The purpose of this Amendment was not merely to destroy chattelism and involuntary servitude" (324), contended Tourgée, but also the "legal condition of subjection to the dominant class," which put the slave "in bondage to the whole white race as well as to his owner" (323).

Tourgée's primary bulwark nonetheless remained the Fourteenth rather than the Thirteenth Amendment. Hence, he devoted his last point, 23, to showing that his interpretation of the Fourteenth Amendment was "in strict accord with the Declaration of Independence," whose immortal words should serve as the "guiding principle" both for interpreting the Fourteenth Amendment and for deciding the *Plessy* case. Did the framers of the Fourteenth Amendment intend "to protect . . . the pursuit of happiness by all," or only "by part of the people?" he asked (326).

Tourgée ended his brief with a powerful appeal to the justices to put themselves in his clients' place. Once again, he did so by undermining the concept of race as a fixed, inalterable biological fact. This time, however, instead of demonstrating the fluidity and indeterminacy of race through a person of mixed ancestry who, like Homer Plessy, could easily pass for white, Tourgée conjured up a scenario reminiscent of his novel *Pactolus Prime*, in which his white-looking title character turns black by a mysterious chemical process:[81]

> Suppose a member of this court, nay, suppose every member of it, by some mysterious dispensation of providence should wake tomorrow with a black skin and curly hair—the two obvious and controlling indications of race—and in traveling through that portion of the country where the "Jim Crow" car abounds, should be ordered into it by the conductor. . . .
>
> What humiliation, what rage would then fill the judicial mind! (326)

Tourgée drove home the message by shifting from the third to the second person, from an abstract "judicial mind" to an embodied "you" facing him in the courtroom: "Why would this sentiment prevail in your minds? Simply because you would then feel and know that such assortment of the citizens on the line of race was a discrimination intended to humiliate and degrade the former subject and dependent class—an attempt to perpetuate the caste distinctions on which slavery rested—a statute in the words of the [1880] Court 'tending to reduce the colored people of the country to the condition of a subject race'" (326). No wonder Elliott has characterized this visionary brief as "an attack on racial segregation unlike any that had ever come before."[82]

Tourgée's Oral Argument

When Tourgée addressed the Court on 13 April, he supplemented his printed brief with several new arguments. First, he pointed out that the Separate Car Law "reduce[d] the whole human family to two grand divisions," "'white' and 'colored,'" which it inaccurately termed "'races.'" It thus created "a new ethnology" derived not from science but from "prejudice based on the lessons of slavery" (329). Second, Tourgée contended that it was "entirely immaterial" whether Plessy was "a colored man or a white one," because neither could be "held liable for violating" an unconstitutional statute (331). Third and most tellingly, he demonstrated the discriminatory thrust of the statute by substituting class for race: "Suppose in one of our northern states or in England a law should be passed requiring one set of cars for 'ladies and gentlemen' and another for 'working people'; should require them to be so labelled; should authorize and command the conductor to assort passengers into these two classes and make it an indictable offence for any one to refuse to obey his direction." Tourgée went on to conjure up the "inextinguishable wrath" of "those who were thus by law classified as non-gentlemen—the clerk, the working man, the 'dinner pail brigade.'" So furiously would they lash out, he predicted, that "no railroad could run such cars" without inciting mob violence "at every station" (333).[83] In translating race into class, Tourgée assumed that however much the "gentlemen" of the Supreme Court looked down on working people, they realized they could not afford to provoke the ire of an entire class amid an era of rampant labor unrest. He clearly hoped the justices would apply the lesson to African Americans.

We do not know how the justices reacted to Tourgée's oral presentation, what questions they raised in response to his brief, or how Tourgée handled the interrogation, for the Court did not yet keep transcripts of its proceedings during this period—"a profound loss," as Elliott has lamented.[84] The only newspaper that covered the hearing, the *Washington Post*, nevertheless conveyed the public mood in the courtroom. Noting that "Judge Tourgée's appearance occasioned some interest and comment" among the spectators in the gallery, the *Post* quoted a wit who described the "famous author" as engaged in "another fool's errand, inasmuch as the practical questions at issue in the case have already been decided in favor of the validity of the law involved."[85]

Tourgée could hardly have avoided sensing this mood. He seems to have left the courtroom feeling that he had failed to sway any of the justices he had once optimistically regarded as undecided. An eerie silence surrounds his assessment of the hearing. Instead of editorializing in the *Basis* on the outcome of the *Plessy* challenge, Tourgée abruptly terminated the organ he had struggled so hard to found and keep afloat. Meanwhile, his previously extensive correspondence suddenly ran dry. No further letters to or from Martinet, Desdunes, or Walker have survived. Although Wells, Smith, and Barnett continued to correspond with Tourgée, none of their letters alluded to his defeat in the *Plessy* case, which by a cruel irony followed on the heels of the Ohio antilynching law's triumphal passage. Cryptic entries in Emma's diary provide the only clues to Tourgée's frame of mind as he awaited the Court's decision after his return from Washington. They suggest that Tourgée had succumbed to a paralyzing depression. "Most distressing, disheartening day," confided Emma on 21 April. "Went to Club,—to get away from the depressing atmosphere, if I might.— So to bed,— so heavy-hearted.— Will no relief ever come!" And then on the twenty-second: "Almost sick and nothing comes to lighten the gloom." We might expect that Emma would at least have recorded a comment on the Court's decision, announced on 18 May, but her sole reference to it on that day—if, indeed, we can interpret it as such—was oblique: "Nothing but disappointments in the mail."[86]

The Court's Verdict

Worse than a disappointment, the Court's seven-to-one verdict upholding the constitutionality of the Separate Car Law, though Tourgée must by now have anticipated it, was a devastating blow from which neither he nor his Creole-of-color clients ever recovered. Justice Henry Billings Brown's formulation of the majority opinion surely heightened Tourgée's bitterness at losing the crusade for racial equality that had defined his career from Reconstruction onward, besides consuming the past five years.

As Elliott points out, Brown "sidestepped most of Tourgée's arguments."[87] For example, he simply denied that segregating passengers by race violated the Thirteenth Amendment. "Slavery implies involuntary servitude," asserted Brown, ignoring Tourgée's contention that the essence of slavery lay rather in an entire people's subjection to another people. Brown similarly refused to grapple with Tourgée's thesis that racial classifications were arbitrary social constructs, based on white supremacist ideology rather than on scientific data. Both color distinctions and social barriers between the races, he emphasized, were rooted "in the nature of things"—a phrase Brook Thomas has identified as a key to the "logic" of the majority for whom Brown spoke. Consequently, Brown dismissed what he called the "underlying fallacy" of Tourgée's argument—"the assumption that the enforced separation of the two races stamps the colored race with a badge of inferiority." The imputation of inferiority did not inhere in the law but arose "solely because the colored race chooses to put that construction upon it," Brown alleged, thus making people of color *themselves* responsible for the humiliation they felt at being treated as pariahs. He concluded, "Legislation is powerless to eradicate racial instincts or to abolish distinctions based upon physical differences."[88]

Unlike Brown's majority opinion, Justice Harlan's eloquent dissent exhibited Tourgée's influence in almost every paragraph. Indeed, many of its most famous pronouncements took inspiration from Tourgée's brief. Notably, Harlan proclaimed, "Our Constitution is color-blind, and neither knows nor tolerates classes among citizens." He agreed that "the arbitrary separation of citizens, on the basis of race, while they are on a public highway, is a badge of servitude wholly inconsistent with the civil freedom and equality before the law established" by the Thirteenth and Fourteenth Amendments. He agreed that the Fourteenth Amendment had fundamentally redefined national and state citizenship. He agreed as well that "everyone" knew the Separate Car Law "had its origin in the purpose, . . . to exclude colored people from coaches occupied by or assigned to white persons" and that the "thin disguise of 'equal' accommodations" would neither "mislead any one, nor atone for the wrong" the Court committed in endorsing it.[89] Yet even Harlan proved unwilling to entertain Tourgée's ideas about the illusoriness of race and the arbitrariness of racial classifications, as Elliott has shown.[90]

Whatever solace Tourgée may have derived from hearing his arguments echoed in Harlan's dissent, he could not have found anything to cheer in his lone judicial ally's confirmation of his own dark forebodings. The *Plessy* decision would prove as "pernicious" as its most infamous predecessor, the *Dred Scott* ruling, Harlan prophesied: "[It] will not only stimulate aggressions, more or less brutal and irritating, upon the admitted rights of colored citizens, but will encourage the belief that it is possible, by means of state enactments, to defeat the beneficient [*sic*] purposes which the people of the United States had in view when they adopted the recent amendments of the Constitution."[91] Harlan's prophecy would turn out to be all too prescient.[92]

The Public Reaction

Despite widespread recognition of its baleful significance, the *Plessy* decision prompted a surprisingly muted public reaction. In contrast to the Court's affirmation of slavery as the law of the land in the 1857 *Dred Scott* case and its overturn in 1883 of the Civil Rights Act, its endorsement of segregation did not trigger an explosion of outrage. Not that the public universally welcomed the decision—quite the reverse "outside of the white South, and not even always there," notes Olsen, who has made the most complete study of the press response.[93] True, the *New Orleans Daily Picayune*, which had vociferously clamored for the Separate Car Law from the very beginning, applauded the victory for segregation. Sounding a theme proslavery apologists had once trumpeted, the *Picayune* alleged that carrying equality too far would lead to "absolute socialism."[94] Less stridently, the *Atlanta Constitution* averred that "the negro himself . . . is thoroughly satisfied with the custom" of separate and equal railway accommodations, which "entails no hardships" for the race.[95]

Northern newspapers, on the other hand, generally distanced themselves from the Court's verdict. Those that endorsed it, such as the *New York Evening Journal*, sought to cast the onus for segregation on African Americans' "objectionable" behavior and to gloss over the erosion of their constitutional rights. "Colored persons . . . frequently exaggerate a denial of special privileges, not necessary to them, though hurtful to others, into rights," claimed the *Evening Journal*. "They are getting their rights; soon they will have their own privileges. They ought to deserve both, then there will be no need to appeal to the courts."[96]

Curiously, given the Democratic press's dismal record of race-baiting, the *Rochester (N.Y.) Democrat and Chronicle* delivered the most vocal rebuke. Under the headline "A Strange Decision," this political newspaper predicted that the Court's ruling would be "received by thoughtful and fair-minded people with disapproval and regret."[97]

From the opposite end of the religious and political spectrum, the *New York Independent* joined in the condemnation but couched it in the accents of its abolitionist heritage and evangelical orientation. Like its original abolitionist editors, the *Independent* invoked the Golden Rule as a higher law than the Constitution and God as a higher authority than the Supreme Court. By these standards, it judged, the "Jim Crow law . . . is a crime before God, no matter whether it does or does not contradict the Constitution of the United States."[98]

Liberal Republican political newspapers struck a markedly more subdued tone. The Court's ruling was "unfortunate, to say the least," bleated the *New York Tribune*, once a bastion of antislavery sentiment.[99] The *Springfield Republican* descended to witticism. Foreseeing that segregationist laws would now "spread like the measles," the *Republican* demanded, "Did the southerners . . . indict the Almighty for allowing negroes to be born on the same earth with white men?"[100] By directing its censure at the South, the paper conveniently overlooked the extent of segregation in the North and exonerated Northern Republican justices of guilt, forgetting that the Court's sole dissenter was a Southerner.

Tourgée's former vehicle, the *Chicago Daily Inter Ocean*, asked in its headline, "Is There a Decline of Republicanism?" Listing the *Plessy* verdict among others tending toward the erosion of African American rights, editor William Penn Nixon admitted that "old-fashioned Republicans" were "inquiring anxiously if anything practical be left of the civil rights bill which marks the climax of Republican legislation." Nixon nevertheless blamed the "disastrous results of Democratic administration" for Republicans' retreat from their own principles and looked forward to an imminent "reawakening of the national conscience," presumably with the election of a Republican president.[101]

African American newspapers and periodicals, of course, unanimously denounced the ruling but revealed some of the same tendencies as their white counterparts. The most militant accents thundered from the *Weekly Blade* of Parsons, Kansas, a region settled by migrants from the Deep South known as "exodusters." Branding the Court's decision a "damnable outrage" and hailing Harlan as "the only one on that bench with grit enough in him to utter a protest" against it, the *Blade* opined that an "august body" so "infernal" and "infamous" deserved to be dismantled and that constitutional amendments so useless might just as well be revoked as "null and void." Like the *Inter Ocean*, however, the *Blade* steered blame away from the Republicans and toward the Democrats. Although Republican justices, of whom four joined in the decision and a fifth abstained, outnumbered Democrats by six to three, the *Blade* accused only the Court's "Democratic majority" of having "wantonly disgraced" the country by betraying its founding creed.[102]

In a departure from its extensive coverage of lynching and its usual militant rhetoric, Smith's *Cleveland Gazette* allotted only two short editorials to "That 'Decision,'" as he called it, putting the word in quotation marks to undermine its legitimacy. In the first, he summarized Brown's majority opinion and Harlan's "very vigorous dissent." In the second, he sarcastically termed the "recent 'civil rights' decision (?) of the supreme court . . . as ridiculous an ultimatum as is to-day Chief Justice Taney's famous alleged statement that 'black men have no rights that white men are bound to respect.'" Yet Smith blunted the edge of his sarcasm by deflecting responsibility from the Republicans to the Democrats, from the six Northern justices who upheld the Separate Car Law to the lone justice from Louisiana he credited with exercising a "'mitey pow'full pull'" over them—a move that aligned the *Gazette* with the *Blade*, the *Inter Ocean*, and the *Springfield Republican*.[103]

Other African American journals recognized the decision as the latest sign of an ominous national trend that cut across party and sectional lines. "No matter what direction the Negro turns opposition stands like a stone wall," editorialized the *Indianapolis Freeman*. "The community, state and country seems to have girt him about with oppression." Under such circumstances, the otherwise secular *Freeman* could only advocate reliance on God: "He, in his own manner, will square up accounts or life is not worth the living."[104]

The *Washington Bee* urged African Americans to save themselves rather than rely on divine intervention or on a Republican Party in which politicians who had been "loyal, true and honest, with the oppressed Afro-American," had been thrust aside by patrons of big business. "We shall no longer play the fool nor shall any more shackles bind the limbs of the once oppressed," fulminated the *Bee*. "We must throw off this mask of humilization [*sic*] and assume an air of independence."[105]

Writing not for an African American publication but for the white Social Gospel monthly *Our Day*, edited by the minister Joseph Cook, who had earlier published Ida B. Wells's "Lynch Law in All Its Phases," Booker T. Washington offered perhaps the most effective response to the Court's sanctioning of Jim Crow: "No race can wrong another race simply because it has the power to do so, without being permanently injured in morals, and its ideas of justice. The negro can endure the temporary inconvenience, but the injury to the white man is permanent. . . . It is for the white man to save himself from this degradation that I plead."[106] Unfortunately, Washington's censure of what he forthrightly called an "unjust law" came too late to undo the damage caused by his "Atlanta Compromise" speech and reached a far smaller audience.

Tourgée's Absence from the Press Reports

A striking omission common to all the newspapers and periodicals cited above, Southern and Northern, white and African American, is that none except the *Washington Post*, whose reporter saw Tourgée in the courtroom, mentions his role in the *Plessy* case—not even the *Inter Ocean* or the *Cleveland Gazette*, whose editors must have known of his involvement in challenging the Separate Car Law.[107] Tourgée's crowning act of advocacy for African Americans thus appears to have gone virtually unnoticed in the press, and the dazzling brief that has attracted so much attention from twentieth- and twenty-first-century scholars seems to have languished unread in the Supreme Court's archives until long after his death. Tourgée himself may have contributed to this effacement, for he had cautioned Martinet and Desdunes not to comment publicly on the case as it was going through the courts, and he had observed the same prohibition himself.

If, as seems likely, the *Crusader* paid tribute to Tourgée in its announcement of the Court's decision, no clippings from the relevant dates have survived. The tribute that has survived is contained in the printed "Statement of the Citizens' Committee," signed by its eighteen members, though probably written by Martinet, and issued after the demise of the *Crusader*. This dignified and moving document shows how the group reacted to losing its lawsuit. Acting "in the name of the people," asserted the signatories, the committee had "battled for equal rights," "protested against" discriminatory laws as "encroachments upon the liberties of the people," and applied "to the courts of the country for redress." The Court had now rendered its judgment, rejecting "our just appeal . . . contrary to our expectations." Nevertheless, the people's representatives refused to accept the legitimacy of a judicial ruling "in direct conflict with the American Declaration of Independence." "We, as freemen, still believe that we were right," they insisted, "and our cause is sacred, when we are encouraged by the indomitable will and noble defence of the Hon. Albion W. Tourgée, and supported by the courageous dissenting opinion of Justice John Harlan in behalf of justice and equal rights." (The reference to Tourgée's "noble defence" suggests that he had sent Martinet a copy of his brief, as would have been appropriate.) The committee's spokesmen added, "In defending the cause of liberty, we met with defeat, but not with ignominy."[108] Ignominy, they implied, would have consisted in yielding without a struggle to second-class citizenship. Much as Desdunes had urged at the outset of the campaign against the Separate Car Law, the Citizens' Committee's valedictory statement adopted an attitude of "noble despair" in the face of the bitter rebuff that "American justice" had dealt people of color.[109]

The statement also expressed "regret at the disappearance of THE CRU-SADER"; gratitude to "the peerless patriot Judge Albion W. Tourgee, for his staunch support and invaluable services to the cause of justice, freely and cheerfully rendered, without compensation"; and further gratitude to the committee's treasurer, Paul Bonseigneur, for his careful stewardship of its legal fund, as well as to all the individuals and groups who had contributed to that fund, listed by name and amount. Of the $2,982.55 collected, $2,762.55 had been expended on legal fees and payments connected to the plaintiffs' arrests. Testifying to the Committee's frugality, a balance of $220 remained, of which $60 went toward purchasing a testimonial to Tourgée—an engraved gold watch, which he treasured for the rest of his life—and $160 toward eight charities.

Despite its brave stance, the Citizens' Committee could not maintain its resistance to Jim Crow after such an overwhelming defeat. The group disbanded, ceased its agitation for racial equality—which had included protest against church segregation, antimiscegenation laws, and exclusion from juries—and terminated the *Crusader*. Under conditions of intensifying oppression, explained Desdunes years later in his homage to his compatriots, *Nos hommes et notre histoire* (1911), many of the former militants believed it would be "not only fruitless, but decidedly dangerous" to continue their crusade, thinking it "better to suffer in silence than to draw attention to their misfortune and their impotence." Desdunes himself never renounced his fighting spirit. "We think it is nobler and worthier to struggle all the same than to show ourselves passive and resigned. Absolute submission increases the power of the oppressor and obscures the sentiment of the oppressed," he maintained, in words reminiscent of Tourgée's.[110] Martinet agreed. In 1898, two years after the *Plessy* debacle, he formed a committee to protest against the exclusion of "colored citizens from service on juries" in Louisiana's U.S. circuit courts. As its corresponding secretary, he wrote a strong letter to the U.S. attorney general, detailing the ways in which "all the rights and privileges that make American citizenship desirable or worth anything are being taken one by one from the colored American in the South" and citing the parallels between antebellum slave laws and turn-of-the-century Jim Crow statutes. A "so-called Constitutional Convention" was even then meeting, Martinet informed the attorney general, "to permanently disfranchise the colored citizen" who had "fought to preserve the Union and the flag" while allowing the "old ex-confederates . . . who fought to disrupt the Union and tear the flag into rags . . . to retain the ballot." According to his family's oral tradition, Martinet remained so militant that his activism endangered his relatives, most of whom sought to protect themselves, either by migrating to California and passing for white or by changing their names.[111]

FIGURE 9 Rodolphe L. Desdunes, member of the New Orleans Citizens' Committee and author of *Nos hommes et notre histoire* (1911), where he wrote, "The population should never forget . . . Tourgée." The photo appears as the book's frontispiece.

Apparently unaware of Martinet's post-*Plessy* agitating, Tourgée died six years before the publication of Desdunes's book, yet he would surely have appreciated its heartfelt acknowledgment not only of his exertions as the committee's lead counsel but of his entire career as a champion of the oppressed. "For more than thirty years," wrote Desdunes, Tourgée had fought for the liberation and uplift of the downtrodden masses, spilling his blood for them on the battlefield, "defending their cause at the risk of his life" during Reconstruction, as depicted in his novel *A Fool's Errand*, and filling the columns of the *Inter Ocean* with his articles on the "conditions of our daily life," which he exposed with "inexorable logic." "The population should never forget" him, Desdunes exhorted readers.[112]

Tourgée's Response to the Court's Decision

What of Tourgée's own response to the Court's decision? Recognizing that the *Plessy* verdict rang the death knell of the crusade for African American rights in his lifetime, he told a Quaker correspondent, "As to the Race Problem I have made up my mind to let it alone."[113] He did not keep his vow, however—at least not yet. Instead, he heaped scorn on the Supreme Court whenever he found an opportunity. In a Memorial Day oration he delivered to Civil War veterans in Boston less than two weeks after the Court issued its ruling, Tourgée warned that although the veterans' sacrifices had overthrown chattel slavery, "caste—the worst element of slavery—the legal subjection of one class to the domination and control of another, still exists; and, under the protection of a supreme court which has always been the consistent enemy of personal liberty and equal right, may for a time triumph in the land."[114] Lest anyone ascribe his caustic assessment of the Court to personal pique, Tourgée studiously avoided mentioning his own role in the *Plessy* case, either in this oration or in any of his subsequent retrospectives.

Tourgée amplified his criticism of the Court in a "Bystander" column of 13 March 1897, ostensibly hailing newly elected president McKinley for saying in his inaugural address, "Lynchings must not be tolerated. Courts, not mobs, must execute the penalties of the law." Immediately after his praise of McKinley's statement, which he called the "boldest" condemnation of lynching "ever uttered by an American President," Tourgée pointed out the limitations of relying on U.S. courts to provide justice for African Americans. "The Supreme Court of the United States has been from its first session to its last the inveterate enemy of equal rights and personal liberty, in its construction of the constitution and the laws of the great republic, built on the foundation stone of human equality," charged Tourgée. "Our soldiers transformed the slave-republic, as they thought, into one of equal right dependent on citizenship. The Supreme Court has re-transformed it into a caste-republic in which the state has an indefeasible power to run the line of right along the boundary of race and color." Attributing the Court's shameful record to "the sad inheritance of prejudice against color which we received from centuries of slavery," Tourgée predicted that even if the president succeeded in winning passage of a national antilynching law, the Court would find "some way . . . to thwart the purpose of the people and decide against" the law's constitutionality. He ended, "It required unnumbered years of praying and four years of fighting to bring the American people to the point of abolishing slavery based on race and color. How many years and how much scourging will it require to enable them to break the bonds of caste based on race and color, which the Supreme Court has riveted upon them? God only knows."[115]

Tourgée offered his most complete postmortem of the *Plessy* case and his most trenchant indictment of the Court's ruling in a "Bystander" column of 29 May 1897, occasioned by the arrival in the mail of the Citizens'

Committee's "flattering testimonial of regard" and its accompanying "final report." He began by reviewing the history of the Separate Car Law and the vigorous resistance it had incited among the "colored people of New Orleans." Once again, Tourgée credited the "ringing utterances of the Crusader" with inspiring the formation of the Citizens' Committee and galvanizing the campaign to test the law's constitutionality. He went on to commend both the thousands of "men, women, and children" who had contributed to the committee's legal fund and the managers of the fund for their "careful thrift." Notwithstanding the failure of the committee's lawsuit, Tourgée emphasized, the endeavor had "proved for their race that it is not only capable, but is inclined to the exercise of peaceful and constitutional means to secure ... the rights they believe themselves entitled to."[116]

Turning in the next section of this article to the Court's verdict, Tourgée implicitly invited comparison between the courageous community of color that had staked so much on the case and the callous white arbiters of the race's fate. "The decision, written by Justice Brown, is the last of a long line of decisions by which the Supreme court of the United States has virtually nullified the fourteenth amendment, declared the fifteenth inoperative, and emasculated the thirteenth," he declared. By restoring "the dogma of 'state sovereignty'" and giving states the power to discriminate at will between citizens of different races, the Court had licensed "that most degrading and inhuman form of oppression—legalized caste, based on race and color." As he plumbed the consequences of the *Plessy* ruling, Tourgée could foresee nothing but harsher and harsher racial oppression. Having deprived the "colored citizen at the South" of "all the rights attaching to self-government and self-protection," the Court had opened the way for "his further and more effectual degradation," prophesied Tourgée. He wound up grimly: "Indeed, it is almost impossible to imagine any form of social, political, or industrial degradation of the colored citizen which this decision does not authorize, encourage, and suggest."[117]

Fittingly, Tourgée addressed his last public statement on the *Plessy* case to people of color through a letter to the *New Orleans Leader*, reprinted and given extensive coverage in the *Cleveland Gazette* of 25 February 1899. As Smith commented in an editorial preface, Tourgée's "indictment against the supreme court [was] terrific and sublime." Deriding the Court for arrogating to itself the power of God by "proclaim[ing] itself omniscient ... and accounting its decisions immutable," Tourgée wrote, "From the very hour of its institution, this court, which the American people have been taught to regard as the very palladium of our national safety, has been the most malignant foe of personal liberty and equality of right that has ever existed on American soil." The Court's latest ruling having blocked all legal and political avenues of redress, however, Tourgée could point to only one remaining consolation: "Thank God, the supreme court of the United States is not omnipotent. . . . God has found a way to overrule the unholy decisions of this court against liberty and in favor of oppression. It required the blood of a million of men to blot out and reverse the specious infamy of the Dred Scott decision. What will it require to obliterate this last judicial crime?"[118] We who live in a secular age may find nothing but "cold comfort" in such an appeal to divine justice, but those who shared Tourgée's Christian faith, as did Smith and other African American editors, did take some solace in the conviction that God would ultimately "overrule" the "cruel sanction of a merciless court." Merging his own voice with Tourgée's, Smith editorialized,

> Says Judge Tourgee, it is just as foolish to try and bind God's justice with the green withes of prejudice-inspired fallacy in 1898 as it was in 1857. Forty years have not changed the Almighty nor made justice dependent on color. At some time and in some way the country will pay, and bitterly, for this judicial effort to enthrone injustice in the constitution by a forced construction of the plainest and simplest, the broadest and strongest, words ever used by a free people in defining the limits of power and describing the parameters of duty of a government toward citizens who had twice earned her gratitude and protection.[119]

A Legacy of Resistance

As Tourgée looked back on the *Plessy* case, did he ever come to regret having encouraged his admirers in New Orleans to test the constitutionality of the Separate Car Law and carry their challenge to the Supreme Court?[120] Did he fear that the endeavor had merely allowed the Court to formulate deleterious legal doctrine sanctioning racism? None of his public comments suggests any such reevaluation. On the contrary, his eulogy of both the Citizens' Committee and the *Crusader* in his "Bystander" column of 29 May 1897 indicates he believed they had not only demonstrated their people's political maturity by asserting their rights through the judicial system but had won honor that African Americans would reap in the future. True, in his letter to Martinet of 31 October 1893, Tourgée had expressed serious misgivings about the long-term negative precedent that an adverse Supreme Court decision would set, but he had advised delaying, not dropping, the case. As he surely realized, dropping it would only have convinced white Southerners that African Americans would supinely accept any wrongs inflicted on them. Such supineness would also have shamed younger generations of African Americans, burdening them with deep psychological scars. Moreover, failure to challenge segregation and disfranchisement, which were mushrooming all over the South in the 1890s, would hardly have prevented or diminished these abuses, though the Court's imprimatur certainly multiplied and extended them. Thus, we need neither fault Tourgée for having pursued the case to the bitter end nor impute to him regrets he did not voice. Rather, we can conclude that like the Citizens' Committee, he, too, felt he had been "right" to defend the "cause of liberty" and to risk "defeat" rather than capitulate to "ignominy."

Even in defeat, both Tourgée and the Citizens' Committee left a legacy of resistance to injustice that the NAACP and a more enlightened Supreme Court would build on more than half a century later. Researching the issue of racial segregation in 1950, Supreme Court justice Robert H. Jackson rediscovered Tourgée's long-buried brief, which he found surprisingly "witty" and prescient. "There is no argument made today that he would not make to the Court," noted Jackson, singling out Tourgée's famous dictum "Justice is pictured blind and her daughter, the Law, ought at least to be color-blind." Four years afterward, in *Brown v. Board of Education,* Jackson voted with a unanimous court to overturn the *Plessy* decision. Ruling that racially segregated schools are "inherently unequal," the Court explicitly "rejected" "any language in *Plessy v. Ferguson* contrary to this finding." As Jackson recognized, Tourgée had at last gained "a post-mortem victory."[121]

CHAPTER SEVEN

The View from Abroad

[The] last few days have been marked by a revival of that most dangerous and horrible feature of American life, a display of race antagonism at the South. . . .
. . . I confess that I am quite unable to advise in regard to the steps necessary or desirable to ameliorate the present condition. . . . It has so cankered the political and moral sentiment of the American people, that no organized resistance to it is possible. . . . I have no doubt that [God] will sometime take it in hand, and it is quite possible that the American Republic may pay the price of its own injustice, by finding in the Race Problem the end of its liberties and the destruction of its organic character.

—Albion W. Tourgée to President William McKinley, 23 November 1898

Writing to President McKinley in response to news of the November 1898 white supremacist coup in Wilmington, North Carolina—during which Democrats, who had lost the election to a biracial Fusion coalition of Republicans and Populists, toppled the government, drove thousands of African Americans out of the city, and massacred an undetermined number—Tourgée struck a markedly different tone than he had in January 1894, when he had exhorted then-governor McKinley to throw his weight behind an antilynching law in Ohio.[1] The dramatic contrast between these two letters reflects the crisis Tourgée underwent in the wake of the *Plessy* debacle. No other political defeat—not even the overthrow of Reconstruction—shook him more profoundly than the Supreme Court's sanctioning of what he called "legalized caste, based on race and color."[2] Although Tourgée never retreated either from his contemptuous denunciation of the *Plessy* verdict or from his passionate commitment to the ideal of racial equality, he could no longer discern a feasible method of combating white racism, as he admitted ruefully to McKinley.

The disastrous outcome of the constitutional challenge in which he had invested five years of agitation through the National Citizens' Rights Association, the "Bystander," and the *Basis*, as well as through the brief he submitted to the Supreme Court, left Tourgée in dire straits. Amid a national mood of indifference to race matters, exacerbated by an economic downturn, publishers and editors rejected his manuscripts, and Tourgée's lecture invitations dwindled to a trickle, cutting off his only sources of income. "I am in effect a Negro so far as literary opportunity is concerned," he complained to an elderly Quaker to whom he recounted his humiliating failure to interest any New York newspaper or magazine in hiring him as a columnist.[3] Tourgée's correspondence bears out his fall from the status of an author who could dictate his terms to the plight of an indigent reduced to begging for scraps. "I fear you did not take the hint when I wrote 'it is snug times for publishers,'" scolded the publisher of the *National Tribune*, who grudgingly accepted a manuscript on condition that Tourgée content himself with a fifty-dollar fee, twenty-five dollars less than he had once been accustomed to earn for each "Bystander" article.[4] Explaining why he had turned down Tourgée's application for an editorial position, an executive of *Frank Leslie's Illustrated Weekly* told him bluntly, as he reported to Emma, "What we wanted . . . was not a thinker or a writer but a skilled editor to select pictures and descriptive matter to go with them." He had tried every outlet and contact he could think of, added Tourgée, but none had panned out.[5] Though publishers put him off with talk of hard times, Tourgée diagnosed his predicament more bleakly. "What is the use when a man is dead[,] walking around and trying to conceal it? I have nothing to say that the world cares to hear," he lamented to Emma.[6]

The Campaign for a Consular Appointment

With his writing and lecturing career at a standstill, Tourgée was exploring another option: a political appointment to a consular position. He had laid the groundwork for such a quest soon after McKinley won the Republican presidential nomination in June 1896, on the heels of the *Plessy* decision. Despite having favored House Speaker Thomas B. Reed of Maine, a staunch ally of African Americans, over McKinley, about whose willingness to fight for racial justice he held few illusions, Tourgée threw himself energetically into campaigning for McKinley. Over an eight-week period, he delivered "more than fifty speeches," sometimes several a day, "all but two in what was considered doubtful territory," as he later reminded the president.[7] For the first time, moreover, Tourgée bowed to party leaders' decree that the race question be kept out of the campaign for the sake of emphasizing economic issues. Accordingly, he focused his speeches on defending "honest money" by upholding the gold standard against Democratic presidential candidate William Jennings Bryan's call for "free silver."[8] McKinley's victory earned Tourgée a letter of thanks from the Republican National Committee for his "eminent services."[9] No doubt with a view toward maintaining the

profile that could best help him parlay these services into a political appointment, Tourgée continued to advocate "sound money" even after the election, not only in his book *The War of the Standards* (1896), sponsored by
the Republican National Committee, but in his "Bystander" column, which
resumed in the *Inter Ocean* on 21 November.

Meanwhile, Tourgée and Emma mobilized his admirers in an all-out
campaign to inundate McKinley with letters recommending him for a consulship.[10] "If it were not a matter of absolute necessity, I would not ask it of
the party. But I am as near starving as a man can be who has three meals a
day," Tourgée avowed to McKinley's newly chosen secretary of the interior,
Cornelius N. Bliss, whom he implored to "say a word for me." He was still
struggling to pay off the last $7,500 of the more than $100,000 debt from his
1884 bankruptcy, Tourgée spelled out. He did not acknowledge the main
reason he was facing "*the wolf*"—that he could no longer sell his writing—
but blamed the problem on his Civil War soldiering, a cause more likely to
garner sympathy from Republicans. His "military services," Tourgée volunteered, had left him with "an almost crushed spine," from which he suffered
constant pain that now compelled him to renounce the "desk-confinement
of a purely literary life."[11]

To collect testimonials from African Americans, Tourgée apparently
relied first and foremost on Harry C. Smith. Ohio African Americans supplied eight out of twelve letters in the packet labeled "Prominent Colored
Men" in the State Department's archives. Besides Smith, whose letter of 26
January 1897 antedated the others by two weeks or more, they included all
the African American members or former members of Ohio's state legislature, as well as Charles W. Chesnutt, a resident of Cleveland. Rounding
out the list were such nationally prominent figures as Booker T. Washington, whose name Smith or Tourgée put at the head of the packet, and AME
bishops Benjamin Tanner and Henry McNeal Turner. "Leading Colored
Citizens of the State of Florida," among them M. M. Lewey, editor of the
Florida Sentinel, contributed further testimonials, as did the pioneering
African American classicist William S. Scarborough, future president of
Wilberforce University in Ohio, and William H. Anderson, editor of the
defunct *Detroit Plaindealer*, which had reprinted so many of Tourgée's
"Bystander" articles. In addition, a Chicago pastor seems to have organized
a letter-writing campaign by his parishioners.[12] Curiously, no testimonials
by Creoles of color or African Americans from New Orleans appear in the
State Department archives, suggesting either that Smith's circle of acquaintances did not extend to Louisiana or that Tourgée did not personally solicit

any of his numerous correspondents there, some of whom later sent congratulatory messages on reading press notices of his appointment.[13]

The depth of affection and appreciation that African Americans felt for
Tourgée shines through their letters of recommendation. Smith struck the
keynote echoed by many: "There is not a man in the United States today
outside of the class itself whose appointment to office would give such general satisfaction to the millions of colored Republicans." The Kentucky clergyman Byron Gunner confirmed that "by his heroic devotion" to protecting
their rights Tourgée had "won the universal esteem and love of the colored
citizens of the United States to an extent not enjoyed by any other man."
The Floridians underscored that Tourgée had "stood alone as a champion"
of black Southerners' "rights, thus bringing down upon his head the male-
dictions of a class in that section which has not yet accepted the results of
the late war as final." The appointment of Tourgée to a consular position
"would be regarded by all colored Americans as a fitting tribute to a grand
and proper man—one of the best friends our race can own in all the wide,
wide world," averred the former Ohio state senator John P. Green. Even
Booker T. Washington, whom Tourgée had so often criticized for preaching accommodation to white supremacy, praised him for having "helped the
Negro race in a potent manner" and asserted that "in helping the Negro he
has thus helped our whole country."[14]

Though featured saliently among the endorsements that Tourgée's application for a consulship received, African Americans' letters constituted
only a small portion of the total that poured in from supporters all over
the nation. Petitions and personal appeals were signed by seven American
authors, six leading publishers, forty influential North Carolinians, fifty
well-known citizens of Osborne, Kansas, fifty "*late Union Soldiers* now members of the Pennsylvania state legislature," a number of college presidents
and faculty members, several governors, eight U.S. senators, and twenty U.S.
congressmen. As Tourgée's biographer Otto H. Olsen comments, "It was as
if a sudden flood of old Civil War idealism was bursting forth in honor of the
famous fool."[15] Fittingly, the tribute that best summed up Tourgée's claims
on his compatriots' gratitude came from the *Inter Ocean*'s former co-owner,
Herbert H. Kohlsaat: "No man in the country has done more than he for the
good of the whole people."[16]

Despite the sheer volume of testimonials, virtually unprecedented "for
such a minor post," as Olsen notes, Tourgée could by no means count on
obtaining the consular appointment he sought. Over his long career of crusading for racial justice and equality, he had made too many enemies by

rebuking Republican politicos and "bosses" for having betrayed the party's abolitionist origins. Not the least of those enemies was Thomas C. Platt, the powerful senator from Tourgée's home state of New York, who controlled its patronage appointments and backed a more loyal candidate for a consulship. Fortunately for Tourgée, however, an incapacitating accident prevented him from going to Washington to lobby in person and forced him to send Emma in his stead. Her tact, persistence, and adroit "plan of campaign," which she had "well thought out" ahead of time, accomplished the mission that his belligerence and bullheadedness might have endangered.[17] To the infinite relief of both, Tourgée was awarded the consulship of Bordeaux, which proved far better suited to his increasingly precarious health than his initial choices of Manchester or Glasgow would have been.

The official announcement in the press unleashed another "flood," this time of congratulations. Speaking for Tourgée's "friends and admirers in Louisiana," L. J. Joubert, a member of the New Orleans Citizens' Committee, and Thomas R. Griffin, an African American clergyman and longtime correspondent, tempered their rejoicing with disappointment that the government had not bestowed a higher honor. "Nothing less than a position on the Supreme Bench of the United States, a cabinet officer [*sic*] or an Embassy will satisfy members of the Grand Army, the A.M.E. Church and the surviving old Abolitionists and other friends," insisted Griffin.[18] T. B. Morton, president of California's Afro-American League chapter, voiced similar sentiments. "My very soul leaped for joy" at the news of Tourgée's nomination, he wrote, but "two regrets" marred his pleasure: "first we can ill afford to lose you, and second we are doubly sorry you didnot [*sic*] secure a far better appointment"—a failure he attributed to Tourgée's championship of "simple justice" for African Americans. "Oh, it does seem sometimes, to be a crime for a man to be a friend of my race," he mourned. To help compensate for Tourgée's departure from the scene, Morton asked for copies of *A Fool's Errand*, *Bricks Without Straw*, and a complete bound run of the *Basis*.[19] Unlike Morton, Ida B. Wells and her husband, Ferdinand L. Barnett, interpreted Tourgée's appointment optimistically, as a sign of "the good feeling of the President towards the colored people." "We are as heartily glad of your success as if it had been one of ourselves. For in you we feel we have an earnest, faithful advocate and representative," wrote Wells. "While I have my full share of race patriotism and am anxiously hoping for a generous recognition of my own race," Barnett elaborated, "still I am free to confess that no appointment accorded to the colored people will give me more pleasure than this deserved recognition of your work."[20]

Reflecting the enthusiasm of Tourgée's African American correspondents, the African American press unanimously hailed his appointment,
which it had vigorously promoted from the moment he announced his application for a consulship.[21] Eulogistic editorials appeared not only in Smith's
Cleveland Gazette, as might be expected, but in the *Indianapolis Freeman*,
the *St. Paul Appeal*, the *Wichita National Reflector*, the *Richmond Planet*, the
Charlotte Star of Zion, and doubtless many other African American newspapers that have not survived. The one that best articulated the African
American community's view of Tourgée was Wells's eloquent tribute in the
Chicago Conservator, which she enclosed with her letter. "Judge Tourgee
has been the most conspicuous exponent of ideal Americanism, which the
nation has known for the past quarter of a century," she proclaimed:

> But no American has known him, nor can appreciate his work as does
> the Negro in whose behalf his tongue and pen have been in constant
> and largely unrequited service. He has been the never failing defender,
> the ever patient counseller [*sic*], the inspiring and candidly critical
> friend. He has told us of our faults and helped us to see ourselves as oth-
> ers see us. He has advised us with sound judgment and wise discretion.
> The nation and our race have been blessed by the patient hopeful work
> of this noble man.[22]

The gratitude that the independent-minded Wells expressed even for
Tourgée's censure of African Americans' "faults"—censure that could at
times be brutally frank, as we have seen—may surprise some readers, yet
she was consciously enunciating a collective judgment. Because African
Americans knew how much Tourgée had sacrificed to fight for them, they
regarded his refusal to flatter them as the mark of a true friend.

For the most part, the white Republican press likewise applauded Tourgée's
appointment as an "eminently fit" gesture toward a man who had done his
utmost to "keep the sentiment in the republican party up to its highest ideal."
Only one white newspaper, however, the *Alton Daily Republican*, reiterated
the widespread African American conviction that Tourgée "merit[ed] a far
better berth than he has received." Qualifying the general approval, the *San
Francisco Chronicle* and the *Jamestown (N.Y.) Journal* remarked that "no one
reads" his books any more, the latter trivializing Tourgée's lifelong preoccupation with the "negro problem" as his "greatest hobby." The Allegheny
County *Republican* opined that this problem, to which Tourgée had conse-
crated more "earnest thought and toil . . . than any other man of the present generation," would be "gradually worked out . . . along other lines than

[he] insisted"—that is, by African Americans' acquisition of "education and property" (as Booker T. Washington maintained). The *Buffalo Evening News* and the *Cleveland Leader* snidely observed that the "Bordeaux consulate" would "pay . . . better" than the *Basis*, showing that for once, Tourgée had not undertaken a "'fool's errand.'" No less snidely, the *Buffalo Express* quoted local citizens who thought Liberia would have been a more appropriate destination than Bordeaux for "such a friend of the negro." Perhaps attesting to the dominance of machine politics in New York, an unidentified local newspaper caviled: "No one seems to question that it was a good appointment, but it came out in such a peculiar way. Who were Judge Tourgee's backers? Nobody appears to know, except that he was indorsed by many of President McKinley's warm friends in various parts of the United States, and it is said that Mrs. Tourgee's personal intervention in her husband's behalf operated to the Judge's great advantage." Whatever reservations the Northern Republican press betrayed, Southern Democratic organs did not share them. The *Louisville Courier and Journal* found only one major "objection" to Tourgée's appointment: that "Bordeaux is not farther away." The *Memphis Commercial Appeal* agreed: "Tourgee is a mighty good man to lose abroad, and it is to be regretted that [George W.] Cable can't be sent along with him."[23] Such editorials proved that Tourgée's works had "not failed to make themselves felt" in the South, wrote an African American correspondent, who relished this evidence that Southern spokesmen "fear[ed]" the power of Tourgée's pen.[24]

From Outsider to Insider

In stepping into the post of U.S. consul to Bordeaux—a post he would occupy until his death in 1905—Tourgée entered on a phase of his career that deviated strikingly from the course he had followed ever since losing his North Carolina judgeship in 1874. After twenty-three years as a political outsider (and arguably more if we recognize that even as a superior court judge, he was reviled by the Southern press and targeted by the Klan), Tourgée now embraced the role of an insider responsible for representing his government abroad. Having devoted his energies almost entirely to crusading for racial equality at home—a mission that entailed relentless excoriation of his country for betraying its founding creed—he shifted his focus to promoting U.S. imperialism, celebrating the nation's emergence as a contender in the race for empire, and burnishing its international image.

How can we account for such an about-face? A letter to McKinley that Tourgée wrote in August 1900 and marked "personal" provides some clues.

First, Tourgée acknowledged having suffered a physical and psychological breakdown when he confronted his impotence against the triumph of racism. "My moral attitude toward the 'Race Problem' in the United States was such," he confessed to McKinley, "that I was driven to despair—utter hopelessness— by the weekly tale of irremediable atrocities which stained our civilization and threatened a future of shame to the country which I have always loved with a passionate devotion not easy to explain even to myself. It was evident that I must escape from this, if I was to conserve my intellectual power for future emergencies." Tourgée recognized that in "accepting the gift of renewed life and restored health" at McKinley's hands, he had incurred a "heavy obligation." No longer could he indulge in the "absolute freedom of expression on all subjects of public interest [that] had been so long as the very breath of his life." Instead, he must resolve never to embarrass the McKinley administration by speaking out against any of its policies, unless his "conscience" imperiously required him to do so, in which case he would resign his post after a private interview with the president.[25]

Buried in Tourgée's very admission of his "despair" over his country's intractable "Race Problem," however, lies a second clue that helps explain why no such conflict between his "conscience" and his "obligation" as a loyal government servant ever arose, notwithstanding the blatantly imperialist policies the McKinley administration pursued. The same patriotic ardor that had impelled Tourgée to right the wrongs of the country he "loved with . . . passionate devotion" also impelled him to applaud its military victories and territorial conquests. It was as if he could not bear indefinitely the spectacle of his country's "shame" and felt a visceral need to seek a source of national pride. How else can we understand why Tourgée claimed that McKinley's administration had "appealed to [his] pride as an American in a peculiar way" and why he believed it would "secure . . . a unique immortality" for inaugurating "a new epoch in the life of [the] Nation" through the "acquisition of new territory and the successful prosecution of a foreign war"?[26]

Tourgée was referring, of course, to the milestones of McKinley's presidency: the annexation of Hawaii; the Spanish-American War of 1898, which began with U.S. intervention in Cuba's Second War of Independence from Spain and culminated in the acquisition from Spain of Cuba (temporarily), Puerto Rico, Guam, and the Philippines; and the prolongation of that war in the Philippines, where American troops brutally crushed another revolution for national independence. As we shall see, Tourgée descanted at length on those events in his "Bystander" column, which provides further clues to the logic he perceived as linking his championship of African American rights with his endorsement of imperialism.

The "Bystander"'s Endorsement of Imperialism

The *Inter Ocean*'s editors agreed with great reluctance to let Tourgée continue his "Bystander" column from Bordeaux—a request he made not only because he prized the column as a creative outlet but because he depended on his weekly *Inter Ocean* check to supplement his modest salary, which other consuls supplemented with "pickins" (bribes).[27] In response, Kohlsaat (still involved in editorial decision-making) pointed out that the Associated Press and European correspondents supplied all the foreign news the paper needed and that Tourgée would not be able to compete with them for up-to-date reports. Moreover, the *Inter Ocean* was still laboring under financial strain—a plea borne out by the paper's bankruptcy in 1912. At best, Kohlsaat warned, he could accept an "occasional article."[28] With his usual pertinacity, however, Tourgée kept on sending weekly contributions until the editors abruptly stopped publishing them in October 1898. Those articles furnish the main record of his political evolution leading up to and encompassing the first sixteen months of his consulship.

Tourgée's earliest statement about the pretext U.S. imperialists initially used to argue for declaring war against Spain—that Cuban revolutionaries deserved U.S. support for the liberation struggle they had been waging since 1895[29]—actually took a stand diametrically opposed to the one he would soon adopt. Asked why "so earnest a lover of liberty as Bystander has nothing to say in behalf of the patriots . . . suffering for the holy cause in Cuba," Tourgée answered in a "Bystander" article of 16 January 1897 that "Spanish rule," with all its defects, offered people of color better conditions than they could hope for "under an American protectorate." In Cuba, as in the various Latin American republics, no color bar existed, alleged Tourgée (erroneously): "The Indian, the negro, and especially the mezzotint, has an opportunity to rise by merit," as exemplified by Antonio Maceo Grajales, the mulatto who held the rank of second-in-command in Cuba's army of independence. "No body of English or American colonists would have permitted a mulatto to attain such rank, no matter what his ability, character, or achievement," Tourgée emphasized, because "racial superiority and racial debasement is the supreme law and all-controlling impulse of our civilization."[30] Tourgée went on to say that if he saw "any prospect of an autonomous republic being established and maintained in Cuba," he would extend his "earnest sympathy" to the rebels, but he feared on the contrary that "Cuba free would soon fall under the dominion of the United States." An influx of white Americans would quickly follow, he prophesied, resulting in a "struggle for . . . race control," a proliferation of "armed 'whitecaps,' 'kuklux,' 'rifle clubs,' and 'regulators,'" and a "slaughter of the colored population terrible to contemplate." In sum, although Cuban revolutionaries were fighting for full independence, Tourgée could envisage only two choices for Cubans: annexation by the United States or continued subjection to Spain. The first would mean living under a civilization that "devote[d] its energies especially to the obliteration of the rights and opportunities of its weak colored elements." The second might eventually mean gaining from Spain both "autonomy" and "equal civil and political privileges to the negroes." Tourgée concluded with "sorrow and humiliation" that "colored Cuban[s]" would be better off as subjects of Spain than as citizens of the United States—an opinion he quoted from a letter a "prominent colored man of the island" had recently addressed to him.[31]

Tourgée's arguments against the annexation of Cuba applied with equal force to Hawaii, where the Native population overwhelmingly opposed the missionary-descended white American oligarchy that had recently taken over the islands and was lobbying for U.S. annexation. Indeed, during the very months when Tourgée was amassing recommendations for a consular appointment, a "monster petition" against annexation, signed by almost all the surviving men and women of Hawaiian ancestry, was receiving wide publicity in Washington, where the islands' deposed queen Lili'uokalani and a delegation of Native Hawaiians maneuvered through an ally to present it to the U.S. Senate.[32]

Nevertheless, barely five weeks after aligning himself with "colored" Cubans who rejected U.S. annexation, Tourgée completely disregarded the views of Native Hawaiians and called for the annexation of the islands, invoking the authority of a member of the white oligarchy, whose letter in favor he quoted at great length. America's "empire-republic needs an outpost in the Pacific," Tourgée contended in his "Bystander" article of 20 February 1897. He cited three geopolitical and commercial reasons: to "preserve our west coast from attack, get and hold our portion of the constantly increasing trade of the Pacific, and continue at peace because we are strategically prepared for war." He reinforced these reasons with warnings against the (nonexistent) threat of Japanese aggression that pro-annexation oligarchs were currently deploying for the same purpose.[33]

Tourgée returned to the issue of Hawaiian annexation in a "Bystander" article of 19 June, timed to influence a Senate debate over the newly concluded annexation treaty. There he addressed the concerns not of Native Hawaiians—nor of the Japanese and Chinese laborers on the islands' white-owned sugar plantations—but of West Coast whites, whose "narrow race antagonism" fueled their fears of absorbing a supposedly unassimilable population that might one day demand citizenship rights. Tellingly, while Tourgée was championing equal citizenship rights for African Americans in "Bystander" articles of the same period,[34] he made no such claims for Japanese, Chinese, or Native Hawaiians. Instead, he implicitly endorsed both the racist government policies that victimized Japanese and Chinese immigrants and the racist stereotypes the white oligarchs were disseminating of Native Hawaiians as ignorant savages. "Very few" Japanese or Chinese would "become citizens" as a result of the annexation treaty, asserted Tourgée. "The Japanese will soon return home"—apparently a reference to the restrictive legislation through which the oligarchy was detaining and turning away shiploads of prospective Japanese plantation laborers—and "the Chinese will soon be eliminated by force of our exclusion acts," acts Tourgée had once criticized but which he now seemed to take for granted.[35] "As to the natives," he added, "we should keep in mind that the present population is what American Christianity and American civilization have made it." Native Hawaiians needed no apologies, however, for they enjoyed widespread literacy and mastery of English, thanks to their education in missionary schools.[36]

Why didn't Tourgée's solidarity with African Americans carry over to the other races that U.S. whites were oppressing? And why didn't his acute insights into the dynamics of white supremacy equip him to contest its manifestations abroad as well as at home? The explanation seems to lie in his inability to replicate the interactions with African Americans that had overcome his youthful anti-black prejudices. Having fought alongside African Americans in the Civil War, worked closely with them during and after Reconstruction, and cultivated extensive personal contacts with them ever since, Tourgée had learned to repudiate demeaning stereotypes of them and to see the race question through African American eyes. Yet the factors that bound him to African Americans could not reshape his assumptions about peoples he had encountered solely through the writings of their white detractors. The virus of racism saturated American culture and its nationalist ideology too thoroughly for Tourgée to escape its contagion where other races were concerned. Thus, he discounted the interests of Native Hawaiians and Japanese and Chinese contract laborers, weighing the benefits of annexation purely from the vantage point of the white ruling class. "It is as an outpost of American power, a citadel in the midst of the Pacific, flying the American flag, that [Hawaii] is of most importance," he trumpeted.[37]

African Americans did not share this view, for their own history predisposed them against whitewashing the subjugation of other colored races. When the white oligarchy seized power in 1893 and began clamoring for Hawaii's annexation by the United States, the *Cleveland Gazette* published a long article by William S. Scarborough arguing that American Christians ought to assign precedence to "ethical" over "commercial" criteria in considering the advisability of annexation. "What right have missionaries or sons of missionaries, after civilizing and Christianizing a heathen people, to take from them either by persuasion or by forcible annexation their possessions as a price for their services?" asked Scarborough. He then foregrounded the contradiction Tourgée would try to sidestep. "We are still struggling with the race question," Scarborough underscored. "We have excluded the Chinese, of whom there are 15,000 more or less, in Hawaii[,] from our shores. We have, by common consent at least, disfranchised the Negro in a large minority of the states, and further than that there have been suggestions made looking toward his deportation. We are now devising measures to prevent the influx of other so-called objectionable nationalities. How can we regard all of this as consistent with the proposition to annex islands distinguished for the heterogeneity of its [*sic*] population?"[38]

It was precisely because the nation's race question remained unresolved and seemingly unresolvable that Tourgée reoriented himself toward the international sphere in June 1897, as he prepared to sail for Bordeaux. "The time is at hand when our relations to the world outside of our borders must engage more of our attention," he wrote. "Having unified the Nation" after more than a century of conflict over slavery culminating in a bloody civil war, "destiny now compels us to assert and maintain its power and prestige."[39] Hitherto, Tourgée had resisted the longing for national reconciliation that had driven most of his white Northern compatriots to abandon the cause of African Americans for the sake of making peace with white Southerners. He could resist it no longer, but he transferred the impulse toward reunifying the nation from the home front, where he despaired of winning justice for African Americans in his lifetime, to the imperialist arena, where he looked forward imminently to glorious successes.

"We have entered on the second stage of empire, an evolution which no great nation can avoid," proclaimed Tourgée. In accents that still reverberate through twenty-first-century U.S. discourse, Tourgée held up a vision of American imperialism as inherently beneficent, in contrast to its European exemplars—the ideology we now call "American exceptionalism." "We have no need of war or conquest; our free institutions, our unprecedented prosperity, our constantly increasing power . . . draw and will continue to draw to us, with the power of irresistible magnetism, related and dependent peoples," Tourgée alleged. Unlike Britain, France, and Spain, the United States would build an empire peacefully, he fantasized, simply by attracting "dependent peoples" into its orbit of their own accord, because they would want to share in its "prosperity" and "free institutions." Tourgée cited Hawaii as his first example. "Hawaii comes to us of her own motion," he insisted, again parroting the islands' white oligarchs and disregarding Native Hawaiians: "She has no alternative except to seek protection under the Stars and Stripes, relapse into barbarism, or become the prize of contending powers."[40]

As his second example, Tourgée cited Cuba, which he predicted would soon "fall into our control"—a prediction John Quincy Adams had likewise made in a famous letter of 1823, which compared Cuba to an apple ready to "fall to the ground" and "gravitate" toward the United States by a "law of nature."[41] Reversing the stand he had taken earlier in his "Bystander" article of 16 January, Tourgée now advocated U.S. intervention in Cuba's Second War of Independence: "We have no quarrel with Spain, but every people struggling for self-government naturally turns to us for succor and support. This we cannot fail to give." It was not "jingoism," Tourgée protested in anticipation of such a charge, to assume that the United States would acquire Cuba by assisting its struggle for "self-government." It was merely "inevitable" and would pave the way toward a "peaceful, prosperous expansion of opportunity," for Cuba and the United States alike.[42] Of course, the U.S. invasion of Cuba would prove neither "peaceful" nor beneficial to the Cuban people.[43] Before it occurred, Tourgée would confront the French analogue of the American "race problem"—an experience that would play a role second only to the *Plessy* verdict in undermining his long-held belief in education as the chief remedy for the racism that blinded whites and kept blacks from achieving equality.

The "Bystander" on French Anti-Semitism and U.S. Racism

When Tourgée debarked in July 1897, France was in the throes of the "Affaire Dreyfus," which convulsed French society for more than a decade, from 1894 to 1906, and reverberated for decades to come.[44] It originated when Captain Alfred Dreyfus, a young Jewish officer whose family had moved to Paris after Germany's conquest of their native province, Alsace, was accused and convicted of treason by a military tribunal on flimsy evidence—a miscarriage of justice triggered by an explosion of anti-Semitism and anti-German xenophobia. By the time Tourgée started commenting on the case in a "Bystander" article of 25 December 1897—the first of many attesting to the impact the "affair" exerted on his thinking—Dreyfus had spent two years in solitary confinement on Devil's Island, and the discovery of evidence incriminating another officer and exonerating Dreyfus had forced the government to conduct a pro forma investigation, which predictably reaffirmed the original verdict. Apparently convinced of Dreyfus's innocence and appalled by the French military tribunal's lack of legal safeguards, Tourgée editorialized, "Guilty or not guilty, Captain Dreyfus could not have been convicted in any American court without the testimony having been so fully published as to prevent any reasonable probability of innocence." The French railroading of Dreyfus should serve as a "potent corrective" to the tendency among Americans to "depreciate our judicial system" for the rights it granted the accused, emphasized Tourgée.[45] Although both the U.S. and British press expressed similar opinions, Tourgée received a reprimand from the State Department for his undiplomatic criticism of the country in which he was serving as U.S. consul, a post that did not allow for a journalist's license.[46]

Six weeks later, Tourgée described writing his "Bystander" column while cries of "'A bas les Juifs!' 'Down with the Jews!' 'Conspuez les Juifs!' 'Spit on the Jews!' 'Conspuez Zola!' 'Spit on the traitors!' echo[ed] through the night."[47] The anti-Semitic riots Tourgée witnessed in Bordeaux, where the "police were barely able to prevent the pillage of Jewish shops," according to the historian Jean-Denis Bredin, engulfed nearly all of France's cities and towns.[48] Erupting in response to the French writer Emile Zola's fiery pamphlet *J'accuse*, which attacked the officers responsible for perpetrating and covering up the judicial "crime" of convicting a man they knew to be innocent, these riots drew four thousand participants in Bordeaux alone and lasted five days there.[49] Tourgée could hardly have avoided comparing the anti-Semitic mobs he saw in Bordeaux to the Ku Klux Klan night riders he had faced in North Carolina and the lynch mobs he had anatomized in so many of his "Bystander" articles. Nor could he have avoided noticing a striking difference between the French and American instances—that unlike their U.S. counterparts, the French police protected the victims of mob violence.

Over the next few weeks, Tourgée devoted several more articles to analyzing French anti-Semitism and comparing it to American racism. "Every class of society appears to have a spite against the Jews and none appears inclined to take up cudgels for them," he noted on 12 February. "One can hardly walk a block during the evening, even in the quietest streets, without hearing the cry, 'Down with the Jews!' or 'Death to the traitors!' . . . No one dissents, no one rebukes. The merchant, the professional man, the ouvrier [worker], seem to occupy a common ground of antagonism to the Jew."[50] Tourgée's observations of French society and his reading of the French press led him to dispute the notion, promulgated in the United States and British press, that "the general and best sentiment of France is in revolt against the sentence of Dreyfus; that the anti-Semitic demonstrations are by irresponsible boys." Those who championed Dreyfus and condemned anti-Semitism represented a "small and practically unimportant minority," much like the American abolitionists who tried to prevent the rendition of fugitive slaves in the 1840s, Tourgée countered on 19 March.[51] Just as the vast majority of Americans had maintained that the "constitutional compact with slavery" must be "carried out to the letter," so the vast majority of French citizens refused to "impugn the infallibility of military tribunals." The lack of "any remonstrance" against "anti-Semitic demonstrations" proved that they reflected general public sentiment, Tourgée underscored. Nevertheless, he reminded Americans, their own country's record was far worse than France's: "We had not one Dreyfus, but 3,000,000 of men and women condemned to hopeless servitude for life. . . . Not only were they innocent, condemned without hearing, but our courts, in the sacred name of liberty, refused to hear their plea at all." Even after abolishing slavery, Tourgée went on, the United States still did not guarantee African Americans "equal enjoyment of political privileges, industrial opportunity, and equal security of civil right." The French courts' condemnation of Dreyfus—and of Zola for championing him—was "no more abhorrent to natural justice, no more absurdly repugnant to the sense of equality and individual right," than the U.S. Supreme Court's endorsement of "the infamous 'Jim Crow car' legislation of the Southern states." Tourgée wound up by accusing the British and American public of exhibiting a hypocritical double standard in its embrace of Dreyfus as a victim of French injustice: "Give Dreyfus a black skin, and hardly a voice in England or America would have been raised in protest or rebuke of any wrong that might have been done to him."[52]

Tourgée returned to this theme for the last time in a "Bystander" article of 9 April 1898. "Is there any reader of The Inter Ocean," he asked, "who believes that the imprisonment of Dreyfus compares in suffering and horror with that of thousands in the prison camps and chain gangs of the South? If he does he is sadly mistaken." No equivalent existed in France, Tourgée added, of the United States' most flagrant offense against humanity—lynching—of which the latest example was Frazier Baker, an African American postmaster appointed by McKinley. As Tourgée recalled, only "a few weeks ago," a mob of "a hundred armed men" had set fire to Baker's house, gunned him down "on his own threshold," and left "his own and his child's body consumed in the flames" and "his wife maimed for life . . . simply because he held the commission of the President of the United States and had a black skin!" Tourgée concluded bitterly, "The anti-Semitism of France is not fit to be mentioned in the same century with the negrophobia which bids defiance to all law and stains the civilization of the United States with a deeper shame than could a thousand cases like that of Dreyfus even if innocent."[53]

This "Bystander" article represented Tourgée's final public statement on the race question. He continued to mull over the causes of American racism, as evidenced both in an unpublished manuscript he wrote the following year, titled "Black and White" (1899), and in many private letters, but after leaving the Dreyfus case behind, he ceased trying to transform his white compatriots' racial attitudes. He explained why in "Black and White." "Like most Americans," confessed Tourgée, he had once harbored a "well-nigh unbound[ed] faith in education as a panacea [sic] for all social and political evils." He had even naively believed in "that most absurd of all antiquated saws, 'Knowledge is power.'" Now, however, he "realize[d] with inexpressible woe that neither education, nor civilization nor christ[i]anity offers any reasonabl[e] hope of a solution of the problem of black and white." What led Tourgée to this "grim" realization was the spectacle of French anti-Semitism, which, unlike anti-black prejudice, could not be attributed to its victims' poverty or ignorance. "The Jews greatly excel in intelligence and wealth, the average of the[ir] countrymen in France," he pointed out. "Yet within a year all France has echoed to the cry 'Mort a[ux] Juifs!' and in every one of its cities thousands have crowded the streets demanding the[ir] spoliation, expu[l]sion or extinction." Although Tourgée had earlier noted the absence of lynching in France, by the time he wrote "Black and White" he had decided that the difference lay merely in whether or not a "restraining power" was applied: "If the hand of power were relaxed a single day, . . . the lynching of Jews would soon become as popular an entertainment as the lynching of negroes with us. With us there is no restraining power."[54]

A few months after setting these thoughts on paper, Tourgée received a letter from Ferdinand L. Barnett asking him to comment on "why in certain States the white man Disfranchises, Lynches, Ignores, and Oppresses the colored man?" In a long reply that Emma spent all day typing up, only to have Tourgée extensively rewrite it, he admitted being unable to supply an answer. All he could say was, "There is nothing to prevent. No law, no party, no public sentiment." Berating himself for having once subscribed to the "fallacy" that by acquiring "wealth and intelligence," African Americans would "appease" white people's "murderous p[h]renzy" against them, Tourgée told Barnett he had since arrived at the opposite conviction: that if every African American adult could "pass an examination" for a bachelor's degree, possessed "an average wealth greater than that of the white people," and was "absolutely without fault before the law," relations between the two races "would be no better and might be even worse than they are now." (Elsewhere Tourgée noted that in the case of whites, "education does not eradicate prejudice, but intensifies it.") As he looked toward the future, Tourgée could conceive of only one solution: African Americans themselves must compel God to intervene in their behalf. He proceeded to conjure up a vision that uncannily evokes the civil rights movement of the 1960s. "Not until every service in every 'colored church,' palpitates with the impassioned demand for Justice, . . . equal rights . . . and equal opportunity" would a God who acted "through human instrumentalities" find a way to complete the unfinished work of emancipation. That consummation would come through an "effective appeal to the brain and conscience either of ALL the white people of the United States or of a portion of them united with practically all the colored people, in some supreme effort for justice." Tourgée expected the struggle to take much longer and to involve much more violence than it ultimately did, however. African Americans might have to furnish "martyrs by the thousand perhaps by the hundred thousand," and they might have to wait until "the year two thousand dawns," he speculated, before their "groans of agony" impelled God to change the hearts of their oppressors.[55]

Tourgée's reply must have disappointed Barnett, indicating as it did that the Bystander had opted out of an active role in the crusade for justice to which he had devoted his life—a crusade both Barnett and Wells pursued until their deaths without seeing its fruition. Yet disappointed or not, the Barnetts preserved Tourgée's last letter to them and chose extracts from it for Wells to read at the memorial service honoring his legacy.

The "Bystander" on the Spanish-American War

While Tourgée was digesting the bitter implications for the American race problem of the anti-Semitic riots he witnessed in Bordeaux, the war fever that had been raging in the American press since before his departure found an outlet, when the U.S. battleship *Maine* blew up in Havana's harbor on 15 February 1898. Although no evidence ever substantiated the charge that a

Spanish mine caused the explosion, sensationalist newspapers and warmongering politicians—chief among them Assistant Navy Secretary Theodore Roosevelt—seized on the incident as a pretext for intervening in Cuba's revolution against Spanish rule. Indeed, Roosevelt's ambitions extended far beyond Cuba, prompting him to dispatch Commodore George Dewey to the Pacific theater "with orders to attack Manila if war came."[56] The cautious McKinley, whom Roosevelt privately accused of having "no more backbone than a chocolate éclair," ultimately succumbed to pressure and asked Congress to authorize military action against Spain.[57] The "splendid little war," as future U.S. secretary of state John Hay famously called it, lasted from mid-April through mid-August. It featured such celebrated American exploits as Dewey's lightning destruction of the Spanish fleet in Manila on 1 May and Roosevelt's iconic charge up San Juan Hill in Cuba on 1 July, where (having resigned his post as assistant navy secretary) he headed a troop of white Rough Riders and African American infantrymen. The war culminated in Spain's ceding Cuba, Puerto Rico, Guam, and the Philippines to the United States on 10 December 1898. In the meantime, Dewey's victory also helped bring about the annexation of Hawaii by demonstrating the strategic usefulness of Pearl Harbor as a berth for America's Pacific fleet.[58]

Tourgée greeted these events with jubilation. From the outset, he perceived the Spanish-American War through the prism of the Civil War.[59] "It is thirty-seven years ago this very week since [the Bystander] stepped out of his college classroom and took his place in the ranks in response to the first call for volunteers to suppress the great rebellion," recalled Tourgée in his column of 15 May, reacting to the news that the United States had declared war on Spain. The memory made him chafe at being "racked with pain on a foreign shore while this wave of patriotic ardor sweeps over the land he loves." Tourgée's conflation of past and present induced him to whitewash the past, omitting the tragic failures that had followed the Civil War and instead tallying up the successes: "Slavery abolished, illiteracy fast being driven to the vanishing point, a nation united in sentiment and civilization, its population doubled, its wealth quadrupled," and two and a half million women "lifted" from the "degradation" of rape and concubinage to "the level of Christian wives and mothers." This "wonderful record" had taught him that "war for a just cause, the extension of human liberty or the maintenance of national honor based on justice and right," is not "an unmixed evil" but rather "is fecund with blessings, individual and collective." Accordingly, Tourgée justified the U.S. invasion of Cuba on the dual grounds of "opening up the 'gem of the Antilles' to civilization, enlightenment, and liberty" and closing it to the European monarchies that perpetually threatened the American Republic.[60]

In subsequent weeks, Tourgée applauded Dewey's feat in Manila as "one of the great naval victories of the world," hailed "the hoisting of Old Glory at Guantanamo," exulted in the status the United States had won in the eyes of the European powers that had previously regarded its military with "profound contempt as a national force," praised McKinley for having achieved the annexation of Hawaii so long blocked by opponents, and inveighed against the anti-imperialist "wise men" who were "reading us a homily on international law, [and] the dangers of extending the territorial limits of the republic," just as their predecessors of the 1860s had warned against the costs of a prolonged civil war and advocated compromising with the South or letting the slave states secede in peace.[61]

As he laid out his own imperialist vision in response, Tourgée inadvertently illustrated the racist consequences of applying his Civil War–era analogy to the countries the United States had conquered from Spain. "We have assumed the obligation to protect the people of Cuba against Spanish barbarity and misrule," he wrote in a "Bystander" article of 29 May.

> We shall have to assume the farther and holier obligation of defending them against themselves—against the inevitable fruits of ignorance and oppression. . . . A successful, self-governing republic cannot be created on an island . . . where but one-tenth of the people are able to read and write; where . . . generations of fractional strife would be certain to follow national independence. The only hope for free Cuba, for a peaceful Cuba, for a prosperous Cuba, for an intelligent, self-governing Cuba, is as an organized territory of the United States, to be prepared by natural and peaceful development to take her place as one of the states of the American Union.[62]

Tourgée was actually prescribing for Cuba a twisted version of Reconstruction that conditioned enfranchisement and statehood for the oppressed and oppressing classes alike on tutelage in American democracy, as well as on universal education—precisely the "panacea" he had recognized as useless in the American South. But in the case of Cuba, he was prescribing it against the wishes of virtually the entire population.

In a "Bystander" article of 10 July, Tourgée unmistakably revealed that he was envisaging for Cuba the Reconstruction policy whose disastrous failure he had chronicled in his novels. "What is required in Cuba," he announced, ". . . is to eradicate not only Spanish rule, but Spanish ideals; to root out the Spanish system of government, of administration, of law, and individual relations."[63] Whether consciously or not, he was substituting the Spanish for the American South's white slaveholding class. Unlike Tourgée's writings on Reconstruction, however, which had consistently portrayed the South's emancipated slaves as readier than their quondam masters for democratic self-government, his reflections on the challenge of transforming Cuba into a "free state" worthy of incorporation into the American Union portrayed its emancipated slaves as fatally handicapped by their racial and cultural heritage: "The population of Cuba, both by race and experience, is about as far removed from healthful self-control as that of any semi-civilized country can be. . . . The practical subjugation of the mixed races has perpetuated the slave relation and its dangers."[64]

The racism discernible in Tourgée's prescription for Cuba is blatant in his prescription for the Philippines, especially as he articulated it in letters to McKinley. Having urged the president as early as 24 June to "claim the whole of the Philippines and establish an American government there *instanter*," Tourgée could "hardly express" his "delight" on learning that McKinley had decided to follow exactly that course, rather than commit the "sacrilege" of "surrender[ing]" to Spain or to any other country the "glorified heaps of twisted junk which Dewey piled up in Manila Bay." Although Tourgée foresaw that "the task of bringing order out of chaos in the Philippines" would prove formidable, he attributed the difficulty not to the brutal methods the U.S. Army would have to use to defeat the Filipino revolutionaries in the ensuing Philippine-American War (1899–1902) but to the savagery of the Filipinos themselves. "No doubt the natives are about as hard material as civilization ever had to deal with," he confided to McKinley in his letter of 5 August. "I do not know what we can do with them, but even if we have to kill them off, it is better than to abandon the relics" of Dewey's victory.[65] Betraying its roots in his culture's racist ideology, Tourgée's rhetoric simultaneously harked back to the Puritans' justifications for their exterminating warfare against Native Americans and anticipated the infamous statement by a U.S. Army spokesman in Vietnam—"It became necessary to destroy the town to save it"—a statement since reapplied to Iraq.[66] Unmoored from the solidarity with African Americans and the mission of liberating them from slavery that had ennobled Tourgée's Civil War experience, his former humanitarian idealism had devolved into naked militarism, and indeed into the very race war against a subjugated people that he had warned against in the South. The toxic fumes of racism and chauvinism, enveloped in idealism gone awry, still befuddle American minds today, rendering them as susceptible as in Tourgée's day to propaganda aimed at dragging the country into imperialist military adventures disguised as liberatory interventions—interventions that inevitably beget atrocities against peoples Americans think they must "civilize."

Tourgée's militaristic bombast reached its peak in his "Bystander" article of 28 August, elicited by the news of Spain's surrender: "What a war it has been! Four months of continuous victory. Never before was the map of the world so changed in so brief an interval. Never before were so many ships of war destroyed without the loss of a single one by the attacking power. Never before were so many killed, wounded, and taken prisoners by one of the powers in a great conflict, and so few by the other." Along with the prefiguration of the body count and shock and awe, so familiar to us from Vietnam and Iraq, Tourgée also sounded themes derived from the Civil War and Reconstruction—themes he proceeded to transmute into the rhetoric of American exceptionalist empire: "Never was the volunteer citizen-soldier so fairly pitted against the conscript. Never was the power of the schoolhouse so well demonstrated in contrast with ignorance and poverty. Never was the Anglo-Saxon system of nation-building so fairly contrasted with the continental system of tributary colonies. Never did the American republic stand so high in the eyes of the world as a naval and military force." The nation must now turn the "prestige" it had won to the end of "redeem[ing]" its newly acquired territories from "Spanish rule" and making them "fit for civilization," urged Tourgée.[67]

The Logic of Racial Egalitarianism versus the Logic of Imperialism

With the discontinuance of his "Bystander" column after 2 October 1898, Tourgée's public commentary on the Spanish-American War and the U.S. imperial mission all but ceased. Tourgée's letters to McKinley and his successor, Theodore Roosevelt, indicate, however, that he never changed his mind about these matters, unlike many other Americans who initially embraced what they misperceived as a humanitarian intervention in Cuba but recoiled from it when the prolonged U.S. occupation of Cuba, and especially the genocide committed against Filipinos, exposed the true nature of U.S. imperialism. Mark Twain provides an illuminating contrast to Tourgée. Explaining why he had turned against the Philippine operation, Twain told a reporter for the *New York World*,

> I thought we should act as [the Filipinos'] protector—not try to get them under our heel. We were to relieve them from Spanish tyranny to

enable them to set up a government of their own, and we were to stand by and see that it got a fair trial. It was not to be a government according to our ideas, but . . . a government according to Filipino ideas. That would have been a worthy mission for the United States. But now— why, we have got into a mess, a quagmire from which each fresh step renders the difficulty of extrication immensely greater.[68]

In a trenchant essay he prudently refrained from publishing, Twain lashed out with particular vehemence against the treachery used to capture the Filipino leader Emilio Aguinaldo and against the massacre of over a million Filipinos, amounting to one-sixth of the islands' population.[69] If these abominations troubled Tourgée, he gave no sign of it. Yet the convergence between Twain's arguments against the war and Tourgée's arguments in favor of it perfectly bears out the thesis of Susan Harris's fine study *God's Arbiters: Americans and the Philippines, 1898–1902*—that "no matter what position they defended," imperialists and anti-imperialists alike "believed that the United States was a nation of white Protestants under a special mandate from God to represent freedom and fair dealing to the rest of the world."[70]

Tourgée weighed in publicly for the last time in the debates over the nation's future during the election of 1900, when Democratic presidential candidate William Jennings Bryan challenged McKinley's imperialist policies by raising the question "Does the Constitution follow the flag?," meaning do the peoples conquered by the United States have the constitutional rights of U.S. citizens. In a letter to the president of the Harvard Republican Club, intended for publication as a campaign document promoting McKinley, Tourgée answered: "[These peoples] are 'citizens' by virtue of the fact that they occupy our territory and are subject to our national jurisdiction" (a formulation that translated the occupying nation into an occupied territory). As citizens by this definition, Tourgée went on, "they have a right to demand protection in their rights of person and property. But this does not carry with it the right to participate in any form of self-government." Self-government could come only when Congress conferred statehood on the conquered provinces, because the power to regulate suffrage derived from the states, contended Tourgée. Echoing the views he had so long criticized when applied to African Americans, he stigmatized the Filipinos as equating the "idea of liberty" with the "license to debauch and oppress." Hence, he recommended delaying the privilege of self-government indefinitely. In contrast to the logic of racial egalitarianism that had informed both his *Plessy* brief and his furious denunciation of the Supreme Court's verdict, the logic of imperialism led Tourgée to anticipate the position the Court would soon take in deciding the *Insular Cases* that denied full constitutional rights to the inhabitants of the United States' newly acquired colonies.[71]

Tourgée's Final Thoughts on the Race Question

Less than a year after McKinley overwhelmingly won reelection, he fell victim to an assassin's bullet. Tourgée had already lived through the assassinations of Lincoln, whom he idolized, and of James A. Garfield, whom he had cherished since his youth as a warm personal friend. Now he reeled under the assassination of the president he credited with having bestowed on him the "gift of renewed life and restored health."[72] Adding to Tourgée's grief and shock, McKinley's death threatened to deprive him of his consulship in Bordeaux, a post that other aspiring political appointees coveted.[73]

For the time being, however, the threat did not materialize. Meanwhile, the "astounding" news that President Theodore Roosevelt had invited Booker T. Washington to dinner at the White House thrilled Tourgée with the hope that this "momentous" gesture portended a "future in which a new civilization and a new Christianity" would no longer "make color the test of right or righteousness." "I am glad that I have lived to know that an American President is brave enough to ask a colored gentleman to his table," Tourgée wrote ecstatically to Roosevelt.[74] Although Roosevelt responded warmly to Tourgée's letter, which "please[d] and touch[ed]" him, he never fulfilled the hopes that his breach of the taboo against "social equality" had kindled. Deluged by denunciations from white Southerners and objections from within Republican ranks, he retreated to the safety of the color line. Indeed, a year after Tourgée's death, Roosevelt would inflict on African Americans the worst betrayal they had yet experienced at the hands of a Republican president, when he unjustly ordered the dishonorable discharge of 167 black soldiers in a regiment stationed in Brownsville, Texas, for infractions they had not committed. Once again, the desire to placate white Southerners trumped all other factors, leading Roosevelt to ignore the testimony of the men's white officers and the pleas of African American leaders, including both Washington and W. E. B. Du Bois.[75]

A far more accurate barometer of contemporary white racial attitudes than Roosevelt's meal with Washington arrived on Tourgée's desk in the spring of 1902. The Presbyterian minister E. H. Johnson, a classmate of Tourgée's from the University of Rochester, sent him a copy of a review he had just published comparing *A Fool's Errand* to the Reverend Thomas

Dixon's recent best seller, *The Leopard's Spots*, an anti-black diatribe, and setting the two works on the same footing as equally biased, but equally valid, representatives of opposing viewpoints. Tourgée replied with what Mark Elliott has called "an extraordinary thirty-eight page analysis [of *The Leopard's Spots*] that constitutes one of the most penetrating commentaries on the history and memory of Reconstruction of the early twentieth century."[76] As remarkable for its honest self-analysis and personal revelations as for its incisive political commentary, Tourgée's letter to Johnson also offers the best summing up of his thinking on the race question as the end of his career loomed.

Dixon's publisher had already sent Tourgée a copy of *The Leopard's Spots*, he informed Johnson, and he had "read it carefully" (356). (As more copies came in the mail, Tourgée "refused to touch the repulsive book but grasped it with tongs and dropped it into the fireplace," according to Olsen.)[77] Tourgée pronounced *The Leopard's Spots* "entirely worthless" as an account of Reconstruction, but "of inestimable value" as "a delineation of the dominant thought of the southern white man of yesterday and today," whose "type" Dixon personified (356–57). He had "known Dixon almost from his boyhood," Tourgée added, though he did not mention that Dixon had sought his literary advice, only to travesty *A Fool's Errand* and *Bricks Without Straw* in *The Leopard's Spots*.[78] He proceeded to refute Dixon point by point, citing his own eyewitness observations of Reconstruction in North Carolina as evidence that Dixon had simply made up incidents out of whole cloth to "defile all things, all classes and all forces" opposed to the Southern white notion of black people's proper status (363). "Annihilation, deportation or eternal and unresisting subjection to the will and pleasure of the white people—these are the only alternatives which a Christian minister offers to the colored people of the United States" (358), Tourgée charged, categorizing the white supremacist Christianity Dixon preached as "the very highest form of blasphemy" (359).

More troubling to Tourgée than Dixon's distortions were Johnson's rationalizations for their nationwide acceptance. "You say, 'The South sees the North self-converted to the Southern political faith,'" Tourgée responded. "In a sense this is quite correct. The love of 'killing a nigger' has spread very widely through the North" (366). Unlike Johnson, however, Tourgée regarded such a development as cause for despair, not as a reason to suspend judgment of the South. Having himself argued against granting suffrage to the natives of the Philippines and Puerto Rico, Tourgée particularly resented Johnson's invoking the laws applied to the newly conquered territories as further "instances of approval of the Southern policy" (367). "There is a world-wide difference between refusing a man the right to vote and taking it away from him after it has once been conferred upon him," especially when it is taken away "by fraud, by terrorism, by murder," he retorted (367).

In the last section of his letter to Johnson, Tourgée turned the lens on himself and addressed the question "If I feel so keenly why do I not raise my voice in protest?" (371). Two motives kept him silent, Tourgée admitted. First, he feared that his country faced the "woe and shame" of a massive uprising or devastating race war, and that far from "awaken[ing] the slumbering sense of justice in the white Christian world," his words of warning "might start the avalanche" (371, 375). Second, and much harder to confess, he was "a coward." In short, Tourgée explained, he wanted to protect his job. "How long do you suppose I would hold my present position or any other under the government if this letter should get into print or even an inkling of my views should become known?" he demanded. "In sending this to you, I am really putting the daily bread of myself and family into your hands. This is why I have marked every page *'Personal and Confidential'*"—and why Tourgée carefully avoided signing his letter to Johnson, contrary to his usual practice (375).

Even to himself, Tourgée could hardly account for having chosen Johnson as a confidant, when "hundreds of colored people and some whites" had written to him "wondering why they do not hear from me upon this question" and he had "put them off with some evasive reply" (376). Perhaps Johnson's equation of *The Leopard's Spots* with *A Fool's Errand* touched a raw nerve. Perhaps the very fact that Johnson did not share his ideals but reflected the mainstream Northern public's susceptibility to the virus of white supremacy made it possible for Tourgée to tell him the truth he would not have been able to tell an African American or white admirer. Perhaps a surge of nostalgia for his "Bystander" audience, or a sense of his mortality, prompted him to wish "someone outside my own family might know my views" (376). Apologizing for the length of his "screed," Tourgée avowed, "I never wrote such a letter before and am never likely to do it again. Indeed, I would destroy it now, but for Mrs. Tourgée, who has gravely decided that I ought to send it" (377)—and who preserved a copy for posterity in her husband's papers.

As he swore, Tourgée never wrote another such letter, but he did unburden himself to another classmate from Rochester, surnamed Gould, who had remained faithful to his abolitionist ideals. He and Tourgée had "cast [their] first ballot together for Lincoln," and Tourgée knew that Gould, too, must be asking himself, "Who could have dreamed that the nation which freed the slave and established universal American citizenship by that grandest charter of Liberty the world ever saw—the 14th Amendment of the Constitution—would have permitted even in the lifetime of those who helped to achieve its glories, the greatest ravishment of human rights ever known in all the world's history?" The Supreme Court not only "coddled" caste, Tourgée railed, but misapplied the Fourteenth Amendment to corporations while refusing to apply it to the protection of "equal rights" for individuals regardless of race. "To day, a negro burned in defiance of law, swathed in cotton saturated with kerosene, constitutes the American idea of 'Liberty Enlightening the World,'" he wound up. Tourgée apparently felt no need to swear Gould to silence, as he had Johnson, but he hinted at the constraints on his own freedom of speech by quoting a famous line from *Hamlet*: "'Break[,] my heart, for I must hold my tongue!'"[79]

The worries about losing his consular post in whose name Tourgée muzzled himself were not imaginary. Bordeaux was a plum location, and others had long been jockeying for it. In fact, what had occasioned Gould's letter was the news that Tourgée had been "promoted" to the consulship of Halifax, Nova Scotia, late in 1903—a promotion he and Emma fiercely resisted. Tourgée's doctors warned that "a transfer to Halifax at the beginning of winter, would be fatal" to his "shattered nervous system."[80] Only at the eleventh hour—after Emma had sailed for New York—did Roosevelt respond to her personal appeal by canceling the reassignment.[81]

Tourgée's physical ailments took an increasing toll during his last eighteen months in Bordeaux. In August 1904 a surgical "excavation" of shrapnel lodged in his hip since the battle of Perryville temporarily relieved the pain he had been suffering. The fall electoral campaign energized him enough to supply some anonymous articles in favor of Roosevelt, which the Republican National Committee praised. By December, however, Tourgée could no longer breathe, sleep, or eat, and Emma was "almost worn out" from nursing him, a duty she alternated with typing up his consular reports and conducting as much of his official business as she could.[82] The end finally came on 21 May, a week after their forty-second wedding anniversary. "My heart is wrung," Emma mourned in her diary. Tourgée's doctors diagnosed the immediate cause of his death as acute uremia, a form of kidney failure, but he and Emma both traced the disease's origin to the probable kidney damage he had sustained at the battle of Bull Run, when a gun carriage had struck him in the back, paralyzing him for months and permanently injuring his spine. In this sense, at least, they believed, he had sacrificed his health and his life for his country, as surely as he had sacrificed political and financial gain for his principles.

White Southern, White Northern, and African American Obituaries

The obituaries Emma pasted into her scrapbook reflected both the controversy Tourgée had aroused in his lifetime and the grudging respect he had won from many of his political enemies. They also confirmed that he had outlived the era in which his advocacy of equal rights for African Americans had any chance of achieving results.

Surprisingly, one of the most eulogistic obituaries appeared in the *Raleigh Daily News and Observer*. Crediting Tourgée with a mind that was "a marvel in its capacity to grasp, absorb, digest and retain" and ranking him as one of North Carolina's "best . . . judges of Law or Equity," the eulogist, Andrew Joyner, recognized that the state was "indebted" to him for its reformed Code of Procedure, a model since adopted across the United States, as well as in England, Ireland, Wales, Australia, and India. If only Tourgée could have renounced his "pet idea of . . . negro suffrage," lamented Joyner, he could have remained in North Carolina, and "his name would today be enrolled among the giants in our history."[83]

The assessments of Southerners from other states were far less charitable. In an obituary titled "Tourgee and the Ku Klux," the *Richmond Times-Dispatch* granted that unlike other carpetbaggers, Tourgée was "an educated man, an able man, an honest man," but claimed that as such, he was "in no danger at the hands of the Ku-Klux Klan, originally one of the noblest and most patriotic of organizations." His "mistake," alleged the *Times-Dispatch*, was that "instead of making a full-fledged Southerner of himself, he tried to make Northerners of full-grown Southerners, and introduce with precipitate speed and suddenness modern progressive Northern ideas among them."[84] Three different Southern papers titled the *News* outdid each other in vilifying Tourgée. The first accused him of having "painted pictures which tended to increase and intensify rather than to abate and rationalize northern sentiment, at a time when mutual confidence and concession were most sorely needed." Left-handedly acknowledging the power of those pictures, the same paper found it a "misfortune" that Tourgée "wrote with such force and impressiveness as to give his books . . . an influence out of all proportion to their political value and broad-minded wisdom."[85] The second

News claimed that had Tourgée "directed" his "vigorous intellect" toward "healing . . . the wounds of war instead of aggravating them in every possible way, the bitterness between the sections would have been over many years earlier." "His name will be odious for all time to come," concluded the second *News*.[86] The third *News* called Tourgée "one of the most bitter of the South-hating carpet-baggers that came this way after the war to feed upon the carcass of the prostrate section, to wax fat upon the pickings, and to heap insult upon the people who were forced to tolerate him."[87] In the same vein, the *New Orleans State* labeled Tourgée "A Traducer of the South" and attributed his "venom" to vindictiveness for having been "kicked out of office in North Carolina."[88]

Northern newspapers presented more balanced appraisals of Tourgée's literary and political contributions but generally relegated him to a past the nation had transcended. Under the title "A Dead Issue Recalled," the *Brooklyn Daily Eagle*, a Democratic organ that was currently serializing Dixon's *The Clansman*, noted that Tourgée's death "receives merely passing mention in to-day's papers," although twenty years earlier it would have "commanded columns of news and editorial comment from one end of the country to the other." Thanks to the "industrial training" offered by schools like Tuskegee, argued the *Eagle*, the "future of the negro is settling itself along industrial lines and in accordance with natural laws." As a result, Tourgée's books now served "merely as a milestone to mark a time of turbulence and uncertainty which the country has happily outgrown."[89] Another Northern newspaper of unidentified provenance, the *Gazette*, similarly remarked that "today the country reads 'Red Rock,' 'The Leopard's Spots,' 'The Clansman' and other books" by Southern authors, which "smooth and soften where Tourgée's irritated and inflamed."[90]

Only a few newspapers gave Tourgée his due. Naturally, the *Inter Ocean* headed the list. When Tourgée was identified as the author of *A Fool's Errand*, recalled the *Inter Ocean*, "he was hailed as the originator of a new school in fiction, as the man who was to write the great American novel." Moreover, "the book reviewers were captured by its vigorous style, its humor, its pathos, as well as aroused by its argument." Tourgée's later novels had invited comparison with those of Dickens, added the *Inter Ocean*.[91] Drawing attention to the "worldwide" reputation Tourgée had acquired through the many translations of *A Fool's Errand*, the *Baltimore American* placed his novels about the struggle for racial justice in a broader literary context, suggesting an analogy with "the work of Victor Hugo in illustrating the economic and political questions of France."[92] Under the title "A Great

Novelist Gone," the *Press* (provenance unidentified) held up Tourgée as a beacon illuminating the "current declension" of the "books . . . which now flood the market." Along with *A Fool's Errand*, the *Press* singled out Tourgée's Social Gospel novel *Murvale Eastman, Christian Socialist* for special praise. "Broad-minded, deeply cultured, widely experienced, he put into his books such an accumulation of power as belongs to few writers of to-day," judged the *Press*.[93] The *Springfield Republican* highlighted Tourgée's "versatile" talents and "many-sided career." The influential antilynching law Tourgée had formulated for Ohio was proving to be a "potent factor in the suppression of lynching," emphasized the *Republican*.[94] The *Cleveland Leader*, which had helped convince Ohio legislators to pass that law, asserted that Tourgée had "earned distinction" not only for his fiction but also for his "legal works," which "would themselves suffice to bring him lasting reputation." Ultimately, predicted the *Leader*, Tourgée would be "best remembered" as "the champion of the enfranchised negro."[95]

As might be expected, the African American press paid Tourgée the warmest tributes, though Emma probably never saw most of them, because her clipping service covered only white newspapers. "Our Best Friend Dead," mourned Harry C. Smith in the *Cleveland Gazette*. "What reader and thinker that does not remember his great race-helps—books—from 'A Fool's Errand' to 'Pactolus Prime' as well as those wonderfully strong weekly letters in our behalf that the Chicago Inter Ocean published for years!" Smith also remembered reading Tourgée's magazine *Our Continent* while in high school and noticing in it "the ground-work for an anti-lynching law" that led him to ask Tourgée to draft one in 1894. Unlike most white commentators, Smith regarded Tourgée's legacy as very much alive in the present. "As the judge lay dying, across the water in France last week," he underscored, "the governor of Illinois was signing an anti-lynching bill" that "embodie[d] the principle" of the one Tourgée had drafted for Ohio. In a separate editorial note, Smith urged every Ohio town with an Afro-American population to "hold a Tourgee memorial meeting."[96] He would reiterate this exhortation for weeks on end.

The *Xenia (Ohio) Standard* followed up by proposing such a memorial meeting in its hometown. Tourgée had differentiated himself from all others as "an aggressive, never-tiring friend," editorialized the *Standard*: "No one, outside of the author of 'Bricks Without Straw,' ever stood up shoulder to shoulder in the ranks of the lowly year after year and fought for the eternal principles of right and justice to all men."[97]

Sounding comparable themes, the *Indianapolis Freeman* likewise invoked a military metaphor: "He gave his ability and his energy toward furthering . . .

the fatherhood of God and the brotherhood of man. His place in history should be greater than that of a general because he led in the forces against injustice and wrong, and lived above prejudice and hate."[98]

Implicitly ranking Tourgée with John Brown and William Lloyd Garrison, the *Appeal* of St. Paul, Minnesota, pronounced him "one of the best friends of the Afro-American people this country has ever produced." In a more detailed obituary published two weeks later, the *Appeal* described *A Fool's Errand* as "filled with thoughts that breathe and words that burn"—qualities that had made the novel a "revelation to the world of the enormities covered up down South by a slight veneering of culture and civilization."[99] "Tourgee for years was the star of hope to the black people of North Carolina, if not of the whole country," testified the *Seattle Republican*. "To black people the world over, his precious and inspiring memory shall be cherished like so many rubies."[100]

The most interesting African American tribute, published in the *Colored American Magazine*, came from the "distinguished North Carolina educator" Charles H. Moore, who had known Tourgée "intimately," having lived "side by side" with him in Greensboro, where Moore's wife had been "raised alongside of Judge Tourgee's children, in his household," and his mother-in-law had been "employed in the Judge's home during Reconstruction." Moore himself had graduated from Amherst College in 1878 and returned home to establish a technical university. As Moore reminisced, Tourgée was "very much beloved . . . by the colored voters of North Carolina. In fact, he was their idol . . . because of the labor and time which he spent trying to indoctrinate them into the principles and duties of American citizenship, which had but recently been imposed upon them by the Federal government." Moore's testimony corroborated that of the white North Carolinian Andrew Joyner:

> His enemies—the democrats—acknowledged him to be a man of great ability, honest, brilliant, and bold. His opponents feared him in joint debate, because he was so resourceful. He was a master of raillery and sarcasm. He stung like a wasp. He could use at will either rapier or bludgeon most skillfully.
>
> Being "a yankee" . . . he was bitterly hated from a political standpoint by those who protested against reconstruction. But in his personal relations he was so clever, good-natured and tactful, that he made, before he pulled up stakes and left this State, many lasting friendships among those formerly opposed to him.[101]

Clearly, Tourgée had left an indelible impression on North Carolinians of both races, and the African Americans he had sought to "indoctrinate" still treasured his memory a quarter century after his departure.

A Host of Memorial Services

While newspapers across the United States were publishing obituaries of Tourgée, Emma was channeling her grief into the rites of death. First, she arranged a funeral service at the English Church in Bordeaux, which the "entire American colony and all the foreign consuls" attended.[102] Then, she accompanied Tourgée's body to Père Lachaise Cemetery in Paris for the cremation ceremony, at which "members of the American embassy and consulate and the Loyal Legion" paid their respects. Before heading home to Mayville, where she planned to organize a memorial service worthy of her husband, Emma and her daughter, Aimée, stopped in England to visit Catherine Impey, who had vainly begged Tourgée to follow in Wells's footsteps by taking his antilynching message to British audiences.[103]

During Emma's travels, Smith tracked the memorial services that African American communities in Chicago and Boston staged for Tourgée and badgered Ohio African Americans to "do your duty!" "If the judge's memory is to be signally honored anywhere on earth, it ought to be right here in Ohio," Tourgée's birthplace and the state whose antilynching law he had fathered, Smith stressed.[104]

The Chicago service, held at the Bethel AME Church the week after Tourgée's death, no doubt owed its impetus to the Barnetts, Bethel's most prominent members. Their pastor, Dr. A. J. Carey, officiated, and Ferdinand Barnett delivered one of the main eulogies, along with Tourgée's editors at the *Inter Ocean*, William Penn Nixon and William H. Busbey. "It was certainly a remarkable meeting," wrote Busbey to Emma, promising to send her the *Inter Ocean*'s brief account of it.[105]

The Boston service, a "large and very earnest gathering of colored people" held on 30 July at Parker Memorial Hall, marked the birth of the militant Niagara Movement, in whose founding Smith had participated a few weeks earlier. Two of the movement's best-known leaders, William Munroe Trotter and W. E. B. Du Bois, sat on the platform, and Du Bois's African American Harvard classmate Clement G. Morgan gave the principal address. In it, Morgan "charged his hearers to ever remember that of all the friends of the black man of the present generation none had quite so real and so keen an interest in him as had Judge Tourgee." He also merged his voice with Tourgée's as he warned that "unless a change takes place in the attitude of the whites toward the colored people in this country a bloody revolution is bound to come," that "the northern negro cannot be secure while the rights of the race are in danger elsewhere in the country," and that "the man who does not complain when his rights are taken away from him is a pretty poor sort of a man."[106]

By 23 September, as Smith reported in his editorial "Our Duty," he had heard from Emma that she was sailing on 4 November, "bringing with her the handful of dust which remains of the 'mortal tenement' of her beloved dead, to be deposited in the base of the monument to be erected to his memory in the cemetery at Mayville, N.Y."[107] Smith immediately began mobilizing as large a contingent of African Americans as possible to attend the event at Mayville, scheduled for 14 November—plans he coordinated with Emma.[108] "Detroit Afro-Americans will charter a [railway] car" for the purpose, he announced on 7 October. (Though Smith did not mention him, William H. Anderson, editor of the defunct *Plaindealer*, surely led the Detroit contingent's initiative.) Whoever wished to join the delegation Cleveland was sending, Smith added, "should notify the editor of *The Gazette* promptly."[109] A few weeks later, the leaders of the Cleveland delegation met in the *Gazette*'s offices, appointing committees to arrange transportation for the group, order a "suitable floral . . . tribute," and draft "resolutions" expressing the community's sentiments. "Many prominent Afro-Americans throughout central and northern Ohio" had already committed themselves to making the trip, the *Gazette* indicated. In addition, Smith had received word that T. Thomas Fortune, editor of the *New York Age*, would head a delegation of the National Afro-American Business Men's League; that the presidents or "other prominent members" of the Niagara Movement, the National Federation of Afro-American Women's Clubs, and the National Afro-American Council would "head delegations from their respective organizations"; and that representatives of African American communities in New York, Buffalo, and "other leading cities" would "materially assist the race in showing due honor and respect."[110]

On 11 November , the day before the Clevelanders were to board a special sleeping car for Mayville, furnished by the Erie Railway, Smith made his final pitch for a creditable African American turnout at the service Emma was hosting: "Very especially do we invite those who have shared a common interest in the cause which was nearest and dearest to [Tourgée's] heart . . . to meet at the grave of our honored dead in renewal of their fidelity . . . to the great principles . . . which he so untiringly labored to promote."[111]

Smith's skillful orchestration paid off with a "Splendid Showing" by the race, as he exulted the following week: "Nearly 50 Afro-Americans, all well known and many very prominent, represent[ed] the race at large, as well as the four national race organizations" at the services, and those who could not attend, including Booker T. Washington, prevented by an earlier commitment, sent letters and telegrams.[112]

One of the most moving letters came from the National Association of Colored Women. "For the race we represent," wrote its president, Josephine Silone Yates, "he was ever ready to work zealously with pen and voice, at a time when to do so was to imperil one's good name and honor, and beyond that, even to risk one's life." Quoting Tourgée's dedication of *Bricks Without Straw*, Yates ended, "To the dear widow, to whose 'unflinching courage, unfaltering faith, unfailing cheer and steadfast love,' [Tourgée] felt he owed much, we especially extend our most loving sympathy and warm regard."[113]

Besides distinguishing themselves by the number of their attendees and messages, African Americans had provided the most "conspicuous" floral tributes, Smith boasted, among them a "broken column" of roses and "an exceptionally large wreath of chrysanthemums and roses, five feet high, mounted on a pedestal and base of ferns and palm leaves." African Americans occupied an equally conspicuous place in the program, which featured addresses by Chesnutt, Wells, Smith, and John W. Thompson, treasurer of the National Afro-American Council. In her address, delivered on behalf of the Illinois Division of the Niagara Movement and the Appomattox Club of Chicago, Wells hailed Tourgée as "a friend whose faith never wavered, whose courage never failed and whose loyalty was free from a 'shadow of turning' to his dying day." She ended by quoting a long extract from Tourgée's last letter to Barnett and offering its "creed to the American people, as a call to duty by a voice from the dead." For his part, Smith, of course, once again highlighted Ohio's antilynching law as Tourgée's ultimate accomplishment. In addition, he emphasized that some of the "Afro-Americans present had traveled hundreds, and, in a few cases, more than a thousand miles to . . . honor the memory of the race's most aggressive, strongest and best friend of the last quarter of a century." In his account of the services, Smith rejoiced that the "excellent showing upon the part of our people was a source of great satisfaction to Mrs. and Miss Tourgee both of whom frankly expressed the warmest appreciation to the editor of *The Gazette*" for his efforts. He proudly noted as well that the local newspaper, the *Jamestown (N.Y.) Post*, had commended the "colored people" for having sent such a "remarkably large and representative delegation . . . to testify publicly to their love and gratitude."[114]

Only the stingy coverage by the *Buffalo Express*, which devoted one line to mentioning the presence at the services of "several Negroes," marred African Americans' pleasure in their achievement, but Wells promptly protested the insult with a letter to the editor correcting his misrepresentation.[115]

Not content with their high-profile participation in Emma's ceremony in Mayville, Smith and his cohorts organized a memorial service of their own in Cleveland on 3 December that the *Gazette* celebrated as "A Grand Success." St. John's AME Church—a larger building than the Methodist Church in Mayville, Smith informed Emma—was filled to capacity "by as intelligent and appreciative an audience of our people, with a fair sprinkling of whites as is rarely gathered together in this or any other city." At Emma's suggestion, the program included a reading of "Be a Man," from Tourgée's book about citizenship, *Letters to a King* (1888), which was "enthusiastically received." Emma herself could not attend because Aimée, who inherited her father's frail health and would die of heart failure at age thirty-eight, was "seriously ill," but she wrote to Smith that she "thought of your memorial services constantly Sunday afternoon," thanked him for sending her the *Gazette*'s write-up of it, and requested extra copies of the program to share with friends.[116] In conjunction with the services, Smith also arranged for an exhibition at the public library of Tourgée's works, which he urged people to "go and see," and then "be sure to . . . read."[117]

Although the Niagara Movement had already commemorated Tourgée in Boston, its Washington, D.C., chapter held its own service on Thanksgiving evening, at which it honored Tourgée along with William Lloyd Garrison as precursors and "friends of freedom." According to the *Washington Bee*, the crowd that filled the Metropolitan AME Church on M Street was "one of the largest" ever gathered at such a "public meeting."[118]

African American tributes to Tourgée continued the following year. Members of Washington, D.C.'s Bethel Literary and Historical Association, hearing that Emma was spending the winter of 1905–6 in their city, invited her and Aimée to attend their meeting at the Metropolitan AME Church, where Professor John L. Love of the M Street High School was going to deliver a eulogy of Tourgée.[119] Love, who had begun corresponding with Tourgée while a student at Oberlin, had recently inquired of Emma how he could obtain a complete run of the "Bystander" column.[120] After her return to Mayville in the spring of 1906, Emma unveiled the obelisk she had ordered as a monument to her husband, engraved with his favorite line— "Write me then / As one who loves his fellow-men"—from Leigh Hunt's "Abou Ben Adhem." Fittingly, she scheduled the event on "Decoration Day" (now called Memorial Day), the national holiday dedicated to the Civil War dead that Tourgée had always marked with such solemnity. For this occasion, African Americans of Cleveland sent an inscribed copper lawn seat and those of Philadelphia an "iron urn," both intended to be "placed by [Tourgée's] grave."[121] A few months later, the Niagara Movement again paid homage to Tourgée, along with his abolitionist predecessors, when it held its second annual meeting at Harpers Ferry.[122]

Tourgée's Continuing Relevance

Tourgée survived in African American memory long after whites had forgotten him. Smith kept his memory alive, both in the *Gazette* and in lectures, such as the one he gave to the Du Bois Club in February 1916, when the group devoted a day to the study of Tourgée's works. He kept up his correspondence with Emma as well and announced her death in the *Gazette*; by a sad coincidence, having outlived her daughter as well as her husband, she died on the day of Smith's Du Bois Club lecture.[123] Smith's columns furnish one barometer of African Americans' fidelity to their great champion. Acknowledgments of Tourgée's legacy by such militants as Wells, Du Bois, and Rodolphe Desdunes furnish another.[124] The young men named for him furnish yet another: the internationally recognized concert pianist Albion Tourgee DeBose, who headed the Music Department of Southern University in Baton Rouge and who passed Tourgée's name on to his son; and the lawyer Albion Tourgee Ricard Jr., who earned his degree in 1952 from Southern University Law School and whose father bore the same name.[125] Perhaps the most telling gauge of the inspiration African Americans continued to find in Tourgée's life and writings, decades after the white literary and historical establishment had consigned them to the dustbin, the *Chicago Defender* published an article in 1932, "A. W. Tourgee's Attitude." Its author, Roberta Thomas, advised African Americans seeking an accurate "picture of conditions . . . during the War of the Rebellion" and a record of one white man's "efforts . . . to help our people" to "read some of the histories and novels by A. W. Tourgee," in particular *A Fool's Errand*, *Bricks Without Straw*, *A Royal Gentleman* (1881), and *An Appeal to Caesar*. Summarizing the messages she distilled from these works—"that the South could be developed by educating blacks and the whites," that "national education is the only way to solve the race problem," and that "the Race would rise" against its oppressors if they did not implement such a policy—Thomas made clear that Tourgée's ideas remained as relevant as ever to her own time.[126]

They remain equally relevant to ours, for the problems with which Tourgée wrestled so tenaciously persist, albeit under different guises. Jim Crow as Tourgée knew it is now dead, thanks to the civil rights movement, whose birth in black churches he predicted. Formal segregation has been outlawed since *Brown v. Board of Education* overthrew the *Plessy* verdict; both the NAACP, which argued the *Brown* case, and the justices who ruled in it built on the foundation Tourgée laid in his *Plessy* brief. Nonetheless, just as the Supreme Court of Tourgée's era reinterpreted the Fourteenth Amendment to mean its opposite, thus legalizing "caste," so the Supreme Court of our era has chipped away affirmative action, thus licensing the growth of informal segregation and discrimination in housing, employment, and education. And just as Jim Crow itself originally emerged to substitute for slavery, so, argues legal scholar Michelle Alexander, the "crumbling" of the old "racial caste" system has given rise to a "new system of control— mass incarceration," which she terms "the new Jim Crow" in her book by that title.[127]

Similarly, black voters no longer meet with violence at the polls or face state laws that bar them outright; instead, some African Americans have risen to the highest offices of the nation as secretaries of state, Supreme Court justices, and even president. Yet hundreds of thousands of others still find themselves disfranchised by felony convictions—a wrong that dates back to the Thirteenth Amendment. Because of laws denying felons the right to vote, in many cases even after they have served out their sentences, "more black men . . . are disenfranchised today," notes Alexander, "than in 1870, the year the Fifteenth Amendment was ratified prohibiting laws that explicitly deny the right to vote on the basis of race."[128] Meanwhile, the opponents of democracy have managed to erect new obstacles to fair elections, such as voter ID laws and polling arrangements that disproportionately hamper working people and racial minorities. Once again, the Supreme Court has favored whites at the expense of racial minorities and the ruling elite at the expense of the vast majority by gutting the Voting Rights Act and removing restrictions on the power of corporations and plutocrats to buy elections. Consequently, Tourgée's searing indictment of the Court as "the inveterate enemy of equal rights and personal liberty, in its construction of the consti- tution," still rings all too true.[129]

The most egregious evil Tourgée battled—lynching—has all but dis- appeared from the public scene but not from the realm of symbolism and discourse. We need only recall the noose that white fraternity boys at Ole Miss tied around the statue of James Meredith, the university's first African

American student, or the notorious claim by Clarence Thomas that the critics protesting against his nomination to the Supreme Court were subjecting him to a "high tech lynching." Far more insidious than such symbolic invocations of lynching, however, are the institutions that have replaced it: mass incarceration and super-max prisons overwhelmingly populated by African Americans and Latinos. As Alexander details, "The system of mass incarceration operates with stunning efficiency to sweep people of color off the streets, lock them in cages, and then release them into an inferior second-class status." Evidencing that grotesque "efficiency"—and showing exactly how mass incarceration operates to replace slavery and the old Jim Crow—"more African American adults are under correctional control today—in prison or jail, on probation or parole—than were enslaved in 1850," and "more black men are imprisoned today than at any other moment in our nation's history."[130] Indeed, as Alexander demonstrates in her chapter "The Color of Justice," today's criminal justice system continues to be almost as heavily biased against people of color—despite increased numbers of black jurors, judges, prosecutors, and governors—as when Tourgée wrote, "The odds are all against [a black defendant] even if innocent. He is poor and black. The judges are all white; the jurors mostly if not entirely white; the prosecuting officers are all white; the chief executives of the States are all white."[131] For these reasons, Tourgée's writings still offer us invaluable resources for combating the injustices that corrode our society.

The remedies Tourgée identified offer us even more precious resources. Contrary to his pessimistic belief that he had erred in advocating education as a solution to the race problem, the transformations wrought over the past few decades have vindicated his original faith, albeit in a deeper and more complex manner than he envisaged. As Tourgée prophesied in his early essay "The South as a Field for Fiction," education enabled "the children . . . of slaves" to "advance American literature to the very front rank," proven by the national and international acclaim African American writers have won in the twentieth and twenty-first centuries.[132] The (re)education that the civil rights and anti–Vietnam War movements afforded, paralleling Tourgée's reeducation as a Civil War soldier, inspired progressives not only to pry open the doors of white universities to African American students and faculty previously excluded from them but also to force major changes in the curriculum. These curricular changes, in turn, have exposed white students to a rich body of literature hitherto ignored by the white academy. The insights students of all races have gained from exploring together texts articulating the viewpoints of authors from diverse cultural backgrounds have resulted in greater mutual understanding and a breakdown of racial barriers. Nothing could testify more convincingly to the soundness of Tourgée's faith in education as a solution to the race problem than the right wing's zealous efforts to undo university affirmative action policies through the Supreme Court.

Tourgée himself exemplified his other main remedy for racism, inequality, and injustice: cross-racial alliances. His vast correspondence with African Americans from all walks of life, unique for an age of white supremacy and racial separatism; his collaboration with Wells and Smith in the campaign against lynching and with Louis A. Martinet in the *Plessy* case; his unfulfilled vision of a movement organ jointly run by a white and a black editor and directed at a biracial audience; and above all his founding of a civil rights organization, the NCRA, that encouraged African Americans and progressive whites to work together for racial equality hold up models we today can profitably emulate as we carry on the struggle to create a just society.

Afterword

The process of rescuing Tourgée from the oblivion to which the triumph of white supremacy consigned him in his lifetime has been long, bumpy, and arduous. Tourgée's two earliest biographers, Roy F. Dibble (1921) and Theodore L. Gross (1963), portrayed him hostilely in the light of the white supremacist ideology and pro-Southern historiography of Reconstruction that dominated the academy in their day. Although a few African American and progressive white scholars paid brief tributes to him,[1] Tourgée did not receive his due until Otto H. Olsen's magnificent biography, *Carpetbagger's Crusade* (1965), revised the history of Reconstruction to reflect the egalitarian values that white and black Radical Republicans of the post–Civil War era shared with their twentieth-century heirs in the civil rights movement. Meanwhile, two other leading revisionist historians, John Hope Franklin and George M. Fredrickson, brought out new editions of *A Fool's Errand* (1961, 1966), and Olsen himself issued a new edition of *Bricks Without Straw* (1969), as well as a collection of documents about the *Plessy v. Ferguson* case (1967), including Tourgée's legal brief and copious extracts from his correspondence with Louis A. Martinet. Simultaneously, Dean H. Keller laid the foundations for further research by organizing, microfilming, and indexing the Albion W. Tourgée Papers (1964), publishing a complete bibliography of Tourgée's writings (1965), reprinting Tourgée's Civil War diary (1965), and microfilming and summarizing his magazine the *Basis* (1965). Despite these promising developments and a flurry of attention from distinguished scholars, the Tourgée revival they seemed to portend did not materialize.[2] Instead, Tourgée fell back into near obscurity.

The hundredth anniversary of the *Plessy* decision and the fiftieth anniversary of the *Brown v. Board of Education* verdict that overthrew it stimulated another burst of scholarship, focused primarily on Tourgée's legal brief and secondarily on his fiction. Since then, the accolades that have greeted Mark Elliott's prizewinning biography, *Color-Blind Justice* (2006); the publication of Elliott and John David Smith's anthology of Tourgée's writings, *Undaunted Radical* (2010), and of my own annotated teaching edition of *Bricks Without Straw* (2009); and the convening of two recent conferences on Tourgée in Westfield, New York (2008), and Raleigh, North Carolina (2011), all fan hope that this time Tourgée may be destined for a lasting revival.

As I have tried to show in *A Refugee from His Race*, however, restoring Tourgée to his rightful place in the history of the struggle for equality involves far more than doing justice to a lone hero. It necessarily entails reconceptualizing that struggle as an alliance between African Americans and the progressive whites who joined them in fighting against racism. Unfortunately, current scholarship does not yet exhibit any sign that such a reconceptualization is underway. Two new books illustrate the separatist paradigm that continues to govern African American Studies—a paradigm that leaves no room for whites, except as racist oppressors or at best paternalistic do-gooders. Both Shawn Leigh Alexander's *An Army of Lions: The Civil Rights Struggle before the NAACP* (2012) and Susan D. Carle's *Defining the Struggle: National Organizing for Racial Justice, 1880–1915* (2013) recuperate the history of the African American organizations that provided models for the NAACP and its strategies of test case litigation and legislative reform—a vital corrective to scholarship that minimizes African Americans' resistance to white supremacy. Both cover the period during which Tourgée founded the National Citizens' Rights Association and collaborated closely with Martinet, Ida B. Wells, Harry C. Smith, William H. Anderson, T. Thomas Fortune, and other African American activists in combating segregation, discrimination, disfranchisement, and lynching. Yet even while detailing these activists' endeavors and quoting their writings, neither Alexander nor Carle acknowledges their collaboration with Tourgée, nor does either recognize the significance of the NCRA as an interracial organization to which all of these activists except Fortune belonged and whose membership roster far exceeded the early NAACP's, as well as other precursors'. Alexander mentions Tourgée only to disparage him for establishing a civil rights association whose "goals or tactics differed [so] little from those of the Afro-American League" that many "wondered why yet another organization had formed."[3] Carle devotes a single sentence to noting that the "African American lawyer Louis Martinet led" a "test case" against Jim Crow transportation in Louisiana, and the "white lawyer and abolitionist Albion Tourgée argued the case to unsuccessful results before the Supreme Court."[4] Both entirely overlook Tourgée's antilynching journalism and omit his authorship of Ohio's influential antilynching law from their accounts of African American activists' campaigns against lynching—an omission that historians of lynching replicate.

My point is not to criticize two otherwise valuable contributions to African American Studies, much less to accuse their (white) authors of racial bias. Rather, I want to underscore the need to modify a separatist paradigm that hampers our understanding of the past and narrows our vision of the future by writing interracial alliances out of the history of civil rights advocacy. In this spirit, I offer my study of Tourgée's alliance with African Americans against white supremacy as an alternative model.

The Tourgée archive itself, on which I have based much of my research, invites an alternative approach to the history of the dark 1890s. A rich source of letters expressing the attitudes of African Americans and attesting to the myriad forms of resistance in which they engaged during an understudied epoch, it cries out to be mined. Indeed, the Tourgée archive constitutes virtually the only source we have for information about Martinet, given the disappearance of the *Crusader,* and the only source of personal information about Anderson, of whom little is known beyond his editorship of the *Detroit Plaindealer* and his coauthorship (with Walter A. Stowers) of the novel *Appointed.* Even for Wells, whose private diary, autobiography, and corpus of antilynching works have inspired an impressive body of scholarship, the dearth of surviving correspondence bids us to pay special heed to the thirteen letters she wrote to Tourgée and Emma.[5] For others, such as Fortune and John Edward Bruce, whose letters are held in important African American collections and who have sometimes been perceived as militant separatists, their letters to Tourgée prompt more nuanced interpretations.[6]

That all of these prominent race men and women were writing to a white radical who carefully preserved their letters, along with some drafts of his answers, sheds precious light on race relations. Their correspondence certainly reveals tensions and misunderstandings, typified by Wells's explanation of why she canceled her planned visit to the Tourgées without notifying them. It likewise reveals Tourgée's occasional manifestations of racial arrogance, notably in refusing to accept African American leaders' judgment that they should support a flawed federal education bill rather than none. And it reveals his sometimes peevish complaints that African Americans did not sufficiently appreciate his sacrifices for them. What emerges most conspicuously from these relatively rare discordant notes in the correspondence, however, is both parties' ability to learn from mistakes and to surmount the formidable obstacles blocking honest communication on an equal basis between the races. Striking the keynote of the archive, African Americans continually reiterated their affection and admiration for Tourgée, their trust in his unswerving allegiance, and their respect for his blunt candor, hurtful though they admittedly found it. Granted, Tourgée hardly represents the norm, either in his passionate commitment to agitating for racial equality or in his cultivation of extensive personal relationships with African Americans, but his example may induce us to reconsider the extent to which the era's extreme segregation prevented progressives from maintaining contacts across the color line.

Tourgée's vast file of correspondence with NCRA members opens another new window into the 1890s. At the very least, the NCRA's peak membership of 250,000 indicates more opposition to white supremacy among both races and greater militancy among Southern blacks, as well as greater confidence in the leadership of a white radical, than we might expect. In addition, the NCRA file may enable researchers to trace members forward, so as to ascertain whether any later joined either the NAACP or the Communist Party. If so, the NCRA may have served as a training ground for organizations that better fulfilled the ideal of interracial solidarity in the pursuit of justice to which Tourgée dedicated his life.

In the final analysis, Tourgée's career dramatizes what is at stake in the writing of history. He vanished from mainstream U.S. history because it could not accommodate his relentless denunciation of the nation's white supremacist ideology and practice. Yet he also remains largely absent from the revisionist history that antiracist scholars have been writing over the last few decades because it has marginalized or excluded the progressive whites who fought alongside people of color. We cannot do full justice to either Tourgée or the still ongoing struggle for a truly egalitarian America until our narratives of the past live up to our aspirations for the future.

Notes

Preface

1. "Death of Judge Tourgee"; *New Orleans Daily States*, 14 June 1892, from scrapbook of press clippings, Albion W. Tourgée Papers (hereinafter AWTP), item #8251.

2. Albion W. Tourgée (hereinafter AWT) to editor, *Raleigh Daily Standard*, 1 February 1870, 2; original in AWTP #1262.

3. Cooper, *Voice from the South*, 188.

4. Olsen, *Carpetbagger's Crusade*, 224; AWTP #9907, scrapbook of obituary clippings, "Judge Tourgee, The Author, Dead," *Baltimore American*, 21 May 1905.

5. Karcher, introduction to *Bricks Without Straw*, by Albion W. Tourgée, 1.

6. Olsen, *Carpetbagger's Crusade*, 281.

7. Tourgée supplies these figures in AWTP #6439, AWT to Phillip C. Garret [*sic*], n.d. [October 1892]. Five years after its founding in 1833, the American Anti-Slavery Society had 1,350 local chapters and approximately 250,000 members, according to Wikipedia, "American Anti-Slavery Society." By comparison, "the NAACP had only a few hundred members" during the "first three years of its existence," according to McPherson, *Abolitionist Legacy*, 389. Moreover, by 1919, NAACP membership was only around 90,000. See Kellogg, *NAACP*, 1:91, 128, 133, 137.

8. [Harris], "Refugee from His Race." Tourgée reprinted and replied to this review in "A Bystander's Notes," 10 May 1890, 4.

9. Quoted in Catherine Impey, editorial, *Anti-Caste*, December 1891, 2–3; AWTP #7614, NCRA (National Citizens' Rights Association) file, Josephine S. P. Ruffin to AWT, 3 December 1891.

10. Cooper, *Voice from the South*, 190, 191.

11. AWTP #5438, W. E. Henry to AWT, 16 March 1891.

12. I am grateful to H. Bruce Franklin and an anonymous reader for the journal *MELUS*, which published an article drawn from this book, for helping me to formulate the distinction offered here between objective and subjective manifestations of racism.

Chapter One

1. AWTP #5374, AWT to J. Gray Lucas, 28 February 1891; housed and recently digitalized at the Chautauqua County Historical Society, these papers are also available on microfilm. In AWTP #5365, J. Gray Lucas to AWT, 24 February 1891, Lucas

mentions that a "few days" previously, he had sent Tourgée a copy of the *Arkansas Gazette* of 21 February containing his speech.

2. AWTP #6481, J. Gray Lucas to AWT, n.d. Though filed with undated letters of late 1892, Lucas's reference to "the movement to organize a 'Citizens Equal Rights Association'" points to November 1891 as the most probable date.

3. John William Graves, "John Gray Lucas," *Encyclopedia of Arkansas History and Culture,* www.encyclopediaofarkansas.net (8 June 2015).

4. Logan, *Betrayal of the Negro.*

5. Quotations are from AWTP #467, AWT to Emma Kilbourne, 6 May 1863; and AWTP #454, AWT to Brothers of the Union, January 1863. For Tourgée's references to his interactions with the fugitive slaves who attached themselves to his regiment, see AWTP #577, Daily Pocket Remembrancer [diary] for 1863, 7 June and 24 October; Keller, "Civil War Diary of Albion W. Tourgée"; and Tourgée, *Story of a Thousand,* 31–34, 83, 87–91, 106–7. For secondary accounts of how Tourgée's Civil War service changed his view of African Americans, see Olsen, *Carpetbagger's Crusade,* chap. 2: "Liberty, Union, and War," especially 24–25; Elliott, *Color-Blind Justice,* chap. 3, especially 85–91; and Karcher, introduction to *Bricks Without Straw,* 6–8.

6. For detailed accounts of Tourgée's role in North Carolina's Reconstruction, see Olsen, *Carpetbagger's Crusade,* chaps. 3–17; Current, *Those Terrible Carpetbaggers,* 46–67, 91–111, 193–289; Elliott, *Color-Blind Justice,* chaps. 4–5; and Karcher, introduction to *Bricks Without Straw,* 8–27. See also Tourgée's own fictionalized account, *A Fool's Errand.*

7. For historical overviews of these developments, see Foner, *Reconstruction,* chaps. 3–7; Hahn, *Nation under Our Feet,* chaps. 4–7; and R. Alexander, *North Carolina Faces the Freedmen.*

8. Current, *Those Terrible Carpetbaggers,* 201–202; Olsen, *Carpetbagger's Crusade,* 152–55; Elliott, *Color-Blind Justice,* 123–32; AWT to editor, *Raleigh Daily Standard,* 1 February 1870, 2; original in AWTP #1262.

9. For detailed historical overviews, see Trelease, *White Terror,* especially chaps. 12, 13, and 21 on North Carolina; Escott, *Many Excellent People,* 152–60; and Escott, "White Republicanism and Ku Klux Klan Terror."

10. For a study tracing and documenting this shift, see Blum, *Reforging the White Republic.* See also Foner, chaps. 10–11; and Gillette, *Retreat from Reconstruction.*

11. AWTP #2249, AWT to Emma Kilbourne Tourgée (hereafter EKT), 9 November 1878.

12. Paraphrased from *Bricks Without Straw,* 352, where Tourgée attributes this sentiment to the Yankee schoolteacher Mollie Ainslee.

13. *Uncle Tom's Cabin* sold 300,000 copies in the United States the first year, according to most sources, but its lifetime sales in the millions of course dwarfed those of *A Fool's Errand.*

14. AWTP #9907, scrapbook containing obituaries; quotations are from "The Fool's Errand," unnamed and undated source, and "Observed about Town," *Utica Observer,* 24 May 1905. On Tourgée's boyhood friendship with Garfield, see AWTP

#10762, in which Tourgée also reminisces about writing *Bricks Without Straw* and about the 1880 campaign.

15. AWTP #10532, EKT, "Memories of the Campaign of 1880," *Buffalo Express*, ca. 31 October 1908.

16. I have omitted Frederick Douglass's "The Heroic Slave" because it is not a full-scale novel and Harriet Wilson's *Our Nig* (1859) and Frances Harper's *Sowing and Reaping* (1876–77) because neither focuses on the collective liberation struggle of the African American community.

17. AWTP #10867, unpublished autobiographical sketch of AWT; Garfield, Inaugural Address, 163–65.

18. Tourgée would live through three presidential assassinations in thirty-six years, the third being William McKinley's in 1901.

19. Fredrickson, *Black Image in the White Mind*, 243.

20. Tourgée, *Appeal to Caesar*, 333–44; Olsen, *Carpetbagger's Crusade*, 250.

21. AWTP #9772, EKT to Adelbert Moot, 17 June 1905 (this letter is misnumbered #9771 in the Chautauqua County Historical Society's digitalized version). Moot was the Tourgées' lawyer, to whom she was writing in the hope that he could help her recover the life insurance Tourgée had signed away to one of his creditors.

22. AWTP #2487, AWT to EKT, 18 February 1886; see also his letters of 4 and 13 February, AWTP #2481, 2484.

23. AWTP #2493, AWT to EKT, 27 February 1886.

24. AWTP #2540, scrapbook, p. 130, clippings from the *Warren Chronicle*, 5 February 1886, and the *Akron Daily Beacon*, 6 February 1886.

25. AWTP #2601 and 3801, Roberts Brothers to EKT, 25 March and 4 November 1887.

26. AWTP #3426, Fords, Howard, and Hulbert to EKT, 22 March 1888; and AWTP #3419, S. S. McClure to AWT, 20 March 1888.

27. Olsen, *Carpetbagger's Crusade*, 281, citing *A History of the City of Chicago* (Chicago: Chicago Inter Ocean Press, 1900), 30, 319.

28. "A Man of Destiny" (13 December 1884–4 March 1885) and "A Child of Luck" (20 March–4 December 1886), partisan attacks on Grover Cleveland published over the pseudonym "Siva"; "The Veteran and His Pipe" (25 April–19 September 1885), in which an anonymous Civil War soldier chides Northerners for pursuing reconciliation with the South at the price of abandoning the ideals of freedom and equal rights he and his comrades had fought for; and "Letters to a Mugwump" (26 September–12 December 1885), addressed to disaffected Republicans who advocated civil service reform and restrictions on voting rights as solutions to government corruption and who repudiated Reconstruction as a prime example of such corruption.

29. The papers are listed in Elliott, *Color-Blind Justice*, 235. I have tracked reprintings of the "Bystander" column in the *Cleveland Gazette* and the *Detroit Plaindealer*.

30. "A Bystander's Notes," 30 June and 14 July 1888, 4.

31. Elliott, *Color-Blind Justice*, 234; see, for example, "A Bystander's Notes," 15 and 22 December 1888, 5 and 12 January 1889.

32. Olsen, *Carpetbagger's Crusade*, 303.

33. AWTP #3929, John Sleicher to AWT, 17 July 1889, solicits an article for *Frank Leslie's* on "What the Colored Man is doing for himself"; AWTP #3939, D. Nicholson to AWT, 29 July 1889, asks Tourgée to write an article of 3,500–5,000 words for the *New York Tribune* on the "character of the colored race in this country and . . . how their position will be affected by their progress in wealth, education and refinement. Also how really to enfranchise that race and secure its representation in Congress."

34. AWTP #4219, AWT to EKT, 14 December 1889.

35. See Elliott, *Color-Blind Justice*, 195–97, on the "mugwumps" and the parallels they drew between the corruption of "Northern urban political machines and Southern Reconstruction governments," as well as between the North's white and Irish proletarians and the South's black masses.

36. Quotations are from Tourgée's "Our Semi-Citizens" and "Shall White Minorities Rule?," quotation from 154. The latter is partially reprinted in Elliott and Smith, *Undaunted Radical*, quotations from 113, 118, and 122.

37. AWTP #3708, P. Blick to AWT, 29 March 1889; AWTP #3760, A. W. Shaffer to EKT, 14 April 1889; AWTP #3775, AWT to EKT, 2 April 1889. See also AWTP #4485, W. L. Curtis to AWT, 20 February 1890, praising Tourgée's article in the *Tribune*.

38. AWTP #4330, scrapbook of clippings, William H. Bernard, "A Screed from an Old Enemy," *Wilmington (N.C.) Morning Star*, 2 April 1889.

39. AWTP #4026, 4077, Charles W. Chesnutt to AWT, 26 September 1889, reprinted in C. Chesnutt, *"To Be an Author,"* 44, and 18 Oct. 1889.

40. AWTP #4124, William T. Green for Wisconsin Civil Rights League to AWT, 7 November 1889.

41. See "The Great Objection," *Detroit Plaindealer*, 11 October 1889, 1–2.

42. AWTP #4043, Robert Pelham Jr. to AWT, 4 October 1889.

43. Tourgée, "The Time Has Come for the Race to Show Itself Worthy of Liberty"; AWTP #4061, "The Time Has Come for the Race to Show Itself Worthy of Liberty," AWT to the editor of the *Plaindealer*, 12 October 1889.

44. "Time Has Come for the Race to Show Itself Worthy of Liberty," *Detroit Plaindealer*. All italics appear in the original sources unless otherwise noted.

45. AWTP #4017, 4160, Harrison Kelly to AWT, 23 September and 26 November 1889. I have followed Kelly's spelling of his name, but both Olsen and Elliott use the spelling "Kelley."

46. AWTP #4023, AWT to Harrison Kelly, 25 September 1889; Olsen, *Carpetbagger's Crusade*, 303; Elliott, *Color-Blind Justice*, 243–44.

47. Olsen, *Carpetbagger's Crusade*, 303–4; Elliott, *Color-Blind Justice*, 243–44. See also AWTP #9906, EKT's diary entries of 20, 21, 22, and 23 March 1890 on Tourgée's appearance before the Election Bill committee and his work on the bill; AWTP #4576 for the draft of Tourgée's testimony before the Election Bill committee; and AWTP #4676, 4688, and 5161 for Tourgée's correspondence with Senator Henry Cabot Lodge as he sought to shape the bill.

48. "A Bystander's Notes," 23 November and 7 December 1889, 8 March 1890, 4.

49. Untitled editorial, *Detroit Plaindealer*, 6 December 1889, 4.

50. AWTP #4857, Alex G. Davis to EKT, 24 July 1890.

51. AWTP #11043, AWT to J. C. Price, n.d.; AWTP #4568, J. C. Price to AWT, 18 March 1890. See also Crofts, "Black Response to the Blair Education Bill," cited in Elliott, *Color-Blind Justice*, 363nn44–45. Crofts mentions T. Thomas Fortune and Harry C. Smith, editors of the *New York Age* and the *Cleveland Gazette* respectively, as criticizing the shortcomings of the Blair bill but castigating Republicans who voted against it (57–61).

52. No doubt with Price in mind, Tourgée asked pointedly, "Can it be that the percentage allowed to [colored] colleges and Normal schools blinds" such educators to their complicity in "increasing the feebleness and dependency of their own race?" "A Bystander's Notes," 8 March 1890, 4.

53. Tourgée, "Negro's View of the Race Problem," quotations from 167. I quote from this speech, though given after the bill's defeat, because it formulates Tourgée's arguments against the bill more succinctly than any of his "Bystander" articles do.

54. AWTP #9906, EKT's diaries, 1889–90, entry for 20 March 1890: "Sat in the gallery and witnessed the defeat of the Blair Bill." The rest of this paragraph is based on Elliott, *Color-Blind Justice*, 245; and Olsen, *Carpetbagger's Crusade*, 304.

55. Tourgée, "Negro's View of the Race Problem," 166–67.

56. Crofts, "Black Response to the Blair Education Bill," 57–61; S. Alexander, *Army of Lions*, 95, 241; Carle, *Defining the Struggle*, 100, 141, 294.

57. Olsen, *Carpetbagger's Crusade*, 305–6; Elliott, *Color-Blind Justice*, 247–48.

58. AWTP #4676, AWT to Henry Cabot Lodge, 30 April 1890. Besides testifying before the Senate Election Committee, Tourgée reworked the election bill and corresponded extensively with Lodge about it, who promised to "make use of" Tourgée's suggestions in the "Republican caucus committee." Lodge's bill apparently did incorporate more of Tourgée's ideas at one stage. Another ally who promised to give "great weight" to Tourgée's views was John C. Spooner of Wisconsin. See AWTP #9906, EKT's diary entry for 23 March 1890; AWTP #4576, Tourgée's testimony before the Election Committee; AWTP #4655, John C. Spooner to AWT, 23 April 1890; AWTP #4688, Henry Cabot Lodge to AWT, 3 May 1890; AWTP #5161, AWT to Henry Cabot Lodge, n.d.; and AWTP #4740, EKT to AWT, 19 May 1890, in which she observes that "Lodge's bill has quite changed character of late. I think the right one will go through and lots of people know whose personality has done it."

59. "A Bystander's Notes," 17 May and 5 July 1890, 4.

60. Olsen, *Carpetbagger's Crusade*, 306; Elliott, *Color-Blind Justice*, 247–48; "A Bystander's Notes," 17 January 1891, 4.

61. Luker, *Social Gospel in Black and White*, 24–25. See also White, *Liberty and Justice for All*, 3–9. Published in his weekly, the *Christian Union*, Abbott's reply to Cable was widely quoted.

62. Untitled editorial, *Detroit Plaindealer*, 20 June 1890, 4.

63. "The Mohonk Conference and the Absence of Afro-Americans" and "Hamlet Left Out," *New York Age*, 21 and 14 June 1890, 2.

64. AWTP #4644, William H. Anderson to AWT, 18 April 1890.

65. AWTP #5147, AWT to William H. Anderson, n.d.

66. AWTP #4738, William H. Anderson to AWT, 19 May 1890.

67. Elliott, *Color-Blind Justice*, 246–47; Tourgée, "Negro's View of the Race Problem," 152–53.

68. *First Mohonk Conference on the Negro Question*, 24–25, 54, 103 (these remarks are not included in Elliott and Smith, *Undaunted Radical*); Olsen, *Carpetbagger's Crusade*, 307.

69. Tourgée, "Negro's View of the Race Problem," 157, 159, 160, 169.

70. AWTP #9906, EKT's diary entry for 6 June 1890; Hayes's journal is quoted in Elliott, *Color-Blind Justice*, 247. "Met and Resolved. The Mohonk Conference Appeals to Christian Sentiment," *Detroit Plaindealer*, 13 June 1890, 1; "Tourgée's Comments on the 'Negro' Conference at Mohonk," *Detroit Plaindealer*, 27 June 1890, 1.

71. AWTP #6365, AWT to "Dear Madame," n.d. [June 1892].

72. AWTP #7005, AWT to "My dear Sir," n.d.

73. AWTP #9190, AWT to Hale Giddings Parker, 8 January 1897. For information on Parker, see Reed, *Black Chicago's First Century*, 1:266. For other examples of African American intellectuals who requested Tourgée's advice on their research projects, see AWTP #6735, Fannie Barrier Williams to AWT, 12 March 1893; AWTP #5220, W. C. McCard to AWT, 10 January 1891; AWTP #5223, James E. Bish to AWT, 11 January 1891; and AWTP #6561, Henry P. Cheatham to AWT, 6 February 1893.

74. AWTP #7633, Charles W. Anderson to AWT, 1 May 1894.

75. AWTP #7746, AWT to Charles W. Anderson, n.d. [between 1 and 9 May 1894].

76. AWTP #7692, Charles W. Anderson to AWT, 9 May 1894.

77. AWTP #7746, AWT to Charles W. Anderson, n.d. [between 1 and 9 May 1894].

78. *Journals of Charles W. Chesnutt*, 124–25.

79. For another interpretation of Chesnutt's literary relationship with Tourgée, see Caccavari, "Trick of Mediation."

80. Tourgée, "South as a Field for Fiction," reprinted in Elliott and Smith, *Undaunted Radical*, quotations on 207, 209, 211. The phrase "compliment paid" comes from Chesnutt's letter of 26 September 1889 in *"To Be an Author,"* 44.

81. Albion W. Tourgée to Charles W. Chesnutt, 8 December 1888, Charles W. Chesnutt Papers, box 2, f. 9. I am grateful to Beth M. Howse for sending me a copy of this letter, which was not preserved among Tourgée's papers at the Chautauqua County Historical Society. McElrath and Leitz, editors of Chesnutt's *"To Be an Author,"* 45n2, 46n6, have partially quoted this letter. However, they have erroneously transcribed "letter" in the first sentence as "letters," which has led them to conclude mistakenly that "Chesnutt's correspondence with [Tourgée] was well advanced" by this date.

82. AWT to Chesnutt, 8 December 1888, Chesnutt Papers.

83. Quotations are from Tourgée, "Claims of Realism," 386, and Tourgée's untitled editorial in the "Migma" column of his weekly magazine *Our Continent*.

84. *Journals of Charles W. Chesnutt*, 139–40.

85. AWT to Chesnutt, 8 December 1888. The word "arena" has been mistranscribed as "medium" by McElrath and Leitz and as "branch" in the typescript that accompanies the handwritten original letter.

86. C. Chesnutt, *"To Be an Author,"* 44–45. This is Chesnutt's first extant letter to Tourgée. Quotations in the next three paragraphs are from this letter.

87. Ibid., 46n6.

88. AWTP #4283, AWT to Charles W. Chesnutt, n.d. [12 October 1889].

89. For an insightful analysis of Chesnutt's literary relationship with Cable, see McElrath and Leitz's introduction to Chesnutt's *"To Be an Author,"* 20–23, and their annotations of Chesnutt's letters to Cable.

90. Charles W. Chesnutt to Susan Chesnutt, 20 July 1891, reprinted in H. Chesnutt, *Charles Waddell Chesnutt*, 65.

91. Charles W. Chesnutt to AWT, 25 April 1896, AWTP #9128, in C. Chesnutt, *"To Be an Author,"* 92.

92. Charles W. Chesnutt to Hon. William McKinley, 2 March 1897, Consular Recommendations, State Department Records, National Archives, College Park, Md.; AWTP #9874, Charles W. Chesnutt to Mrs. Albion W. Tourgée, 14 December 1905; Joseph R. McElrath and Robert C. Leitz III, introduction to *"To Be an Author": Letters of Charles W. Chesnutt, 1889–1905*, ed. Joseph R. McElrath and Robert C. Leitz III (Princeton: Princeton University Press, 1997), 20; Sally Ann H. Ferguson, introduction to *The Colonel's Dream*, by Charles Waddell Chesnutt (1905; New Milford, Conn.: Toby Press, 2004), xi–xix.

93. C. Chesnutt, *Colonel's Dream*, 280. If Chesnutt knew Tourgée's novel *Figs and Thistles* (1879), for which there is no evidence one way or the other, the applicability of this comment to Tourgée would be indisputable.

94. Gaines, *Uplifting the Race*, xiv.

95. AWTP #7801, William H. Anderson to AWT, 1 June 1894.

96. William H. Anderson, "A Truthful Indictment. The Two Phases of the Race Problem. Part II. The Solution," *Detroit Plaindealer*, 18 April 1890, 1. Part 1 appeared on 11 April. The article had originally appeared in *America*, a weekly pamphlet published in Chicago, on 27 March and 3 April. Tourgée received a copy of it from Anderson before it appeared in the *Plaindealer* (see AWTP #4763, William H. Anderson to AWT, 19 May 1890).

97. AWTP #5143, AWT to [William H. Anderson], n.d. Anderson's reply to "yours of the 11th" supplies the date of this letter. See AWTP #4644, cited below.

98. AWTP #4644, William H. Anderson to AWT, 18 April 1890. Quotations in the next paragraph are also from this letter.

99. Gaines, *Uplifting the Race*, 127.

100. AWTP #5147, AWT to William H. Anderson, n.d. [before 19 May 1890].

101. William H. Anderson to Hon. William McKinley, 15 March 1897, Consular Recommendations, State Department Records, National Archives, College Park, Md.

102. AWTP #6269, William H. Anderson to AWT, 25 May 1892; AWTP #8733, William H. Anderson to AWT, 8 August 1895; AWTP #8618, William H. Anderson to

AWT, 11 July 1895. The books he recommended were Thomas Jay Hudson's *The Law of Psychic Phenomena* and Mary Baker Eddy's *Science and Health*.

103. AWTP #7850, AWT to [William H. Anderson], n.d. [before 14 June 1894]; "A Bystander's Notes: Colored Men and the Democratic Party," 4 August 1894, 12–13. The review of *Appointed* is included in this article, as was typical of Tourgée's practice in his "Bystander" column.

104. AWTP #7801, William H. Anderson to AWT, 14 June 1894; AWTP #7950, William H. Anderson to AWT, 6 August 1894.

105. Republican Party Platform of 1888, The Presidency Project, www. presidency. ucsb.edu/ws (10 June 2015).

106. AWTP #11043, AWT to J. C. Price, n.d. [before 18 March 1890].

107. AWTP #7552, AWT to T. Thomas Fortune, n.d. [14 November 1893].

108. AWTP #6680, AWT to T. Thomas Fortune, n.d. [before 6 February 1893]. The editorial itself is no longer extant, because files of the *New York Age* for 1893 have not been preserved. See also AWTP #6685, AWT to [unknown], n.d. In this letter, marked "Personal," Tourgée likewise warns that "it would not be advisable for me to publicly express an opinion with regard to the subject of your editorial, received today," but reiterates what he told Fortune: "I am very glad to see colored men and colored journals estimating the quality and character of public men by their attitude toward your race. . . . [S]o long as the colored man is any where distinguished against in right, privilege or opportunity—just so long every colored man ought to base his approval or condemnation on the attitude of such men towards his race; and he should express that approval or condemnation with openness and emphasis."

109. AWTP #6680, AWT to T. Thomas Fortune, n.d. [before 6 February 1893]. Tourgée's "Bystander" column of 11 February 1893 did not, in fact, quote "Fortune's" editorial, but it made many of the same points in more temperate language; in particular, it similarly connected Harrison's inaction on lynching with his appointment of a states' rights white Democrat to the Supreme Court.

110. AWTP #6564, T. Thomas Fortune to AWT, 6 February 1893; AWTP #6573, T. Thomas Fortune to AWT, 8 February 1893.

111. AWTP #6674, clipping from *Troy Press*, 13 February 1893; again, the original editorial in the *New York Age* is no longer extant. Tourgée would report the incident concerning the denial of a judgeship to an African American applicant almost a decade later in a letter of 21 October 1901 to Theodore Roosevelt, Theodore Roosevelt Papers, Library of Congress, reprinted in Elliott and Smith, *Undaunted Radical*, 353. Even here, however, he did not name the president he quoted; thus, Elliott and Smith have identified Garfield rather than Harrison as the subject of Tourgée's reminiscence.

112. AWTP #6666, T. Thomas Fortune to AWT, 27 February 1893.

113. AWTP #6703, AWT to T. Thomas Fortune, n.d. [2 March 1893].

114. Ibid.

115. AWTP #6708, T. Thomas Fortune to AWT, 4 March 1893.

116. For a detailed analysis of their relationship, see Karcher, "White 'Bystander' and the Black Journalist 'Abroad.'"

117. *Memphis Diary of Ida B. Wells*, 52.

118. Ibid., 21.

119. *Memphis Commercial*, 15 December 1892, quoted in McMurry, *To Keep the Waters Troubled*, 177; and in Giddings, *Ida*, 245.

120. AWTP #6645, Ida B. Wells to AWT, 22 February 1893; for Wells's initial request, see AWTP #6582, 10 February 1893.

121. AWTP #6687, AWT to Ida B. Wells, n.d.

122. AWTP #6645, Ida B. Wells to AWT, 22 February 1893. As scholars have noted, Wells's *Memphis Diary* records indiscretions with men that subjected her to gossip and might indeed have been used against her. See *Memphis Diary of Ida B. Wells*, 9–10, 37–38, 44, 110, 112–16; Giddings, *Ida*, chap. 4; and Goldsby, *Spectacular Secret*, chap. 2.

123. AWTP #6646 and 6707, Ferdinand L. Barnett to Albion W. Tourgée, 23 February and 4 March 1893. Wells's views on consensual sexual relations between white women and black men will be discussed in chapter 5.

124. AWTP #6687, AWT to Ida B. Wells, n.d.; AWTP #6645, Ida B. Wells to AWT, 22 February 1893.

125. Even Anderson, who preened himself on his contacts with his church's white parishioners, admitted, "Of course the social life of the home is not free." AWTP #7801, William H. Anderson to AWT, 14 June 1894.

126. AWTP #8530, Ida B. Wells to EKT, 19 May 1895. Except for one heavily revised draft of which Emma no doubt typed up a fair copy, none of the Tourgées' letters to Wells survive because a catastrophic house fire destroyed all of her personal papers.

127. For details on the Tourgées' adoption of Adaline Patillo, see Elliott, *Color-Blind Justice*, 136–38; and Woods, "Adaline and the Judge" (Woods is the great-grandson of Adaline). Emma was still corresponding with Adaline in the 1890s.

128. AWTP #8530, Ida B. Wells to EKT, 19 May 1895.

129. Ibid.

130. AWTP #8801, Ida B. Wells to EKT, 26 August 1895.

131. AWTP #9838, "In Memoriam: Tribute of Respect by Colored Citizens of Chicago to the Memory of Judge Albion W. Tourgee, Adopted by the Illinois Division of the Niagara Movement and The Appomattox Club and Presented on the occasion of the funeral obsequies at Mayville, New York, November 15, a.d. 1905, by Mrs. Ida B. Wells-Barnett, representing the above named organizations."

132. AWTP #9842, Ida B. Wells-Barnett to EKT, 18 November 1905; AWTP #10984, Ida B. Wells-Barnett to EKT, n.d. [ca. 1906].

133. I use this term to distinguish Creoles of color both from the white French-descended elite that also claimed the designation Creole and from African Americans.

134. According to Brian Martinet, a descendant of Louis Martinet's brother, Martinet's estranged wife destroyed his papers after his death. E-mail communication, 24 April 2014.

135. The "Biographical Sketch" in the Louis A. Martinet Records, New Orleans Notarial Archives, http://www.notarialarchives.org/martinet.htm (25 April 2011), describes Martinet's mother as a freeborn woman of color, but Brian Martinet

informs me that she was a slave. Her husband bought her and their child from their owner, and the couple married in 1862, when it became legal to do so. E-mail communication, 7 May 2014.

136. AWTP #6377, Louis A. Martinet to AWT, 4 July 1892, not reprinted in Olsen, *Thin Disguise.*

137. "Biographical Sketch," Martinet Records, New Orleans Notarial Archives; AWTP #6377, Louis A. Martinet to AWT, 4 July 1892, not reprinted in Olsen, *Thin Disguise.*

138. AWTP #5760, Louis A. Martinet to AWT, 5 October 1891, partially reprinted in Olsen, *Thin Disguise*, 55–60, quotations from 58–59.

139. Martinet Records, New Orleans Notarial Archives. Although this biographical sketch asserts that Martinet graduated from Straight University Law School, a letter by Martinet to the *Southwestern Christian Advocate*, 2 April 1885, 4, titled "How Admitted to the Bar," corrects this widespread belief. Martinet explains that he began the study of law at Straight University and was one of the founders of its first law class but that he subsequently withdrew from the university to study law independently. After his admission to the bar in December 1875, he was awarded an honorary bachelor of laws degree by Straight in May 1876 as an acknowledgment of his role in starting the class.

140. AWTP #8958, AWT to William E. Chandler, n.d. [before 4 February 1896]. For additional information about Martinet, see Medley, *We as Freemen*, 103–9, 112–13; Scott, "Public Rights, Social Equality, and the Conceptual Roots of the *Plessy* Challenge," 795–98; and Elliott, *Color-Blind Justice*, 249–51, 294.

141. AWTP #6377, Louis A. Martinet to AWT, 4 July 1892, partially reprinted in Olsen, *Thin Disguise*, 61–66, quotations from 63, 64, and 66.

142. Ibid., partially reprinted in Olsen, *Thin Disguise*, 59.

143. Ibid., not reprinted in Olsen, *Thin Disguise*. Tourgée laments his inadequacies as a wage earner in AWTP #2487, AWT to EKT, 18 February 1886: "I am sorry that I recovered my health for I am only able to bring sorrow and suffering to those I love—." For entries in Emma's diary reflecting the strains in their marriage, see AWTP #9906, 30 September 1892: "My 52 birthday I awoke with a heavy depressed spirit, overwhelmed with the amount of work Albion has on hand and promised,— which he seems to regard so lightly. . . . [W]rote several Association [NCRA] letters"; 31 August 1893: "Began copying Circulars for Albion, with a heavy heart.—seeing nothing but disaster in the scheme if he attempts it alone. He will listen to no reason or persuasion on my part—"; and especially 7 November 1893: "Albion wrote again to Bishop Turner. I have no faith in what he is doing.—merely wasting time which should be given to other work, whereby we could have something to live on. My heart is very heavy." According to the Martinet Records in the New Orleans Notarial Archives, Martinet and his wife "divorced sometime around 1900." Although this source renders his wife's name as Leona, her name is given as Leonora in the inventory of Martinet's succession. Both the inventory and Martinet's death certificate refer to the couple as married rather than divorced, but this may be because as Catholics, they could not officially divorce. See Nils R. Douglas Papers, box 1, folder 8.

144. Desdunes, *Nos hommes et notre histoire*, 191. I have provided a literal translation of the French quotation.

145. AWTP #6377, Louis A. Martinet to AWT, 4 July 1892, last two sentences reprinted in Olsen, *Thin Disguise*, 64.

146. AWTP #5837, Louis A. Martinet to AWT, 7 December 1891. Martinet would repeat this assertion seven years later in a letter complaining to the U.S. attorney general of Jim Crow practices in Louisiana: "We beg leave to say, Mr. Attorney General, that there are people here who care for their rights, who are not office seekers nor are they interested in office seekers. We belong to that class and we contend for justice only." See Louis A. Martinet to the Honorable Attorney General, 8 February 1898, 55th Congress, Records of the U.S. Senate, Record Group 46, Committee Papers, Senate Judiciary Committee, Sen 55A-F15, National Archives, Washington, D.C.

147. AWTP #6377, Louis A. Martinet to AWT, 4 July 1892, partially reprinted in Olsen, *Thin Disguise*, 64.

148. "What We Meant to Say," *New Orleans Crusader*, 2 June 1891, Charles B. Rousseve Papers, box 2, folder 17, clipping.

149. AWTP #5768, Louis A. Martinet to AWT, 25 October 1891.

150. The Amistad Research Center in New Orleans holds a complete issue of the *Crusader* dated 19 July 1890 in the Nils R. Douglas Papers and two nearly complete issues dated 22 March 1890 and 19 May 1894, as well as a scattering of clippings from other issues in the Rousseve Papers, but very few of the editorials are by Martinet. Xavier University, New Orleans, holds a large number of clippings from the *Crusader* by Rodolphe L. Desdunes in the Desdunes Family *New Orleans Crusader* Clippings collection in its Archives and Special Collections.

151. Martinet, "Plead for the Crusader," editorial, and Tourgée, untitled fragment, *New Orleans Crusader*, 19 May 1894, 1, 2, Rousseve Papers, box 1, folder 9.

152. AWTP #6998, Louis A. Martinet to AWT, 30 May 1893.

153. Ibid.

154. "A Bystander's Notes," 12 August 1893, 12. See chapter 3 for a detailed discussion of Tourgée's quotations from this passage.

155. AWTP #7197, Louis A. Martinet to AWT, 4 August 1893, refers to "the plan you suggested to me in Chicago."

156. AWTP #7593, AWT to Louis A. Martinet, n.d.

Chapter Two

1. AWTP #3699, AWT to H. S. Harrison, 26 March 1889; for Harrison's end of the correspondence, see AWTP #3691, 3696, 3704, H. S. Harrison to AWT, 23, 26, and 28 March 1889. Quotations at the beginning of the paragraph are from these letters.

2. AWTP #3801, AWT to Anna E. Hahn, 4 May 1889, in answer to AWTP #3759, Anna E. Hahn to AWT, 14 April 1889.

3. Tourgée, *Pactolus Prime*, 290. Subsequent page references will be given parenthetically in the text. Tourgée eliminated the subtitle "The White Christ" from the book version and added six chapters to it, including "A True Record." He sandwiched

five of them between the two halves of the serial's last chapter, titled "'And Fate at Length Was Kind'" and "What It Is to Be a Hero." The *Advance*'s reviewer commented, "As the story now appears, supplementary chapters, mainly in the form of a journal left by Prime, answer those questions which sprang up at the former conclusion of the story"; see AWTP #8251, Tourgée's scrapbook of press clippings.

4. *Dansville (N.Y.) Advertiser* and *Newark Advertiser*, AWTP #8251.

5. Quotations are from Tourgée, *Bricks Without Straw*, 206; and "A Bystander's Notes: Colored People and Christianity," 27 October 1894, 12.

6. Cooper, *Voice from the South*, 189; the review originally appeared in the *Southland* 2, no. 2 (April 1891): 175–80 and was revised for the book. The quoted passage appears in both, with slight differences in wording. Little is known about the *Southland*, of which I have found only the number containing this review. No record exists of when or if Cooper and Tourgée met, but because Cooper taught at the M Street High School in Washington, D.C., she probably attended at least one of the lectures Tourgée later gave at the city's African American institutions. After Tourgée's death, she invited Emma, who was spending the winter in Washington, to attend a celebration of Frederick Douglass's life at the M Street school; see AWTP #9943, A. J. Cooper to Mrs. A. W. Tourgée, 13 February 1906.

7. B. Thomas, *American Literary Realism*, 201.

8. On Tourgée's Civil War injuries, see Elliott, *Color-Blind Justice*, 80–81, 83–84; and Olsen, *Carpetbagger's Crusade*, 16, 19.

9. Tourgée describes the battle of Missionary Ridge in *Story of a Thousand*, chap. 22; see also Elliott, *Color-Blind Justice*, 97. In *Pactolus Prime* he calls it "Mission Ridge."

10. Tourgée recalls his experiences as a POW in "A Bystander's Notes," 15 February 1890, 4. Quoting the same line from it as Pactolus does (124), he describes "The Battle Hymn of the Republic" as "the favorite good-night song of those who might never see the morning."

11. See Patterson, *Slavery and Social Death*.

12. "A Bystander's Notes. Colored Men and the Democratic Party," 4 August 1894, 12.

13. AWTP #9543, Charles H. Williams to AWT, 14 July 1897. Williams quotes what Tourgée had written to him in a no-longer-extant letter.

14. See B. Thomas, "Legitimacy of Law in Literature," on Tourgée's use of fiction to develop and test legal arguments; Thomas discusses *Pactolus Prime*'s anticipation of *Plessy* on 176–77.

15. Benny apparently shares the philosophy of Frances Harper's phenotypically white heroine Iola Leroy, who "see[s] no necessity for proclaiming" her race "on the house-top" when applying for a job but who is "resolved that nothing shall tempt [her] to deny it" if asked. See Harper, *Iola Leroy*, 208. The whole of chapter 24 shows Iola confronting Northern race prejudice as she is fired each time her employers or fellow employees learn that she is "colored."

16. In the same letter to the editor of the *Advance* partially quoted in the epigraph to this chapter, Tourgée described *Pactolus Prime* as "a realistic picture of one possible day in the life of a half dozen actual types." Tourgée considered himself a realist,

even though he disagreed vehemently with William Dean Howells's definition of realism as limited to the "commonplace." See, for example, AWTP #7748, AWT to [S. S. McClure], n.d. [May 1894]: "You know I am a realist, in a much broader sense than those who claim the name." See also the contrast Tourgée draws, in the correspondence quoted in chapter 1, between the "realism" for which he praised Chesnutt's stories and the "so-called realism" of Howells's "narrow rules." Granted, some might object that the plot of *Pactolus Prime*—which Tourgée reluctantly tacked onto his original magazine story, as I have noted—is sensational rather than realistic. Yet in the masterful chapter of *American Literary Realism* comparing *Pactolus Prime* with Mark Twain's *Pudd'nhead Wilson*, Brook Thomas points out that "a realist aesthetic cannot be distinguished simply at the level of plot" (199) and that "the realists themselves were not completely free of sentimentalism" (336n63)—or, I might add, of sensationalism, which certainly marks Twain's novels. Thomas judges Tourgée's aesthetic (at least as regards *Pactolus Prime*) "outmoded" in comparison with that of Twain and other realists (208), but I would argue that Tourgée's definition of his aesthetic in the statements I quote at the beginning of this chapter ought to modify such a judgment.

17. As H. Bruce Franklin has suggested to me in a personal communication (13 July 2012), Herman Melville used this technique "brilliantly" in *The Confidence-Man: His Masquerade* (1857)—a novel Tourgée surely did not know and probably would not have liked. *Pactolus Prime* lacks the symbolic resonance and enigmatic quality that twentieth- and twenty-first-century critics have found so fascinating in *The Confidence-Man*, but it succeeds on its own terms and would have succeeded even better had Tourgée not compromised his original plan.

18. For a historical account of the ex-slave reparations movement that began in the late 1890s, see Berry, *My Face Is Black Is True*. For the continuing modern debate, see the "Reparations for Slavery" article on Wikipedia and other Internet sources.

19. McKinley, *Appeal to Pharaoh*. McKinley quotes Tourgée on pp. 8 and 199–200; the publishers advertised Tourgée's books in the back pages of McKinley's. Tourgée, "Shall We Re-Barbarize the Negro?," 411, AWTP #4192. Tourgée also replied in his "Bystander" column to two other proponents of deportation, one by a "Northern scientific negrophobist," the other by a Southern Republican. See "A Bystander's Notes," 13 July and 24 August 1889, 4.

20. For parallel statements by Tourgée in his own voice, see AWTP #10812, "The Elevation of the Negro," *The Citizen*, n.d. [ca. 1885], which asserts, "The Negro race undoubtedly did thrive under the institution of slavery. . . . Not only physically but morally and intellectually the colored race made marvellous progress under the influences of slavery. The difference between the American Negro of to-day and his congener of the African coast is the true measure of that development." See also "A Bystander's Notes: The Dissatisfied Elements," 2 June 1894, 12–13: "The only class who really gained anything by slavery was the slave himself. He gained patience, strength, civilization."

21. Washington, *Up from Slavery*, 37.

22. Crofts, "Black Response to the Blair Education Bill," 56.

23. Ibid., 57–58; "Afro-American League." It was a delegate from Indiana who defended Price's position with those words. In reporting on the debate among League members over whether or not to endorse the Blair bill, the *Gazette* quoted its editor Harry C. Smith, who proposed endorsing the Taylor bill instead, noting that it not only lacked the "objectionable features" of the Blair bill but had "received the encouragement and support of a large number of the race's friends, headed by Judge Albion W. Tourgee."

24. B. Thomas, *American Literary Realism*, 214.

25. "Afro-American League."

26. AWTP #4406, AWT to unknown, n.d. [ca. February–March 1890] (Tourgée mentions that he is "just now correcting the proof of a new book, 'Pactolus Prime,' which will be out in a few days").

27. See, for example, Charles W. Chesnutt, *The House behind the Cedars* (1900), Alice Dunbar-Nelson, "The Stones of the Village" (ca. 1910), James Weldon Johnson, *Autobiography of an Ex-colored Man* (1912), and Nella Larsen, *Passing* (1929).

28. "Tourgee Again," Memphis *Commercial*, n.d., AWTP #8251, scrapbook of press clippings. Emma identified the newspapers in handwritten inserts; when these are too faint to decipher, I refer to the newspapers as unidentified. Unfortunately, almost none of the clippings are dated. Where possible, I have tracked down the originals in order to date them.

29. [Harris], "Refugee from His Race." Tourgée reprinted and replied to this review in "A Bystander's Notes," 10 May 1890, 4. "There is something very comical to the average mind in the solemnity with which the Southern champion imputes personal malice and individual hate to every man who is so unfortunate as to intimate that the conditions of Southern life are not altogether perfect," he wryly commented in his reply.

30. AWTP #8251, "New Novels," *New York Daily Tribune*, 13 April 1890, 14. The *Tribune* ends by saying, "Judge Tourgee's book is often moving and tragic, but the sadness of the situation described is not lightened by strong hopes."

31. "Minor Novels," *San Francisco Chronicle*, 4 May 1890, 7 (ProQuest Historical Newspapers, www.proquest.com/products-services/pq-hist-news.html); this appears as an unidentified clipping in AWTP #8251.

32. AWTP #8251: unidentified, and "The Latest Books. Under the Guise of Fiction," *New York Commercial Advertiser*, 12 May 1890, 4.

33. AWTP #8251, "Recent Literature," *Chicago Times*, 12 April 1890, 12.

34. Reviews commenting on the "hopelessness" of African Americans' condition are AWTP #8251: *Philadelphia Inquirer*, 14 April 1890, 6; *New York Daily Tribune*, 13 April 1890, 14; *Newark Advertiser*, n.d.; unidentified, n.d.; "Recent Fiction," *Nation*, 4 September 1890, 195.

35. AWTP #8251: unidentified, n.d.; *Newark Advertiser*, n.d.; *Christian Union*, 24 April 1890, 595.

36. "Talk about New Books," *Catholic World* 55 (July 1892), 606–7. This review was not in Tourgée's file of clippings. See http://quod.lib.umich.edu/cgi/t/text/pageviewer (23 March 2011).

37. "Literary . . . New Publications," *Chicago Daily Inter Ocean*, 19 April 1890, 12.

38. AWTP #8251: *Harrisburg Telegraph*, n.d.; "Literary Review," *Congregationalist*, 17 April 1890, 6; *Philadelphia Bulletin*, n.d. The clipping from the *Rochester Herald* is identical with those found in the *Buffalo Christian Advertiser*, n.d., the *Omaha Bee*, n.d., and the *Philadelphia Inquirer*, 17 February 1890, 6; the date of the original in the *Inquirer* indicates that it is an advance notice rather than a review and may thus have been written by Tourgée himself.

39. "Current Literature. Fiction Longer and Shorter," *Springfield Republican*, 10 April 1890, 2.

40. AWTP #8251: Quotations are from the *Chicago Times*, the *New York Tribune*, and the *Christian Union*. Referring to Tourgée's previous novels, Joel Chandler Harris acknowledged in "A Refugee from His Race" that his nemesis "wrote with such graphic power, and with such vivid coloring that he found many readers." He added that *Pactolus Prime* "is written in the same old vein" (*Atlanta Constitution*, 23 April 1890).

41. AWTP #8251: *Chicago Daily Inter Ocean*, 19 April 1890, 12; *Harrisburg Telegraph*, n.d.; *Rochester Herald*, n.d.; *Omaha Bee*, n.d.; *Boston Traveller*, n.d.; *Jamestown (N.Y.) Journal*, n.d.; "Current Literature. 'Pactolus Prime,'" *San Francisco Daily Evening Bulletin*, 12 April 1890, 5.

42. AWTP #8251: *New York Daily Tribune*, 13 April 1890, 14; *New York Commercial Advertiser*, 12 May 1890, 4; *Baltimore Sun*, 11 April 1890, supplement, 4.

43. AWTP #8251: "Recent Fiction," *Independent*, 8 May 1890, 21; the *Chicago Times* also contended that "Judge Tourgee's book goes too far, in respect of using for characters to work out its teachings negroes with so little negro blood that only an expert could detect it" (12 April 1890, 12).

44. See AWTP #8251. The two African American reviews are "Judge Tourgee's New Book," from an unidentified paper, but apparently extracted without attribution from the *Detroit Plaindealer*, and one in the *Cleveland Gazette*, 17 May 1890, 2, which quotes the most favorable sentences from the *New York Tribune*'s review and exhorts subscribers to "purchase copies of Judge Tourgee's books and read them carefully."

45. AWTP #4740, EKT to AWT, 19 May 1890.

46. AWTP #5878, W. H. A. Morse to EKT, 28 December 1891. Unfortunately, most numbers of the *Age* from September 1891 to 1900 are missing, and the few extant numbers do not contain the reviews in question.

47. [Anderson], "Tourgee's Book. Afro-American Claims on the Republic. . . ."

48. Cooper (A. J. C.), "'Pactolus Prime'—Tourgee's Last Novel," quotation on 177. Cooper dropped her summary of the plot, including her criticism of the denouement, from the version of the review she reprinted in *A Voice from the South*.

49. Cooper, *Voice from the South*, 199.

50. AWTP #5629, Anna Julia Cooper to AWT, 5 June 1891. This is actually a reply to AWTP #5690, discussed below. Cooper's first letter has not survived.

51. The same number featured her pathbreaking feminist article "The Higher Education of Women." This is the only number of the *Southland* that I have found.

52. AWTP #5690, AWT to [Anna Julia Cooper], n.d. The quotations in the following paragraph are also from this letter.

53. AWTP #5629, Anna Julia Cooper to AWT, 5 June 1891; "A Bystander's Notes," 8 April 1893, 4.

54. Untitled editorial note, *Christian Recorder*, 10 July 1890, 4, http://www.accessible-archives.com (23 March 2011).

55. AWTP #5729, J[ohn] E[dward] Bruce to AWT, 27 July 1891. Bruce also urged his friend T. Thomas Fortune to buy and read *Pactolus Prime*, saying, "[I]t will give you inspiration and intensify your contempt for that thing called the christian civilization of the Western world." See J. E. Bruce to T. Thomas Fortune, John Edward Bruce Collection, Microfilm 1, B 14. Reflecting the impact that *Pactolus Prime* had on Bruce, he cited the novel eight years later in an editorial in the *Colored American*, quoted in S. Alexander, *Army of Lions*, 86.

56. AWTP #4764, Mack W. Caldwell to AWT, 29 May 1890; AWTP #5788, Alexander S. Jackson to AWT, 13 November 1891. Another African American correspondent sent Tourgée a dollar for a copy of the novel, saying that "from what I have heard of the book it relates my experience. I have been a salve [*sic*], sold for 1000$ at New Orleans, after the fall of Sumpter [*sic*] sent South to prevent learning my letters, placed in prison because I wanted to learn, . . . following the army during the first of the war, enlisting in the Navy advanced to a first class petty officer, finally entering the U.S. Army as a commissioned officer ranking the son of my mother's former master, etc."; see AWTP #6438, Allen Allensworth to AWT, 29 August 1892.

57. "Never Emigrate, Says Senator John P. Green Who Is Now in London, England. Portions of Judge Albion W. Tourgee's Book, 'Pactolus Prime,' Reviewed . . . ," *Cleveland Gazette*, 3 March 1894, 1.

58. Charles W. Chesnutt to George Washington Cable, 5 June 1890, reproduced in H. Chesnutt, *Charles Waddell Chesnutt*, 58–59. For the version of this letter in Cable's papers, dated 13 June 1890, see C. Chesnutt, *"To Be an Author,"* 65–66.

59. *Journals of Charles W. Chesnutt*, 92–93.

60. In "A Bystander's Notes," 12 June 1897, Tourgée quoted Chesnutt without naming him: "The most eminent writer of fiction yet developed among the colored people of the United States said to the Bystander not many weeks ago: 'Just as soon as I can arrange my affairs, sell my property, and my daughters have completed their education, I am going to become a citizen of France. I look forward with horror to their living under the conditions that await them in the United States.'"

61. Chesnutt to Cable, 5 June 1890, draft, in H. Chesnutt, *Charles Waddell Chesnutt*, 57. In his foreword to Chesnutt's *Mandy Oxendine*, published for the first time in 1997, William L. Andrews suggests that the rejection of this novel may have "helped convince Chesnutt that to get his version of the novel of passing into print, he would have to tone down and conventionalize" his portrayal of the eponymous mulatto heroine and better "accommodate . . . to the protocols of 'tragic mulatta' fiction," as he did in *The House behind the Cedars*. See also Andrews's extended discussion of Chesnutt's revisions of "Rena Walden" to make it palatable to white critics in what became *The*

House behind the Cedars: Andrews, *Literary Career of Charles W. Chesnutt*, 23–30, 122–23, 145–50. Andrews's comparisons of Chesnutt's novels of passing with Tourgée's are relevant as well (153–57).

62. AWTP #4662, Rev. J[eremiah] E. Rankin to AWT, 26 April 1890.

63. AWTP #4677, AWT to Dr. J. E. Rankin, 30 April 1890.

64. Tourgée, "Claims of Realism," 387.

65. See "Literary Coincidence," in which the author remarks on the similarities between *An Imperative Duty* and *Pactolus Prime* and speculates about whether Howells had "read 'Pactolus Prime,' a novel by Albion W. Tourgée, published nearly two years ago." See also B. Thomas, *American Literary Realism*, 198–99.

66. Howells, *Imperative Duty*, 44, 85, 87, 88, 142, 148–50. For differing interpretations of the racial views the novel expresses, see Cady, *Realist at War*, 156–63; Berzon, *Neither White nor Black*, 109–14; Kinney, *Amalgamation!*, 137–41; Warren, *Black and White Strangers*, 65–70, 118–19; Rosenthal, "White Blackbird"; Belluscio, *To Be Suddenly White*, 55–87; and B. Thomas, *American Literary Realism*, 156–59.

67. Cooper, *Voice from the South*, 203, 206–7, 208.

68. AWTP #4662, Rev. J[eremiah] E. Rankin to AWT, 26 April 1890.

69. *Iola Leroy* and *A Voice from the South* are reviewed together in the *Christian Recorder* and the New York *Independent*; see notes below.

70. Harper, *Iola Leroy*, 232–33, 235, 239–40, 262–63. Iola's refusal to pass represents a clear rejection of her mother's choice to pass, which the novel's plot reveals as disastrous for the entire family. *Iola Leroy* and *A Voice from the South* are reviewed together by the Rev. J. C. Embry, "Two New Books from the Hand of Representative Ladies of Our Race." Though Embry ranks *Iola Leroy* "among the very best of [Harper's] productions, in prose," he complains that "the quadroon and creole girl, suffering the misfortunes and hardships incident to slavery, has become a totally worthless subject to set before the public in the name of Afro American well being, or in plea of the rights and dignity attached to free citizenship."

71. See, for example, Warren, *Black and White Strangers*, 67; B. Thomas, *American Literary Realism*, 157; Rosenthal, "White Blackbird," 511–17; and Belluscio, *To Be Suddenly White*, 55–87.

72. Harper, *Iola Leroy*, 58–60, 230–36. For insightful analyses of *Iola Leroy*, see Carby, *Reconstructing Womanhood*, 62–94; Tate, *Domestic Allegories of Political Desire*, 144–49, 168–72; Ammons, *Conflicting Stories*, 20–33; Foster, *Written by Herself*, 183–86; Peterson, "Further Liftings of the Veil"; Young, *Disarming the Nation*, 195–231; Rosenthal, "White Blackbird," 510–17; and Belluscio, *To Be Suddenly White*, 55–87.

73. AWTP #3699, AWT to H. S. Harrison, 26 March 1889.

74. Harper, *Iola Leroy*, 282 (the last words of the novel).

75. *"Iola Leroy; or, Shadows Uplifted,"* *Independent*, 5 January 1893, 2; "Recent Fiction," *Nation*, 23 February 1893, 146–47; these two reviews are quoted by Hazel Carby in her introduction to the 1987 Beacon Press edition of *Iola Leroy*, but without specifying their exact dates. Although Tourgée read the *Independent* regularly, he clearly did not see this review, which would surely have attracted his interest in

the novel. The reviewer identifies Harper as "certainly one of the most accomplished literary women the colored race has numbered among its members," mentions her extensive "personal contact with colored people in the South" and the "unrivaled" material she has amassed on their lives and incorporated into the novel, and refers to "thrilling scenes and episodes of the War." He ends by saying, "The book does not treat of a dead issue, but pleads the cause of a race whose needs were never more pressing than now, and whose destiny is now more closely interwoven with those of the nation than ever"—precisely Tourgée's own views.

Chapter Three

1. "A Bystander's Notes," 21 April 1888, 4. I have not succeeded in identifying either the "ancient chronicler" or the quotation.

2. Mott, *American Journalism*, 463.

3. See chapter 1 on the impact of *A Fool's Errand* and *Bricks Without Straw*. Tourgée's documentary history of the Klan, *The Invisible Empire*, was published as an appendix to the second edition of *A Fool's Errand* (1880). His now little-known novel *Figs and Thistles: A Romance of the Western Reserve* (1879) was mistaken by many readers at the time for a fictionalized campaign biography of Garfield.

4. "The Veteran and His Pipe" (25 April–19 September 1885) aimed to restore the Civil War's meaning as a crusade against slavery; "Letters to a Mugwump" (26 September–12 December 1885) addressed defectors whose disillusionment with the corruption they attributed to an ignorant electorate led them to repudiate egalitarian ideals and align themselves with Southern Democrats; and the twin sequences of letters signed "Siva" (after the Hindu god of destruction), "A Man of Destiny" (13 December 1884–4 March 1885) and "A Child of Luck" (20 March–4 December 1886), castigated the newly elected Democratic president Grover Cleveland for denying pensions to Union veterans while catering to the "Solid South" and pampering mammoth corporations.

5. See Foner, *Free Soil*; and Foner, *Reconstruction*, chap. 6.

6. *Dictionary of American Biography*; AWTP #3918, William Penn Nixon to AWT, 13 July 1889; AWTP #7501, William H. Busbey to EKT, 17 November 1893; Elliott, *Color-Blind Justice*, 232.

7. Elliott, *Color-Blind Justice*, 232.

8. Ibid., 232–33. See AWTP #6383, William Penn Nixon to AWT, 7 July 1892; AWTP #7969, William H. Busbey to EKT, 13 August 1894; and AWTP #7983, William H. Busbey to AWT, 20 August 1894. These letters are all quoted and discussed near the end of this chapter.

9. For typical notations in Emma's diary, see AWTP #9906: "Bystander, written, copied and mailed this afternoon" (24 September 1891); "Sent next Bystander off. . . . Mailed Bystander written last week" (10 November 1891); "Copied Bystander, but did not get it done in time for mailing today" (25 November 1891).

10. AWTP #3525, AWT to EKT, 23 January 1889.

11. "A Bystander's Notes," 28 April 1888, 4.

12. The words "solid, respectable" derive from Mott, *American Journalism*, 463. Most historians cite the figure of 186,000, rather than 225,000, African American soldiers. The contrast Tourgée draws between law-abiding African Americans and unruly European immigrants—a recurrent theme in his "Bystander" column—will remind many readers of Booker T. Washington's 1895 Atlanta Exposition Address, which famously affirms that African Americans have done the work of the South "without strikes and labor wars"; see his *Up from Slavery*, chap. 14. Both Tourgée and Washington emphasize that blacks deserve patronage not only because they are "peaceful, industrious, sober" (as Tourgée puts it) but also because they are fellow Americans, not foreigners. Unlike Washington, however, Tourgée did not oppose unions or strikes, whether by African Americans or by European immigrants. Although he condemned anarchism as a threat to American democracy and consistently equated it with the types of mob violence that prevailed in the South, his 1890 novel *Murvale Eastman, Christian Socialist* expressed considerable sympathy for at least one form of socialism.

13. "A Bystander's Notes," 5 May 1888, 4.

14. Ibid., 30 June 1888, 4.

15. Ibid., 24 November 1888, 4.

16. Ibid., 14 July 1888, 4.

17. Ibid., 4 August 1888, 4. See also 14 July 1888, 4.

18. Ibid., 17 November 1888, 4.

19. Elliott, *Color-Blind Justice*, 234.

20. Ibid., 361n11; untitled editorial, *Cleveland Gazette*, 28 July 1888, 2; "Ohio's Ku Klux—the White Caps" and "Fighting for Rights in Felicity," *Cleveland Gazette*, 8 December 1888, 2, http://dbs.ohiohistory.org/africanam/page.cfm (26 April 2012).

21. "A Bystander's Notes," 15 December 1888, 4.

22. Ibid., 22 December 1888, 4. Quotations in the next three paragraphs are all drawn from this column. The oscillation the passage here quoted exhibits between phrases in which Tourgée "merges his own voice" with the Southern propagandist's ("the barbarous brutality of black demons") and comically "exaggerates" the propagandist's language ("innocent and saintly whites," "lovely" civilization) perfectly exemplifies Mikhail M. Bakhtin's description of how parody functions. See Bakhtin's *Dialogic Imagination*, 302.

23. "A Bystander's Notes," 5 January 1889, 4. Tourgée quotes the Southern newspaper's accusation in his column of 29 December 1888, 4.

24. Ibid., 2 March 1889, 4.

25. Ibid., 4 May 1889, 4. Around the same time, Tourgée began supplementing his reportage on Southern atrocities by invoking the testimony of African American spokesmen. His column of 18 May 1889, for example, used a speech by the well-known Episcopalian minister Alexander Crummell, later celebrated in W. E. B. Du Bois's *The Souls of Black Folk* (1903), to moralize on two recent incidents targeting African Americans in New Orleans.

26. "A Bystander's Notes," 29 June 1889, 4. See also ibid., 5 July 1890, 4, where Tourgée warned that a white man who spoke or acted in favor of the election bill Republicans had proposed would be subjected "at the very least" to a "social and business boycott" and might find himself "set upon by unknown parties and killed." Tourgée's autobiographical persona in *A Fool's Errand* escapes several attempts on his life, and one of the white characters in *Bricks Without Straw* who allies himself with blacks is publicly whipped.

27. AWTP #3868, William Penn Nixon to AWT, 14 June 1889.

28. AWTP #3916, AWT to William Penn Nixon, 11 July 1889.

29. AWTP #3980, William Penn Nixon to AWT, 23 August 1889.

30. AWTP #3986, AWT to William Penn Nixon, 29 August 1889.

31. "A Bystander's Notes," 31 August 1889, 4.

32. Ibid., 21 September 1889, 4. For a modern historical account of the episode that white Southerners referred to as the "recent race trouble" and that African Americans and their supporters called the "Leflore massacre," see Hahn, *Nation under Our Feet*, 422–23, 444. As Hahn documents, the organizers Tourgée discusses in this "Bystander" article belonged to the Colored Farmers' Alliance movement.

33. "A Bystander's Notes," 22 February 1890, 4. Kennan's articles, later compiled in his two-volume *Siberia and the Exile System* (1891), were published serially in *Century* magazine from November 1886 through November 1891.

34. "Judge Tourgee Says That Intelligence and Justice Will Solve the Problem. . . . ," *Cleveland Gazette*, 3 August 1889, 1. For the original, see "A Bystander's Notes," 20 July 1889, 4.

35. "Judge Tourgee Advises the Organization of a League. . . . ," *Cleveland Gazette*, 23 November 1889, 1; "An Important Matter of No Party, but an Appeal to the Conscience of the Land. . . . ," *Detroit Plaindealer*, 15 November 1889, 1; Tourgée preserved this clipping in his papers, AWTP #11166a. For the original, see "A Bystander's Notes," 2 November 1889, 4.

36. For Tourgée's replies to correspondents who asked him to explain his positions on the Blair and Lodge bills, see "A Bystander's Notes," 23 November and 7 December 1889, 8 and 29 March 1890, 17 May 1890, 5 July 1890, and 2 August 1890.

37. AWTP #3916, AWT to William Penn Nixon, 11 July 1889; AWTP #3918, William Penn Nixon to AWT, 13 July 1889; "A Bystander's Notes," 13 July 1889, 4. Tourgée uses the term "Scientific Negrophobist" in the above-cited letter.

38. "A Bystander's Notes," 19 July 1890, 4. For a modern historical study of late nineteenth-century scientific racism that discusses Shaler, see Haller, *Outcasts from Evolution*.

39. "A Bystander's Notes," 19 July 1890, 4.

40. Ibid., 17 January 1891, 4.

41. AWTP #5207, A. O. Coffin to AWT, 4 January 1891. For further information about Coffin, see the entry by Robert Fikes in BlackPast.org and the sources he cites: *Who's Who of the Colored Race* (Chicago: F. L. Mather, 1915); *Harry H. Greene, Holders of Doctorates Among American Negroes* (Boston: Meador, 1946); and http://

webfiles.uci.edu/mcbrown/display/coffin.html and http://www.blackpast.org/aah/coffin-alfred-0-1861#sthash.

42. "A Bystander's Notes," 11 April 1891, 4.

43. Ibid., 25 April 1891, 4. None of the quoted letters can be definitively traced to originals in Tourgée's papers, but for similar passages, see AWTP #5521, A. M. Middlebrooks to AWT, 18 April 1891: "We have been true when called on both in time of war and Peace. . . . The colored people were asked to help Mrs. John Brown and they did so to the best of their ability and you know as much about the action of the colored People towards the raising of money for the erection of a monument to Abraham Lincoln as any body and they were very Patriotic in their actions." See also AWTP #5533, W. C. Carter to AWT, 23 April 1891: "We have fought for this Nation's liberty in all of its wars; we have been faithful to all of this Nation's interests; we we [*sic*] have been true to the Republican party, whose underlieing [*sic*] principles are liberty and justice, and yet foreigners are treated better than we are if their skin is white. . . . We sometimes think this government is ungrateful."

44. For a similar letter, see AWTP #5510, J. L. Love to AWT, 13 April 1891:

There are times even in Oberlin when the prospect seems gloomy and discouraging. At such times the 'Bystanders Notes' have penetrated the darkness like a flood of light awakening courage, and inciting to new endeavor. And I weep with joy at the fact that all the friends of justice have not gone.

I almost despair some times at the constantly growing indifference on the part of the young white men of our country in regard to a matter of such vital interest as National Citizenship. . . . Some, however, are true to whom the recital of pledges broken, of rights ignored, of the constitution nullified, of the restriction of opportunities and privileges because of *color* is a serious matter, and not a provocation for "sickness" or "weariness."

45. "A Bystander's Notes," 25 April 1891, 4.

46. Ibid., 15 August 1891, 4.

47. Ibid., 12 September 1891, 4. Martinet's editorial is no longer extant.

48. Ibid.

49. AWTP #5748, Ferdinand L. Barnett to AWT, 12 September 1891. No files of the *Conservator* for this period remain extant. Fairbank was also featured as a "Living Martyr" in the *Cleveland Gazette*, which urged readers to buy his book. See "Rev. Calvin Fairbank," *Cleveland Gazette*, 21 March 1891, 1. See also the untitled editorial of 20 August 1892, 2, directing readers to the letter from Fairbank on the same page, under the heading "Purchase One": "No member of the race who is able to send Rev. Calvin Fairbank $1.50 at once should fail to do so for two reasons, namely, because it is a duty and also because his book, 'HOW THE WAY WAS PREPARED,' is of special and great interest to every Afro-American."

50. See, for example, Blum, *Reforging the White Republic*; Blight, *Race and Reunion*; and Silber, *Romance of Reunion*.

51. AWTP #5752, AWT to Ferdinand L. Barnett, 16 September 1891. At least some of Tourgée's African American admirers shared his perception that he did not receive

sufficient gratitude for his devotion to their people's cause. See the quotations in chap. 5 from the editorial "'Twas Ever Thus" in the *Cleveland Gazette*, 4 January 1896, 2, which reprints an earlier statement by the *Gazette* along with a comment on it by the *New Orleans Crusader*.

52. AWTP #5752, AWT to Ferdinand L. Barnett, 16 September 1891; AWTP #5748, Ferdinand L. Barnett to AWT, 12 September 1891.

53. "A Bystander's Notes," 15 August 1891, 4.

54. AWTP #5729, J. E. Bruce to AWT, 27 July 1891.

55. AWT to J. E. Bruce, 31 July 1891, John Edward Bruce Collection, reel 1, letters T 7.

56. AWTP #5743, J. E. Bruce to AWT, 1 September 1891.

57. AWTP #4061–4062, "The Time Has Come for the Race to Show Itself Worthy of Liberty," AWT to the editor of the *Plaindealer*, 12 October 1889; *Detroit Plaindealer*, 18 October 1889, 4.

58. AWTP #5743, J. E. Bruce to AWT, 1 September 1891.

59. AWTP #5744, J. E. Bruce to AWT, 1 September 1891.

60. *Selected Writings of John Edward Bruce*, 32. For information about Bruce, see editor Peter Gilbert's introduction (1–9) to Bruce's *Selected Writings*; Seraile, *Bruce Grit*; and Crowder, *John Edward Bruce*. Bruce ended his career as an adherent of Marcus Garvey.

61. "A Bystander's Notes," 9 May 1891, 4.

62. AWTP #5548, A. M. Middlebrooks to AWT, 29 April 1891. I have been unable to ascertain Middlebrooks's full name or to learn much more about him, but the Black History Archives of Arkansas list an A. M. Middlebrooks (1855–?) as a minister, politician, and businessman. See http://uca.edu/archives/p2-black-history/.

63. "A Bystander's Notes," 11 July 1891, 4. This column was reprinted in the *Cleveland Gazette* under the title "Judge Tourgee on the Political Outlook in Ohio—Dissatisfied Afro-American Voters," 25 July 1891, 1. In an article that may have influenced Tourgée, the *Gazette* had previously reported on the protest movement among Cincinnati African Americans; see "A Decided Kick. The Afro-American Republicans of Cincinnati Are More Dissatisfied Than Those in Cleveland," 4 July 1891, 1.

64. "A Bystander's Notes," 7 February 1891, 4, and 2 May 1891, 5.

65. Medley, *We as Freemen*, 118–27; "A Bystander's Notes," 3 October 1891, 4.

66. "A Bystander's Notes," 17 and 24 October 1891, 4.

67. Ibid., 31 October 1891, 4.

68. Ibid.

69. No originals exist in Tourgée's papers for any of the letters quoted in these columns.

70. "A Bystander's Notes," 7 November 1891, 4.

71. Ibid., 14 November 1891, 4.

72. Ibid., 21 November 1891, 4.

73. Ibid., 7 and 14 November 1891, 4.

74. Ibid., 21 November 1891, 4.

75. See, for example, ibid., 5 December 1891, 4; 16 January 1892, 4; and 4 June 1892, 12.

76. Ibid., 28 November 1891, 4.

77. Ibid., 12 December 1891, 4. No originals for these letters have survived in Tourgée's papers.

78. Ibid.

79. Ibid., 19 and 26 December 1891, 4.

80. Ibid., 16 April 1892, 4. The subject Tourgée most often raised when he was not discussing the NCRA was lynching. See chapter 5.

81. Ibid., 14 May 1892, 4.

82. See, for example, ibid., 5 March, 14 May, and 28 May 1892, 4.

83. Ibid., 18 June 1892, 4.

84. Ibid., 30 July 1892, 4. Quotations in the next paragraph are also from this article.

85. Ibid., 3 September 1892, 4.

86. Ibid., 12 November 1892, 4.

87. Ibid., 19 November 1892, 4. See also the "Bystander" of 3 December 1892, in which Tourgée continues this method of involving readers in a collective postmortem of the election.

88. Ibid., 10 December 1892, 4. For the original article Tourgée quotes, see Caldwell, "The Order System. How the Southerner Manages to Keep the Afro-American Poor." Quotations in the next paragraph are also from this "Bystander" column. Eight letters from Caldwell survive in Tourgée's papers. I have been unable to find out anything more about him.

89. "A Bystander's Notes," 7 January 1893, 4. Quotations in the next paragraph are also from this column. Martinet's original editorial has been lost, along with all but a few scattered remnants of the *Crusader*.

90. Ibid., 24 June 1893, 12. The editorial page on which Tourgée's column continued to appear was shifted from p. 4 to p. 12 in May 1893.

91. "A Bystander's Notes: The Parting of the Ways," 10 June 1893, 12.

92. Ibid., 17 June 1893, 12.

93. AWTP #6973, William W. Bates to AWT, 20 May 1893.

94. "A Bystander's Notes," 12 August 1893, 12. Quotations in this and the next few paragraphs are all drawn from this column.

95. AWTP #6998, Louis A. Martinet to AWT, 30 May 1893.

96. Tourgée slightly revised Martinet's original wording. Martinet had actually written: "All I want is my civil rights & privileges as a citizen, and simple justice for all who are denied it." In the sentence that follows, Martinet underlined only "enjoy" and "tolerated" where Tourgée italicized whole phrases.

97. "A Bystander's Notes," 12 August 1893, 12. For Martinet's request, see AWTP #7197, Louis A. Martinet to AWT, 4 August 1893. For the text of the pamphlet, see Louis A. Martinet, ed., *The Violation of a Constitutional Right* (New Orleans: Citizens' Committee, 1893), quotation on 10, Rousseve Papers, box 1, folder 12.

98. The words "unceremoniously dropped" are Elliott's, *Color-Blind Justice,* 278.

99. AWTP #6133, William Penn Nixon to AWT, 21 March 1892.

100. AWTP #6383, William Penn Nixon to AWT, 7 July 1892. For the typescript of the column Nixon returned to Tourgée, see AWTP #6386, "A Bystander's Notes." Similar criticisms of Tourgée's prophecy (which he had also made orally in a press interview) were made by conservative African Americans. See untitled editorial and "As to Judge Tourgée," *Indianapolis Freeman*, 2 and 9 July 1892, 4; the latter charges Tourgée with "unbalanced, untimely zeal" and "indiscretion." See also Robert Purvis and Isaac C. Wear, quoted in "Won't Indorse Tourgee—Leading Colored Men Regard Him as an Alarmist." For discussion of these men's criticisms of Tourgée, see chapter 5.

101. AWTP #6379, AWT to William Penn Nixon, 7 July 1892. (The date is unclear and may be 9 July.) This is a draft written at white heat, full of deletions and insertions. In the absence of Nixon's papers, for which I have so far searched in vain, there is no way of knowing whether it is identical with the typed copy Emma mailed.

102. AWTP #7107, AWT to William Penn Nixon, 6 July 1893.

103. AWTP #7120, William Penn Nixon to AWT, 12 July 1893.

104. AWTP #7133 and 7134, AWT to William Penn Nixon, 15 July 1893; AWTP #7135, EKT to William Penn Nixon, 15 July 1893; AWTP #7209, William Penn Nixon to AWT, 8 August 1893; AWTP #7219, William Penn Nixon to EKT, 11 August 1893; AWTP #7288 and 7289, AWT to William Penn Nixon, n.d., after 8 August 1893.

105. AWTP #7107, AWT to William Penn Nixon, 6 July 1893; AWTP #7294, Joseph Cook to AWT, 1 September 1893.

106. AWTP #7305, Sarah A. Farley to editor, *Chicago Daily Inter Ocean*, 5 September 1893.

107. AWTP #7361, S. Fillmore Bennett, MD, to editor, *Chicago Daily Inter Ocean*, 28 September 1893.

108. AWTP #7614, NCRA file, F. E. Cobb to AWT, 11 October 1893.

109. AWTP #7456, G. H. Hill to AWT, 3 November 1893.

110. AWTP #7501, William H. Busbey to EKT, 17 November 1893. A letter from at least one NCRA member to Tourgée does give the impression that he may have encouraged a letter-writing "campaign." See AWTP #7614, NCRA file, Herbert M. Woodward to AWT, 4 December 1893: "I did write the Editor of the Inter Ocean asking him why the Bystander's Notes did not appear any more . . . and he never answered my letter. It may be that I offended the gentleman for I made the remark in my letter that the Inter Ocean was not worth half price since Tourgee's articles were left out."

111. On the first condition, see Elliott, *Color-Blind Justice*, 278; on the second, see AWTP #7679, William H. Busbey to EKT, 13 August 1894, discussed below.

112. "A Bystander's Notes: The Approaching Economic Crisis—Protection to the Citizen," 5 May 1894, 12–13.

113. "A Bystander's Notes: The Theory of Malthus and Its Bearing on the Question of Wages," 12 May 1894, 12. The quotations in the rest of this paragraph come from this article.

114. "A Bystander's Notes: Wage Tyrants and Profit Tyrants," 14 July 1894, 12–13; "A Bystander's Notes: To Prevent Strikes by Removing the Inducement to Strike," 21 July

1894, 12–13. For the *Inter Ocean*'s perspective on the strike, see the editorials of 7 July 1894, 12: "The Strong Arm," "Altgeld to Cleveland," and "Mr. Debs and Arbitration"; also the news article on p. 4: "Anarchy Is Doomed. The President Sees Something Like Rebellion at Chicago. He Will Suppress It. Every Rifle in the Nation Will Be Used if Necessary. Governor Altgeld is Denounced and His Letter Is Designated as State's Rights Gone Mad."

115. "A Bystander's Notes: Colored Men and the Democratic Party," 4 August 1894.

116. AWTP #7969, William H. Busbey to EKT, 13 August 1894. For the text of the passage cut, see AWTP #7965. For the article as published, in a form much shorter than usual, see "A Bystander's Notes: The Evolution of Parties," 11 August 1894, 12.

117. AWTP #7983, William H. Busbey to AWT, 20 August 1894.

118. AWTP #8082, William Penn Nixon to AWT, 5 October 1894.

119. AWTP #8164, AWT to William Penn Nixon, n.d. [after 5 October 1894].

120. AWTP #8437, William H. Busbey to AWT, 25 March 1895, enclosing the published letter, titled "Tourgee and His Bystander Notes."

121. Untitled editorial, *Cleveland Gazette*, 2 February 1895, 2.

122. See, for example, the "Bystander" articles subtitled "The President and the Tariff Bill" (18 August 1894, 12–13); "The Blasted Counsels of the Brave" (1 September 1894, 12–13); "The Markets of the World" (29 September 1894, 12–13); "The Theoretical Free Trader and His Assumption" (6 October 1894, 12–13); and "Free Trade as an Economic Theory—Reciprocity and Its Effect" (13 October 1894, 12–13).

123. "A Bystander's Notes: Colored People and Christianity," 27 October 1894, 12–13. Quotations in this paragraph and the next are all from this article.

124. "A Bystander's Notes: White-Line Republicans in the Southern States," 5 January 1895, 12–13. Quotations in this paragraph and the next two are all from this article.

Chapter Four

1. AWTP #5256, AWT to M[arriott] Brosius, 24 January 1891. Brosius, whose name is misspelled in the index to the Albion W. Tourgee Papers, was first identified by Olsen, *Carpetbagger's Crusade*, 295n. According to "Marriott Henry Brosius," Wikipedia, he was a Civil War Union veteran from Lancaster County, Pennsylvania, and served in Congress from 1889 until his death in 1901.

2. "A Bystander's Notes," 17 October 1891, 4.

3. Tourgée supplies these figures in AWTP #6439, AWT to Phillip C. Garret [*sic*], n.d. [ca. October 1892].

4. Quotations from AWT to Rev. Benton, n.d. [ca. November 1891], and AWT to Philip C. Garrett, n.d. [ca. October 1892], AWTP #5897, 6439.

5. Most of the correspondence relating to the NCRA is contained in AWTP #7614, which I will refer to as the NCRA file. Unfortunately, this file is neither indexed nor organized chronologically, making the letters from which I will be quoting almost impossible to locate individually.

6. AWTP #5760, Louis A. Martinet to AWT, 5 October 1891; AWTP #5768, Louis A. Martinet to AWT, 25 October 1891.

7. See Andrew J. Gholson to AWT, 19 November 1891: "I here with enclose you a clipping from the [']Free Speech' a paper published in Memphis, Tenn—Being fully in sympathy with the contents contained therein which you will readily perceive by my having filled out the blanks [in the application form] as requested"; also Ida B. Wells to EKT, 3 November 1892: "The ladies of New York and Brooklyn wish to know more about the National Citizens Rights Association," and Wells requests Emma to forward "all circulars pamphlets and other matter" to one of them; both letters from AWTP #7614, NCRA file.

8. *Cleveland Gazette*, 21 November 1891, 2, and 4 June 1892, 1; *Detroit Plaindealer*, 27 May 1892, 4, and 3 June 1892, 1, 8.

9. AWTP #7614, NCRA file, enclosures in Charles Whitefield (St. Louis, Mo.) to AWT, 13 September 1892; George R. Nevels (Detroit, Mich.) to AWT, 5 October 1892; and H. G. Newsom (Akron, Ohio?) to AWT, n.d.

10. AWTP #5788, Alexander S. Jackson to AWT, 13 November 1891.

11. AWTP #7614, NCRA file, S. T. Clanton to AWT, 21 December 1891.

12. Ibid., Charles W. Cansler to AWT, 15 June [1892?].

13. Ibid., Jno M. Nimocks to AWT, 7 July 1892; and Jno G. Monroe to AWT, 26 November 1891; AWTP #5255, A. M. Middlebrooks to AWT, 24 January 1891.

14. AWTP #7614, NCRA file, Rodolphe L. Desdunes to AWT, 5 February 1892.

15. AWTP #4726, Thomas R. Griffin to AWT, 5 May 1890.

16. AWTP #7614, NCRA file, F. B. Hood to AWT, 15 March 1892.

17. See AWTP #5217, A. M. Middlebrooks to AWT, 9 January 1891; and AWTP #7614, NCRA file, AWT to A. M. Middlebrooks, 19 December 1891.

18. AWTP #7614, NCRA file, S. R. Kendrick to AWT, 4 July 1892.

19. Ibid., A. P. Hood to AWT, 9 May 1892. Here and in all other letters from NCRA correspondents, I have retained the idiosyncratic spelling, capitalization, punctuation, and grammar found in the original documents.

20. Ibid., F. B. Hood to AWT, 15 March 1892.

21. AWTP #8846, A. P. Hood to AWT, 10 December 1895. F. B. Hood's murder was reported in an untitled editorial in the *Cleveland Gazette* of 4 August 1894, 2, that Tourgée seems to have overlooked:

> Frank B. Hood, of Liberty, Miss., a school teacher, shot and killed the leader and several of the mob that came to his home at mid-day on July 2 to take him out and whip him for writing a sharp reply to the white superintendent of schools of that place. May Hood's kind of Afro-Americans increase. He is a martyr—for he was finally killed by the mob, several of whom also sleep the long sleep of death. When a few more such defenses are made the lawless element in the south will be checked in its mad career and whippings and lynchings will not be of such frequent occurrence.

No information is available regarding the discrepancies between the two accounts.

22. AWTP #7614, NCRA file, S. R. Kendrick to AWT, 4 July 1892.

23. Ibid., H. W. Winans (Lake Village, Ark.) to AWT, 24 March 1892; S. R. Kendrick to AWT, 4 July 1892.

24. Ibid., Henry A. Fowler to AWT, 28 December 1891.

25. Ibid., A. N. Jackson to AWT, 23 March 1892.

26. Ibid., Jam[es?] Mosly to AWT, 24 February 1892.

27. Ibid., Jane and Minnie Evans to AWT, 17 December 1891.

28. See, for example, AWTP #7779, [unknown] to AWT, 10 June 1894. This correspondent wrote "My No is" but failed to provide a number.

29. AWTP #7614, NCRA file, "John Branch" to AWT, 28 March 1892.

30. Ibid., Walter H. Griffin to AWT, 7 June 1892.

31. Ibid., A. A. Tompkins and Pliny A. Weels to AWT, 7 and 24 September 1892.

32. Ibid., Willis Reese to AWT, 17 September 1892.

33. Ibid., F. Bass, W. C. Freeman, and J. H. Johnson to AWT, 21 April 1892.

34. "A Bystander's Notes," 15 October 1892, 4.

35. AWTP #7614, NCRA file, J. A. Swanson, Mason Woodard, and Dudley Steuard to AWT, 9 October, 11 July, and 15 August 1892. Steuard's letter is reprinted in Olsen, "Albion W. Tourgee and Negro Militants of the 1890's," 199–200, which identifies Steuard as a "frequent correspondent and active organizer, whose freedom was secured." See "A Bystander's Notes," 1 October 1892, 4, for additional details about Steuard.

36. AWTP #7614, NCRA file, M. W. Walker, W. R. Linck, Henry Williams, William Mayfield, and [illegible] to AWT, 13 June, 30 July, 10 August, 20 September, and n.d. September 1892.

37. Ibid., AWT to M. W. Walker, n.d., attached to Walker's letter of 13 June 1892.

38. AWTP #6297, AWT to [Charlotte Forten Grimké], n.d. [after 18 May 1892]. Tourgée is referring to Nathaniel Southgate Shaler's "Science and the African Problem," *Atlantic Monthly* 66 (July 1890): 36–45. For Tourgée's critique of Shaler's article and refutation of his pseudoscientific theories, see "A Bystander's Notes," 19 July 1890, 4.

39. AWTP #6240, Charlotte F[orten] Grimké to AWT, 18 May 1892; AWTP #7614, NCRA file, Charlotte F[orten] Grimké to AWT, 27 May and 7 June 1892.

40. AWTP #5904, AWT to Florence A. Lewis, n.d.; AWTP #7614, NCRA file, AWT to Florence A. Lewis, 30 November 1891; AWTP #5816 and 5940, Florence A. Lewis to AWT, 2 December 1891 and 11 January 1892; AWTP #7614, NCRA file, Florence A. Lewis to AWT, 25 February 1892. Kevin K. Gaines has identified the *A.M.E. Church Review* as the "leading black thought journal of the day"; see his *Uplifting the Race*, 94. No article by Florence Lewis about the NCRA appears in any 1892 number.

41. Quotations are from the 18 November 1891 *Philadelphia Press* interview with Mossell that he enclosed in his letter to Tourgée of that date, AWTP #7614, NCRA file.

42. AWTP #7614, NCRA file: Nathan F. Mossell to AWT, 18 November 1891; H. O. Tanner to AWT, 31 July, 3 August, 30 August, and 10 October 1893; AWTP #5814, AWT to [Nathan F. Mossell], n.d. [after 18 November 1891].

43. AWTP #7614, NCRA file, AWT to Ed[itor,] "Courant," 16 November 1891.

44. Ibid., Josephine S. P. Ruffin to AWT, 3 December 1891.

45. AWTP #5900, AWT to Ed[i]t[or]s, *Courant*, n.d. For evidence of Ruffin's continuing support of Tourgée, see *Woman's Era*, 1 May 1894, 13, and AWTP #9243, Josephine S. P. Ruffin to AWT, 24 February 1897.

46. AWTP #7614, NCRA file, Timothy G. Tynes to AWT, 27 February [1892].

47. Ibid., Mack W. Caldwell to AWT, 14 February, 1 May, and 25 May 1892. For further information about Caldwell, see chapter 3, in which Tourgée quotes extensively in his "Bystander" column from an article Caldwell published in the *Detroit Plaindealer,* as documented in n. 88.

48. AWTP #7614, NCRA file, William Lewis Martin to AWT, 1 January 1892.

49. Ibid., Robert McCoomer to AWT, 19 March 1892.

50. Tourgée, "'Tourgeeism!' A Personal Letter to Afro-Americans, from Judge Tourgée"; Tourgée, "'Tourgeeism.' What the National Citizens' Rights Association Is. Why Every Afro-American Should Become a Member." The *Conservator* and the *Courant* likely published this letter as well.

51. "'Tourgeeism!'" and untitled editorial, *Detroit Plaindealer,* 3 June 1892, 4. In a letter marked "Personal," Tourgée objected: "Isn't it unjust to your people to intimate that they favor the Association because a white man is the head of it?" The NCRA had "no 'leader,'" he claimed. See AWTP #6495, AWT to [William H.] Anderson, n.d. [after 3 June 1892].

52. AWTP #7614, NCRA file, AWT to "Dear Sir," n.d. For other views on why Northern African Americans did not join the NCRA in greater numbers, see Olsen, *Carpetbagger's Crusade,* 318–20; and Elliott, *Color-Blind Justice,* 273–76.

53. AWTP #7614, NCRA file, Arthur B. Lee to AWT, 19 December 1891; AWTP #5940, Florence Lewis to AWT, 11 January 1892.

54. AWTP #7614, NCRA file, Samuel G. Hicks to AWT, 10 March 1892.

55. Ibid., AWT to Samuel J. [*sic*] Hicks, 12 March 1892.

56. Ibid., D. D. Weaver to AWT, 15 July 1893, and AWT to [D. D. Weaver], n.d. [after 15 July 1893]; see also C. M. Tanner and H. O. Tanner to AWT, 14, 15, and 31 July 1893; and Thomas Green to AWT, 19 July 1893.

57. See chapter 5 on Tourgée's antilynching advocacy. For the two most detailed accounts to date of Tourgée's collaboration with Wells in her campaign against lynching, see Karcher, "White 'Bystander' and the Black Journalist 'Abroad'"; and Karcher, "Ida B. Wells and Her Allies against Lynching."

58. AWTP #7614, NCRA file, AWT to [D. D. Weaver], n.d. [after 15 July 1893].

59. See, for example, Quarles, *Black Abolitionists,* 47–55; Pease and Pease, *They Who Would Be Free,* chaps. 1 and 5; Harding, *There Is a River,* 124–28; and Friedman, *Gregarious Saints,* chap. 6.

60. See Logan, *Betrayal of the Negro*; Blight, *Race and Reunion*; and Blum, *Reforging the White Republic.*

61. See Gaines, *Uplifting the Race.*

62. See Thornbrough, "National Afro-American League." According to Thornbrough, "Fortune's plan was to organize local and state leagues before attempting to effect a national organization. In the months following his initial proposal [of 28 May 1887], local leagues of varying size and strength were formed—in New England, Pennsylvania, New York, Illinois, Minnesota, and even in distant San Francisco. In the South organizations were attempted in Virginia, Texas, North Carolina, Tennessee,

and Georgia" (498). See also S. Alexander, *Army of Lions*, chap. 2; and Carle, *Defining the Struggle*, chap. 3.

63. "A Bystander's Notes," 2 November 1889, 4, partially reprinted in Elliott and Smith, *Undaunted Radical*, 246–51, quotations from 248, 256, 257; AWTP #4408, undated fragment. Fortune's speech detailing the objectives of the league is reprinted in full in "The League Convention. A National Organization Perfected at Chicago," *New York Age*, 25 January 1890, 1–2.

64. AWTP #11043, AWT to J. C. Price, n.d. [before 18 March 1890]; AWTP #4568, J. C. Price to AWT, 18 March 1890. For detailed reports on the convention, see "The League Convention," *New York Age*, 25 January 1890, 1–3; and "A Gratifying Success. Afro-Americans in National Convention Organize a National League," *Detroit Plaindealer*, 24 January 1890, 1. The *Age* does not mention the debate over returning Tourgée's letter and simply reports that it was received, but an editorial note on p. 2 comments: "The letter of Judge ALBION W. TOURGEE, to the League Convention, was worthy of the man, who has never wavered in his fight for a square deal for Afro-Americans." According to the *Plaindealer*, the two convention members who wanted the letter returned unread were Rev. J. E. Haynes of South Carolina and Rev. J. A. Brockett of Massachusetts. In addition to Price, Rev. W. H. Heard of Pennsylvania defended Tourgée. Fortune apparently did not participate in the discussion, perhaps because he was not on the committee handling messages.

65. AWTP #11043, AWT to J. C. Price, n.d. Interestingly, Emma noted in her diary that she "did not approve" of this letter and forced him to "modif[y]" it "so it is not so objectionable." See AWTP #9906, entries for 25 and 26 January 1890.

66. See AWTP #5147, AWT to Wm H. Anderson, n.d. [after 18 April 1890]; and AWTP #4764, Mack W. Caldwell to AWT, 29 May 1890. Tourgée's dissatisfaction with Price was echoed by at least two African American radicals, Wells and Harry C. Smith. Smith quoted Wells as commenting in the *Memphis Free Speech* on the National Afro-American League meeting held in Knoxville, "'Dr. (Rev. J. C.) Price is a great and good man, but I can not recall one thing he has said or done for the league during his year of presidency. . . . That he has not fulfilled the hopes predicted of him on his election a year ago is much to be regretted." Smith editorialized: "Very true—every word of the excerpt." See "Make the League a Power," *Cleveland Gazette*, 1 August 1891, 2.

67. AWTP #7614, NCRA file, AWT to "Dear Sir," n.d. See also Renfro, "Is the Afro-American League a Failure?" Renfro explicitly argues against allowing whites to participate in the Afro-American League: "Our experience with white men all along has taught us to observe that no matter how friendly, and brotherly, and Christian-like they may be, when Caucasians come into an Ethiopian assembly, like a band of conquerors they seize upon the highest seats, or are elevated by the servility and pusillanimity of the dark-hued followers. . . . Let the League discard the reliance upon the arm and heart of any save its own proud Afro-American. Let it avoid an association that cannot be beneficial" (13).

68. AWTP #5760, Louis A. Martinet to AWT, 5 October 1891. For further details on the ACERA, see Elliott, *Color-Blind Justice*, 249–52; and Kelley, *Right to Ride*, 62–69.

69. Thornbrough, "National Afro-American League," 500, 501; S. Alexander, *Army of Lions*, 63–65 (Alexander mentions John Mercer Langston, Blanche K. Bruce, and Frederick Douglass among the African American politicians, or "race leaders," who failed to give adequate support to the league); Carle, *Defining the Struggle*, 69–71.

70. AWTP #6473, AWT to Louis A. Martinet, n.d. [before 7 December 1891]. This undated letter has been miscataloged among letters of late 1892. Martinet's reply of 7 December 1891, AWTP #5837, establishes its probable date.

71. The quotation is from AWTP #6377, Louis A. Martinet to AWT, 4 July 1892, partially reprinted in Olsen, *Thin Disguise*, 61–66, quotation on 64–65; Martinet specifically mentioned "Douglas, Pinchback, & the like." For analogous criticisms by Wells, see Giddings, *Ida*, 204: "'Where are our leaders when the race is being burnt, shot and hanged?' the *Free Speech* taunted. . . . No doubt thinking of the likes of John Langston, Blanche K. Bruce, and P. B. S. Pinchback, all maneuvering in a presidential election year, Wells concluded, 'A few big offices and the control of a little Federal patronage is not sufficient recompense for the lives lost, the blood shed, and the rights denied the race.'" Such criticisms of black leaders can also be found in the *Cleveland Gazette*; see, for example, "Sick of Bruce," 14 February 1890, 2: "May the good Lord save us from any more of Bruce, Lynch, Milton Holland, Douglass, Pinchback and the rest of that set of professional Negro office-seekers and holders, political barnacles." When the *New York Age* objected to this disparagement of black leaders, the *Gazette* replied:

> The men named have enjoyed office almost continuously since the close of the war upon the strength of their connection with the race and the claim that they were leaders. What has the race received from them in return? *Nothing*, absolutely *nothing*. . . . The Age wants to know how many of the other editors of the race subscribe to what we have written. *Every one* who does not wear one of these men's "collars" and who *dares* to speak for his race. All loyal and true Afro-Americans will subscribe to it because they know we speak the truth.

See "Be True to the Race," *Cleveland Gazette*, 7 March 1891, 2. In an untitled editorial of 23 April 1892, 2, Smith reiterated his aspersions on "our so-called leaders," branding them as "creatures-in-office and toadies" of "tricky" white politicians and accusing them of attempting to "hoodwink, fool, mislead and play upon the credulity of our people." In another untitled editorial of 26 November 1892, 2, Smith quoted and praised an editorial in the *Crusader* titled "Too Many Douglasses," in which Martinet contrasted the generous contribution of Wells to the New Orleans Citizens' Committee's fund for challenging the Separate Car Law with the refusal of Douglass to contribute, noting that "Miss Wells, at the time, hardly knew where her next dollar was coming from, while Mr. Douglass was and is worth at least $200,000." Smith editorialized: "The race needs, and badly too, a far different leadership. Intelligent, broad-minded, unselfish, energetic, honest and intensely loyal must be the leaders of the future." For further speculation about which leaders Tourgée had in mind, see Elliott, *Color-Blind Justice*, 273–75. Elliott shows that Tourgée tried in vain to obtain Douglass's endorsement of the NCRA.

72. George Arnold, "In Tourgée's Defense," letter to the editor of the *Plaindealer*, 6 May 1892, 4, preserved in AWTP #7614, NCRA file; Arnold identified himself as having known Tourgée since his days in North Carolina and said that Tourgée "was then the same upright, brave, bold, courageous, outspoken friend of humanity, that he has shown to be as 'Bystander.'" He added: "For God's sake don't mention it that there is on this green earth an Afro-American who does not honor and value Judge Tourgée." The paragraph about Hackley in the *Plaindealer*, to which Arnold refers in his letter, was reprinted from the *Conservator* on 29 April 1892, 4, under the "Current Comment" column, which typically published extracts from African American and some white newspapers. The 6 May "Current Comment" column also included an extract from the *Boston Republican*: "It sounds exceedingly strange to the colored men in sections of the country that have produced some of the strongest and most devoted white friends of our people, to hear other colored men speak in a belittling way of such individuals." The *Republican* praised Tourgée as a "noble and worthy" successor of Garrison and Phillips and credited him with "working harder for the colored people than we are doing for ourselves." It concluded: "We pray for more Tourgees. . . . Long live 'Tourgeeism,' and may it find its way into every home and hamlet in the world." See also the *Cleveland Gazette*, "Color Not Considered," 18 June 1892, 2, which quoted Hackley's reply to Arnold and commented, "The ridiculousness of the idea that 'we err grievously in looking to or *following* any *white* man's efforts for our material salvation,' is made all the more apparent when it is known that the above is a direct thrust at perhaps the race's truest and best friend of to day—Judge Albion W. Tourgée. . . . The assistance of such white men as Messrs. Tourgee and Cable is absolutely indispensable."

73. Quoted in Olsen, *Carpetbagger's Crusade*, 318–19. Hackley's views are summarized and criticized in the *Plaindealer* on 15 April 1892, 4; the *Plaindealer* of 3 June 1892, 8, also allowed Hackley to make his own case in his "Open Letter" replying to George Arnold and other critics.

74. For editorials attacking Tourgée in the *Indianapolis Freeman, An Illustrated Colored Newspaper,* see "The Colored Ministry," 31 October 1891, 4; "Negroes as Partisans," 9 April 1892, 4; and "Judge Tourgée's Ill-Seasoned Vaporings," 25 June 1892, 4. The *Freeman* of 19 March 1892 did, however, publish on its front page a eulogistic article sent from Chicago: "Negro Oppression. The National Citizen's Rights Association—Its Mission."

75. Tourgée editorial, *Basis*, 29 June 1895, 388.

76. AWTP #6473, AWT to Louis A. Martinet, n.d. [before 7 December 1891]. Tourgée asked Martinet whether he agreed with the choice of Desdunes or would like the position himself. According to Elliott, the names of Administrative Council members appeared on the NCRA's official letterhead; see *Color-Blind Justice*, 255.

77. AWTP #6297, AWT to [Charlotte Forten Grimké], n.d. [after 18 May 1892]: "The National Citizens' Rights Association has on its roll today ten white names for one colored"; AWTP #6439, AWT to Hon. Phillip C. Garret [*sic*], n.d. [ca. October 1892]: "We have 250,000, or thereabouts; probably 200,000 of them white and about that number at the North."

78. AWTP #6297, AWT to [Charlotte Forten Grimké], n.d. [after 18 May 1892]. See also AWTP #5900, AWT to Ed[itor]s, *Boston Courant*, n.d. [after 3 December 1891]: "I dread to see the intelligent colored man of the North behind the white people and his less intelligent fellows of the South, in what is of such vital import to the colored citizen everywhere."

79. See McPherson, *Abolitionist Legacy*.

80. AWTP #7614, NCRA file, H. Farmer to AWT, 12 February 1892. See also ibid., Adrian Reynolds to AWT, 19 October 1892: "My father was an abolitionist as long ago as 1820, in Guilford County, N.C. where he was born and lived until 1856." Reynolds mentions that he has read *A Fool's Errand* and *Bricks Without Straw* and that as a boy he studied with David Hodgin, one of Tourgée's Quaker allies during his years in Guilford County.

81. Ibid., A. Ryall to AWT, 18 December 1891.

82. Ibid., J. H. Wimpey to AWT, 20 November 1891.

83. Ibid., Jannice Page to AWT, 22 October 1891.

84. AWTP #9907, scrapbook of obituary clippings, *Baltimore American*, 21 May 1905: "As a lecturer Judge Tourgee has in one or two brief tours won a popularity second to none. Especially in the West is he a prime favorite. Fond of young people and the best of story tellers, he always manages to spend an hour when in a college town with the students." The article is dated 21 May but appeared on 22 May.

85. AWTP #7614, NCRA file, F. W. Meyers to AWT, 6 March 1892; and AWT to Students of the State University of Iowa, n.d.

86. AWTP #6221, Charles L. Fitch and Charles D. Seaton to AWT, 7 May 1892.

87. AWTP #7614, NCRA file, A. Ryall to AWT, 18 December 1891.

88. AWTP #6025, AWT to A. Royall [*sic*], 14 February 1892. For a similar diagnosis of the NCRA's limitations, see Olsen, *Carpetbagger's Crusade*, 324: "Altogether, the simplicity of the N.C.R.A. and its domination by the Judge had been both a source of its rapid growth and strength and of its weakness. It had never been much more than a list of names, a personal possession of Tourgée's that added to, but was also dependent upon, his prestige and power." Citing Olsen, McPherson blames the collapse of the NCRA on "Tourgée's autocratic insistence on running the whole show himself" (*Abolitionist Legacy*, 317).

89. AWTP #5814, AWT to [Nathan F. Mossell], n.d. [after 18 November 1891].

90. See AWTP #7614, NCRA file: Timothy G. Tynes to AWT, 27 February [1892]; J. W. Shavers to AWT, 16 July 1892; Henry Williams (No 29951, Stovall, Miss.) to AWT, 30 July 1892; J. J. Jones to AWT, 27 July 1893; and Henry O. Tanner to AWT, 3 August 1893. On the Administrative Council's lack of responsibilities, see AWTP #6439, AWT to Hon. Phillip C. Garret [*sic*], n.d. [ca. October 1892]; AWTP #5818 and 5862, George W. Cable to AWT, 3 and 19 December 1891.

91. AWTP #6495, AWT to William H. Anderson, n.d.; AWTP #6025, AWT to A. Royall [*sic*], 14 February 1892; AWTP #5814, AWT to [Nathan F. Mossell], n.d. [after 18 November 1891].

92. AWTP #5814, AWT to [Nathan F. Mossell], n.d. [after 18 November 1891]; AWTP #7614, NCRA file, AWT to [Henry O. Tanner], n.d. [after 10 October 1893].

93. AWTP #6439, AWT to Hon. Phillip C. Garret [*sic*], n.d. [ca. October 1892]. See also AWT to J. E. Bruce, 17 November 1891, John Edward Bruce Collection, reel 1, letters T 8: "This method dispen[s]es with meetings, prevents discord and envy and does not scare any one with the idea of social equality."

94. AWTP #6362, AWT to [unknown], n.d.; AWTP #6439, AWT to Hon. Phillip C. Garret [*sic*], n.d. [ca. October 1892]; "A Bystander's Notes," 4 June 1892. On the Union Leagues of the Reconstruction era, see Foner, *Reconstruction*, 283–85.

95. AWTP #6492, AWT to [unknown], n.d.

96. See AWTP #7614, NCRA file, Mack W. Caldwell to AWT, 14 February 1892: "I am deeply involved in two lawsuits now. One because a restaurant keeper refused to serve me a glass of milk and a piece of apple pie on account of my color and another because my wife and three babies was made to ride 476 miles in a smoking car on the East Tennessee, Virginia and Georgia Ry when they had paid first class fare."

97. *Is Liberty Worth Preserving?* (1892), reprinted in Elliott and Smith, *Undaunted Radical*, 252–75. Quotations are from 256, 257, 272, 273.

98. AWTP #5814, AWT to [Nathan F. Mossell], n.d. [after 18 November 1891].

99. AWTP #6025, AWT to A. Royall [*sic*], 14 February 1892.

100. Olsen, *Carpetbagger's Crusade*, 320; AWTP #6500, AWT to Thomas B. Reed, n.d.

101. AWTP #6009, AWT to Wm Penn Nixon, 4 February 1892; AWTP #7614, NCRA file, John Hammon "To Bystander," 13 May 1892; "A Bystander's Notes," 7 May 1892.

102. AWTP #7614, NCRA file, John Hammon "To Bystander," 13 May 1892; Hammon had asked Tourgée to supply him with the names of the African American delegates. See also AWTP #6341, George W. Gaines to AWT, 22 June 1892; and AWTP #6350, AWT to Rev. George W. Gaines, 24 June 1892. Tourgée defended the African American delegates to Gaines, on the grounds that they were not voting against Reed but against Harrison's main rival, James G. Blaine, whose record on African American rights was far worse than Harrison's.

103. Olsen, *Carpetbagger's Crusade*, 321; AWTP #6383, William Penn Nixon to AWT, 7 July 1892; AWTP #6379, AWT to William Penn Nixon, 9 July 1892. For the 1892 Republican Party platform, see the American Presidency Project, http://www .presidency.ucsb.edu/ws/print (21 January 2010).

104. AWTP #6360, AWT to E. H. Bowman, n.d. [after 24 June 1892].

105. AWTP #6377, Louis A. Martinet to AWT, 4 July 1892, partially reprinted in Olsen, *Thin Disguise*, 61–67, quotation on 65.

106. AWTP #6379, AWT to William Penn Nixon, 9 July 1892. On the history of the Liberty, Free Soil, and Republican Parties, see Filler, *Crusade against Slavery*, chaps. 7–8; and Foner, *Free Soil*.

107. AWTP #6350, AWT to Rev. Geo. W. Gaines, 24 June 1892. Although Tourgée addresses him as Reverend, Gaines is identified in his first letter to Tourgée as a member of the law firm of Ferdinand L. Barnett and S. Laing Williams; see AWTP #6123, George W. Gaines to AWT, 18 March 1892.

108. AWTP #6366, AWT to W. E. Turner, n.d. [after 18 June 1892].

109. AWTP #6273, AWT to Prof. Jencks [*sic*], 26 May 1892.

110. AWTP #6364, AWT to C. Spalding, Manager *Atlanta Times*, n.d. [after 6 June 1892]. In a "Bystander" column of 8 July 1892 that the *Inter Ocean* refused to publish, Tourgée refers to this correspondence and identifies Spalding (without naming him) as a well-intentioned Southern Democrat; see AWTP #6386 for the typescript of this column.

111. "A Bystander's Notes," 21 May 1892, 4.

112. Olsen, *Carpetbagger's Crusade*, 321. Martinet took a more cynical view of the Methodists' response. "What have the splendid memorials you addressed to the M.E. Church General Conference & the Nat[ional] Rep[ublican] Convention, in effect, amounted to?" he asked. "The Conference it is true adopted resolutions denunciatory of Southern outrages, but it discharged Dr. Albert as editor of the Southwestern Christian Advocate for a man *less* aggressive, *more* conservative. The Convention did absolutely nothing." See AWTP #6377, Louis A. Martinet to AWT, 4 July 1892, partially reprinted in Olsen, *Thin Disguise*, 65–66.

113. AWTP #6240, Charlotte F[orten] Grimké to AWT, 18 May 1892; AWTP #6297, AWT to [Charlotte Forten Grimké], n.d. [after 18 May 1892]; Olsen, *Carpetbagger's Crusade*, 321.

114. AWTP #5760, Louis A. Martinet to AWT, 5 October 1891.

115. AWTP #5813, AWT to [Louis A. Martinet], n.d. [after 5 October 1891].

116. "A Bystander's Notes," 29 July 1893, 12.

117. AWTP #7197, Louis A. Martinet to AWT, 4 August 1893.

118. AWTP #6377, Louis A. Martinet to AWT, 4 July 1892, partially reprinted in Olsen, *Thin Disguise*, 65.

119. AWTP #5813, AWT to [Louis A. Martinet], n.d. [after 5 October 1891]; AWTP #7438, AWT to Louis A. Martinet, 31 October 1893; "A Bystander's Notes," 12 March 1892, 4.

120. AWTP #7614, NCRA file, AWT to F. J. Loudin, n.d. [before 27 November 1893].

121. "A Bystander's Notes," 8 April 1893, 4; AWTP #7513, Charles W. Chesnutt to AWT, 21 November 1893, reprinted in C. Chesnutt, *"To Be an Author,"* 79–80. Chesnutt is replying to Tourgée's letter of 20 November 1893, Chesnutt Papers.

122. AWTP #7527, AWT to Charles W. Chesnutt, 23 November 1893.

123. AWTP #7537, Charles W. Chesnutt to AWT, 27 November 1893, reprinted in C. Chesnutt, *"To Be an Author,"* 81–82. Editors McElrath and Leitz note that in light of this letter, "it appears that Chesnutt did not visit Mayville in November, despite Tourgée's 23 November invitation to do so" (80n5). In *Color-Blind Justice*, however, Elliott contends that Chesnutt did travel to Mayville "to discuss the position with Tourgée in person" (258).

124. AWTP #7614, F. J. Loudin to AWT, 27 November 1893. According to Olsen, House Speaker Thomas B. Reed of Maine, the most prominent political backer of the NCRA, had suffered equally "heavy depression losses," making it impossible for him to fulfill a pledge to support the *National Citizen*; see *Carpetbagger's Crusade*, 323.

125. AWTP #7552, AWT to T. Thomas Fortune, n.d. [14 November 1893]. Tourgée wisely deleted the sentence in which he confessed that he had "once had a certain distrust of" Fortune but had since changed his mind—a confession he must have realized Fortune would find offensive.

126. AWTP #7499, T. Thomas Fortune to AWT, 16 November 1893. Fortune indicates that he is replying to Tourgée's "important favor of the 14th instant . . . received today."

127. AWTP #7510, AWT to T. Thomas Fortune, 20 November 1893; AWTP #7433, AWT to Bishop Henry McNeal Turner, n.d. Tourgée mentions the *National Era* in his letter to Fortune but elaborates on why he regards it as a model in his letter to Turner. Fortune reprinted Tourgée's letter to Turner in the *New York Age*, as he informs Tourgée in his letter of 23 November 1893, AWTP #7502.

128. AWTP #7510, AWT to T. Thomas Fortune, 20 November 1893. Tourgée's biographers both attribute his refusal to lingering distrust of Fortune; see Olsen, *Carpetbagger's Crusade*, 322, and Elliott, *Color-Blind Justice*, 277. Yet the avowal Tourgée crossed out in the draft of his 14 November letter to Fortune—"I once had a certain distrust of you, but your course for the past few years has not only removed it, but given me the firmest confidence in your high purpose and sincere conviction"—strikes me as conclusively disproving this explanation. Had Tourgée not excised the sentence, one might interpret it as an attempt to flatter Fortune; because he did excise it, we can safely read it as a sincere expression of his revised estimate of Fortune.

129. *Journals of Charles W. Chesnutt*, 139–40 (entry of 29 May 1880).

130. AWTP #7510, AWT to T. Thomas Fortune, 20 November 1893. Elliott comments: "Thus, somewhat paradoxically, Tourgée seemed to conclude that only with a white man as general editor could his publication truly be viewed as 'a journal of citizenship without regard to color'"; see *Color-Blind Justice*, 277.

131. AWTP #7510, AWT to T. Thomas Fortune, 20 November 1893; AWTP #7522, T. Thomas Fortune to AWT, 23 November 1893.

132. Olsen, *Carpetbagger's Crusade*, 322.

133. Elliott, *Color-Blind Justice*, 277.

134. On the financial difficulties Fortune was facing and the failure of either the Afro-American League or the Afro-American Council to gain a mass following among black Northerners, see Thornbrough, "National Afro-American League," 500–501, 505; S. Alexander, *Army of Lions*, 63–65, 136–37, 241; Carle, *Defining the Struggle*, 69–71, 120–21; and Moglen's introduction to his reprint edition of Fortune's *Black and White*, xi–xiii.

135. Hahn, *Nation under Our Feet*, 317–63, extensively documents and analyzes the surge of interest in emigration.

136. AWTP #7438, AWT to Louis A. Martinet, 31 October 1893, partially reprinted in Elliott and Smith, *Undaunted Radical*, 282–88, quotations on 284–85.

137. AWTP #7433, AWT to Bishop [Henry McNeal] Turner, 30 October 1893. It is striking that Turner was the first to whom Tourgée wrote about his intention to found the *National Citizen*, even before Martinet. For further information on Turner and emigration, see Redkey, "Bishop Turner's African Dream."

138. AWTP #7454, H[enry] M[cNeal] Turner to AWT, 2 November 1893.

139. AWTP #7471, AWT to Rev. Bishop [Henry McNeal] Turner, 7 November 1893.

140. AWTP #7464, J. C. Embry, publisher of the *Christian Recorder*, to AWT, 6 November 1893; AWTP #7502, T. Thomas Fortune to AWT, 17 November 1893. Embry at first proposed giving the letter wider circulation by having it published in the *Philadelphia Sunday Press*, an idea Tourgée rejected because he thought it safer for progressives to debate matters among themselves rather than to air their disagreements before the general public. See also AWTP #7523, C. R. Harris to AWT, 23 November 1893, an enthusiastic response by a subscriber to the *Christian Recorder*.

141. AWTP #7547, J. C. Hartzell to AWT, 29 November 1893.

142. I am indebted to conversations with Mark Elliott for drawing my attention to Emma's diary. See *Color-Blind Justice*, 272–73, where he details how "conflict with Emma ate away at Albion's commitment to the NCRA." For pertinent entries in Emma's 1893 diary, see AWTP #9906, 7, 14, 15, 28 July; 10 and 31 August; 1 September; 1, 4, and 7 November; and 25 December. The fullest account of the *Continent* debacle and its financial impact on the Tourgées can be found in AWTP #9772, EKT to Adelbert Moot, 17 June 1905, written to the family's lawyer after Albion's death; this letter is apparently misnumbered #9771 in the Chautauqua County Historical Society's digitalized version.

143. AWTP #7537, Charles W. Chesnutt to AWT, 27 November 1893, reprinted in C. Chesnutt, *"To Be an Author,"* 81–82; AWTP #7501, William H. Busbey to Mrs. A. W. Tourgee, 17 November 1893. Emma had apparently written to ask Busbey what the chances were that the "Bystander" column might be restored.

144. AWTP #9906, EKT diary, 5 and 7 April 1894; AWTP #8235, AWT to "Gentlemen" [McGerald & Son], n.d. [August 1894]; Elliott, *Color-Blind Justice*, 277. Tourgée explains the circumstances in a "Bystander" column written for the inaugural issue of the *Basis*, 20 March 1895, 9: "Before arrangements could be completed for its [the *National Citizen*'s] publication, the Bystander was prostrated with what was supposed to be a fatal illness. . . . The Bystander . . . returned the money subscribed for stock, notified those who had subscribed for the journal that it would not be published, folded his arms and prepared for the end. There were months of doubt, but in the end health came instead of death."

145. Elliott, *Color-Blind Justice*, 294–95.

146. For evidence of African American efforts to promote the *Basis*, see AWTP #8677, Louis A. Martinet to AWT, 24 July 1895; AWTP #8826, Charles W. Chesnutt to AWT, 3 September 1895; AWTP #8444, William H. Anderson to AWT, 27 March 1895; AWTP #8543, 8581, Thomas R. Griffin to AWT, 6 and 30 June 1895; untitled editorial, *Cleveland Gazette*, 2 March 1895, 2; "The Basis! The Basis!," *Cleveland Gazette*, 19 October 1895, 2; AWTP #9194, Harry C. Smith to AWT, 3 March 1896; untitled editorial, *Cleveland Gazette*, 7 March 1896, 2; "It Passed. Ohio's Anti-Lynching Bill Passes the Senate"; and AWTP #8871, John Q. Johnson to AWT, n.d. [soon after 29 June 1895]. Quotations are from "For Colored Writers," *Basis*, 20 March 1895, 30, repeated in successive issues.

147. Letter from "A Colored Farmer," *Basis*, 25 May 1895, 233.

148. "The Federation of Women's Clubs," ibid., 20 April 1895, 10; "'A Meeting of Negresses,'" ibid., 10 August 1895, 555; "The Color Line in Boston" and "Race Prejudice in Connecticut," ibid., March 1896, 191–92.

149. The same lack of funds severely hampered the work of the Afro-American League, the Afro-American Council, and other race organizations that paved the way for the NAACP; see S. Alexander, *Army of Lions*, 136–38, 141, 164–65, 167, 172; and Carle, *Defining the Struggle*, 122–25.

150. For accounts of these racial conflicts, see Wells, *Crusade for Justice*, chap. 37; Giddings, *Ida*, 473–80; Lewis, *W. E. B. Du Bois*, chap. 14; and Kellogg, *NAACP*, 1:21–23.

Chapter Five

1. Tourgée, *Fool's Errand*, 206.

2. Brown, *Clotel*, 98–99.

3. Christopher Waldrep contests the assumption, accepted by most historians, that "whites only rarely lynched slaves" and argues that further historical research would uncover many more examples of slave lynchings; see Waldrep, *Lynching in America*, 3, 68. Some of the examples he provides stretch the definition of lynching, however. Even if one accepts his claim that the beating to death of a slave by an overseer and two white accomplices should be defined as a lynching, one must concede that mob murders of African Americans skyrocketed after emancipation, involving far greater numbers of white perpetrators and black victims.

4. "A Bystander's Notes," 12 March 1892, 4.

5. Tourgée, *Fool's Errand*, 202.

6. For Tourgée's explanation of Outlaw's lynching, see AWTP #1366, "Ku Klux War in North Carolina," August 1870, 13 (draft of article submitted to the abolitionist weekly *National Standard* but rejected because too long).

7. "A Bystander's Notes," 12 March 1892, 4.

8. See Gerber, "Lynching and Law and Order," 48.

9. On the Ohio law, see ibid. For a more recent account that does discuss Tourgée as "one of two leading figures in the Ohio campaign," see Barton, "'Necessity of an Example': Chesnutt's *The Marrow of Tradition* & the Ohio Anti-Lynching Campaign," especially 38–41; even this article nevertheless minimizes Tourgée's role and overlooks his long-term editorializing against lynching and its possible influence on Chesnutt, as well as Tourgée's collaboration with Wells and other African American antilynching activists. For a standard history of lynching that fails to mention Tourgée, see Dray, *At the Hands of Persons Unknown*. For other relevant examples, see Williamson, *Crucible of Race*; Brundage, *Lynching in the New South*; Brundage, *Under Sentence of Death*; Pinar, *Gender of Racial Politics and Violence in America*; Rosen, *Terror in the Heart of Freedom*; and Berg, *Popular Justice*. Waldrep, *Many Faces of Judge Lynch*, discusses Tourgée's Reconstruction-era campaign against Ku Klux Klan terrorism but not his later antilynching work. Waldrep's otherwise excellent edited collection, *Lynching in*

America, includes not a single selection by Tourgée. Grant, *Anti-lynching Movement,* 33, devotes a paragraph to the NCRA, which he cites as exemplifying the "slow entry of whites into the anti-lynching reform." S. Alexander, *Army of Lions,* and Carle, *Defining the Struggle,* omit Tourgée entirely from their accounts of African American leaders' agitation against lynching and efforts to secure antilynching legislation.

10. Of Wells's many biographers, the only one to devote significant attention to her relationship with Tourgée is Giddings, *Ida.* For other recent studies that discuss the alliance between Wells and Tourgée, see Karcher, "White 'Bystander' and the Black Journalist 'Abroad'"; Karcher, "Ida B. Wells and Her Allies against Lynching"; and Elliott, *Color-Blind Justice,* 238–42. Elliott also updates Gerber's article on the Ohio antilynching law and provides a fresh perspective on the law's efficacy; see 237–38.

11. "A Bystander's Notes," 15 December 1888, 4, partially reprinted in Elliott and Smith, *Undaunted Radical,* 237, 239.

12. Ibid., 23 March 1889, 4. Tourgée was responding to those who, like Ohio governor Joseph B. Foraker, defended the White Caps as "men of the highest respectability." See ibid., 19 January 1889, 4.

13. "A Bystander's Notes. The Policy of the Republican Party in Congress," 1 December 1894, 12–13.

14. Goldsby, *Spectacular Secret,* 62, quoting an entry of 4 September 1886 in Wells's *Memphis Diary,* 102. Goldsby is the first to have read this diary entry as "the closest transcription we have of [Wells's] no longer extant article."

15. Royster, *Southern Horrors and Other Writings,* 70.

16. "White-Caps Warn Us." The integration battle is described in "Fighting for Rights in Felicity."

17. *Selected Writings of John Edward Bruce,* 31–32.

18. Fortune's editorial in the *New York Freeman* and the article by "B" in the *Indianapolis Freeman* are reprinted in Waldrep, *Lynching in America,* 116–19. For Edward E. Cooper's criticisms of Tourgée in the *Indianapolis Freeman,* see chap. 4, n. 74, in the present book.

19. Quotations are from "A Bystander's Notes," 23 March 1889, 4; 7 September 1889, 4; and 28 December 1889, 4.

20. Ibid., 7 September 1889, 4.

21. See "A Bystander's Notes: Lynching as a Fad," 24 November 1894, 12–13: "It is now four years since the Bystander began, in the columns of THE INTER OCEAN, a systematic crusade against this new form of barbarism."

22. Editorials and articles about lynching, untitled except where indicated, appeared in the *Cleveland Gazette* on the following dates: 20 April 1889, 2; 11 May 1889, 1; 18 May 1889, 3; 22 June 1889, 2; "An Infernal Outrage," 12 October 1889, 2; 18 January 1890, 2; and 25 January 1890, 2, 4. Smith also reprinted Senator Chandler's letter to the *Tribune* and hailed him as "one of our best friends"; see "Barnwell. Detailed List of the Suffering Survivors at the Scene of the Tragedy. That Terrible Massacre in Which Eight Innocent Men Lost Their Lives. Senator Chandler Tells of the Terror and Despair of the Afro-Americans and the Whites' Brutal Indifference."

23. Untitled editorial, *Cleveland Gazette*, 20 April 1889, 2. For parallels, see Royster, *Southern Horrors and Other Writings*, 57, where Wells quoted the "Bystander" article of 1 October 1892 in which Tourgée expounded on the lynching of Edward Coy. See also Alexander Manly, "Mrs. Fellows's Speech."

24. Untitled editorial, *Cleveland Gazette* 22 June 1889, 2.

25. "'Iola' Wells. An Interesting Biographical Sketch—A Forcible Writer."

26. For the most complete discussion of Wells's apprentice journalism, see Giddings, *Ida*, 133–34, 143–44, 149–210. See also two earlier biographies: McMurry, *To Keep the Waters Troubled*; and Schechter, *Ida B. Wells-Barnett and American Reform*.

27. "A Bystander's Notes," 15 August 1891, 4.

28. Ibid., 5 September 1891, 4; quotations in the following paragraph are also drawn from this article. The postcard photo and message on the back are reproduced in chapter 4, "Lynch Law," of Wells, *The Reason Why the Colored American Is Not in the World's Columbian Exposition*, collected in the volume *Selected Works of Ida B. Wells-Barnett*, compiled by Trudier Harris, 88–89; and in chapter 5, "Lynched for Anything or Nothing," of Wells, *A Red Record*, also found in Harris's compiled volume, 198–99.

29. "A Bystander's Notes," 5 September 1891, 4.

30. Ibid., 26 September 1891, 4.

31. Ibid., 5 December 1891, 4.

32. The figure 241 comes from the *Chicago Tribune*'s table of lynchings, on which Wells relied. See "Lynching Record" in Royster, *Southern Horrors and Other Writings*, 206.

33. "A Bystander's Notes," 12 March 1892, 4. Quotations in the next few paragraphs are from this article.

34. Jacquelyn Dowd Hall originated this phrase in *Revolt against Chivalry*, xx; since then it has been quoted by many others.

35. See S. Alexander, *Army of Lions*, 136–37, 164–65.

36. "A Bystander's Notes," 19 March 1892, 4.

37. See, for example, ibid., 7 September and 28 December 1889, 4.

38. "Those Memphis Murders."

39. "The Government Must Act." According to Giddings, "The dailies, especially the *Appeal-Avalanche* and the *Memphis Commercial*, wrote up the murders in such harrowing detail that it was clear the reporters had been called in advance to witness the lynching"; see *Ida*, 182–83. Wells makes the same charge less explicitly in *Crusade for Justice*, 50.

40. Wells, *Crusade for Justice*, 50–51, 64.

41. Royster, *Southern Horrors and Other Writings*, 52; quotations in the rest of the paragraph are from the same page. No numbers of the *Free Speech* survive, and *Southern Horrors* and *Crusade for Justice* provide the only extant texts of Wells's editorial.

42. AWTP #6374, Ida B. Wells to AWT, 2 July 1892.

43. "A Bystander's Notes," 25 June 1892, 4–5.

44. See Smith's untitled editorial, *Cleveland Gazette*, 20 April 1889, 2, quoted earlier.

45. Royster, *Southern Horrors and Other Writings*, 53–54. Quotes from the next paragraph are also from this source, p. 55. Compare "A Bystander's Notes," 5 September 1891, 4, quoted earlier.

46. Royster, *Southern Horrors and Other Writings*, 57. Wells gives 1 October as the date of Tourgée's article, a discrepancy that may arise from citing the weekly rather than the daily *Inter Ocean*. See "A Bystander's Notes," 24 September 1892, 4.

47. Mrs. H. Davis to AWT, 16 March 1892, Benjamin Harrison Papers.

48. AWT to Benjamin Harrison, 28 March 1892, ibid.

49. Mrs. H. Davis to President B. Harrison, 17 March 1892, ibid.

50. Benjamin Harrison to Mrs. H. Davis, 1 April 1892, ibid.

51. AWT to Benjamin Harrison, 12 April 1892, ibid.

52. AWTP #6170, Mrs. H. Davis to AWT, 5 April 1892.

53. "A Bystander's Notes," 23 April 1892, 4.

54. Ibid., 30 April 1892, 4.

55. Ibid., 17 September 1892, 4.

56. Smith reprinted Tourgée's article of 17 September in full under the headlines "Judge Tourgee Treats Two Branches of a Subject Touched upon by the President's Letter of Acceptance. The Most Momentous Question with Which the American Republic Has to Deal. The Afro-American's Terrible Situation at the South— Robbed, Outraged, Mobbed, Murdered and Denied Citizen Rights and Protection." Impey provided a partial reprint; see "A By-stander's Notes" in *Anti-Caste* 5 (October 1892): 1–2. Her version omitted the section relating to Harrison's acceptance speech (too parochial for the British public) and reorganized the remaining sections, so that the article ended with the paragraph blaming the government's failure to act on a lack of political will. Impey used an equals sign in place of a hyphen on the front page of every number of *Anti-Caste*.

57. See, for example, Blackett, *Building an Antislavery Wall*; and Peterson, *"Doers of the Word,"* 137–45.

58. AWTP #4785, Catherine Impey to AWT, 16 June 1890; *Anti-Caste. Devoted to the Interests of Coloured Races* 1 (March 1888): 1. This inaugural number also featured a reprint of Fortune's prospectus for "The Proposed Afro-American League," originally published in his newspaper the *New York Freeman* (4 June 1887), and a "List of Books, by Popular American Authors, Illustrating the Condition of the Freedmen since the War of the Union"; *Bricks Without Straw* and *A Fool's Errand* headed the list. In her January 1893 "Editor's Address to the Friends of Anti-Caste," 5, Impey cites her "intimate acquaintance with leading coloured Americans" as a prime strength of the magazine. For more information about Impey, see Ware, *Beyond the Pale*, 173–75, 184–96; and Bressey, *Empire, Race, and the Politics of Anti-Caste*.

59. AWTP #6415, Catherine Impey to AWT, 19 July 1892.

60. "A Bystander's Notes," 24 September 1892, 4.

61. "America Re-visited," 3. The phrase "horrors of Negro life in the South," below, is also from this article.

62. AWTP #6700, Catherine Impey to AWT, 3 January–2 March 1893.

63. "America Re-visited."

64. Wells, *Crusade for Justice*, 82.

65. AWTP #6583, Ida B. Wells to EKT, 10 February 1893.

66. The phrase "terrible race war" is from "A Bystander's Notes," 24 September 1892, 4; Impey reprinted it in small capitals in the preface to her extracts from "A Bystander's Notes," 8 October 1892, 4, which she retitled "Outbreak of Race Persecution in the United States." Quotations in the rest of the paragraph are from Caldwell's article, as reproduced by Tourgée in "A Bystander's Notes," 8 October 1892, 4, and by Impey in *Anti-Caste*, November 1893, 5–7.

67. "A Bystander's Notes," 8 October 1892, 4; "Outbreak of Race Persecution in the United States," *Anti-Caste*, November 1892, 5–7. I have quoted only those passages of the article reprinted in *Anti-Caste*.

68. "A Lynching Scene in Alabama"; "Our Picture."

69. Wells, *Crusade for Justice*, 86.

70. Wells, *Crusade for Justice*, 96, 99, quoting a press report and a letter to the editor from the *Birmingham Daily Post*.

71. Gilroy, *Black Atlantic*, 48, 186. For a fuller discussion of Wells's deployment of "insider-outsider duality" as a rhetorical strategy, see Karcher, "Ida B. Wells and Her Allies against Lynching," 141–45.

72. Wells, *Crusade for Justice*, 99–101, quoting her own letter to the editor of the *Birmingham Daily Post*. This letter is particularly important because it allows us to hear Wells's own voice, unlike the news reports she quotes, which merely paraphrase or summarize her lectures.

73. Wells, *Crusade for Justice*, 100–101.

74. Ibid., 95, 96, 128.

75. AWTP #7069, Catherine Impey to AWT and EKT, 24 June 1893.

76. Wells, *Crusade for Justice*, 128.

77. Untitled editorial, *Cleveland Gazette*, 3 June 1893, 2. Although one would think that Wells must have at least kept the *New York Age* abreast of her reception in British cities, the disappearance of the *Age*'s files for the years 1892 to 1900 makes it impossible to verify such a surmise, and the lack of reprints from the *Age* about Wells in other African American newspapers may indicate a paucity of material sent from England. Other than announcements of her departure for England, I found no articles about Wells's British lectures in the *Detroit Plaindealer*, and only two one-sentence references to them in the *Indianapolis Freeman*, the first under the Woman's World column, 3 June 1893, 7, the second under the "Race Gleanings" column, 10 June 1893, 6. The latter reports: "Miss Ida B. Wells, the modern Joan of the race, is meeting with unqualified success in her lectures in England and Scotland."

78. Giddings, *Ida*, 268, 690n43, cites the *Memphis Appeal-Avalanche*, 23 April 1893, but I could find no article about Wells in the *Appeal-Avalanche* of that date.

79. "Our Civilization's Shame."

80. "A Bystander's Notes," 11 February 1893, 4.

81. "Whew!!! Judge Tourgee All but Skins President Harrison Alive for Appointing a Southern Democrat Associate Justice of the United States Supreme Court Almost at the Very Time Southern 'Chivalry' Was Torturing to Death a Texas Afro-American."

82. "A Bystander's Notes," 11 February 1893, 4; quotations in the rest of this paragraph are from this article. For Tourgée's prediction, see ibid., 12 March 1892, 4, on the lynching of Edward Coy.

83. Preface to "Whew!!!" and untitled editorial note, *Cleveland Gazette*, 18 February 1893, 1, 2.

84. AWTP #6616, F. J. Loudin to AWT, 16 February 1893.

85. "Indorses a Good Idea. Now Let There Be Action and Less Talk—Mr. Loudin Sounds the Key-Note"; "Mr. Loudin's Open Letter." Quotations are from the latter. See also "The Pamphlet Idea," where Smith again asserts that he had made a similar suggestion "many months ago."

86. AWTP #6616, F. J. Loudin to AWT, 16 February 1893.

87. AWTP #6740, F. J. Loudin to AWT, 13 March 1893. Tourgée's letter has been lost, but its content can be inferred from Loudin's reply to it.

88. AWTP #6810, AWT to F. J. Loudin, n.d. [after 13 March 1893].

89. "Our World's Fair Effort. Every Afro-American Should Contribute Something— Amount Already Subscribed"; "Our World's Fair Representation"; "The Pamphlet Idea."

90. AWTP #7093, Ida B. Wells to AWT, 1 July 1893.

91. Ibid.

92. "Miss Ida B. Wells Informs Our Readers as to the Condition of the World's Fair Pamphlet Movement. What the Pamphlet Will Be—The Amount of Cash in Hand and Subscribed—Ohio Afro-Americans Should Do Their Duty at Once and Forward Something to Aid the Movement."

93. See "The Pamphlet Idea" on the *Freeman's* opposition; untitled editorial, *Cleveland Gazette*, 8 July 1893, 2, on Fortune's failure to endorse the project; and "Miss Ida B. Wells Informs Our Readers" on Loudin's promise to send his contribution "soon."

94. Untitled editorial, *Cleveland Gazette*, 23 September 1893, 2.

95. AWTP #8530, Ida B. Wells to EKT, 19 May 1895. For more extensive analysis of this letter, see chapter 1 and Karcher, "White 'Bystander' and the Black Journalist 'Abroad,'" 107–9.

96. Quotations are from "A Bystander's Notes: A Typical Compromise," 22 July 1893, 12. In *Reason Why*, Wells similarly wrote: "Confident of his innocence, Miller remained cool while hundreds of drunken, heavily armed men raged about him" (87).

97. Wells, *Reason Why*, 90.

98. "A Bystander's Notes: A Typical Compromise," 22 July 1893, 12. For the article in which Tourgée previously recommended such a law, see "A Bystander's Notes," 19 March 1892, 4.

99. Untitled editorial, *Cleveland Gazette*, 23 September 1893, 2.

100. "Now a Law. The 'Smith' Bill Amending the State Civil Rights Law, Which Passed the House Last Week, Is Passed in the Senate This Week.... That West Union

Lynching"; "Bad Candy ... The West Union Lynching and How Gov. McKinley Feels and Talks."

101. Tourgée, "That Lynching. Judge Tourgee Writes Gov. McKinley and the Editor of 'The Gazette,' and Suggests That Ohio Take the Lead in a Crusade against Such Crime. The Judge's Suggestions Relative to a Law to Stop Lynching, Etc.—The Letter of Prime Interest to All Afro-Americans."

102. Ibid., reprinted in Elliott and Smith, *Undaunted Radical*, 289–90.

103. "Lynch Bills. The Two Cuyahoga County, Ohio, Afro-American Representatives Introduced. Judge Albion W. Tourgee, the Race's Great and Good Friend, Passes upon Them. ..."; the phrase "fatal negligence" is from Tourgée's letter to McKinley, in Elliott and Smith, *Undaunted Radical*, 294.

104. See, for example, "Why No Lynch Law"; untitled editorial, *Cleveland Gazette*, 24 November 1894, 2; and "Willie's Wail."

105. "A Bystander's Notes: The Law and the Mob," 19 May 1894, 12–13.

106. In his first letter to Tourgée, Barnett refers him to "Mr Nixon and Mr Kohlsaat [then co-owner] of the Inter-Ocean" for testimony as to his "standing" in Chicago; see AWTP #5748, Ferdinand L. Barnett to AWT, 12 September 1891. Nixon's openness to hiring Wells is consistent with his "reputation for extreme friendliness toward the colored race"; see AWTP #7501, William H. Busbey to EKT, 17 November 1893. Unlike Tourgée, moreover, Wells did not criticize the Republican Party.

107. Wells, *Crusade for Justice*, 125. Wells probably chose the term "regular paid correspondent" to differentiate herself from African Americans who were already publishing in the white press, some of whom are mentioned by Penn in *Afro-American Press and Its Editors*, 375, 516–17.

108. "Ida B. Wells Abroad," *Chicago Daily Inter Ocean*, 2 April 1894, 12; 23 April 1894, 10; and 19 May 1894, 16. In *Manliness and Civilization*, Gail Bederman further explicates Wells's strategy: "Wells represented herself and her mission as modeling African Americans' civilized refinement, in marked contrast to white Americans' barbarism"; in describing the "massive support she received from the most prominent, civilized British dignitaries," Wells used "British Anglo-Saxons to pressure American Anglo-Saxons" (62–63).

109. Wells, *Crusade for Justice*, 137–38; original "Ida B. Wells Abroad. Speaking in Liverpool against Lynchers of Negroes. British Sentiment. How the Chicago of England Learned a Lesson. A Photograph Sent Out by Lynchers Brought Up in Evidence against Them," *Chicago Daily Inter Ocean*, 9 April 1894, 8.

110. Wells, *Crusade for Justice*, 135; original "Ida B. Wells Abroad. Speaking in Liverpool against Lynchers of Negroes." For comparable statements by Wells's black abolitionist predecessors in England, see Blackett, *Building an Antislavery Wall*, 40–41.

111. Wells, *Crusade for Justice*, 131, 151–52, 154–55; originals "Ida B. Wells Abroad. The Nemesis of Southern Lynchers Again in England," *Chicago Daily Inter Ocean*, 2 April 1894, 12; "Ida B. Wells Abroad. The Bishop of Manchester on American Lynching. Its Horrible Cruelties. England Sympathizes with the African Race. Attitude of Moody and Miss Willard to the Negroes. ...," *Chicago Daily Inter Ocean*,

23 April 1894, 10; and "Ida B. Wells Abroad. Lectures in Bristol, England, on American Lynch Law. Audiences Are Shocked. . . . Cordial Receptions from Churches of All Denominations—Horrified at Cruelties Perpetrated," *Chicago Daily Inter Ocean*, 19 May 1894, 16. Compare Wells's statement about the "silence" of American churches to Tourgée's in his "Bystander" article of 12 March 1892, quoted and paraphrased earlier: "The press, pulpits, and people of the South—the wealth, intelligence, and white Christianity of the South—have been silent. . . . The churches of the North are silent."

112. Wells, *Crusade for Justice*, 146; original "Ida B. Wells Abroad. The Bishop of Manchester on American Lynching."

113. Wells, *Crusade for Justice*, 151, 156; originals "Ida B. Wells Abroad. The Bishop of Manchester on American Lynching" and "Ida B. Wells Abroad. Lectures in Bristol."

114. *New York Independent*, untitled editorial notes, 28 June 1894, 828; and 12 July 1894, 897. The *Independent* pointedly took issue with the *Congregationalist*, quoted below.

115. *Congregationalist*, 5 July 1894, 9.

116. *New York Sun*, reprinted in *Literary Digest*, 11 August 1894.

117. H. F., "Church Scorned by Wales"; "British Anti-Lynchers." Reactions to Wells in the white U.S. press were not uniformly negative, however. The *Literary Digest* of 11 August 1894 also includes two favorable comments on Wells by Republican newspapers, the *Advertiser* of New York City and the *Chronicle* of Rochester.

118. *Memphis Daily Commercial*, 26 May 1894, 4–5, partially quoted in Giddings, *Ida*, 304–5. The editorial "The Ida B. Wells Case" appears on p. 4 and the article "Career of Ida B. Wells. The Record of This Notorious Courtesan. A Few Plain Facts Which Will No Doubt Open the Eyes of the People of England, Where She Is 'Lecturing' and Lying about Memphis" appears on p. 5. The *Daily Commercial* for this period is not available on microfilm or online but only in bound volumes.

119. Wells, *Crusade for Justice*, 181–83, 187; original "Ida B. Wells Abroad. Her Reply to Governor Northen and Others. The Lynching Record. Effect in England of Abuse by Memphis Papers. The English Papers and People Resent the Attack on a Woman," *Chicago Daily Inter Ocean*, 7 July 1894, 13.

120. "Tillman and Miss Wells."

121. Untitled editorial, *Cleveland Gazette*, 28 July 1894, 2; "Miss Ida B. Wells," *Cleveland Gazette*, 4 August 1894, 1. The 4 August number also praised Wells in two untitled editorials on p. 2. For more articles in the *Gazette* about Wells, see "The English Speak," "A Negro Adventuress," and untitled editorial, 16 June 1894, 1, 2; "Ida B. Wells Writes of Her Wonderful Success in England" and untitled editorials, 30 June 1894, 1, 2; and "Ida B. Wells" and untitled editorials, 14 July 1894, 1–2.

122. Untitled editorial, *Cleveland Gazette*, 4 August 1894, 2.

123. Ibid., 18 August 1894, 2.

124. "A Bystander's Notes: In the Glass of English Opinion," 16 June 1894, 12–13.

125. [Harris], "Refugee from His Race."

126. "A Bystander's Notes. Christian Thought and the Inherent Rights of Colored Citizens," 28 July 1894, 12–13. For Wells's statistics on the proportion of lynching

victims charged with rape, see her chapter "Lynch Law" in *The Reason Why*, found in Trudier Harris's compiled volume *Selected Works of Ida B. Wells-Barnett*, 76. Though Wells repeats these statistics in other works, Tourgée most likely saw it in his copy of *The Reason Why*.

127. "A Bystander's Notes. Republicans and Populists in the South," 8 September 1894, 12–13. The first part of this article commented with the same dismissiveness on the recent fusion of Republicans with Populists in North Carolina. Tourgée proved wrong in discounting the significance of the two groups' fusion but right in that its ultimate outcome—a bloody coup against the victorious fusionists, accompanied by a massacre of African Americans in Wilmington, North Carolina—justified his prediction that "the Democrats . . . would not permit" a government including Republicans, much less African American Republicans, to exercise power.

128. "A Bystander's Notes. Lynching and Mob Law in the South and North," 15 September 1894, 12–13.

129. "A Bystander's Notes. Reed and the Democrats—The Louisiana Sugar Planters and Republicans," 22 September 1894, 12–13.

130. Epstein, *Politics of Domesticity*, 115–20, credits Willard with vastly increasing the membership of the WCTU and bringing conservative women into the suffrage movement by linking the issues of temperance, home protection, and suffrage. She traces the growth of the WCTU from 73,000 members with locals in forty-two states in 1883 to 168,000 members with representation in all states by the turn of the century (120).

131. Gilmore, *Gender and Jim Crow*, 46–59.

132. Royster, *Southern Horrors and Other Writings*, 140; the quotation is from *Red Record*, where Wells details her quarrel with Willard in chapter 8, "Miss Willard's Attitude." The statement defending Willard and signed by Douglass, Turner, and white abolitionist stalwarts is reprinted in the African American feminist journal *Woman's Era*, July 1895, 6, and endorsed by Josephine Silone Yates, a prominent African American feminist.

133. Willard as quoted by Wells in "Miss Willard's Attitude," 139. Willard presented her side of the dispute in the editorial "An Unwise Advocate," which reprinted the exculpatory interview Lady Somerset conducted with her, also referred to by Wells in chapter 8 of *Red Record* (see note 132, above). For a direct account of the Cleveland WCTU convention, see the *Union Signal*, which reprinted the proceedings in special numbers of 16, 17, 19, 21, and 22 November 1894, besides summarizing the highlights of the convention in the 29 November and 6 December numbers. The proceedings mentioned Wells only briefly in the 20 November number, euphemistically reporting that she "asked the assistance of the women in this convention for the suppression of lawlessness toward their race" (8). Willard's "Annual Address" indirectly acknowledged Wells's critique of the WCTU by admitting, "Much misapprehension has arisen in the last year concerning the attitude of our unions towards the colored people," and by providing an "official explanation" of the organization's racial policies (*Union Signal*, 16 November 1894, 3). The portion of Willard's speech quoted by Wells is not printed in the *Union Signal*. For a nuanced analysis of Well's dispute with Willard, see Ware, *Beyond the Pale*, 198–221.

134. Willard, "Notes from Temperance Meetings."

135. AWTP #8217, Frances E. Willard to AWT, 21 December 1894.

136. "A Bystander's Notes. Lynching as a Fad," 24 November 1894, 12–13.

137. AWTP #8202, Ida B. Wells to AWT, 27 November 1894. Though dated three days after the column appeared, Wells wrote that she had just read it. She used the word "grateful" twice and reiterated her thanks at the end of her letter for "these and all other words in behalf of justice."

138. "A Bystander's Notes. Lynching as a Fad," 24 November 1894, 12–13.

139. Untitled editorials, *Cleveland Gazette*, 27 October and 24 November 1894, 2.

140. According to Gerber, "Lynching and Law and Order," 46, the Ohio state legislature began "meeting biennially rather than yearly after the 1894 session."

141. Untitled editorial, *Cleveland Gazette*, 24 November 1894, 2.

142. "Frances, a Temporizer."

143. "Miss Wells Lectures. 'Colored' Women Who Side with Miss Willard as against Miss Wells. That Annual Address and Its Attack upon Our Anti-Lynching Champion, Miss Wells."

144. Wells, *Crusade for Justice*, 220, 222–23.

145. AWTP #8251, scrapbook of newspaper clippings, "Won't Indorse Tourgée—Leading Colored Men Regard Him as an Alarmist"; "A Bystander's Notes," 25 June 1892, 4. Tourgée reiterated this prophecy often. According to Mott, *American Journalism,* 451, the *Philadelphia Times,* founded and edited by Alexander K. McClure, "set a new example of aggressive journalism" in the city. McClure may have regarded debunking Tourgée as a form of muckraking. Washington, *Up from Slavery,* 147.

146. A Negro, "Rights of Negroes. Many of Them Lynched for Crimes They Did Not Commit. . . . Judge Tourgee's Opinions Discussed."

147. "A Bystander's Notes. Reed and the Democrats—The Louisiana Sugar Planters and Republicans," 22 September 1894, 12–13.

148. The Massachusetts Anti-Lynching League is briefly mentioned by McPherson, *Abolitionist Legacy,* 304, and by Harriet Hyman Alonso, *Growing Up Abolitionist,* 280, but I could find no further information about it.

149. The facsimile title page of *Red Record* lists no publisher except Wells. The last page invites "friends of the cause" to "lend a helping hand" in the book's distribution, directs those interested in obtaining copies to the "Central Anti-Lynching League" at 128 Clark St., Chicago, and promises that orders will be promptly filled. See Royster, *Southern Horrors and Other Writings,* 73, 157. Giddings, *Ida,* confirms that *Red Record* "failed to pay for itself" (352) and did not succeed in its goal of "reignit[ing]" Wells's "flagging" antilynching campaign (346, 348). I have searched the *Cleveland Gazette* and Tourgée's the *Basis* in vain for reviews or even brief mentions of *Red Record.*

150. Smith began to advertise the *Basis* in the *Gazette* with an untitled editorial of 2 March 1895, 2, announcing that it would debut on 10 April and would include the "Bystander" column. For further advertisements, see "The Basis! The Basis!," 19 October 1895, 2; 7 March 1896, 2; 11 April 1896, 1. See also AWTP #9194 (*Basis* correspondence file), H. C. Smith to AWT, 3 March 1896: "We make editorial mention

of 'The Basis' this week (in 'The Gazette.') I also called quite a good sized audience's attention to it, in a speech made in Cleveland, last evening." On the circulation of the *Basis*, see AWTP #9194, AWT to E. C. Fisk and Willis H. Tennant, 27 November 1895: "THE BASIS now has a bona fide paid subscription list of 1,200 copies per issue." On the circulation of the *Inter Ocean*, see Olsen, *Carpetbagger's Crusade*, 281, which in turn cites the Chicago Inter Ocean Press, *A History of the City of Chicago* (Chicago, 1900), 30, 319.

151. Untitled editorial, *Cleveland Gazette*, 19 January 1895, 2.

152. Ibid., 2 February 1895, 2.

153. Ibid., 2 March 1895, 2.

154. Ibid., 20 July 1895, 2.

155. Ibid., 17 August 1895, 2.

156. "Queer Christianity"; this editorial partially reprinted and commented on a section of Tourgée's "Bystander" column of 24 November praising Wells.

157. "Judge Tourgee on Prof. Washington."

158. Untitled editorial, *Cleveland Gazette*, 14 December 1895, 2; "'Twas Ever Thus."

159. "At the Front. Where His Own Efforts Have Placed Hon. H. C. Smith. An Orator and Writer. He Has Been Very Successful Along Both Lines. . . . Two Years in the General Assembly and on the Road to Two More," reprinted from the *Cleveland Leader*.

160. See "Civil Rights and Lynching" and "The Anti-Lynch Law."

161. "Gov. M'Kinley, the Man of the Hour"; "Massachusetts against Lynch 'Law'"; "Killing the Innocent"; "A Disgraceful Lynching"; "The Lynching Question"; "The Lynchings of 1895."

162. Gerber, "Lynching and Law and Order," 47; "Political Snaps . . . The Anti-Lynch Bill—Other Notes"; "To Stop Them. The Anti-Lynching Bill Again Introduced in the Ohio Legislature. . . ."; untitled editorial, *Cleveland Gazette*, 25 January 1896, 2. During Smith's legislative terms in Columbus, he supplied long, front-page newsletters to the *Gazette*.

163. "That True Friend. Judge Tourgee Going to Columbus to Help Pass the Anti-Lynching Bill. Representatives Stewart and Parham Doing Splendid Work— The Three Afro-American Legislators Unite— . . . The Amendments, Etc."

164. "Judge Tourgee Makes a Telling Argument for Ohio's Anti-Lynching Bill. Hundreds of Assembly Members, Citizens and Ladies, Gather to Hear Him. The Distinguished Author and Jurist, the Race's Greatest White Friend, on the Majesty of the Law." See also Smith's reminiscences in "Poor Old John, Still 'Knocking,'" where he specifies that he paid Tourgée's expenses on the trip "out of his own pocket."

165. Untitled editorial, *Cleveland Gazette*, 8 February 1896, 2.

166. Ibid., 22 February 1896, 2.

167. Ibid., 29 February 1896, 2.

168. Gerber, "Lynching and Law and Order," 47–48; "Press Comment on the Careful Consideration Given the Anti-Lynching Bill."

169. These editorials from the *Lexington (Ky.) Standard*, the *Indianapolis Freeman*, and the *Chicago Conservator* are reprinted under the title "Ohio's Anti-Lynching Bill."

See also untitled editorial, *Cleveland Gazette*, 29 February 1896, 2, reprinted on 7 and 14 March, and another untitled editorial on 21 March. African American editors' complaints about their people's apathy seem to corroborate similar complaints Tourgée made in his correspondence about the inadequate representation of Northern blacks in the NCRA (see chapter 4).

170. "Pass the Bill"; "It Ought to Pass"; "It Passed. Ohio's Anti-Lynching Bill Half Way through the Assembly."

171. Gerber, "Lynching and Law and Order," 48.

172. "It Passed. Ohio's Anti-Lynching Bill Half Way through the Assembly."

173. "It Passed. Ohio's Anti-Lynching Bill Passes the Senate."

174. "Light from Ohio," *Basis*, April 1896, 215. Tourgée discontinued the *Basis* immediately after the U.S. Supreme Court issued its adverse decision in the *Plessy* case on 18 May.

175. "Judge Tourgee Makes a Telling Argument for Ohio's Anti-Lynching Bill."

176. Wells Barnett, "Open Letter to the Chicago Daily Chronicle."

177. "A Bystander's Notes," 12 June 1897, part 2, 13.

178. "Not Guilty. 'Click' Mitchell, the Unfortunate Afro-American Lynched at Urbana, Was Clearly Innocent of the Crime Charged, and His Willingly Surrendering Himself to the Officers Goes Far toward Establishing the Fact—His Side—The Truth at Last," special report addressed to Smith as editor.

179. "Judge Tourgee Writes a Caustic Letter in Reply to an Attack"; Gerber, "Lynching and Law and Order," 48–49.

180. AWTP #10527, H. C. Smith to EKT, 12 October 1908. Smith was replying to an inquiry from Emma, prompted by a reference to the Ohio law in a letter to the editor of the *New York Tribune*, which she enclosed for Smith; see AWTP #10525, EKT to H. C. Smith, 9 October 1908.

181. Gerber, "Lynching and Law and Order," 48; Elliott, *Color-Blind Justice*, 237–38.

Chapter Six

1. AWTP #5760, Louis A. Martinet to AWT, 5 October 1891, partial reprint in Olsen, *Thin Disguise*, 55–61, quotation on 55–56. I use the word "extant" because Martinet refers to a previous letter he wrote to Tourgée, possibly one in which he requested Tourgée to serve as counsel for the committee.

2. "Protest of the American Citizens' Equal Rights Association of Louisiana against Class Legislation," reprinted in Olsen, *Thin Disguise*, 47–50. In *Color-Blind Justice*, Mark Elliott points out that the ACERA protest "foreshadowed several lines of argument that Tourgée would later develop in the *Plessy* case" (250). For the text of the "separate car bill," see http://railroads.unl.edu/documents/viewdocument (17 July 2015).

3. "The Separate Car Bill," *Crusader*, 19 July 1890, 3, Nils R. Douglas Papers, box 2; this is the only surviving complete issue of the *Crusader*.

4. AWTP #4872 and 4895, Eli C. Freeman to AWT, 4 August and 26 August 1890. Neither Tourgée's letter nor the number of the *Crusader* in which it appeared has

survived. Olsen, *Thin Disguise*, 11, and Elliott, *Color-Blind Justice*, 249–50, have pieced together the story of how Freeman contacted Tourgée for advice.

5. See Desdunes, "Forlorn Hope and Noble Despair," in which Desdunes quotes and replies to this correspondent.

6. Ibid.

7. See chap. 3 on the dialogue between Tourgée and Martinet reflected in "Bystander" articles of 15 August and 12 September 1891.

8. "A Bystander's Notes," 15 August 1891, 4.

9. AWTP #5760, Louis A. Martinet to AWT, 5 October 1891, partial reprint in Olsen, *Thin Disguise*, 56.

10. Desdunes, "To Be or Not to Be."

11. *Report of Proceedings for the Annulment of Act 111 of 1890*, 2, 8–10. On the "networks and solidarities registered in Martinet's notarial records" that underlie the list of contributors, see Scott, "Public Rights, Social Equality, and the Conceptual Roots of the *Plessy* Challenge," 797–98.

12. "A Bystander's Notes," 17 October 1891, 4. The main author of this libel was the paleontologist Nathaniel Southgate Shaler, whose pseudoscientific theories Tourgée had refuted in "A Bystander's Notes," 19 July 1890, 4.

13. Ibid., 12 September and 3 October 1891, 4; AWTP #5760, Louis A. Martinet to AWT, 5 October 1891, partial reprint in Olsen, *Thin Disguise*, 55–56. In this letter Martinet also asserted that Tourgée's public praise of the *Crusader* had increased its circulation. The quotations in the next few paragraphs are all from this letter.

14. Dean H. Keller's *Index to the Albion W. Tourgée Papers in the Chautauqua County Historical Society* lists twenty-four letters between Tourgée and Martinet, to which should be added a twenty-fifth addressed by Tourgée to an unnamed recipient identifiable as Martinet by internal evidence.

15. Kelley, *Right to Ride*, 11.

16. Elliott, *Color-Blind Justice*, 266, quotes and refutes Cheryl I. Harris, whose "influential 1993 *Harvard Law Review* article" made this charge in a footnote based only on another secondary source. Elliott's accompanying footnote cites C. Vann Woodward, Kevin Gaines, David W. Bishop, and Eric Sundquist as scholars who have voiced similar criticisms. I cite these and other scholars below, where relevant to my argument.

17. Trevigne, "World Will Move."

18. Desdunes, "To Be or Not To Be."

19. AWTP #5763, Louis A. Martinet to AWT, 11 October 1891.

20. Kelley, *Right to Ride*, 61. For an in-depth analysis of that legacy, see Scott, "Public Rights, Social Equality, and the Conceptual Roots of the *Plessy* Challenge."

21. Medley, *We as Freemen*, the most detailed study of the Citizens' Committee, describes Martinet as "labor[ing] in the trenches" to prepare the legal challenge; for his summary of Martinet's responsibilities, see 134, 139, and 152.

22. AWTP #5837, Louis A. Martinet to AWT, 7 December 1891.

23. AWTP #5877, Louis A. Martinet to AWT, 28 December 1891.

24. AWTP #5722 and 5837, Louis A. Martinet to AWT, 28 October and 7 December 1891.

25. AWTP #5768 and 5837, Louis A. Martinet to AWT, 25 October and 7 December 1891.

26. AWTP #6547 and 6998, Louis A. Martinet to AWT, 2 February and 30 May 1893.

27. On Langston, see AWTP #5768, Louis A. Martinet to AWT, 25 October 1891. For Tourgée's and Martinet's views on the race's "so-called 'leaders,'" see AWTP #6473, AWT to Louis A. Martinet, n.d. [before 7 December 1891]; and AWTP #5837, 6377, Louis A. Martinet to AWT, 7 December 1891 and 4 July 1892, partial reprint in Olsen, *Thin Disguise*, 64–65.

28. AWTP #5837, Louis A. Martinet to AWT, 7 December 1891; Elliott, *Color-Blind Justice*, 266.

29. AWTP #5788, Alexander S. Jackson to AWT, 13 November 1891.

30. AWTP #5877, Louis A. Martinet to AWT, 28 December 1891.

31. Elliott, *Color-Blind Justice*, 266. As Elliott points out, although the Reverend Jackson's remarks have been cited by historians as evidence of the black community's opposition to the strategy of challenging segregation through a near-white plaintiff, Tourgée had not yet publicly suggested this strategy when Jackson (supposedly) voiced his complaints about the Citizens' Committee.

32. AWTP #5760, Louis A. Martinet to AWT, 5 October 1891.

33. See AWTP #5837, Louis A. Martinet to AWT, 7 December 1891: "The plan is for us to put a colored passenger interstate on board & the conductor to direct him *or her, for we may have a lady*, to the Jim Crow car, and on refusal to go into it to enforce the law by legal means, that is to make the proper affidavit against the passenger, under the specific act" (italics mine).

34. Elliott, *Color-Blind Justice*, 265.

35. *Report of Proceedings for the Annulment of Act 111 of 1890*, 4.

36. "Justice Wins. The Jim Crow Car Laws Ditched and Will Remain So."

37. Lofgren, Plessy *Case*, 41.

38. AWTP #6377, Louis A. Martinet to AWT, 4 July 1892, partially reprinted in Olsen, *Thin Disguise*, 63; Medley, *We as Freemen*, 154.

39. See, for example, criticisms of this strategy by Elliott, *Color-Blind Justice*, 265; and Olsen, *Thin Disguise*, 13. AWTP #6377, Louis A. Martinet to AWT, 4 July 1892, partially reprinted in Olsen, *Thin Disguise*, 64.

40. The *Crusader* of June 1892, as quoted in Medley, *We as Freemen*, 146.

41. AWTP #5915, James C. Walker to AWT, 2 January 1892.

42. AWTP #6086, James C. Walker to AWT, 6 March 1892.

43. AWTP #6058, James C. Walker to AWT, 25 February 1892.

44. AWTP #6101, AWT to James C. Walker, n.d. [after 6 March 1862].

45. See Medley, *We as Freemen*, 159: "Meanwhile, the *Times Democrat* continued to clamor for segregation at every level of society, as newspapers in New Orleans openly encouraged and applauded vigilantism."

46. AWTP #6058, James C. Walker to AWT, 25 February 1892.

47. AWTP #6073, AWT to James C. Walker, 1 March 1892.

48. Ibid.; AWTP #6096, James C. Walker to AWT, 8 March 1892; AWTP #6104, AWT to James C. Walker, 12 March 1892.

49. Lofgren, Plessy *Case*, 41.

50. Ibid., 43.

51. Elliott, *Color-Blind Justice*, 117, 269; Lofgren, Plessy *Case*, 148–49.

52. AWTP #7197, Louis A. Martinet to AWT, 4 August 1893.

53. In AWTP #7428, James A. Walker to AWT, 27 October 1893, Walker informed Tourgée that Judge Ferguson, with whom he was on friendly terms, had "had a private interview with" Louisiana's attorney general "in the hope of prevailing upon him to join in our application to advance the Plessy case in the Supreme Court," but that "nothing has come of it so far."

54. AWTP #7438, AWT to Louis A. Martinet, 31 October 1893, partially reprinted in Olsen, *Thin Disguise*, 78. B. Thomas, *Plessy v. Ferguson: A Brief History with Documents*, 179–85, provides helpful biographical sketches of the justices who decided the case. Commenting on Tourgée's letter, Thomas writes, "It is not possible to know with certainty which justices Tourgée aligned with which positions. The justice who was rethinking his ruling on the *Civil Rights Cases* was most likely Samuel Blatchford, who left the Court in 1893. . . . One can only guess who Tourgée thought could be won over by argument. . . . He might . . . have had in mind two new Republicans: George Shiras Jr. and Henry Billings Brown, who eventually wrote the majority opinion but years later somewhat reconsidered his position. . . . Another possibility," adds Thomas, "is David Josiah Brewer, who had not been on the Court for the *Civil Rights Cases* and who came from a missionary family with a strong antislavery tradition," but Brewer did not participate in oral arguments and thus did not vote. Meanwhile, notes Thomas, the two justices who joined the Court between the date of Tourgée's letter and the hearing, both Democrats appointed by Grover Cleveland, were Edward Douglass White of Louisiana, reputedly a former member of the Ku Klux Klan, and Rufus Wheeler Peckham, a wealthy corporate lawyer.

55. AWTP #7438, AWT to Louis A. Martinet, 31 October 1893, partially reprinted in Olsen, *Thin Disguise*, 78–79.

56. AWTP #9014, Louis A. Martinet to AWT, 4 March 1896; see also his telegram to the same effect, AWTP #8953, Louis A. Martinet to AWT, 29 January 1896.

57. Elliott, *Color-Blind Justice*, 278. See also B. Thomas, *Plessy v. Ferguson: A Brief History with Documents*, 28: "Although Washington himself was not in favor of equal-but-separate laws, his metaphor helped to confirm arguments for segregation." For Washington's speech, see *Up from Slavery* in *Three Negro Classics*, quotation on 148.

58. AWTP #9071, Samuel F. Phillips to AWT, 1 April 1896. Tourgée's letter to the Supreme Court clerk is quoted in Elliott, *Color-Blind Justice*, 280–81; also partially quoted in Lofgren, Plessy *Case*, 151. Although Tourgée refers to three other attorneys who planned to join him in oral arguments, only Walker and Martinet are listed by the Citizens' Committee.

59. AWTP #9081, James H. McKenney to AWT, 7 April 1896; Lofgren, Plessy *Case*, 151; Elliott, *Color-Blind Justice*, 280.

60. See AWTP #8936, 8969, 9071, Samuel F. Phillips to AWT, 20 January, 4 February, and 1 April 1896.

61. AWTP #9091, James C. Walker to AWT, 9 April 1896; Medley, *We as Freemen*, 214.

62. AWTP #9014, Louis A. Martinet to AWT, 4 March 1896. An entry for 6 April 1896 in Emma's diary indicates: "Wrote to Walker & Martinet about case to be argued the 13"; see AWTP #9906, diary for 1895–98. For Martinet's telegram of congratulations on learning of Tourgée's appointment as U.S. consul to Bordeaux, see AWTP #9383, 12 May 1897.

63. B. Thomas, Plessy v. Ferguson: *A Brief History with Documents*, 181–85; see also Olsen, *Thin Disguise*, 17–18. Of the four Democrats, one (Field) was nominated by Lincoln, the other three by Grover Cleveland. Of the five Republicans, one (Harlan) was nominated by Rutherford B. Hayes, one by Chester A. Arthur, and the other three by Benjamin Harrison.

64. Elliott, *Color-Blind Justice*, 281–82. Unlike Elliott, Olsen finds that "Tourgée may have erred in the degree to which he attacked earlier, related court decisions rather than concentrating upon [the] one obvious, remaining protection" the Court still recognized; yet Olsen indirectly acknowledges that opting for a narrower approach would not have helped after all, because the Court's decision "revealed its ability to circumvent even" this protection (*Thin Disguise*, 16).

65. Elliott and Smith, *Undaunted Radical*, 312. I quote this text of Tourgée's 1895 "Brief of Plaintiff in Error," rather than the one in AWTP #8250, because it is the most readily accessible. Subsequent page references to this edition of the brief will be given parenthetically in my text.

66. Curtis, *No State Shall Abridge*, 215. Especially in chapters 2, 3, and 7, readers will find a superb interpretation of the Fourteenth Amendment in historical context and a sharp analysis of its distortion by the courts soon after its framing. See also Curtis's "Reflections on Albion Tourgée's 1896 View of the Supreme Court."

67. In what follows, I offer a comprehensive close reading of Tourgée's brief that highlights his rhetorical strategies by analyzing his arguments in the order in which he presented them. None of the scholars I have consulted has adopted this approach, although I have learned much from all of them. In addition to those cited elsewhere in the notes, see Kull, *Color-Blind Constitution*; Fiss, *Troubled Beginnings of the Modern State*, chap. 12; Fireside, *Separate and Unequal*; and Hoffer, "*Plessy v. Ferguson*: The Effects of Lawyering."

68. Woodward, *American Counterpoint*, 212–33, quotation on 224. See also Olsen, *Thin Disguise*, 19–20; Elliott, *Color-Blind Justice*, 288; and Douglas, "'Most Valuable Sort of Property,'" especially 881–96.

69. Douglas, "'Most Valuable Sort of Property,'" 887, 891.

70. Woodward, "Birth of Jim Crow," 101. This influential essay is reprinted in slightly revised form in Woodward's *American Counterpoint*. See also Sundquist,

To Wake the Nations, 247: "Apparently hoping to fool the property-minded justices into recognizing an element of color that would destroy Jim Crow by rendering it chaotic, Tourgée opened himself to the irony that such an argument would in reality protect only those who could pass—the mulatto elite—and define equal protection just as restrictively and negatively as the Court already had, only locating it at a different mark on the color line." And see Kelley, *Right to Ride*, 80: "Tourgée's argument undercut the notion that African Americans, regardless of skin color, deserved protection under the banner of equitable citizenship. It undermined the claim that systematic exclusion degraded black citizenship no matter how white an individual's heritage might be." For scholars who argue, as I do, that Tourgée instead intended to highlight the "arbitrariness of racial classifications," see Elliott, *Color-Blind Justice*, 286; Douglas, "'Most Valuable Sort of Property'"; and Golub, "*Plessy* as 'Passing.'" Golub, in particular, offers "an interpretation of passing in *Plessy* as a radical critique of the legal institutions of white supremacy" rather than an attempt to "extend the benefits of whiteness to light-skinned blacks" (565).

71. See also Elliott, *Color-Blind Justice*, 288: "This claim invoked a tradition that harkened back to such mainstream antislavery novels as *Uncle Tom's Cabin* that highlighted slavery's violation of family bonds."

72. Douglas, "'Most Valuable Sort of Property,'" 917–18, cites two cases in which the "casual scrutiny" of a conductor resulted in lawsuits for defamation by white women who had been taken for "Negro."

73. I am quoting the Fourteenth Amendment itself, not Tourgée's formatting of it, which divides it into "affirmative" and "restrictive" provisions and separates it into "constituent clauses"; see Elliott and Smith, *Undaunted Radical*, 298, for Tourgée's formatted version.

74. For an interpretation by a legal historian who concurs with Tourgée, see Curtis, *No State Shall Abridge*, 2: "A reasonable reader might conclude that the Fourteenth Amendment was intended to change things so that states could no longer violate rights in the federal Bill of Rights. The reader might think this was what was intended by the language, 'No state shall make or enforce any law which shall abridge the privileges or immunities of citizens of the United States.' I believe that the reader would be right." Curtis goes on to say, however, that this "thesis is intensely controversial" and has "never . . . been accepted by the United States Supreme Court."

75. B. Thomas, *Plessy v. Ferguson: A Brief History with Documents*, 19; "The Slaughter-House Cases" article on Wikipedia.

76. Elliott, *Color-Blind Justice*, 285.

77. For a dramatic account of the Colfax massacre, see Lemann, *Redemption*, 12–22.

78. B. Thomas, *Plessy v. Ferguson: A Brief History with Documents*, 21–22.

79. Elliott, *Color-Blind Justice*, 285, quoting the Court's ruling; see also B. Thomas, *Plessy v. Ferguson: A Brief History with Documents*, 21–22. In "Legitimacy of Law in Literature," 180–81, Thomas points out that Tourgée highlights the importance of the Colfax massacre in his novel *Bricks Without Straw*, whose hero Nimbus emerges from it with his "spirit . . . broken," and that Tourgée "rebuts the Court's argument"

regarding the massacre by counterarguing in his novel *A Fool's Errand* that because white supremacist groups "attacked the authority of the nation, the nation was justified in passing legislation allowing a national response."

80. See, for example, Gaines, *Uplifting the Race*, 29.

81. As B. Thomas indicates in "Legitimacy of Law in Literature," *Pactolus Prime* provides another example of the ways in which Tourgée uses literature "to try to change the law" by using the "imaginative space" literature offers "to rehearse various legal arguments, that, when the opportunity arises, he can use in court" (172, 176).

82. Elliott, *Color-Blind Justice*, 270. Tourgée's brief certainly differed strikingly from that of his friend Phillips, which took a much more pragmatic approach. Although Phillips, too, maintained that the Separate Car Law violated the Fourteenth Amendment, he claimed that to disallow segregated transportation did not necessitate abolishing segregated schools. The state had a right to safeguard the institutions of marriage and the family by imposing separate schools for the two races, reasoned Phillips, but it did not have the right to prevent any group of people from traveling in "common carriers." Significantly, Tourgée eschewed such pragmatic concessions to popular sentiment in his own brief. Willing to countenance separate schools as long as they received equal funding, as we saw with the alternative he presented to the Blair bill, Tourgée was not willing to compromise the moral tenor of his brief by accommodating deathless constitutional principles to current prejudices. For a partial reprint of Phillips's brief, see Olsen, *Thin Disguise*, 103–8, quotations from 103. For analyses of Phillips's arguments, see Lofgren, *Plessy Case*, 164–69; B. Thomas, *Plessy v. Ferguson: A Brief History with Documents*, 30–31; and Elliott, *Color-Blind Justice*, 289.

83. "Oral Argument of A. W. Tourgée," in Elliott and Smith, *Undaunted Radical*, quotations from 329, 331, 333. I have corrected misprints in this text by referring to the original, AWTP #6472.

84. Elliott, *Color-Blind Justice*, 281.

85. "Capitol Chat."

86. AWTP #9906, EKT's diary for 1895–98, entries for 21 and 22 April and 18 May 1896, also quoted in Elliott, *Color-Blind Justice*, 291.

87. Elliott, *Color-Blind Justice*, 291; see also Lofgren, *Plessy Case*, 176: "[Brown's] . . . comments skirted any serious attempt to grapple either with Tourgée's argument based on the Thirteenth Amendment or with Justice Harlan's similar contention in dissent."

88. As many scholars have noted, Brown is here echoing Massachusetts Supreme Court chief justice Lemuel Shaw's verdict in the *Roberts* case of 1849, which legitimized school segregation and introduced the "separate but equal" doctrine into U.S. jurisprudence. Brown's majority opinion is reproduced in B. Thomas, *Plessy v. Ferguson: A Brief History with Documents*; quotations are from 32 (Thomas's analysis), 42, 44, 50, and 51.

89. Harlan's dissent is reproduced in ibid.; quotations are from 55, 57, 59.

90. Elliott, *Color-Blind Justice*, 293: "[W]hile Justice Brown needlessly endorsed the notion of 'racial instincts' to separate, Harlan gratuitously reassured whites that

'amalgamation' would not result, nor white supremacy become 'imperilled,' by contact with blacks on public conveyances." See also Gaines, *Uplifting the Race*, xiii: "While claiming the Constitution as the color-blind, classless guarantor of formal equality before the law, Harlan regarded white dominance as axiomatic and eternal." Elizabeth Mertz makes a similar point in "Consensus and Dissent in U.S. Legal Opinions": "Harlan is careful throughout his dissent to reassure white citizens that his proposed solution would not upset the current balance of power between races" (382); "Harlan challenges neither the authority of the court nor the ultimate hegemony of white domination" (384).

91. B. Thomas, *Plessy v. Ferguson: A Brief History with Documents*, 57.

92. Olsen points out: "Enforced segregation soon seriously impeded the struggle against racism by making it next to impossible for more enlightened whites publicly to work together with Negroes. Before long even this hindrance was extended when the Supreme Court upheld state laws prohibiting integrated activities that were privately conducted"; see *Thin Disguise*, 25.

93. Ibid.

94. *New Orleans Daily Picayune*, 19 May 1896, reprinted in Olsen, *Thin Disguise*, 123; also in B. Thomas, *Plessy v. Ferguson: A Brief History with Documents*, 128. For a proslavery diatribe equating abolitionism with socialism, see Fitzhugh, *Sociology for the South*.

95. *Atlanta Constitution*, 22 May 1896, 4 (ProQuest Historical Newspapers). Olsen notes, however, that a few of the South's religious organs "ventured some criticism of racial segregation"; see *Thin Disguise*, 27.

96. *New York Evening Journal*, 20 May 1896, reprinted in B. Thomas, *Plessy v. Ferguson: A Brief History with Documents*, 131–32; also under the title *New York Journal* in Olsen, *Thin Disguise*, 128–29. Weaker endorsements appeared in the *Duluth (Minn.) News Tribune*, 22 May 1896, reprinted in Olsen, *Thin Disguise*, 126; and the *Rochester (N.Y.) Union Advertiser*, 19 May 1896, reprinted in B. Thomas, *Plessy v. Ferguson: A Brief History with Documents*, 129. The majority of newspapers surveyed by Olsen greeted the decision with varying degrees of disapproval.

97. "A Strange Decision," *Rochester (N.Y.) Democrat and Chronicle*, 20 May 1896, reprinted in Olsen, *Thin Disguise*, 123–25; also in B. Thomas, *Plessy v. Ferguson: A Brief History with Documents*, 129–30. For another surprising critique by an Irish Catholic Democratic organ, see untitled editorial, *Donahoe's Magazine*, July 1896, 100–101, reprinted under the title "A Sad Spectacle" in Olsen, *Thin Disguise*, 127–28.

98. Untitled editorial, *Independent*, 21 May 1896, 12 (American Periodicals), cited, but not reprinted, in Olsen, *Thin Disguise*, 30n27.

99. "The Unfortunate Law of the Land," *New York Daily Tribune*, 19 May 1896, reprinted in Olsen, *Thin Disguise*, 130; also in B. Thomas, *Plessy v. Ferguson: A Brief History with Documents*, 128.

100. *Springfield Republican*, 20 May 1896, reprinted in Olsen, *Thin Disguise*, 127; also in B. Thomas, *Plessy v. Ferguson: A Brief History with Documents*, 131.

101. "Is There a Decline of Republicanism?"; the *Chicago Daily Inter Ocean* briefly announced the decision on 19 May, 5: "Legalizes the Line. United States Supreme Court Renders a Color Decision. 'Jim Crow' Cars Upheld. Law of Louisiana Is Declared Constitutional."

102. *Parsons (Kans.) Weekly Blade*, 30 May 1896, reprinted in Olsen, *Thin Disguise*, 129; also in B. Thomas, Plessy v. Ferguson: *A Brief History with Documents*, 133–34.

103. "That 'Decision'" and untitled editorial, *Cleveland Gazette*, 30 May 1896, 2.

104. "The Jim Crow Case." See also "The Supreme Court Decision," *A.M.E. Church Review*, 156–62, partially reprinted in Olsen, *Thin Disguise*, 125–26; also in B. Thomas, Plessy v. Ferguson: *A Brief History with Documents*, 134.

105. "Why Should We Care?"

106. "Who Is Permanently Hurt?," *Our Day*, June 1896, reprinted in B. Thomas, Plessy v. Ferguson: *A Brief History with Documents*, 135. Cook had demonstrated his commitment to racial integration when he had refused to attend the 1890 Mohonk Conference on the Negro because it excluded African Americans.

107. The *Post* mentioned Tourgée only in its brief account of the hearing, not in its announcement of the verdict; see "Capitol Chat" and "Separate Coach Law Upheld. The Supreme Court Decides a Case from Louisiana." It is particularly telling that the *A.M.E. Church Review*, which provided a detailed summary of Tourgée's arguments, attributed those arguments to "Mr. Plessy"; see "The Supreme Court Decision," 157–58 (section not reprinted by either Olsen or Thomas).

108. "Statement of the Citizens' Committee," in *Report of Proceedings for the Annulment of Act 111 of 1890*, 7–8.

109. Desdunes, "Forlorn Hope and Noble Despair."

110. Desdunes, *Nos hommes et notre histoire*, 192, my translation. The French original reads: "Nous croyons qu'il est plus noble et plus digne de lutter quant même, que de se montrer passif et résigné. La soumission absolue augmente la puissance de l'oppresseur et fait douter du sentiment de l'opprimé." Compare the wording of Tourgée's "Bystander" article of 15 August 1891, quoted at the beginning of this chapter: "Submission to oppression stimulates the desire to oppress."

111. E-mail communication from Brian Martinet, 7 May 2014. I am indebted to Nicholas Buccola, who contacted me regarding his projected book on Lydia Maria Child's political ideas, for putting me in touch with his Martinet relatives and to Brian Martinet for directing me toward the records of the U.S. Senate Judiciary Committee at the National Archives, where Martinet's letter is held; see Louis A. Martinet to the Honorable Attorney General, 8 February 1898, 55th Congress, Records of the U.S. Senate, Record Group 46, Committee Papers, Senate Judiciary Committee, Sen 55A-F15, National Archives, Washington, D.C.

112. Desdunes, *Nos hommes et notre histoire*, 186, my translation.

113. AWTP #9543, Charles H. Williams to AWT, 14 July 1897, quoting a letter Tourgée had written to him on 28 May.

114. "On the Common. . . . Soldiers' and Sailors' Monument Decorated by Members. . . . Hon. Albion W. Tourgee of New York Made the Oration," quoted in Olsen, *Carpetbagger's Crusade*, 334. In his "Reflections on Albion Tourgée's 1896 View

of the Supreme Court," Curtis tests this indictment against a large number of cases; he concludes that if we qualify Tourgée's sweeping language by substituting the word "usually" for "always" and "consistent," his thesis holds true (20).

115. "A Bystander's Notes," 13 March 1897, 6–7. Tourgée also praised McKinley directly in a personal letter for denouncing lynching in his inaugural address; see AWT to Honorable William McKinley President, 5 March 1897, William McKinley Papers. In this letter he urged McKinley to follow up the example he had set in Ohio by becoming "the leader of a movement for [lynching's] extinction in the Nation." Perhaps referring to this "Bystander" column, which he also praised in a private letter, AME bishop Reverdy Ransom of Chicago's Bethel Church noted that Tourgée, "a white man," had been "protest[ing] . . . more forcibly . . . than any Negro in the country" against the "recent infamous decision of the Supreme Court." In contrast, he complained, most African Americans had greeted the judicial endorsement of segregation with "apathy" rather than with the "storm of protest" it should have aroused. See Ransom, "May God Give Aim to Shoot the Enemy on the Spot! Are the Startling Words Uttered by Bishop Turner. . . ." See also AWTP #9262, Reverdy Ransom to AWT, 13 March 1897.

116. "A Bystander's Notes," 29 May 1897, 12–13.

117. Ibid.

118. "Judge Albion W. Tourgee," *Cleveland Gazette*, 25 February 1899, 2.

119. "The Supreme Court in the Conspiracy." This editorial seems to paraphrase sections of Tourgée's letter to the *New Orleans Leader* that Smith did not reprint. See also "The Jim Crow Case." The words "cold comfort" are Elliott's, *Color-Blind Justice*, 295, commenting on the same quotation from Tourgée's letter to the *Leader*.

120. According to Elliott, *Color-Blind Justice*, 295, "Tourgée's retirement from civil rights agitation and his self-censorship on race issues after *Plessy* suggest that he regarded the case as a terrible mistake." Elliott reads Tourgée's letter of 31 October 1893 as implying "they should either delay or drop the case. For the present, his advice was to delay" (271). In contrast, Olsen notes that far from ceasing his civil rights agitation after *Plessy*, Tourgée "saw fit to urge upon McKinley a national campaign against lynching" at the very moment when his own desperate quest for a consular appointment from the president dictated that he refrain from alienating Republican Party leaders who wanted to bury the race question; see *Carpetbagger's Crusade*, 338. As we shall see in chapter 7, Tourgée continued to speak out against American racism in the "Bystander" articles he sent to the *Inter Ocean* from France, although the main focus of these articles shifted to European affairs and the Spanish-American War.

121. Woodward, *American Counterpoint*, 232, was the first to cite Jackson's letter; see also Elliott, *Justice Deferred*, 3–4.

Chapter Seven

1. AWT to President William McKinley, 23 November 1898, William McKinley Papers; and "That Lynching,'" reprinted in Elliott and Smith, *Undaunted Radical*, 291–95, 343–45. The reprint has omitted a line that I have restored.

2. "A Bystander's Notes," 29 May 1897, 12–13.

3. AWTP #9543, Charles H. Williams to AWT, 14 July 1897, quoting a no-longer-extant letter Tourgée had written to him on 28 May. Williams also refers to and comments on this letter in AWTP #9515, Charles H. Williams to AWT, 10 June 1897.

4. AWTP #9508, Byron Andrews (*National Tribune*) to AWT, 10 June 1897.

5. AWTP #9174, AWT to EKT, 19 November 1896.

6. AWTP #9172, AWT to EKT, 11 November 1896.

7. AWT to Wm. McKinley, President, 5 March 1897, Consular Recommendations, State Department Records, National Archives and Records Administration, College Park, Md.

8. An interview Tourgée gave to the *Baltimore Sun* while campaigning in Maryland indicates that he did not entirely muzzle himself, however. Asked "what he thought of the new South," Tourgée replied, "There is no new South. I find very little change in the conditions of the South from those which prevailed when I made my home there." He also praised the progress African Americans had made since emancipation. Regarding "the future of the South," nonetheless, Tourgée no longer ventured any predictions. See "Tourgee on the South. Visit of a Well-Known Speaker and Writer to Advocate Honest Money. An Interesting Interview. . . . ," *Baltimore Sun*, 6 October 1896, 10 (ProQuest Historical Newspapers).

9. AWTP #9165, Powell Clayton, Chairman, Speakers Bureau, New York Headquarters, Republican National Committee, to AWT, 5 November 1896.

10. For evidence of Emma's role in requesting letters of recommendation for Tourgée, see H. H. Kohlsaat to EKT, 27 February 1897: "Your letter of the 26th is just at hand. . . . If you wish, you may send this letter to Major McKinley with your other letters of endorsement." Consular Recommendations, State Department Records, National Archives.

11. AWT to Cornelius N. Bliss, date illegible, Consular Recommendations, State Department Records, National Archives.

12. Consular Recommendations, State Department Records, National Archives. Most of the letters are grouped together in packets labeled with a cover listing the contents. See "Prominent Colored Men"; "Petition Urging the APPOINTMENT of Hon. Albion W. Tourgee, of Mayville, N.Y. to the Consular Service at Glasgow Signed by—Leading Colored Citizens of the State of Florida." Others, including the batch from Chicago, seem to have been submitted individually. For further evidence of a church letter-writing campaign, see AWTP #9406, Ida B. Wells-Barnett to AWT, 15 May 1897: "Altho Dr. Bently did not give us [a] chance to sign the petition he was to circulate, the members of Bethel A.M.E. Church passed a resolution and sent many individual letters to Washington making request for the English consulship."

13. For congratulatory messages from New Orleans, see AWTP #9378, Thomas R. Griffin to AWT, 12 May 1897; AWTP #9379, L. J. Joubert to AWT, 12 May 1897; and AWTP #9383, L. A. Martinet to AWT, 12 May 1897.

14. See "Prominent Colored Men" for letters by Smith, Gunner, Green, and Washington and "Petition . . . by Leading Colored Citizens . . . of Florida," Consular Recommendations, State Department Records, National Archives.

15. Olsen, *Carpetbagger's Crusade*, 337. I have based the numbers on my own count of the names listed in the available State Department Records. However, a clipping from the *Grape Belt*, titled "Chautauqua Honored" and dated 18 May 1897, in AWTP #9471, cites far higher numbers: "At least one-half the United States Senate; a dozen or more college presidents and whole faculties of several universities; nearly all the Methodist bishops of the country; . . . sixty members of the Pennsylvania legislature; [and] the whole Maryland delegation in Congress." According to this source, endorsements came from "not less than forty-two out of the forty-five states of the Union."

16. H. H. Kohlsaat to EKT, 27 February 1897, "Letters endorsing Hon. Albion W. Tourgée of Mayville, N.Y., for Consul at Glasgow, Scotland, from leading Republicans," Consular Recommendations, State Department Records, National Archives. Kohlsaat suggested that Emma send this letter to McKinley, since he had promised that he would "never write a letter of endorsement or sign a petition for office."

17. For the inside story, "How the Office Was Obtained," see Emma's reminiscences in AWTP #10865, ca. 1910; also Olsen, *Carpetbagger's Crusade*, 338.

18. AWTP #9378 and 9379, Thomas R. Griffin and L. J. Joubert to AWT, 12 May 1897. Griffin went on to say that he had urged a number of leaders to demand a more fitting recognition for Tourgée and that he himself would "esteem it a happy privilege" for himself or his fifteen-year-old son to serve Tourgée "in any capacity at nominal wages" during his stint abroad. In comparison with these effusions—and with his "Statement of the Citizens' Committee," quoted in chapter 6—Martinet's telegram of "sincere congratulations" sounds surprisingly cold. See AWTP #9383, L. A. Martinet to AWT, 12 May 1897.

19. AWTP #9399, T. B. Morton to AWT, 14 May 1897. See also AWTP #9402, H. P. Slaughter to AWT, 14 May 1897; as evidence that *A Fool's Errand* and *Bricks Without Straw* had "ma[d]e themselves felt" in the South, Slaughter cited the *Louisville Courier Journal*'s "chief objection" to Tourgée's appointment: "that Bordeaux was not farther away."

20. AWTP #9406 and 9441, Ida B. Wells-Barnett and Ferdinand L. Barnett to AWT, 15 and 24 May 1897.

21. See, for example, "Hon. Albion W. Tourgee Has Been Announced as an Applicant for a Consulship. He Desires to Represent the United States at Glasgow, Scotland— The Race Urged to Endorse Him—Michigan's Negro Bureau." Interestingly, this article mentions that Tourgée "served as counsel for the citizens' committee of New Orleans in its fight to have the Separate Car law declared unconstitutional, without pay." Pointing out that Tourgée's advocacy of African American rights had made him "many enemies among the whites," the author emphasizes that "our appreciation can not be better shown than by endorsing and petitioning for his appointment" and suggests using still extant campaign organizations for this purpose.

22. "Honor Well Won," *Chicago Conservator*, 15 May 1897, AWTP #9471. The editorials from the *Richmond Planet* and the *Star of Zion* have been preserved in the same scrapbook of press clippings. The other African American newspapers cited

are available in digital form in America's Historical Newspapers, http://www.readex.com/content/americas-historical-newspapers.

23. All of these press clippings come from Tourgée's scrapbook, AWTP #9471. The first two quotations are from the *Springfield Republican* and the Cerro Gordo County *Republican*. For other wholly complimentary notices, see the *Chicago Inter Ocean*, the *Grape Belt*, the *Alton Daily Republican*, and the *Washington Evening Star*.

24. AWTP #9402, H. P. Slaughter to AWT, 14 May 1897.

25. AWT to William McKinley, 19 August 1900, William McKinley Papers.

26. Ibid. Regarding the expansionism that "swept the United States" in the 1890s, the historian Hugh Thomas asks, "Was this expansionism an excuse, explicit or implicit, for a failure to assure the unity of the races in the U.S. itself? Imperialism helped to heal surviving sores between old Confederates and Union men. . . . But it seems also to have diverted North Americans away from any serious attempt at integration of the Negro race in the U.S. at a time when it was perhaps possible." See H. Thomas, *Cuba or the Pursuit of Freedom*, 312–13. Tourgée, of course, had learned that such integration was not possible at the time, but Thomas's insight into the connection still applies.

27. In "How the Office Was Obtained," AWTP #10865, Emma mentions that consuls usually supplemented their incomes with what they called "pickins"—bribes for enabling people to evade regulations. Tourgée instead became "*persona non grata*" for enforcing regulations, she notes.

28. AWTP #9451, William H. Busbey to AWT, 25 May 1897; AWTP #9493, H. H. Kohlsaat to EKT, 5 June 1897; AWTP #9509, William H. Busbey to EKT, 10 June 1897. On the *Inter Ocean*'s bankruptcy and reacquisition by Kohlsaat in 1912, see the article "H. H. Kohlsaat" on Wikipedia.

29. For a detailed account of the war for independence that began in 1895 and of the U.S. press's role in fomenting intervention fever, also stoked by Cuban exiles in the United States, see H. Thomas, *Cuba or the Pursuit of Freedom*, 316–66.

30. Although Maceo's rank reflected the values of the revolutionaries he led—one of whose goals was to abolish the color bar—rather than of Cuban society at large, no African American attained a comparable position within the abolitionist movement, for example.

31. "A Bystander's Notes," 16 January 1897, 6. Tourgée's "colored" Cuban correspondent remains unidentified.

32. See Coffman, *Nation Within*, 263–82.

33. "A Bystander's Notes," 20 February 1897, 6–7. I have not succeeded in identifying the correspondent whose pro-annexation letter Tourgée quotes, but later a doctor named E. S. Goodhue thanked Tourgée for writing this article, informed him that "three of our best men went to Washington in time to attend the Inauguration for the purpose of submitting an Annexation treaty," and expressed the wish that Tourgée could be appointed "Minister to Hawaii"; see AWTP #9296, E. S. Goodhue to AWT, 2 April 1897.

34. See, for example, "A Bystander's Notes," 12 June 1897, part 2, 13, quoted in chapter 5; and ibid., 13 March 1897, 6–7; and 29 May 1897, 12–13, quoted in chapter 6.

35. Tourgée, "Veto of the Chinese Bill." Pointing out the limitations of this critique, Elliott and Smith note, "Tourgée nonetheless seems to accept some of the claims of the anti-Chinese supporters of the [exclusion] bill in regard to the alleged morally 'degraded' condition of the predominately male Chinese immigrant population." In fairness to Tourgée, he reiterated his opposition to Chinese exclusion in a "Bystander" column of 15 January 1898, 6. On the white oligarchy's treatment of Japanese immigrants and deliberate provocation of the Japanese government, see Coffman, *Nation Within*, 188–204.

36. "A Bystander's Notes," 20 February 1897, 6–7; ibid., 19 June 1897, 13; Coffman, *Nation Within*, 13.

37. "A Bystander's Notes," 19 June 1897, 13.

38. "The Hawaiian Question Ably Discussed by Prof. W. S. Scarborough of Wilberforce, O. Missionaries and Their Sons Morally Wrong in Their Attempt at Annexation. . . ."

39. "A Bystander's Notes," 19 June 1897, 13.

40. Ibid.

41. Quoted in H. Thomas, *Cuba or the Pursuit of Freedom*, 101; I thank Jane Franklin for this reference and for recommending Thomas's book to me.

42. "A Bystander's Notes," 16 January 1897, 6; 19 June 1897, 13.

43. For an assessment of the economic and human devastation the war wreaked on Cuba, see the chapter "Cuba Prostrate" in H. Thomas, *Cuba or the Pursuit of Freedom*, 417–35.

44. For authoritative accounts of the Dreyfus case, see Bredin, *Affair*; and Burns, *France and the Dreyfus Affair*.

45. "A Bystander's Notes," 25 December 1897, 13.

46. For examples of British and U.S. press accounts, see the London *Times*, 24 December 1894, reprinted in Burns, *France and the Dreyfus Affair*, 46–49; and "Zola and the Dreyfus Mystery" (editorial). On the State Department's reprimand, see Olsen, *Carpetbagger's Crusade*, 341.

47. "A Bystander's Notes," 5 February 1898, 6. "Conspuez" actually means "hoot," rather than "spit."

48. Bredin, *Affair*, 285–86.

49. Ibid., 286; the text of *J'accuse* is reprinted in translation in Burns, *France and the Dreyfus Affair*, 93–102.

50. "A Bystander's Notes," 12 February 1898, 6.

51. Tourgée's assessment was correct until the publication of *J'accuse*, but according to Bredin, "Zola's manifesto had the almost immediate result of encouraging and almost imposing a commitment on the part of all those—writers, teachers, scientists, and artists—who until then had hesitated to plunge into a judicial, military, or political struggle that did not concern them directly" (*Affair*, 275). Thereafter, a split occurred between "Dreyfusard" and "anti-Dreyfusard" intellectuals. Zola's pamphlet also emboldened the socialist leader Jean Jaurès to take a strong stand in favor of Dreyfus, which ultimately brought the whole Socialist Party into the Dreyfusard camp.

52. "A Bystander's Notes," 19 March 1898, 6.

53. Ibid., 9 April 1898, 6. For a brief account of the Baker case, see Dray, *At the Hands of Persons Unknown*, 116–18. The rest of this "Bystander" article impugns the motives of Zola, whom Tourgée accused of having defended Dreyfus for the sake of notoriety rather than of justice—a charge retailed by the anti-Semitic and ultranationalist French press. Tourgée's animus against Zola—a writer with whose martyrdom in the cause of truth one might expect him to identify—derived from his Victorian distaste for *Nana* (1880) and the other novels in which Zola exposed the sexual corruption of French bourgeois society.

54. AWTP #9627, "Black and White" (1899). There is no way of determining whether Tourgée ever submitted this article for publication. The many typographical errors in the typescript give the impression of an uncorrected draft.

55. AWTP #9665, AWT to Ferdinand L. Barnett, 6 August 1900, partially reprinted in Elliott and Smith, *Undaunted Radical*, 346–50. Quotations are both from unreprinted portions of this letter and from 348, 349, and 350. The quotation in parentheses is from AWT to Theodore Roosevelt, 21 October 1901, Theodore Roosevelt Papers, reprinted in Elliott and Smith, *Undaunted Radical*, 352.

56. H. Thomas, *Cuba or the Pursuit of Freedom*, 355.

57. Ibid., 364.

58. Coffman, *Nation Within*, 302–11.

59. Tourgée was not alone in this. See H. Thomas, *Cuba or the Pursuit of Freedom*, on the influence that the precedent of the Civil War and Reconstruction exerted on the "North American officers who constituted the military government" the United States imposed on Cuba. For example, "these officers sought with dedication and without sparing themselves, to recast Cuban society, such as it was, in the mould of North America; all the corruption, the incompetence and makeshift devices lying between law and custom were to be swept immediately away; and from this well-meant effort much ill was later to flow" (436).

60. "A Bystander's Notes," 15 May 1898, 19.

61. For the sources of these quotations and paraphrases, see, in order, ibid., 29 May 1898, 19; 10 July 1898, 13; 14 August 1898, 19; 7 August 1898, 19; 26 June 1898, 19; and 5 June 1898, 19.

62. Ibid., 29 May 1898, 19.

63. Ibid., 10 July 1898, 13.

64. "A Bystander's Notes: Pacification of Cuba Greater Task Than the Conquest. . . . Anglo-Saxon Law and Even-Handed Justice Will Establish a Worthy Civilization," 21 August 1898, 19. The phrase "free state" comes from the "Bystander" article of 29 May quoted above.

65. AWT to President William McKinley, 24 June and 5 August 1898, William McKinley Papers.

66. Quoted in Franklin, *Vietnam and Other American Fantasies*, 123. For the reapplication to Iraq, see *New York Times*, 5 July 2006, 1.

67. "A Bystander's Notes: Never Did War Make Such a Sudden Change on the Map. Glory All on Our Side. Most Wonderful Conflict in Many Respects. Our Duty

Will Not Be Fully Performed until Islands Are Made Fit for Civilization," 28 August 1898, 19.

68. *Mark Twain's Weapons of Satire*, 4.

69. Ibid., 103, 106–7.

70. Harris, *God's Arbiters*, 13.

71. AWTP #9668, AWT to Harry B. Kirtland, President Harvard Republican Club, 14 September 1900; Tourgée, "Does Not Follow Flag. A. W. Tourgee Points Out Limits to the Constitution. Author of 'Fool's Errand,' 'Bricks Without Straw,' and Other Political Novels in a Letter from Bordeaux, France, Declares That the States Alone Regulate the Suffrage and That McKinley's Policy in the Philippines Is Right." For illuminating analyses of "The Legal and Literary Complexities of U.S. Citizenship Around 1900," see Brook Thomas's article by that title; also B. Thomas, "Constitution Led by the Flag."

72. AWT to William McKinley, 19 August 1900, William McKinley Papers.

73. In his last letter to McKinley, Tourgée reported having learned from a colleague "that there is to be a free fight over diplomatic and consular places during your next term, and that if I wish to remain in the service, I must, as he says, 'begin to hustle.'" See AWT to William McKinley, 21 January 1901, William McKinley Papers.

74. AWT to Theodore Roosevelt, 21 October 1901, Theodore Roosevelt Papers, reprinted in Elliott and Smith, *Undaunted Radical*, 351–55, quotations on 351, 354–55.

75. For Roosevelt's letter, see Theodore Roosevelt to AWT, 8 November 1901, Theodore Roosevelt Papers. For a thoughtful analysis of the differences between Tourgée's racial views and those Roosevelt articulates in his letter, see Elliott, *Color-Blind Justice*, 303–6. On the Brownsville incident, see Lewis, *W. E. B. Du Bois*, 330–33.

76. Elliott, headnote to Tourgée's "Letter to E. H. Johnson (1902)," in Elliott and Smith, *Undaunted Radical*, 356. Page references to quotations from the letter, as reprinted 356–78, will be given parenthetically in the text. I have corrected misprints against the original text, AWTP #9671, AWT to E. H. Johnson, 15 May 1902.

77. Olsen, *Carpetbagger's Crusade*, 346.

78. AWTP #3368, Thomas Dixon to AWT, 25 February 1888; Elliott, *Color-Blind Justice*, 307.

79. AWTP #9743, AWT to "My dear Gould," 23 November 1904. The quotation is from *Hamlet*, act 1, scene 2.

80. AWTP #9725, AWT to "My dear Gould," 17 September 1903.

81. Olsen, *Carpetbagger's Crusade*, 349.

82. Emma chronicles his day-to-day condition in her diary entries for December 1904 through May 1905, AWTP #9906. The quotation is from the entry for 27 December 1904. The word "excavation" is from AWTP #9743.

83. AWTP #9761, Andrew Joyner, "The Real Hero of 'A Fool's Errand': Albion Tourgee's Life in North Carolina. Brave and True Man. If He Could Have Seen His Error in Blind Adhesion to the Negro Suffrage Idea His Name Would Be Written High," *Raleigh Daily News and Observer*, 28 May 1905.

84. AWTP #9907, scrapbook of obituary clippings, "Tourgee and the Ku Klux," *Richmond Times-Dispatch*, n.d.

85. AWTP #9907, "The Late Judge Tourgee," *News*, 22 May 1905. There are three newspapers titled the *News* in Emma's scrapbook of obituary clippings, none of which identifies the city of origin. Emma jotted down a list of identifications that includes the *Savannah News* and the *Atlanta News*, but I have not succeeded in tracing the articles in her scrapbook to either of these newspapers. The third *News* remains unidentified.

86. AWTP #9907, "The Death of Albion Tourgee," *News*, n.d.

87. AWTP #9907, untitled editorial, *News*, 24 May 1905.

88. AWTP #9907, "A Traducer of the South," *New Orleans State*, 4 June 1905.

89. AWTP #9907, "A Dead Issue Recalled," *Brooklyn Daily Eagle*, 22 May 1905, 4. See also the obituary titled "'The Fool's Errand,'" from an unknown newspaper, apparently Democratic. Citing Tourgée's novel as an illustration of "the difference between fame and ephemeral popularity," this paper pronounced it "now chiefly interesting, if interesting at all, as a proof that when the fever of politics is in their veins, a great many otherwise rational people are not quite sane."

90. AWTP #9907, "Death of Tourgee," *Gazette*, 23 May 1905.

91. AWTP #9907, "Judge Tourgee," *Chicago Daily Inter Ocean*, 23 May 1905, 6. A late photo of Tourgée appears on the preceding page. See also "Albion W. Tourgee, Noted Writer, Dead," *Chicago Daily Inter Ocean*, 22 May 1905, 3. The latter inaccurately reports that Tourgée lived in Chicago during his association with the *Inter Ocean*.

92. AWTP #9907, "Judge Tourgee, the Author, Dead: A Novelist Whose Reputation Was Worldwide," *Baltimore American*, 22 May 1905, 3.

93. AWTP #9907, "A Great Novelist Gone," *Press*, 25 May 1905. Neither the *Cleveland Press* nor the *Philadelphia Press* contains this article.

94. AWTP #9907, "Death of Albion W. Tourgee. A Versatile Author Gone. His Interesting and Many-Sided Career—Death Came at Bordeaux, France, Where He Was Consul," *Springfield Republican*, 22 May 1905, 12.

95. AWTP #9907, "Judge Tourgee," *Cleveland Leader*, 23 May 1905.

96. "Our Best Friend Dead," 2. For Smith's repeated calls for memorial meetings throughout Ohio, see the editorial notes of 10 and 24 June, 2 (America's Historical Newspapers).

97. "Tourgee Memorial Meeting."

98. "Albion W. Tourgee," *Indianapolis Freeman*, 27 May 1905, 4 (America's Historical Newspapers).

99. "Death of Judge Tourgee"; "Judge Albion W. Tourgee," *St. Paul (Minn.) Appeal*, 10 June 1905, 2 (America's Historical Newspapers).

100. "Albion W. Tourgee," *Seattle Republican*, 23 June 1905, reprinted from *Colored American Magazine* (African American Newspapers, www.readex/content/african-american-newspapers-1827-1998).

101. Moore, "Albion Westbray [*sic*] Tourgee." The information about Moore's family connection with Tourgée comes from the editor's headnote. Moore's wife may

have been the sister of Adaline Pattillo, the former slave the Tourgées adopted at age thirteen. For information about Adaline, see Woods, "Adaline and the Judge"; and Elliott, *Color-Blind Justice*, 135–39, 149–52.

102. AWTP #9907, "Consul Tourgee's Funeral. Ceremonies in the English Church at Bordeaux This Morning," unknown newspaper, 23 May 1905.

103. AWTP #8044, Catherine Impey to AWT, 23 September 1894: "Do you not make room in your thoughts for coming this side? If you could but come to speak your whole heart out here, what might it not do. . . . It is what we now want I believe—a white American champion of their cause to silence" skeptics who would not believe an African American's testimony. Both Tourgée's health and his finances precluded his making the trip. Emma describes her visit with Impey in two letters to her friend "Damie": AWTP #9803 and #9806, EKT to [Mrs. Diadama K. Hall], 24 and 29 September 1905.

104. Untitled editorial notes, *Cleveland Gazette*, 10 and 24 June 1905, 2 (America's Historical Newspapers).

105. AWTP #9907, "In Memory of Judge Tourgee," *Chicago Daily Inter Ocean*, 29 May 1905; AWTP #9782, William H. Busbey to EKT, 19 July 1905. Emma had apparently written to Busbey, asking him to send her whatever reports of the meeting were published in the Chicago papers. He offered to ask Barnett to send a copy of the *Conservator*'s account, if available.

106. "Honor His Name: Negroes Speak of the Late Judge Tourgee."

107. "Our Duty"; "Tribute to Judge Tourgee."

108. See AWTP #9828, Harry C. Smith to EKT, 8 November 1905: "*I have invited a number of prominent Afro-Americans to be present at the services on Tuesday* & would like to have one of the number read a set of resolutions and one or two deliver *short* addresses. . . . Can you see that provision for these are made by the Committee in charge & let me know positively as soon as possible this week that I may complete arrangements? With greatest respect & highest (love &) esteem."

109. *Cleveland Gazette*, untitled note under column of African American news items, 7 October 1905, 3 (America's Historical Newspapers).

110. "Arranging to Attend the Tourgee Funeral Services."

111. "Judge Albion W. Tourgee," *Cleveland Gazette*, 11 November 1905, 2; Smith mentions the special sleeping car in an untitled note on 18 November 1905, 2 (America's Historical Newspapers).

112. "Judge Tourgée! Splendid Showing Made at the Memorial Services on Tuesday in His Honor. Many Beautiful Floral Tributes, Resolutions, Letters and Telegrams Sent by Afro-Americans—The Program—Participants—Other Notes"; untitled editorial note, *Cleveland Gazette*, 18 November 1905, 2.

113. AWTP #9823, Officers of the National Association of Colored Women to EKT, 30 October 1905. A shorter letter of sympathy was signed by other prominent members of the association, including Lucy Thurman, Mary C. Terrell, and Mrs. Booker T. Washington. See AWTP #9832, National Association of Colored Women to EKT, 10 November 1905.

114. "Judge Tourgée! Splendid Showing Made at the Memorial Services on Tuesday in His Honor. . . .'"; AWTP #9838, "In Memoriam: Tribute of Respect by Colored Citizens of Chicago to the Memory of Judge Albion W. Tourgee" (Wells had her memorial tribute printed and sent a copy to Emma).

115. "Mrs. Ida Wells Barnett Writes of the Negroes' Part in the Tourgee Memorial Exercises at Mayville, N.Y., Nov. 14, 1905." Neither Wells nor Smith mentions any delegation from New Orleans among the fifty African Americans who came from New York, Pennsylvania, Ohio, Michigan, Illinois, and North Carolina.

116. "A Grand Success Were the Memorial Services in Honor of Judge Albion W. Tourgee, Held at St. John's A.M.E. Church Last Sunday Afternoon"; AWTP #9865, Harry C. Smith to EKT, 5 December 1905; EKT to Harry C. Smith, 7 December 1905, reprinted in *Cleveland Gazette*, 16 December 1905, 3.

117. Untitled, *Cleveland Gazette*, 16 December 1905, 3 (America's Historical Newspapers).

118. "The Niagara Movement"; "Honor Garrison and Tourgee. Negroes Hear Addresses upon These Emancipators of Their Race." Although Douglass is usually listed as a precursor with Tourgée and Garrison, he is not mentioned in these articles.

119. AWTP #9967, #10011, Shelby J. Davidson and M. Grant Lucas to EKT, 25 February and 18 March 1906.

120. AWTP #9899, J. L. Love to EKT, 31 December 1905. For his early correspondence with Tourgée, see AWTP #5510, J. L. Love to AWT, 13 April 1891.

121. AWTP #10057, #10059, Harry C. Smith to EKT, 1 and 4 June 1906; AWTP #9896, #10031, #10051, George W. Mitchell to EKT, 28 December 1905, 6 March [1906], and 15 May 1906; AWTP #10055, Address of Adelbert Moot at Dedication of Tourgée Monument, 30 May 1906; "Albion W. Tourgee. Soldier, Jurist, Author, Humanitarian, Statesman," unknown newspaper account of dedication ceremony, 7 June 1906; "The Tourgee Monument. Unveiled—Appropriate Exercises—A Beautiful Shaft." Both the lawn seat and the urn have since disappeared, and only the obelisk now remains.

122. Farmer, "The Afro-Americans Are Admonised [*sic*] to Grasp the Passing Opportunities to Comemorate [*sic*] the Memories of Those Noble Men and Women Who Have So Unselfishly Championed the Cause of the Race in the Past."

123. Tourgée is briefly mentioned in the following *Cleveland Gazette* articles: "Foraker! Successor to Sumner, Garrison and Tourgée"; "Helping Tillman and Dixon"; "Constitutional Delegate"; "Poor Old John, Still 'Knocking'"; untitled note on the Du Bois Club lecture, 12 February 1916, 2; "Obituary," 26 February 1916, 2; and "Senator Foraker."

124. For Wells's references to Tourgée, see *Crusade for Justice*, 110, 120–21, 138, 151, and 156; for Desdunes's, see *Nos hommes et notre histoire*, 186; for Du Bois's, see his essay "Reconstruction and Its Benefits," 796, in which he quotes Tourgée's "Bystander" column of 26 December 1890; the same quotation appears in Du Bois's magnum opus, *Black Reconstruction in America*, 621. I am indebted to Elliott, *Color-Blind Justice*, 310, for the Du Bois reference.

125. On Albion Tourgee DeBose, see Adams, "In the World of Music," and the website of the DeBose Foundation; on Albion Tourgee Ricard Jr., see "Louisiana to Get New Negro Lawyers"; the latter article is signed "A Negro Congressman."

126. R. Thomas, "A Little about Everything."

127. M. Alexander, *New Jim Crow*, 22.

128. Ibid., 180.

129. "A Bystander's Notes," 13 March 1897, 6.

130. M. Alexander, *New Jim Crow*, 103, 180.

131. "A Bystander's Notes," 5 September 1891, 4.

132. Tourgée, "South as a Field for Fiction," 211.

Afterword

1. See, for example, S. Brown, *Negro in American Fiction*; Becker, "Albion W. Tourgée"; and Cowie, *Rise of the American Novel*, 521–35.

2. Among the distinguished scholars who published early articles or book chapters on Tourgée are Wilson, *Patriotic Gore*, 529–48; Woodward, "Birth of Jim Crow," revised and expanded in his *American Counterpoint*, 217–33; and Aaron, *Unwritten War*, 193–203.

3. S. Alexander, *Army of Lions*, 55.

4. Carle, *Defining the Struggle*, 138.

5. A catastrophic house fire destroyed most of Wells's personal papers, including her file of the *Conservator*. The largest other source of her letters is the Frederick Douglass Papers in the Library of Congress, Manuscript Division.

6. Fortune's letters are held in the Booker T. Washington Papers, Library of Congress, among others. Bruce cofounded the Schomburg Center for Research in Black Culture, which holds a collection of his papers.

Bibliography

This bibliography covers works cited in the text and the endnotes; it does not include works merely mentioned, which can be found in the index. Nor does it include all of Tourgée's works. Tourgée's "Bystander" articles are not listed individually here but are cited in the endnotes. The same applies to the reviews and obituaries drawn from his scrapbooks and to the correspondence drawn from the Albion W. Tourgée Papers. This method applies as well to untitled editorials from African American newspapers and to documents drawn from other manuscript collections.

Manuscript Collections

John Edward Bruce Collection, Schomburg Center for Research in Black Culture, New York Public Library
Charles W. Chesnutt Papers, John Hope and Aurelia E. Franklin Library, Fisk University, Nashville, Tenn.
Desdunes Family *New Orleans Crusader* Clippings, Archives and Special Collections, Xavier University, New Orleans
Nils R. Douglas Papers, Amistad Research Center, New Orleans
Frederick Douglass Papers, Manuscript Division, Library of Congress
James A. Garfield Papers, Manuscript Division, Library of Congress
Benjamin Harrison Papers, Manuscript Division, Library of Congress
National Archives and Records Administration, College Park, Md.
    Consular Recommendations, State Department Records
National Archives and Records Administration, Washington, D.C.
Theodore Roosevelt Papers, Manuscript Division, Library of Congress
Charles B. Rousseve Papers, Amistad Research Center, New Orleans
Albion W. Tourgée Papers (AWTP), Chautauqua County Historical Society, Westfield, N.Y.

Newspapers

Anti-Caste
Chicago Daily Inter Ocean
Cleveland Gazette
Detroit Plaindealer

Indianapolis Freeman
New York Age
New York Daily Tribune
Washington Bee
Woman's Era

Works of Albion W. Tourgée (listed chronologically)

BOOKS

[Henry Churton]. *'Toinette: A Novel.* New York: J. B. Ford, 1874.

Figs and Thistles: A Romance of the Western Reserve. New York: Fords, Howard, and Hulbert, 1879.

[Anonymous]. *A Fool's Errand. By One of the Fools.* New York: Fords, Howard, and Hulbert, 1879.

The Invisible Empire. 1880. Edited by Otto H. Olsen. Baton Rouge: Louisiana State University Press, 1989.

Bricks Without Straw: A Novel. 1880. Edited by Carolyn L. Karcher. Durham, N.C.: Duke University Press, 2009.

An Appeal to Caesar. New York: Fords, Howard, and Hulbert, 1884.

Letters to a King. New York: Phillips and Hunt, 1888.

Pactolus Prime. New York: Cassell, 1890.

The Story of a Thousand, Being a History of the Service of the 105th Ohio Volunteer Infantry, in the War for the Union, from August 21, 1862 to June 6, 1865. 1896. Edited by Peter C. Luebke. Kent: Kent State University Press, 2011.

Undaunted Radical: The Selected Writings and Speeches of Albion W. Tourgée. See Elliott and Smith under Other Primary and Secondary Sources.

NEWSPAPER SERIES

[Siva]. "A Man of Destiny." *Chicago Daily Inter Ocean.* 13 December 1884–4 March 1885.

[Anonymous]. "The Veteran and His Pipe." *Chicago Daily Inter Ocean.* 25 April–19 September 1885.

[Trueman Joyce]. "Letters to a Mugwump." *Chicago Daily Inter Ocean.* 26 September–12 December 1885.

[Siva]. "A Child of Luck." *Chicago Daily Inter Ocean.* 20 March–4 December 1886.

"A Bystander's Notes." *Chicago Daily Inter Ocean.* 21 April 1888–12 August 1893; 5 May 1894–5 January 1895; 21 November 1896–2 October 1898.

EDITED JOURNAL

The Basis: A Journal of Citizenship. 20 March–9 November 1895 (weekly); December 1895–April 1896 (monthly).

ARTICLES AND PUBLISHED LETTERS

AWT to editor. *Raleigh Standard,* 1 February 1870, 2.

"The Veto of the Chinese Bill." 1882. In *Undaunted Radical,* edited by Elliott and Smith, 88–90.

Untitled editorial. *Our Continent,* 23 May 1883, 669.

"The Elevation of the Negro." *The Citizen,* n.d. [ca. 1885]. AWTP #10812.

"The South as a Field for Fiction." *Forum* 6 (December 1888): 404–13. In *Undaunted Radical,* edited by Elliott and Smith, 203–11.

"The Claims of Realism." *North American Review* 148 (March 1889): 386–88.

"Shall White Minorities Rule?" *Forum* 7 (April 1889): 143–55. In *Undaunted Radical*, edited by Elliott and Smith, 112–22.

"Our Semi-Citizens." *Frank Leslie's Illustrated Newspaper*, 28 September 1889, 122.

"The Time Has Come for the Race to Show Itself Worthy of Liberty. Mr. Tourgee on the League. . . ." *Detroit Plaindealer*, 18 October 1889, 4.

"Shall We Re-Barbarize the Negro?" *Congregationalist*, 5 December 1889, 411–16.

"The Negro's View of the Race Problem." 1890. In *Undaunted Radical*, edited by Elliott and Smith, 152–70.

"'Tourgeeism!' A Personal Letter to Afro-Americans, from Judge Tourgee." *Detroit Plaindealer*, 3 June 1892, 1, 8.

"'Tourgeeism.' What the National Citizens' Rights Association Is. Why Every Afro-American Should Become a Member." *Cleveland Gazette*, 4 June 1892, 1.

"Judge Tourgee Treats Two Branches of a Subject Touched upon by the President's Letter of Acceptance. . . ." *Cleveland Gazette*, 24 September 1892, 1–2.

"A By-stander's Notes." *Anti-Caste* 5 (October 1892): 1–2.

"Outbreak of Race Persecution in the United States." *Anti-Caste* 5 (November 1892): 5–7.

"That Lynching. Judge Tourgee Writes Gov. McKinley and the Editor of 'The Gazette.' . . ." *Cleveland Gazette*, 3 March 1894, 1–2. In *Undaunted Radical*, edited by Elliott and Smith, 289–95.

AWT to President William McKinley, 23 November 1898. William McKinley Papers, Manuscript Division, Library of Congress. In *Undaunted Radical*, edited by Elliott and Smith, 343–45.

AWT to Ferdinand L. Barnett, 6 August 1900, AWTP #9665. Partially reprinted in *Undaunted Radical*, edited by Elliott and Smith, 346–50.

"Does Not Follow Flag. A. W. Tourgee Points Out Limits to the Constitution. . . ." *Chicago Daily Tribune*, 8 October 1900, 4 (ProQuest Historical Newspapers, www.proquest.com/products-services/pq-hist-news.html).

AWT to Theodore Roosevelt, 21 October 1901. Theodore Roosevelt Papers. Reprinted in *Undaunted Radical*, edited by Elliott and Smith, 351–55.

"Letter to E. H. Johnson (1902)." In *Undaunted Radical*, edited by Elliott and Smith, 356–78.

Contemporaneous Newspaper Articles (Exclusive of Untitled Editorials)

Adams, Wellington A. "In the World of Music." *Washington Bee*, 8 February 1921, 7.

"An Afro-American League." *Cleveland Gazette*, 25 January 1890, 1–2.

"Albion W. Tourgee." *Indianapolis Freeman*, 27 May 1905, 4 (America's Historical Newspapers, http://www.readex.com/content/americas-historical-newspapers).

"Albion W. Tourgee." *Seattle Republican*, 23 June 1905 (African American Newspapers, www.readex.com/content/

african-american-newspapers-1827-1998). Reprinted from *Colored American Magazine*.

"America Re-visited." *Anti-Caste* 5 (October 1892): 3–4.

[Anderson, William H.]. "Tourgee's Book. Afro-American Claims on the Republic. . . ." *Detroit Plaindealer*, 30 May 1890, 1.

"The Anti-Lynch Law." *Cleveland Gazette*, 14 December 1895, 2.

"Arranging to Attend the Tourgee Funeral Services." *Cleveland Gazette*, 28 October 1905, 1.

"At the Front. Where His Own Efforts Have Placed Hon. H. C. Smith. . . . Two Years in the General Assembly and on the Road to Two More." *Cleveland Gazette*, 5 October 1895, 1.

"Bad Candy . . . The West Union Lynching and How Gov. McKinley Feels and Talks. . . ." *Cleveland Gazette*, 20 January 1894, 1.

"Barnwell. Detailed List of the Suffering Survivors at the Scene of the Tragedy. . . ." *Cleveland Gazette*, 15 March 1890, 1.

"British Anti-Lynchers." *New York Times*, 2 August 1894, 4.

Caldwell, M[ack] W. "The Order System. How the Southerner Manages to Keep the Afro-American Poor." *Detroit Plaindealer*, 4 November 1892, 3.

"Capitol Chat." *Washington Post*, 14 April 1896, 6 (ProQuest Historical Newspapers, www.proquest.com/products-services/pq-hist-news.html).

"Career of Ida B. Wells. The Record of This Notorious Courtesan. . . ." *Memphis Daily Commercial*, 26 May 1894, 5.

"Civil Rights and Lynching." *Cleveland Gazette*, 16 November 1895, 2.

"Constitutional Delegate." *Cleveland Gazette*, 21 October 1911, 2.

"Death of Judge Tourgee." *St. Paul (Minn.) Appeal*, 27 May 1905, 2 (America's Historical Newspapers, http://www.readex.com/content/americas-historical-newspapers).

Desdunes, Rodolphe L. "Forlorn Hope and Noble Despair." *New Orleans Crusader*, 15 August 1891. Charles B. Rousseve Papers, box 2, folder 20, Amistad Research Center.

———. "To Be or Not to Be." *New Orleans Crusader*, 4 July 1891. Charles B. Rousseve Papers, box 1, folder 8, Amistad Research Center.

"A Disgraceful Lynching." *Cleveland Gazette*, 21 December 1895, 2.

"Editor's Address to the Friends of *Anti-Caste*." 6 (January 1893): 4–5.

Embry, J. C. "Two New Books from the Hand of Representative Ladies of Our Race." *Christian Recorder*, 12 January 1893, 3.

"The English Speak. . . ." *Cleveland Gazette*, 16 June 1894, 1.

Farmer, Walter M. "The Afro-Americans Are Admonised [*sic*] to Grasp the Passing Opportunities to Comemorate [*sic*] the Memories of Those Noble Men and Women Who Have So Unselfishly Championed the Cause of the Race in the Past." *Chicago Broad Ax*, 15 September 1906, 1 (America's Historical Newspapers).

"Fighting for Rights in Felicity." *Cleveland Gazette*, 8 December 1888, 2 (The African American Experience in Ohio, 1850–1920, http://dbs.Ohiohistory.org/africanam/page.cfm).

"Foraker! Successor to Sumner, Garrison and Tourgée." *Cleveland Gazette,* 16 February 1907, 1.

"Frances, a Temporizer." *Cleveland Gazette,* 24 November 1894, 2.

"The Government Must Act." *Cleveland Gazette,* 26 March 1892, 2.

"Gov. M'Kinley, the Man of the Hour." *Cleveland Gazette,* 23 November 1895, 2.

"A Grand Success Were the Memorial Services in Honor of Judge Albion W. Tourgee, Held at St. John's A.M.E. Church Last Sunday Afternoon." *Cleveland Gazette,* 9 December 1905.

H. F. "Church Scorned by Wales." *New York Times,* 29 April 1894, 1.

[Harris, Joel Chandler]. "A Refugee from His Race." *Atlanta Constitution,* 23 April 1890, AWTP #8251.

"The Hawaiian Question Ably Discussed by Prof. W. S. Scarborough of Wilberforce, O. . . ." *Cleveland Gazette,* 22 April 1893, 1.

"Helping Tillman and Dixon." *Cleveland Gazette,* 11 March 1911, 2.

"Hon. Albion W. Tourgee Has Been Announced as an Applicant for a Consulship. . . . The Race Urged to Endorse Him. . . ." *Indianapolis Freeman,* 6 March 1897, 3.

"Honor Garrison and Tourgee. Negroes Hear Addresses upon These Emancipators of Their Race." *Washington Post,* 1 December 1905, 4 (America's Historical Newspapers).

"Honor His Name: Negroes Speak of the Late Judge Tourgee." *Boston Daily Globe,* 31 July 1905, 4 (ProQuest Historical Newspapers).

"The Ida B. Wells Case." *Memphis Daily Commercial,* 26 May 1894, 4.

"Ida B. Wells. . . . The English Papers and People Resent the Attack on Miss Wells." *Cleveland Gazette,* 14 July 1894, 1.

"Ida B. Wells Writes of Her Wonderful Success in England." *Cleveland Gazette,* 30 June 1894, 1.

"Indorses a Good Idea. Now Let There Be Action and Less Talk—Mr. Loudin Sounds the Key-Note." *Cleveland Gazette,* 25 February 1893, 2.

"An Infernal Outrage." *Cleveland Gazette,* 12 October 1889, 2.

"*Iola Leroy; or, Shadows Uplifted.*" *Independent,* 5 January 1893, 2.

"'Iola' Wells. An Interesting Biographical Sketch—A Forcible Writer." *Cleveland Gazette,* 6 July 1889, 1.

"Is There a Decline of Republicanism?" *Chicago Daily Inter Ocean,* 20 May 1896, 6.

"It Ought to Pass. . . ." *Cleveland Gazette,* 21 March 1896, 1.

"It Passed. Ohio's Anti-lynching Bill Half Way through the Assembly." *Cleveland Gazette,* 28 March 1896, 1.

"It Passed. Ohio's Anti-Lynching Bill Passes the Senate," *Cleveland Gazette,* 11 April 1896, 1.

"The Jim Crow Case." *Indianapolis Freeman,* 23 May 1896, 4.

"Judge Albion W. Tourgee." *Cleveland Gazette,* 25 February 1899, 2.

"Judge Albion W. Tourgee." *Cleveland Gazette,* 11 November 1905, 2.

"Judge Albion W. Tourgee." *St. Paul (Minn.) Appeal,* 10 June 1905, 2 (America's Historical Newspapers).

"Judge Tourgee Makes a Telling Argument for Ohio's Anti-Lynching Bill. . . ." *Cleveland Gazette,* 8 February 1896, 1.

"Judge Tourgee on Prof. Washington." *Cleveland Gazette*, 19 October 1895, 2.

"Judge Tourgée! Splendid Showing Made at the Memorial Services on Tuesday in His Honor...." *Cleveland Gazette*, 18 November 1905, 1.

"Judge Tourgee Writes a Caustic Letter in Reply to an Attack." *Cleveland Gazette*, 29 May 1897, 1.

"Justice Wins. The Jim Crow Car Laws Ditched and Will Remain So." *Cleveland Gazette*, 13 August 1892, 1, reprinted from the *Crusader.*

"Killing the Innocent." *Cleveland Gazette*, 21 December 1895, 2.

"Legalizes the Line. United States Supreme Court Renders a Color Decision. 'Jim Crow' Cars Upheld. Law of Louisiana Is Declared Constitutional." *Chicago Daily Inter Ocean*, 19 May 1896, 5.

"A Literary Coincidence." *Chicago Daily Inter Ocean*, 1 November 1891, 12.

"Lynch Bills.... Judge Albion W. Tourgee, the Race's Great and Good Friend, Passes upon Them...." *Cleveland Gazette*, 5 May 1894, 1.

"The Lynching Question." *Cleveland Gazette*, 4 January 1896, 2.

"A Lynching Scene in Alabama." *Anti-Caste* 6 (January 1893): 1.

"The Lynchings of 1895." *Cleveland Gazette*, 11 January 1896, 2.

Manly, Alexander. "Mrs. Fellows's Speech." In *Lynching in America*, edited by Waldrep, 146–47.

"Massachusetts against Lynch 'Law.'" *Cleveland Gazette*, 23 November 1895, 2.

"Miss Ida B. Wells Informs Our Readers as to the Condition of the World's Fair Pamphlet Movement.... Ohio Afro-Americans Should Do Their Duty at Once and Forward Something to Aid the Movement." *Cleveland Gazette*, 22 July 1893, 1.

"Miss Wells Lectures. 'Colored' Women Who Side with Miss Willard as against Miss Wells. That Annual Address and Its Attack upon Our Anti-Lynching Champion, Miss Wells." *Cleveland Gazette*, 24 November 1894, 1.

Moore, Charles H. "Albion Westbray [*sic*] Tourgee." *Colored American Magazine*, 1 June 1905, 336–37 (African American Periodicals).

"Mr. Loudin's Open Letter." *Cleveland Gazette*, 25 February 1893, 2.

"Mrs. Ida Wells Barnett Writes of the Negroes' Part in the Tourgee Memorial Exercises at Mayville, N.Y., Nov. 14, 1905." *Cleveland Gazette*, 23 November 1905, 1, reprinted from the *Buffalo Express.*

A Negro. "Rights of Negroes. Many of Them Lynched for Crimes They Did Not Commit.... Judge Tourgee's Opinions Discussed." *Pittsburgh Dispatch*, 24 June 1892, AWTP #8251.

"'A Negro Adventuress.'" *Cleveland Gazette*, 16 June 1894, 2.

"The Niagara Movement." *Washington Bee*, 9 December 1905, 5.

"No Objection Is Raised by the Negro." *Atlanta Constitution*, 22 May 1896, 4 (ProQuest Historical Newspapers).

"Not Guilty. 'Click' Mitchell, the Unfortunate Afro-American, Lynched at Urbana, Was Clearly Innocent of the Crime Charged....," *Cleveland Gazette*, 3 July 1897, 1.

"Now a Law. The 'Smith' Bill Amending the State Civil Rights Law, Which Passed the House Last Week, Is Passed in the Senate This Week. . . . That West Union Lynching. . . ." *Cleveland Gazette*, 3 February 1894, 1.

"Ohio's Anti-Lynching Bill." *Cleveland Gazette*, 21 March 1896, 1.

"On the Common. . . . Soldiers' and Sailors' Monument Decorated by Members. . . . Hon. Albion W. Tourgee of New York Made the Oration." *Boston Daily Globe*, 31 May 1896, 16 (ProQuest Historical Newspapers).

"Our Best Friend Dead." *Cleveland Gazette*, 27 May 1905, 3, and 3 June 1905, 2.

"Our Civilization's Shame." *Cleveland Gazette*, 2 April 1892, 2.

"Our Duty." *Cleveland Gazette*, 23 September 1905, 2.

"Our Picture." *Anti-Caste* 6 (January 1893): 5.

"Our World's Fair Effort. Every Afro-American Should Contribute Something. . . ." *Cleveland Gazette*, 18 March 1893, 2.

"Our World's Fair Representation." *Cleveland Gazette*, 18 March 1893, 2.

"The Pamphlet Idea." *Cleveland Gazette*, 22 April 1893, 2.

"Pass the Bill. . . ." *Cleveland Gazette*, 14 March 1896, 1.

"Political Snaps. . . . The Anti-Lynch Bill—Other Notes." *Cleveland Gazette*, 18 January 1896, 1.

"Poor Old John, Still 'Knocking.'" *Cleveland Gazette*, 29 May 1915, 2.

"Press Comment on the Careful Consideration Given the Anti-Lynching Bill." *Cleveland Gazette*, 7 March 1896, 1.

"Queer Christianity." *Cleveland Gazette*, 15 December 1894, 2.

Ransom, Rev. Reverdy C. "May God Give Aim to Shoot the Enemy on the Spot! Are the Startling Words Uttered by Bishop Turner. . . ." Letter to the editor, *Indianapolis Freeman*, 3 April 1897, 2 (America's Historical Newspapers).

"Senator Foraker." *Cleveland Gazette*, 19 May 1917, 2 (America's Historical Newspapers).

"Separate Coach Law Upheld. The Supreme Court Decides a Case from Louisiana." *Washington Post*, 19 May 1896, 6 (ProQuest Historical Newspapers).

"The Supreme Court Decision." *A.M.E. Church Review*, 156–62, partially reprinted in Olsen, *Thin Disguise*, 125–26.

"The Supreme Court in the Conspiracy." *Cleveland Gazette*, 25 February 1899, 2.

"That 'Decision.'" *Cleveland Gazette*, 30 May 1896, 2.

"That True Friend. Judge Tourgee Going to Columbus to Help Pass the Anti-Lynching Bill. . . ." *Cleveland Gazette*, 1 February 1896, 1.

Thomas, Roberta. "A Little about Everything: A. W. Tourgee's Attitude." *Chicago Defender*, 26 November 1932, 15 (ProQuest Historical Newspapers).

"Those Memphis Murders." *Cleveland Gazette*, 19 March 1892, 2.

"Tillman and Miss Wells." *Cleveland Gazette*, 9 June 1894, 2.

"To Stop Them. The Anti-Lynching Bill Again Introduced in the Ohio Legislature. . . ." *Cleveland Gazette*, 25 January 1896, 1.

"Tourgee Memorial Meeting." *Cleveland Gazette*, 17 June 1905, 2, reprinted from *Xenia (Ohio) Standard*.

"The Tourgee Monument. Unveiled—Appropriate Exercises—A Beautiful Shaft." *Cleveland Gazette*, 23 June 1906, 1.

Trevigne, Paul. "The World Will Move." *New Orleans Crusader*, 19 July 1890, 1. Nils R. Douglas Papers, box 2, Amistad Research Center.

"Tribute to Judge Tourgee." *Cleveland Gazette*, 30 September 1905, 2.

"'Twas Ever Thus." *Cleveland Gazette*, 4 January 1896, 2, reprinted from the *Crusader*.

Wells-Barnett, Ida B. "Open Letter to the Chicago Daily Chronicle." Chicago *Daily Inter Ocean*, 12 June 1897, part 2, 1.

"What We Meant to Say." *New Orleans Crusader*, 2 June 1891, Charles B. Rousseve Papers, box 2, folder 17, Amistad Research Center.

"Whew!!! Judge Tourgee All But Skins President Harrison Alive. . . ." *Cleveland Gazette*, 18 February 1893, 1–2.

"The White-Caps Warn Us." *Cleveland Gazette*, 12 January 1889, 2.

"Why No Lynch Law." *Cleveland Gazette*, 19 May 1894, 2.

"Why Should We Care?" *Washington Bee*, 23 May 1896, 4.

Willard, Frances E. "Notes from Temperance Meetings." *Union Signal*, 21 March 1889, 2.

[———]. "An Unwise Advocate." *Union Signal*, 21 June 1894, 8–9.

"Willie's Wail." *Cleveland Gazette*, 8 December 1894, 2.

"Won't Indorse Tourgee—Leading Colored Men Regard Him as an Alarmist." *Philadelphia Times*, 18 June 1892. AWTP #8251.

"Zola and the Dreyfus Mystery" (editorial). *Chicago Daily Inter Ocean*, 12 February 1898, 6.

Unpublished Manuscripts

Martinet, Louis A. to the Honorable Attorney General, 8 February 1898, 55th Congress, Records of the U.S. Senate, Record Group 46, Committee Papers, Senate Judiciary Committee, Sen 55A-F15, National Archives, Washington, D.C.

Roosevelt, Theodore. Theodore Roosevelt to AWT, 8 November 1901, Theodore Roosevelt Papers, Manuscript Division, Library of Congress.

Tourgée, Albion W. "Ku Klux War in North Carolina." August 1870. AWTP #1366.

———. AWT to Hon. William McKinley President, 5 March 1897, William McKinley Papers, Manuscript Division, Library of Congress.

———. AWT to President William McKinley, 24 June 1898, William McKinley Papers, Manuscript Division, Library of Congress.

———. AWT to President William McKinley, 5 August 1898, William McKinley Papers, Manuscript Division, Library of Congress.

———. "Black and White" (1899). AWTP #9627.

———. AWT to William McKinley, 19 August 1900, William McKinley Papers, Manuscript Division, Library of Congress.

———. AWT to William McKinley, 21 January 1901, William McKinley Papers, Manuscript Division, Library of Congress.

Other Primary and Secondary Sources

BOOKS

Aaron, Daniel. *The Unwritten War: American Writers and the Civil War*. New York: Alfred A. Knopf, 1973.

Alexander, Michelle. *The New Jim Crow: Mass Incarceration in the Age of Colorblindness*. Rev. ed. New York: New Press, 2012.

Alexander, Roberta Sue. *North Carolina Faces the Freedmen: Race Relations during Presidential Reconstruction, 1865–67*. Durham, N.C.: Duke University Press, 1985.

Alexander, Shawn Leigh. *An Army of Lions: The Civil Rights Struggle before the NAACP*. Philadelphia: University of Pennsylvania Press, 2012.

Alonso, Harriet Hyman. *Growing Up Abolitionist: The Story of the Garrison Children*. Amherst: University of Massachusetts Press, 2002.

Ammons, Elizabeth. *Conflicting Stories: American Women Writers at the Turn into the Twentieth Century*. New York: Oxford University Press, 1992.

Anderson, William H., and Walter H. Stowers [Sanda, pseud.]. *Appointed: An American Novel*. 1894. New York: AMS Press, 1977.

Andrews, William L. *The Literary Career of Charles W. Chesnutt*. Baton Rouge: Louisiana State University Press, 1980.

Bakhtin, Mikhail M. *The Dialogic Imagination: Four Essays*. Edited by Michael Holquist. Translated by Caryl Emerson and Michael Holquist. Austin: University of Texas Press, 1981.

Bederman, Gail. *Manliness & Civilization: A Cultural History of Gender and Race in the United States, 1880–1917*. Chicago: University of Chicago Press, 1995.

Belluscio, Stephen J. *To Be Suddenly White: Literary Realism and Racial Passing*. Columbia: University of Missouri Press, 2006.

Berg, Manfred. *Popular Justice: A History of Lynching in America*. Chicago: Ivan R. Dee, 2011.

Berry, Mary Frances. *My Face Is Black Is True: Callie House and the Struggle for Ex-slave Reparations*. New York: Alfred A. Knopf, 2005.

Berzon, Judith R. *Neither White Nor Black: The Mulatto Character in American Fiction*. New York: New York University Press, 1978.

Blackett, R. J. M. *Building an Antislavery Wall: Black Americans in the Atlantic Abolitionist Movement, 1830–1860*. Baton Rouge: Louisiana State University Press, 1983.

Blight, David W. *Race and Reunion: The Civil War in American Memory*. Cambridge, Mass.: Belknap Press of Harvard University Press, 2001.

Blum, Edward J. *Reforging the White Republic: Race, Religion, and American Nationalism, 1865–1898*. Baton Rouge: Louisiana State University Press, 2005.

Bredin, Jean-Denis. *The Affair: The Case of Alfred Dreyfus*. Translated by Jeffrey Mehlman. 1983. New York: George Braziller, 1986.

Bressey, Caroline. *Empire, Race, and the Politics of Anti-Caste*. London: Bloomsbury, 2013.

Brown, Sterling. *The Negro in American Fiction*. Washington, D.C.: Associates in Negro Folk Education, 1937.

Brown, William Wells. *Clotel; or, The President's Daughter: A Narrative of Slave Life in the United States*. Edited by Robert S. Levine. 1853. Boston: Bedford/St. Martin's, 2000.

Bruce, John Edward. *The Selected Writings of John Edward Bruce: Militant Black Journalist*. Edited by Peter Gilbert. New York: Arno Press and New York Times, 1971.

Brundage, W. Fitzhugh. *Lynching in the New South: Georgia and Virginia, 1880–1930*. Urbana: University of Illinois Press, 1993.

————, ed. *Under Sentence of Death: Lynching in the South*. Chapel Hill: University of North Carolina Press, 1997.

Burns, Michael, ed. *France and the Dreyfus Affair: A Documentary History*. Boston: Bedford/St. Martin's, 1999.

Cady, Edwin H. *The Realist at War: The Mature Years, 1885–1920, of William Dean Howells*. Syracuse, N.Y.: Syracuse University Press, 1958.

Carby, Hazel V. *Reconstructing Womanhood: The Emergence of the Afro-American Woman Novelist*. New York: Oxford University Press, 1987.

Carle, Susan D. *Defining the Struggle: National Organizing for Racial Justice, 1880–1915*. New York: Oxford University Press, 2013.

Chesnutt, Charles Waddell. *The Colonel's Dream*. 1905. Introduction by Sally Ann H. Ferguson. New Milford, Conn.: Toby Press, 2004.

————. *The Conjure Woman and Other Conjure Tales*. Edited by Richard H. Brodhead. Durham, N.C.: Duke University Press, 1993.

————. *The House behind the Cedars*. 1900. New York: Macmillan, 1969.

————. *The Journals of Charles W. Chesnutt*. Edited by Richard H. Brodhead. Durham, N.C.: Duke University Press, 1993.

————. *Mandy Oxendine*. Ca. 1896. Edited by Charles Hackenberry. Urbana: University of Illinois Press, 1997.

————. *The Marrow of Tradition*. 1901. Edited by Eric J. Sundquist. New York: Penguin, 1993.

————. "The Sheriff's Children." In *The Wife of His Youth and Other Stories of the Color Line*, 60–93. 1899. Ann Arbor: University of Michigan Press, 1968.

————. *"To Be an Author": Letters of Charles W. Chesnutt, 1889–1905*. Edited by Joseph R. McElrath Jr. and Robert C. Leitz III. Princeton: Princeton University Press, 1997.

Chesnutt, Helen M. *Charles Waddell Chesnutt: Pioneer of the Color Line*. Chapel Hill: University of North Carolina Press, 1952.

Coffman, Tom. *Nation Within: The History of the American Occupation of Hawai'i*. Rev. ed. Kihei, Hawai'i: Koa Books, 2009.

Cooper, Anna Julia. *A Voice from the South*. 1892. Introduction by Mary Helen Washington. New York: Oxford University Press, 1988.

Cowie, Alexander. *The Rise of the American Novel*. New York: American Book Company, 1951.

Crowder, Ralph L. *John Edward Bruce: Politician, Journalist, and Self-Trained Historian of the African Diaspora.* New York: New York University Press, 2004.

Current, Richard Nelson. *Those Terrible Carpetbaggers.* New York: Oxford University Press, 1988.

Curtis, Michael Kent. *No State Shall Abridge: The Fourteenth Amendment and the Bill of Rights.* Durham, N.C.: Duke University Press, 1986.

Desdunes, R[odolphe] L. *Nos hommes et notre histoire: Notices biographiques accompagnées de reflexions et de souvenirs personnels.* Montreal: Arbour and Dupont, 1911.

Dray, Philip. *At the Hands of Persons Unknown: The Lynching of Black America.* New York: Modern Library, 2002.

Du Bois, W. E. B. *Black Reconstruction in America, 1860–1880.* 1935. New York: Atheneum, 1977.

Dunbar-Nelson, Alice. "The Stones of the Village," ca. 1910. In *The Works of Alice Dunbar-Nelson,* edited by Gloria T. Hull, 3:3–33. 3 vols. New York: Oxford University Press, 1988.

Elliott, Mark. *Color-Blind Justice: Albion Tourgée and the Quest for Racial Equality from the Civil War to* Plessy v. Ferguson. New York: Oxford University Press, 2006.

——. *Justice Deferred: Albion Tourgée and the Fight for Civil Rights.* Guide to Chautauqua County Historical Society Tourgée exhibition (catalog). Foreword by Carolyn L. Karcher. Westfield, N.Y.: Chautauqua County Historical Society, 2008.

Elliott, Mark, and John David Smith, eds. *Undaunted Radical: The Selected Writings and Speeches of Albion W. Tourgée.* Baton Rouge: Louisiana State University Press, 2010.

Epstein, Barbara Leslie. *The Politics of Domesticity: Women, Evangelism, and Temperance in Nineteenth-Century America.* Middletown, Conn.: Wesleyan University Press, 1981.

Escott, Paul D. *Many Excellent People: Power and Privilege in North Carolina, 1850–1900.* Chapel Hill: University of North Carolina Press, 1985.

Filler, Louis. *The Crusade against Slavery, 1830–1860.* New York: Harper and Brothers, 1960.

Fireside, Harvey. *Separate and Unequal: Homer Plessy and the Supreme Court Decision That Legalized Racism.* New York: Carroll & Graf, 2004.

First Mohonk Conference on the Negro Question, Held at Lake Mohonk, Ulster County, New York, June 4, 5, 6, 1890. Edited by Isabel C. Barrows. Boston: George H. Ellis, 1890.

Fiss, Owen M. *Troubled Beginnings of the Modern State, 1888–1910.* Vol. 8 of Oliver Wendell Holmes Devise, *History of the Supreme Court of the United States.* New York: Cambridge University Press, 2006.

Fitzhugh, George. *Sociology for the South, or the Failure of Free Society.* 1854. New York: Burt Franklin, n.d.

Foner, Eric. *Free Soil, Free Labor, Free Men: The Ideology of the Republican Party before the Civil War.* New York: Oxford University Press, 1970.

———. *Reconstruction: America's Unfinished Revolution, 1863–1877.* New York: Harper & Row, 1988.

Fortune, T. Thomas. *Black and White: Land, Labor, and Politics in the South.* 1884. Edited by Seth Moglen. New York: Washington Square Press, 2007.

Foster, Frances Smith. *Written by Herself: Literary Production by African American Women, 1746–1892.* Bloomington: Indiana University Press, 1993.

Franklin, H. Bruce. *Vietnam and Other American Fantasies.* Amherst: University of Massachusetts Press, 2000.

Fredrickson, George M. *The Black Image in the White Mind: The Debate on Afro-American Character and Destiny, 1817–1914.* New York: Harper and Row, 1971.

Friedman, Lawrence J. *Gregarious Saints: Self and Community in American Abolitionism, 1830–1870.* Cambridge: Cambridge University Press, 1982.

Gaines, Kevin K. *Uplifting the Race: Black Leadership, Politics, and Culture in the Twentieth Century.* Chapel Hill: University of North Carolina Press, 1996.

Giddings, Paula J. *Ida: A Sword Among Lions; Ida B. Wells and the Campaign against Lynching.* New York: Amistad-HarperCollins, 2008.

Gillette, William. *Retreat from Reconstruction, 1869–1879.* Baton Rouge: Louisiana State University Press, 1979.

Gilmore, Glenda Elizabeth. *Gender and Jim Crow: Women and the Politics of White Supremacy in North Carolina, 1896–1920.* Chapel Hill: University of North Carolina Press, 1996.

Gilroy, Paul. *The Black Atlantic: Modernity and Double Consciousness.* Cambridge, Mass.: Harvard University Press, 1993.

Goldsby, Jacqueline. *A Spectacular Secret: Lynching in American Life and Literature.* Chicago: University of Chicago Press, 2006.

Grant, Donald L. *The Anti-lynching Movement: 1883–1932.* San Francisco: R. and E. Research Associates, 1975.

Hahn, Steven. *A Nation under Our Feet: Black Political Struggles in the Rural South from Slavery to the Great Migration.* Cambridge, Mass.: Belknap Press of Harvard University Press, 2003.

Hall, Jacquelyn Dowd. *Revolt against Chivalry: Jessie Daniel Ames and the Women's Campaign against Lynching.* 1979. Rev. ed. New York: Columbia University Press, 1993.

Haller, John S., Jr. *Outcasts from Evolution: Scientific Attitudes of Racial Inferiority, 1859–1900.* Urbana: University of Illinois Press, 1971.

Harding, Vincent. *There Is a River: The Black Struggle for Freedom in America.* 1981. New York: Vintage, 1983.

Harper, Frances E[llen] W[atkins]. *Iola Leroy; or, Shadows Uplifted.* 1892. Introduction by Hazel V. Carby. Boston: Beacon Press, 1987.

Harris, Susan K. *God's Arbiters: Americans and the Philippines, 1898–1902.* New York: Oxford University Press, 2011.

Howells, William Dean. *An Imperative Duty. A Novel*. New York: Harper and Brothers, 1891.

Johnson, James Weldon. *Autobiography of an Ex-colored Man*. 1912. Reprinted in *Three Negro Classics*. Introduction by John Hope Franklin. New York: Avon, 1965.

Keller, Dean H. *An Index to the Albion W. Tourgée Papers in the Chautauqua County Historical Society, Westfield, New York*. Research Series 7, *Kent State University Bulletin* 52, no. 5. Kent: Kent State University, 1964.

Kelley, Blair L. M. *Right to Ride: Streetcar Boycotts and African American Citizenship in the Era of* Plessy V. Ferguson. Chapel Hill: University of North Carolina Press, 2010.

Kellogg, Charles Flint. *NAACP: A History of the National Association for the Advancement of Colored People*. 2 vols. Baltimore: Johns Hopkins University Press, 1967.

Kinney, James. *Amalgamation! Race, Sex and Rhetoric in the Nineteenth-Century American Novel*. Westport, Conn.: Greenwood Press, 1985.

Kull, Andrew. *The Color-Blind Constitution*. Cambridge, Mass.: Harvard University Press, 1992.

Larsen, Nella. *Passing*. 1929. In *Quicksand* and *Passing*. Edited by Deborah E. McDowell. New Brunswick, N.J.: Rutgers University Press, 1986.

Lemann, Nicholas. *Redemption: The Last Battle of the Civil War*. New York: Farrar, Straus and Giroux, 2006.

Lewis, David Levering. *W. E. B. Du Bois: Biography of a Race, 1868–1919*. New York: Henry Holt, 1993.

Lofgren, Charles A. *The* Plessy *Case: A Legal-Historical Interpretation*. New York: Oxford University Press, 1987.

Logan, Rayford W. *The Betrayal of the Negro from Rutherford B. Hayes to Woodrow Wilson*. Introduction by Eric Foner. New York: Da Capo Press, 1997. Originally published in 1954 as *The Negro in American Life and Thought: The Nadir, 1877–1901*.

Luker, Ralph E. *The Social Gospel in Black and White: American Racial Reform, 1885–1912*. Chapel Hill: University of North Carolina Press, 1991.

McKinley, Carlyle. *An Appeal to Pharaoh: The Negro Problem and Its Radical Solution*. New York: Fords, Howard, and Hulbert, 1889.

McMurry, Linda O. *To Keep the Waters Troubled: The Life of Ida B. Wells*. New York: Oxford University Press, 1998.

McPherson, James M. *The Abolitionist Legacy: From Reconstruction to the NAACP*. Princeton: Princeton University Press, 1975.

Medley, Keith Weldon. *We as Freemen*: Plessy v. Ferguson. Gretna, La.: Pelican, 2003.

Mott, Frank Luther. *American Journalism, A History: 1690–1960*. 3rd ed. New York: Macmillan, 1962.

Olsen, Otto H. *Carpetbagger's Crusade: The Life of Albion Winegar Tourgée*. Baltimore: Johns Hopkins University Press, 1965.

————, ed. *The Thin Disguise: Turning Point in Negro History:* Plessy v. Ferguson, *A Documentary Presentation (1864–1896)*. New York: Humanities Press, 1967.

Patterson, Orlando. *Slavery and Social Death: A Comparative Study*. Cambridge, Mass.: Harvard University Press, 1982.

Pease, Jane H., and William H. Pease. *They Who Would Be Free: Blacks' Search for Freedom, 1830–1861*. 1974. Urbana: University of Illinois Press, 1990.

Penn, I. Garland. *The Afro-American Press and Its Editors*. 1891. New York: Arno Press and New York Times, 1969.

Peterson, Carla L. *"Doers of the Word": African-American Women Speakers and Writers in the North (1830–1860)*. New York: Oxford University Press, 1995.

Pinar, William F. *The Gender of Racial Politics and Violence in America: Lynching, Prison Rape, & the Crisis of Masculinity*. New York: Peter Lang, 2001.

Quarles, Benjamin. *Black Abolitionists*. 1969. New York: Da Capo Press, 1991.

Reed, Christopher Robert. *Black Chicago's First Century*. Columbia: University of Missouri Press, 2005.

Report of Proceedings for the Annulment of Act 111 of 1890, by the Citizens' Committee, New Orleans, LA. N.d. [1897]. Charles B. Rousseve Papers, box 1, folder 13, Amistad Research Center.

Rosen, Hannah. *Terror in the Heart of Freedom: Citizenship, Sexual Violence, and the Meaning of Race in the Postemancipation South*. Chapel Hill: University of North Carolina Press, 2009.

Royster, Jacqueline Jones, ed. *Southern Horrors and Other Writings: The Anti-Lynching Campaign of Ida B. Wells, 1892–1900*. Boston: Bedford/St. Martins, 1997.

Schechter, Patricia A. *Ida B. Wells-Barnett and American Reform, 1880–1930*. Chapel Hill: University of North Carolina Press, 2001.

Seraile, William. *Bruce Grit: The Black Nationalist Writings of John Edward Bruce*. Knoxville: University of Tennessee Press, 2003.

Silber, Nina. *The Romance of Reunion: Northerners and the South, 1865–1900*. Chapel Hill: University of North Carolina Press, 1993.

Stowe, Harriet Beecher. *Uncle Tom's Cabin; or, Life among the Lowly: Authoritative Text, Backgrounds and Context, Criticism*. 1852. Edited by Elizabeth Ammons. New York: W. W. Norton, 1994.

Sundquist, Eric J. *To Wake the Nations: Race in the Making of American Literature*. Cambridge, Mass.: Belknap Press of Harvard University Press, 1983.

Tate, Claudia. *Domestic Allegories of Political Desire: The Black Heroine's Text at the Turn of the Century*. New York: Oxford University Press, 1992.

Thomas, Brook. *American Literary Realism and the Failed Promise of Contract*. Berkeley: University of California Press, 1997.

————, ed. Plessy v. Ferguson: *A Brief History with Documents*. Boston: Bedford/St. Martin's, 1997.

Thomas, Hugh. *Cuba or the Pursuit of Freedom*. Updated ed. New York: Da Capo Press, 1998.

Trelease, Allen W. *White Terror: The Ku Klux Klan Conspiracy and Southern Reconstruction*. Baton Rouge: Louisiana State University Press, 1971.

Twain, Mark. *Mark Twain's Weapons of Satire: Anti-imperialist Writings on the Philippine-American War.* Edited by Jim Zwick. Syracuse: Syracuse University Press, 1992.

Waldrep, Christopher. *The Many Faces of Judge Lynch: Extralegal Violence and Punishment in America.* New York: Palgrave MacMillan, 2002.

———, ed. *Lynching in America: A History in Documents.* New York: New York University Press, 2006.

Ware, Vron. *Beyond the Pale: White Women, Racism and History.* London: Verso, 1992.

Warren, Kenneth. *Black and White Strangers: Race and American Literary Realism.* Chicago: University of Chicago Press, 1993.

Washington, Booker T. *Up from Slavery.* 1901. Reprinted in *Three Negro Classics.* Introduction by John Hope Franklin. New York: Avon, 1965.

Wells, Ida B. *Crusade for Justice: The Autobiography of Ida B. Wells.* Edited by Alfreda M. Duster. Chicago: University of Chicago Press, 1970.

———. *The Memphis Diary of Ida B. Wells.* Edited by Miriam DeCosta-Willis. Foreword by Mary Helen Washington. Afterword by Dorothy Sterling. Boston: Beacon Press, 1995.

———. *The Reason Why the Colored American Is Not in the World's Columbian Exposition: The Afro-American's Contribution to Columbian Literature.* 1893. Reprinted in *Selected Works of Ida B. Wells-Barnett.* Compiled by Trudier Harris. New York: Oxford University Press, 1991.

———. *A Red Record: Tabulated Statistics and Alleged Causes of Lynchings in the United States, 1892–1893–1894.* 1895. Reprinted in *Selected Works of Ida B. Wells-Barnett.* Compiled by Trudier Harris. New York: Oxford University Press, 1991.

———. *Southern Horrors and Other Writings: The Anti-lynching Campaign of Ida B. Wells, 1892–1900.* Edited by Jacqueline Jones Royster. Boston: Bedford/St. Martin's, 1997.

White, Ronald C., Jr. *Liberty and Justice for All: Racial Reform and the Social Gospel (1877–1925).* San Francisco: Harper and Row, 1990.

Williamson, Joel. *The Crucible of Race: Black-White Relations in the American South since Emancipation.* New York: Oxford University Press, 1984.

Wilson, Edmund. *Patriotic Gore: Studies in the Literature of the American Civil War.* New York: Oxford University Press, 1962.

Woodward, C. Vann. *American Counterpoint: Slavery and Racism in the North-South Dialogue.* Boston: Little, Brown, 1971.

Young, Elizabeth. *Disarming the Nation: Women's Writing and the American Civil War.* Chicago: University of Chicago Press, 1999.

ARTICLES

Andrews, William L. Foreword to *Mandy Oxendine,* by Charles W. Chesnutt. Edited by Charles Hackenberry. Urbana: University of Illinois Press, 1997.

Barton, John Cyril. "'The Necessity of an Example': Chesnutt's *The Marrow of Tradition* and the Ohio Anti-lynching Campaign." *Arizona Quarterly* 67, no. 4 (Winter 2011): 27–58.

Becker, George J. "Albion W. Tourgée: Pioneer in Social Criticism." *American Literature* 19 (March 1947): 59–72.

Caccavari, Peter. "A Trick of Mediation: Charles Chesnutt's Conflicted Literary Relationship with Albion Tourgée." In *Literary Influence and African-American Writers: Collected Essays,* edited by Tracy Mishkin, 129–53. New York: Garland, 1996.

Cooper, Anna Julia (A. J. C.). "'Pactolus Prime'–Tourgée's Last Novel." *Southland,* 2, no. 2 (April 1891): 175–80.

Crofts, Daniel W. "The Black Response to the Blair Education Bill." *Journal of Southern History* 37, no. 1 (February 1971): 41–65.

Curtis, Michael Kent. "Reflections on Albion Tourgée's 1896 View of the Supreme Court: A 'Consistent Enemy of Personal Liberty and Equal Right'?" *Elon Law Review* 5, no. 1 (April 2013): 19–87.

Douglas, J. Allen. "The 'Most Valuable Sort of Property': Constructing White Identity in American Law, 1880–1940." *San Diego Law Review* 40 (August–September 2003): 881–946.

Du Bois, W. E. B. "Reconstruction and Its Benefits." *American Historical Review* 15, no. 4 (July 1910): 781–99.

Elliott, Mark. "Race, Color Blindness, and the Democratic Public: Albion W. Tourgée's Radical Principles in *Plessy v. Ferguson.*" *Journal of Southern History* 67, no. 2 (May 2001): 287–330.

Escott, Paul D. "White Republicanism and Ku Klux Klan Terror: The North Carolina Piedmont during Reconstruction." In *Race, Class, and Politics in Southern History: Essays in Honor of Robert F. Durden,* edited by Jeffrey J. Crow, Paul D. Escott, and Charles L. Flynn Jr., 3–34. Baton Rouge: Louisiana State University Press, 1989.

Garfield, James A. Inaugural Address, Friday, 4 March 1881. In *Inaugural Addresses of the Presidents of the United States from George Washington 1789 to George Bush 1989.* Bicentennial ed. Washington: U.S. Government Printing Office, 1989, 163–65.

Gerber, David A. "Lynching and Law and Order: Origin and Passage of the Ohio Anti-lynching Law of 1896." *Ohio History* 83, no. 1 (Winter 1974): 33–50.

Golub, Mark. "*Plessy* as 'Passing': Judicial Responses to Ambiguously Raced Bodies in *Plessy v. Ferguson.*" *Law and Society Review* 39, no. 3 (September 2005): 563–600.

Hoffer, William James. "*Plessy v. Ferguson*: The Effects of Lawyering on a Challenge to Jim Crow." *Journal of Supreme Court History* 39 (March 2014): 1–21.

Karcher, Carolyn L. "Ida B. Wells and Her Allies against Lynching: A Transnational Perspective." *Comparative American Studies* 3, no. 2 (2005): 131–51.

———. "The White 'Bystander' and the Black Journalist 'Abroad': Albion W. Tourgée and Ida B. Wells as Allies against Lynching." *Prospects* 29 (2005): 85–119.

Keller, Dean H., ed. "A Civil War Diary of Albion W. Tourgée." *Ohio History* 74 (Spring 1965): 99–131.

Mertz, Elizabeth. "Consensus and Dissent in U.S. Legal Opinions: Narrative Structure and Social Voices." *Anthropological Linguistics* 30, no. 3/4 (Fall–Winter 1988): 369–94.

A Negro Congressman. "Louisiana to Get New Negro Lawyers." *Philadelphia Tribune*, 8 July 1952, 3.

Olsen, Otto H. "Albion W. Tourgee and Negro Militants of the 1890's: A Documentary Selection." *Science and Society* 28, no. 2 (Spring 1964): 183–208.

Peterson, Carla L. "'Further Liftings of the Veil': Gender, Class, and Labor in Frances E. W. Harper's *Iola Leroy*." In *Listening to Silences: New Essays in Feminist Criticism*, edited by Elaine Hedges and Shelley Fisher Fishkin, 97–112. New York: Oxford University Press, 1994.

"Recent Fiction." *Nation*, 23 February 1893, 146–47.

Redkey, Edwin S. "Bishop Turner's African Dream." *Journal of American History* 54, no. 2 (September 1967): 271–90.

Renfro, Herbert. "Is the Afro-American League a Failure?" *A.M.E. Church Review*, July 1892, 9–18.

Rosenthal, Debra J. "The White Blackbird: Miscegenation, Genre, and the Tragic Mulatta in Howells, Harper, and the 'Babes of Romance.'" *Nineteenth-Century Literature* 56, no. 4 (2002): 495–517.

Scott, Rebecca J. "Public Rights, Social Equality, and the Conceptual Roots of the *Plessy* Challenge." *Michigan Law Review* 106 (March 2008): 777–804.

Thomas, Brook. "A Constitution Led by the Flag: The *Insular Cases* and the Metaphor of Incorporation." In *Foreign in a Domestic Sense: Puerto Rico, American Expansion, and the Constitution*, edited by Christina Duffy Burnett and Burke Marshall, 82–103. Durham, N.C.: Duke University Press, 2001.

———. "The Legal and Literary Complexities of U.S. Citizenship around 1900." *Law and Literature* 22, no. 2 (2010): 307–24.

———. "The Legitimacy of Law in Literature." *Elon Law Review* 5, no. 1 (April 2013): 171–97.

Thornbrough, Emma Lou. "The National Afro-American League, 1887–1908." *Journal of Southern History* 27, no. 4 (November 1961): 494–512.

Woods, Naurice Frank, Jr. "Adaline and the Judge: An Ex-slave Girl's Journey with Albion W. Tourgée." *Elon Law Review* 5, no. 1 (April 2013): 199–222.

Woodward, C. Vann. "The Birth of Jim Crow." *American Heritage* 15 (April 1964): 52–55, 100–103.

Index